Lecture Notes in Computer Sci

Edited by G. Goos, J. Hartmanis and J. van L

T0238321

Springer

Berlin
Heidelberg
New York
Barcelona
Hong Kong
London
Milan
Paris
Singapore
Tokyo

Paolo Ciancarini   Alexander L. Wolf (Eds.)

Coordination
Languages and Models

Third International Conference
COORDINATION '99
Amsterdam, The Netherlands, April 26-28, 1999
Proceedings

 Springer

Series Editors

Gerhard Goos, Karlsruhe University, Germany
Juris Hartmanis, Cornell University, NY, USA
Jan van Leeuwen, Utrecht University, The Netherlands

Volume Editors

Paolo Ciancarini
Dipartimento di Scienze dell'Informazione
Università di Bologna
Mura Anteo Zamboni, 7, I-40127 Bologna, Italy
E-mail: ciancarini@cs.unibo.it

Alexander L. Wolf
Department of Computer Science, University of Colorado
Boulder, CO 80309-0430, USA
E-mail: alw@cs.colorado.edu

Cataloging-in-Publication data applied for

Die Deutsche Bibliothek - CIP-Einheitsaufnahme

Coordination languages and models : third international conference,
coordination '99, Amsterdam, The Netherlands, April 26 - 28, 1999 ;
proceedings / Paolo Ciancarini ; Alexander L. Wolf (ed.). - Berlin ;
Heidelberg ; New York ; Barcelona ; Hong Kong ; London ; Milan ;
Paris ; Singapore ; Tokyo : Springer, 1999
   (Lecture notes in computer science ; Vol. 1594)
   ISBN 3-540-65836-X

CR Subject Classification (1998): D.1.3, C.2.4, F.1.2, D.2.4, I.2.11

ISSN 0302-9743
ISBN 3-540-65836-X Springer-Verlag Berlin Heidelberg New York

Typesetting: Camera-ready by author
SPIN: 10704698   06/3142 – 5 4 3 2 1 0   Printed on acid-free paper

Foreword

We welcome you to Coordination '99, the third in a series of conferences dedicated to an important perspective on the development of complex software systems. That perspective is shared by a growing community of researchers interested in models, languages, and implementation techniques for coordination.

The last decade has seen the emergence of a class of models and languages variously termed "coordination languages", "configuration languages", "architectural description languages", and "agent-oriented programming languages". These formalisms provide a clean separation between individual software components and their interaction within the overall software organization. This separation makes complex applications more tractable, supports global analysis, and enhances the reuse of software components.

The proceedings of the previous two conferences on this topic were published by Springer as Lecture Notes in Computer Science 1061 and 1282. This issue of LNCS containing the papers presented at Coordination '99 continues the tradition of carefully selected and high quality papers representing the state of the art in coordination technology. In response to the call for papers, we received 67 submissions, from which 26 papers were accepted. These proceedings also contain abstracts for posters presented at the conference. This year's program features invited talks by Rocco De Nicola and Danny B. Lange.

Reading through the papers, we expect that you may be surprised by the variety of disciplines within computer science that have embraced the notion of coordination. In fact, we expect this trend to continue, and hope that you will contribute to the on-going exploration of its strengths, weaknesses, and applications.

We thank all the contributors, the members of the program committee, and additional reviewers of submissions. A special thanks goes to local organizers at CWI, especially Farhad Arbab and Joost Kok. The following organizations provided helpful sponsorship and cooperation for the conference: the EU-funded ESPRIT Working Group "Coordina", the Institute for Programming Research and Algorithmics (IPA); the Royal Dutch Academy of Sciences (KNAW); and the Association for Computing Machinery Special Interest Group in Software Engineering (ACM SIGSOFT).

February 1999   Paolo Ciancarini and Alexander L. Wolf

Program Committee

Paolo Ciancarini (Bologna, Italy), co-chair
Alexander L. Wolf (Colorado, USA), co-chair

Farhad Arbab (CWI/NL)
Martin Boasson (Signaal/NL)
Nick Carriero (Yale/USA)
Georges Gonthier (INRIA/F)
Roberto Gorrieri (Bologna/I)
Chris Hankin (IC/UK)
Paola Inverardi (L'Aquila/I)
Valerie Issarny (IRISA/F)
Suresh Jagannathan (NEC/USA)
Joost Kok (U.Leiden/NL)

Jeff Kramer (IC/UK)
Claudia Linnhoff-Popien (Aachen/D)
Jose Meseguer (SRI/USA)
Dewayn Perry (BellLab/USA)
Antonio Porto (U.Lisbon/P)
G. Catalin Roman (S.Louis/USA)
Richard Taylor (UCI/USA)
Robert Tolksdorf (TU.Berlin/D)
Mike Woolridge (QMC/UK)

Organizing Committee

Farhad Arbab (CWI/NL)
Joost Kok (U.Leiden/NL)

List of additional reviewers

Greg Bolcer
Marcello Bonsangue
Nadia Busi
Mario Bravetti
Michel Chaudron
Flavio Corradini
P. Dechering
Pierpaolo Degano

Edwin de Jong
Rocco De Nicola
H. Goeman
Kenneth Goldman
Dan Hirsch
Arthur S. Hitomi
Peter J. Kammer
Rohit Khare

Cosimo Laneve
Daniel Le Metayer
G. Michele Pinna
Marco Roccetti
Sebastian Uchitel
Jim Whitehead
Martin Wirsing
Gianluigi Zavattaro

Table of Contents

Posters

Coordination and Access Control
of Mobile Agents

Rocco De Nicola

Dipartimento di Sistemi e Informatica
Università degli Studi di Firenze

Abstract

KLAIM (*a Kernel Language for Agents Interaction and Mobility*) [1] is an experimental programming language specifically designed for programming mobile agents that supports a programming paradigm where both processes and data can be moved across different computing environments. The language relies on the use of explicit localities, and on allocation environments that associate logical localities to physical sites. The language consists of core Linda with multiple located tuple spaces and of a set of process operators, borrowed from Milner's CCS. KLAIM tuple spaces and processes are distributed over different localities, which are considered as first-class data. Linda operations are indexed with the locations of the tuple space they operate on. This allows programmers to distribute/retrieve data and processes over/from different nodes directly. Programmers share their control with what we call the *net coordinators*. Net coordinators describe the distributed infrastructure necessary for managing physical distribution of processes, allocation policies, and agents mobility.

KLAIM provides direct support for expressing and enforcing security policies that control access to resources and data. In particular, KLAIM uses types to protect resources and data and to establish policies for access control. The type system guarantees that the operations that processes intend to perform at various network sites comply with the processes' access rights [2, 3]. Types are used to describe the intentions (read, write, execute, ...) of processes relative to the different localities that they are willing to interact with, or that they want to migrate to. Type checking then determines whether processes comply with the declared intentions, and whether they have been assigned the necessary rights to perform the intended operations at the specified localities. The KLAIM type system encompasses both subtyping and recursively defined types. The former occurs naturally when considering hierarchies of access rights, while the latters are needed to model migration of recursive processes.

We are actually working on extending both the language and the type system for introducing types for tuples (record types), notions of multi–level security (by structuring localities into levels of security) and public or shared keys to model dynamic transmission of access rights. Other ongoing research is considering the extension of the language to deal with "open" systems and with hierarchical nets. The interested reader is referred to [4] for written material about our project, for related software (a Java implementation of the topic of KLAIM is available), and for forthcoming additional written documentation.

References

1. De Nicola,R., Ferrari,G.-L., Pugliese,R. Klaim: a Kernel Language for Agents Interaction and Mobility *IEEE Trans. on Software Engineering*, Vol. 24 (5), pp. 315-330, 1998.
2. De Nicola,R., Ferrari,G.-L., Pugliese,R. "Types as Specifications of Access Policies", In *Secure Internet Programming: Security Issues for Distributed and Mobile Objects* (J. Vitek, C. Jensen, Eds.), Lectures Notes in Computer Science, Springer, 1999. To appear.
3. De Nicola,R., Ferrari,G.-L., Pugliese,R., Venneri,B. Types for Access Control. *Theoretical Computer Science*, to appear.
4. Web site for the Klaim project - http://rap.dsi.unifi.it/klaim.html.

Characteristics of an Agent Scripting Language and Its Execution Environment

Danny B. Lange

General Magic, Inc.
Sunnyvale, California, U.S.A
danny@acm.org, http://www.acm.org/~danny

Abstract

Experience gained from IBM's Aglets project[1] has led us to the conclusion that Java is far from being a language ideal for agent development. We discovered significant deficiencies in Java related to agent mobility, messaging, and security. Most importantly, we recognized that the Java programming language and Java-based agent frameworks do not provide a sufficient set of high-level abstraction mechanisms for efficient agent development. At last but not least, we also found the Aglets system put an undesirable emphasis on code mobility which is only required in a certain class of agent-based applications.

Consequently, we have taken steps to address these issues in the creation of new agent scripting language and an associated execution environment. This new scripting language is based on the XML Internet standard. That is, the scripting language is optimized for manipulating and producing XML data and it is itself represented in the XML format. Drawing ideas from from popular *Tcl* and *LISP*, it is an extensible, persistent, and adaptive scripting language for creating agent-based applications.

The execution environment consists of a network of communicating agent servers based on the HTTP and TCP/IP protocols. Agents can safely be hosted in this environment which has been built to support long-term hosting of agents. The environment also provides a graphical agent workbench for developing and testing agents. The execution environment is in its entirety written in Java for optimal portability.

References

1. Lange, D.B. and Oshima, M.: Programming and Deploying Java™ Mobile Agents with Aglets™, Addison-Wesley, 1998.

A Coordination Model for Agents Based on Secure Spaces

Ciarán Bryce, Manuel Oriol, and Jan Vitek

Object Systems Group, University of Geneva

Abstract. Shared space coordination models such as Linda are ill-suited for structuring applications composed of erroneous or insecure components. This paper presents the *Secure Object Space* model. In this model, a data element can be locked with a key and is only visible to a process that presents a matching key to unlock the element. We give a precise semantics for Secure Object Space operations and discuss an implementation in JAVA for a mobile agent system. An implementation of the semantics that employs encryption is also outlined for use in untrusted environments.

1 Introduction

Coordination languages based on shared data spaces have been around for over fifteen years. Researchers have often advocated their use for structuring distributed and concurrent systems because the mode of communication that they provide, sometimes called *generative communication*, is **associative** and **uncoupled**. Communication is associative in that processes do not explicitly *name* their communication partners, but rather specify the kinds of messages that they are interested in reading. Communication is uncoupled in that no links are established between communicating partners; a message placed in the space may be read at any time and by any process interested in it. These properties make it straightforward to code resource discovery protocols that match up clients with servers based on their respective offers [27], to program in an event-driven style [23] and to dynamically configure running systems [17].

Our goal is to use shared data spaces to coordinate applications made up of potentially **erroneous** and **malicious** components. In particular, we want to use shared data spaces as the main communication model in a mobile agent system called JAVASEAL [29]. *Mobile agents* are programs that carry out distributed computations by communicating locally with resources on a site, and migrating to a remote site to gain access to resources there [24, 12, 30, 5]. A key issue for agent programming is *how to structure and regulate communication between agents*. Our experience with JAVASEAL has shown that a standard message passing model is cumbersome. An agent that arrives in a foreign environment might not know the naming conventions of that environment; it is more convenient for that agent to specify the attributes of the resources that it needs rather than the actual names — hence the utility of associative communication. Further, since agents might migrate in the midst of a protocol, communication must be strongly uncoupled. We identified three design goals for agent communication in JAVASEAL which we use for the model presented in this paper:

- **Efficiency**: Frequent communication patterns require low overhead.
- **Controlled Communication**: A message exchanged between agents is subject to a security policy that verifies whether the message is allowed.
- **Privacy**: The secrecy of messages sent between agents must be preserved.

These requirements highlight shortcomings of the shared space model. The model works well when all processes with access to the shared space have been designed carefully and are well-behaved. Unfortunately, mistakes are easily made — the simplest example being reading an entry which is part of another protocol [27, 18] — and nothing prevents malicious processes from spying or even corrupting the data exchanged over the common space. Moreover, denial of service attacks can easily be mounted by flooding the space with requests.

In this paper we present a coordination model, called the Secure Object Space model (SECOS), that meets the above mentioned requirements. In a SECOS, entries in the shared space are locked using *keys*. These keys are used to query the data space and to hide the contents of the data space entries: that is, the contents of the locked object remain hidden until the correct key is presented. In Section 3, we give a precise semantics to SECOS operations in the context of a small programming language derived from the π calculus. Locking is enforced by dynamic typing. In Section 4, we give an overview of the implementation of SECOS in JAVA, and cite an example of its use within the JAVASEAL agent platform. Finally, since it is not possible to rely on typing to protect space entries in untrusted or open environments, we describe a cryptographic implementation of SECOS in Section 5.

2 Shared Spaces

Linda is probably the most widely known shared space coordination model [13]. The model is based on the concept of generative communication; two processes can communicate if one process generates a message tuple, posts it to a Linda tuple space, from where it can be read by the second process. The basic model consists of three primitive operations: out to write a tuple, in to perform a destructive read, and read to perform a non-destructive read.

The Linda input operations are associative since the reader process need only provide a partial description of the value to be retrieved. It can specify some of the tuple fields and leave others blank. Using our syntax, $in(\langle ?, 3 \rangle, x)$ is a Linda operation that retrieves a two element tuple with integer 3 in the second position, and any value in the first position (? represents the wild card). In Linda, a template specifies the number of fields a matching tuple should have as well as the value of each field when a wild card is not used.

While Linda is adequate for coordinating closed parallel systems, coordinating potentially erroneous or malicious components is more challenging. Consider the following two examples:

1. *Secure logical channels*: In a client-server protocol, the reply channel used to send the result of a query to the client must be protected from interference. In a Linda implementation there is no way to guarantee that a tuple containing a server's reply will not be accidentally or willfully read by another process.
2. *Secure garbage collection*: In a long-lived agent environment, migration is frequent and tuple spaces can be littered with "garbage" tuples. These are tuples that are no longer needed, or worse, tuples that have been output as part of a denial of service attack. Thus a garbage collector is needed. Since there can be no clear cut criteria for deciding which tuples are garbage, the garbage collector will rely on heuristics coded at the user-level. Privacy of data being one of the requirements for agent communication, a *secure* garbage collector is defined as a plain process that is trusted to extract tuples from the space according to some policy, but not to access the contents of the extracted tuples. Linda does not distinguish the removal of a tuple from the reading of its fields.

Multiple data spaces have been used to address the access control problem [7, 13, 15, 26] by fulfilling the role of protection domains. In this approach, agents are granted access to a space if they are trusted to manipulate the data in that space and to interact with other agents that have access to the same space. The problem with this approach is that it supposes that each domain is independent, whereas some resources must be visible in several domains. Managing multiple spaces where agents may appear in several spaces is complex. Moreover, this approach does not protect the values stored in the data space, as is required for secure garbage collection. Our model uses multiple data spaces for convenience, but they do not represent an essential part of our proposal.

Another important issue in an agent environment is the treatment of distribution. We have not considered distributed shared spaces on the grounds of efficiency and scalability. Agent systems are meant to be distributed over the Internet. The size and connectivity involved in large scale networks render an efficient implementation of a shared space difficult, if not impossible. From the viewpoint of security, distributed spaces require a trusted implementation (on all nodes) which may be difficult. We therefore prefer to rely on mobile agents for distributed interaction and to keep shared spaces for local, fast and secure communication.

3   Secure Object Spaces

Secure Object Spaces (SECOS) extends Linda in three respects. Firstly, an SECOS system consists of multiple, disjoint, shared object spaces. Secondly, SECOS entries are sequences of *locked* values. Finally, matching is performed on locked entries. We will introduce these features by examples before giving their semantics.

A SECOS entry is called an *object*. It consists of an unordered sequence of *locked fields* – pairs of values and labels. Labels will be referred to as locks or keys. The following is an example of a process that outputs an objects with two fields; we use SECOS syntax.

$$\mathbf{out}(\langle a: \text{"Tom's number is"} , b_c: \text{"233 349"}\rangle)@\text{main} \qquad (1)$$

Assuming that there is a SECOS space named main, the term (1) evaluates by depositing the object $\langle a: \text{"Tom's number is"} , b_c: \text{"233 349"}\rangle$ in main. We consider this to be an object composed of values "Tom's number is" and 233 349 locked under the keys a and b_c respectively. Keys serve two purposes in SECOS. First, they filter entries from a SECOS space. When performing an input operation, the template must specify the keys of fields on which associative matching is to be effected. A request for an object from the space main is written

$$\mathbf{in}(\langle a: \text{"Tom's number is"} , c_b: \text{"233 349"}\rangle, x)@\text{main} \qquad (2)$$

The effect of evaluating this term is to retrieve an object matching template $\langle a: \text{"Tom's number is"} , c_b: \text{"233 349"}\rangle$, and to bind x to the result. The expression $x.a$ denotes the value "Tom's number is" and $x.c_b$ denotes 233 349.

The second purpose of keys is to provide security. A key for a locked object must be presented in order for a match on that field to succeed. There are two types of keys in SECOS: *symmetric* keys and *asymmetric* keys. A key is symmetric if it both locks and also unlocks an object; in the example above, the key a is symmetric. A key is asymmetric if it belongs to an asymmetric key pair, that is one of the keys of the pair is used to lock a field, and the other key is used to unlock it. The keys (b_c, c_b) form an asymmetric key pair: b_c is used to lock 233 349, and only c_b can unlock it.

Keys modify the notion of matching. Instead of the positional matching of Linda, SECOS relies on key directed matching. We say that a template object matches a target if for every field in the template, there is a matching field in the target. Two fields match if (1) they have been locked with compatible keys, and (2) if their values are equal or if the template's value is "?". Key compatibility is defined as follows. Two symmetric keys are compatible if they are equal (*e.g.*, a is compatible with a); two asymmetric keys are compatible if they belong to the same pair (a_b is compatible with b_a).

The definition of matching we have just given differs from Linda in that matching does not require the number of fields of the template and target to be equal. In SECOS, a shorter object can match a longer object. To illustrate this, the following table lists all of the templates that match the object of line (1).

out	$\langle a: \text{"Tom's number is"} , b_c: \text{"233 349"}\rangle$
in	$\langle a: \text{"Tom's number is"} , c_b: \text{"233 349"}\rangle$, $\langle c_b: \text{"233 349"} , a: \text{"Tom's number is"}\rangle$, $\langle a: \text{"Tom's number is"} , c_b: ?\rangle$, $\langle c_b: \text{"233 349"} , a: ?\rangle$, $\langle a: ? , c_b: \text{"233 349"}\rangle$, $\langle c_b: ? , a: \text{"Tom's number is"}\rangle$, $\langle a: ? , c_b: ?\rangle$, $\langle a: \text{"Tom's number is"}\rangle$, $\langle c_b: \text{"233 349"}\rangle$, $\langle a: ?\rangle$, $\langle c_b: ?\rangle$, $\langle\rangle$

An implication of this approach is that an empty template, $\langle\rangle$, matches everything. A simple-minded garbage collector whose goal is to match with any element can be written as follows:

$$! \ \mathbf{in}(\langle\rangle, x)@\mathsf{main} \qquad (3)$$

The repetition operator, $!$, indicates that the command will be executed in a loop. Line (3) will repeatedly use the empty template to retrieve an arbitrary object from the space main. Nevertheless, an important property of the model is that *matching of objects happens without the identity of any entry being revealed*. The garbage collector must present a key to select a value locked with the corresponding key. This shows that it is possible to implement a user-level collector that cannot peek in other people's garbage; this was one of the requirements outlined in Section 2.

Another feature of the model is that *objects can be extended without revealing their contents*.

$$\langle a : \text{"22"}\rangle \oplus b : \text{"High"} \qquad \text{yields} \qquad \langle a : \text{"22"}, b : \text{"High"}\rangle$$

An implication of extension on a template, denoted by $\oplus$, is that the template becomes more specific, and can thus match with fewer objects. This technique can be used to implement a security policy on data. For instance, a security policy may designate a process as being low-level or high-level. All in and out requests from a process have the locked field (b:level) appended to the template, where level is "high" or "low". This means that a process can only match with objects of the same security group.

3.1 The SECOS programming language

The remainder of this section gives a semantics for the SECOS model. The SECOS language is a process calculus based on the asynchronous π-calculus [14, 4, 3] which is known to be very expressive, supporting many programming idioms and Turing-complete. To π we add a notion of objects and change the communication rules to use object spaces instead of channels.

Although we are interested in coordinating mobile agents, the language presented here does not allow the exchange of code in object spaces. A treatment of mobility can be found in [30, 6]. The calculi could be merged at the cost of some complexity, but we prefer to leave this as a topic of future investigation. The syntax of the calculus is now given.

Names and Labels We take an infinite set $\mathcal{N}$ of *names* ranged over by metavariables $a, b, c, \ldots$ (except e, k, t, v). Object spaces and fields are named; names play the role of variables, as in the π-calculus. The infinite set $\mathcal{L}$ of *labels* consists of names (symmetric keys), and pairs of names (asymmetric keys) written a_b. Labels are ranged over by ℓ. We define the *co-label* function $\overline{\cdot}$ as $\overline{a_b} = b_a$ and $\overline{a} = a$.

Objects Basic values are taken from the set of labels extended with a distinguished void element, ?, and are ranged over by v. The values communicated amongst processes are *objects*, ranged over by t. An object $\langle \ell_1 : v_1, \ldots \ell_i : v_i \rangle$ is a possibly empty sequence of fields where field labels are distinct.

Expressions The syntactic category of *expressions*, ranged over by e, includes basic values, objects, selection expressions and extension expressions.

$$
\begin{array}{lll}
e ::= v & & \text{basic value} \\
\quad t & & \text{object} \\
\quad e.e & & \text{selection} \\
\quad e \oplus e : e & & \text{extension}
\end{array}
$$

Processes The syntactic category of *processes*, ranged over by P, Q, follows the asynchronous π up to the communication primitives. The empty process $\mathbf{0}$ has no behavior; it is the inert process. Processes can be composed in parallel, $P \mid Q$, and replicated $!\,P$.

$$
\begin{array}{lll}
P ::= \mathbf{0} & \text{inactivity} \\
\quad P \mid Q & \text{composition} \\
\quad !\,P & \text{replication} \\
\quad \ldots
\end{array}
$$

There are two communication primitives: $\mathbf{in}(e, a)@e.P$ for input and $\mathbf{out}(e)@e$ for output. $\mathbf{in}(e_1, a)@e_2.P$ tries to extract an object matching the template e_1 from the object space e_2 and binds the result to variable a. The operation is blocking, P cannot execute until the match succeeds. $\mathbf{out}(e_1)@e_2$ outputs the object denoted by e_1 into object space e_2.

$$
\begin{array}{lll}
P ::= \ldots & \\
\quad \mathbf{in}(e, a)@e.P & \text{input} \\
\quad \mathbf{out}(e)@e & \text{output} \\
\quad \ldots
\end{array}
$$

The restriction operator $(\mathbf{new}\,a)$ introduces a fresh name. In our case we also view it as key generation; $(\mathbf{new}\,a)P$ means that a is valid only in P.

$$
\begin{array}{lll}
P ::= \ldots & \\
\quad (\mathbf{new}\,a)P & \text{new name creation}
\end{array}
$$

We use alpha conversions of bound names in expression evaluation. The free name function is denoted $fn(\_)$.

3.2 Matching, Keys and Dynamic Typing

We now turn to object types and matching. The notion of matching is somewhat similar to standard notions of subtyping. Asymmetric key pairs introduce an asymmetry that leads to the definition of the type-matching relation ($\trianglelefteq$) which is related to subtyping, but which has significantly different mathematical properties.

Definition 1 (SECOS object type) *An object $t = \langle \ell_1 : v_1 \ldots, \ell_n : v_n \rangle$ is of type $\mathcal{T} = \{\ell_1, \ldots, \ell_n\}$, written $t \in \mathcal{T}$. The co-type of $\mathcal{T}$ is $\overline{\mathcal{T}} = \{\overline{\ell}_1, \ldots, \overline{\ell}_n\}$.*

Intuitively, $\mathcal{T}$ type-matches $\mathcal{T}'$ if each field $\overline{\ell}$ of $\mathcal{T}'$ is compatible with a field ℓ of $\mathcal{T}$. Note that $\mathcal{T}'$ may have more fields than $\mathcal{T}$.

Definition 2 (type-matching) *The* match *relation* $\trianglelefteq$ *relates types*, $\mathcal{T} \trianglelefteq \mathcal{T}'$ *iff for all $\ell \in \mathcal{T}$ there exists $\overline{\ell} \in \mathcal{T}'$.*

We now define the matching procedure which takes a template object t and a candidate object t' and determines whether t' meets the specification of t.

Definition 3 (matching) *Let $t \in \mathcal{T}$ and $t' \in \mathcal{T}'$, we say that t matches t', written $t \lessapprox t'$, iff (1) $\mathcal{T} \trianglelefteq \mathcal{T}'$ and (2) if $\ell : v \in t$ and $\overline{\ell} : v' \in t'$ implies either $v = ?$ or $v = v'$.*

Thus matching can be implemented by a combination of a dynamic type checks and a sequence of field value tests.

3.3 Reduction semantics

The semantic definition of the calculus is a *reduction semantics*, a one-step reduction relation $P \to P'$, indicating that P reduces in one step of internal computation to P'. We first define two auxiliary notions: *structural congruence* and *evaluation*. Structural congruence, $\equiv$, is the least congruence on processes satisfying the axioms and rules given in Figure 1. The evaluation relation ($\downarrow$) yields the result of field selection and object extension expressions. The reduction relation $\to$ is the least relation on processes that satisfies the axioms and rules defined in Figure 1.

Reduction does not proceed for nonsensical terms. While these terms can be avoided by the introduction of a type system, there is little benefit in the present discussion to add one. Trailing inert processes are elided; thus $\mathbf{in}(t, x)@e \cdot \mathbf{0}$ becomes $\mathbf{in}(t, x)@e$. The notation for capture avoiding substitution is $P\{t/x\}$. We write $\ell : x \in \langle \ell : x, \ell_1 : x_1, \ldots, \ell_n : x_n \rangle$.

3.4 Examples of SECOS Programming

We now give some programming examples; we assume the presence of additional data types and meaningful space names.

Secure channels

One of the goals of SECOS is to support secure logical channels between processes. Consider an example in which Bob wants to speak with Alice and does not wish anyone else to listen in on their exchange, or even know that the exchange took place. We assume that Bob knows Alice's public key Alice_x. The

Reduction

$$\frac{P \to Q}{(\mathbf{new}\,a)P \to (\mathbf{new}\,a)Q} \qquad \frac{P \to Q}{P \mid R \to Q \mid R} \qquad \frac{P \equiv P' \quad P' \to Q' \quad Q' \equiv Q}{P \to Q}$$

$$\frac{e_2 \downarrow a \quad e_4 \downarrow a \quad e_1 \downarrow t \quad e_3 \downarrow t' \quad t' \gtrsim t}{\mathbf{out}(e_1)@e_2 \mid \mathbf{in}(e_3, b)@e_4 \,.\, P \to P\{^t\!/_b\}}$$

Evaluation

$$\frac{}{v \downarrow v} \qquad \frac{e \downarrow t' \quad t \equiv t'}{e \downarrow t} \qquad \frac{t \equiv \langle e_1 : e_2, \ldots \rangle \quad e_1 \downarrow \ell \quad e_2 \downarrow v \quad e \downarrow \bar{\ell}}{t.e \downarrow v}$$

Structural congruence

$$P \mid Q \equiv Q \mid P$$
$$P \mid 0 \equiv P$$
$$(P \mid Q) \mid R \equiv P \mid (Q \mid R)$$
$$!P \equiv P \mid !P$$
$$(\mathbf{new}\,a)(\mathbf{new}\,b)P \equiv (\mathbf{new}\,b)(\mathbf{new}\,a)P$$
$$a \notin \mathit{fn}(P) \;\Rightarrow\; (\mathbf{new}\,a)(P \mid Q) \equiv P \mid (\mathbf{new}\,a)Q$$

$$\langle \ell : v, \ell_1 : v_1, \ldots \ell_n : v_n \rangle \equiv \langle \ell_1 : v_1, \ldots \ell_n : v_n, \ell : x \rangle$$
$$\ell \notin \langle \ell_1 : v_1, \ldots \ell_n : v_n \rangle \;\Rightarrow\;$$
$$\langle \ell_1 : v_1, \ldots \ell_n : v_n \rangle \oplus \ell : v \equiv \langle \ell : v, \ell_1 : v_1, \ldots \ell_n : v_n \rangle$$

Figure 1: SECOS reduction semantics.

protocol is fairly standard: Bob generates an object which contains his public key (Bob_y) locked under Alice's public key. When Alice retrieves the object, she may select Bob's key. In this way, Alice can send private messages to Bob and vice versa.

$\mathsf{Bob} = \mathbf{out}((\mathsf{Alice}_x : \mathsf{Bob}_y, \mathsf{req} : \text{"let's talk"}))@\mathsf{main} \mid \mathbf{in}((\langle y_{\mathsf{Bob}} : ?\rangle, z)@\mathsf{main}\,.\,P$

$\mathsf{Alice} = \mathbf{in}((\langle x_{\mathsf{Alice}} : ?, \mathsf{req} : \text{"let's talk"}\rangle, z)@\mathsf{main}\,.\,\mathbf{out}((\langle z.x_{\mathsf{Alice}} : \text{"ok"}\rangle))@\mathsf{main}$

When Bob and Alice are composed in parallel, the following reductions occur:

$\mathbf{out}((\langle \mathsf{Alice}_x : \mathsf{Bob}_y, \mathsf{req} : \text{"let's talk"}\rangle))@\mathsf{main} \mid \mathbf{in}((\langle y_{\mathsf{Bob}} : ?\rangle, z)@\mathsf{main}\,.\,P \mid$
$\mathbf{in}((\langle x_{\mathsf{Alice}} : ?, \mathsf{req} : \text{"let's talk"}\rangle, z)@\mathsf{main}\,.\,\mathbf{out}((\langle z.x_{\mathsf{Alice}} : \text{"ok"}\rangle))@\mathsf{main}$

$\equiv \mathbf{out}((\langle \mathsf{Alice}_x : \mathsf{Bob}_y, \mathsf{req} : \text{"let's talk"}\rangle))@\mathsf{main} \mid$
$\mathbf{in}((\langle x_{\mathsf{Alice}} : ?, \mathsf{req} : \text{"let's talk"}\rangle, z)@\mathsf{main}\,.\,\mathbf{out}((\langle z.x_{\mathsf{Alice}} : \text{"ok"}\rangle))@\mathsf{main} \mid$
$\mathbf{in}((\langle y_{\mathsf{Bob}} : ?\rangle, z)@\mathsf{main}\,.\,P$

$\to \mathbf{out}((\langle\langle \mathsf{Alice}_x : \mathsf{Bob}_y, \mathsf{req} : \text{"let's talk"}\rangle.x_{\mathsf{Alice}} : \text{"ok"}\rangle))@\mathsf{main} \mid$
$\mathbf{in}((\langle y_{\mathsf{Bob}} : ?\rangle, z)@\mathsf{main}\,.\,P$

$\to P\{^{(\mathsf{Bob}_y\,:\,\text{"ok"})}/_z\}$

Private Store

An agent may store private information in a SECOS without having to be concerned about this data being read by another agent. For instance, an agent that regularly visits a site may leave partial results in a SECOS of the site; the matching semantics prevent the data from being matched, accidentally or on purpose by other agents.

The solution relies on creating a fresh symmetric key to lock an object. The process shown below creates a new name a and deposits an object locked by a into space main.

$$(\textbf{new } a)\big(\textbf{out}(\langle a : \langle name : \text{``joe''}, cookie : 19990212184523\rangle\rangle)@main \mid P\big) \mid Q$$

Since the name a is restricted, composition with an arbitrary Q is possible, and we know that Q may not match on a. Thus if $P = \textbf{in}(\langle a : ?\rangle, x)@main . P'$ then a reduction can take place:

$$(\textbf{new } a)\big(\textbf{out}(\langle a : \langle name : \text{``joe''}, cookie : 19990212184523\rangle\rangle)@main \mid$$
$$\textbf{in}(\langle a : ?\rangle, x)@main . P'\big) \mid Q$$

$$\rightarrow (\textbf{new } a)\big(P\{^{\langle a\,:\,\langle name\,:\,\text{``joe''}, cookie\,:\,19990212184523\rangle\rangle}/_x\}\big) \mid Q$$

Another way to obtain a similar result is to use a private SECOS, that is, a space with a restricted name.

Care must be taken when matching with the empty object, $\langle\rangle$, as it may retrieve any object indiscriminately from a shared space.

Interposition

Untrusted agents should not be granted direct access to a shared space. The technique of interposition allows us to filter SECOS requests emitted by an agent without revealing the contents of the objects being manipulated.

Interposition relies on mediating access to the main object space by filter processes that implement an access control policy. We show one implementation of this idea below. A filter is a process that reads requests deposited in a space called from-space and reroutes them to a space called to-space. A client process deposits an object $\langle i : t\rangle$ in from-space to request that the filter perform an input in to-space using t as a template. The result x of the input is then deposited back into from-space as an object $\langle r : x\rangle$. An output can be requested by depositing an object $\langle o : t\rangle$ into from-space. The filter process, parameterized over the two space names, is defined as

$Filter(\text{from-space}, \text{to-space}) =$
$\quad !\,\textbf{in}(\langle i : ?\rangle, x)@\text{from-space} . \textbf{in}(x.i, y)@\text{to-space} . \textbf{out}(\langle r : y\rangle)@\text{from-space}$
$\quad \mid !\,\textbf{in}(\langle o : ?\rangle, x)@\text{from-space} . \textbf{out}(x.o)@\text{to-space}$

Thus, the following configuration will perform an output of object $\langle a : 1\rangle$ in space main, and then an input of that object. Space buf is used as the from-space.

$\quad \textbf{out}(\langle o : \langle a : 1\rangle\rangle)@buf \mid \textbf{out}(\langle i : \langle a : ?\rangle\rangle)@buf \mid \textbf{in}(\langle r : ?\rangle, x)@buf . P$
$\quad \mid (\textbf{new } main)(Filter(buf, main))$

This system will reduce to $P\{^{\langle r\,:\,\langle a\,:\,1\rangle\rangle}/_x\} \mid (\textbf{new } main)(Filter(buf, main))$.

Garbage collection

We can implement a time-based garbage collector agent (GCA) as a process that mediates access to an object space by interposition. Every output request is extended by the GCA with some GC specific information before inserting the object into the space. For a time-based garbage collector this information may simply be a time-to-live field. This is coded in the calculus as

$$\mathbf{in}(\langle\rangle, x)@a \,.\, \mathbf{out}(x \oplus \mathsf{TTL}:y)@b$$

assuming that a denotes a space in which insertion requests are placed and b denotes the actual SECOS used for communication. Further, y is some time stamp. The evaluation rule decrees that the extension expression $x \oplus \mathsf{TTL}:y$ returns an object with a TTL field, here TTL is a shared key which we assume to be known only to the GCA.

When a time stamp ceases to be valid, the following process collects the garbage

$$!\,\mathbf{in}(\langle \mathsf{TTL}:y\rangle, x)@b$$

using the rule that only objects stamped at time y are extracted.

This examples reiterates the main properties of SECOS. The GCA is a user level agent which does not gain any knowledge about the content of the objects it manipulates. Secondly, we may have several different GCAs with different policies mediating the same space. Thirdly, GC information is not visible in normal communication; processes may retrieve time stamped objects as before but will not see the GC information.

Linda

It is straightforward to model Linda in SECOS. Linda uses positional notation for matching and does not have any equivalent to our locking primitives. A Linda tuple $\langle x, y, z \rangle$ is represented as an object $\langle 1:x, 2:y, 3:z \rangle$ where **1**, **2** and **3** are globally scoped names that stand for positions in the obvious way. A Linda output operation $\mathbf{out}(\langle x, y \rangle)@a$ is translated in SECOS to $\mathbf{out}(\langle 1:x, 2:y \rangle)@a$. A Linda $\mathbf{in}(\langle ?v, y \rangle, a)@ \,.\, P$ is translated to $\mathbf{in}(\langle 1:?, 2:y \rangle, u)@a \,.\, P'$ where all occurrences of v in P are replaced by $u.\mathbf{1}$.

4 SECOS on JAVA

We implemented SECOS over JAVA for the JAVASEAL agent system [29]. As was the case with the programming language proposal, typing is used to implement tuple locking. Encryption of objects is not necessary for protection so long as the objects remain with the confines of the JAVA virtual machine.

Implementing SECOS within an object-oriented language required careful treatment of two points: inheritance and aliasing. Regarding **inheritance**, SECOS matching requires that the value fields be compared. In an object-oriented language we may either use a default hard-wired comparison operation or allow objects to customize this code by inheritance. The advantage of inheritance is that the meaning of *match* can be adapted to the application. The problem is that extensions introduce security risks. An attacker could program a match method of an object that loops, thereby blocking the thread of the SECOS and subjecting the system to a denial of service attack.

In Jada [9] the match can be extended. In JavaSpaces [23] an object written to the shared space is first transformed to a serialized java.rmi.MarshalledObject; the equals method of MarshalledObject is used for the match, which the user has no possibility of overwriting. In SECOS we also chose a fixed match.

Aliasing occurs when an object can be reached by following different sequences of references. Aliasing is the key to dynamic information sharing, and is pretty much unavoidable as JAVA uses references for parameter passing. The problem with aliasing is that it undermines the role of the space as the sole communication mechanism between communicating agents. Objects placed within an SECOS must not introduce aliases between agents. We use JAVA serialization - the JAVA deep object copy mechanism - in the implementation of the in and out operations to satisfy this constraint.

4.1 Classes

We briefly look at the main classes needed to implement SECOS; helper classes are not described. We model SECOS labels with three classes: an abstract Key class, and two final subclasses AsymKey and SymKey which represent the asymmetric and symmetric keys respectively.

The Key class defines the common attributes of keys. The match method compares two key instances.

The class SymKey represents shared keys. Its match method expects its argument to be this, *i.e.*, the same key is used in actual encryption and decryption.

The class ASymKey represents asymmetric keys. This class contains the dual key that is needed to match with it. Its constructor is protected since an asymmetric key is created indirectly. A user first creates a KeyPair helper class, which creates the two asymmetric keys. In this way, one is sure that each asymmetric key has a dual.

The SecOSObject class implements the object space entries. Recall that the notion of subtyping and type matching defined relied on the notion of structural subtyping. This differs from the JAVA type system since structural subtyping does not require an explicit type hierarchy (such as the hierarchy in JAVA explicitly defined using extends in declarations), and structural subtyping naturally allows for multiple supertypes for any given type. The implementation of matching is thus done dynamically in the match() method which is a final method. For the purpose of matching, null (the "empty" value for pointers) plays the role of ?. A SecOSObject instance is created with a set of key-value pairs. Keys are checked to be either of type SymKey or AsymKey; a user-defined key type is automatically rejected. The select operation has a method that takes a key as parameter and returns the object if the key is the correct key, or null if no matching object is found in the SecOSObject. The extend method returns a new object obtained by extending the target with a key-value pair. The operation fails if the pair is already present in the SecOSObject. The match method returns true if the argument SecOSObject matches. This requires that the keys of both SecOSObjects match, and that the values match.

The SecureObjectSpace class represents the SECOS itself. It provides associative addressing and the methods in, out and read. The latter is a non-destructive version of in (modeled as the atomic execution of an in followed by an out). Both of these are blocking. The out operation is synchronized to guarantee mutual exclusion. The SECOS represents an object in serialized form within the space; thus out serializes the value component of each SecOSObject, in and read deserialize it.

4.2 Coordinating Agents

Our implementation platform for SECOS is the JAVASEAL agent platform [29, 28]. The main characteristic of JAVASEAL is that each agent executes within a *protection domain*, meaning that the agent cannot directly view or modify the data of another agent; communication between agents must use the system provided *channels*. Protection domains are structured in a hierarchy; the root of the hierarchy is the JVM. An agent protection domain can only send a message to its parent domain or to its direct children. Hence, a message sent between two domains must be routed through the common ancestor of the domains.

HyperNews [19] is an agent-based newspaper application that runs over JAVASEAL. Articles are downloaded in the form of agents to client sites; these agents contain code that verify receipt of payment and which only decrypts articles when payment is made. A client site contains an *area* allocated for each newspaper provider; article agents belonging to that provider reside in the provider's area. A basic security requirement is that a provider may not interfere with the articles of another provider. In the JAVASEAL implementation of HyperNews, the root seal of the hierarchy contains the core of the application. A child protection domain is allocated for each provider *proxy*; within each proxy, a child domain is allocated to each article of that provider.

In JAVASEAL, the SECOS is implemented within the root domain of the hierarchy. An in or out message generated by an agent is sent to the root seal via the channel mechanism. A message can be treated at each level of the hierarchy. For instance, an article can publish its contents by sending an out message to the SECOS. To protect articles from other providers, the root domain which intercepts all messages enforces a security policy. It does this by appending a *password* field to each out and in request. The password varies for each proxy; the extension of each request is transparent to the agent that generates the message and it implements the $\oplus$ operator introduced in Section 3. In JAVASEAL, this is implemented with the following code segment.

```
SymKey AgentKey = new SymKey() ;
```

```
String password = new String( "KeepMeSecretTimes" ); // Password for Times
...
public SecOSObject in( SecOSObject request ) { // Request on Times Channel
    SecOSObject extRequest = request.extend( AgentKey , password );
    return sos.in( extRequest );
}
public SecOSObject out( SecOSObject request ) {// Request on Times Channel
    SecOSObject extRequest = request.extend( AgentKey , password );
    return sos.out( extRequest );
}
```

5   A Cryptographic Implementation of SECOS

It should be obvious that keys and locks in SECOS are analogous to cryptographic keys. The crucial difference is that cryptography is based on the transformation of data from clear-text to cipher-text, and involves heavy-weight mathematical procedures. SECOS locking on the other hand is enforced by dynamic typing, thus making protected communication cheap. However, the protection afforded by types breaks down as soon as values leave the trusted runtime of the SECOS system. This can happen whenever an object is stored on disk, transferred on the network, or used on malicious platforms.

In this section, we consider how to retain the semantics of SECOS in a hostile environment. We begin with a look at some relevant facts about cryptography, and then explain how the locking primitives can be implemented.

5.1   Cryptography

There are two fundamental cryptography schemes. *Symmetric schemes* use shared keys: the same key encrypts and decrypts data from clear-text to cipher-text and back [20]. *Asymmetric schemes*, or public-key cryptography, use key pairs [22]; one key is used to encrypt data, the other to decrypt. The syntax for cryptographic operations is summarized in the following table:

Scheme	Encryption	Decryption
symmetric	$K_a(v)$	$K_a^{-1}(K_a(v))$
asymmetric	$PK_{a_b}(v)$	$PK_{b_a}^{-1}(PK_{a_b}(v))$

In the remainder we make some standard assumptions about cryptography (*c.f.*, [2]): (1) The only way to decrypt a value is to know the corresponding key. (2) An encrypted packet does not reveal the key under which it was encrypted. (3) There is sufficient redundancy in messages so that the decryption algorithm can detect whether the cipher-text was encrypted with a given key.

5.2   Implementing Locking in Open Environments

An implementation of locking in open environments is subject to the following requirements: (R1) Locked values should remain protected while in transit, on secondary media, or while in a third-party shared space. By protection we mean that only a process possessing a matching key may access fields. (R2) Matching should not reveal actual values or keys. (R3) It should not be possible to falsify entries.

In other words, (R1) implies that values should be, and remain, encrypted until fields are selected with the appropriate keys. (R2) implies that matching is performed on encrypted values. (R3) implies that if malicious site sees a request, it should not be possible for it to fabricate an object that matches it. This requirement is the hardest to satisfy.

We outline the proposed solution. Each symmetric lock key ℓ is represented by a pair (a, r) in which a is a symmetric cryptographic key and r is a random number. A compatible key $\overline{\ell}$ is the pair (a, r). A field $\ell : v$ locked under ℓ, is represented as the pair $K_a(v), r$. Each asymmetric lock key ℓ is represented by a triple (a_b, c_d, e) in which a_b and c_d are asymmetric cryptographic keys and e is a symmetric cryptographic key. The matching key $\overline{\ell}$ is (b_a, d_c, e). A field $\ell : v$ locked under asymmetric key ℓ is represented as the triple $(c_d, PK_{c_d}(a_b), PK_{a_b}(K_e(v)))$. Conversely, the value locked by $\overline{\ell}$ is $(d_c, PK_{d_c}(b_a), PK_{b_a}(K_e(v)))$. We require that $K_e(?) = null$ so that the server can recognize a request containing ?, but $PK_{b_a}(null) \neq null$ so that we can hide the fact that a request contains ? and thus prevent a replay attack by someone who sees the request and tries to reuse the key to fake further requests.

Fields are only decrypted during field selection, when a matching key is presented, e.g., $o.\overline{\ell}$. Otherwise objects are cryptographically protected.

Matching is performed on ciphertext values, the matching rules differ only on the determination of compatible fields. Here we say that fields are compatible if (1) in the case of symmetric locks: (1a) the encrypted fields are equal, (1b) the template is $(null, r)$ and the target is $(K_a(v), r)$. (2) For asymmetric keys, (2a) if the template is $(c_d, PK_{c_d}(a_b), PK_{a_b}(K_e(v)))$ and the target is $(d_c, PK_{d_c}(b_a), PK_{b_a}(K_e(v)))$ or (2b) if the template is $(c_d, PK_{c_d}(a_b), null)$ and the target is $(d_c, PK_{d_c}(b_a), PK_{b_a}(K_e(v)))$.

Clearly (R1) and (R2) are respected, but (R3) is only partially met. For a symmetric key, any process that sees a request may $K_a(v), r$ may create a false request $null, r$ that matches everything. For asymmetric keys we fare a little better, as seeing $(c_d, PK_{c_d}(a_b), PK_{a_b}(K_e(v)))$ does not suffice for an attacker to guess $(d_c, PK_{d_c}b_a, PK_{b_a}(K_e(v)))$, $(d_c, PK_{d_c}(b_a), PK_{b_a}(null))$ or $(c_d, PK_{c_d}(a_b), PK_{a_b}(null))$. But, seeing two different requests $(c_d, PK_{c_d}(a_b), PK_{a_b}(K_e(v_1)))$ and $(d_c, PK_{d_c}(b_a), PK_{b_a}(K_e(v_2)))$ is sufficient to be able to generate $(d_c, PK_{d_c}(b_a), PK_{b_a}(null))$ which represents an entry with a ? argument.

The solution means that we can give a cryptographic interpretation SECOS primitive, but their semantics is slightly weaker than in the typed interpretation. Of course, it is costly, since for every match at least one encryption and one decryption can take place. However, optimizations are possible. One does not program an internet application in the same way that one programs a local system. The programmer is likely to impose conventions on his use of remote spaces. For instance, he may decide to only send objects to sites that are trusted.

Alternatively, he might only send requests when the destination space is statically known; in this situation he encrypts each request with the public key of the destination host for that request [31]; this makes the need for the second pair of asymmetric keys (c_d, d_c) redundant since one can no longer identify requests containing ?. Fundamentally though, preventing replay attacks and thus avoiding the need for the extra encryption means employing mechanisms for protecting agent data from malicious hosts; this is still an open research area.

6 Related Work

The work of Gordon and Abadi has inspired some aspects of the theoretical treatment of SecOS. In the spi calculus, they extend the π-calculus to employ cryptography for messages sent over named channels [2]. Abadi also equates the security of a protocol to its type correctness [1]. While this is clearly applicable to protocols that consists of a predefined set of message exchanges, we do not see a direct relation to dynamic communication environments such as SecOS.

The Klaim language takes another approach to security. There, a process requires access rights (read or write) to use a tuple space [11]. Access rights are represented as types, and a *static* type analysis is sufficient to determine if a process attempts to read or write a tuple space without possessing the right. This approach complements our proposal. While dynamic checking is necessary in a mobile agent context, it is also important to investigate the class of security properties that can be verified in SecOS using a static approach such as Klaim's.

The role of typing in the matching process has received much attention recently. The Laura system, for instance, is a WAN service architecture based on the shared space model [27]. One reason why the shared space paradigm is exploited is that it allows services to join and leave the system dynamically. Services place offers in the space which are matched with requests. An offer or request is an *interface* form that matches if the type of the service is a subtype of the requestor's. Alice is the type system employed for matching these interfaces [25]. Dami also investigates type inference for generative communication [10].

As regards implementing the shared object paradigm in JAVA, we have already cited JavaSpaces [23] and Jada [9]. Jada is one example of the shared space paradigm being used to coordinate mobile agents: it is employed in the PageSpace agent architecture. More generally, neither Jada nor JavaSpaces were designed with security issues in mind. Though keys can be employed to protect items in the tuple from agents, this can only be done using encryption algorithms, even for agents executing within the same JVM which is too inefficient for generalized use.

Apart from JAVA, the shared space paradigm, usually in its Linda variant, has been integrated into several languages, C, Prolog [8], C++ [21], SmallTalk [18] and Eiffel [16]. Interestingly, the papers that treat object-oriented languages have not considered the security issues posed by inheritance and user defined matching.

7 Conclusions

In this paper, we have considered coordination support for independent and mistrusting software components that cooperate by means of shared object spaces. To this end, we presented a model that integrates the notion of keys into the shared space model. Security is enforced through typing. Further, the model can be implemented in JAVA provided that some care is taken with respect to aliasing and inheritance. Finally, we discussed the implementation of SECOS semantics using encryption for objects that leave a trusted SECOS environment, for instance, when they are transferred over a network or stored on disk.

References

1. M. Abadi. Secrecy by Typing in Security Protocols. *Theoretical aspects of Computer Software*, September 1998.
2. M. Abadi and A. D. Gordon. A calculus for cryptographic protocols: The Spi calculus. In *Proceedings of the Fourth ACM Conference on Computer and Communications Security, Zürich, April 1997*, 1997.
3. R. M. Amadio, I. Castellani, and D. Sangiorgi. On bisimulations for the asynchronous π-calculus. In U. Montanari and V. Sassone, editors, *CONCUR '96*, volume 1119 of *LNCS*, pages 147–162. Springer-Verlag, Berlin, 1996.
4. G. Boudol. Asynchrony and the π-calculus (note). Rapport de Recherche 1702, INRIA Sofia-Antipolis, May 1992.
5. L. Cardelli. Abstractions for mobile computations. Manuscript, Microsoft Research, 1998.
6. L. Cardelli and A. D. Gordon. Mobile ambients. In *Proc. of Foundations of Software Science and Computation Structures (FoSSaCS), ETAPS'98, LNCS 1378*, Mar. 1998.
7. N. Carriero, D. Gelernter, and L. Zuck. Bauhaus Linda. In P. Ciancarini, O. Nierstrasz, and A. Yonezawa, editors, *Object-Based Models and Languages for Concurrent Systems*, volume 924 of *LNCS*, pages 66–76. Springer-Verlag, Berlin, 1995.
8. P. Ciancarini. Distribued Programming with Logic Tuple Spaces. Technical Report UBLCS-93-7, The Technical University of Berlin, April 1993.
9. P. Ciancarini and D. Rossi. Jada: Coordination and Communication for Java Agents. In J. Vitek and C. Tschudin, editors, *Mobile Agent Systems: Towards the Programmable Internet*, volume 1222 of *LNCS*, 1997.
10. L. Dami. Type Inference and Subtyping in Higher-Order Generative Communication. In D. Tsichritzis, editor, *Object Applications*. University of Geneva, 1996.
11. R. DeNicola, G. Ferrari, and R. Pugliese. Coordinating Mobile Agents via Blackboards and Access Rights. In *Proc. 2nd Int. Conf. on Coordination Models and Languages*, volume 1282 of *LNCS*, September 1997.
12. C. Fournet, G. Gonthier, J.-J. Lévy, L. Maranget, and D. Rémy. A calculus of mobile agents. In *CONCUR96*, 1996.
13. D. Gelernter. Multiple Tuple Spaces in Linda. In E. Odijk, M. Rem, and J. Syre, editors, *Proc. Conf. on Parallel Architectures and Languages Europe (PARLE 89)*, volume 365 of *LNCS*. Springer-Verlag, Berlin, 1989.
14. K. Honda and M. Tokoro. On asynchronous communication semantics. In M. Tokoro, O. Nierstrasz, and P. Wegner, editors, *Object-Based Concurrent Computing. LNCS 612*, pages 21–51, 1992.

15. S. Hupfer. Melinda: Linda with multiple tuple spaces. Technical Report RR YALEU/DCS/R-766, Dept. of Computer Science, Yale University, New Haven, CT, 1990.

16. R. Jellinghaus. Eiffel Linda: an Object Oriented Linda Dialect. *ACM Sigplan Notices*, 25(12), December 1990.

17. G. Matos and J. Purtilo. Reconfiguration of hierarchical tuple spaces: Experiments with Linda-polylith. Technical report, University of Maryland.

18. S. Matsouka and S. Kawai. Using Tuple Space Communication in Distributed Object Oriented Languages. In *Proc. ACM Object Oriented Programming, Systems, Languages and Applications (OOPSLA 88)*, 1988.

19. J.-H. Morin and D. Konstantas. Hypernews: A MEDIA application for the commercialization of an electronic newspaper. In *Proceesings of SAC '98 - The 1998 ACM Symposium on Applied Computing*, Marriott Marquis, Atlanta, Georgia, U.S.A, Feb. 27 - Mar. 1 1998.

20. N. B. of Standards. The Data Encryption Standard. Technical Report Publication 46, Federal Information Processing Standards, January 1977.

21. A. Polze. The Object Space Approach: Decoupled Communication in C++. In *Proc. Technology of Object-Oriented Languages and Systems (TOOLS 93)*, 1993.

22. R. Rivest, A. Shamir, and L. Aldeman. A Method for Obtaining Digital Signatures and Public-Key Cryptosystems. *CACM*, 21(2), 1978.

23. Sun MicroSystems. JavaSpaces Specification. Technical report, Sun MicroSystems Inc., July 1998.

24. D. Tennenhouse. Active networks. In USENIX, editor, *2nd Symposium on Operating Systems Design and Implementation (OSDI '96), October 28–31, 1996. Seattle, WA*, 1996.

25. R. Tolksdorf. Alice - Basic Model and Subtyping Agents. Technical Report 1993/7, The Technical University of Berlin, 1993.

26. R. Tolksdorf. Coordinating Java Agents with Multiple Coordination Languages on the Berlinda Platform. In *IEEE Workshops on Enabling Technologies: Infrastructure for Collaborative Enterprises (WETICE)*, 1997.

27. R. Tolksdorf. Laura: A Service-Based Coordination Language. *Science of Computer Programming*, 31, 1998.

28. J. Vitek and C. Bryce. Secure Mobile Code: The JavaSeal experiment. In *submitted for publication*, 1999.

29. J. Vitek, C. Bryce, and W. Binder. Designing JavaSeal: or How to make Java safe for agents. In D. Tsichritzis, editor, *Electronic Commerce Objects*. University of Geneva, 1998.

30. J. Vitek and G. Castagna. A calculus of secure mobile computations. In *Proceedings of the IEEE Workshop on Internet Programming Languages, (WIPL)*. Chicago, Ill., 1998.

31. B. S. Yee. A sanctuary for mobile agents. Technical Report CS97-537, UC San Diego, Department of Computer Science and Engineering, Apr. 1997.

Coordination with Attributes

Alan Wood

Department of Computer Science
University of York
wood@cs.york.ac.uk

Abstract. This paper addresses the opportunities for, and effects of, incorporating object attributes in LINDA-like tuple-space systems. The focus is on exploring how the coordination attributes are affected by this enhancement, and investigating in what ways the classical LINDA model needs to be modified. Particular emphasis is placed on the potential *practical* gains to be expected in both performance and expressibility, with consideration being given to methods for implementing attribute frameworks in open distributed systems.

1 Introduction

The concept of coordination could not be claimed to be 'new' — even in the narrow domain of computing, and its sub-domain of concurrency, the need to coordinate things has been around a long time. However, it is only relatively recently that coordination has been identified as a topic for independent study, and which promises to unify several apparently disparate fields in computing.

In their 1992 paper [6], Carriero and Gelernter crystalised this idea by identifying the *two* functions of a "full" programming language as *computation* and *coordination*, and suggesting that these two aspects of a language are *orthogonal*. Consequently, the study of coordination may be undertaken *independently of* any host computation technology.

Once the idea of coordination being distinct from computation is accepted, the question arises as to what the coordination *structures* are. These would be analogous to the control and data structures in the *computation* half of a language. Some coordination structures have been in common use for many years: semaphores, monitors, signals (in the UNIX sense). Others have been emerging from the increased *use* of parallel and distributed architectures ... examples might be light-weight threads, message-passing, or barrier-synchronisation.

This paper addresses coordination problems in *open distributed systems*, which are to be contrasted with *closed* systems. The distinction lies in the fact that in an open system agents (processes) can 'join' or 'leave' during the lifetime of the system with no prior knowledge of their (potential) existence necessarily being available to the other agents. From the point of view of a programmer, or more importantly a *compiler*, full information about the behaviour of the system while his/her/its process is executing cannot be determined. In a closed system, however, such information is in principle available, and can be used by a compiler, say, to optimise the process ensemble. The open system model is that of the internet; the closed system is that of a subset of processors in a box, with only a single parallel program running.

1.1 Object Attributes

Objects have a number of properties associated with them — indeed, it is the set of properties that *define* an object. In a computational context, perhaps the most fundamental properties are *value* and *type*. However, there are other properties which are normally associated with objects including their *scope* (or visibility), updatability, or other accessibility features. Although these are some obvious concrete examples, attributes should be seen as a collection of abstract properties associated with objects. This view admits the possibility of having attributes which may be user-defined (and, consequently, would need to be user-maintained), rather than fixed by the system.

1.2 LINDA

Since this paper addresses some *general* aspects of coordination, while suggesting practical ways of implementing them, trying to relate the ideas to the diversity of current coordination languages would almost certainly obscure the issues. Therefore, only one coordination system will be used as a focus for the ideas presented — LINDA. There are two main reasons for choosing LINDA. Firstly, it is (probably) the earliest explicitly 'coordinative' language, and (certainly) one of the best-known of the current coordination languages. Secondly, it is a very flexible model which subsumes most others (although, as shall be seen later, it still has some deficiencies in its coordinative features).

However, many of the issues raised here are not LINDA-specific — indeed, much of the point of the paper is in identifying 'purely' coordinative issues which exist independently of any specific coordination model.

The LINDA model considered here is the 'classical' one [5], with in, out, rd, and eval primitives extended to work with multiple tuple spaces.

1.3 Motivation

In LINDA-like systems, agents (processes) coordinate by means of *generative communication* [8]. This term is intended to suggest that the 'carrier particles' of coordination are created by agents, but then have existence independent of their creators.[1] Using this medium, LINDA is able to provide (nearly) all the coordination mechanisms normally used in parallel processing situations. There are other ways of achieving coordination which do not fall neatly into the category of data communications, as will be seen later. However, why should they be needed? There are two reasons:

---

[1] This is in contrast to conventional synchronous message-passing communication models in which the message only has a fleeting existence at the instant of synchronisation. It therefore cannot exist independently of the sender and receiver.

1. There are coordination tasks which are *not* supported by the model.
2. There are also some coordination tasks arising quite naturally which, although supported in the 'classical' LINDA framework, give rise to significant inefficiencies[2] under the classical model. This in itself is not a sufficient reason to support any proposed modifications to the LINDA model, since any change introduces extra complexity which must be weighed carefully against the potential benefits.

Examples of both of these types of task will be described in Sect. 2.1.

2 The Design Space

The objects that we shall be concentrating on are *tuple-spaces*, and *tuples*, although it is possible also to consider tuple *elements* as being candidates for attribute-based coordination. There is a wide variety of possible object attributes that could be incorporated in an attribute-based coordination scheme, and some of the more unusual candidates might include persistence and fault-tolerance, types, and costs. However, in this paper we shall focus on the widely-understood access attributes, which are analogous to those found in conventional file-systems.

The choice of objects, together with the set of attributes gives rise to a 'design space' formed from the object and attribute 'axes'. This space then enables the issues of semantics, implementability, expressibility etc. to be addressed when assessing which modifications to the LINDA model are required.

2.1 Access-control Attributes in LINDA

The object axis of the design space is clearly defined above — tuples, tuple-spaces, and tuple elements. The attributes will include the right to perform the appropriate LINDA access operations on the objects — in, rd, and out — which approximately correspond to read and write permissions on files in conventional systems.[3] However there are other operations which are performed on objects in a LINDA-like system which must also be considered.

Figure 1 displays the part of the design space determined by these objects and attributes. A tick ($\checkmark$) implies that a sensible meaning can be assigned to that attribute:object pair; a bullet ($\bullet$) suggests that that pairing is incompatible; a question mark (?) indicates those pairings for which it is not clear that there is a sensible use, but might prove useful in some situations.

---

[2] Here, 'inefficiency' is to be taken in a broad sense, which will include run-time performance, but will also encompass *programming* or *software engineering* inefficiencies. An example of the latter would be a perceived need for tuples output by an agent to have additional information 'just in case' some other agent *might* require this extra information.

[3] This correspondence is not exact since there is now a distinction between copying content from an object, and *removing* content, which has no direct analogue for file systems.

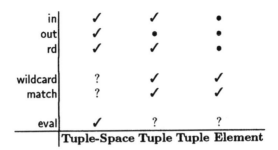

	Tuple-Space	Tuple	Element
in	✓	✓	•
out	✓	•	•
rd	✓	✓	•
wildcard	?	✓	✓
match	?	✓	✓
eval	✓	?	?

Fig. 1. The design space

The attributes can be placed in the following groups based on their effects:

out, in, rd It is easy to see that out, rd and in attributes applied to tuple-spaces make sense — if a tuple-space has that attribute then an agent can access it accordingly, otherwise that type of access is prevented.

With individual *tuples*, only in and rd can apply — corresponding to permission to remove or copy that tuple, respectively — since outing to a tuple is not defined.[4] Similarly, neither in nor rd nor out can be applied to tuple elements.

wildcard and match

The lack of wildcard permission on a tuple element would prevent an in or rd operation form retrieving that tuple if the operation's template specified a *formal* for that element. By extension, this would be applicable to whole tuples and tuple-spaces, affecting actual:formal matching on all elements of a tuple, and all tuples, respectively.

The match attribute is the dual of wildcard: its lack would imply that *only* actual:formal matches would succeed, and actual:actual matching would not.

eval

Permission to place an active tuple into a tuple-space is controlled by the eval attribute. This is clearly meaningful when applied to tuple-spaces, although it can also be of use when applied to individual tuples, as will be discussed later.

2.2 Semantic Implications

Extending the LINDA model with an attribute framework will of course change the semantics — there now exist properties that could not be achieved previously. However, these attributes might be purely *extensions*, that is they do not modify the semantics of the underlying model, or they might necessitate a revision of the underlying semantics.

In the first group — those which do *not* change the model — are all of the 'ticked' entries in the first five rows of the design space, except for the out attribute. For instance, due to the non-determinism in LINDA, a process would not

---

[4] If there were some sort of update operator, then this attribute could be applied to a tuple — it would prevent or allow updating.

be able to detect the difference between a rd which is blocked due to a tuple being unavailable in tuple-space, and being blocked due to a tuple (or tuple-space) denying rd permission. Similarly for the in, wildcard, and match attributes. However, with out the situation is different. If a tuple-space denies out permission to a process, then one of two outcomes could result depending on the implementation. Either the out operation *fails*, in which case the host *computational language* must have some exception mechanism to deal with this, or the operation *blocks*. Both of these represent changes to the user's view of the model's semantics. In the first case, the independence of the computational and coordination languages is broken. In the second, a fundamental alteration in the semantics of out has been forced — out *never blocks* in the standard LINDA model. Unfortunately, there is no clear choice between the two alternatives — to rely on integrating the LINDA coordination system with a host's exception mechanism would, at least, mean that existing LINDA programs would need modifying. On the other hand, enforcing a 'blocking out' semantics would introduce subtle (and not so subtle) problems in using existing techniques for analysing and designing LINDA process ensembles.[5] The problem of choosing between the two alternatives will be side-stepped in this paper by considering that processes are so well-behaved that there will be no attempt to do an operation that would be prevented by an attribute. In this way we shall be able to concentrate on the new coordination structures made available by incorporating an attribute framework into LINDA. There is, therefore, further work to be done in this area.

The following sections will consider only the basic access-control attributes in the examples. However, it is hoped that by discussing some of the other aspects of the basic 'design space', a feel for the potential improvements in expressiveness brought about by the introduction of an attribute framework can be gained.

3 Attribute-Supported Coordination Structures

The purpose of a coordination language is to enable the expression of coordination structures in the same way that a computation language supports the definition of control and data structures — both are means for specifying *algorithmically* the interactions between component objects that are composed to achieve a task. Deciding what constitutes a coordination structure is, however, rather awkward since there is no body of coordination theory to compare with the theory of computation. Consequently, an informal definition will be used here — a coordination structure describes and governs the temporal and spatial interactions between agents, without reference to their internal computational structure.

This formulation leaves some 'grey areas' at the interface between computation and coordination, but will suffice for the purposes of this paper since the examples used will be firmly coordinative.

Given the the difficulty in defining what constitutes a coordination structure, it is perhaps rather unfair to suggest that LINDA is deficient in its ability to ex-

---

[5] It would, for instance, affect questions of deadlock and termination.

press some coordination structures — it could be argued that such structures are *not* coordination structures, and therefore that LINDA is not deficient. However, at least one facility which appears in other non-LINDA coordination languages (for example IWIM [3]), the provision of private or point-point communication, cannot be implemented using the classical LINDA model. Consequently, there is a *prima facie* case that the classical LINDA model requires some enhancement. The rest of this section investigates such an enhancement.

The following two sections give examples of the types of coordination patterns or structures that become available once an attribute system is incorporated into LINDA. The first section addresses those structures that are generated by the basic access-control attributes discussed in Sect. 2.1. Section 3.2 touches on attributes which do not address access control, but which may affect the ways in which a process ensemble behaves.

As mentioned before, all these coordination patterns can be split into those which could be achieved before but are now more efficient, and those which were previously unavailable.

3.1   Access-control Attributes

In this section, two attribute-supported coordination structures are described. In order to do so without preempting the discussion in Sect. 4 on implementation choices, the notation used for expressing attributes is simplistic: only the attributes applicable to the structures are shown, and these are in, rd, and out, which are represented by their initial letters. Attributes are grouped into the two *domains* which are applicable — the owner or creator, and all others, respectively. In a full system there could be a large number of domains, defined in a variety of ways (see the discussion in Sect. 4).

In the code examples, tuples are assigned access attributes by decorating the out operation's tuple parameter with the required attributes. Tuple-spaces are created with the `tsc` primitive, which is extended to take an attribute set as a parameter.

Private Channels — a new coordination structure in LINDA It is often the case that (subsets of) agents need to establish means by which they can communicate without any interference from other agents in the system. Many coordination languages have explicit structures for setting up such 'private channels' — indeed, private, point-to-point communication is the *only* means of coordination in most common coordination systems. In LINDA-like systems, however, the coordination model is based on *broadcast* communication through tuple spaces which is more general, but less 'secure'. The lack of security can be demonstrated by considering a pair of agents which wish to coordinate by the communication of some tuple. Agent 1 outs the tuple into a tuple-space, and Agent 2 ins the tuple, *by specifying a matching template*. Unfortunately (for the purposes of a private conversation), there is nothing to prevent a third agent removing the tuple — and this could happen *accidentally* (as well as maliciously).

This problem is not solved by the mere addition of multiple tuple-spaces — some means has to be provided to make such tuple spaces *privately scoped*. The solution is to make use of access control attributes. It will be seen that attributes attached to both tuples and tuple-spaces will be needed.

A sketch of the core of the method is shown in Fig. 2, with the skeleton of the required code (in a C-like syntax) given in Fig. 3. One agent (process P_1 in the example) broadcasts that fact that it is willing to engage in a private conversation by placing a tuple containing a reference to a tuple-space (of which it is the creator) in UTS. The tuple has rd-only access to all other agents. This prevents any accidental or malicious *removal* of the tuple, which is the first part of the guarantee against interference in setting up the private channel.

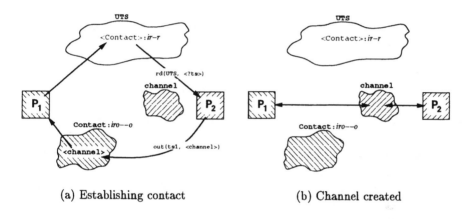

(a) Establishing contact   (b) Channel created

Fig. 2. Creating a private channel using access attributes (shading matches a tuple-space with its creator.)

The tuple-space, Contact, is intended to be the means by which the other agent (P_2) informs P_1 of a reference to the private-channel (which is a tuple-space known only to the two agents involved). Contact is created with out-only access with respect to all other agents, so that its contents cannot be altered by any other agent. This gives the second part of the guarantee against accidental or malicious interference in the process of setting up a private channel — no third-party would be able to gain knowledge of a reference to the 'private-channel' tuple space which is passed in a tuple in Contact.

Once channel has been created and its reference passed to P_1 via Contact, P_1 and P_2 have a secure means for coordination.

Global Software Distribution — an application of access attributes
This example of the use of access-control attributes shows how private channels, scoped tuple-spaces and controlled access to tuples can be combined to

```
Contact = tsc( iro--o );              channel = tsc( iroiro );
out( UTS, <Contact>:ir-r);            contact = rd( UTS, <?ts> );
channel = in(Contact, <?ts>);         out( Contact, <channel>:irir );
/* Use channel */                     /* Use channel */
```

(a) Process P_1 (b) Process P_2

Fig. 3. Skeleton code for Fig. 2

provide an architecture for the 'hard media free' distribution of software. In addition, if some further technological problems were to be solved together with the opportunities for *caching*, this architecture could provide a platform for the fully distributed operating systems of the 'Network Computer' type [16], or the 'Millennium Project' [4].

When a user acquires a piece of software from a producer, whether by paying money to a commercial supplier or by copying it from a free source, several things must happen. Firstly, the potential user must know *how* to acquire it — its existence, who can supply it, how to contact the supplier, etc. Secondly, a request for the software must be made to the supplier — this will involve different protocols depending on whether or not money must change hands, whether the software is shareware or freeware, whether or not a formal licence is required, etc. Next, the user must obtain a copy of the software — normally on hard media if commercial, or electronically if free/shareware. Finally the user must install it.

This method of distribution works reasonably well, but it has several problems including:

- Bug fixes — as bugs are found, all previously distributed copies must be replaced. In practice this is so difficult logistically, and commercially, that it is never done.
- Media Waste — each new customer requires a new piece of media which is often discarded after installation.
- Piracy — any distributable medium, and its contents, can be cloned.

Now consider how a tuple-space based system, with access-control attributes, might be used to overcome these problems, while admitting some new possibilities. Figure 4 outlines the skeleton of such a system.

The configuration in the lower part of Fig. 4, involving the customers C_1 and C_2, the Production agent (part of the vendor), and tuple-space V1, represents the goal — a number of users of version 1 of the software, which is stored as a set of tuples in V1. V1 can only be modified by Production, and is only known to the vendor and the authorized customers.

The upper part of the figure shows how a new customer would acquire access to the software. The situation shown is that C_3 wants version 2 of the software, in

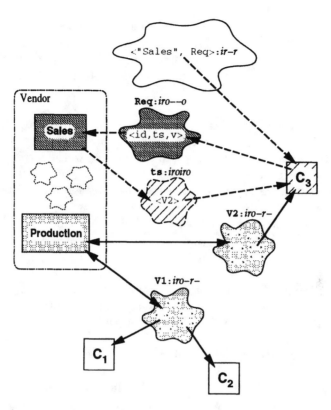

Fig. 4. The use of access attributes in a global software distribution system. (Shading is used to associate tuple spaces with their creator.)

which case it would communicate with the Sales agent of the vendor via a private channel established using the protocol described in Sect. 3.1. The information passed to Sales would be the customer's id, the version of the software wanted, and the private-channel tuple-space reference. Once Sales is satisfiedthat C_3 is entitled to the software, it would obtain a reference to the appropriate tuple-space from Production (using private channels local to the Vendor), and pass this to the customer. Then C_3 would be in a situation similar to customers C_1 and C_2, but with access to version 2.

This method for distribution does not depend on the actual representation of the software as tuples in the tuple-space. In the simplest case it would be possible to have the entire piece of software as an element of a tuple. Then authorized customers (those with a reference to the tuple-space) could either copy the software to local storage, or run the software from the tuple-space (in effect 'copying' it by means of their system's program loader). This would require no fundamental alteration to the way in which the software would be installed and used ... only the method of delivery would have changed.

However, by representing the software as a *set* of tuples, a number of novel possibilities for software architectures can be considered. The tuples might then correspond to library routines (as in pre-'object-oriented' systems), objects, or services (as in operating systems). Some of the potential advantages of this arrangement are:

Bug fixes. When modifications to the software are required that don't imply a new full release, only those components that require correcting need be replaced. An *update* of a tuple (routine or object) would correspond to the Production agent removing the original version (using an in), and outing the replacement. Therefore, a completely up to date version of the software would always be available to both existing and new customers — management of bug-fixes by the vendor would become relatively trivial.

Copy protection. A degree of copy protection — more accurately, copy *discouragement* — becomes available. It is likely that most of the tuples accessed by customers would contain 'interface' routines, or 'wrappers' which call other services/objects. Within a tuple-space based system, these lower-level routines would be accessed via tuple-space operations as would the routines that they require. Consequently, it would not be necessary to have the *complete* code for the software existing in the customer-accessible tuple-space — much of the system could exist in tuple-spaces local to the vendor which is only accessed by the *code* of the routines contained in the customer tuple-space. This has two effects. Firstly, since only the 'interface' tuples formats need be made known to the user, it would be practically difficult to take a copy of the *entirety* of the tuple-space, since this would require being able to specify templates to match *every* tuple, and this would not in general be possible. Secondly, even if a complete copy of the tuple-space's contents were able to be made, which is doubtful, there would be no simple way of obtaining copies of the lower-level routines.[6]

The execution model resulting from this system is similar to demand-paging — the routine (code) for the required service is loaded by rding the appropriate tuple. When the execution of this routine caused the retrieval of the contents of further tuples this would be equivalent to 'demand' loading the required code — the newly loaded code could then retrieve code-tuples itself, and so on. This could form the basis of a Network Computer style of operating system in which the operating system's services were represented as code contained in tuples.

However, currently this execution model would not be feasible since it implies a *single* source of the code, which would be frequently accessed by a very large number of agents. A single tuple-space could not cope. For this to work a very efficient caching and replication scheme would need to be implemented.

---

[6] This would at least require disassembling the routines' code to determine all the references to vendor's local tuple-spaces. Even then this would not necessarily be the end of the unethical copier's task, as the routines thus copied could call the contents of tuples in yet other unknown tuple spaces.

If the caching and replication problems were satisfactorily solved, then this execution model could be comparable in efficiency to the disk-based demand-paging schemes in common use.

3.2 Other Attributes

The previous sections have shown, in detail, how *access-control* attributes can be used to significantly enhance a system's coordinative vocabulary. It has been argued that, despite focusing on LINDA-like systems, incorporating such an attribute framework is *generally* useful in any coordination language. However, once the notion of attribute-based coordination is admitted, there are many attributes other than access-control that might be considered — often these will be more or less specific to the actual coordination platform being used. Two examples, which are of particular interest in LINDA systems are:

Ordering It is sometimes the case that the order of insertion of tuples into a tuple-space is important to an agent retrieving those tuples. For instance, if the tuple-space were to represent a keyboard buffer, then the order in which the tuples are inserted would reflect the order in which the keys were pressed. Consequently, the tuple-space (or its controlling LINDA kernel) would need to maintain sequence information. This could be specified as an attribute of the tuple space.

In the absence of attribute-supported ordering, this would have to be emulated when needed by the inserting agent producing a sequence number as an extra element in the tuples that it outs.

Other coordination systems will have similar examples.

Non-determinism LINDA's associative access mechanism is *non-deterministic*. However, this is not the same thing as *random* access, which is related to the *fairness* attributes of the system. Consider a process which repeatedly executes a rd of a tuple-space containing several tuples which match the rd's template. LINDA's non-determinism ensures that the process cannot predict which tuple it will receive, but LINDA's semantics does not prevent the kernel supplying the *same* tuple every time.[7]

A random access scheme, on the other hand, would identify *all* candidate tuples and randomly choose one to be returned. This would guarantee fairness over a sufficiently large number of repeated accesses. In some circumstances an improved *performance* can be obtained with a random system compared with a purely non-deterministic implementation [7], Therefore, 'random choice' is an example of a useful behaviour-modifying attribute.

---

[7] This is not only semantically valid, but highly likely in practice — the 'natural' way for a LINDA kernel to represent a tuple-space is as a list. Then a retrieval operation would return the first tuple in the list that matches. Repeating the operation would merely find the same tuple again.

4   Implementation Considerations

So far attributes have been represented abstractly as a set of flags attached to representations of the objects. This has enabled discussion of the issues without being concerned with how the abstractions are actually to be implemented. In fact, if the only attributes were access-control, and it were only necessary to distinguish an object's creator from other agents, then the implementation would follow this representation. However, in the context of open distributed systems, it will be necessary to provide a level of attribute control that is both more general, and finer, than can be achieved with this simple model. This section discusses the implementation issues and alternatives in the open system environment.

4.1   Conventional Approaches

There are two approaches to the implementation of access (and other) attributes described in the standard operating systems literature (see for example [12, 17, 18]).

Access Control Lists The first approach is essentially that assumed in the earlier sections of this paperin which an object, generally a file or device, has attached to it a list of sets of attributes. Each set in the list represents the attributes that are appropriate for a given *domain* of agents when accessing the object. In UNIX there are three domains — the owner, a 'group', and all others. This method of implementing attributes is called the *Access Control List* (ACL). The exact means by which the domains are defined and maintained will vary from system to system.

Capabilities In the second method, each domain holds rights to the object's attributes that it requires, rather than the object maintaining a list of domains' attribute rights. If a domain needs to perform some action on an object, it requests the right to do so from the object. If the request is granted, the object returns an unforgeable 'passport' — a *capability*[8] — which identifies the domain, the object, and the rights granted. When an element of the domain (a process) needs to perform some action on the object, it presents the object with a copy of the capability along with the access request so the object can determine whether the process possesses the right to do the requested action.

Although the technique still encompasses the idea of a domain consisting of several elements, in practice it is normal to have a capability *per process* and to identify domains with processes.

These two techniques have several complementary attributes. Summarising the pros and cons (+ and − respectively) of ACLs and capabilities:

---

[8] As far as the domain's elements (processes) are concerned this would be some 'opaque' bit-string. For full details of how this is implemented, see the references [18].

ACLs

+ **Applicable to un-named objects.** Therefore they can be used with tuples, tuple elements, and tuple-spaces.
- **Require distributed domain management.** This limits the flexibility and increases complexity.
- **Require arbitrarily large lists attached to each object.** This is not practical, *especially* in an open system.
- **The set of applicable attributes is fixed by the system,** since each ACL element must account for the attribute *set* for that domain.

Capabilities

+ **Easily implemented in an open distributed system.** Agents store their own set of capabilities, putting no storage overhead on the objects to which they refer.
- **Cannot easily *withdraw* permission,** or otherwise modify a capability once granted.
- **Cannot be used with anonymous objects.** This limits their use to tuple-spaces alone.

Therefore there is no clear choice between the two methods for an open distributed tuple-space system, and so a compromise solution must be found. Since there is no choice but to use ACLs for tuples and tuple elements, it is proposed that the simple, two domain ACL system implicitly used in Sect. 3 be implemented — the domains being *creator*, and *others*.

For tuple-spaces, however, a capability system should be used for several reasons:

Firstly, the lack of 'domain flexibility' inherent in the use of ACLs for tuple-space contents can be overcome by designing process ensembles to use tuple-spaces (with capabilities) as the prime means of attribute-control thereby regaining access to the richness of domains that is a feature of capability-based systems. Secondly, user-defined attributes can easily be handled — a kernel needs only to know that an attribute *exists* in order for it to be able to grant, and verify, a capability for that attribute. Finally, a capability-based scheme is not restricted to a fixed set of attributes — this set may change over time, which is essential for an open system since its life-span might be very long. The protocols described in the literature for managing capabilities are quite straight-forward, and are easily transferred to a tuple-space based system.

Secondly, there are four important features that this capability scheme has which positively affect the implementation:

1. The kernel is only involved in generating and checking capabilities — initially deciding whether or not an agent is to be granted some attribute rights to an object is the responsibility of the object's creator.
2. All the information required to generate capabilities (object identity, agent identity, etc.) would naturally exist in any 'conventional' LINDA kernels.

3. Since all LINDA operations must be serviced by the kernel, the only overhead involved in incorporating a capability-based scheme is the extra communication costs due to the need to provide the capability in addition to the other parameters in an operation.
4. No information regarding capabilities need be stored in the kernel — the information contained in the capability itself is sufficient for the kernel to asses its validity for the specified object.

The remaining problem with capabilities is more awkward to solve — withdrawing an agent's capability for an object is difficult. Several methods have been reported which all result in revoking the capability of *all* agents for a particular object. Any finer degree of control seems very difficult to achieve. However, it is most likely that, in a LINDA-like system, the only need to revoke a capability would be when the creator (or one of its proxies — agents which have been given creator capability) needs to block access temporarily — for example, if it needs to 'freeze' a tuple-space when doing a series of operations. In this case, a request to the kernel to temporarily withdraw non-creator access permission would be sufficient — all processes would merely block until the permission were reinstated.

5 Related Work

The deficiencies in LINDA, in particular the inability to express directed, or point to point, communication have been noted by several authors. In general the response has been to propose entirely new systems (or existing systems extended to work in a distributed environment) which overcome the perceived deficiencies, but at the expense of losing the advantages that LINDA-like systems have over many of the proposals in the area of open systems.

An example of an attempt to solve the LINDA problems by improving LINDA, is that of Pinakis's Joyce-Linda [13]. The focus was solely on the directed communication (private channels) problem, and developed a solution which was based on a type of public-key encryption technique inspired by the capability-like 'port' concept in an early version of the Amoeba operating system. There are, therefore, strong links with the ideas presented in Sect. 4 regarding implementation of the attribute framework. However, Pinakis's solution had difficulties in communicating "tickets" (his proto-capabilities) through tuple-space securely, since a basic attribute of ticket values was that they could not be matched by formals in templates. Consequently he had to resort to the rather unsatisfactory solution of introducing a second special data type (tickets being the first) to which ticket values could be coerced, and hence matched by formals. Hence it can be seen that his implementation incorporated some of the attributes of the capability-based implementation of the attribute framework discussed here. Finally, the Joyce-Linda system "relies on the compiler and runtime system", and therefore would be difficult to adapt to the *open* systems problems addressed in this paper.

Two proposals taking the more radical approach to the LINDA deficiencies are those of Law Governed LINDA [11], and ActorSpace [2]. Minsky and Leichter's motivation in developing Law Governed LINDA was to address LINDA's "inherent lack of safety", specifically citing its inability to support "pair-wise communication" (private channels). The reason why they do not abandon LINDA completely is that they regard it as "particularly suitable as a coordination model for open systems", and that it is by implication merely the lack of safety that prevents it from being more widely used. They identify the principal safety problem as the need for component processes in an ensemble to rely on "voluntary conventions" regarding tuple/template formats and hence tuple-space accessing. This mode of operation is just acceptable for closed systems, but cannot be expected to work in open systems. Therefore they propose to replace these voluntary rules with globally enforceable 'laws'. This is to be achieved by the system assigning a 'controller' to *each process* which mediates between the process and the system, thereby ensuring adherence to the built-in law.

Again there are parallels with the attribute framework described in earlier sections — in this case there is a rough duality between LGL and the attribute framework. Whereas LGL's integrity is maintained by the *agents* (or their controllers in conjunction with the system), in the attribute framework the control resides with the *objects* (in conjunction with the kernel). Which system has the performance/resource advantage would depend on the relative complexities of the controlling components and the relative numbers of objects and agents.

The LGL system is very powerful and the laws that can be expressed are extremely general. The authors do comment, however, that the efficiency of the system is still to be determined.

The ActorSpace proposal of Agha and Callsen [2] also criticises LINDA for its insecurity, but makes no attempt to fix LINDA, preferring to develop Agha's Actors [1] to work in the open distributed environment. The result is a new coordination language, rather more complex than LINDA, in which the focus is on a 'generalized' direct (point to point) communication based on a pattern matching mechanism. The patterns which are involved in the match in essence define attributes in the sense used in this paper. In their proposal, the authors make the case for attribute-based control of system activity, and choose to provide security by means of capabilities. Their work is therefore in several ways directly comparable to that described in this paper, only using a different coordination basis.

6 Conclusion

It has been argued that an attribute framework is necessary for complete coordination in open distributed systems. In particular, access-control attributes have been shown to be *essential* for LINDA-like tuple-space systems to be able to provide at least one coordination structure — private channels — that could not be achieved previously. Other desirable coordination attributes also emerge from such an attribute framework.

The implementation proposed is a mixed system combining both Access Control Lists when necessary, with Capabilities when possible. It has been argued that a capability-based implementation is particularly natural in the context of LINDA.

The ideas discussed in this paper are being implemented in the latest in the series of LINDA kernels [14, 15] developed at York. This will also incorporate recent advances in distributed resource management (in particular, garbage collection [9]) and the confluence of Input/Output with the LINDA model [10].

References

[1] G. Agha. *Actors: A Model of Concurrent Computation in Distributed Systems.* MIT Press, 1986.

[2] G. Agha and C.J. Callsen. ActorSpace: An Open Distributed Programming Paradigm. *SIGPLAN Notices*, 28(7):23–32, 1993.

[3] F. Arbab. The IWIM Model for Coordination of Concurrent Activities. In P. Ciancarini and C. Hankin, editors, *Coordination Languages and Models*, volume LNCS-1061, pages 34–56. Springer-Verlag, 1996.

[4] W.J. Bolosky, R.P. Draves, R.P. Fitzgerald, C.W. Fraser, M.B. Jones, T.B. Knoblock, and R. Rashid. Operating System Directions for the Next Millennium. http://www.research.microsoft.com/research/os/Millennium/mgoals.html, 1996.

[5] N. Carriero and D. Gelernter. *How to Write Parallel Programs: A First Course.* MIT Press, 1990.

[6] N. Carriero and D. Gelernter. Coordination Languages and their Significance. *Communications of the ACM*, 35(2):97–106, 1992.

[7] D. Edwards. Genetic Algorithms in LINDA. Technical report, University of York, Department of Computer Science, 1997.

[8] D. Gelernter. Generative Communications in LINDA. *ACM Trans. Programming Languages and Systems*, 7:80, 1985.

[9] R. Menezes and A. Wood. Garbage Collection in Open Distributed Tuple-Space Systems. In *Proc. 15th Brazilian Computer Networks Symposium — SBRC'97*, 1997.

[10] R. Menezes and A. Wood. Incorporating Input/Output Operations in Linda. In *submitted to 30th Hawaii International Conference on System Science*, 1998.

[11] N.H. Minsky and J. Leichter. Law-Governed Linda as a Coordination Model. In P. Ciancarini, O. Nierstrasz, and A. Yonezawa, editors, *Object-Based Models and Languages for Concurrent Systems*, volume LNCS-924, pages 125–146, 1995.

[12] J.L. Petersen and A. Silberschatz. *Operating System Concepts.* Addison-Wesley, 1985.

[13] J. Pinakis. Providing Directed Communication in LINDA. In *Proc. 15th Australian Computer Science Conference*, pages 731–743, 1992.

[14] A. Rowstron, A. Douglas, and A.Wood. A distributed LINDA-like kernel for PVM. In *Proc. Euro PVM*, pages 107–112. Hermes, 1995.

[15] A. Rowstron and A.M. Wood. An Efficient Distributed Tuple Space Implementation for Networks of Workstations. In L. Bougé, P. Fraigniaud, A. Mignotte, and Y. Robert, editors, *EuroPar'96*, volume LNCS-1123, pages 510–513. Springer-Verlag, 1996.

[16] D. Simpson. Who Needs a Network Computer. *Datamation*, 42(16):96–99, 1996.

[17] A.S. Tanenbaum. *Modern Operating Systems.* Prentice Hall, 1992.

[18] A.S. Tanenbaum. *Distributed Operating Systems.* Prentice Hall, 1995.

MobiS: A Specification Language for Mobile Systems

Cecilia Mascolo

Department of Computer Science, University of Bologna,
Mura Anteo Zamboni ,7, I-40127 Bologna (Italy)
phone: +39 51 354871, fax: +39 51 354510
e-mail: {mascolo}@cs.unibo.it

Abstract. New formal languages have been proposed for the specification of mobility aspects of systems and for understanding the recent devised technologies for mobile computing.

In this paper we introduce MobiS, a specification language based on a tuple-spaces based model which specifies coordination by multiset rewriting. We show how MobiS can be flexibly used to specify architectures containing mobile components and give formalization of some common mobility paradigms.

We explore the styles we introduce showing how they model the software architecture of a "Purchasing System", a case study in electronic commerce.

1 Introduction

Modern network technologies based on mobile computers and devices, and programming languages for the Internet like Java require novel software design techniques. An important feature in network-aware applications is mobility. Since there are several kind of entities that can be mobile, like for instance data, code, agents, operating environments, an issue designers have to face is the description of the entities that can move and the justification of why and when they should move. New formal languages are being proposed in order to specify mobile entities; a short list includes Bauhaus [3], Ambit [2], Join Calculus [8], Klaim [6], and Mobile Unity [13]. These languages can be used to describe and analyze software architectures including mobile entities. Mobility can range from mobility of data, as in client-server architectures, to mobility of code, as in applications including Java applets, to mobility of agents, as in some applications for virtual shopping, to mobility of whole operating environments, as in platforms including mobile hardware. The increasing diffusion of systems including mobile components suggests the formalization of new architectural styles based on mobility paradigms [9], using special languages for specifying mobile systems [7].

In this paper we study some architectural styles for mobility. We present such styles using MobiS, a specification language based on a coordination model with hierarchical tuple-spaces and multiset rewriting. We show how MobiS can be used for specifying and reasoning on different mobile entities, clarifying their properties and features.

We introduce an original classification aiming at precisely defining several different types of mobile entities. The paper [9] defines a general taxonomy for systems including mobility; the paper shows a classification of mobility in three dimensions: technologies, paradigms, and applications. We focus on paradigms and present a more fine grained taxonomy merging the handling of code and execution state mobility to the handling of the data (this is the terminology in [9]).

This paper has the following structure. In Section 2 we introduce the MobiS language. Section 3 contains the description of the mobile paradigms and their MobiS formal specification. Section 4 contains the specification of the software architecture of a Purchasing System as an instance of some mobility styles we define. In Section 5 we list some related work, draw conclusions and illustrate our current work.

2 Overview of MobiS

MobiS is an extended version of PoliS, a specification language based on multiple tuple spaces [5]. MobiS specifications are hierarchically structured: a MobiS specification denotes a tree of nested spaces that dynamically evolves in time. Spaces are first class entities, and can move, namely they can change their position in the tree.

The typical structure of a MobiS specification is graphically shown in Figure 1 (First Step). In such a figure the structure of the tree represents the hierarchical structure of the nested tuple-spaces. The environment contains two "Hosts" (*Host*1 and *Host*2). "Host1" contains an "Agent". Formally, a MobiS space can contain three types of tuples: *ordinary tuples*, which are ordered sequences of values, *program tuples*, which represent code, and *space tuples*, which represent spaces.

A program tuple can modify a space removing and adding tuples (and therefore spaces). However, a program tuple can only handle the tuples of the space it belongs to *and* the tuples of its parent space. This constraint defines both the "input" and the "output" environment of any tuple. The action of the program tuple is performed atomically. A program tuple ("*r*" : *R*) refers to a rule *R* that defines which reaction can take place. A rule can act either on the tuples of the space in which it resides or on the tuples of the parent space: we call these spaces the *rule scope*. A rule reads and consumes tuples in its scope, performs a sequential computation, and produces new tuples in its scope. Formally, a rule consists of a *preactivation*, a *local computation*, and a *postactivation*. The preactivation is a multi-set of tuples to be found in its scope; the local computation is any sequential computation which does not modify the tuple space; the postactivation consists of a multi-set of tuples to be produced in its scope. The preactivation can include *formal tuples*, that are tuples whose fields can be identifiers; moreover, it includes the primitive **ask**, that permits to check the values that are assigned to the identifiers of a formal tuple matched against a tuple in the space. When a rule is activated in a space, a reaction takes place: the tuples to be locally consumed are removed, the tuples to be consumed externally are removed from the parent space, the local computation is performed, and finally some tuples are created. A tuple in the preactivation must be read if the symbol "?" is put in front of it and must be consumed otherwise; a read or consume operation involves the parent space if the symbol "↑" is put in front of a tuple and involves the local space if the symbol is missing; a tuple in the postactivation must be produced in the parent space if the symbol " ↑" is put in front of it and must be produced locally otherwise.

Spaces are represented as space tuples ("*name*" ∗ *SP*) where *name* is the name of the space. *SP* is the specification of the contents of the space. A space is a multi-set of tuples. Spaces are first class entities in MobiS. In fact, they are themselves part of spaces (as space tuples) as program tuples, are and they can be read, consumed or produced just like ordinary tuples. A program tuple has the form ("*rule_id*": *rule*) where *rule_id* is a rule identifier and *rule* is a MobiS rule. While a space tuple has the form ("*name*" ∗ *SP*) where *name* is the name that identifies the space, and *SP* is the space configuration. Program and space tuples have an identifier which simplifies reading or consuming program and space tuples ("*rule_id*" and "*name*"). Whenever disjoint multi-sets of tuples satisfy the activation preconditions of a set of rules, such rules can be executed independently and simultaneously: every rule modifies only the portion of space containing the tuples that must be read or consumed and therefore other rules can modify other tuples in the space or other spaces. Tuples representing messages are put in a space shared by components which have to communicate. Hence, communication is decoupled because components do not know each other, since they access tuples by pattern matching. Since messages have no destination address, their contents determine the set of possible receivers, (communication is property driven).

Mobility. As they are first class entities, spaces can move. Actually, a whole subtree (referring to the space tree of the MobiS specification) can migrate from a node to another. Mobility in MobiS consists of consuming and producing space tuples. As the scope of the rules is the local space and the parent space, the moving is performed "step by step", from a space to its parent and so on.

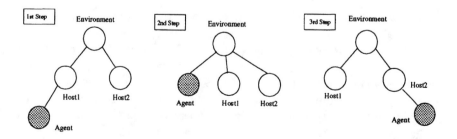

Fig. 1. An Agent Moves

$$\text{---------- } Environment \text{ ----------}$$
$$Environment = \{\!| \, (\text{``create''} : CREATE) \, |\!\}$$

$$CREATE = \{\!| \, (\text{``create''} : CREATE) \, |\!\} \longrightarrow \{\!| \, (\text{``H1''} * Host1), (\text{``H2''} * Host2) \, |\!\}$$

$$\text{---------- } Host1 \text{ ----------}$$
$$Host1 = \{\!| \, (\text{``name''}, k), (\text{``send''} : SEND), (\text{``agent''} * AGENT) \, |\!\}$$

$$SEND = \{\!| \, (\text{``agent''} * AGENT) \, |\!\} \longrightarrow \{\!| \, \uparrow(\text{``agent''} * AGENT), (\text{``wait''}) \, |\!\}$$

$$\text{---------- } AGENT \text{ ----------}$$
$$AGENT = \left\{\!\left| \begin{array}{l} (\text{``name''}, k), (\text{``code''} : CODE), \\ (\text{``authorize''} : AUTHORIZE), (\textbf{invariant} : END) \end{array} \right|\!\right\}$$
$$AUTHORIZE = \{\!| \, ?(\text{``name''}, j) \, |\!\} \longrightarrow \{\!| \, \uparrow(\text{``name\_agent''}, j) \, |\!\}$$
$$CODE = \{\!| \, \uparrow(\text{``go''}), \uparrow(\text{``data''}, d) \, |\!\} \xrightarrow{\;(r) \leftarrow f(d)\;} \{\!| \, (\text{``result''}, r) \, |\!\}$$
$$\textbf{where } f(dat) = (res)$$
$$END = \{\!| \, \uparrow(\text{``data''}, \text{''}1000\text{''}) \, |\!\} \longrightarrow \{\!| \, \uparrow(\text{``agent\_expired''}) \, |\!\}$$

$$\text{---------- } Host2 \text{ ----------}$$
$$Host2 = \left\{\!\left| \begin{array}{l} (\text{``name''}, k), (\text{``getag''} : GET), (\text{``kill''} : KILL), \\ (\text{``recognize''} : RECOGNIZE), (\text{``data''}, \text{''}d\text{''}) \end{array} \right|\!\right\}$$

$$GET = \{\!| \, \uparrow(a * AGENT) \, |\!\} \longrightarrow \{\!| \, (a * AGENT) \, |\!\}$$
$$RECOGNIZE = \{\!| \, (\text{``name\_agent''}, j), \textbf{ask}(j \leq 100) \, |\!\} \longrightarrow \{\!| \, (\text{``go''}) \, |\!\}$$
$$KILL = \{\!| \, (\text{``name\_agent''}, j), \textbf{ask}(j > 100), (a * AGENT) \, |\!\} \longrightarrow \{\!| |\!\}$$

Table 1. Specification of a System including a Mobile Agent

A simple example helps in explaining both MobiS syntax and semantics. Let us consider a system with two hosts: Host1 sends an agent performing some actions to Host2 site. Host2 accepts the agent sent from Host1. Host2 can kill the agent if it performs some "illegal actions". The two hosts can be described by two distinct spaces both included in a main space representing an "environment". The agent space, that initially is located inside the Host1 space, moves from the Host1 space to the Host2 space. Such a movement is graphically shown in Figure 1. Table 1 contains the specification of the system. The *Environment* space is the main space, that contains the program tuple (*"create"* : *CREATE*). The program tuple indicates that the rule *CREATE*, specified below in Table 1, is contained in the main space. The rule $CREATE$ creates two spaces $H1$ and $H2$ containing the tuples describing Host1 and Host2 respectively: their specification is included in the table. $Host1$ contains the host name ($"name", k$), the program tuple ($"send" : SEND$) that refers to the rule $SEND$ specified below in the table, and the space tuple ($agent * AGENT$), that refers to a space AGENT that is specified in the table as well. The rule $SEND$ moves the agent space from the host space to the main space ($\uparrow("agent" * AGENT)$) and sets the host state to "wait" emitting the tuple ($"wait"$). The $agent$ space is described below in the same table: it contains a name tuple, the code to be executed and three rules. The rule $AUTHORIZE$ emits a tuple containing the name of the agent into the external space in order to let the Host2 recognize it. The rule $CODE$ is enabled when the agent is authorized by the Host2 with the tuple ($"go"$). It exploits some data from the Host2 space and executes the code computing a result. The function f on the top of the arrows computes the result: its parameters are specified in the **where** clause, at the end of the rule. $Host2$ initially contains its name, some data, and three rules: the rule GET checks if an agent is present in the main space, then moves it in the local space. The rule $RECOGNIZE$ verifies the identity of the agent checking its name (e.g.. we check that the name is a number smaller than 100), and emits the tuple ($"go"$), granting the agent the permission to move.

Spaces can be terminated by external rules (as rules can consume space tuples) as the rule $KILL$ in the Host2 space, that terminates the agent when its name is not an authorized one (e.g.. a number greater than 100): the primitive **ask** checks the value; or spaces can terminate themselves by *invariant* rules.

The preactivation of an *invariant* rule defines a constraint that must hold for all the tuple space lifetime. Whenever an invariant is violated, the tuple space terminates and disappears; its sub-spaces disappear as well. A MobiS invariant is a condition on the tuple space contents: it asserts that the space will never contain a given multi-set of tuples. Invariant rules can only read tuples locally (the tuples that must not belong to the tuple space) and produce tuples in the parent space. When the tuples to be read are in the space, the reaction specified by the invariant takes place in the usual way. Local computation and tuple production are used to communicate possible results to the parent space and then the space dies. Invariants are given by means of special program tuples whose names are replaced by the keyword **invariant**. MobiS rules cannot consume the space in which they are. For this purpose the specifier should use the *Invariant* rules. An example is the invariant rule END in the $AGENT$ space that kills the agent when the data tuple ($"data", "1000"$) is in the external space. It emits a tuple ($"agent\_expired"$) to signal the termination of the space.

In summary, a space represents at the same time both a component performing a (reactive) computation and a persistent, multicast channel supporting communication among the components it contains. The coordination model underlying MobiS can easily encode different mobile entities: in the next section we introduce a fine grained classification of mobile entities.

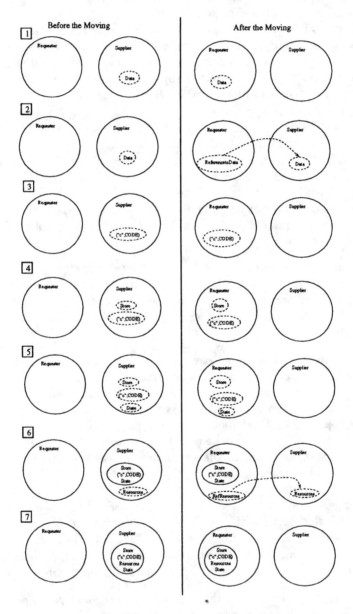

Fig. 2. A Classification of Mobility

3 Specification of Architectural Styles for Mobility

$$\text{Environment}$$
$$Environment = \{\!\!\{\,(\text{``}R\text{''} * Requester), (\text{``}S\text{''} * Supplier)\,\}\!\!\}$$

$$\text{Requester}$$
$$Requester = \left\{\!\!\left\{ \begin{array}{l} (\text{``}name\text{''}, k), (\text{``}refreq\text{''}, req), (\text{``}request\text{''} : REFREQ), \\ (\text{``}get\text{''} : GET)(\text{``}code\text{''} : CODE), (\text{``}data\text{''}, d), (\text{``}state\text{''}, s) \end{array} \right\}\!\!\right\}$$

$$REFREQ = \{\!\!\{\, ?(\text{``}refreq\text{''}, req)\,\}\!\!\} \longrightarrow \{\!\!\{\, \uparrow(\text{``}refreq\text{''}, req)\,\}\!\!\}$$

$$GET = \{\!\!\{\, \uparrow(\text{``}refdata\text{''}, rd), (\text{``}refreq\text{''}, req)\,\}\!\!\} \longrightarrow \{\!\!\{\, (\text{``}refdata\text{''}, rd)\,\}\!\!\}$$

$$CODE = \{\!\!\{\, ?(\text{``}refdata\text{''}, rd), ?(\text{``}state\text{''}, s),\,\}\!\!\} \xrightarrow{(s') \leftarrow f(s, rd)} \{\!\!\{\, (\text{``}state\text{''}, s')\,\}\!\!\}$$
$$\textbf{where } f(dataref, state) = (nstate(data, state))$$

$$\text{Supplier}$$
$$Supplier = \{\!\!\{\, (\text{``}name\text{''}, k), (\text{``}data\text{''}, d), (\text{``}put\text{''} : PUT), (\text{``}getreq\text{''} : GETREQ)\,\}\!\!\}$$

$$GETREQ = \{\!\!\{\, \uparrow(\text{``}refreq\text{''}, req), ?(\text{``}data\text{''}, d)\,\}\!\!\} \longrightarrow \{\!\!\{\, (\text{``}refreq\text{''}, req)\,\}\!\!\}$$

$$PUT = \{\!\!\{\, (\text{``}refreq\text{''}, req), ?(\text{``}data\text{''}, d)\,\}\!\!\} \xrightarrow{(rd) \leftarrow f(d)} \{\!\!\{\, \uparrow(\text{``}refdata\text{''}, rd)\,\}\!\!\}$$
$$\textbf{where } f(x) = (referenceto(x))$$

Table 2. MobiS specification of the Reference paradigm

An architectural style is an abstract skeleton which helps in designing, understanding, and analyzing actual software architectures, said *instances* of such a style.

There are at least three reasons why it is important and useful to systematically study architectural styles:

- to help designers to choose a specific style in a given design situation; the definition and classification of common architectural styles with clearly defined properties supports both design and code reuse;
- to build a library of styles, so that software designers can choose the most appropriate one;
- to support analysis methods and tools suitable to deal with style instances, namely concrete software architectures, understanding and reasoning on their properties.

We have defined a basic set of architectural styles for mobility. We catalog these *mobile architectural styles* in terms of *what is moving,* namely which entities move with respect to an infrastructure including at least two immobile entities:

a *requester* entity and a *supplier* entity. The requester asks the supplier for a service, and the supplier provides the service. These two entities are actually part of the styles as they characterize the structure of the environment. Both these immobile entities can be thought of as two Internet sites connected by some channel able to transport mobile entities from a site to another.

In figure 2 we have illustrated the different paradigms for mobility described below. The dashed arrows show the reference links among entities. The non-dashed circles represent the spaces, while the dashed ones represent the tuples. The figure shows, for each style, the location of the tuples/spaces before and after the moving.

We now describe a number of architectural styles including different mobile components and give some concrete examples of their use.

1. **Data Style**: This is the simplest kind of mobility to understand. The mobile entities are data from a supplier to a requester. A typical example is a client-server architecture based on a protocol like HTTP: HTTP servers send to HTTP clients data in form of HTML pages (HTML being a not Turing complete language).

2. **Reference Style**: in this case what moves from the supplier to the requester is only a reference to some entity, not data or programs. An example of a mobile reference is an URL address: a requester receives an URL and can "move" its browser to the referred page.

3. **Code Style**: in this case some executable code can move from a site to an other. Java applets are based on code mobility.

4. **Code&Store Style**: in this case both some code and the values of the variables it refers to (a *store*) move. This kind of mobility is usually termed *agent mobility* and it is the form of mobility offered by current Java mobile agent systems.

5. **Code, Store&State Style**: in this case code, store, and scheduling state (threads) of an agent can move. Referential transparency is the main goal of this kind of mobility, as the execution continues on a different site from the exact point it had been suspended on the other site. This style of mobility has been implemented in Telescript.

6. **Closure Style**: In this case an agent (code+store) moves and maintains its links to resources which were local to its source location and become remote in its destination. As an example we quote Obliq [1], that uses exactly this kind of mobility.

7. **Ambient Style**: this style describes the moving of the whole ambient involved in a computation. Ambients can contain other ambients that are moved too. In this way it is possible to model, for instance, the moving of a set of programs from a workstation to a laptop. At the moment no languages exist allowing this kind of mobility. However, Cardelli and Gordon have proposed a programming language based on this paradigm [2].

MobiS allows the specification of architectural styles for mobility. Architectural styles are abstractions including components, connectors [14]. Components

$$\boxed{\quad\text{Environment}\quad}$$

$$Environment = \{\!|\,(\text{``R''} * Requester), (\text{``S''} * Supplier)\,|\!\}$$

$$\boxed{\quad\text{Requester}\quad}$$

$$Requester = \left\{\!\left|\begin{array}{l}(\text{``name''}, k), (\text{``codereq''}, req), (\text{``request''} : CODEREQ),\\ (\text{``get''} : GET), (\text{``store''}, st), (\text{``state''}, s)\end{array}\right|\!\right\}$$

$$CODEREQ = \{\!|\, ?(\text{``codereq''}, req)\,|\!\} \longrightarrow \{\!|\, \uparrow(\text{``codereq''}, req)\,|\!\}$$

$$GET = \{\!|\, \uparrow(\text{``serializedcode''}, sc), (\text{``codereq''}, req)\,|\!\} \xrightarrow{(c)\leftarrow f(sc)} \{\!|\, (\text{``code''}, c)\,|\!\}$$
$$\textbf{where } f(x) = (f_{code}(x))$$

$$\boxed{\quad\text{Supplier}\quad}$$

$$Supplier = \{\!|\,(\text{``name''}, k), (\text{``c''} : CODE), (\text{``put''} : PUT), (\text{``getreq''} : GETREQ)\,|\!\}$$

$$GETREQ = \{\!|\, \uparrow(\text{``codereq''}, req), ?(\text{``code''}, c)\,|\!\} \longrightarrow \{\!|\, (\text{``codereq''}, req)\,|\!\}$$

$$PUT = \{\!|\, (\text{``codereq''}, req), ?(\text{``code''}, c)\,|\!\} \xrightarrow{(sc)\leftarrow f(c)} \{\!|\, \uparrow(\text{``serializedcode''}, sc)\,|\!\}$$
$$\textbf{where } f(x) = (serialize(x))$$

$$CODE = \left\{\!\left|\begin{array}{l}?(\text{``store''}, st),\\ ?(\text{``state''}, s),\end{array}\right|\!\right\} \xrightarrow{(s',st)\leftarrow f(s,st)} \left\{\!\left|\begin{array}{l}(\text{``state''}, s'),\\ (\text{``store''}, st')\end{array}\right|\!\right\}$$
$$\textbf{where } f(store, state) = (nstate(store, state))$$

Table 3. MobiS specification of Code Paradigm

are computation loci, while connectors define the interactions among components. In MobiS components can be specified as spaces (that can also be nested): new components can be generated (i.e. spaces can be created), eliminated (i.e. spaces can be consumed), or can migrate (i.e. spaces can be consumed and recreated elsewhere). The way in which MobiS models software architectures [12] is similar to the one described in [10] where the CHAM coordination model is used. The coordination allows flexible moving of components and extensibility of the model. Our model, where rules and spaces as first class entities, provides a framework in which encoding all the different styles listed above. The concept of connector in MobiS is in some sense implicit (as in [11, 10]): components interactions are defined by the coordination model, whereas communication is specified using the asynchronous mechanism of multiset rewriting.

We now specify some mobility styles using MobiS. Table 2 contains the specification of the **Reference style**. The main space contains two spaces, a "Requester" and a "Supplier". The *Requester* space contains a data reference request tuple, the code, and the state. The rule *REFREQ* sends a reference request to the main space. The rule *GET* gets from the main space the data reference. The rule *CODE* formalizes the execution of the requester code using the reference to the data. Notice that as the spaces are organized in a tree it is quite easy to specify the access to the referenced data: spaces have names in form of paths. In table 4 where the closure style is specified, the spaces maintain some knowledge of the remote location of the resources exploiting the tree structure of the spaces as in the Join Calculus [8].

$$\text{--- } Environment \text{ ---}$$
$$Environment = \{\!| \,(\text{``R''} * Requester), (\text{``S''} * Supplier) \,|\!\}$$

$$\text{--- } Requester \text{ ---}$$
$$Requester = \left\{\!\left| \begin{array}{l} (\text{``name''}, k), (\text{``req''}, req), (\text{``request''} : REQ), (\text{``get''} : GET), \\ (\text{``name''}, \text{``Requester''}) \end{array} \right.\right\}$$

$$REQ = \{\!| \,?(\text{``req''}, req) \,|\!\} \longrightarrow \{\!| \,\uparrow(\text{``req''}, req) \,|\!\}$$

$$GET = \left\{\!\left| \begin{array}{l} \uparrow(j * Closure), (\text{``name''}, u) \\ (\text{``req''}, req) \end{array} \right.\right\} \xrightarrow{\;(k) \leftarrow f(j,u)\;} \{\!| \,(k * Closure) \,|\!\}$$
$$\textbf{where } f(x,y) = (concat(x,y))$$

$$\text{--- } Supplier \text{ ---}$$
$$Supplier = \{\!| \,(\text{``name''}, k), (k.Cl * Closure), (\text{``resource''}, r), (\text{``put''} : PUT) \,|\!\}$$

$$PUT = \left\{\!\left| \begin{array}{l} \uparrow(\text{``req''}, req), ?(\text{``name''}, i), \\ (k * Closure), \\ (\text{``ready''}), ?(\text{``resource''}, r) \end{array} \right.\right\} \xrightarrow{\;(j) \leftarrow f(i,k)\;} \{\!| \,\uparrow(j * Closure) \,|\!\}$$
$$\textbf{where } f(x,y) = (diff(x,y))$$

$$\text{--- } Closure \text{ ---}$$
$$Closure = \left\{\!\left| \begin{array}{l} (\text{``name''}, k), (\text{``c''} : CODE), (\text{``store''}, st), \\ (\text{``state''}, s), (\text{``tr''} : TRANSF) \end{array} \right.\right\}$$

$$TRANSF = \left\{\!\left| \begin{array}{l} ? \uparrow(\text{``name''}, k), ?(\text{``c''} : CODE), \\ ?(\text{``store''}, st), ?(\text{``state''}, s), \\ ? \uparrow (\text{``resources''}, r), \\ (\text{``tr''} : TRANSF) \end{array} \right.\right\} \longrightarrow \left\{\!\left| \begin{array}{l} (\text{``remote\_res''}, k), \\ \uparrow(\text{``ready''}) \end{array} \right.\right\}$$

$$CODE = \left\{\!\left| \begin{array}{l} ?(\text{``store''}, st), ?(\text{``state''}, s), \\ ?(\text{``remote\_res''}, r) \end{array} \right.\right\} \xrightarrow{\;(s', st') \leftarrow f(r,s,st)\;} \left\{\!\left| \begin{array}{l} (\text{``store''}, st'), \\ (\text{``state''}, s') \end{array} \right.\right\}$$
$$\textbf{where } f(res, store, state) = (nstate(res, store, state), nstore(res, store, state))$$

Table 4. MobiS specification of Closure paradigm

A *Supplier* space contains the data and two rules. The rule *GET REQ* accepts requests of data references while the rule *PUT* emits a reference tuple the main space in order to let the requester to catch the required reference to data.

We omit the formalization of the **Data style**, in fact it is quite similar to the *Reference style*: the only difference being that the supplier has to send data to the requester and not simply references to data.

Table 3 contains the formalization of the **Code style**: The *Requester* space contains a code-request tuple, the state, and the store. The rule *CODEREQ* sends a code request in the main space. The rule *GET* gets from the main space the serialized code sent by the supplier. The rule *CODE* formalizes the execution of code updating the values of the state and the store. The *Supplier* space contains the code and two rules. The rule *GET REQ* accepts a request of code from the main space, and the rule *PUT* emits the serialized code in the main space.

We omit the formalization of **Code & Store Style** and **Code, Store, & State style** as their formalizations can be easily derived from the **Code Style** specification (Table 3).

The following two styles fully exploit the power of MobiS as they are based on the mobility of spaces. Table 4 contains the formalization of the **Closure style**: a closure is a group of entities, that we model as a space. The *Supplier* space contains the tuple with its name (location), a tuple indicating the subspace ("*k.Cl*" * *Closure*), and two rules (*GET REQ* and *PUT*). The *Closure* space is specified below in the table and *k.Cl* is the name of the subspace, indicating the location of the subspace in the space tree. The rule *PUT* puts the closure space in the main space, when ready. It also updates the location of the subspace, eliminating the name of the supplier space from the location path of the name of the closure space (*diff* function in the **where** clause has this role). The *Closure* space contains its name, the code, the state, and the store. The *TRANSF* rule is activated only once (it consumes itself). It creates a reference to the resources of the supplier space and emits a tuple ("*ready*") in the supplier space, indicating that the closure is ready to be moved elsewhere. The *CODE* rule executes the code exploiting the resources of the supplier space, no matter if the closure space is not located in the supplier site anymore. The *Requester* space contains the rule *GET* that gets the closure space from the parent space and updates its location adding the requester name in the name path of the closure space (function *concat* in the **where** clause does it).

Table 5 contains the specification of the **Ambient style**. The *Supplier* space contains two rules and an *Ambient* subspace. The rule *PUT* transfers the ambient space outside. It changes the location of the ambient as in the Closure style. The *Ambient* space contains the code, the state, the store, and some resources.The rule *CODE* executes the code using the local resources to the ambient, no matter where the ambient is located. The *Requester* rule *GET* gets the *Ambient* space from the parent space and updates its location name.

$$\boxed{\begin{array}{l} \rule{0pt}{0pt}\hspace{3cm}\textit{Environment}\hspace{3cm} \\ Environment = \{\!\!\{\, (\text{``}R\text{''} * Requester), (\text{``}S\text{''} * Supplier)\, \}\!\!\} \end{array}}$$

$$\boxed{\begin{array}{l} \rule{0pt}{0pt}\hspace{3cm}\textit{Supplier}\hspace{3cm} \\ Supplier = \{\!\!\{\, (a * Ambient), (\text{``}name\text{''}, k)(\text{``}put\text{''} : PUT)\, \}\!\!\} \\[2ex] \hline \\ PUT = \left\{\!\!\!\left\{ \begin{array}{l} \uparrow(\text{``}req\text{''}, req), ?(\text{``}name\text{''}, i), \\ (a * Ambient) \end{array} \right\}\!\!\!\right\} \xrightarrow{(z)\leftarrow f(a,i)} \{\!\!\{\, \uparrow(z * Ambient)\, \}\!\!\} \\[2ex] \textbf{where } f(x,y) = (diff(x,y)) \end{array}}$$

$$\boxed{\begin{array}{l} \rule{0pt}{0pt}\hspace{3cm}\textit{Ambient}\hspace{3cm} \\ Ambient = \left\{\!\!\!\left\{ \begin{array}{l} (\text{``}name\text{''}, k), (\text{``}data\text{''}, d), (\text{``}state\text{''}, s), \\ (\text{``}c\text{''} : CODE), (\text{``}resources\text{''}, r) \end{array} \right\}\!\!\!\right\} \\[2ex] \hline \\ CODE = \left\{\!\!\!\left\{ \begin{array}{l} ?(\text{``}store\text{''}, st), \\ ?(\text{``}state\text{''}, s), (\text{``}resource\text{''}, r) \end{array} \right\}\!\!\!\right\} \xrightarrow{(s',st')\leftarrow f(r,s,st)} \left\{\!\!\!\left\{ \begin{array}{l} (\text{``}store\text{''}, st'), \\ (\text{``}state\text{''}, s') \end{array} \right\}\!\!\!\right\} \\[2ex] \textbf{where } f(res, store, state) = (nstate(res, store, state), nstore(res, store, state)) \end{array}}$$

$$\boxed{\begin{array}{l} \rule{0pt}{0pt}\hspace{3cm}\textit{Requester}\hspace{3cm} \\ Requester = \{\!\!\{\, (\text{``}req\text{''}, req), (\text{``}request\text{''} : REQ), (\text{``}get\text{''} : GET), (\text{``}name\text{''}, k)\, \}\!\!\} \\[2ex] \hline \\ REQ = \{\!\!\{\, ?(\text{``}req\text{''}, req)\, \}\!\!\} \longrightarrow \{\!\!\{\, \uparrow(\text{``}req\text{''}, req)\, \}\!\!\} \\[2ex] GET = \left\{\!\!\!\left\{ \begin{array}{l} \uparrow(a * Ambient), (\text{``}req\text{''}, req), \\ ?(\text{``}name\text{''}, z) \end{array} \right\}\!\!\!\right\} \xrightarrow{(j)\leftarrow f(z,a)} \{\!\!\{\, (j * Ambient)\, \}\!\!\} \\[2ex] \textbf{where } f(x,y) = (concat(x,y)) \end{array}}$$

Table 5. MobiS specification of the Ambient style

4 Application of the Styles to the Architecture of a Mobile System

We consider the software architecture of a system and apply these styles to see how these paradigms can be used.

As a case study we consider an electronic commerce application. With the advancements in the network technology new kinds of applications are now possible. A purchaser is trying to buy items at the best available prices on the network. The purchaser travels on the network looking for the best selling-price. We have simplified the problem supposing that the purchaser is looking for the best price of a single object. We exploit the mobility styles defined in Section 3 to specify the software architecture of the *Purchasing System*.

Using the **Data style** the purchaser can be seen as a requester that asks for the items prices from different stores. The stores send prices of the items

$$\boxed{\begin{array}{l} \text{----------------- } \textit{Environment} \text{ -----------------} \\ \textit{Environment} = \{\!|\ (\text{``s1''} * \textit{Shop}), (\text{``s2''} * \textit{Shop}), (\text{``agent''} * \textit{Ambient}) \,|\!\} \end{array}}$$

$$\boxed{\begin{array}{l} \text{------------- } \textit{Shop} \text{ -------------} \\ \textit{Shop} = \left\{\!\!\left|\ \begin{array}{l} (\text{``name''}, k)(\text{``put''} : PUT), (\text{``req''}, req), \\ (\text{``request''} : REQ), (\text{``get''} : GET)(\text{``catalog''}, l) \end{array}\ \right|\!\!\right\} \end{array}}$$

$PUT = \{\!|\ \uparrow(\text{``req''}, req), ?(\text{``name''}, i), (a * Ambient)\ |\!\}\ \xrightarrow{(z) \leftarrow f(a,i)}\ \{\!|\ \uparrow(z * Ambient)\ |\!\}$
where $f(x, y) = (diff(x, y))$

$REQ = \{\!|\ ?(\text{``req''}, req)\ |\!\}\ \longrightarrow\ \{\!|\ \uparrow(\text{``req''}, req), (\text{``wait''})\ |\!\}$

$GET = \left\{\!\!\left|\ \begin{array}{l} \uparrow(a * Ambient), (\text{``wait''}), \\ ?(\text{``name''}, z), ?(\text{``catalog''}, l) \end{array}\ \right|\!\!\right\}\ \xrightarrow{(j) \leftarrow f(z,a)}\ \{\!|\ (j * Ambient)\ |\!\}$
where $f(x, y) = (concat(x, y))$

$$\boxed{\begin{array}{l} \text{----------------- } \textit{Ambient} \text{ -----------------} \\ \textit{Ambient} = \left\{\!\!\left|\ \begin{array}{l} (\text{``name''}, k), (\text{``state''}, s), (\text{``bestpricefound''}, b), \\ (\text{``printer''}, p), (\text{``update''} : UPDATE), (\text{``print''} : PRINT) \end{array}\ \right|\!\!\right\} \end{array}}$$

$UPDATE = \left\{\!\!\left|\ \begin{array}{l} ?(\text{``bestpricefound''}, b), \\ ?(\text{``state''}, s), \\ \uparrow(\text{``catalog''}, l), \\ \mathbf{ask}(l < b) \end{array}\ \right|\!\!\right\}\ \xrightarrow{(s',b') \leftarrow f(s,l)}\ \left\{\!\!\left|\ \begin{array}{l} (\text{``bestpricefound''}, b'), \\ (\text{``state''}, s') \end{array}\ \right|\!\!\right\}$
where $f(s, l) = (compute(s', l), l))$

$PRINT = \{\!|\ ?(\text{``bestpricefound''}, b), \uparrow(\text{``printer''}, p)\ |\!\}\ \longrightarrow\ \{\!|\ (\text{``outonprinter''}, b)\ |\!\}$

Table 6. Specification of the Purchasing Architecture in the Ambient Style

to the purchaser that can remotely check the prices and choose the lower one. The use of the **Reference style** is very similar: the stores do not send directly the prices of the items, but they send references to their catalogs. The purchaser still does not move, and it can remotely check the prices on the catalogs. In the **Code style** solution we imagine the purchaser migrating from a store site to an other moving its code. Every store puts an advertisement request tuple, (*"newsellingprice"*, *reqselling*), in the main space. The store containing the code of the purchasing agent emits the code tuple in the main space and the store that puts the advertisement can obtain the purchasing code. However this solution is not suitable for the purchasing system, because the purchaser has to remember the best price found every time it moves. With the **Code&Store style** every node has the function of both requester and supplier. The purchaser code and a tuple for storing the best price found till that moment, (*"bestprice"*, *price*), are sent from a store to another whenever a new advertisement tuple is received. This solution fits better the purchasing system than the one with the **Code**

style, in fact it allows the store (the best price found) to be moved with the code, letting the purchaser do its job. The new $CODE$ rule (that has to instance the rule $CODE$ of the code&store style) updates the store of the purchaser, with a new best price, if the price offered by the local space is better than the one in the previous store. **Code, Store, & State style** is not suitable, in fact the same procedure has to be applied on every node in order to find the best price. We are not interested in transparently continuing the execution of the purchaser on different sites. The **Closure style** allows the references to remote resources. It would be useful, for instance, if the purchaser, while moving, has to communicate its temporary best price found to its company: it could for example print the offered price of every store on the company (remote) printer. Using the **Ambient style** we imagine a mobile "agent" traveling with all its data and exploiting its resources (printer, modem, cellular phone, ...) on different selling-stores looking for the best price for an item. The purchaser could, for example, use its printer to print the temporary best price found till that moment.

We give the specification of the architecture of the Purchasing System in the Ambient style in table 6. The Shops are Requester and Supplier at the same time. The resources in the Ambient Style shown in Table 5 are now portable resources (i.e. a printer, a scanner, ...). The rules PUT, REQ, and GET do the same operations. The Ambient stores the best price found and contains two rules refining the $CODE$ rule in Table 5: the rule $PRINT$ prints the best price temporary found on the portable printer.

These paradigms could also be composed. For instance in Table 5 we allows the agent to read from the shop catalog (i.e to access to some external resources). Therefore, the resulting architecture is a mixture among Code,State&Store style and Ambient style. The $UPDATE$ rule updates the best price found if the catalog of the shop offers a better price. These architectures offer different advantages and some of them are better than the other for particular requirements. The designer knows the requirements of the systems that she wants to implement and can choose on the basis of these requirements the most suitable style of mobility. The resulting architecture could also be an integration among different paradigms.

5   Related work and Conclusions

We have studied different kinds of mobile entities, and shown how we specify software architectures including these mobile entities. MobiS language has been used for the formal specification. An architecture of a simplified purchasing system has been described exploiting the different architectural styles formalized.

Other formal languages have been proposed for the specification of mobility aspects of systems. In [4, 9] a general classification is given on mobility paradigms, technologies, and applications. We present a catalog where the handling of data and code is merged, We also have formalized with MobiS the paradigms defined in the classification.

In [13] a formalization of some mobility paradigms is given using Mobile Unity. Mobile Unity is expressive enough to specify the different mechanisms of mobility and the Unity logic can be used in order to reason on the specifications. However, the unit of mobility is a complete UNITY program and there is no distinction between active and inactive programs: instead, we differentiate the sending of code or data from the sending of processes with execution state.

Obliq [1] and the Ambient calculus [2] are specification languages for mobility: they both offer a particular approach to mobility based on a particular style (respectively *Closure* and *Ambient*). The Ambient Calculus is based on the movement of spaces (ambients). Whenever there is a need for movement, an ambient is created, and what has to be moved is placed inside. The whole ambient is moved. The movement is performed step by step like in MobiS. "It is not realistic to imagine that an agent can migrate from any point A to any point B on the Internet ... Access information is controlled at many levels" [2]. Also in MobiS mobility is quite realistic: an entity can move only between spaces which are parent and son. A complete travel is composed of many of these single steps movements.

Several research efforts have been devoted to address mobility using the π-calculus and its extensions, that are process algebras where processes communicate using mobile channel references. The distributed Join-calculus [8] is an extension of the π-calculus which introduces the explicit notions of named localities and distribution failure.

Klaim [6] and Bauhaus [3] are specification languages based on multiple tuple spaces, like MobiS. Bauhaus spaces can be nested as in MobiS while in Klaim spaces are not nested. Klaim includes a process algebra and uses a type system to perform some security checks. Differently from MobiS, Klaim and Bauhaus do not provide mobility of spaces.

The coordination model of MobiS is quite similar to the semantics framework of the CHAM, a notation that has been exploited to specify software architectures [10]. However, the CHAM does not provide mobility of solutions (that are the CHAM equivalent of MobiS spaces).

We are developing a logic for reasoning on MobiS specification, in particular we are adapting the CTL logic we used for the ancestor of MobiS: PoliS [5]. The automatic verification of properties in another goal: we plan to enhance the PoliS model checker [5] in order to deal with MobiS mobility of spaces.

We are working on the integration of MobiS inside UML. UML offers support for the specification of many different approaches to design of systems, while MobiS is a formal language for the specification of the mobility of components. The integration of the two models offers the possibility to inspect different aspects of architectures that contains mobile components.

Acknowledgments: I would like to thank Paolo Ciancarini for the helpful suggestions and for the stimulating discussion.

References

1. L. Cardelli. A language with distributed scope. In *Proc. 22nd ACM Symposium on Principles of Programming Languages (POPL)*, pages 286–298, 1995.
2. L. Cardelli and A. Gordon. Mobile Ambients. In M. Nivat, editor, *Proc. of Foundations of Software Science and Computation Structures (FoSSaCS), European Joint Conferences on Theory and Practice of Software (ETAPS'98)*, volume 1378 of *Lecture Notes in Computer Science*, pages 140–155, Lisbon, Portugal, 1998. Springer-Verlag, Berlin.
3. N. Carriero, D. Gelernter, and L. Zuck. Bauhaus Linda. In P. Ciancarini, O. Nierstrasz, and A. Yonezawa, editors, *Object-Based Models and Languages for Concurrent Systems*, volume 924 of *Lecture Notes in Computer Science*, pages 66–76. Springer-Verlag, Berlin, 1995.
4. A. Carzaniga, G. Picco, and G. Vigna. Designing Distributed Applications with Mobile Code Paradigms. In *Proc. 19th Int. Conf. on Software Engineering (ICSE)*, pages 22–32, Boston, Ma, May 1997.
5. P. Ciancarini, F. Franzé, and C. Mascolo. A Coordination Model to Specify Systems including Mobile Agents. In *Proc. 9th IEEE Int. Workshop on Software Specification and Design (IWSSD)*, pages 96–105, Japan, 1998.
6. R. DeNicola, G. Ferrari, and R. Pugliese. KLAIM: A kernel Language for Agents Interaction and Mobility. *IEEE Transactions on Software Engineering*, 24(5):315–330, 1998.
7. G. DiMarzoSerugendo, M. Muhugusa, and C. Tschudin. An Survey of Theories for Mobile Agents. *World Wide Web*, 1(3):139–153, 1998.
8. C. Fournet, G. Gonthier, J. Levy, L. Maranget, and D. Remy. A Calculus of Mobile Agents. In U. Montanari and V. Sassone, editors, *Proc. 7th Int. Conf. on Concurrency Theory (CONCUR)*, volume 1119 of *Lecture Notes in Computer Science*, pages 406–421, Pisa, Italy, August 1996. Springer-Verlag, Berlin.
9. A. Fuggetta, G. Picco, and G. Vigna. Understanding Code Mobility. *IEEE Transactions on Software Engineering*, 24(5):342–361, 1998.
10. P. Inverardi and A. Wolf. Formal Specification and Analysis of Software Architectures Using the Chemical Abstract Machine Model. *IEEE Transactions on Software Engineering*, 21(4):373–386, April 1995.
11. J. Kramer and J. Magee. Exposing the skeleton in the coordination closet. In D. Garlan and D. LeMetayer, editors, *Proc. 2nd Int. Conf. on Coordination Models and Languages*, volume 1282 of *Lecture Notes in Computer Science*, pages 18–31, Berlin, Germany, September 1997. Springer-Verlag, Berlin.
12. P.Ciancarini and C.Mascolo. Software architecture and mobility. In D. Perry and J. Magee, editors, *Proc. 3rd Int. Software Architecture Workshop (ISAW-3)*, ACM SIGSOFT Software Engineering Notes, pages 21–24, Orlando, FL, November 1998.
13. G. Picco, G. Roman, and P. McCann. Expressing Code Mobility in Mobile Unity. In M. Jazayeri and H. Schauer, editors, *Proc. 6th European Software Eng. Conf. (ESEC 97)*, volume 1301 of *Lecture Notes in Computer Science*, pages 500–518. Springer-Verlag, Berlin, 1997.
14. M. Shaw and D. Garlan. *Software Architecture. Perspectives on an Emerging Discipline*. Prentice-Hall, 1996.

Coordinated Roles: Promoting Re-usability of Coordinated Active Objects Using Event Notification Protocols[1]

Juan M. Murillo, Juan Hernández, Fernando Sánchez, Luis A. Álvarez

Departamento de Informática. Universidad de Extremadura
Escuela Politécnica. Avenida de la Universidad s/n 10.071 - Cáceres
{juanmamu, juanher, fernando, luisalva}@unex.es

Abstract. Nowadays, the need for developing more and more complex applications with distributed capabilities has promoted the development of coordination models. The goal of these models is to express the synchronized interaction among the different components of a distributed application. Whilst the Concurrent Object Oriented Programming (COOP) paradigm has revealed special adaptation to the modeling of distributed applications, the integration of this paradigm with current coordination models results in a reduction of the potential re-usability of classes that negates the capital benefit of object orientation. The main contributions of this paper are twofold. Firstly, the Event Notification Protocols, a mechanism that permits the transparent monitoring of active objects, are presented. Secondly, Coordinated Roles, a general-purpose coordination model based on the event notification protocols is proposed. Coordinated Roles is integrated with the COOP paradigm in such a way that the reduction of re-usability is avoided. In addition, it provides flexibility, composability, polymorphism, distribution, and dynamic change of coordination patterns.

1 Introduction

In recent years, the need for developing more and more complex software, supporting more services and for wider application domains, together with advance in the net technology, have motivated the development of distributed applications.

The most complex task in the design of such applications is to specify the coordination that must exist among the components. To make this task easier for the programmer, the research community has devoted great efforts to produce *coordination models and languages*. The goal of a coordination model is to let the programmer specify the synchronized interaction among components in a distributed application, in such a way that it:

1. Provides the highest expressive power to specify any coordination pattern ([15], [16]). These patterns detail the order in which the tasks developed by each component of the distributed application have to be executed. The state of the

---

[1] This work is supported by CICYT under contract TIC 98-1049-C02-02 and Junta de Extremadura under contract IPR98A041.

global computation determines the set of tasks that can be performed in each instant.

2. Promotes the re-usability not only of coordinated components, but also of coordination patterns ([3], [6], [9], [13], [15], [16]). The coordinated components could be used in any other application in which their functionality behaviour is required, apart from the coordination pattern that directs them. The same holds for the coordination patterns that could be used in a different application, managing a different group of components with different behaviour, different interfaces, but the same coordination needs.

Coordination models must be implemented in a self-contained coordination language [11]. This language must allow the expression of coordination constraints separately from the components that have to be coordinated ([4], [6], [11], [13], [15], [16]). To enhance the re-usability of components, coordination constraints must be *transparent* to them. By *transparency* we mean that components should not have actions associated with them in order to be coordinated. Transparency requires *separation*. Besides, separation provides *modularization* and modularization makes the reasoning about coordination patterns easier.

The Concurrent Object Oriented Programming paradigm has revealed a special adaptation to model distributed applications. However, the integration of this paradigm with current coordination models leads to a reduction in the potential re-usability of classes that negates the main benefit of object orientation. The reason is that only few coordination models satisfy the separation and transparency requirements simultaneously, although both are essential when a coordination model is integrated with this programming paradigm[2]. In some cases ([3], [5], [6], [7], [8], [9], [10], [12], [14]) although separation is achieved, the provided mechanisms for coordination are not transparent. The coordinated objects have to start those mechanisms and, so, only those objects that have been previously programmed for such a task can be coordinated. In other cases ([15], [20]) although separation and transparency are achieved, the expressive power provided is limited so they can not be used to solve all coordination problems in a natural way.

With the aim of circumventing this deficiency, we propose two innovations. Firstly, we introduce the *event notification protocols* as a mechanism allowing the specification of coordination patterns in a transparent and separate way. Secondly, we present *Coordinated Roles*, a coordination model for active objects based on the event notification protocols. This model not only offers good integration with the COOP paradigm but it also provides some other advantages such as flexibility, polymorphism, extensibility, composability, distribution, and the dynamic change of coordination patterns.

In section 2, problems arising in the integration of the mentioned coordination models with the COOP paradigm are detailed. In section 3, the event notification protocols are described. The Coordinated Roles model is introduced in section 4. Lastly, conclusions and future work are presented.

---

[2] Separation and transparency are essential for the COOP paradigm due to the reduction in re-usability that this paradigm generates as a consequence of the mixing of aspects (coordination among them) ([1], [19], [23]). The code implementing the functionality that these classes were designed for is contaminated with constraints induced by the concurrent dimension. This fact limits class re-usability. The solution to this problem is the separation of aspects ([1], [17], [18], [24]).

2 Background and Motivation

A concurrent object-oriented application is composed of several active and possibly distributed objects in a computer network. Every object has a set of methods and a runtime system that controls its internal state. Objects interact with one another invoking methods through message passing. When an object receives the invocation of a method, its runtime system can decide between executing it or delaying it, according to the state it is in. Besides, when an active object is instantiated, it can execute internal activities that do not correspond to the processing of any message. Coordination models have to cope with these issues. However, some of them do not focus on all the problems inherent to the coordination of active objects. A simple example will be used to show some of these problems.

The proposed case study is the functionality of a car park. Before entering the car park, drivers have to obtain a ticket from a ticket machine and, only then, they are allowed to pass a barrier. Both the ticket machine and the barrier are controlled by active objects. Each of these objects has associated with it a car-detecting sensor. A possible implementation of this scenario would be the use of the message passing mechanism as shown in Figure 1. The ticket machine is sent a *Give a ticket* message when its object sensor detects a car. Once the ticket has been produced the ticket machine sends a *Given* message to the barrier. When the object sensor of the barrier detects a car it sends an *Elevate* message to the barrier. Only when the barrier has received both messages, will it elevate. The barrier will not elevate if it has not received a *Given* message.

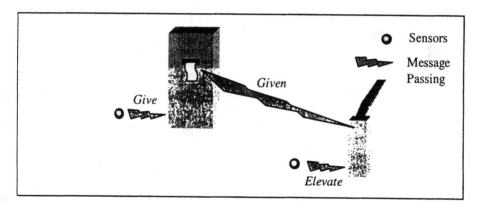

Fig. 1. Coordination among objects controlling the access to a car park

This situation highlights the problems explicit communication mechanisms have in expressing coordination (some of them have been previously identified in [3]):
1. The Ticket Machine object has to be programmed to send a *Given* message. Besides, the Barrier object must incorporate in its abstract interface this method, although it does not add anything to its functionality. Consequently, only those ticket machine and barrier objects specially coded for the car park can be used.

2. The code of the coordination pattern is dispersed among the objects and, therefore, will not be able to be used in any other application (for instance, controlling the access of passengers to the subway).

3. The message passing mechanism creates strong interdependencies among the objects. None of them in Figure 1 can be used without the other.

4. The message passing mechanism offers no flexibility. What happens if it is necessary to insert new objects in the scenario? For instance, suppose we are interested in putting a traffic light after the barrier in order to control the flow of pedestrians. In this case a new constraint arises: the ticket machine can not give tickets and the barrier can not elevate if the traffic light is red. Unfortunately, both the ticket machine and the barrier would have to be recoded to be synchronized with the new object.

To solve these problems, coordination models propose alternative mechanisms to message passing. These models can be classified as *endogenous* and *exogenous* [4]. The endogenous models provide primitives, which have to be included in the functional code of the methods of the objects for their coordination. For instance, Linda [10] and all the models which have arisen from it (for example [5], [8], [9] to name a few) propose the tuple space as an alternative mechanism for coordination. Objects have to put and get tuples from a certain space of tuples through the primitives *in* and *out*. Because there can be some producers and consumers associated with the same space of tuples, the sender and receiver are not fixed in the primitives of communication. In LO [7], the computational unit is the agent. The use of blackboards and message broadcasting let abstract the receiver in the communication inside an agent as well as among agents. These capabilities are improved in COOLL [12]. In these models, an object does not have to specify the group of objects it is going to be coordinated with. In fact, this group is only determined at runtime. Thanks to these features, problems 3 and 4 are solved, but 1 and 2 persist. The reason is that, although those models have liberated the coordination code from the set or number of coordinated objects, they have not succeeded in separating the coordination policies from the body of the methods of the objects.

In contrast, the exogenous models introduce separation providing coordination primitives that can be used from different entities from those which are being coordinated. In [6] it is showed how to design tools which can work with any other. The idea is to separate the specification of the inter-operability among the tools in components called *Toolbus*. The tools do not communicate directly, but through the Toolbus. In this setup, when a tool is coded, the set of tools one is going to work with do not have to be specified and, in addition, the coordination code is separated in specific components to express interoperability. The work described in [14] also gets to abstract the sender and receiver in the communications. In this case the mechanisms used are *Tuple Channels*. A Tuple Channel can be seen as an ordered sequence of tuples shared by several processes. These processes can send and receive tuples trough the Tuple Channels. The Tuple Channels can be interconnected in a dynamic way by *connectors*. The connection pattern is specified outside of the processes that are coordinated, separating the coordination code. Manifold [3], based on the IWIM communication model goes a step further. Manifold gets to abstract the sender and receiver in the communications by means of input and output ports connected by streams. Streams can be connected, disconnected and reconnected to ports. The specification of this connection and reconnection pattern is specified in components different from those that are coordinated. In this way, the separation of the coordination code is achieved. Also, coordinated components can raise events that are broadcasted to all the components in their environment. A component can pick up an event if it has been tuned to do it. All these models solve problems 2, 3, and 4: problems 3 and 4 are solved in the same way as they are for the analysed endogenous models. Moreover, as the coordination pattern is now specified in separated components that can be used in different applications, 2 is also solved. Nevertheless, 1 is still unsolved. In our case study, the ticket machine needs to communicate that a ticket has been given (through the toolbus, or a tuple channel, or a stream, or raising an event) to the barrier. In conclusion, the problem of these models is that, although they got to separate the coordination code from the objects that are coordinated, the mechanisms used are not transparent.

Other models provide separation and transparency simultaneously. For instance, [15] and [20] are based in the interception of messages. They capture the coordination constraints in separate components designed to monitor the events that occur in an object according to those messages (reception, processing, etc.). Every component has a series of coordination constraints associated with every event. In all the cases, the monitoring of events is made in a transparent way to the objects. With these features the previous problems are solved. However, these models still present some limitations. The exclusive use of the interception of messages limits the expressive power [16] because it leaves the events, which take place in the objects as a result of the execution of internal activities which do not respond to the invocation of messages, out of the scope of the coordination constraints. For instance, imagine a traffic light object that rules traffic and crossing. This traffic light changes its state periodically by an internal activity but also, offers the use of a button to pedestrians who want to cross. With the use of these models, the traffic could only be coordinated with the change of state produced by a request from a pedestrian. On the other hand, all the changes of state which are controlled by the internal activity are outside the scope of the coordination code, unless the internal activity has been coded to send the object itself a message communicating the change of state. So although internal activities can be coordinated it is certainly less intuitive to picture, to program or to maintain.

This survey permits us to conclude that, although the analysed coordination models present good features, they could be improved so that their integration in the COOP paradigm was achieved without any reduction in re-usability or expressive power.

3 Event Notification Protocols

In this section, a mechanism allowing the specification of coordination constraints on a group of active objects in a transparent way is presented. From the analysis of section 2 we deduce that such a mechanism has to address the following issues:
- If the mechanism has to be transparent, the objects of the group that is being coordinated have not to make an explicit use of it.
- If the coordination patterns have to be applicable to (re-usable for) different classes, the mechanism not only has to express those patterns as something outside the objects but, also, it must not refer to the class or kind of objects that are going to be coordinated.

- If the coordination patterns have to act by executing a series of actions answering the events that occur in the coordinated object, then, to get the highest possible expressive power, the group of events they can react to has to be as large as possible, including not only those which have relation with the reception and processing of messages, but also with the internal changes that occur in the objects. The recognition of the occurrence of those kind of events without a violation of encapsulation, can be obtained if the model of active objects support the concept of *abstract states* ([16], [22]) as part of the object interface together with the methods. *Abstract states* are those relevant states of execution of an object; for example, the traffic light object of the previous example could have three abstract states: red, amber and green. The abstract states are not excluding, that is to say, an object can be found in several states simultaneously.
- If the coordinated environment has to be an open system, the mechanism to make the binding between the coordination pattern and the group of objects must be dynamic so that both objects and patterns can be reconfigured dynamically.

As a mechanism that satisfies all these requirements, this paper proposes the *event notification protocols*, which take advantage of the runtime system of the objects. Through this mechanism, an object, A, (the coordinator) can request from another, B, (the coordinated) to communicate to it the occurrence of an event E. The runtime system of B accepts and processes the request in such a way that, when E occurs, it communicates it to A. Several objects can ask for the notification of the same event. A request is active until the requesting object cancels it. While a request is active, all the event occurrences will be notified.

The events we can ask for notification of are, the reception of a message, start or the end of the processing of a message, or when a certain abstract state is reached. The first three events are introduced for the utility they have exhibited in the coordination models based on the interception of messages, while the fourth one solves the lack of expressive power of those models. All the notifications can be asked for in an asynchronous or synchronous way, although, as we will see in Section 4.4, great care must be taken in the use of the last one. The protocol followed for the notification of every kind of event is as follows:

1. *Receipt Message (RM):* With the notification of this event, an object can know when another one receives a message in order to execute a particular method. The requesting object will have some actions associated with the event that will be executed when the notification is produced. Besides, if the notification was asked for in a synchronous way, the requesting object (requester) can re-route the message to a target different to the original one. The protocol for this is as follows: the notifying object communicates the occurrence of the event and waits for a response from the requester. If the response is positive, the message is queued and the object will execute it, if it is negative message is not queued, the requested object will ignore it, and then the requester can re-route the message to another object.

2. *Start of Processing (SoP):* This event informs the requester when an object is going to process a message. The requester could then execute the appropriate actions. If the notification was asked in a synchronous way, the requester will be able to abort the dispatch. As several objects might be waiting for the notification of this event, the protocol followed in this case is similar to the Two Phases Commit of the transactional systems. When the event is produced, the notifying

object communicates it to all the requesters and waits for confirmation. Each requester sends its response and waits for confirmation from the notifying object. If there is a negative response from one of the requesters, the notifying object sends a stop signal to every requester and aborts the dispatch. If every response is positive the notifying object sends a proceed signal and waits for the confirmation of all the requesters to execute the dispatch. In this way it is guaranteed that requesters will execute their synchronisation actions before dispatching.

3. *End of Processing (EoP)*: This event informs an object when another has finished processing a message. If the notification is applied in a synchronous way, the notifying object waits for the confirmation of the requester to proceed.

4. *State Reached (SR)*: When the object asks for notification of this event, it is informed of when another has reached a certain abstract state. The requesting object has to specify the abstract state that it wants to be notified of, and the notifier has to introduce this abstract state as part of its interface. If the notification is synchronous, the object waits for confirmation from the requester without executing any action in order to prevent the objects leaving the notified state. This guarantees that the object stays in the same state while the notification takes place. To support this feature the runtime system of the object has to provide mechanisms to post up the relevant states of the object in its interface, otherwise encapsulation would be violated.

The event notification protocols have the required features mentioned at the beginning of this section:

− The treatment of notifications is transparent to object *B*. All the notification requests are accepted and processed by the *B* Runtime System. Consequently, *B* does not have to be coded in any special way to treat those requests.

− The applying object (*A*) codes the coordination pattern with the actions associated with every event. In this way, this pattern is built as something isolated from the coordinated objects. Also, the notification request process is executed in such a way that *A* does not specify the class of *B*, it simply requires that it has the method or abstract state associated with the requested notification.

− Thanks to the State Reached Events, it is possible to request an object for notification of the fact that it has reached a certain abstract state. This provides the event notification protocols with the necessary expressive power to be able to monitor the events that take place in an object as a result of internal activities. Thus we are not limited to events associated with the interception and processing of messages.

− The binding between the coordination pattern and the coordination object is done in a dynamic way through the notification request process once that *A* and *B* have been instantiated. *A* can request notifications from objects and, afterwards, some of these notifications request can be cancelled. This allows the group of monitored objects to be modified in a dynamic way.

4 Coordinated Roles

In this section *Coordinated Roles*, a coordination model based on the event notification protocols, is presented. Firstly, we offer a general description of the model. Following this we introduce the concept of compounds events, and present some examples to exhibit the advantages it provides. Finally, we briefly describe the first built prototype. So as not to lengther this paper yet further, the linguistic support for the model is not given in full but it can be found in [21].

4.1 The model: Roles and Coordinated Roles

The design of the model is motivated by the behaviour of large business organisations. These are usually ruled by the leader hierarchy criterion. The structure of coordination patterns in Coordinated Roles is similar. A pattern is organised as a hierarchy of coordination components. Every component can have under its charge several groups of work and coordination components. The task of every component is to impose the laws of internal behaviour on every group it has under its charge and to coordinate the whole behaviour of all the groups and leaders that depend on it. In the lowest level of the hierarchy there are always groups of workers.

Every coordination component implements a coordination pattern prepared to impose constraints on working groups and other coordination components. Every work group or coordination component controlled by another one becomes a *role* in the imposed pattern. The coordination components are called *coordinators of roles* or simply *coordinators*.

4.2 Coordinators and hierarchies of coordinators

The mission of every coordinator is to monitor every component under its charge through the event notification protocols. To code a coordinator, the programmer simply specifies the groups of workers and coordinators upon which the coordinator imposes its constraints, and the events it reacts to jointly with the actions it executes in every case.

The members of every monitored group of work are active objects. Every active object incorporates in its interface some methods and abstract states. So, the events that can be monitored for every member of a group are the RM, SoP, and EoP, corresponding to the invocation of every one of these methods, and the SR events of every of their abstract states.

Each coordinator is implemented as another active object in the model. So, coordinators can also implement abstract states. The events a coordinator can monitor of another coordinator are those that the latter observes of its subordinates plus the State Reached Events of every of its abstract states. A requested notification event made in a synchronous way by a coordinator can always be observed asynchronously by a superior in the hierarchy. However, the opposite situation is not possible: a superior cannot observe synchronously an asynchronously propagated notification because synchronous notification requires that the notifier waits for confirmation and in this case the notifier is not waiting.

In order to build coordination hierarchies and to impose coordination patterns on objects, the programmer simply instantiates coordinator and worker objects and places some coordinators under the control of others. To achieve these tasks, every coordinator object implements the methods *Add_Object* or *Eliminate_Object* to add or eliminate active objects from the groups of work, and *Connect_Coordinator* or

Disconnect_Coordinator to place a coordinator under the control of another or free a coordinator from another's control.

4.3 Compound events

Besides the simple events described in Section 3, a coordinator can monitor compound events. A compound event is a group of simple events to which a sequence of actions that will only be executed when all the events of the group have occurred is associated. To declare a compound event, the programmer gives it a symbolic name, associates with it a series of notification requests as asynchronous or synchronous simple events and, finally, specifies the sequence of operations to be executed when all notifications have taken place.

If a synchronous request is associated with a compound event, its treatment will be delayed until all the notifications of the compound event have been produced and the associated actions have been executed. In this way, we can express mutual interdependencies among different objects [15] (the object *A* cannot execute the action *P* unless *B* executes *Q* and vice versa).

4.4 Some simple examples

In order to illustrate the benefits of the proposed model, in this section the example outlined in Section 2 is implemented with Coordinated Roles.

4.4.1 The car park

Here we first outline the ATOM[3] [22] code for the ticket machine and the barrier classes of this example. Subsequently we give the coordination pattern for these classes coded with Coordinated Roles and, finally, the construction of the coordination hierarchy using the composition syntax. The classes are specified in ATOM as follows.

```
CLASS Ticket_Machine              CLASS Barrier
     (ActiveObjectSupport):       (ActiveObjectSupport):

   METHODS = [Give]                 METHODS = [Elevate]

   DEF Give (self):                 DEF Elevate (self):
      #  Give a ticket                 # Elevate the barrier
```

It can be noted that none of the classes to be coordinated contain code for coordination purposes. They do not implement anything more than their expected

---

[3] ATOM is an active object model built as a Python extension. We use it here because the first protoype of Coordinated Roles was built for ATOM. This language supports the definition of abstract states in the objects and the event notification mechanism. This mechanism, although different from the Reached State Notification protocol, has the same goal: to let an object know when the other one has reached a certain state.

functionality: giving tickets and raising the barrier. Both classes inherit from *ActiveObjectSupport* which converts the instances of those classes into *ATOM* active objects. The variable *METHODS* specifies in *ATOM* those methods that can be concurrently invoked. The code for the coordinator would be:

```
CLASS Serializer (Coordinator):
    TO COORDINATE
            ROLE Obj1 FOR OBJECT WITH METHODS [MObj1 ];
            ROLE Obj2 FOR OBJECT WITH METHODS [MObj2 ];
    AS

    DECLARE ASYNCHRON EoP EVENT
        MObj1_Terminated FOR MObj1 AS
      EXECUTE Termination_MObj1;

    DECLARE SYNCHRON SoP EVENT
        Request_MObj2  FOR MObj2 AS
      CONSTRAINED BY  MObj1_Processed?;

    DEF Termination_MObj1 (self):
        MObj1_Processed = 1;
    DEF MObj1_Processed? (self):
      Aux = MObj1_Processed;
      MObj1_Processed = 0;
      RETURN Aux
```

The coordinator for the car park will be an instance of the class *Serializer*. This class inherits from *Coordinator*, which makes it a coordinator of Coordinated Roles. This coordinator oversees two roles (*Obj1* and *Obj2*) and only requires two methods, symbolically called *MObj1* and *MObj2*, to be declared in the interface of the roles. The coordinator serializes the execution of these methods and to achieve this monitors the end of the processing event of the method MObj1. When this event occurs, the coordinator executes the *Termination_MObj1* method. This event is exported to the interface of the coordinator with the name *MObj1_Terminated*. The coordinator also monitors the SoP event of the method *Mobj2*. On the triggering of this event, the execution of *Mobj2* will be aborted in *Obj2* if *Mobj1_Processed?* returns false. This event is exported to the interface of the coordinator with the name *Request_MObj2*. The code to start the application is the following:

```
TM1 = ActiveObject (Ticket_Machine)
B1 = ActiveObject (Barrier)
Car_Park = Coordinator_Object (Serializer)
Car_Park.ADD_OBJECT (TM1 TO Obj1 With Give AS MObj1)
Car_Park.ADD_OBJECT (B1 TO Obj2 With Elevate AS MObj2)
```

First, the objects and the coordinator are instantiated. Then, the *Ticket_Machine* is associated with the role *Obj1* making the necessary binding between its method *Give* and the method *MObj1* of the role. This is made invoking the method *ADD_OBJECT* of the coordinator. Lastly, the *Barrier*, is associated with the role making the appropriate binding.

4.4.2 Introducing coordinators extensibility

Let us suppose now that a new constraint is introduced in the access control of the car park, namely that the ticket machine can not give tickets if the car park is full. To manage this new constraint a new class to control the state of the car park is introduced and *Serializer* is extended through inheritance:

```
CLASS Car_Park_State (ActiveObjectSupport):

    METHODS = [In,out]

    STATES = [Full, notFull]
        #Relevant states observable in the instances of
        this class

    #Implementation of methods and abstract states (not
    shown)


CLASS Serializer_II (Serializer):
    TO COORDINATE
        ROLE Obj3 FOR OBJECT WITH STATE [Lock, Unlock];
    AS

    DECLARE SYNCHRON SR EVENT
        Lock_Reached FOR Lock AS
        EXECUTE Locked;

    DECLARE SYNCHRON SR EVENT
        Unlock_Reached FOR Unlock AS
        EXECUTE Unlocked;

    DECLARE SYNCHRON SoP EVENT
        Request_MObj1  FOR MObj1 AS
        CONSTRAINED BY Operation_Locked?;

    DEF Locked (self):
        Lc = 1;
    DEF Unlocked (self):
        Lc = 0;
    DEF Operation_Locked? (self):
        RETURN Lc;
```

Serializer_II extends *Serializer* in two ways. First of all, a new role is introduced. This role corresponds to the object that manages the state of the car park. This object has two methods, *In* (to enter the car park) and *Out* (to exit the car park), and two abstract states indicating whether the car park is full or not. Secondly, the *Obj1* role is extended with a new event. This event constrains the execution of the *MObj1* method. The following sentences indicate the way in which the application can be started:

```
P1 = ActiveObject (Car_Park_State)
Car_Park2= Coordinator_Object (Serializer_II)
Car_Park2.ADD_OBJECT (P1 TO Obj3 With Full AS Lock AND
                     notFull AS Unlock)
Replace (Car_Park BY Car_Park2)
```

Note how *Car_Park2* replaces the *Car_Park* coordinator from Section 4.4.1. The semantics of the *Replace* command transfer the state and the object/role bindings from the old coordinator to the new one. This feature allows the model to dynamically change the coordination policies.

4.4.3 Introducing shared objects among several coordinators

Several coordinators can monitor an object at the same time. For example, let us consider the introduction of a new entrance to the car park. To deal with this new constraint it is necessary to create a new *Ticket_Machine*, a new *Barrier* and a new coordinator. However, the *Car_Park_State* will be the same as in the last section. The new coordinator will share *Car_Park_State* with the coordinator *Car_Park2*. To add this restriction to the application of the last section, the following code needs to be included:

```
TM2 = ActiveObject (Ticket_Machine)
B2 = ActiveObject (Barrier)
Car_Park3 = Coordinator_Object (Serializer_II)
Car_Park3.ADD_OBJECT (TM2 TO Obj1 With Give AS MObj1)
Car_Park3.ADD_OBJECT (B2 TO Obj2 With Elevate AS MObj2)
Car_Park3.ADD_OBJECT (P1 TO Obj3 With Full AS Lock AND
                     notFull AS Unlock)
```

4.4.4 Introducing composability, polymorphism, and distribution of coordination patterns

A coordinator can be monitored by other coordinators. This feature allows the composition of complex coordination policies from fine grain coordination components. To illustrate it, we introduce a further constraint to the car park scenario. A traffic light is now installed after the barrier *B1* in order to let pedestrians pass. Now *B1* can not be raised if the traffic light coordinating the crossing of pedestrians is on green[4]. To manage this constraint a new coordinator is needed. This coordinator will monitor the abstract states (*Open* or *Closed*) of the object controlling the traffic light and the event *Request_MObj2* of the *Car_Park2* coordinator. In this case, it is not necessary to implement a new coordinator, the behaviour coded in the *Serializer_II* coordinator can be reused. The following code illustrates this fact. Note that we can use only just part of the global functionality of the coordinator:

```
TL = ActiveObject (Traffic_Light) (*not  shown *)
Barrier_Locker = Coordinator_Object (Serializer_II)
Barrier_Locker.ADD_OBJECT (Car_Park2 TO Obj1 With
```

---

[4] For the sake of simplicity, other situations such as the existence of the *amber* state in the traffic light object and the constraint "the light should not turn green if the barrier is up" have been ignored. However, they can be easily implemented.

```
                     Request_MObj2 AS Request_MObj1)
Barrier_Locker.ADD_OBJECT (TL TO Obj3 With Open AS Lock
                     AND Closed AS Unlock)
```

The event *Request_MObj2* (request to raise the barrier) is observed by *Barrier_Locker* as the event *Request_Mobj1* (attempt to execute a method that now will be constrained by the state of the traffic light). When the SoP event for the *Elevate* method is triggered by the object *B1* (the barrier) the coordinator *Car_Park2* will examine the associated constraint but, before letting control proceed to the barrier, it will propagate the event to the *Barrier_Locker* coordinator. Now, *Barrier_Locker* will be responsible for control proceeding to the barrier *B1*.

Note that it is not necessary to use the entire functionality coded for the coordinator. In this way, the model provides the polymorphism of the coordination patterns, in that the same coordination pattern can be used to coordinate different objects from different classes. In addition, coordinator hierarchies provide the possibility to distribute coordination patterns, in that coordinators are objects that can be instantiated in different computers.

4.4.5 Introducing the flexibility of the model

By flexibility of the model we mean the facilities the model provides to the programmer for coding the same coordination pattern with different coordination hierarchies. For example, the constraint added in Section 4.4.4 could be coded in several ways which achieve the same behaviour. For instance, the coordinator *Barrier_Locker* could have been introduced directly monitoring the barrier *B1*:

```
TL = ActiveObject (Trafic_Light) (* not shown *)
Barrier_Locker = Coordinator_Object (Serializer_II)
Barrier_Locker.ADD_OBJECT (B1 TO Obj1 With Request_MObj2
                     AS Request_MObj1)
Barrier_Locker.ADD_OBJECT (TL TO Obj3 With Open AS Lock
                     AND Closed AS Unlock)
```

Or simply, the coordinator *Serializer_II* could have been extended to manage the new constraint (not shown). Although the three methods define the same behaviour, they provide different features. For example, the first two promote code re-usability but are not as efficient as the last (because they have a synchronous event monitored by two coordinators at the same time). In contrast, the coordinator in the last implementation is more efficient but is less re-usable than the coordinators in the first two implementations. In general, depth coordination hierarchies are better for coordination policies with little synchronisation whereas wide coordination hierarchies without shared objects among coordinators are better for coordination policies specifying greater synchronisation.

4.5   Coordinated Roles in ATOM

As it was mentioned in Section 4.4, the first prototype of Coordinated Roles was developed for ATOM [22]. In this version of Coordinated Roles, the coordinators were implemented as active objects inheriting from the special class *Coordinator*.

This class implements the methods needed to manage the state notification requests corresponding to the associated objects of each role.

Although the prototype has confirmed the viability of this model, it still presents several problems. Firstly, ATOM does not support the notification protocols of events related to the reception and processing of messages. These protocols have been simulated through state notification. In order to achieve this, it was necessary to implement a mechanism to define three abstract states for any method in every coordinated object. These abstract states correspond to "true" when a message is received, the method is going to be dispatched or the execution of the method has finished. Secondly, the original version of ATOM does not support distribution and this forced us to build a distributed version of it based in ILU. Lastly, ATOM is not very efficient and led to poor performance of the prototype. In order to solve these problems we developed ActiveJava [2], a model of distributed active objects supporting the event notification protocols.

5 Related works

Although in Section 2 it has been presented a brief background on coordination models, here we discuss the similarities of Coordinated Roles with some of them. In [15] coordination patterns are expressed as *Synchronizers*, a kind of components that have to be added to concurrent object oriented languages. These components are also designed to monitor a group of objects imposing a set of constraints over them. In contrast, Synchronizers let only monitor SoP events. RM, EoP and SR events are out of its scope. Moreover, a synchronizer can not monitor other synchronizers. This restriction makes difficult the composition of coordination policies.

More are the similarities between Coordinated Roles and IWIM/Manifold [3]. Both models give two kind of entities, coordinators and coordinated. In both models, a coordinator can monitor others coordinator, react to events, reconfigure the communication patterns between the coordinated entities in a dynamic way. Nevertheless, Manifold do not provides total transparency in the sense presented in this paper (events must be raised explicitly using the RAISE primitive). A regular process specifies the name of the events it is tuned for, so diminishing the re-usability of such a process. In Manifold, the events pending to be handled by a regular process are manage as a set (if an event is raised twice before it has been handled, the event is handled once). Moreover, Manifold only deals with asynchronous events.

6 Conclusions and Future Work

In this paper the event notification protocols have been presented. This mechanism permits the monitoring of events that occur in an active object and exhibits two important properties: it is transparent to the monitored objects and it does not violate their encapsulation. Based on this mechanism Coordinated Roles has been presented, a coordination model that, apart from offering good integration with the COOP paradigm, also provides good power of expression and promotes re-usability, not only of the coordinated objects, but also of the coordination patterns. In addition, the use of

Coordinated Roles provides a high degree of flexibility, polymorphism, extensibility, composability, and dynamic change of coordination patterns.

Nowadays, the second prototype of Coordinated Roles based on ActiveJava is being implemented. Based on this version a software architecture to coordinate Java applets in the WWW will be developed. The idea is to have hierarchies of distributed coordinators in web servers so that applets inserted in HTML documents could instantiate ActiveJava objects and put them under the control of the coordinators placed in the servers from which these documents come.

Acknowledgments

We would like to thank Alberto Gómez, Arthur Pewsey, Antonio Vallecillo, Pascal Poizat and the anonymous referees for their helpful comments.

References

1. M. Aksit, B. Tekinerdogan, L. Bergmans. Achieving Adaptability through separation and composition of concerns, In Max Mühlhäuser editor, *Special Issues in Object-Oriented Programming, Workshop Reader of the ECOOP'96.* Dpunkt-Verlag, 1997.
2. L. A. Álvarez, J. M. Murillo, F. Sánchez, J. Hernández. ActiveJava: Un modelo de programación concurrente orientado a objetos, *III Jornadas de Ingeniería del Software,* Murcia (Spain) 1998.
3. F. Arbab. The IWIM Model for Coordination of Concurrent Activities. P. Ciancarini, C. Hankin (Eds.). *First International conference Coordination'96.* LNCS 1061. Springer-Verlag. 1996.
4. F. Arbab. What Do You Mean Coordination? Bulletin of the Dutch Association for Theoretical Computer Science (NVTI). March'98.
5. M. Banville. Sonia: An adaptation of Linda for Coordination of Activities in Organisations. P. Ciancarini, C. Hankin (Eds.). *First International conference Coordination'96.* LNCS 1061. Springer-Verlag. 1996.
6. J. A. Bergstra, P. Klint. The ToolBus Coordination Architecture. P. Ciancarini, C. Hankin (Eds.). *First International conference Coordination'96.* LNCS 1061. Springer-Verlag. 1996.
7. M. Bourgois, J.M. Andreoli, R. Pareschi. Concurrency and Communication: Choices in Implementing the Coordination Language LO. R. Guerraoui, Oscar Nierstrasz and Michel Riveill, editors. *Proceedings of ECOOP'93 Workshop in Object-Based Distributed Programming,* Kaiserslautern, Germany. LNCS 791, Springer-Verlag. July 1993.
8. K. De Bosschere, Jean-Marie Jacquet. μ^2Log: Towards Remote Coordination. P. Ciancarini, C. Hankin (Eds.). *First International conference Coordination'96.* LNCS 1061. Springer-Verlag. 1996.
9. C. Callsen, G. Agha. Open Heterogeneus Computing in ActorSpace. Journal of Parallel and Distributed Computing, Special issue on Heterogeneus Processing, 21:289-300, 1994.
10. N. Carreiro, D. Gelernter. LINDA in Context. *Communications of the ACM,* vol 32, pp. 444-458, 1989.
11. N.Carreiro, D. Gelenter. Coordination languagues and their significance. *Communications of the ACM,* 35 (2):97-107, Febraury 1992.
12. S. Castellani, Paolo Ciancarini. Enhancing Coordination and Modularity for a Languague with Objects-as-Multisets. P. Ciancarini, C. Hankin (Eds.). *First International conference Coordination'96.* LNCS 1061. Springer-Verlag. 1996.
13. M. Chaudron, Edwin de Jong. Towards a Compositional Method for Coordinating Gamma Programs. P. Ciancarini, C. Hankin (Eds.). *First International conference Coordination'96.* LNCS 1061. Springer-Verlag. 1996.

14. M. Díaz, M. Rubio, J.M. Troya. The Tuple Channel Coordination Model. *Workshop on Software Engineering for Parallel and Distributed Systems (PDSE'97).* IEEE Computer Society Press, pp. 95-106. Boston, USA. May 1997.

15. S. Frølund. Coordinating Distributed Objects. An Actor-Based Approach to Synchronization. *The MIT Press.* 1996.

16. J. Hernández, M. Papathomas, J.M. Murillo, F. Sánchez. Coordinating Concurrent Objects: How to deal with the coordination aspect? *Aspect Oriented Programming Workshop of the 11th. European Conference on Object-Oriented Programming, ECOOP'97.*

17. D. Holmes, James Noble, John Potter. Aspects of Synchronisation. *Proceedings of TOOLS Pacific'97.* IEEE Press 1998.

18. W. L. Hürsch, C. Videira Lopes. Separation of Concerns. *College of Computer Science,* Northeastern University, February 1995.

19. S. Matsuoka, A. Yonezawa. Inheritance anomaly in Object-Oriented Concurrent Programming. In *Research Directions in Concurrent Object Oriented Languages.* G. Agha, P. Wegner and A. Yonezawa Eds. The MIT Press. April 1993.

20. M. Mukherji, D. Kafura. Specification of Multi-Object Coordination Schemes Using Coordinating Environments. *ftp://actor.cs.vt.edu/pub/kafura/ce.ps,* 1995.

21. J.M. Murillo, J. Hernández, F. Sánchez, L.A. Álvarez. Coordinated Roles: un modelo de coordinación transparente no basado en la interceptación de mensajes. *Technical Report TR-4/98. Department of Computer Science. University of Extremadura.* November 1998.

22. M. Papathomas, J. Hernández, J. M. Murillo, F. Sánchez. Inheritance and Expressive Power in Concurrent Object-Oriented Programing, *Proceedings of the LMO'97 Conference.* Roscoff, France. October 1997.

23. F. Sánchez, J. Hernández, M. Barrena, J. M. Murillo, A. Polo. Issues in Composability of Synchronization Constraints in Concurrent Object-Oriented Languages. In Max Mühlhäuser editor, Special Issues in Object-Oriented Programming, *Workshop Reader of the ECOOP'96,* Dpunkt-Verlag, 1997.

24. F. Sánchez, J. Hernández, J.M. Murillo, E. Pedraza. Run-time Adaptability of Synchronization Policies in Concurrent Object-Oriented Languages. *Position Paper in ECOOP'98 workshop on Aspect-Oriented Programming,* May 1998.

Pipelining the Molecule Soup:
A Plumber's Approach to Gamma

Martin Weichert

Göteborg University and Chalmers University of Technology,
Department of Computing Science, S-412 96 Göteborg, Sweden
martinw@cs.chalmers.se

Abstract. Gamma is a language based on multiset rewriting aimed at separating coordination from computation. The "pipelining" technique turns a producer-consumer-type Gamma program with sequential composition into a parallel one, preventing the data from erroneously "flowing back" from the consumer to the producer. The resulting parallel composition offers more freedom to coordinate the computation and to choose an appropriate refinement later on. This paper extends a previous paper by Hankin, Le Métayer and Sands. It identifies conditions for the pipelining transformation of atomic programs and proves it correct under these conditions with relational reasoning. It also proves refinement in the other direction correct with respect to a stronger refinement relation, statebased simulation, and strengthens it further to a precongruence using Chaudron's "convex simulation" and the new notion of "data-equivalent" simulation". [1]

1 Introduction

1.1 The Gamma Model

The unique data structure of Gamma is a multiset of data items, called a *state*. A Gamma program consists of a set of *atomic programs*. These are *rewrite rules* (also called *reaction rules*) r of the form

$$r : lhs \rightarrow f(lhs), \text{ if } cond(lhs)$$

which states that whenever elements matching *lhs* in the multiset satisfy condition *cond*(*lhs*), they may be replaced in the multiset by the result of applying the function f to *lhs*. A result (not "the" result!) is obtained when a stable state is reached, i.e., when no more reaction can take place. For example the Gamma program consisting of just the following rule *max* computes the maximum element of a non-empty multiset, whereas the following *add* sums up the elements of a non-empty multiset:

$$max : \quad x, y \rightarrow y, \quad \text{ if } x \leq y$$
$$add : m, n \rightarrow m + n, \text{ if } true$$

---

[1] A longer version of this paper, with detailed proofs, appears as a technical report and can be reached via <http://www.cs.chalmers.se/~martinw/papers/>.

The semantics of an atomic Gamma rule r is thus determined by a binary relation $\mathcal{R}_r$ between states: $\langle M, M' \rangle \in \mathcal{R}_r$ iff state M can be changed into M' by one application of rule r.

Atomic Gamma programs can be combined into bigger ones with sequential and parallel composition [6], which we write $p; q$ and $p \| q$.

The semantics of a composed Gamma program p is given in form of an unlabelled transition system $\rightarrow$ on pairs of a program and a state, and a *termination predicate* $\sqrt{}$ ("immediate convergence") on such pairs. The semantics of p is derived from the semantics $\mathcal{R}$ of its atomic programs by the set of Structured Operational Semantics rules:

$$\frac{\langle M, M' \rangle \in \mathcal{R}_r}{\langle r, M \rangle \rightarrow \langle r, M' \rangle} \ (\mathbf{at}_\rightarrow) \qquad \frac{\not\exists M' : \langle M, M' \rangle \in \mathcal{R}_r}{\langle r, M \rangle \sqrt{}} \ (\mathbf{at}_\sqrt{})$$

$$\frac{\langle p, M \rangle \rightarrow \langle p', M' \rangle}{\langle p; q, M \rangle \rightarrow \langle p'; q, M' \rangle} \ (\mathbf{Seq}_\rightarrow) \qquad \frac{\langle p, M \rangle \sqrt{}}{\langle p; q, M \rangle \rightarrow \langle q, M \rangle} \ (\mathbf{Seq}_\sqrt{})$$

$$\frac{\langle p, M \rangle \rightarrow \langle p', M' \rangle}{\begin{array}{c} \langle p \| q, M \rangle \rightarrow \langle p' \| q, M' \rangle \\ \langle q \| p, M \rangle \rightarrow \langle q \| p', M' \rangle \end{array}} \ (\mathbf{Par}_\rightarrow) \qquad \frac{\langle p, M \rangle \sqrt{} \quad \langle q, M \rangle \sqrt{}}{\langle p \| q, M \rangle \sqrt{}} \ (\mathbf{Par}_\sqrt{})$$

Gamma is thus an instance of a *composed reduction system* [9], which are all systems with a sequential and a parallel composition that behave according to this set of rules, independently of the underlying data structure $State$ or the way the one-step relations $\mathcal{R}_r$ are defined.

1.2 Refinement Relations

Gamma programs are related to each other by different forms of **refinement**. A simple Gamma program can be seen as a very nondeterministic (pre-)algorithm. A refinement step can make the program more specific and more deterministic. A program may (but need not necessarily) be refined into a completely deterministic algorithm. If a program p is a refinement of a program q, written $p \leqslant q$, then p is considered a correct implementation of q.

Sometimes however, as in the "pipelining transformation" of this paper, we are also interested in "refining" in the other direction: from a more deterministic p to a more general q, maybe in order to refine q into a different p' later on.

There are a variety of possible ways to describe the "behaviour" of a transition system, which also give rise to different refinement relations.

One such description which is often relevant is that of **input-output behaviour**. For any given input, we are interested in which output(s) the system can produce, and consider two systems equivalent if for every given input they will produce the same (set of) output(s). Mathematically, the semantics of the system is a relation between inputs and outputs (or a function in the deterministic case). In the case of a transition system as we have here, with transitions between program-state pairs, we can consider a state M as the input to a program p and consider all the transition sequences that start with $\langle p, M \rangle$. If such a transition sequence leads to $\langle p', M' \rangle$ and $\langle p', M' \rangle$ cannot do any further transitions (it has *terminated*, written as $\langle p', M' \rangle \sqrt{}$), then we consider the state M' an output of program p to the input M. Thus we can define the *behaviour* of a program p as the relation:

$$IO(p) = \{\langle M, M' \rangle \mid \langle p, M \rangle \rightarrow^* \langle p', M' \rangle \wedge \langle p', M' \rangle \sqrt{}\}$$

and define a program p to be an *IO refinement* of q if its IO behaviours are included in those of q:

$$p \leqslant^{io} q \Leftrightarrow IO(p) \subseteq IO(q)$$

Now the behaviour of the sequential composition of two programs is the relational composition of their behaviours:

$$IO(p; q) = IO(p) \cdot IO(q) \tag{1}$$

and IO refinement can be substituted under sequential composition ("sequential compositionality"):

$$\text{If } p \leqslant^{io} p_2 \text{ and } q \leqslant^{io} q_2 \text{ then } p; q \leqslant^{io} p_2; q_2$$

A characteristic property of this description is that it *abstracts away from the intermediate states* that the program passes through during execution. This description is perfectly adequate in a large number of situations. It however breaks down under the context of (shared-state) parallel composition. In the case of parallel composition with shared state, it is precisely those intermediate states that can make a difference. Programs that have the same IO behaviour and may be substitutable under sequential composition may behave quite differently under parallel composition: $p \leqslant^{io} p_2$ and $q \leqslant^{io} q_2$ but not $p \| q \leqslant^{io} p_2 \| q_2$. So if we want to make any statements about the behaviour of parallel compositions, we need a more detailed description that takes the intermediate states into account, and an equivalence $\leqslant^\times$ based on that more detailed description, which should have the "parallel compositionality" property:

$$\text{If } p \leqslant^\times p_2 \text{ and } q \leqslant^\times q_2 \text{ then } p \| q \leqslant^\times p_2 \| q_2$$

Refinement by simulation **does** take the intermediate states into account, and so does the one by *transition trace semantics* [9], which also gives similar results.

1.3 Producer-Consumer Systems

A typical class of problems in Gamma are a kind of "producer-consumer" systems. Let *prod* be a Gamma program that produces a multiset from some *input*, and *cons* a program that consumes the elements coming from *prod*, to produce the final *output*. The whole computation of *output* from *input* is thus done by the sequentially composed Gamma program *prod; cons*.

Examples for this kind of Gamma programs are Fibonacci numbers [5, 8, 7], sorting [7], prime factorisation [2, 7], and many others. We will look at one of these examples in more detail in Sect. 4.

Pipelining. Now since Gamma is all about parallelism, we would like to "refine" this into $prod \| cons$. In fact, under certain conditions (explored in this paper) the following *statebased refinement* (see Sect. 2.1) holds:

$$prod; cons \leqslant^{sb} prod \| cons$$

With this refinement we can conclude correctness of the left hand side from the correctness of the right hand side, going from the more nondeterministic, more parallel, to the more deterministic, more sequential, from a larger set of correct behaviours to a subset.

However, we cannot conclude correctness in the other direction, going from the more deterministic, more sequential $prod; cons$ to the less deterministic, more parallel $prod \| cons$, where we may receive additional behaviours, possibly incorrect behaviours. To conclude that we would need some refinement:

$$prod \| cons \leqslant prod; cons$$

Now, under some more conditions on $cons$ and $prod$ we will even get the desired refinement to hold, at least for IO behaviours:

$$prod \| cons \leqslant^{io} prod; cons$$

Thus even the more nondeterministic program will not produce any more outputs than the more deterministic one. We will however not be able to make this refinement true when considering intermediate states as well. The program $prod \| cons$ *does* have additional intermediate states (where $cons$ has already started working before $prod$ has finished) that $prod; cons$ doesn't; and if those intermediate states interfere with the environment of the program, expressed as another program env that is put in parallel with the program in question, we may get

$$(prod \| cons) \| env \not\leqslant^{io} (prod; cons) \| env$$

Proper plumbing for producer-consumer systems. If we replaced $prod; cons$ by $prod \| cons$ and let $cons$ start before $prod$ is finished, then basically two things could "go wrong". Firstly, $cons$ could wrongly consume elements that belong to the *input* and should have been consumed by $prod$ instead. Secondly, $cons$ could even produce *output* that $prod$ could wrongly consume. Thus we would like the following conditions to hold: $(\star)$ the input of $cons$ and the input of $prod$ should be disjoint, to prevent the first risk, and $(\star\star)$ the output of $cons$ and the input of $prod$ should be disjoint, to prevent the second one.

More precisely, in terms of the transition systems of two atomic programs $prod$ and $cons$ (some results can be generalised to non-simple programs):

If condition $(\star)$ holds, we get a strong confluence property: whenever $M_1 \xrightarrow{prod} M_2$ and $M_1 \xrightarrow{cons} M_3$, then $M_2 \xrightarrow{cons} M_4$ and $M_3 \xrightarrow{prod} M_4$. (The lower half of a diamond in a transition graph can be completed from the upper half.) One consequence of this confluence property is the following:

$$\text{"}cons \text{ cannot disable } prod\text{"} \tag{2}$$

that is, whenever *prod* and *cons* are both enabled at the same state, then *prod* will still be enabled in every state that *cons* leads to.

Further, if condition (⋆⋆) holds, we get another diamond property: whenever $M_1 \xrightarrow{cons} M_3 \xrightarrow{prod} M_4$, then $M_1 \xrightarrow{prod} M_2 \xrightarrow{cons} M_4$. (The diamond in the transition graph can be completed sideways.) Equivalently,

$$\text{"}cons \text{ can be postponed until after } prod\text{"} \tag{3}$$

Property (3) implies the following weaker property: Whenever *prod* is enabled after *cons*, it must already have been enabled before (and it will not disable *cons*). Or the other way round, whenever *prod* is disabled, it will not become (re)enabled by *cons*:

$$\text{"}cons \text{ cannot re-enable } prod\text{"} \tag{4}$$

When both (2) and (3) hold, we say:

$$\text{"}prod \text{ is independent of } cons\text{"} \tag{5}$$

One important result of this paper is that whenever property (4) holds, then the refinement $prod; cons \leqslant^{sb} prod \,\|\, cons$ is valid. But even $\leqslant^{sb}$ is still a weak refinement relation and is not respected by $\|$. With a process *env* in parallel we could get: $(prod; cons) \,\|\, env \not\leqslant (prod \,\|\, cons) \,\|\, env$. Therefore the next step we do is to explore *convex simulation* $\leqslant^\diamond$ and find some additional conditions which will ensure that $(prod; cons) \,\|\, env \leqslant^\diamond (prod \,\|\, cons) \,\|\, env$ holds. It turns out that the extra condition we need is just this: "*env* cannot reenable *prod*".

Property (3), will ensure that any path containing $\ldots \xrightarrow{cons} \xrightarrow{prod} \ldots$ can be replaced with an equivalent one containing $\ldots \xrightarrow{prod} \xrightarrow{cons} \ldots$ that leads to the same final state. Furthermore, if also property (2) holds, "*cons* cannot disable *prod*", then in that final state *prod* will be disabled, and so will be $prod \,\|\, cons$. Therefore the process $prod \,\|\, cons$ cannot add any new IO behaviour that is not already contained in $prod; cons$, and we get refinement also in the opposite direction, $prod \,\|\, cons \leqslant^{io} prod; cons$, at least for the weaker IO refinement relation $\leqslant^{io}$. Because of the additional intermediate states of $prod \,\|\, cons$ we cannot expect parallel compositionality to hold for this refinement.

2 Simulations: Tools for Formal Refinement

2.1 Statebased and Stateless Simulations

The central notion of refinement we are going to use is *simulation*, which is a well-known comparison relation between transition systems. We will start by defining *statebased simulation*, and step by step we will extend this basic notion to adjust it to different needs.

Definition 1 (Statebased Simulation).
$\mathcal{R} \subseteq (\mathcal{P}rog \times State) \times (\mathcal{P}rog \times State)$ *is a statebased simulation if for all* $p, q \in \mathcal{P}rog$, $M, N \in State$, *such that* $\langle p, M \rangle \, \mathcal{R} \, \langle q, N \rangle$:

- $M = N$
- Whenever $\langle p, M \rangle \to \langle p', M' \rangle$ then there exists a q', N' such that $\langle q, N \rangle \to^*$ $\langle q', N' \rangle$, and $\langle p', M' \rangle \, \mathcal{R} \, \langle q', N' \rangle$.
- Whenever $\langle p, M \rangle \surd$ then there exists a q', N' such that $\langle q, N \rangle \to^* \langle q', N' \rangle$, $\langle p, M \rangle \, \mathcal{R} \, \langle q', N' \rangle$, and $\langle q', N' \rangle \surd$.

Note that we allow one step of p to be matched by several, or even zero, steps of q. The two programs may thus progress "at different speeds". This "matching different speeds" is sometimes called a "weak" simulation (or "jumping", [4]).

Unlike *bisimulation*, simulation needs an extra clause for matching termination, otherwise any program could be refined into one that does nothing at all.

Statebased simulation is usually presented in contrast with the stronger *stateless simulation*. Stateless simulation can actually be seen as just a specific instance of statebased simulation:

Definition 2 (Stateless Simulation).

A stateless simulation is a relation $\mathcal{R} \subseteq \mathcal{P}rog \times \mathcal{P}rog$ such that $\mathcal{R} \times \mathcal{I}d$ is a statebased simulation.

$\mathcal{R} \times \mathcal{I}d$ is defined in the obvious way: $\langle p, M \rangle \, (\mathcal{R} \times \mathcal{I}d) \, \langle q, N \rangle$ iff $p \, \mathcal{R} \, q$ and $M = N$.

2.2 State-dependent Statements

As the name implies, a stateless refinement $p \leqslant^{sl} q$ between two programs is independent of any state. Most other refinement relations that we will use are state-dependent: they can be true for one state but false for another (they are predicates on states). We use the following uniform notation for state-dependent properties A property φ that holds *for a particular state* M will be written as $M \models \varphi$. Specifically, we use the following state-dependent properties:

- $M \models p \surd$ holds iff $\langle p, M \rangle \surd$
- $M \models p \leqslant^{sb} q$ holds iff $\langle p, M \rangle \leqslant^{sb} \langle q, M \rangle$, that is, iff $\langle \langle p, M \rangle, \langle q, M \rangle \rangle \in \mathcal{R}$ for some statebased simulation $\mathcal{R}$.
- $M \models p \leqslant^{io} q$ holds iff for all M': whenever $\langle M, M' \rangle \in IO(p)$ then $\langle M, M' \rangle \in IO(q)$, that is, every output M' of program p on input M is also an output of program q on the same input.

These notations are extended to sets of states by defining

$$A \models \varphi \text{ iff } M \models \varphi \text{ for all } M \in A$$
$$\models \varphi \text{ iff } M \models \varphi \text{ for all } M$$

Note that we can express the refinement $\leqslant^{io}$ with relational operators:

$$A \models p \leqslant^{io} q \text{ iff } \mathcal{I}d(A) \cdot IO(p) \subseteq IO(q)$$

Other notations that are used for state-dependent properties are for example $P \leqslant_E Q$ in [7], Sect. 2.2, which is called "constrained refinement" and which corresponds to $Multi(E) \models p \leqslant^{io} q$ in our notation, or the definition $s \leqslant_M t \Leftrightarrow \langle s, M \rangle \leqslant \langle t, M \rangle$ in [3], which thus corresponds to $M \models s \leqslant t$ in our notation.

With the notation $M \models \varphi$ state-dependent properties can be combined with different boolean and *modal* operators. A particularly useful one is the modal "forall" operator [_], which can be read as "for all successors". For any binary relation $\mathcal{R}$, the meaning of $[\mathcal{R}]$ is given by:

- $M \models [\mathcal{R}]\varphi$ holds iff for all M' such that $\langle M, M' \rangle \in \mathcal{R}$, $M' \models \varphi$ holds.

Thus in particular: $M \models [IO(p)]\varphi$ holds iff for all p', M' such that $\langle p, M \rangle \rightarrow^* \langle p', M' \rangle \surd$, $M' \models \varphi$ holds.

Relating different refinements. Our first result relates two refinement relations:

Proposition 3. *Statebased refinement implies IO refinement:*
  If $M \models p \leqslant^{sb} q$ then $M \models p \leqslant^{io} q$.

2.3 Congruence, Compositionality

It is a standard result that all Gamma operators respect stateless simulation:

$$\frac{p \leqslant^{sl} q \quad p_2 \leqslant^{sl} q_2}{p; p_2 \leqslant^{sl} q; q_2} \qquad \frac{p \leqslant^{sl} q \quad p_2 \leqslant^{sl} q_2}{p \,\|\, p_2 \leqslant^{sl} q \,\|\, q_2}$$

but not statebased. For example, the following conclusion does *not* hold:

$$\frac{M \models p \leqslant^{sb} q \quad M \models p_2 \leqslant^{sb} q_2}{M \models p; p_2 \leqslant^{sb} q; q_2} \quad wrong!$$

The reason this goes wrong is that when p_2 starts executing in $p; p_2$ the state has already changed from M to some M'. So we need the refinement $M \models p_2 \leqslant^{sb} q_2$ to hold not in the state M, but in some other state M'. Actually, we need it to hold in *all* possible output states of $\langle p, M \rangle$ – but this is nothing other than saying $M \models [IO(p)]p_2 \leqslant^{sb} q_2$! Therefore we can express and prove the following:

Proposition 4 (Compositionality of Statebased Refinement).

$$\frac{M \models p \leqslant^{sb} q \quad M \models [IO(p)]p_2 \leqslant^{sb} q_2}{M \models p; p_2 \leqslant^{sb} q; q_2}$$

A similar discussion and result is given in Sect. 4.3.2 in [3] for *schedules*, a coordination language for Gamma.

The same property holds if we replace statebased by IO refinement, although the proof technique is different: by relational reasoning instead of by simulation.

Proposition 5 (Compositionality of IO Refinement).

$$\frac{M \models p \leqslant^{io} q \quad M \models [IO(p)]p_2 \leqslant^{io} q_2}{M \models p; p_2 \leqslant^{io} q; q_2}$$

2.4 Convex Simulation

Convex simulation is introduced in [3]. The statement $M \models p \leqslant^\phi q$ expresses the idea that the refinement between p and q is "robust" under all possible interferences of the kind ϕ, where ϕ is a binary relation on states, called the "interference relation". Especially, if programs p and q are to be put in an "environment" that is represented by a program env, then the refinement $M \models p \leqslant^{\Diamond env} q$ is "robust" under all interferences that could possibly be caused by a program env.

Definition 6 (Interference Relation).
For any program p, we define $\Diamond p$, the interference relation induced by p, as

$$\Diamond p = \{\langle M', M'' \rangle \mid \langle p, M \rangle \to^* \langle p', M' \rangle \to^* \langle p'', M'' \rangle\}$$

For any set of atomic programs S (called a sort), we define $\Diamond S = (\bigcup_{a \in S} \mathcal{R}_a)^*$.

For simple programs and finite sorts these two notions coincide:
$\Diamond(a_1 \| \ldots \| a_n) = \Diamond\{a_1, \ldots, a_n\}$.

Definition 7 (ϕ-Simulation, Convex Simulation).
For a given relation $\phi \subseteq State \times State$ (called interference relation),
$\mathcal{R} \subseteq (Prog \times State) \times (Prog \times State)$ *is a ϕ-simulation if*

- $\mathcal{R}$ *is a statebased simulation, and*
- *the inclusion $\widehat{\phi}(\mathcal{R}) \subseteq \mathcal{R}$ holds, where $\widehat{\phi}(\mathcal{R})$ is defined as:*

$$\widehat{\phi}(\mathcal{R}) = \{\langle \langle p, M' \rangle, \langle q, M' \rangle \rangle \mid \langle p, M \rangle \mathcal{R} \langle q, M \rangle \wedge M \phi M'\}$$
$$= (\mathcal{I}d \times \phi^{-1}) \cdot \mathcal{R} \cdot (\mathcal{I}d \times \phi) \cap (\top \times \mathcal{I}d)$$

For any program p, a $\Diamond p$-simulation is called a convex simulation for program p. For any sort S, a $\Diamond S$-simulation is called a convex simulation for sort S.

The inclusion condition $\widehat{\phi}(\mathcal{R}) \subseteq \mathcal{R}$ can be spelled out as: For all p, q, M and M': Whenever $\langle p, M \rangle \mathcal{R} \langle q, M \rangle$ and $M \phi M'$, then $\langle p, M' \rangle \mathcal{R} \langle q, M' \rangle$. It is explained in detail in [3].

Convex refinement is weaker than stateless but stronger than statebased refinement. One good property of it is that – like statebased and unlike stateless refinement – it can be used to express local properties. Another good property is that – like stateless and unlike statebased refinement – it is is respected by sequential and parallel composition in many circumstances, as the following proposition shows:

Proposition 8 (Compositionality of Convex Refinement).
Convex simulation for any sort S is respected under both sequential and parallel composition by all programs s such that $atoms(s) \subseteq S$, where $atoms(s)$ is the set of atomic programs in s.

$$\frac{M \models p \leqslant^{\Diamond S} q \quad atoms(s) \subseteq S}{\begin{array}{c} M \models s; p \leqslant^{\Diamond S} s; q \\ M \models p; s \leqslant^{\Diamond S} q; s \\ M \models p \| s \leqslant^{\Diamond S} q \| s \end{array}} \tag{6}$$

Proof. By $\Diamond S$-simulations. □

We can read these rules as: If $M \models p \leqslant^{\Diamond S} q$, i.e., the refinement $p \leqslant q$ is "robust" under all possible interferences of the sort S, then the refinement will still hold within any (sequential or parallel) context that has only interferences from S.

Corollary 9 (Precongruence of Convex Refinement).
Given p, p_2, q, q_2 such that $atoms(p)$, $atoms(p_2)$, $atoms(q)$, $atoms(q_2) \subseteq S$:

$$\frac{M \models p \leqslant^{\Diamond S} p_2 \quad M \models q \leqslant^{\Diamond S} q_2}{\begin{array}{c} M \models p;q \leqslant^{\Diamond S} p_2;q_2 \\ M \models p \| q \leqslant^{\Diamond S} p_2 \| q_2 \end{array}} \tag{7}$$

2.5 Data-equivalent Simulation

We are going to extend the well-estalished notion of simulation with one adaptation to make it suitable to compare transition systems with different data representation.

For all of this section, let $\prec$ be an arbitrary relation (not necessarily an equivalence relation) between states, called *data-equivalence*, where $M \prec N$ is meant to express that M and N represent the same data values. Then we extend the definitions and propositions from the previous sections as follow:

Definition 10 (Simulation modulo $\prec$).
$\mathcal{R} \subseteq (Prog \times State) \times (Prog \times State)$ *is a statebased simulation modulo $\prec$ if for all $p, q \in Prog$, $M, N \in State$, such that $\langle p, M \rangle \mathcal{R} \langle q, N \rangle$:*

- $M \prec N$
- *Whenever $\langle p, M \rangle \to \langle p', M' \rangle$ then $\exists q', N'$ such that $\langle q, N \rangle \to^* \langle q', N' \rangle$, and $\langle p', M' \rangle \mathcal{R} \langle q', N' \rangle$.*
- *Whenever $\langle p, M \rangle \surd$ then $\exists q', N'$ such that $\langle q, N \rangle \to^* \langle q', N' \rangle$, $\langle p, M \rangle \mathcal{R} \langle q', N' \rangle$, and $\langle q', N' \rangle \surd$.*

A stateless simulation modulo $\prec$ is a relation $\mathcal{R} \subseteq Prog \times Prog$ such that $\mathcal{R} \times (\prec)$ is a statebased simulation modulo $\prec$.

We write $\langle p, M \rangle \leqslant^{sb}_{\prec} \langle q, N \rangle$ or short $MN \models p \leqslant^{sb}_{\prec} q$ for "$\langle \langle p, M \rangle, \langle q, N \rangle \rangle \in \mathcal{R}$ for some statebased simulation $\mathcal{R}$ modulo $\prec$". State-dependent properties $MN \models \varphi$ now depend on data-equivalent pairs $M \prec N$ of states. All the previous results, like statebased refinement implies IO refinement and compositionality of refinement, go through with data-equivalence as well.

Now we arrive at our most general definition of simulation, by combining of ϕ-simulation and convex simulation with the idea of data-equivalence as well. The complete definition looks rather complicated, because it extends the concept of simulation in two directions at the same time: with a *data-interference* relation [3], and with a *data-equivalence* relation (introduced here for the first time).

Data-equivalence relates states "horizontally", that is, states on different sides of a refinement relation, whereas *data-interference* relates states "vertically", that is states before and after a transition on the same side of a refinement relation. They are "orthogonal" in the sense that they can be used independently.

Definition 11 (Simulation with ϕ and $\prec$).
   For a given relation $\prec \subseteq State \times State$ (called data-equivalence*), and a given relation $\phi \subseteq State \times State$ (called* interference relation*),*
   $\mathcal{R} \subseteq (Prog \times State) \times (Prog \times State)$ is a ϕ-simulation (modulo $\prec$) if

- *$\mathcal{R}$ is a statebased simulation (modulo $\prec$), and*
- *the inclusion $\widehat{\phi_\prec}(\mathcal{R}) \subseteq \mathcal{R}$ holds, where $\widehat{\phi_\prec}(\mathcal{R})$ is defined as:*

$$\widehat{\phi_\prec}(\mathcal{R}) = \{\langle\langle p, M'\rangle, \langle q, N'\rangle\rangle \mid \langle p, M\rangle \mathcal{R} \langle q, N\rangle \wedge M\phi M' \wedge N\phi N' \wedge M' \prec N'\}$$
$$= (\mathcal{I}d \times \phi^{-1}) \cdot \mathcal{R} \cdot (\mathcal{I}d \times \phi) \cap (\top \times \prec)$$

   For any program p, a $\Diamond p$-simulation (modulo $\prec$) is called a convex simulation *(modulo $\prec$) for program p. (Analogous for sorts.)*

3 The Pipelining Transformations

This section states several conditions which ensure correctness of pipelining.

3.1 Statebased Refinement

Proposition 12. *Let prod and cons be atomic programs that satisfy (4), "cons cannot re-enable prod". Then the following statebased refinement holds:*

$$\models prod; cons \leqslant^{sb} prod \| cons \tag{8}$$

Proof. By showing statebased simulation

$$\mathcal{R} = \{\langle\langle prod; cons, M\rangle, \langle prod \| cons, M\rangle\rangle\}$$
$$\cup \{\langle\langle cons, M\rangle, \langle prod \| cons, M\rangle\rangle \mid M \models prod\sqrt{}\}$$

A program p is called "simple" if it contains no sequential composition.

Corollary 13. *Proposition 12 holds also for all simple programs prod and cons.*

Proof. If p is simple, i.e., $p = r_1 \| \ldots \| r_n$, then the behaviour of p is the same as that of an atomic program r such that $\mathcal{R}_r = \mathcal{R}_{r_1} \cup \ldots \cup \mathcal{R}_{r_n}$. Thus all results proved about the behaviour of atomic programs lift to simple programs. □

   This result can be extended to non-simple programs as well. If *prod* is non-simple, then it may have transformed by some passive steps into a different program $\underline{prod}$ by the time it terminates. This program $\underline{prod}$ is called the *residual* of *prod* and is independent of M, uniquely determined only by *prod*'s syntactic structure. It can be computed recursively by the following equalities:

$$\underline{r} = r \qquad \underline{p;q} = \underline{q} \qquad \underline{p\|q} = \underline{p}\|\underline{q}$$

Now it is this residual part of *prod* that shall not become reenabled.

If *cons* is non-simple, we take "*cons* cannot reenable $\underline{prod}$" to mean:

$$\models \underline{prod}\surd \Rightarrow [IO(cons)]\underline{prod}\surd \tag{9}$$

With these definitions we get:

Proposition 14. *Let prod and cons be general programs that satisfy (9), "cons cannot re-enable $\underline{prod}$". Then the following statebased refinement holds:*

$$\models prod; cons \leqslant^{sb} prod \| cons \tag{10}$$

This result strengthens Theorem 11 in [7] from IO to statebased refinement.

3.2 IO Equivalence

Proposition 15. *Let prod and cons be atomic programs such that "prod is independent of cons" (5). Then the following IO equivalence holds:*

$$\models prod; cons =^{io} prod \| cons \tag{11}$$

Proof. First, recall that the "postpone" property (3) implies the "not re-enable" property (4). By Propositions 12 and 3 follows the refinement $prod; cons \leqslant^{io} prod \| cons$.

Second, we show the other direction, $prod \| cons \leqslant^{io} prod; cons$, by relational reasoning:

Let us write $\dagger\mathcal{R}_r$ for the identity relation on all states where the atomic program r is disabled. With this notation the IO behaviour of all simple programs can be easily written as a relational expression:

$$IO(r) = (\mathcal{R}_r)^* \cdot \dagger\mathcal{R}_r \tag{12}$$
$$IO(r_1 \| r_2) = (\mathcal{R}_{r_1} \cup \mathcal{R}_{r_2})^* \cdot \dagger(\mathcal{R}_{r_1} \cup \mathcal{R}_{r_2}) \tag{13}$$

... and so on for more than two.

The "postpone *cons*" property (3) is equivalent to

$$\mathcal{R}_{cons} \cdot \mathcal{R}_{prod} \subseteq \mathcal{R}_{prod} \cdot \mathcal{R}_{cons} \tag{14}$$

This property enables us to push all the *cons*'s after the *prod*'s: By induction over n we can prove

$$\forall n \geq 0 : (\mathcal{R}_{prod}{}^* \cdot \mathcal{R}_{cons}{}^*)^n \subseteq \mathcal{R}_{prod}{}^* \cdot \mathcal{R}_{cons}{}^*$$

and from that:

$$(\mathcal{R}_{prod} \cup \mathcal{R}_{cons})^* = (\mathcal{R}_{prod}^* \cdot \mathcal{R}_{cons}^*)^* \subseteq \mathcal{R}_{prod}^* \cdot \mathcal{R}_{cons}^* \qquad (15)$$

Similarly, the "not disable" property (2) is expressed relationally as

$$\mathcal{R}_{cons} \cdot \dagger\mathcal{R}_{prod} \subseteq \dagger\mathcal{R}_{prod} \cdot \mathcal{R}_{cons}$$

This lets us then similarly push the $\mathcal{R}_{cons}$ terms after the $\dagger\mathcal{R}_{prod}$ terms:

$$\mathcal{R}_{cons}^* \cdot \dagger\mathcal{R}_{prod} \subseteq \dagger\mathcal{R}_{prod} \cdot \mathcal{R}_{cons}^* \qquad (16)$$

This gives us:

$$
\begin{aligned}
& IO(prod \,\|\, cons) \\
by\ (13) = &\ (\mathcal{R}_{prod} \cup \mathcal{R}_{cons})^* \cdot \dagger\mathcal{R}_{prod} \cdot \dagger\mathcal{R}_{cons} \\
by\ (15) \subseteq &\ \mathcal{R}_{prod}^* \cdot \mathcal{R}_{cons}^* \cdot \dagger\mathcal{R}_{prod} \cdot \dagger\mathcal{R}_{cons} \\
by\ (16) \subseteq &\ \mathcal{R}_{prod}^* \cdot \dagger\mathcal{R}_{prod} \cdot \mathcal{R}_{cons}^* \cdot \dagger\mathcal{R}_{cons} \\
by\ (12) = &\ IO(prod) \cdot IO(cons) \\
by\ (1) = &\ IO(prod; cons)
\end{aligned}
$$

$\square$

Theorem 16. *Proposition 15 holds also for all simple programs prod and cons.*

For simple programs, our Theorem 16 (actually just a corollary) coincides with Theorem 16 in [7]. That theorem however claims the same result even for non-simple *prod* and *cons*, which does not hold in general, because of the possibility that *prod* terminates prematurely. See Sect. 4.2 for a counterexample. Some even stronger conditions will be needed to achieve correct pipelining even for non-simple programs. Another possible approach would include modifying the semantics of the parallel operator, as in [4].

3.3 Convex Refinement

Proposition 17. *Let prod and cons be atomic programs that satisfy (4), "cons cannot re-enable prod". Additionally, let env ("the environment") be an atomic program that satisfies "env cannot re-enable prod".*

Then the following convex refinement holds:

$$\models prod; cons \leqslant^{\Diamond env} prod \,\|\, cons \qquad (17)$$

Proof. By showing that under the given conditions, the statebased simulation in the proof of Prop. 12 is a $\Diamond env$-simulation. $\square$

From Prop. 8 then follows:

Corollary 18. *Under the conditions of Prop. 17, the following holds:*

$$\models (prod; cons) \,\|\, env \leqslant^{\Diamond env} (prod \,\|\, cons) \,\|\, env \qquad (18)$$

We conjecture that Prop. 17 can be generalised from simple to general programs.

4 Applying the Pipelining Transformations

4.1 Tagging and Trimming

Section 1.3 stated the following conditions on two (atomic) Gamma programs *prod* and *cons*: ($\star$) the input of *cons* and the input of *prod* should be disjoint, and ($\star\star$) the output of *cons* and the input of *prod* should be disjoint. Together they guarantee independence of *prod* from *cons*. Now how can we establish conditions ($\star$) and ($\star\star$) in Gamma?

In [7] condition ($\star$) is called "separable". Both conditions together are called "left exclusive". They present the idea of *tagging* the data of a Gamma program in order to achieve left-exclusive-ness. We follow this idea, and we show how the program transformations achieved with tagging (and trimming) can be proved correct with simulation modulo data-equivalence.

Some definitions. For any Gamma rule r, we define the sets $input(r)$ and $output(r)$ of all elements that can possibly be input and be output by r, by $input(r) = \bigcup\{M \mid \langle M, M' \rangle \in \mathcal{R}_r\}$ and $output(r) = \bigcup\{M' \mid \langle M, M' \rangle \in \mathcal{R}_r\}$, that is, the union over all multisets (seen as sets) that appear on the left hand side, resp. right hand side, of any transitions by r.

To get ($\star$): Consider a Gamma rule *prod* with the property that whenever *prod* is disabled, then $M \cap input(prod) = \emptyset$. (In particular, this is true if the lhs of *prod* always is a singleton multiset.) Thus the *cons* in *prod*; *cons* only gets started in a multiset M where $M \cap input(prod) = \emptyset$ holds. In such a multiset M we can replace the rule

$$cons : lhs \to f(lhs), \text{ if } cond(lhs)$$

with the "trimmed" rule *cons* $\upharpoonright_{prod}$ which simply ignores all input from $input(prod)$ and which is defined as:

$$cons \upharpoonright_{prod} : lhs \to f(lhs), \text{ if } cond(lhs) \land (lhs \cap input(prod) = \emptyset)$$

The trimmed rule *cons* $\upharpoonright_{prod}$ has the desired property $input(prod) \cap input(cons \upharpoonright prod) = \emptyset$. Both rules *cons* and *cons* $\upharpoonright_{prod}$ can do the same transitions in any state M where *prod* is disabled. We would like to conclude $M \models cons =^{sb} (cons \upharpoonright_{prod})$ for all such M, but for this it is necessary that *prod* cannot become enabled again by *cons*, which is guaranteed by ($\star\star$).

To get ($\star\star$): If $input(prod) \cap output(cons) \neq \emptyset$, then *prod* in *prod* $\|$ *cons* might become (re)enabled on the wrong elements. To prevent this, we can replace *cons* by a modified rule $cons^\tau$ which attaches a distinct *tag* to all output elements such that *prod* will not react to any tagged elements at all, whereas $cons^\tau$ treats tagged input elements just like untagged ones. For any rule *cons* as above, $cons^\tau$ is defined as:

$$cons^\tau : lhs \to tag(f(untag(lhs))), \text{ if } cond(untag(lhs))$$

where function *tag* attaches a tag to every element in its argument and function *untag* removes the tags from all tagged elements in its argument and leaves all others unchanged. This gives us $\models cons =^{sb}_{\prec} cons^{\tau}$, i.e. $cons^{\tau}$ is equivalent to $cons$ modulo the data-equivalence $\prec$ defined as $M \prec N$ iff $M = untag(N)$.

For $prod$ to work correctly it is necessary that the initial multiset does not contain already tagged elements. Hence we define $Init = \{\langle M, N \rangle \mid M \prec N, N = untag(N)\}$. We can show that $Init \models prod =^{sb}_{\prec} prod$, which gives us the first refinement step of $prod; cons$, modulo data-equivalence:

$$Init \models prod; cons =^{sb}_{\prec} prod; cons^{\tau} \qquad (19)$$

The tagged rule $cons^{\tau}$ has the desired property $input(prod) \cap output(cons^{\tau}) = \emptyset$. Hence $cons^{\tau}$ cannot reenable $prod$, and thus the refinement $M \models cons^{\tau} =^{sb} (cons^{\tau} \upharpoonright_{prod})$ holds for all M where $prod$ is disabled. That in turn implies the refinement

$$\models prod; cons^{\tau} =^{sb} prod; (cons^{\tau} \upharpoonright_{prod}) \qquad (20)$$

by Prop. 4 (sequential compositionality), under the condition $\models [IO(prod)]\, prod\surd$, which holds since $prod$ is simple.

Since $prod$ cannot become reenabled by $cons^{\tau}$, and thus not by the trimmed rule $cons^{\tau} \upharpoonright_{prod}$ either, we can apply the pipelining transformation by Prop. 12:

$$\models prod; (cons^{\tau} \upharpoonright_{prod}) \leqslant^{sb} prod \,\|\, (cons^{\tau} \upharpoonright_{prod}) \qquad (21)$$

For the weaker IO refinement, the refinement step holds in both directions by Prop. 15:

$$\models prod; (cons^{\tau} \upharpoonright_{prod}) =^{io} prod \,\|\, (cons^{\tau} \upharpoonright_{prod}) \qquad (22)$$

Finally, an "untagging rule"

$$untag : a \to untag(a), \text{ if } a \text{ is tagged}$$

may be appended after the parallel composition to remove the tags after the end of the pipelined operation. On multisets that are finite (which we assume all our multisets to be), rule $untag$ is equivalent to an empty program modulo the equivalence relation $\succ \cdot \prec$. (Note that $M \succ \cdot \prec N$ is the same as $untag(M) = untag(N)$.) We get the following refinement:

$$\mathcal{I}d \models prod \,\|\, (cons^{\tau} \upharpoonright_{prod}) =^{sb}_{\succ \cdot \prec} (prod \,\|\, (cons^{\tau} \upharpoonright_{prod}))\,; untag \qquad (23)$$

which expresses that when programs $prod \,\|\, (cons^{\tau} \upharpoonright_{prod})$ and $(prod \,\|\, (cons^{\tau} \upharpoonright_{prod}))\,; untag$ start in equal states, they exhibit matching behaviour and will maintain equivalent – but not necessarily equal – states throughout.

Using transitivity of refinement, we can put it all together to get:

$$Init \models prod; cons =^{io}_{\prec} (prod \,\|\, (cons^{\tau} \upharpoonright_{prod})); untag \qquad (24)$$

Using the fact that $IO(untag) = (\succ)$, this result can even be strengthened from $=^{io}_{\prec}$ to $=^{io}$ with relational reasoning.

4.2 Pipelining: the CGZ Example

Ciancarini, Gorrieri and Zavattaro [4] present the following example. Let $cons = max; ones; add$ be a program that computes the number of occurrences of the maximum value among the non-negative elements of a set of numbers, where:

$$
\begin{aligned}
max : \quad & x, y \to y, \quad && \text{if } 0 \leq x < y \\
ones : \quad & x \to 1, \quad && \text{if } 0 \leq x \neq 1 \\
add : \quad & m, n \to m + n
\end{aligned}
$$

Suppose we have a multiset with both negative and positive values and want to use this program for computing the maximum *absolute value*. We can do this by prepending the following program $prod = abs$:

$$
abs : x \to -x, \ \text{if } x < 0
$$

The sequential composition $prod; cons = abs; max; ones; add$ does what we want, so it can serve as our specification.

It is easy to check that the program satisfies the condition "$cons$ cannot reenable $prod$" for pipelining. Thus, by Prop. 12, the statebased refinement

$$
\models abs; (max; ones; add) \leqslant^{sb} abs \parallel (max; ones; add)
$$

holds for all states. Now we would however like to achieve refinement in the other direction, at least with respect to IO behaviours. As is pointed out in [4], the desired IO refinement

$$
\models abs \parallel (max; ones; add) \leqslant^{io} abs; (max; ones; add)
$$

does **not** hold, due to the fact that max could terminate prematurely in a state where it is temporarily disabled (but would have become re-enabled by abs later on).

This also gives us a counterexample to [7], Theorem 16. If we replace add in the example above by the trimmed rule $add' = add \lceil_{abs}$:

$$
add' : m, n \to m + n, \ \text{if } 0 \leq m, n
$$

then $input(add') \cap input(abs) = \emptyset$, and $Lex(max; ones; add', abs)$ holds, which is the precondition for Theorem 16 in [7]. However, $abs \parallel (max; ones; add')$ still has the same undesired behaviour with max ending prematurely, and therefore the IO refinement does not hold.

If we want to get valid refinement in both directions, we can still safely apply their or our Theorem 16 to atomic programs like abs and max to get $\models abs \parallel max =^{io} abs; max$. By compositionality of IO refinement, Prop. 5, this implies

$$
\models (abs \parallel max); ones; add =^{io} abs; max; ones; add
$$

5 Conclusions

We have presented several different refinement relations for Gamma programs and shown how they are interrelated. Besides the well-known refinement of IO behaviours, statebased and stateless refinement, the relatively new idea of convex simulation has been adapted from schedules [3] to Gamma programs, and our own new notion of simulation modulo data-equivalence has been presented. These different refinements show themselves to be useful in proving several pipelining transformations correct. We have identified several conditions for correct pipelining with respect to different refinement relations, by reasoning both on the level of Gamma programs and on the level of Composed Reduction Systems, which are clearly kept apart. The conditions "*cons* cannot disable *prod*", "*cons* cannot enable *prod*" and "*cons* can be postponed after *prod*" give clear and easy-to-handle characterisations for establishing correctness of pipelining transformations, for example in connection with *tagging* [7], and *trimming* of Gamma rules.

A theorem about IO refinement from [7] is strengthened to statebased refinement, which allows further strengthening to convex refinement. Another theorem from [7] is shown to be not correct in general, and it is partly reestablished.

References

[1] J.-M. Andreoli, C. Hankin, and D. Le Métayer, editors. *Coordination programming: mechanisms, models and semantics*. IC Press, London, 1996.

[2] J.-P. Banâtre and D. Le Métayer. The Gamma model and its discipline of programming. *Science of Computer Programming*, 15:55–77, 1990.

[3] Michel Chaudron. *Separating Computation and Coordination in the Design of Parallel and Distributed Programs*. PhD thesis, Rijksuniv. Leiden, May 1998. ISBN 90-9011643-5.

[4] P. Ciancarini, R. Gorrieri, and G. Zavattaro. An alternative semantics for the parallel operator of the calculus of Gamma programs. In *[1]*, pages 232–248. 1996.

[5] S. J. Gay and C. L. Hankin. A program logic for Gamma. In *[1]*, pages 171–194. 1996.

[6] C. Hankin, D. Le Métayer, and D. Sands. A calculus of Gamma programs. In U. Banerjee, D. Gelernter, A. Nicolau, and D. Padua, editors, *Languages and Compilers for Parallel Computing, 5th International Workshop*, number 757 in Lecture Notes in Computer Science, pages 342–355. Springer-Verlag, August 1992.

[7] C. Hankin, D. Le Métayer, and D. Sands. Refining multiset transformers. *Theoretical Computer Science*, 192:233–258, 1998.

[8] Mark Reynolds. Temporal semantics for Gamma. In *[1]*, pages 141–170. 1996.

[9] David Sands. Composed reduction systems. In *[1]*, pages 211–231. 1996.

Erratic Fudgets:
A Semantic Theory for an Embedded Coordination Language

Andrew Moran, David Sands, and Magnus Carlsson

Department of Computing Science
Chalmers University of Technology and the University of Gteborg
S-412 96 Gteborg, Sweden
{andrew,dave,magnus}@cs.chalmers.se

Abstract. The powerful abstraction mechanisms of functional programming languages provide the means to develop domain-specific programming languages within the language itself. Typically, this is realised by designing a set of combinators (higher-order reusable programs) for an application area, and by constructing individual applications by combining and coordinating individual combinators. This paper is concerned with a successful example of such an embedded programming language, namely Fudgets, a library of combinators for building graphical user interfaces in the lazy functional language Haskell. The Fudget library has been used to build a number of substantial applications, including a web browser and a proof editor interface to a proof checker for constructive type theory. This paper develops a semantic theory for the non-deterministic stream processors that are at the heart of the Fudget concept. The interaction of two features of stream processors makes the development of such a semantic theory problematic:

(i) the sharing of computation provided by the lazy evaluation mechanism of the underlying host language, and

(ii) the addition of non-deterministic choice needed to handle the natural concurrency that reactive applications entail.

We demonstrate that this combination of features in a higher-order functional language can be tamed to provide a tractable semantic theory and induction principles suitable for reasoning about contextual equivalence of Fudgets.

1 Introduction

Fudgets are a collection of combinators for developing graphical user interfaces in the lazy functional programming language Haskell. Typical fudget programs exhibit the clean separation between *computation* (the standard Haskell code) and *coordination* (the management of the user interface) that is the hallmark of the so-called coordination languages.

This paper is concerned with the semantics of fudgets, or rather, with the semantics of the high-level language of stream processors that lie at the heart of fudgets. A stream processor is a higher-order process that communicates with its surroundings through a single input stream and a single output stream.

The implementation of stream processors used in the Fudget library could serve as a semantic basis for formal reasoning about stream processor and fudget programs. But as a semantics, the current implementation itself leaves a lot to be desired. For one thing, it is implemented deterministically, and as a consequence many intuitively correct transformation laws, such as symmetry of parallel composition, are in fact unsound. We aim to develop a more abstract semantics of stream processors, which better captures their conceptually concurrent, non-deterministic nature, and which relates to concrete implementations by a notion of refinement.

We build our semantic theory for fudgets on top of a lazy functional language with erratic non-deterministic choice. Erratic choice is a simple internal choice operator. In modelling non-determinism with erratic choice, we are choosing to ignore aspects of fairness. This can be viewed as a shortcoming of our model since we can neither express a bottom-avoiding merge operator for streams, nor prevent starvation when merging streams.

Despite the simplicity of erratic choice, it exhibits a nontrivial interaction with lazy evaluation. By *lazy evaluation* we mean to the standard *call-by-need* implementation technique for non-strict languages whereby the argument in each instance of a function application is evaluated at most once. In the standard semantic theories of functional languages this evaluation mechanism (also known as graph reduction) is modelled by the much simpler *call-by-name* evaluation, in which an argument is evaluated as many times as it is required. In the presence of non-determinism, there is an observable difference between these evaluation mechanisms, and so a semantic theory must take care to model these details accurately. Consider the following desirable equivalence:

$$2 * x \cong x + x$$

This doesn't hold in a call-by-name theory when non-determinism is present. To see this, consider the situation when x is bound to $3 \oplus 4$, where $\oplus$ is erratic choice. The righthand side may evaluate to 6, 7, or 8, but the lefthand side may result in 6 or 8, but *not* 7. However, the equivalence *does* hold in a call-by-need theory for non-determinism, since the result of $3 \oplus 4$ will be shared between both occurrences of x in the righthand side. So while the call-by-need theory may lack arbitrary β-reduction, it does retain other useful equivalences.

1.1 Contributions

We develop an operational theory for $\Lambda^{\oplus}_{\text{NEED}}$, a call-by-need lambda calculus with recursive lets, constructors, case expressions, and an erratic choice operator. The stream processor calculus of [CH98] is presented and a translation into $\Lambda^{\oplus}_{\text{NEED}}$ is given. We show that congruences and reductions in the stream processor calculus are equivalences and refinements, respectively, in the theory. Some specific contributions are:

- A *context lemma* for call-by-need and non-determinism, meaning we can establish equivalence and refinement by considering just computation in a restricted class of contexts, the evaluation contexts;
- A rich inequational theory for call-by-need and non-determinism;
- A *unique fixed-point induction* proof rule, which allows us to prove properties of recursive programs, and
- Validation of congruences and reductions in the stream processor calculus proposed by Carlsson and Hallgren [CH98].

1.2 Organisation

The remainder of the paper is organised as follows. We begin with a discussion of related work in section 2. Then section 3 introduces stream processors and the stream processor calculus. The language $\Lambda_{\text{NEED}}^{\oplus}$ is presented, along with the translation from stream processor calculus into $\Lambda_{\text{NEED}}^{\oplus}$. The operational semantics of $\Lambda_{\text{NEED}}^{\oplus}$ is presented in section 4. This is used to define notions of *convergence* and *divergence*, leading to contextual definitions of *refinement* and *observational equivalence*. The context lemma is then stated, and a number of laws from the inequational theory are presented. An equivalence sensitive to the cost of evaluation is defined, leading to the statement of the unique fixed-point induction rule. Section 5 deals with the correctness of the translation of stream processors into $\Lambda_{\text{NEED}}^{\oplus}$[1]. Section 6 concludes, and we discuss of future avenues of research.

2 Related Work

2.1 Fudget Calculi

The Fudgets thesis [CH98] introduces a calculus of stream processors, which is presented in the Cham-style as a collection of structural congruences and a set of reduction rules. Independently of this work, Colin Taylor has developed theories of "core fudgets" using two approaches: an encoding into the pi calculus, and a direct operational semantics of "core fudgets" [Tay98a,Tay98b]. Taylor is somewhat dismissive of his earlier pi-calculus approach, since (like many pi calculus semantics) it suffers from the rather low-level nature of the encoding. In particular he notes that "the pi calculus encodings are often large and non-intuitive". Taylor's direct approach [Tay98b] is based on a labelled transition system in which the core fudget combinators such as parallel composition are given a direct operational interpretation. The theory which is built on top of this is based on higher-order bisimulation. Taylor's theory can be seen to verify many of the congruence rules of Carlsson and Hallgren's calculus. The difference with our theory stems from the fact that Taylors calculus completely abstracts away the underlying functional language. This abstraction presupposes that the semantics

---

[1] These results are stated without proof; there is an extended version [MSC98] of this paper which not only contains proofs of these results, but also summarises the technical development of the theory and presents the proofs of the main theorems.

of the combinators is orthogonal to the underlying functional computations. As we have argued, in the presence of call-by-need computation, there is an observable interaction between the sharing present in the functional computation, and the non-determinism implied by the concurrency of parallel composition.

2.2 Other functional GUIs

There are at least two other functional approaches to GUI in a functional language for which an underlying theory exists (for a "core" language). The toolkit eXene, by Reppy and Gansner [GR91] is written on top of Concurrent ML (CML) [Rep91], a multi-threaded extension to Standard ML. A number of authors have considered the semantics for a fragment of CML, *e.g.* [FH95,FHJ96,NN96].

The GUI library *Haggis* [FPJ95], which is built upon *Concurrent Haskell* [PJAF96]. Fudgets have been implemented in Haggis, and a theory for concurrent Haskell has been outlined in [PJAF96]. This suggests that a theory of fudgets could be developed using this route.

2.3 Non-Determinism in Functional Languages

One usually gives meaning to non-deterministic constructs via *powerdomain* constructions [Plo76,Smy78,Smy83,Bro86,SS92,Cli82], domain-theoretic analogues of the powerset operator. The Plotkin, or convex, powerdomain [Plo76] models erratic choice very well, but like all powerdomain semantics, ignores the issue of sharing. An alternative to erratic choice is McCarthy's *amb*, a bottom-avoiding non-deterministic operator which embodies a certain kind of fairness, but the denotational approach has well-documented problems modelling McCarthy's *amb* (see *e.g.* [Mor98]). The only serious attempt at a denotational semantics for McCarthy's *amb*, that due to Broy [Bro86], is developed for a first-order language only, and doesn't consider sharing.

Lassen and Moran [LM98] also consider McCarthy's *amb*, in the context of a call-by-name lambda calculus. Though able to construct a powerful equational theory for that language (including proof rules for recursion) by taking an operational approach, the language in question is not call-by-need. The choice operator considered in this article is simpler (and arguably less useful) and thus we are able to build on the semantic theory for deterministic call-by-need developed in [MS99].

Kutzner and Schmidt-Schauß [KSS98] recently presented a reduction-calculus for call-by-need with erratic non-determinism based on an extension of the call-by-need lambda calculus of [AFM+95]. We believe that our theory of equivalence subsumes the calculus of Kutzner and Schmidt-Schauß's in the same way that the deterministic part is subsumed by the improvement theory of [MS99]. Kutzner and Schmidt-Schauß's theory is inadequate for our purposes. Firstly, it only considers a pure lambda calculus with no constructors. Secondly it does not consider cyclic recursion (so it cannot, for example, express the cyclic Y-combinator). Thirdly, and most importantly, it does not include any proof principles for reasoning about recursive definitions. Our semantic theory has none of these deficiencies.

3 The Essence of Fudgets

The Fudget library is implemented in the purely functional language Haskell [PH97], in which all computations are deterministic. Conceptually, a fudget program should be regarded as a set of concurrent processes exchanging messages with each other and the outside world. In a style that is typical for a higher-order, functional programming language, combinators in the Fudget library are used to express high-level communication patterns between fudgets.

Taking an abstract view, the essence of the fudget concept is the *stream processor*, which has truly parallel and non-deterministic properties.

3.1 The stream processor calculus

A stream processor can be seen as a process that consumes messages in an input stream, producing messages in an output stream. However, the streams are not manipulated directly by the process, only the messages are (a more appropriate name would actually be *message processor*). There are seven ways of constructing a stream processor:

$$
\begin{array}{lll}
S, T, U ::= & S\,!\,T & (Put) \\
\mid & x\,?\,S & (Get) \\
\mid & S <\!\cdot\, T & (Feed) \\
\mid & S \ll T & (Serial) \\
\mid & S \mid T & (Parallel) \\
\mid & \ell\, S & (Loop) \\
\mid & x & (Var)
\end{array}
$$

The first three forms are stream processors that deal with input and output of single messages. $S\,!\,T$ outputs the message S and then becomes the stream processor T. $x\,?\,S$ waits for a message, and binds the variable x to that message (in S) and then becomes S. $S <\!\cdot\, T$ feeds the message T to S, that is, T is the first message that S will consume on its input stream.

The following three constructions are used for coordinating the message flow between stream processors (see also figure 1). $S \ll T$ connects the output stream of T to the input stream of S, and thus acts as a serial composition. $S \mid T$ puts the stream processors S and T in parallel: consumed messages are broadcast to both S and T, and messages produced by S and T are merged into one stream. Feedback can be introduced in a network of stream processors by $\ell\, S$, which feeds all messages output from S back to its input.

Finally, variables (that is, messages) can be used as stream processors, which makes the calculus higher order: stream processors can be sent as messages from one stream processor and "plugged in" in another stream processor.

The stream processor calculus defines a number of congruence rules to be used freely in order to enable application of the reaction rules to follow. In

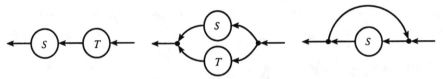

Fig. 1. Composing stream processors: serial and parallel composition, and loop.

addition to the commutativity of | and the associativity of | and $\ll$, we have the following congruences (where M and N range over stream processors used as messages):

$$(S \ll T) <\cdot M \sim S \ll (T <\cdot M) \qquad (Input\text{-}\ll)$$
$$S \ll (M \,!\, T) \sim (S <\cdot M) \ll T \qquad (Internal\text{-}\ll)$$
$$(M \,!\, S) \ll T \sim M \,!\, (S \ll T) \qquad (Output\text{-}\ll)$$
$$(S \,|\, T) <\cdot M \sim (S <\cdot M) \,|\, (T <\cdot M) \qquad (Input\text{-}|)$$
$$(M \,!\, S) <\cdot N \sim M \,!\, (S <\cdot N) \qquad (Output\text{-}<\cdot)$$
$$(x \,?\, S) <\cdot M \sim S[M/_x] \qquad (Input\text{-}?)$$

When used in a left-to-right fashion, these rules mirror propagation of messages in a network of stream processors.

Whereas the congruence rules in the last section can be freely used in any direction without changing the behaviour of a stream processor, the reaction rules are irreversible, and introduce non-determinism. The reason is that by applying a reaction rule, we make a choice of *how the message streams should be merged*. There are two places where merging occurs, in the output from a parallel composition, and in the input to a stream processor in a loop.

$$(M \,!\, S) \,|\, T \to M \,!\, (S \,|\, T) \qquad (Output\text{-}|)$$
$$\ell \, (M \,!\, S) \to M \,!\, \ell \, (S <\cdot M) \qquad (Output\text{-}\ell)$$
$$(\ell \, S) <\cdot M \to \ell \, (S <\cdot M) \qquad (Input\text{-}\ell)$$

Remember that we defined | to be commutative, which means that we only need one output rule for |. Note also that there is one congruence rule that one might find tempting to include, which we do not:

$$(S \,|\, T) \ll U \sim (S \ll U) \,|\, (T \ll U)$$

On the left hand side, S and T will receive the same input stream. On the right-hand side, U is duplicated, and there is no guarantee that the two occurrences produce the same stream of messages, so S and T may be passed different input streams.[2]

The stream processor equivalences and reduction rules can be viewed as a *chemical abstract machine*-style operational semantics [BB92] for the language of

---

[2] This rule is already a classic; it has been mistakenly included by both Moran [Mor98] and Taylor [Tay98b]. Taylor retracts the rule in his PhD thesis [Tay98a].

stream processors. With this as a basis, one could develop a theory of equivalence, *e.g.* based on bisimilarity, with which to further investigate the language. This is essentially the approach taken by Taylor [Tay98b] (using a more conventional SOS-style definition). However, as we have mentioned, this approach ignores interactions with the features of the language in which the stream processors are embedded, namely a lazy functional language. Instead of considering the stream processor calculus in isolation, we show how it can be realised by simple encodings into a call-by-need functional language with an additional erratic non-deterministic choice operator. By developing the theory of contextual equivalence for this language, we will show that the laws of the calculus are sound with respect to this implementation, and that the reduction rules are refinements. First we must introduce our language and its operational semantics.

3.2 Implementing the Stream Processors

We will embed the stream processors into an untyped lambda calculus with recursive let bindings, structured data, case expressions, and a non-deterministic choice operator. We work with a restricted syntax in which arguments to functions (including constructors) are always variables:

$$L, M, N ::= x \mid \lambda x.M \mid M\,x \mid c\,\vec{x} \mid M \oplus N$$
$$\mid \text{let } \{\vec{x} = \vec{M}\} \text{ in } N \mid \text{case } M \text{ of } \{c_i\ \vec{x}_i {\rightarrow} N_i\}.$$

The syntactic restriction is now rather standard, following its use in core language of the Glasgow Haskell compiler, *e.g.*, [PJPS96,PJS98], and in [Lau93,Ses97]. We call the language $\Lambda^{\oplus}_{\text{NEED}}$.

All constructors have a fixed arity, and are assumed to be saturated. By $c\,\vec{x}$ we mean $c\,x_1 \cdots x_n$. The only values are lambda expressions and fully-applied constructors. Throughout, x, y, z, and w will range over variables, c over constructor names, and V and W over values. We will write let $\{\vec{x} = \vec{M}\}$ in N as a shorthand for let $\{x_1 = M_1, \dots, x_n = M_n\}$ in N, where the $\vec{x}$ are distinct, the order of bindings is not syntactically significant, and the $\vec{x}$ are considered bound in N *and* the $\vec{M}$ (so our lets are recursive). Similarly we write case M of $\{c_i\ \vec{x}_i {\rightarrow} N_i\}$ for case M of $\{c_1\ \vec{x}_1 {\rightarrow} N_1 \mid \cdots \mid c_m\ \vec{x}_m {\rightarrow} N_m\}$, where each $\vec{x}_i$ is a vector of distinct variables, and the c_i are distinct constructors. In addition, we will sometimes write *alts* as an abbreviation for case alternatives $\{c_i\ \vec{x}_i {\rightarrow} N_i\}$.

For examples, working with a restricted syntax can be cumbersome, so it is sometimes useful to lift the restriction. Where we do this it should be taken that $M\,N \equiv \text{let } \{x = N\} \text{ in } M\,x$, where x is fresh, whenever N is not a variable. Similarly for constructor expressions. We will encode streams using the "cons" constructor, written in the Haskell-style infix as $M{:}N$ (read as M "consed onto" N). The nil-stream (the empty stream) is written as nil.

We use two kinds of definition in this section. The notation $f\,x_1 \cdots x_n \overset{\text{def}}{=} M$ means that $f\,x_1 \cdots x_n$ should be considered as a synonym for M, and the x_i are bound in M. The notation $f\,x_1 \cdots x_n = M$ will be used when f occurs free in

M to denote a recursive definition of f; f should be considered to be defined by a recursive let thus: let $\{f = \lambda x_1, \ldots , x_n.M\}$ in f.

Erratic Merge. The parallel combination of stream processors will depend upon the ability to merge incoming streams. We define *erratic merge* thus:

$$merge\ xs\ ys = \begin{pmatrix} \text{case } xs \text{ of} \\ \text{nil} \quad \to ys \\ z{:}zs \to z{:}merge\ zs\ ys \end{pmatrix} \oplus \begin{pmatrix} \text{case } ys \text{ of} \\ \text{nil} \quad \to xs \\ z{:}zs \to z{:}merge\ xs\ zs \end{pmatrix}$$

Essentially, *merge* non-deterministically chooses which of its operands to evaluate first. This is not fair: it may lead to starvation of a branch (since the same stream may be chosen *ad infinitum*). Neither is it bottom-avoiding: divergence in either input stream can lead to divergence for the merge as a whole.

Translating Stream Processors. We implement stream processors by translating them into $\Lambda^{\oplus}_{\text{NEED}}$. Fundamental stream processors have simple translations. All variables introduced on the right hand sides are assumed to be fresh:

$$[\![x]\!] = \lambda i.x\,i$$
$$[\![M\,!\,S]\!] = \lambda i.[\![M]\!]{:}([\![S]\!]\,i)$$
$$[\![x\,?\,S]\!] = \lambda i.\text{case } i \text{ of}$$
$$\text{nil} \quad \to \text{nil}$$
$$x{:}xs \to [\![S]\!]\,xs$$
$$[\![S <\cdot M]\!] = \lambda i.[\![S]\!]\,([\![M]\!]{:}i)$$

Note that in $x\,?\,S$, x may be free in S. The three combinator forms are as follows:

$$[\![S \ll T]\!] = \lambda i.[\![S]\!]\,([\![T]\!]\,i)$$
$$[\![S\,|\,T]\!] = \lambda i.merge\,([\![S]\!]\,i)\,([\![T]\!]\,i)$$
$$[\![\ell\,S]\!] = \lambda i.\text{let } \{o = [\![S]\!]\,(merge\,o\,i)\} \text{ in } o$$

Serial composition is just function composition. We use erratic merge to merge the output streams for parallel composition, and to merge the incoming stream with the feedback stream for the loop construct.

4   The Operational Theory

The operational semantics is presented in the form of an abstract machine semantics that correctly describes both sharing and erratic non-determinism. Using this semantics to define notions of *convergence* and *divergence*, we define what it means for one term to be *refined* by another, and what it means for two terms to be equivalent. These definitions are contextual in nature, which makes proving refinement or equivalence difficult (since one must prove the relationship holds

$$\langle \Gamma\{x = M\},\ x,\ S \rangle \rightarrow \langle \Gamma,\ M,\ \#x : S \rangle \qquad\qquad (Lookup)$$

$$\langle \Gamma,\ V,\ \#x : S \rangle \rightarrow \langle \Gamma\{x = V\},\ V,\ S \rangle \qquad\qquad (Update)$$

$$\langle \Gamma,\ M\,x,\ S \rangle \rightarrow \langle \Gamma,\ M,\ x : S \rangle \qquad\qquad (Unwind)$$

$$\langle \Gamma,\ \lambda x.M,\ y : S \rangle \rightarrow \langle \Gamma,\ M[y/x],\ S \rangle \qquad\qquad (Subst)$$

$$\langle \Gamma,\ \text{case } M \text{ of } alts,\ S \rangle \rightarrow \langle \Gamma,\ M,\ alts : S \rangle \qquad\qquad (Case)$$

$$\langle \Gamma,\ c_j\ \vec{y},\ \{c_i\ \vec{x}_i \rightarrow N_i\} : S \rangle \rightarrow \langle \Gamma,\ N_j[\vec{y}/\vec{x}_j],\ S \rangle \qquad\qquad (Branch)$$

$$\langle \Gamma,\ \text{let } \{\vec{x} = \vec{M}\} \text{ in } N,\ S \rangle \rightarrow \langle \Gamma\{\vec{x}=\vec{M}\},\ N,\ S \rangle \quad \vec{x} \cap \mathrm{dom}(\Gamma, S) = \emptyset \quad (Letrec)$$

$$\langle \Gamma,\ M \oplus N,\ S \rangle \rightarrow \langle \Gamma,\ M,\ S \rangle \qquad\qquad (Left)$$

$$\langle \Gamma,\ M \oplus N,\ S \rangle \rightarrow \langle \Gamma,\ N,\ S \rangle \qquad\qquad (Right)$$

$$\langle \Gamma,\ x,\ S \rangle \rightarrow \langle \Gamma,\ x,\ S \rangle \quad x \in \mathrm{dom}\, S \qquad\qquad (Black\ Hole)$$

Fig. 2. The abstract machine semantics for non-deterministic call-by-need.

for *all* program contexts). However, we are able to show that one need only prove that the relationship holds for a much smaller set of contexts, the so-called *evaluation contexts*. This result is then used to validate a set of algebraic laws. Lastly, we introduce the notion of *cost equivalence*, which is a cost-sensitive version of contextual equivalence. A powerful unique fixed-point proof rule is shown to be valid for cost equivalence. It is this proof rule that will allow us to establish the properties of erratic merge required to prove the correctness of the list-based implementation of stream processors.

4.1 The Abstract Machine

The semantics presented in this section is essentially Sestoft's "mark 1" abstract machine for laziness [Ses97], augmented with rules for erratic choice.

Transitions are over configurations consisting of a heap, containing bindings, the expression currently being evaluated, and a stack. The heap is a partial function from variables to terms, and denoted in an identical manner to a collection of let-bindings. The stack may contain variables (the arguments to applications), case alternatives, or *update markers* denoted by $\#x$ for some variable x. Update markers ensure that a binding to x will be recreated in the heap with the result of the current evaluation; this is how sharing is maintained in the semantics.

We write $\langle \Gamma,\ M,\ S \rangle$ for the abstract machine configuration with heap Γ, expression M, and stack S. We denote the empty heap by $\emptyset$, and the addition of a group of bindings $\vec{x} = \vec{M}$ to a heap Γ by juxtaposition: $\Gamma\{\vec{x}=\vec{M}\}$. The stack written $b : S$ will denote the a stack S with b pushed on the top. The empty stack is denoted by ϵ, and the concatenation of two stacks S and T by ST (where S is on top of T).

We will refer to the set of variables bound by Γ as $\mathrm{dom}\,\Gamma$, and to the set of variables marked for update in a stack S as $\mathrm{dom}\,S$. Update markers should be thought of as binding occurrences of variables. A configuration is *well-formed* if dom Γ and dom S are disjoint. We write dom (Γ, S) for their union. For a configuration $\langle \Gamma, M, S \rangle$ to be closed, any free variables in Γ, M, and S must be contained in dom (Γ, S).

The abstract machine semantics is presented in figure 2; we implicitly restrict the definition to well-formed configurations. There are seven rules, which can grouped as follows. Rules (*Lookup*) and (*Update*) concern evaluation of variables. To begin evaluation of x, we remove the binding $x = M$ from the heap and start evaluating M, with x, marked for update, pushed onto the stack. Rule (*Update*) applies when this evaluation is finished; we update the heap with x bound to the resulting value. It is this rules that lies at the heart of laziness: all subsequent uses of x will now share this value.

Rules (*Unwind*) and (*Subst*) concern function application: rule (*Unwind*) pushes an argument onto the stack while the function is being evaluated; once a lambda expression has been obtained, rule (*Subst*) retrieves the argument from the stack and substitutes it into the body of that lambda expression.

Rules (*Case*) and (*Branch*) govern the evaluation of case expressions. Rule (*Case*) initiates evaluation of the case expression, with the case alternatives pushed onto the stack. Rule (*Branch*) uses the result of this evaluation to choose one of the branches of the case, performing substitution of the constructor's arguments for the branch's pattern variables.

Rule (*Letrec*) adds a set of bindings to the heap. The side condition ensures that no inadvertent name capture occurs, and can always be satisfied by a local α-conversion.

The evaluation of choice expressions is described by rules (*Left*) and (*Right*). This is *erratic* choice, so we just pick one of the branches.

The last rule, (*Black Hole*), concerns self-dependent expressions (such as let $x = x$ in x). If we come to evaluate x when it is bound in S (*i.e.* there is an update marker for x on the stack S), then x is self-dependent[3]. By rewriting a self-dependent configuration to itself, we identify black holes with non-termination, which simplifies the development to follow.

Definition 1 (Convergence). *For closed configurations* $\langle \Gamma, M, S \rangle$,

$$\langle \Gamma, M, S \rangle \Downarrow^n \stackrel{\text{def}}{=} \exists \Delta, V. \langle \Gamma, M, S \rangle \to^n \langle \Delta, V, \epsilon \rangle,$$

$$\langle \Gamma, M, S \rangle \Downarrow \stackrel{\text{def}}{=} \exists n. \langle \Gamma, M, S \rangle \Downarrow^n.$$

We will also write $M \Downarrow$ and $M \Downarrow^n$ identifying closed M with the initial configuration $\langle \emptyset, M, \epsilon \rangle$.

Closed configurations which do not converge simply reduce indefinitely. For this language, this is the same as having arbitrarily long reduction sequences[4].

---

[3] An alternative definition would be to check whether or not x is bound in Γ. However, the underlying technical development relies upon the extension of the operational semantics to *open* terms. If the side-condition was instead $x \notin$ dom Γ then open terms would also diverge.

[4] This is due to the fact that $\to$ is finitely-branching. If we were working with a fair choice like McCarthy's *amb*, this definition would not be sufficient.

Definition 2 (Divergence). *For closed configurations* $\langle \Gamma, M, S \rangle$,

$$\langle \Gamma, M, S \rangle \Uparrow \overset{\text{def}}{=} \forall k. \langle \Gamma, M, S \rangle \rightarrow^k .$$

Since the language is non-deterministic, a given expression may have many different convergent and divergent behaviours.

4.2 Program Contexts

The starting point for an operational theory is usually an approximation and an equivalence defined in terms of *program contexts*. Program contexts are usually introduced as "programs with holes", the intention being that an expression is to be "plugged into" all of the holes in the context. The central idea is that to compare the behaviour of two terms one should compare their behaviour in all program contexts. We will use contexts of the following form:

$$\mathbb{C}, \mathbb{D} ::= [\cdot] \mid x \mid \lambda x.\mathbb{C} \mid \mathbb{C}\, x \mid c\ \vec{x} \mid \mathbb{C} \oplus \mathbb{D}$$
$$\mid \ \mathsf{let}\ \{\vec{x} = \vec{\mathbb{C}}\}\ \mathsf{in}\ \mathbb{D} \mid \mathsf{case}\ \mathbb{C}\ \mathsf{of}\ \{c_i\ \vec{x}_i \rightarrow \mathbb{D}_i\}.$$

Our contexts may contain zero or more occurrences of the hole, and as usual the operation of filling a hole with a term can cause variables in the term to become captured.

An *evaluation context* is a context in which the hole is the target of evaluation; in other words, evaluation cannot proceed until the hole is filled. Evaluation contexts have the following form:

$$\mathbb{E} ::= \mathbb{A} \mid \mathsf{let}\ \{\vec{x} = \vec{M}\}\ \mathsf{in}\ \mathbb{A}$$
$$\mid \ \mathsf{let}\ \{\vec{y} = \vec{M}, x_0 = \mathbb{A}_0[x_1], x_1 = \mathbb{A}_1[x_2], \dots, x_n = \mathbb{A}_n\}$$
$$\quad \mathsf{in}\ \mathbb{A}[x_0]$$
$$\mathbb{A} ::= [\cdot] \mid \mathbb{A}\, x \mid \mathsf{case}\ \mathbb{A}\ \mathsf{of}\ \{c_i\ \vec{x}_i \rightarrow M_i\}.$$

$\mathbb{E}$ ranges over evaluation contexts, and $\mathbb{A}$ over what we call *applicative contexts*. Our evaluation contexts are strictly contained in those mentioned in the letrec extension of Ariola and Felleisen [AF97]: there they allow $\mathbb{E}$ to appear anywhere we have an $\mathbb{A}$. Our "flattened" definition corresponds exactly to configuration contexts (with a single hole) of the form $\langle \Gamma, [\cdot], S \rangle$.

4.3 Refinement and Observational Equivalence

We define refinement and observational equivalence via contexts in the following way.

Definition 3 (Refinement). *We say that M is refined by N, written $M \overset{\sim}{\lesssim} N$, if for all $\mathbb{C}$ such that $\mathbb{C}[M]$ and $\mathbb{C}[N]$ are closed,*

$$\mathbb{C}[N]\Downarrow \implies \mathbb{C}[M]\Downarrow \ \wedge \ \mathbb{C}[N]\Uparrow \implies \mathbb{C}[M]\Uparrow.$$

$$(\lambda x.M)\, y \cong M[\sqrt[y]{x}] \qquad\qquad (\beta)$$

$$\text{case } c_j \ \vec{y} \text{ of } \{c_i \ \vec{x}_i{\to}M_i\} \cong M_j[\vec{y}/\vec{x}_j] \qquad\qquad (case\text{-}\beta)$$

$$\text{let } \{x = V, \vec{y} = \vec{D}\,[x]\} \text{ in } \mathbb{C}[x] \cong \text{let } \{x = V, \vec{y} = \vec{D}\,[V]\} \text{ in } \mathbb{C}[V] \qquad\qquad (value\text{-}\beta)$$

$$\mathbb{E}[\text{case } M \text{ of } \{pat_i{\to}N_i\}] \cong \text{case } M \text{ of } \{pat_i{\to}\mathbb{E}[N_i]\} \qquad\qquad (case\text{-}\mathbb{E})$$

$$\text{let } \{\vec{x} = \vec{L}, \vec{y} = \vec{M}\} \text{ in } N \cong \text{let } \{\vec{y} = \vec{M}\} \text{ in } N, \quad \text{if } \vec{x} \cap FV\,(\vec{M}, N) = \emptyset \qquad (gc)$$

$$M \oplus N \cong N \oplus M \qquad\qquad (\oplus\text{-}comm)$$

$$L \oplus (M \oplus N) \cong (L \oplus M) \oplus N \qquad\qquad (\oplus\text{-}assoc)$$

$$\mathbb{E}[M \oplus N] \cong \mathbb{E}[M] \oplus \mathbb{E}[N] \qquad\qquad (\oplus\text{-}\mathbb{E})$$

$$M \oplus N \underset{\sim}{\lesssim} M \qquad\qquad (\oplus\text{-}left)$$

Fig. 3. Selected laws of the equational theory.

Whenever $M \underset{\sim}{\lesssim} N$, then N's convergent behaviours can be matched by M and N does not exhibit divergent behaviours not already present in M. We say that M and N are *observationally equivalent*, written $M \cong N$, when $M \underset{\sim}{\lesssim} N$ and $N \underset{\sim}{\lesssim} M$.

This definition suffers from the same problem as any contextual definition: to prove that two terms are related requires one to examine their behaviour in *all* contexts. For this reason, it is common to seek to prove a *context lemma* [Mil77] for an operational semantics: one tries to show that to prove M observationally approximates N, one only need compare their behaviour with respect to a much smaller set of contexts.

We have established the following context lemma for call-by-need and erratic choice:

Lemma 1 (Context Lemma). *For all terms M and N, if for all evaluation contexts $\mathbb{E}$ such that $\mathbb{E}[M]$ and $\mathbb{E}[N]$ are closed,*

$$\mathbb{E}[N]\Downarrow \implies \mathbb{E}[M]\Downarrow \quad \wedge \quad \mathbb{E}[N]\Uparrow \implies \mathbb{E}[M]\Uparrow$$

then $M \underset{\sim}{\lesssim} N$.

The context lemma says that we need only consider the behaviour of M and N with respect to evaluation contexts. Despite the presence of non-determinism, the language has a rich equational theory. A selection of laws is presented in figure 3. Throughout, we follow the standard convention that all bound variables in the statement of a law are distinct, and that they are disjoint from the free variables.

4.4 Unique Fixed-Point Induction

The context lemma allows a number of basic equivalences to be established. But the basic equivalences thus provable are typically insufficient to prove anything interesting about recursively defined entities. One can directly apply the context lemma, although reasoning this way is somewhat tedious. An alternative is to develop an operational counterpart to the denotational fixed-point induction rule, which characterises a recursive function (say) in terms of its "finite approximations". In [MS99], Moran and Sands show that call-by-need supports a fixed-point induction rule, based on a cost-sensitive preorder. This work could be adapted to the present setting by studying a convex-approximation relation[5].

We will focus instead on a rather different proof rule for recursion based on unique fixed-points. A well-known proof technique in *e.g.* process algebra involves syntactically characterising a class of recursion equations which have a unique solution. Knowing that a recursive equation has a unique fixed point means that one can prove equivalence of two terms by showing that they both satisfy the recursion equation. The usual syntactic characterisation is that of *guarded recursion*: if recursive calls are syntactically "guarded" by an observable action then the fixed-point of the definition is unique.

In a functional language the use of unique fixed-points is rather uncommon. The natural notion of "guard" is a constructor; however many recursive definitions are "unguarded" – for example, the standard *filter* function, which selects all elements from a list which satisfy a predicate. Additionally, the presence of destructors make the usual notions of guardedness rather ineffective. Consider, for example, the equation

$$x \cong 1 : (\text{tail } (\text{tail } x)).$$

Despite the fact that on the right-hand-side, x is guarded by the cons-constructor, there are many deterministic solutions for this equation. For example, both $1 : \bot$ and the infinite list of ones are solutions.

To recover a usable unique fixed-point theorem, we work with a finer, more intentional theory of equivalence. The motivation is that using a finer equivalence will give us fewer solutions to recursive equations, which in turn will give us a unique fixed-point proof rule. The finer equivalence we use is called *cost equivalence* [San95].

Definition 4 (Cost Equivalence). *We say that M is* cost equivalent *to N, written $M \doteq N$, if for all $\mathbb{C}$ such that $\mathbb{C}[M]$ and $\mathbb{C}[N]$ are closed,*

$$\mathbb{C}[M]{\Downarrow}^n \iff \mathbb{C}[N]{\Downarrow}^n \quad \wedge \quad \mathbb{C}[M]{\Uparrow} \iff \mathbb{C}[N]{\Uparrow}.$$

Clearly $\doteq$ is contained in $\cong$. The point is that cost equivalence equations have unique solutions – provided that the recursion is guarded by at least one computation step. To make this precise, we need to introduce a very useful syntactic representation/characterisation of a computation step, the *tick*:

$$\checkmark M \stackrel{\text{def}}{=} \text{let } \{\} \text{ in } M.$$

---

[5] The present refinement relation does not support a fixed-point induction principle since divergence is not a bottom element in this ordering.

Clearly, $\checkmark$ adds one unit to the cost of evaluating M without otherwise changing its behaviour, so that $M \cong \checkmark M$. Note that:

$$M \Downarrow \iff \checkmark M \Downarrow \qquad\qquad M \Downarrow^n \iff \checkmark M \Downarrow^{n+1}$$

We will write $^{k\checkmark}M$ to mean that M has been slowed down by k ticks. As an example of a cost equivalence involving the tick, we have the following:

$$(\lambda x.M)\, y \doteq\, ^{2\checkmark}M[{}^y\!/_x] \tag{β}$$

Now we are in a position to state the unique fixed-point induction principle, which is a variation on the proof rule of "improvement up to context" [San98], and Lassen and Moran's cost equivalence induction [LM98,Mor98]:

Theorem 1 (Unique Fixed-Point Induction). *For any M, N, $\mathbb{C}$, and substitution σ, the following proof rule is sound:*

$$\frac{M \doteq\, \checkmark\mathbb{C}[M\sigma] \quad N \doteq\, \checkmark\mathbb{C}[N\sigma]}{M \doteq N}$$

It may seem at first sight that cost equivalence is too fine to be applicable. The reason that this appears not to be the case in practice is that firstly, proof techniques such as the context lemma extend in a very straightforward manner to cost equivalence, and secondly, for every equivalence in figure 3, there is a corresponding cost equivalence which can be obtained by adding an appropriate number of ticks (in appropriate places) to the left and right hand sides. We saw one example of this above (β). Rather than list all of these we take just a couple of examples:

$$\text{case } c_j\; \vec{y} \text{ of } \{c_i\; \vec{x}_i \to M_i\} \doteq\, ^{2\checkmark}M_j[{}^{\vec{y}}\!/_{\vec{x}_j}] \tag{$case\text{-}\beta$}$$

$$cE[\text{case } M \text{ of } \{pat_i \to N_i\}] \doteq \text{case } M \text{ of } \{pat_i \to E[N_i]\} \tag{$case\text{-}E$}$$

Collectively we refer to these rules as the *tick algebra*. An example use of the tick algebra, in conjunction with unique fixed-point induction is the proof of the commutativity of merge, is to be found in the extended version.

5 Correctness of the Translation

The calculus of stream processors presented in section 3 (and introduced in [CH98]) represents the designers' intuition regarding the "essence of fudgets". The purpose of this section is to demonstrate that the semantics we have given to this calculus in terms of the non-deterministic lazy language is consistent with the laws and reductions of the calculus: every congruence is an equivalence, and each reduction rule is a refinement. More precisely,

Theorem 2. *For any stream processors S and T,*

(i) $S \sim T \implies [S] \cong [T]$,
(ii) $S \to T \implies [S] \lesssim [T]$.

5.1 Properties of Merge

In order to establish the lemmata we will need to prove theorem 2, we will need the following properties of erratic merge: it is commutative, associative, and we may choose to propagate the head of either input stream (yielding a refinement).

Proposition 1.

$$merge\ xs\ ys \cong merge\ ys\ xs \qquad\qquad (merge\text{-}comm)$$
$$merge\ xs\ (merge\ ys\ zs) \cong merge\ (merge\ xs\ ys)\ zs \qquad (merge\text{-}assoc)$$
$$merge\ (x{:}xs)\ ys \lesssim x{:}merge\ xs\ ys \qquad\qquad (merge\text{-}eval)$$

5.2 The Congruences

The commutativity and associativity of $|$ follow in a straightforward way from the corresponding properties of $merge$. The associativity of $\ll$ simply follows from the associativity of function composition. In the sequel we make the following overloaded use of the combinators of the stream processor calculus:

$$x\,!\,s \overset{\text{def}}{=} \lambda i.x{:}(s\,i)$$
$$x\,?\,M \overset{\text{def}}{=} \lambda i.\text{case}\ i\ \text{of}\ \{nil \to nil \mid x{:}xs \to M\ xs\} \qquad i, xs \notin \text{FV}\,(M)$$
$$s < \cdot\, x \overset{\text{def}}{=} \lambda i.s\,(x{:}i)$$
$$s \ll t \overset{\text{def}}{=} \lambda i.s\,(t\,i)$$
$$s \mid t \overset{\text{def}}{=} \lambda i.merge\,(s\,i)\,(t\,i)$$
$$\ell\,s \overset{\text{def}}{=} \lambda i.\text{let}\ \{o = s\,(merge\,o\,i)\}\ \text{in}\ o$$

Lemma 2. *For any terms S and T and variables x and y,*

(i) $(S \ll T) < \cdot\, x \cong S \ll (T < \cdot\, x)$.
(ii) $S \ll (x\,!\,T) \cong (S < \cdot\, x) \ll T$.
(iii) $(x\,!\,S) \ll T \cong x\,!\,(S \ll T)$.
(iv) $(S \mid T) < \cdot\, x \cong (S < \cdot\, x) \mid (T < \cdot\, x)$.
(v) $(x\,!\,S) < \cdot\, y \cong x\,!\,(S < \cdot\, y)$.
(vi) $(x\,?\,S) < \cdot\, y \cong \lambda i.S[y/x]\,i$.

5.3 The Reduction Rules

Throughout, we will use the syntactic equivalences for application and constructors mentioned in section 3.2 without reference, but only where such usage does not obscure the calculation in question.

Lemma 3. *For any terms S and T and variables x,*

(i) $(x\,!\,S) \mid T \lesssim x\,!\,(S \mid T)$.
(ii) $\ell\,(x\,!\,S) \lesssim x\,!\,(\ell\,(S < \cdot\, x))$.
(iii) $(\ell\,S) < \cdot\, x \lesssim \ell\,(S < \cdot\, x)$.

The proof of the main theorem now follows from the above lemmata by an easy induction on the structure of the stream processors. The only other properties needed in the proof are that (i) the image of the translation $[\![\cdot]\!]$ is always a lambda abstraction, and that (ii) the refinement and congruence relation are closed under substitution of values for variables.

6   Conclusions and Future Work

We have presented a semantic theory of the stream processors at the heart of the Fudgets toolkit. The theory is built upon a call-by-need language with erratic non-deterministic choice. Our semantic theory correctly models sharing and its interaction with non-deterministic choice, and still contains proof principles for reasoning about recursive programs. We have shown that in this theory, the congruences and reduction rules of Carlsson and Hallgren's proposed stream processor calculus are equivalences and refinements, respectively. The semantic model improves on the calculus of Kutzner and Schmidt-Schauß, and unlike Taylor's theory of core fudgets it models the effects of shared computation.

Making Parallel Composition Fair. As it stands, parallel composition is not fair: if either operand fails to produce output, then so may the composition as a whole, and an operand's output may never appear as output from the composition. This is because the merging of output streams is erratic. There are three different kinds of "fair" merge one might consider instead: with *fair merge*, every element of the input streams xs and ys appears eventually (with relative order preserved) in the output; with *bottom-avoiding merge*, if one of xs or ys is finite or partial, then every element of the other appears in the output, and with *infinity-fair merge*, if one of xs or ys is infinite, then every element of the other appears in the output. The ideal merge for our purposes is the first: it is fair with respect to infinite lists (*i.e.* it avoids starvation in both operands), and is also able to avoid non-termination associated with partial streams. The second can avoid non-termination associated with partial lists, but may starve one of its input streams, if both streams are infinite. The third, infinity-fair merge, does not starve infinite input streams, but cannot avoid the divergence inherent in partial streams.

The first merge cannot be implemented with McCarthy's *amb* [PS88], and would require study in its own right. However, the last two can be implemented by *amb* (see *e.g.* chapter 2 of [Mor98]). A call-by-need theory for *amb* would have all of the advantages of the current theory, as well as yielding bottom-avoiding implementations of | and ℓ. As stated elsewhere, *amb* is a much more difficult operator to model. The technical development outlined in appendix B of the extended version of this paper does not carry through for *amb*: the divergence relation is far less tractable. Nevertheless, *amb* warrants further study.

Streams as Data Structures. In the current implementation, Fudgets are represented by a continuation-like data structure. An interesting difference from the rather direct stream representation used here is that it permits a stream processor to be unplugged from its point of use and moved to another location.[6] This has been used in the Fudget library to implement interaction by drag-and-drop, where the user can actually move a fudget from one place in the program to another. The feature can even be pushed further, allowing stream processors to migrate over networks to implement mobile agents in the full sense. Although the present theory allows stream processors to be passed as data, it does not permit this degree of freedom. We see no particular obstacle in working with this more concrete representation – although it is likely that we would need to impose a type discipline in order to be able to establish the expected laws.

References

[AF97]   Z. M. Ariola and M. Felleisen, *The call-by-need lambda calculus*, Journal of Functional Programming **7** (1997), no. 3, 265–301.

[AFM+95] Z. Ariola, M. Felleisen, J. Maraist, M. Odersky, and P. Wadler, *A call-by-need lambda calculus*, Proc. POPL'95, ACM Press, January 1995, pp. 233–246.

[AHS93]   F. Arbab, I. Herman, and P. Spilling, *An overview of* MANIFOLD *and its implementation*, Concurrency: Practice and Experience **5** (1993), no. 1, 23–70.

[BB92]   G. Berry and G. Boudol, *The chemical abstract machine*, Theoretical Computer Science **96** (1992), no. 1, 217–248.

[Bro86]   M. Broy, *A theory for nondeterminism, parallelism, communication, and concurrency*, Theoretical Computer Science **45** (1986), no. 1, 1–61.

[CH98]   M. Carlsson and T. Hallgren, *Fudgets — Purely Functional Processes with Applications to Graphical User Interfaces*, Ph.D. thesis, Department of Computing Sciences, Chalmers University of Technology and University of Gothenburg, Gothenburg, Sweden, March 1998.

[Cli82]   W. Clinger, *Nondeterministic call by need is neither lazy nor by name*, Lisp and Functional Programming, August 1982, pp. 226–234.

[FH95]   W. Ferreira and M. Hennessy, *Towards a semantic theory of CML (extended abstract)*, Proc. of MFCS'95 (J. Wiedermann and P. Hajek, eds.), LNCS, vol. 969, Springer-Verlag, August 1995.

[FHJ96]   W. Ferreira, M. Hennessy, and A. Jeffrey, *A theory of weak bisimulation for core CML*, Proc. ICFP'96, ACM Press, May 1996, pp. 201–212.

[FPJ95]   S. Finne and S. Peyton Jones, *Composing Haggis*, Proc. of the 5th Eurographics Workshop on Programming Paradigms in Graphics, September 1995.

[GR91]   E. R. Gansner and J. H. Reppy, *eXene*, Proceedings of the 1991 CMU Workshop on Standard ML (Carnegie Mellon University), September 1991.

[KSS98]   A. Kutzner and M. Schmidt-Schauß, *A non-deterministic call-by-need lambda calculus*, Proc. ICFP'98, ACM Press, September 1998, pp. 324–335.

---

[6] This opens the possibility to dynamically change the topology of a running program, an important feature in other coordination languages such as MANIFOLD [AHS93].

[Lau93]   J. Launchbury, *A natural semantics for lazy evaluation*, Proc. POPL'93, ACM Press, January 1993, pp. 144–154.

[LM98]   S. B. Lassen and A. K. Moran, *An operational theory for McCarthy's Amb*, Submitted for publication, 1998.

[Mil77]   R. Milner, *Fully abstract models of the typed λ-calculus*, Theoretical Computer Science **4** (1977), 1–22.

[Mor98]   A. K. Moran, *Call-by-name, call-by-need, and McCarthy's Amb*, Ph.D. thesis, Department of Computing Sciences, Chalmers University of Technology, Gothenburg, Sweden, September 1998.

[MS99]   A. K. Moran and D. Sands, *Improvement in a lazy context: An operational theory for call-by-need*, Proc. POPL'99, ACM Press, January 1999, pp. 43–56.

[MSC98]   A. K. Moran, D. Sands, and M. Carlsson, *Erratic Fudgets: A semantic theory for an embedded coordination language (extended version)*, Extended version of this paper; available from authors, 1998.

[NN96]   F. Nielson and H. R. Nielson, *From CML to its process algebra*, Theoretical Computer Science **155** (1996), no. 1, 179–219.

[PH97]   J. Peterson and K. Hammond, *The Haskell Report, Version 1.4*, Tech. report, Yale University, 1997.

[PJAF96]   S. Peyton Jones, A.Gordon, and S. Finne, *Concurrent Haskell*, Proc. POPL'96, ACM Press, January 1996, pp. 295–308.

[PJPS96]   S. Peyton Jones, W. Partain, and A. Santos, *Let-floating: moving bindings to give faster programs*, Proc. ICFP'96, ACM Press, May 1996, pp. 1–12.

[PJS98]   S. Peyton Jones and A. Santos, *A transformation-based optimiser for Haskell*, Science of Computer Programming **32** (1998), no. 1–3, 3–47.

[Plo76]   G. D. Plotkin, *A powerdomain construction*, SIAM Journal on Computing **5** (1976), no. 3, 452–487.

[PS88]   P. Panangaden and V. Shanbhogue, *McCarthy's amb cannot implement fair merge*, Tech. Report TR88-913, Cornell University, Computer Science Department, May 1988.

[Rep91]   J. H. Reppy, *CML: A Higher-Order Concurrent Language*, Proc. PLDI'91, vol. 26, SIGPLAN Notices, no. 6, ACM Press, June 1991, pp. 294–305.

[San95]   D. Sands, *A naïve time analysis and its theory of cost equivalence*, Journal of Logic and Computation **5** (1995), no. 4, 495–541.

[San98]   D. Sands, *Improvement theory and its applications*, (A. D. Gordon and A. M. Pitts, eds.), Publications of the Newton Institute, Cambridge University Press, 1998, pp. 275–306.

[Ses97]   P. Sestoft, *Deriving a lazy abstract machine*, Journal of Functional Programming **7** (1997), no. 3, 231–264.

[Smy78]   M. B. Smyth, *Power domains*, Journal of Computer and System Sciences **16** (1978), no. 23–26, 23–35.

[Smy83]   M. B. Smyth, *Power domains and predicate transformers: A topological view*, ICALP '83, LNCS, vol. 154, 1983, pp. 662–676.

[SS92]   H. Søndergaard and P. Sestoft, *Non-determinism in functional languages*, The Computer Journal **35** (1992), no. 5, 514–523.

[Tay98a]   C. Taylor, *Formalising and Reasoning about Fudgets*, Ph.D. thesis, School of Computer Science and Information Technology, University of Nottingham, October 1998.

[Tay98b]   C. Taylor, *A theory for Core Fudgets*, Proc. ICFP'98, ACM Press, September 1998, pp. 75–85.

Coordination of Synchronous Programs[*]

Reinhard Budde[1], G. Michele Pinna[1,2], and Axel Poigné[1]

[1] GMD-SET, Schloß Birlinghoven, D-53754 Sankt Augustin, Germany
[2] Dipartimento di Matematica, Università di Siena, I-53100 Siena, Italy
{reinhard.budde,pinna,poigne}@gmd.de

Abstract. We propose to extend the synchronous language Esterel by coordination primitives and by an asynchronous parallel composition operation on the level of modules. This is to program reactive systems such that subsystems may proceed at their own speed without enforcing a global knowledge of time. We intend is to stick with the synchronous language paradigm as close as possible since we aim for properties such as local determinism (each agent/control unit should have a predictable behaviour) or global deadlock detection, though we want to enhance modularity and flexibility of system design.

1 Introduction

Synchronous languages [2, 7] have been developed to program reactive systems, i.e. systems that continuously interact with the environment. The basic hypothesis of these languages is that of *perfect synchrony*: the reaction to an external stimulus is instantaneous, it coincides, in terms of time, with the external stimulus. Its duration is "zero", or rather, the delay is so small that the environment is not able to observe it.

Moreover, these languages support real concurrency. Communication is based on instantaneous *broadcast*. This implies that "time"[1] is global. Often there is explicit basic clock (for instance, the tick for Esterel [3], or the basic clock of a Lustre node [8]). The basic clock is assumed to be fast enough to detect changes of input signals. At each instant a signal can have two status: either it is *present* or it is *absent*. Both informations can be used. A signal can, of course, be present for many instants, but this implies that the same signal is emitted at each instant.

Though being an extremely useful design paradigm (as, for instance, well known from hardware), synchrony is not easy to establish for distributed systems (often only at prohibitive costs by introducing a very fast clock), nor is it flexible with regard to addition and deletion of subcomponent from a system.

Asynchronous languages (such as CSP [6]) do much better in this respect. Components evolve loosely coupled at their one speed, and synchronize only

---

[*] Partly funded by the ESPRIT IIM-Project CRISYS "Critical Instrumentation of Control System"), EP 25.514
[1] Time should be understood as the perception of it: one detects that an instant has elapsed because a change can be observed.

when communicating. Communication is done via message passing or rendez-vous: a channel is established between the components which want to communicate. A communication can last an impredictable amount of time. It is "synchronous" or, rather, blocking in that components, if engaged in a communication, cannot proceed on their own. Messages can *only* be sensed for presence (unlike as for synchronous computations).

Sending message can be seen as the counterpart of the signal emission, the main difference is that we can only say when a message is present and we cannot say that, if the message is not present, then it is *absent*, as it could be that the sent message is not yet arrived. Also in the synchronous approach communication is synchronous: agents send out signals (in Esterel terminology emit), but it is non-blocking: agents don't care to know whether there was someone waiting for their signals. In fact the adjectives asynchronous or synchronous together with languages are used to describe how the computation proceeds and then has nothing to do with the kind of communication adopted.

In many distributed reactive systems (especially for safety critical control ones) one would like to use both synchronicity in the behaviour of a single component (a unit of such a control system can be considered as a synchronous program, as it should have a clear understanding of the flowing of time, should be reactive and it should be deterministic) and some asynchronicity in the overall behaviour of the system, avoiding to enforce a global notion of time.

This asynchronicity can be achieved via allowing other communications capabilities besides the instantaneous broadcasting. The first proposal in this respect is the Calculus of Reactive Processes (CRP) of Berry, Ramesh and Shymasundar [4] supports both the broadcast synchronous communication (this is the basic communication mechanism inside a module) and a channel based synchronous communication (a randezvous is implemented). As there is a rendezvous communication, in their case processes are blocked awaiting to accomplish the communication. This could lead to unpleasant situations when programming a distributed reactive system. To be practical, consider an airplane flying and passing the boundaries of closed air spaces. The units responsible for an air space are equipped with surveillance equipments for boundaries of the air space. Once detected that an airplane leaves an air space the responsible unit communicates to other units that it should reach a certain air space within a given time. After sending out the message the unit has to continue the monitoring activity. The communication to other units has the characteristic of asynchronicity: the sender does not care to know *when* the message will be received, it continues its own activity. The only assumption is that the message *will* be received (if the system behaves correctly). This example shows that it could be convenient to introduce asynchronous communication between reactive processes.

1.1 Our proposal

We propose to add to a synchronous language some coordination primitives and an asynchronous parallel composition operator (here asynchronous is used for denoting the way of computing). We obtain in this way an asynchronous communication between the various module, that in the perspective of our previous discussion can be considered a broadcast asynchronous communication.

In fact, *coordinations* primitives are well suited to allow exchange of informations (making coordination between several parallel activities possible) without any regards for common knowledge of time.

A key notion in the coordination world is the so called *tuple space*, that we adapt to our purpose[2]. Here rather then tuple space, we consider blackboards, where messages can be put and taken away. One important feature of our notion of blackboards is that there is always some delay between the receiving of a message and the *availability* of the message itself. Moreover we assume that a blackboard is always ready to receive messages from other system components.

We experiment our ideas with Esterel. We try to add as few as possible: in fact we want still stay as close as possible to the synchronous language paradigm, as we are interested in the holding of properties like local determinism (each agent/control unit should have a predictable behaviour) or global deadlock detection. However we achieve asynchronous communication and modularity.

To sum up, our contribution is twofold: we investigate the consequences of adding coordination primitives to synchronous languages and we study an asynchronous model for dealing with distributed control systems.

The paper is organized as follows: we first discuss (in section 2) in some detail the motivating system architecture. Then we present Esterel with the coordination primitives and the asynchronous parallel composition (section 3 and then we introduce its behavioural semantics (section 4). In section 5 we discuss briefly the properties enjoyed by our proposal and finally we draw some conclusion and discuss briefly the perspective of our proposal.

We finish this section with a brief comparison with related works.

1.2 Related Works

To the best of our knowledge the line of research we are pursuing, i.e. to extend synchronous languages with coordination primitives, is novel. There are however some analogies, or at least similar motivations, in other approaches, that we review briefly. Our approach has some similarity with the SL synchronous language of Boussinot and de Simone [5] as they do not allow to check the presence of signal, or better forbid drawing conclusions from the absence of a signal. Similarly, we do not allow to check for absence of messages. There the concern is rather how to add a piece of code assuring that the overall program is still correct, whereas our is how to spread the control still retaining some of the typical features of these kind of languages.

The other approach we plan to compare is the timed concurrent constraint approach ([10]) where a notion of blackboard as store is present. Quite clearly our

---

[2] In fact, coordination primitives (and coordination languages as well) have been introduced in a totally different setting, namely distributed programming. There is in this realm the need of coordinating different activities and data structures, hence the notion of a space where tuples can lives together, each tuple belonging to a template.

notion of blackboard has nothing to do with their notion of constraint systems, nevertheless a comparison is worthwhile.

2 Underlying Architecture

We illustrate the basic idea. Synchronous languages assume that two processes operate on the same frequency

while we require that both the processes should operate on different frequencies, e.g.

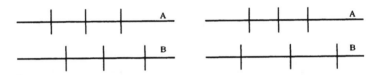

We make our idea a bit more precise assuming that the language is Esterel and that the coordination between these activities is obtained by with emit and await. Let us introduce a notation such as

$$\dots \text{ emit a } \dots // \dots \text{await a}; P \dots$$

to refer to a computation on different, a priori unrelated, frequencies, and let us discuss consequences.

The first case of the two picture above may suggest to introduce a time delay δ. Apart from still a global knowledge of time being present the second picture demonstrates the restrictions. Even if we assume that both frequencies are quite similar such a situation may arise due to small deviations in the frequency. In such a case a second message may overwrite a first one, or even worse many messages may get lost in

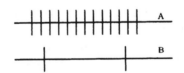

Experience suggests that either the processes should be synchronized (what we did) or that a buffer is needed (as a particular kind of blackboard) to keep track of the messages, hence have a picture of the form

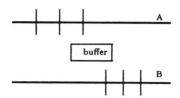

We believe that the following picture

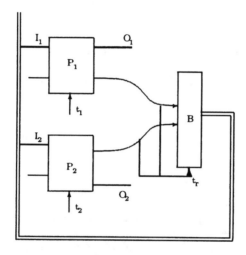

gives a fairly clear account of the architecture. Processes only communicate via a blackboard. The spaces of other signals are disjoint. Each process operates on its own frequency (t_1, t_2). A blackboard must synchronize with a process whenever the latter puts data to or fetches data from the blackboard. A process may put, read or fetch a message whenever it wants. However, a process has to read a message addressed to it whenever the message is present. Hence processes are the driving force which cannot be blocked, and messages are guaranteed to be delivered.

We consider a blackboard as a synchronous component with a precedence of reading before writing. This implies that data can be read only one instant after being written (similar to the Statemate semantics of Statecharts [9]). The blackboard operates on a kind of local clock but which is restricted by the processes communicating with it: given that, for instance, process 1 writes or fetches data at an instant, a reaction of the blackboard must take place before the next instant of process 1. This is sort of indicates by the trigger wire indexed by r. However, process 2 may read, write or fetch concurrently. Now it depends, in terms of "real" time, how long the delay δ between the reaction of process 1 and the reaction of the blackboard is. If the reaction of process 2 is in between its reaction depends on the "old" status of the blackboard as in picture 1 below.

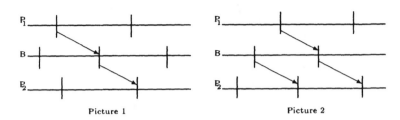

Picture 1   Picture 2

Otherwise its reaction may depend on the updated blackboard as in picture 2. Since process 1 and process 2 operate on different frequencies we do not know what will happen. Note that on the other side the reactions are perfectly predictable given that the delay δ and a relation between the frequencies is given. Note that messages are going to be delivered, as we claimed, but not necessarily instantaneously. It will be the task of a system designer that a process is rather stable with regard to this fuzzyness of when a message is delivered. In system like the one sketched above where sending of messages is sparse with regard to the driving frequencies due the the restrictions of the physics of the system, this should be fairly simple.

3 Esterel with Coordination Primitives

We briefly present Esterel ([3]) and we discuss the new coordination primitives and the asynchronous parallel composition operator devised in the introduction.

There are two basic objects: *signals* and *messages*. Signals are used for communication with the environment whereas messages are used to communicate between the various modules. The main difference between these two objects is that messages are persistent, whereas signal are not. A kind of persistence can be achieved also with signals stipulating that a given signal is emitted at each instant, but this is not the kind of persistence we are interested in, hence we go for the more flexible notion of message.

3.1 Modules and interface

Modules are the basic programming units. A module has an interface which defines its input and outputs signals, the accessible blackboards, and a body of executable statements:

```
module M:
input list of input signals;
output list of output signals;
common names of the common spaces;
input relations
statement
end module
```

The only difference between our definition of module and the usual one is that we provide now names of the blackboards.

At execution time, a module is activated by giving to it a *input event* that consists of a set (possibly empty) of input signals (assumed to be present) and a set (again possibly empty) of messages (if not empty, assumed to be present in some blackboards). The module reacts by executing its body and outputs the emitted output signals and the messages to be delivered to some blackboard. We assume, as usual, that the reaction is instantaneous (or perfectly synchronous, in the sense that outputs are produced in no time). As in Esterel, we require that the reaction in a module is deterministic.

3.2 Statements

We list Esterel statements. Besides the ones listed here, there are a number of derived ones, that can be used to write more user friendly programs, and these are just macro expanded to primitive ones. The kernel statements are:

nothing	$stat_1 \| stat_2$
halt	trap T in *stat* end
emit S	exit T
$stat_1; stat_2$	signal S in *stat* end
loop *stat* end	do *stat* watching S
present S then $stat_1$ else $stat_2$	

These statement are imperative in nature and most of them are now standard. We omit here a detailed explanation of these statements referring to [3] or [4], but we give a rough description of them. The emit instantaneously emit a signal. For the others, we simply give the intuition of how the control flows. The nothing does nothing, and let the control flowing, whereas the statement halt does nothing but retains the control forever. In $stat_1; stat_2$ first $stat_1$ is executed and when it is terminated $stat_2$ is executed. loop *stat* end retains the control forever and the statement *stat* is executed, when it terminates its execution is started again. It is required to be not instantaneous. In present S then $stat_1$ else $stat_2$ one of the branches is executed according to presence, at the execution instant, of the signal S. signal S in *stat* end allows for local signal declaration and trap T in *stat* end with exit T define weak preemption mechanisms (suited for exceptions handling): the body of the trap is executed normally until the exit is encountered, and then the whole trap terminates. This preemption mechanism is weaker with respect to the one implemented by the do *stat* watching S, where the body is executed and if it doesn't terminate and the signal S is present then the whole do watching is terminated as parallel branches are aborted as well. In the parallel $stat_1 \| stat_2$ the control is split and the two statements are executed concurrently. It terminates when both branches terminate.

3.3 The Coordination Primitives

We add to the kernel statements of Esterel the following coordination (or communication) primitives:

out m(v) - for writing in the blackboard,

read m   - reading from the blackboard, and

fetch m - for reading from the blackboard and deleting the read entry.

To give an intuition of how these primitives work, we resume the airplane example: as soon as the airplane is detected in the controlled area, a message with some relevant information is "posted" and the surveillance is continued till the plane leaves the controlled area. This may be expressed by the following piece of code

```
loop
  await ENTER_AIR_SPACE_1;
  :
  await LEAVE_AIR_SPACE_1;
  out PREDICTION(expected_time);
end
```

Another module can have then the following piece of code:

```
loop
 trap PLANE_OK
   do
     fetch PREDICTION;
     trap PLANE_COMES
      do
        await ENTER_AIR_SPACE_2;
        exit PLANE_COMES;
      watching ?PREDICTION TICK;
      emit ALARM_LOST;
     end;
     emit OK;
     exit PLANE_OK;
   watching IN_2;
   emit ALARM_PHANTOM;
  end;
end
```

where, if the message is not posted, and a plane is detected, then an alarm rings. If the message is read then if, after a certain delay, the plane has not appeared then another alarm rings. Locally a message behaves like a valued signal in that, if it present at an instant, its value persist till the next time it is present. Hence the statement 'do P watching ?PREDICTION TICK' states that P is preempted after as many instants as communicated by the message as expected_time.

The intuitive semantics of these statement is just as expected a small variation on the emit and await[3] for what concern signals. In the case of read and fetch the control is retained until the message is present in the blackboard. We stress again that there is a relevant difference between messages and signals, as

---

[3] await S is a shorthand for do halt watching S.

in the case of signals the perfect synchronicity implies that at a given instant a signal is present or absent: a decision can be taken on both possibilities, whereas the *presence* of a message can be only positively observed.

3.4 Blackboards

The blackboard is a process running in parallel (asynchronously) with the other components. On execution of an out-statement, it starts, from the next instant, to sustain a *signal* with the same name as the message posted. Fetching a message causes the deletion of the message on the blackboard. We assume that, if two parallel processes wish to fetch the same message, both can do. Our choice is based on the assumption that the blackboards themselves are synchronous and that deletion of a messages takes place only at the end of an instance.

The intuitive semantics of a blackboard is as follows: as soon as a message is delivered to the blackboard, a (kind of) process sustaining a special signal is started and this process can be killed by any other process. We do not place any limitation in the number of processes bearing the same message, as they have, so to say, different pids. This has some similarity with the **exec** statement illustrated in [4] with a relevant difference: there the control is retained till the accomplishment of the asynchronous task, whereas here it not retained. Due to this, we give a more abstract account of a blackboard.

Let $M \subseteq S$ be a set of message identifiers. A blackboard $\mathcal{B}$ consists of a mapping $\mathcal{B} : M \to V_B$ of message identifiers to the value type V_B of $\mathcal{B}$. The latter is equipped with three operations: $o : V_B \to V$ - reading out, $p : V \times V_B \to V_B$ - adding, and $d : V_B \to V_B$ - deleting. For example, V_B may be a queue with obvious operations.

For each message $m \in M$, we have signals pm - put to the blackboard, and dm - delete from the blackboard. These signals are different from the other signals in the sense that it is not allowed to use them in a statement.

In order to avoid cumbersome definitions for the asynchronous parallel composition, blackboard will be ranged over by $\mathcal{B}$ or M (as they are in fact special kind of reactive modules).

3.5 Asynchronous Parallel Composition

The final operation we have to describe is the *asynchronous* parallel composition. Similarly to CRP, a system is described by a network

$$M_1 /\!/ M_2 /\!/ \ldots /\!/ M_n$$

of Esterel modules (reactive programs, each having its own input/output signals and its own notion of instant), and blackboards. The only inter-process communication is achieved via blackboards.

The intuitive semantics of the asynchronous parallel composition is as follows: a module proceeds at its own speed provided that there is no interaction with a blackboard, otherwise it has to *synchronize* with the blackboard. The rules will be given later one.

To finish off with the intuitive semantics, we now consider the computations of the two pieces of programs seen before asynchronously composed (they will be ranged by s and t respectively, moreover the blackboard is written on a side, and m is a shorthand for the prediction message PREDICTION($expected\_time$)):

$$(s, t, \langle\rangle) \xrightarrow[I_1]{O_1, \emptyset} (s', t, \langle m \rangle) \xrightarrow[I_2]{O_2, \{m\}} (s', t', \langle\rangle) \Longrightarrow \cdots$$

$$\cdots \Longrightarrow (s^i, t^j, \langle m, m \rangle) \xrightarrow[I_k]{O_k, \{m\}} (s^i, t^{j+1}, \langle m \rangle)$$

4 Behavioural Semantics

We define the behavioural semantics of the enriched language. The behavioural semantics defines transitions of the form $M \xrightarrow[I]{O} M'$, where M is a module, I are inputs events, O are output eventsand M' is the new module that will correctly react to the next inputs events. The transition is computed using an auxiliary relation which defines the micro steps of the form

$$stat \xrightarrow[E]{E', k} E stat'$$

following the definition of *Esterel* in [1]. The *event* E consists of a set of *valued signals* of the form $s(v)$, or s in case of a pure signal, with $s \in S$ being a signal and v being a value of appropriate type, or signals pm, dm. The set $E' \subseteq E$ specifies the emitted signals, and k is the termination level (0 - terminates instantaneously, 1 - never terminates and $k > 1$ are used in traps).

We have

$$M \xrightarrow[I]{O} M' \quad \text{if} \quad M \xrightarrow[E]{O, k} I \cup O M' \quad \text{for some } k.$$

We concentrate here on the new statements and notions. The rules for Esterel are recalled in the appendix.

4.1 Blackboards

The behaviour of a blackboard is defined by the following rule

$$\mathcal{B} \xrightarrow[E]{E', 1} \mathcal{E} \mathcal{B}'$$

where $E' = \{m(o(\mathcal{B}(m))) \mid m \in M\}$, and $\mathcal{B}'$ is defined by

$$\mathcal{B}'(m) = \begin{cases} p(v, d(\mathcal{B}(m))) \text{ if} & pm(v) \in E, \text{ and } dm \in E \\ p(v, \mathcal{B}(m)) & \text{if} & pm(v) \in E, \text{ and } dm \notin E \\ d(\mathcal{B}(m)) & \text{if} & pm(v) \notin E, \text{ and } dm \in E \\ \mathcal{B}(m) & \text{else} \end{cases}$$

One should note that put and delete messages affect the blackboard only in the next instant. As stated in the introduction, we assume that it is always possible to write on the blackboard, hence the clock is determined by the various modules writing out messages on the blackboard.

One relevant limitation on blackboard is that the status of the blackboard cannot be tested. This limitation, together with the fact that messages are present in the next instant, give us the possibility of avoiding causality cycles and allow us for separate compilation.

4.2 Coordination Primitives

The coordination primitives have very simple behaviours:

$$\text{read } m \xrightarrow[E]{\emptyset,0} E \text{nothing} \qquad \text{if } m(v) \in E$$

$$\text{read } m \xrightarrow[E]{\emptyset,1} E \text{read } m \qquad \text{if } m(v) \notin E$$

$$\text{out } m(v) \xrightarrow[E]{\{pm(v)\},0} E \text{nothing}$$

$$\text{fetch } m \xrightarrow[E]{\{dm\},0} E \text{nothing} \qquad \text{if } m(v) \in E$$

$$\text{fetch } m \xrightarrow[E]{\emptyset,1} E \text{fetch } m \qquad \text{if } m(v) \notin E$$

It can be observed that the control is retained if the desired message is not present in the blackboard.

4.3 Asynchronous Parallel Composition

The crucial operator is that of asynchronous composition which will turn out (with slight but common modification [6]) the one of process algebra. The modification is such that synchronization of communication is restricted to messages. The first set of rules states that modules are not allowed to react on their own if they write to a blackboard: let $\downarrow M = \{pm(v) \mid m \in M, v \in V\} \cup \{pm \mid m \in M\}$. Then

$$\left.\begin{array}{c} \dfrac{M \xrightarrow[I]{O} M'}{M/\!/M_1 \xrightarrow[I]{O} M'/\!/M_1} \\[2em] \dfrac{M \xrightarrow[I]{O} M'}{M_1/\!/M \xrightarrow[I]{O} M_1/\!/M'} \end{array}\right\} \text{ only if } (I \cap O) \cap \downarrow M = \emptyset$$

Otherwise processes have to synchronize:

$$\dfrac{M_1 \xrightarrow[I_1 \cup O_2]{O_1} M_1' \quad M_2 \xrightarrow[I_2 \cup O_1]{O_2} M_2'}{M_1/\!/M_2 \xrightarrow[I_1 \cup I_2]{O_1 \cup O_2} M_1'/\!/M_2'}$$

Let us analyze the different extensions of the latter rule.

- If $(I_1 \cup I_2 \cup O_1 \cup O_2) \cap M = \emptyset$ then both the processes do not synchronize since $I_1 \cap I_2 = \emptyset$. They may have proceeded on their own as well.
- If, for instance, $pm(v) \in O_1 \cup O_2$ then the processes have to synchronize in writing to a blackboard, meaning that you can write the same message only once to a blackboard at an instant[4].
- $pm(v), dm \in I_1 \cup I_2$ cannot happen as well as $m(v) \in I_1 \cup I_2$) since a message identifier relates only to one blackboard.
- If, for instance, $m(v) \in I_1 \cup I_2$ then both processes read the messages at the same time from a blackboard. However, the subprocesses may have moved and read on their own due to the other rules.
- If, for instance, $dm \in O_2$ then a subprocess of M_1 must be a blackboard from which m is fetched. Similarly, if $m(v) \in O_2$ then a subprocess of M_2 must be a blackboard which sustains $m(v)$.

The reader may check that the rules cover the phenomenon illustrated by the pictures 1 and 2.

We assume that messages are local. Messages are meant just for the communication between components of a system. Hence the interaction of system of modules is determined by the relation

$$ M_1 /\!/ \ldots /\!/ M_n \xLeftrightarrow[I]{O} M'_1 /\!/ \ldots /\!/ M'_n $$

where I and O only consist of signals.

5   Properties and Perspectives

We briefly investigate on the properties of our programs.

As each module can be an Esterel program without coordination primitives it is clear that Esterel is subsumed.

We can observe that the communication possibilities we have added are not too powerful:

Property 1. It is impossible to simulate a rendezvous with the added coordination primitives.

In fact, as it is not allowed to check the status of blackboards and because there is always a delay in the interprocess communication, due to the fact that blackboards have delays, it is impossible to establish a channel between two processes (as processes are synchronous programs).

Because of this property, it holds also that

Property 2. The systems are free of causality-cycle.

---

[4] This is an hidden but natural assumption: every message identifier relates only to one blackboard.

Another property we want to stress is that the rules for the asynchronous parallel composition are deterministic (this is a consequence of the fact that is a message is available and it can be taken that it is).

Property 3. The rules for the asynchronous parallel composition are deterministic.

This can be easily checked inspecting the rules.

The above property does not imply that the system as a whole is deterministic, as there is a source of non determinism, namely the different clocks of the various modules. However this non determinism can be equated to the so called external non determinism of CSP, where the source of the choice is external to the agent performing the choice[5].

We consider now the notion of deadlock. This situation can arise when all the agents want to read or fetch a message that has been not posted yet (and cannot be, as all the agents are waiting for it). This situation is completely different from the causality-cycle, as in that case a causal dependence arises, whereas here, due to the possible different speeds of the agent, an undesired situation can arise. The nice point is that it is possible to detect deadlocks. In fact, to each agent (which is a synchronous program) a finite state automaton corresponds, and this one can be seen as a Petri net. Blackboards can be represented via places connecting the different nets (better some transitions of these) and the kind of arcs connecting the *blackboard* places and these transitions are either the classical one (in-going if the message has to be written or out-going if the message has to fetched) or the so called *test* arc (if the message has to be read). The resulting system is still a Petri net for which it is possible to prove reachability of certain markings which represent the deadlock of the system.

Property 4. Deadlock is decidable.

We finally show that the semantic of our parallel operator is compositional. The semantics we consider for each module is the usual one: via the behavioural semantics we obtain an *history*, i.e. a sequence of input output pairs (the same applies for blackboards, inputs being the signals coming from agents and the outputs are the name of messages available). Formally we have the following sequences $(I_1^i, O_1^i), \ldots, (I_n^i, O_n^i), \ldots$ for the i-th module. The sequences can be combined according to the rules devised in the previous section (we denote these sequences with H_i):

$$H_i//H_j = \begin{cases} (I_1^i, O_1^i), \overline{H}_i//H_j \cup (I_1^j, O_1^j), H_i//\overline{H}_j & \text{only if } (I \cap O) \cap \downarrow M = \emptyset \\ (I_1^i \cup I_1^j, O_1^i \cup O_1^j), \overline{H}_i//\overline{H}_j & \text{otherwise} \end{cases}$$

where $(I_1^k, O_1^k), \overline{H}_k = H_k$, with $k = i, j$. Denoting the histories of a module with $D[\![M]\!]$ we have

---

[5] It can be argued that this is not a *choice*, but we are not here interested in such debatte.

Property 5. $D[\![M_i/\!/M_j]\!] = D[\![M_i]\!]/\!/D[\![M_j]\!]$, i.e. the semantic is compositional.

Finally we have the following property.

Property 6. Modules can be added to a system, i.e. the language supports modular design.

5.1 Perspectives

As we showed above, our proposal have a number of properties we consider relevant, for instance a consequence of modularity is that we allow the separate compilation of the various modules, preserving the possibility of proving that the system behaves correctly.

These properties need a deeper investigation. Moreover we plan to study the consequence of adding full fledged coordination primitives to such languages.

We feel confident in the usefulness of this approach in reality. This is justified by the fact that our proposal is *minimal*, in fact we believe to have added as little expressive power as possible.

References

1. G. Berry. Esterel on hardware. *Philosophical Transation Royal Society of London*, A:87–104, 1992.
2. G. Berry and A. Benveniste. The synchronous approach to reactive and real-time systems. *Another Look at Real Time Programming, Proceedings of IEEE*, 79:1270–1282, 1991.
3. G. Berry and G. Gonthier. The ESTEREL synchronous programming language: design, semantics, implementation. *Science of Computer Programming*, 19(2):87–152, 1992.
4. G. Berry, S. Ramesh, and R. K. Shyamasundar. Communicating reactive processes. In *Conference Record of the Twentieth Annual ACM SIGPLAN-SIGACT Symposium on Principles of Programming Languages*, 1993.
5. F. Boussinot and R. de Simone. The SL synchronous language. *IEEE Transactions on Software Engineering*, 22(4):256–266, 1996.
6. S. D. Brookes, C. A. R. Hoare, and A. W. Roscoe. A theory of communicating sequential processes. *Journal of the ACM*, 31(3):560–599, 1984.
7. N. Halbwachs. *Synchronous Programming of Reactive Systems*. The Kuwler International Series in Engineering and Computer Science. Kuwler Academic Publisher, 1993.
8. N. Halbwachs, P. Caspi, P. Raymond, and D. Pilaud. The synchronous dataflow programming language lustre. *Proceedings of the IEEE*, 79(9):1305–1320, 1991.
9. D. Harel, H. Lachover, A. Naamad, A. Pnueli, M. Politi, R. Sherman, A. Shtull-Trauring, and M. B. Trakhtenbrot. STATEMATE: A working environment for the development of complex reactive systems. *IEEE Transactions on Software Engineering*, 16(4):403–414, April 1990.
10. V. Saraswat, R. Jagadeesan, and V. Gupta. Foundations of timed concurrent constraint programming. In *Proceedings, Ninth Annual IEEE Symposium on Logic in Computer Science*, pages 71–80. IEEE Computer Society Press, 1994.

Appendix

For the sake of self containedness, we list the behavioural semantics rules of Esterel.

$$\text{nothing} \xrightarrow[E]{\emptyset,0} \text{nothing} \qquad\qquad \text{halt} \xrightarrow[E]{\emptyset,1} \text{halt}$$

$$\text{emit } S \xrightarrow[E]{\{S\},0} \text{nothing}$$

$$\frac{stat_1 \xrightarrow[E]{E'_1,0} stat'_1 \quad stat_2 \xrightarrow[E]{E'_2,k_2} stat'_2}{stat_1; stat_2 \xrightarrow[E]{E'_1 \cup E'_2, k_2} stat'_2} \qquad \frac{stat_1 \xrightarrow[E]{E'_1,k_1} stat'_1 \quad k_1 > 0}{stat_1; stat_2 \xrightarrow[E]{E_1,k_1} stat'_1; stat_2}$$

$$\frac{stat \xrightarrow[E]{E',k} stat' \quad k > 0}{\text{loop } stat \text{ end} \xrightarrow[E]{E,k} stat'; \text{loop } stat \text{ end}}$$

$$\frac{stat_1 \xrightarrow[E]{E'_1,k_1} stat'_1 \quad S \in E}{\text{present } S \text{ then } stat_1 \text{ else } stat_2 \xrightarrow[E]{E'_1,k_1} stat'_1}$$

$$\frac{stat_2 \xrightarrow[E]{E'_2,k_2} stat'_2 \quad S \notin E}{\text{present } S \text{ then } stat_1 \text{ else } stat_2 \xrightarrow[E]{E'_2,k_2} stat'_2}$$

$$\frac{stat \xrightarrow[E]{E',k} stat'}{\text{do } stat \text{ watching } S \xrightarrow[E]{E',k} \text{present } S \text{ else do } stat' \text{ watching } S}$$

$$\frac{stat_1 \xrightarrow[E]{E'_1,k_1} stat'_1 \quad stat_2 \xrightarrow[E]{E'_2,k_2} stat'_2}{stat_1 \| stat_2 \xrightarrow[E]{E'_1 \cup E'_2, max\{k_1,k_2\}} stat'_1 \| stat'_2}$$

$$\text{exit } T^k \xrightarrow[E]{\emptyset,k} \text{halt} \qquad \frac{stat \xrightarrow[E]{E',k} stat' \quad k = 0 \text{ or } k = 2}{\text{trap } T \text{ in } stat \text{ end} \xrightarrow[E]{E',0} \text{nothing}}$$

$$\frac{stat \xrightarrow[E]{E',k} stat' \quad (k = 1 \text{ and } k' = 1) \text{ or } (k > 2 \text{ and } k' = k - 1)}{\text{trap } T \text{ in } stat \text{ end} \xrightarrow[E]{E',k'} \text{trap } T \text{ in } stat' \text{ end}}$$

Composing Specifications for Coordination

Carlo Montangero[1] and Laura Semini[2]

[1] Dipartimento di Informatica, Università di Pisa, `monta@di.unipi.it`
[2] Dip. di Sistemi e Informatica, Università di Firenze, `semini@dsi.unifi.it`

Abstract. We introduce Oikos_adtl, a specification language for distributed systems based on asynchronous communication via remote writings. The language is designed to support the composition of specifications. It allows expressing the global properties of a system in terms of the local properties of the components and of *coordination templates*.
Oikos_adtl is based on an asynchronous, distributed, temporal logic, which extends Unity to deal with components and events.
We present the specification language and its semantics, introduce a number of compositionality theorems, and discuss some coordination templates. A fragment of a standard case study is used to validate pragmatically the approach, with respect to expressiveness and work-ability.

1 Introduction

The design of quality software for distributed systems is becoming more and more critical, due to the current impact of software on every technical accomplishment, and the fact that networks pervade any current application. The problem has two facets: the complexity of the systems under development, and the need of continuous update to keep the pace with moving requirements. To avoid old errors and face complexity, we need a design process that helps in getting the *right* system architecture *right* from the outset, rather than rely *only* on afterwards checks. Besides, to cope with change better, the process should naturally support the recording of the complete justification of the development, for future reference.

A design process based on formal refinements, centered on the system architecture, when applied in the early phases of development, would mitigate the problems related to both complexity and change. So, a long term goal of ours is to extend the refinement calculi, traditionally applied to programming in the small [2], to programming in the large. The approach can be effective only if it comes with simple, workable concepts and notations. A key strategy to cope with complexity, also in design, is "divide and conquer": express the global properties of a system in terms of the properties that are local to its components and of *coordination templates* that make it easier for the designer to *compose* specifications. The other way round, once valuable composition templates are available, they can be exploited to devise *refinement templates*, to be used top-down in the design.

The work reported here is a first step towards a distributed refinement calculus that integrates in a natural way local refinements (i.e. within a single component) and coordination templates. Our previous work [21] can readily be adapted to work locally. The compositionality results of this paper represent the main ingredient to develop useful coordination, and hence refinement, templates.

To exploit our past experience, we circumscribe our field of application and consider distributed systems that consist of loosely coupled asynchronous long running services, like work-flow systems. These systems are conveniently modeled as multiple data-spaces interacting via remote writings. The multiple data-spaces paradigm is widely regarded as interesting for coordination applications [4, 8, 10]. Brogi and Jacquet [5] argue convincingly for the relevance of asynchronous communications. Still, there is a lack of satisfactory design and analysis techniques for these systems.

We introduce Oikos_adtl, a specification language for distributed systems based on asynchronous communication via remote writings. The language is designed to support the composition of specifications. It allows expressing the global properties of a system in terms of local properties and of *coordination templates*. The former are properties exposed by a single component, the latter describe the approach taken to control the interactions of the components. Oikos_adtl is based on an asynchronous, distributed, temporal logic, which extends Unity [6] to deal with components and events.

The structure of the paper is the following. Section 2 presents the specification language and its semantics. Section 3 introduces a number of composition theorems, and discusses some coordination templates. A fragment of a standard case study from the COORDINA working group is used in Section 4 to show the expressiveness of the language and to validate the selected theorems and templates, pragmatically. Before some concluding remarks, Section 5 discusses related work.

2   Oikos_adtl

The extensions to Unity that allows Oikos_adtl to deal with *events*, are taken from Oikos_tl [21]. This paper works out the extension to distributed components first proposed in [20, 17].

A component has a name, and it is specified by liveness (something good will happen) and safety (nothing bad will happen) properties of the evolution of its state. An event occurs when a given condition is established in a component. Operators CAUSES_C, CAUSES, NEEDS, BECAUSE_C, and BECAUSE permit to deal with events. The first two express liveness conditions, the latter express safety conditions. Suffixe c stands for *closely*, CAUSES relates an event and a condition, and specifies that the occurrence of the event is sufficient to arrive in a state in which the condition holds; CAUSES_C requires also the condition to occur in the state in which the event occured, or in the next one. NEEDS requires a condition to hold when an event occurs; BECAUSE also relates an event and a condition, and specifies that the condition is necessary for the event to occur: the condition must hold sometime before the event occurs. BECAUSE is weaker than NEEDS, which entails that the conditions it relates are synchronous. BECAUSE_C lays in between: the condition enabling the event happened in the *close past*, i.e. it must hold in the same or in the previous state (this notions will be made precise in Sect. 2.2). Operators LEADS_TO, UNLESS, STABLE, and INV extend consistently the corresponding operators of Unity.

The specification of a distributed system in Oikos_adtl shapes $\mathcal{M}:\ll \mathcal{F} \gg$, where $\mathcal{M} = M^1, \ldots, M^n$ is a set of component names and $\mathcal{F}$ is a set of *properties*, i.e. a set of formulae with the structure given in Table 1. A property F can be *local* or *distributed*. In the first case it refers to a single component, in the second case to a set of components. Most operators can be distributed: a notable exception is NEEDS, which can be used only locally. Indeed, for NEEDS to hold, the event and its enabling condition must be synchronous, and this notion is defined only locally in an asynchronous world.

Components interact via *remote writings*, as in multiple tuple-spaces [4, 8, 10]. They are denoted in Oikos_adtl by expressions like $n : q@m$, meaning that component n has caused condition q to be established in component m. Remote writings introduce temporal ordering among the states of different components.

Table 1. Oikos_adtl syntax.

F	::=	$M: Local \mid Distr$ with M component name
$Local$	::=	$State$ UNLESS $State \mid Atomic$ NEEDS $State$
$Distr$	::=	INIT $DiState \mid$
		$M: Atomic$ BECAUSE_C $DiState \mid M: Atomic$ BECAUSE $DiState \mid$
		$M: Atomic$ CAUSES_C $DiState \mid M: Atomic$ CAUSES $DiState \mid$
		$M: State$ LEADS_TO $DiState$
$DiState$	::=	$M: State \mid DiState \wedge DiState \mid DiState \vee DiState$
$State$	::=	$Atomic \mid \neg State \mid State \wedge State$
$Atomic$	::=	$n * p \mid p@M$ with $n \in \mathbb{N}$, p a term

Two local operators are derived: $M :$ STABLE $A \overset{def}{=} M : A$ UNLESS $false$

$$M : \text{INV } A \overset{def}{=} \text{INIT } M : A \wedge M : \text{STABLE } A$$

Let us consider, as an example, a very common coordination template, namely the *moderated publish-subscribe* template. There are $n + 1$ components, one of which is the *moderator* M. The other components are interested in publishing $(pub\_int(X))$ and being notified of new items $(notif(X))$. The moderator can reject an item $(rej(X))$, in ways unsaid at this level of abstraction. The specification in Table 2 captures the template. The first property defines liveness: it states that each event carrying an intention to publish will be honored, either by a rejection or by notifying everybody. The other properties state essential safety conditions. The second one requires that a notification event occurs only if somebody manifested an intention to publish. The last properties express the weakest form of consistency: a reject event cannot occur in presence of a matching notification, and viceversa. Stronger conditions may be needed in specific applications of the template and must be dealt with case by case. E.g., one can say that once an item has been rejected it can no longer be notified, adding the clause STABLE $rej(X)$.

Other examples of specifications will be discussed in Sections 3 and 4.

Table 2. A specification example.

$M, PS^1, \ldots, PS^n : \ll \quad$ (for all i.)

$$PS^i : pub\_int(X) \text{ CAUSES } M : (rej(X)@PS^i \lor \land_j notif(X)@PS^j), \quad (1)$$

$$PS^i : notif(X) \text{ BECAUSE } (\lor_j PS^j : pub\_int(X)), \quad (2)$$

$$PS^i : rej(X) \text{ NEEDS } \neg notif(X), \qquad PS^i : notif(X) \text{ NEEDS } \neg rej(X) \gg \quad (3)$$

2.1 The Computational Model

A system Σ is characterized by a list $\mathcal{M}$ of component names, and a set $\mathcal{T}$ of state transitions, where each transition is associated to a component in $\mathcal{M}$. A computation of a system $\langle \mathcal{M}, \mathcal{T} \rangle$ is an acyclic oriented graph of states like the one in Fig. 1 (dotted arrows denote multiple transitions, plain arrows single transitions or remote writings). We allow actions towards the environment.

Fig. 1. Computation of a system with three components

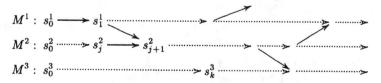

We call s_j^i the jth state of component M^i. A state is a multiset of terms: standard terms p, and terms of the form $p@M$. A computation satisfies:

$$s^i_{j+1} = \begin{cases} t_i(s^i_j), & \text{for some } t_i \in \mathcal{T} \qquad\qquad\qquad \text{or} \\ s^i_j \cup p & \text{and there are } s^k_{l-1},\ s^k_l \text{ s.t. } s^k_l = t_k(s^k_{l-1}) \text{ for some } t_k \in \mathcal{T}, \\ & \text{with } p@M^i \notin s^k_{l-1} \text{ and } p@M^i \in s^k_l. \end{cases}$$

A state of component M^i is either the result of the application of a local transition, say t_i (as the local write of q in Fig. 2), or the result of a remote write originated in a distinguished component M^k by a transition t_k. Moreover, the application of t_k causes, in M^k, the appearance of a term of the form $p@M^i$.

Fig. 2. Example of Computation.

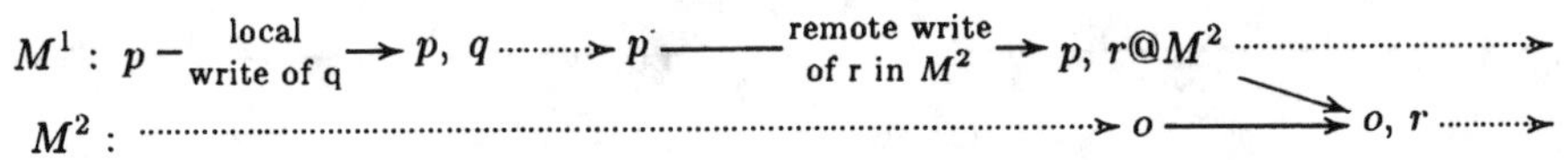

Finally, we define the parallel composition $\langle \mathcal{M}_1, \mathcal{T}_1 \rangle \parallel \langle \mathcal{M}_2, \mathcal{T}_2 \rangle$ of a pair of systems with $\mathcal{M}_1 \cap \mathcal{M}_2 = \emptyset$, as the system $\langle \mathcal{M}_1 \cup \mathcal{M}_2, \mathcal{T}_1 \cup \mathcal{T}_2 \rangle$.

2.2 Oikos_adtl Semantics

Formulae are interpreted on computations. Transitions and remote writings define the *next state* relation $\mathcal{N}$. States in computations are also related by the *future state* relation $\geq$ which is the reflexive and transitive closure of relation $\mathcal{N}$. Since the underlying graph is acyclic, the future state relation is antisymmetric and thus a partial order.

For instance, the computations:

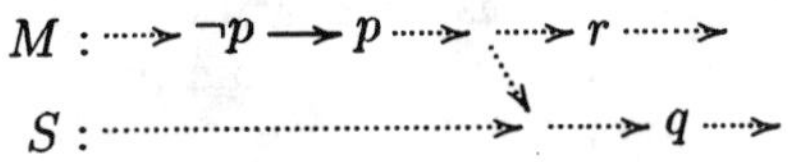

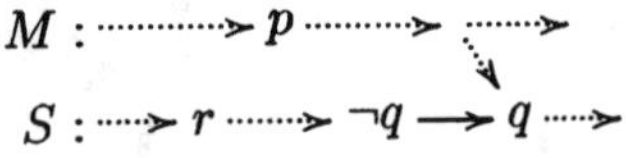

are, respectively, models of:

$$M{:}p \text{ CAUSES } (S{:}q \wedge M{:}r) \qquad \text{and} \qquad S{:}q \text{ BECAUSE } (M{:}p \wedge S{:}r)$$

Formally, given a formula F and a computation S of $\langle \mathcal{M}, \mathcal{T} \rangle$, S is a model of F if and only if: *(a)* $M^i \in \mathcal{M}$ for each sub-formula $M^i : F'$ of F, and *(b)* the states in S satisfy appropriate conditions given by cases on the structure of F in Table 3.

Finally, a system $\langle \mathcal{M}, \mathcal{T} \rangle$ satisfies a specification $M' :\ll \mathcal{F} \gg$ if and only if $\mathcal{M} = \mathcal{M}'$ and all its computations are models of all the formulae in $\mathcal{F}$.

Table 3. Oikos_adtl semantics. The semantics defines the conditions a computation S of a system $\langle \mathcal{M}, \mathcal{T} \rangle$ has to verify to be a model for F, given by cases on the structure of formula F. Note that $p@M^k$ holds if p *has been* sent to M^k, i.e., it holds in a state s_j^i whenever a state $s_k^i \leq s_j^i$ exists in which the remote writing has been performed.

$M^i : A$ UNLESS B	$: \forall j \geq 0.\ s_j^i \models A \wedge \neg B \rightarrow s_{j+1}^i \models A \vee B$
$M^i : A$ NEEDS B	$: \forall j \geq 0.\ s_j^i \models A! \rightarrow s_j^i \models B$
INIT DS	$: s_0^i \models$ BEGIN DS for some i
$M^i : A$ BECAUSE_C DS	$: (s_0^i \models A \rightarrow s_0^i \models$ BEGIN DS) and
	$(\forall k > 0.\ s_k^i \models A! \rightarrow s_k^i \models$ C_PAST DS)
$M^i : A$ BECAUSE DS	$: (s_0^i \models A \rightarrow s_0^i \models$ BEGIN DS) and
	$(\forall k > 0.\ s_k^i \models A! \rightarrow s_k^i \models$ PAST DS)
$M^i : A$ CAUSES_C DS	$: \forall k \geq 0.\ s_k^i \models A! \rightarrow s_k^i \models$ C_FUT DS
$M^i : A$ CAUSES DS	$: \forall k \geq 0.\ s_k^i \models A! \rightarrow s_k^i \models$ FUT DS
$M^i : A$ LEADS_TO DS	$: \forall k \geq 0.\ s_k^i \models A \rightarrow s_k^i \models$ FUT DS

Where:

$s_j^i \models n * p$	iff s_j^i contains at least n occurrences of p
$s_j^i \models p@M^k$	iff $(\forall l \geq j.\ p@M^k \in s_l^i)$ and
	$[(M^k \in \Sigma$ and $s_{j-1}^i \not\models p@M^k) \rightarrow (\exists s_l^k.(s_j^i, s_l^k) \in \mathcal{N}$ and $s_l^k \models p)]$
$s_j^i \models \neg A$	iff $s_j^i \not\models A$
$s_j^i \models A \wedge B$	iff $s_j^i \models A$ and $s_j^i \models B$
$s_j^i \models A!$	iff $(s_j^i \models A$ and $s_{j-1}^i \not\models A)$ or $(j = 0$ and $s_0^i \models A)$
$s_0^i \models$ BEGIN $M^k : A$	iff $s_0^k \models A$
$s_j^i \models$ C_PAST $M^k : A$	iff $(i = k$ and $s_j^i \models A)$ or $(\exists s_l^k.\ (s_l^k, s_j^i) \in \mathcal{N}$ and $s_l^k \models A)$
$s_j^i \models$ PAST $M^k : A$	iff $\exists s_l^k \leq s_j^i.\ s_l^k \models A$
$s_j^i \models$ C_FUT $M^k : A$	iff $[i = k$ and $(s_j^i \models A$ or $s_{j+1}^i \models A)]$ or $[s_{j+1}^i \models A@M^k]$
$s_j^i \models$ FUT $M^k : A$	iff $\exists s_l^k \geq s_j^i.\ s_l^k \models A$
$s_j^i \models$ OP $DS \wedge DS'$	iff $s_j^i \models$ OP $DS \wedge$ OP DS'
$s_j^i \models$ OP $DS \vee DS'$	iff $s_j^i \models$ OP $DS \vee$ OP DS'
	for OP $\in \{$ BEGIN , C_PAST , PAST , C_FUT , FUT $\}$

2.3 Composing Specifications

We discuss how to prove that a single component satisfies its specification else-where [21]. Here we show how to derive the properties satisfied by a larger system from the properties satisfied locally by its components. More in general, we want to derive the specification $\mathcal{M}_1, \mathcal{M}_2 :\ll \mathcal{F} \gg$ of a system $\Sigma_1 \parallel \Sigma_2$ from the specifications $\mathcal{M}_1 :\ll \mathcal{F}_1 \gg$ and $\mathcal{M}_2 :\ll \mathcal{F}_2 \gg$ of Σ_1 and Σ_2, respectively.

We assert:

$$\vdash_{\mathcal{M}} \mathcal{F}$$ iff, for any $\mathcal{T}$, $\langle \mathcal{M}, \mathcal{T} \rangle$ satisfies $\mathcal{F}$, i.e. iff all its computations are models of all the formulae in $\mathcal{F}$;

$$\frac{\vdash_{\mathcal{M}} \mathcal{F}}{\vdash_{\mathcal{M}} F}$$ iff any $\langle \mathcal{M}, \mathcal{T} \rangle$ satisfying $\mathcal{F}$, also satisfies formula F;

$$\frac{\vdash_{\mathcal{M}_1} \mathcal{F}_1}{\vdash_{\mathcal{M}_1, \mathcal{M}_2} F}$$ iff, for any system $\langle \mathcal{M}_1, \mathcal{T}_1 \rangle$ satisfying $\mathcal{F}_1$ and for any $\mathcal{T}_2$, $\langle \mathcal{M}_1 \cup \mathcal{M}_2, \mathcal{T}_1 \cup \mathcal{T}_2 \rangle$ satisfies F;

$$\frac{\vdash_{\mathcal{M}_1} \mathcal{F}_1 \quad \vdash_{\mathcal{M}_2} \mathcal{F}_2}{\vdash_{\mathcal{M}_1, \mathcal{M}_2} F}$$ iff, for any pair $\langle \mathcal{M}_1, \mathcal{T}_1 \rangle$, $\langle \mathcal{M}_2, \mathcal{T}_2 \rangle$, satisfying $\mathcal{F}_1$ and $\mathcal{F}_2$, respectively, $\langle \mathcal{M}_1 \cup \mathcal{M}_2, \mathcal{T}_1 \cup \mathcal{T}_2 \rangle$ satisfies F.

Thus, given Σ_1 and Σ_2 satisfying $\mathcal{M}_1 :\ll \mathcal{F}_1 \gg$ and $\mathcal{M}_2 :\ll \mathcal{F}_2 \gg$ respectively, $\Sigma_1 \parallel \Sigma_2$ satisfies $\mathcal{M}_1, \mathcal{M}_2 :\ll \mathcal{F} \gg$ iff every $F \in \mathcal{F}$ satisfies the last condition above.

2.4 Composition Theorems

In this section we discuss some useful theorems, that can be proved exploiting the semantics in Table 3 and the definitions in the previous subsection. We distinguish liveness (Table 4, 4–8) and safety (Table 4, 9–15). Most theorems refer to the new operators, and only few of them refer to Unity operators: the former are those needed to prove the refinement templates presented in this paper.

(4) *Reliable Communication:* this theorem characterizes remote writings, linking the sufficient cause in the sender to the effect in the recipient.
(5) *Causes/Leads_To:* there will always be a state in which B holds after C holds, hence the consequence.
(6) *Preserve Causes_Closely:* the essential points here are: *a)* the syntax for CAUSES_C restricts A to be positive; *b)* each component can only add to the others: therefore, the new component N cannot falsify the sufficient condition A in M; *c)* a similar property does not hold for CAUSES, A CAUSES B in M might be mediated by some negative intermediate clause, i.e. it might hold because (5) applies, with $C = \neg D$. Hence, N might invalidate it, by sending D. The fact that A and B are close in CAUSES_C avoids this possibility.
(7) *Causes Introduction:* CAUSES is weaker than CAUSES_C.

Table 4. Composition Theorems.

——————————————— **Liveness** ———————————————

$$\vdash_{M,N} \; M : B@N \; \text{CAUSES\_C} \; N : B \tag{4}$$

$$\frac{\vdash_{\mathcal{M}} \; M : A \; \text{CAUSES} \; O : C \quad \vdash_{\mathcal{M}} \; O : C \; \text{LEADS\_TO} \; N : B}{\vdash_{\mathcal{M}} \; M : A \; \text{CAUSES} \; N : B} \tag{5}$$

$$\frac{\vdash_{\mathcal{M}} \; M : A \; \text{CAUSES\_C} \; O : B}{\vdash_{N,\mathcal{M}} \; M : A \; \text{CAUSES\_C} \; O : B} \tag{6}$$

$$\frac{\vdash_{\mathcal{M}} \; M : A \; \text{CAUSES\_C} \; O : B}{\vdash_{\mathcal{M}} \; M : A \; \text{CAUSES} \; O : B} \tag{7}$$

$$\frac{\vdash_{\mathcal{M}} \; M : A \; \text{CAUSES} \; O : C \quad \vdash_{\mathcal{M}} \; O : C \; \text{CAUSES} \; N : B \quad \vdash_{\mathcal{M}} \; O : C \; \text{BECAUSE} \; M : A}{\vdash_{\mathcal{M}} \; M : A \; \text{CAUSES} \; N : B} \tag{8}$$

——————————————— **Safety** ———————————————

$$\vdash_{\mathcal{M}} \; M : \; \text{STABLE} \; p@N \tag{9}$$

$$\frac{\vdash_{\mathcal{M}} \; M : (A \wedge \neg B) \; \text{UNLESS} \; O : C \quad \vdash_{N} \; N : \; \text{INV} \; \neg B@M \quad A \; \text{conjunction of atomic formulae}}{\vdash_{N,\mathcal{M}} \; (M : A \wedge \neg B) \; \text{UNLESS} \; O : C} \tag{10}$$

$$\frac{\vdash_{\mathcal{M}} \; M : A \; \text{NEEDS} \; B \quad \vdash_{N} \; N : \; \text{INV} \; \neg A@M}{\vdash_{N,\mathcal{M}} \; M : A \; \text{NEEDS} \; B} \tag{11}$$

$$\frac{\vdash_{\mathcal{M}} \; M : A@O \; \text{NEEDS} \; B}{\vdash_{N,\mathcal{M}} \; M : A@O \; \text{NEEDS} \; B} \tag{12}$$

$$\frac{\vdash_{\mathcal{M}} \; M : A \; \text{NEEDS} \; B}{\vdash_{\mathcal{M}} \; M : A \; \text{BECAUSE\_C} \; M : B} \quad \frac{\vdash_{\mathcal{M}} \; M : A \; \text{BECAUSE\_C} \; N : B}{\vdash_{\mathcal{M}} \; M : A \; \text{BECAUSE} \; N : B} \tag{13}$$

$$\frac{\vdash_{\mathcal{M}} \; M : A \; \text{BECAUSE\_C} \; N : B}{\vdash_{O,\mathcal{M}} \; M : A \; \text{BECAUSE\_C} \; (N : B \vee O : A@M)} \tag{14}$$

$$\frac{\vdash_{\mathcal{M}} \; M : A \; \text{BECAUSE} \; N : B \quad \vdash_{\mathcal{M}} \; N : B \; \text{BECAUSE} \; O : C}{\vdash_{\mathcal{M}} \; M : A \; \text{BECAUSE} \; O : C} \tag{15}$$

$$\frac{\vdash_{N} \; N : A \; \text{NEEDS} \; false \quad \vdash_{M} \; M : B@N \; \text{NEEDS} \; \neg A@N \quad \vdash_{N} \; N : B \; \text{NEEDS} \; false \quad \vdash_{M} \; M : A@N \; \text{NEEDS} \; \neg B@N}{\vdash_{M,N} \; N : A \; \text{NEEDS} \; \neg B} \tag{16}$$

---

(8) *Causes Weak Transitivity*: CAUSES is only weakly transitive. Indeed, consider a computation in which first C becomes true, then B appears and disappears before A becomes true, while C keeps holding: it satisfies the first two premises, but not the consequence. Hence the last premise.

(9) *Committing Communication*: something sent cannot be retracted: the sender has committed itself.

(10) *Preserve Unless*: the added component N cannot falsify A, restricted to be positive by the side condition. The second condition guarantees that N does not falsify B.

(11) *Preserve Needs*: the argument is similar to *Preserve Unless*. N must be constrained so that it does not interfere with the computations of the components in M, that will not establish A in the absence of B.

(12) *Preserve Communication Conditions*: this is an important specialization of the previous one: the communication event cannot be generated from outside component M.

(13) *Because_Closely and Because Introduction*: BECAUSE is weaker than BE-CAUSE_C, which is weaker than NEEDS.

(14) *Preserve Because_Closely*: the new component can be an unforeseen cause for A.

(15) *Because Transitivity*: if B is necessary for event A, B must hold before or when A becomes true; if also C is necessary for event B, C must hold before or when B becomes true. Therefore, C is necessary for event A, i.e. C holds before or when A becomes true.

(16) *Preserve Mutual Exclusion*: the premises guarantee that N cannot generate neither A nor B locally, and that M can send at most one of them. Stability of $B@N$ is crucial here.

3 Coordination Templates

To specify and prove the global coordination properties of a distributed system is often a complex task. A coordination template defines a specification schema for a set of components, and derives global properties of their parallel composition. Once valuable composition templates are available, they can be used to simplify the design process. We introduce two such templates, *broadcast* and *moderated publish-subscribe*.

3.1 Broadcast

This template consists of the parallel composition of a sender S and n receivers R^i ($i \in \{1, \ldots, n\}$) specified, respectively, by:

$$S : \ll S : req(X) \text{ CAUSES\_C } S : \wedge_j notif(X)@R^j, \tag{17}$$

$$\text{(for all } j) \ S : notif(X)@R^j \text{ NEEDS } req(X) \gg \tag{18}$$

$$R^i : \ll R^i : notif(X) \text{ NEEDS } false, \qquad (19)$$

$$(\text{for all } j) \; R^i : notif(X)@R^j \text{ NEEDS } false \gg \qquad (20)$$

The sender component has to notify all the receivers of any new item X it is requested to publish (17). Besides, it sends a notification only upon request (18). Nothing is said here on the request originator. Receivers can neither produce nor send notifications (19 and 20).

Proposition 1. *The parallel composition of sender and receivers has the property that receivers will be notified of all the items following a request, and only of those:*

$$S, R^1, \ldots, R^n : \ll \; S : req(X) \text{ CAUSES } \wedge_i R^i : notif(X), \qquad (21)$$

$$(\text{for all } i) \; R^i : notif(X) \text{ BECAUSE } S : req(X) \; \gg \qquad (22)$$

Proof. To prove (21), we apply *Causes Weak Transitivity* (8). The two first premises are obtained by lifting (17) and (4) to the level of the composed system: to lift, we use *Preserve Causes_Closely* (6). The third premise, call it *TP*, is obtained from (18) by application of *Preserve Communication Conditions* (12), and *Because Introduction* (13). Property (22) is proved by first fifting (19) by *Because_Closely Introduction* (13) and *Preserve Because_Closely* (14), and then applying *Because Transitivity* (15), with *TP* being the second premise.

□

3.2 Moderated Publish–subscribe

We now reconsider the publish–subscribers template (see Sect. 2), and provide, in Table 5, the local specifications of the moderator and the other components PS^i.

The moderator reacts to a publication request $req(X, PS^j)$ by rejecting it and informing PS^j of the rejection, or by notifying X to everybody (23). The moderator sends a notification only in the presence of the corresponding request and if the request was not already rejected (26). Two identical notifications cannot be sent (27). The moderator rejects X only in the presence of a publication request for X and if X has not already been notified (25). Finally, the moderator does not fake requests (24).

The publish–subscribers send a publication request to the moderator for every new publication intention (28), and only for those (29). They do not send more than a request for the same item (30), nor produce or send any notification or rejection (31–34). Finally, subscribers do not fake requests (35).

Table 5. Local specifications of the publish–subscribers template

---

$M : \ll$ (for all j)

$$M : req(X, PS^j) \text{ CAUSES\_C } M : rej(X)@PS^j \vee \wedge_i notif(X)@PS^i, \quad (23)$$

$$M : req(X, PS^j) \text{ NEEDS } false \quad (24)$$

$$M : rej(X)@PS^j \text{ NEEDS } (req(X, PS^j) \wedge \wedge_i \neg notif(X)@PS^i), \quad (25)$$

$$M : notif(X)@PS^j \text{ NEEDS } \vee_i (req(X, PS^i) \wedge \neg rej(X)@PS^i), \quad (26)$$

$$M : 2 * notif(X)@PS^j \text{ NEEDS } false \gg \quad (27)$$

$PS^i : \ll$

$$PS^i : pub\_int(X) \text{ CAUSES\_C } PS^i : req(X, PS^i)@M, \quad (28)$$

$$PS^i : req(X, PS^i)@M \text{ NEEDS } PS^i : pub\_int(X), \quad (29)$$

$$PS^i : 2 * req(X, PS^i)@M \text{ NEEDS } false, \quad (30)$$

$$PS^i : notif(X) \text{ NEEDS } false, \quad (31)$$

$$\text{(for all } j) \; PS^i : notif(X)@PS^j \text{ NEEDS } false, \quad (32)$$

$$PS^i : rej(X) \text{ NEEDS } false, \quad (33)$$

$$\text{(for all } j) \; PS^i : rej(X)@PS^j \text{ NEEDS } false \quad (34)$$

$$\text{(for all } j \neq i) \; PS^i : \text{ INV } \neg req(X, PS^j)@M \gg \quad (35)$$

Proposition 2. *The parallel composition of the systems in Table 5 yields a system that satisfies the specification in Table 2.*

Proof. We need to prove that the properties in Table 2 are satisfied by the system composed of M and the PS^is running in parallel. We first deal with liveness. The natural way to prove (1) is by *Causes Introduction* (7) and *Causes Weak Transitivity* (8) from (28) and (23), since they can be lifted from local to global, by multiple applications of *Preserve Causes_Closely* (6).

We are left with proving the third premise of (8):

$$\vdash_{M,PS^1,...,PS^n} PS^i : req(X, PS^i)@M \text{ BECAUSE } PS^i : pub\_int(X)$$

which follows from (29), by multiple applications of (12), followed by BECAUSE_C and BECAUSE introductions (13).

To prove that (2) is satisfied by the composed system, we first apply *Preserve Because_Closely* (14) to lift the local properties to the level of the composed system, then *Because Introduction* (13), and finally *Because Transitivity* (15). To prove (3), we apply *Preserve Mutual Exclusion* (16). □

These proofs show a general pattern: first lift local properties to the global level, and then apply transitivity, or other composition theorems.

4 Case Study

The problem we address in this section is a fragment of the "Conference Management on the Internet"' case study from the COORDINA working group [9]. The case study addresses the coordination of all the activities and people involved in the preparation of a conference proceedings volume, starting from the submission of the drafts. The geographical distribution of the partners, and the use of e-mail to carry over their tasks, are naturally modelled in the asynchronous distributed paradigm used in Oikos_adtl.

We consider a fragment dealing with the allocations of the submitted papers to the PC members, for reviewing. We assume that the task is accomplished in two phases and that m reviewers are needed for each paper. In phase one, each PC member can express some preferences. If a preferred paper is assigned, all the other PC members are notified. To be fair, a maximum of n papers can be assigned to each PC member in this phase: a preference is rejected if the PC member has already been assigned n papers, or if the selected paper is already assigned to m reviewers. Moreover, a paper cannot be assigned twice to the same PC member. In phase two, all the papers not yet assigned are fairly distributed by the PC chair. This phase can be naturally modelled by instantiating the broadcast coordination template, with the PC chair as the sender and the PC members as the receivers.

The model is realistic only if no PC member is the author of a submitted paper. However, the changes to the specification needed to accommodate such a case consist in strengthening some conditions.

Phase one can be modelled by instantiating the moderated publish–subscribe template, with the program committee members P^i acting as the publisher-subscribers, and a coordination component acting as the moderator M. The instance renames the components in the template. Besides, since notifications here state the assignment of a paper to a PC member, the term $ass(W, P)$ substitutes X: W identifies a paper, and P a PC member.

A new property is added to the specification of the moderator, expressing the causes for rejection, which are specific for this case:

$$M : rej(ass(W,P))@P^i \text{ NEEDS}$$
$$\bigvee_j (m * notif(ass(W,\_))@P^j \ \vee \ n * notif(ass(\_,P))@P^j) \tag{36}$$

According to the template, the global properties holding in phase one are those of Table 2, suitably renamed. Rejections should be constrained at the global level too. The following proposition states how.

Proposition 3. *At the conference level we have:*

$$P^i : rej(ass(W,P)) \text{ BECAUSE } M : \bigvee_j$$
$$(m*notif(ass(W,\_))@P^j \ \lor \ n*notif(ass(\_,P))@P^j) \qquad (37)$$

Proof. We apply the general schema: first, we lift (33), i.e.

$$\vdash_{P^i} P^i : rej(ass(W,P)) \text{ NEEDS } false$$

to

$$\vdash_{P^1,...,P^n} P^i : rej(ass(W,P)) \text{ BECAUSE\_C } P^i : false$$

via *Preserve Needs* (11) ($n-1$ times) and *Because_Closely Introduction* (13). Then via *Preserve Because_Closely* (14) we get:

$$\vdash_{M,P^1,...,P^n} P^i : rej(ass(W,P)) \text{ BECAUSE\_C } M : rej(ass(W,P))@P^i$$

Similarly, we lift (36) to the global level by repeated applications of *Preserve Communication Conditions* (12). We introduce BECAUSE and get our result by applying *Because Transitivity*. $\Box$

5 Related Work

Ciancarini et al. [8] present a formal method for construction and verification of open systems whose architecture is modeled by multiple data-spaces. The approach features a theoretical coordination model, PoliS, and rules to translate PoliS specifications in Lamport's TLA [15]. The advantage is that tools available for TLA, like TLP, can be exploited to reason about PoliS specification, albeit at the price of the somewhat cumbersome translation. To our taste, however, PoliS, in line with Lamport's original goals for TLA, is too operational as a specification language. Besides, the approach does not show the desired properties of composition: the proofs take into account the evolution of the system as a whole, rather than decomposing the task into simpler proofs, dealing with local properties and their composition, separately. Finally, it has to be noted that PoliS deals with open systems, while Oikos_adtl does not.

Compositional issues for multiple tuple spaces were discussed by Chen and Montangero [7], albeit in an operational setting.

Goeman et al. introduce the ImpUnity framework [13] to reason on coordination programs. These are written in ImpUnity, a programming language based on Unity, action systems, and the tuple space model of communication. The language permits to declare private variables in programs, and these declarations are used to refine the programs compositionally. As for Swarm and for our approach, program properties are derived using assertion on the form of Hoare triples, but no formal definition of the axiomatic semantics is given.

Compositionality results for programs based on tuple spaces have been proposed also by Jacquet and De Bosschere. In [14], they discuss a methodology based on a logical approach. Program properties are expressed in Unity, properties of the composition of programs are obtained with a rely–guarantee reasoning similar to the one proposed in [1]. However, they only consider compositions of programs acting on a single component.

The main difference between our approach and other proposals of distributed logic relies in the "amount" of knowledge a component can have of the others components in the system. In the logic underlying TROLL [11] non–local assertion are possible only at communication time. In the n–agent logic [16, 19] non–local knowledge is gained at communication time and then kept. In either cases, communications are synchronous handshakings. Besides, non–local assertions can include remote properties which have not been caused, directly or indirectly, by the component in which the assertion is made. We think that Oikos_adtl conservative approach in this respect is more realistic. An interesting issue would be to compare the different approaches by expressing their modalities in terms of the knowledge modalities of [12], as it is partly done in [18].

6 Conclusions

We introduced Oikos_adtl, a specification language for distributed systems with components communicating via asynchronous remote writings. The language is based on a distributed temporal logic, and extends smoothly Oikos_tl, which has been used to specify single components viewed as tuple spaces [21]. We presented a semantic definition of the language, and discussed a number of composition theorems, that can be used to justify coordination templates. This work provides the basis of a refinement calculus to design distributed systems. To sketch how to proceed towards this goal, we glimpse specification refinement. A specification can be refined either by decomposing a system in two or more subsystems, or by refining its properties $\mathcal{F}$, finding $\mathcal{F}'$ such that $\vdash_{\mathcal{M}} \mathcal{F}'$ justifies $\vdash_{\mathcal{M}} F$, for all F in $\mathcal{F}$. The composition templates we discussed above, provide examples of decomposition templates, that in general shape

$$M^1, \ldots, M^n : \ll \mathcal{F} \gg$$

$$\sqsubseteq \quad \frac{\vdash_{M^1, \ldots, M^i} \mathcal{F}' \quad \vdash_{M^{i+1}, \ldots, M^n} \mathcal{F}''}{\vdash_{M^1, \ldots, M^n} \mathcal{F}}$$

$$M^1, \ldots, M^i : \ll \mathcal{F}' \gg \ \| \ M^{i+1}, \ldots, M^n : \ll \mathcal{F}'' \gg$$

The refinement templates have to be proved once for all using the composition theorems: to apply the template, the designer has only to verify that the premises hold. We have purposefully used the term template in this paper, given the somewhat ad hoc nature of the examples. However, we expect our approach to be useful to capture the essence of coordination *patterns*, i.e. coordination templates that are documented to be used in practice.

To validate the approach we plan to deal with more substantial case studies, like the coordination model for distributed control systems presented in [3]. Besides, a challenging and interesting issue is the extension to cope with open and mobile systems.

Acknowledgements

This work was partly supported by the ESPRIT W.G. 24512 COORDINA.

References

1. M. Abadi and L. Lamport. Composing Specifications. In J.W. de Bakker, W.P. de Roever, and G. Rozenberg, editors, *Proc. Stepwise Refinement of Distributed Systems*, volume 430 of *Lecture Notes in Computer Science*, pages 1–41. Springer-Verlag, 1989.
2. R.J.R. Back and J. von Wright. *Refinement Calculus. A Systematic Introduction.* Graduate texts in computer science. Springer-Verlag, 1998.
3. M. M. Bonsangue, J.N. Kok, M. Boasson, and E. de Jong. A software architecture for distributed control systems and its transition system semantics. In *Proc. ACM Symp. on Applied Computing SAC'98*, pages 159–168, Atlanta, 1998. ACM press.
4. K. De Bosschere and J.-M. Jacquet. μ^2 Log: Towards Remote Coordination. In P. Ciancarini and C. Hankin, editors, *Proc. Coordination Languages and Models, First International Conference, COORDINATION 96*, volume 1061 of *Lecture Notes in Computer Science*, pages 142–159, Cesena, April 1996. Springer-Verlag.
5. A. Brogi and J.-M. Jacquet. Modelling Coordination via Asynchronous Communication. In D. Garlan and D. LeMetayer, editors, *Proc. 2nd Int. Conf. on Coordination Models and Languages*, volume 1282 of *Lecture Notes in Computer Science*, pages 238–255, Berlin, Germany, September 1997. Springer-Verlag, Berlin.
6. K.M. Chandy and J. Misra. *Parallel Program Design: A Foundation.* Addison-Wesley, Reading Mass., 1988.
7. X.J. Chen and C. Montangero. Compositional Refinements of Multiple Blackboard Systems. *Acta Informatica*, 32(5):415–458, 1995.
8. P. Ciancarini, M. Mazza, and L. Pazzaglia. A logic for a coordination model with multiple spaces. *Science of Computer Programming*, 31(2–3):231–261, July 1998.
9. P. Ciancarini, O. Nierstrasz, and R. Tolksdorf. A case study in coordination: Conference management on the internet. Available at: http://malvasia.di.fct.unl.pt/activity/coordina/working/case–studies, 1998.
10. R. DeNicola, G. Ferrari, and R. Pugliese. A kernel Language for Agents Interaction and Mobility. *IEEE Transactions on Software Engineering*, 24(5):315–330, 1998.
11. H.-D. Ehrich, C. Caleiro, A. Sernadas, and G. Denker. Logics for specifying concurrent information systems. In J. Chomicki and G. Saake, editors, *Logic for Databases and Information Syustems*, pages 167–198. Kluver Academic Publishers, 1998.

12. R. Fagin, J. Halpern, Y. Moses, and M. Vardi. *Reasoning about knowledge*. MIT Press, 1995.
13. H. Goeman, J.N. Kok, K. Sere, and R. Udkin. Coordination in the ImpUnity Framework. *Science of Computer Programming*, 31(2-3):313–334, Jul. 1998.
14. J.-M. Jacquet and K. De Bosschere. On Composing Concurrent Logic Processes. In L. Sterling, editor, *Proc. 12th Int'l Conf. on Logic Programming, ICLP'95*, pages 531–545, Tokio, 1995. The MIT Press, Cambridge, Mass.
15. L. Lamport. The Temporal Logic of Actions. *ACM Transactions on Programming Languages and Systems*, 16(3):872–923, May 1994.
16. K. Lodaya, R. Parikh, R. Ramanujam, and P.S. Thiagarajan. A Logical Study of Distributed Transition Systems. *Information and Computation*, 119(1):91–118, 1995.
17. C. Montangero and L. Semini. Refining by Architectural Styles or Architecting by Refinements. In L. Vidal, A. Finkelstein, G. Spanoudakis, and A.L. Wolf, editors, *2nd International Software Architecture Workshop, Proceedings of the SIGSOFT '96 Workshops, Part 1*, pages 76–79, San Francisco, CA, Oct 1996. ACM Press.
18. R. Ramanujam. Local knowledge assertions in a changing world. In *Proc. TARK IV*, pages 1–17. Morgan Kaufmann, 1996.
19. R. Ramanujam. Locally linear time temporal logic. In *Proc. 11th IEEE Symp. on Logic In Computer Science*, pages 118–127. IEEE Computer Society, 1996.
20. L. Semini. *Refinement in Tuple Space Languages*. PhD thesis, Dipartimento di Informatica, Università di Pisa, 1996. TD 10–96.
21. L. Semini and C. Montangero. A Refinement Calculus for Tuple Spaces. To appear in Science of Computer Programming.

On the Expressiveness of Coordination Models

Antonio Brogi[1] and Jean-Marie Jacquet[2]

[1] Department of Computer Science, University of Pisa, Italy
[2] Institut d'Informatique, Facultés Universitaires de Namur, Belgium

Abstract. A number of different coordination models for specifying inter-process communication and synchronisation rely on a notion of shared dataspace. Many of these models are extensions of the Linda coordination model, which includes operations for adding, deleting and testing the presence/absence of data in a shared dataspace.

We compare the expressive power of three classes of coordination models based on shared dataspaces. The first class relies on Linda's communication primitives, while a second class relies on the more general notion of multi-set rewriting (e.g., like Bauhaus Linda or Gamma). Finally, we consider a third class of models featuring communication transactions that consist of sequences of Linda-like operations to be executed atomically (e.g., like in Shared Prolog or PoliS).

1 Introduction

1.1 Motivations

As motivated by the constant expansion of computer networks and illustrated by the development of distributed applications, the design of modern software systems centers on re-using and integrating software components. The corresponding paradigm shift from stand-alone applications to interacting distributed systems calls for well-defined methodologies and tools for integrating heterogeneous software components.

One of the key issues in this perspective is a clear separation between the *interaction* and the *computation* aspects of software components. Such a separation was advocated by Gelernter and Carriero in [19] as a promising approach to master the complexity of large applications, to enhance software reusability and to ease global analysis. The importance of separating interaction and computation aspects may be also summarised by Wegner's provocative argument that "interaction is more important than algorithms" [27].

Accordingly, the last decade has seen an increasing attention towards models and languages which support a neat separation of the design of individual software components from their interaction. Such models and languages are often referred to as *coordination models and languages*, respectively [13, 18].

Linda [10] was the first coordination language, originally presented as a set of inter-agent communication primitives which may be virtually added to any programming language. Besides process creation, this set includes primitives for adding, deleting, and testing the presence/absence of data in a shared dataspace.

A number of other coordination models have been proposed after Linda. Some of them extend Linda in different ways, for instance by introducing multiple dataspaces and meta-level control rules (e.g., Bauhaus Linda [11], Bonita [23], μLog ([20]), PoliS [12], Shared Prolog [6]), by addressing open distributed systems (e.g., Laura [26]), middleware web-based environments (e.g., Jada [14]), or mobility (e.g., KLAIM [16]). A number of other coordination models rely on a notion of shared dataspace, e.g., Concurrent Constraint Programming [24], Gamma [3], Linear Objects [2] and Manifold [1], to cite only a few. A comprehensive survey of these and other coordination models and languages has been recently reported in [22].

The availability of a considerable number of coordination models and languages stimulates a natural question:

Which is the best language or model for expressing coordination issues?

Of course the answer depends on what we mean by the "best" model. A formal way of specifying this question is to reformulate it in terms of the expressive power of models and languages.

1.2 Comparing the expressive power of coordination languages

As pointed out in [15], from a computational point of view all "reasonable" sequential programming languages are equivalent, as they express the same class of functions. Still it is common practice to speak about the "power" of a language on the basis of the expressibility or non-expressibility of programming constructs. In general [17], a sequential language L is considered to be more expressive than another sequential language L' if the constructs of L' can be translated in L without requiring a "global reorganisation of the program", that is, in a compositional way. Of course the translation must preserve the meaning, at least in the weak sense of preserving termination.

When considering concurrent languages, the notion of termination must be reconsidered as each possible computation represents a possible different evolution of a system of interacting processes. Moreover *deadlock* represents an additional case of termination. De Boer and Palamidessi introduced in [15] the notion of *modular embedding* as a method to compare the expressive power of concurrent languages.

In this paper we use the notion of modular embedding to compare the relative expressive power of three classes of coordination languages that employ data-driven communication primitives. The first family, denoted by $\mathcal{L}_L$, is based on a set of communication primitives à la Linda: *tell, get, ask,* and *nask* for respectively adding, deleting, and checking the presence and the absence of data in a shared dataspace. The second family, denoted by $\mathcal{L}_{MR}$, adopts an alternative view of these primitives by considering them as the rewriting of pre- and post-conditions on a shared data space, namely as multi-sets of *tell, get, ask,* and *nask* operations. The third family, denoted by $\mathcal{L}_{CS}$, imposes an order on the evaluation of the primitives, hence introducing communication sequences to be evaluated atomically as "all-or-nothing" transactions.

All the languages considered contain sequential, parallel and choice operators. For each family (viz., $\mathcal{L}_L$, $\mathcal{L}_{MR}$, $\mathcal{L}_{CS}$) we consider three different languages that differ from one another in the set $\mathcal{X}$ of communication primitives used, syntactically denoted by a set parameter. For instance, if $\mathcal{X}$ is the set $\{ask, tell\}$ then the language $\mathcal{L}_L(\mathcal{X})$ is Linda restricted to ask and $tell$ operations, and it corresponds to a basic form of concurrent constraint programming [24]. Analogously (set brackets will be omitted for the ease of reading), $\mathcal{L}_L(ask, get, tell)$ corresponds to non-monotonic concurrent constraint programming [4], while $\mathcal{L}_L(ask, nask, get, tell)$ corresponds to Linda without process creation. Moreover, $\mathcal{L}_{MR}(ask, get, tell)$ corresponds to Gamma [3], $\mathcal{L}_{MR}(ask, nask, get, tell)$ extends Gamma with negative (non-local) pre-conditions , while $\mathcal{L}_{CS}(ask, nask, get, tell)$ generalises the communication transactions introduced in Shared Prolog [6].

As just suggested, the families $\mathcal{L}_L$, $\mathcal{L}_{MR}$, and $\mathcal{L}_{CS}$ are thus representatives of a substantial amount of coordination languages. We turn in this paper to an exhaustive pair-wise comparison of the expressive power of the languages obtained by taking $\mathcal{X}$ as $\{ask, tell\}$, $\{ask, get, tell\}$, and $\{ask, nask, get, tell\}$, for each of the three classes.

1.3 Results of the comparisons

It is easy to see that a number of (modular) embeddings can be trivially established by considering sub-languages. For instance, for any considered class of languages (viz., for any possible subscript of $\mathcal{L}$):

$$\mathcal{L}(ask, tell) \ \leq \ \mathcal{L}(ask, get, tell) \ \leq \ \mathcal{L}(ask, nask, get, tell)$$

holds, where $L' \leq L$ denotes that L' can be (modularly) embedded by L. However, the most interesting results are *separation* results, where a language is shown to be strictly more powerful than another language, and *equivalence* results, where two languages are shown to have the same expressive power.

An expected result proved in the paper is that the above disequalities are strict in the sense that, on the one hand, it is not possible to simulate the destructive get primitives via ask and $tell$ operations and, on the other hand, it is not possible to reduce $nask$ tests to ask, get, and $tell$ primitives. Hence for instance concurrent constraint programming languages are strictly less expressive than their non-monotonic versions, which are in turn strictly less expressive than Linda.

Another interesting result is that, for any subset $\mathcal{X}$ of communication primitives, $\mathcal{L}_L(\mathcal{X}) < \mathcal{L}_{MR}(\mathcal{X})$. This establishes that Linda without $nask$ operations is strictly less expressive than Gamma. Similarly, for each $\mathcal{X}$, $\mathcal{L}_L(\mathcal{X}) < \mathcal{L}_{CS}(\mathcal{X})$, which shows that the introduction of communication transactions strictly increases the expressive power of languages. However, $\mathcal{L}_L(ask, nask, get, tell)$ and $\mathcal{L}_{MR}(ask, get, tell)$ are incomparable, which proves that full Linda and Gamma are incomparable.

It is interesting to observe that communication transactions get more and more expressiveness as they are enriched with primitives, as evidenced by the following relations:

$$\mathcal{L}_{CS}(ask, tell) < \mathcal{L}_{MR}(ask, tell)$$
$$\mathcal{L}_{CS}(ask, get, tell) = \mathcal{L}_{MR}(ask, get, tell)$$
$$\mathcal{L}_{CS}(ask, nask, get, tell) > \mathcal{L}_{MR}(ask, nask, get, tell)$$

Finally, it worth observing that $\mathcal{L}_{CS}(ask, nask, get, tell)$ is the most expressive languages of the nine languages under study.

Our study of the languages is complete in the sense that all possible relations between pairs of languages have been analysed. For each pair of languages we have established whether they have the same expressive power ($L = L'$), or one is strictly more powerful than the other ($L < L'$), or none of the above two cases holds (i.e., L and L' are incomparable).

This study provides useful insights for both the theory and the practice of coordination-based approaches. Indeed, the resulting hierarchy depicted in figure 4 shows the equivalence of different models and indicates which extensions may be worth considering because of their additional expressive power.

1.4 Related work

The specificities of our work may be highlighted by contrasting it with related work. The closest pieces of work are [29] and [28].

The expressiveness of four coordination languages is analysed in [29]. Using our terminology, they are obtained by enriching the language $L_0 = \mathcal{L}_L(get, tell)$ with three forms of negative tests: $nask(a)$ which tests for the absence of a, $t\&e(a)$ which instantaneously produces a after testing that a is not present, and $t\&p(a, b)$ which atomically tests for the absence of a and produces an instance of b. Consequently, the first extension L_1 is $\mathcal{L}_L(nask, get, tell)$, which is proved equivalent in [7] to $\mathcal{L}_L(ask, nask, get, tell)$. The second extension L_2 is a restricted version of the language $\mathcal{L}_{CS}(nask, get, tell)$ reduced by considering as communication primitives operations of the form $[get(t)]$, $[tell(t)]$, and $[nask(t); tell(t)]$, where the $[\cdots]$ construct denotes a communication transaction. Finally, the third extension L_3 is obtained by allowing communication transactions of the form $[nask(t); tell(u)]$ for possibly different data t and u. In [29] the languages are compared on the basis of three properties: compositionality of the encoding with respect to parallel composition, preservation of divergence and deadlock, and a symmetry condition. It is worth noting that the resulting hierarchy $L_0 < L_1 < L_2 < L_3$ is consistent with our results. Similar properties are used in [28] to establish the incomparability of Linda and Gamma.

Compared to our work, we shall use compositionality of the encoding with respect to sequential composition, choice, and parallel composition operator. We will use the preservation of termination marks too, and require an element-wise decoding of the set of observables. However, in contrast to [29] and [28], we shall be more liberal with respect to the preservation of termination marks in requiring these preservations on the store resulting from the execution from the empty store of the coded versions of the considered agents and not on the same store. In particular, these ending stores are not required to be of the form $\sigma \cup \sigma$ if this is so for the stores resulting from the agents themselves. Moreover, as the reader may appreciate, this paper presents a wider comparison of a larger class of languages, which requires new proof techniques at the technical level.

The paper [5] compares nine variants of the $\mathcal{L}_L(ask, nask, get, tell)$ language. They are obtained by varying both the nature of the shared data space and its structure. On the one hand, one distributed model and two centralised models, preserving or not the order in which data values are produced, are proposed. On the other hand, a multi-set structure, a set structure, and a list structure of the dataspace are considered. Rephrased in the [15] setting, this amounts to considering different operational semantics. In contrast, we fix an operational semantics and compare different languages on the basis of this semantics. The goals are thus different, and call for completely different treatments and results.

In [9], a process algebraic treatment of a family of Linda-like concurrent languages is presented. A lattice of eight languages is obtained by considering different sets of primitives out of ask, get, $tell$ primitives, cited above, and conditional ask and get variants. The authors also show that this lattice collapses to a smaller four-points lattice of different bisimulation-based semantics. Again, compared to our work, different semantics are considered whereas we shall stick to one semantics and compare languages on this basis. Different goals are thus aimed, which call also for different results and treatments.

Busi, Gorrieri and Zavattaro also recently studied in [8] the issue of Turing-completeness in Linda-like concurrent languages. They define a process algebra containing Linda's communication primitives and compare two possible semantics for the $tell$ primitive: an ordered one, with respect to which the execution of $tell$ is considered to be finished when the data has reached the dataspace, and an $unordered$ one for which $tell$ terminates just after having sent the insertion request to the dataspace. The main result presented in [8] is that the process algebra is not Turing-complete under the second interpretation of $tell$, while it is so under the first interpretation. Besides the fact that we tackle in this paper a broader class of languages, including among others the $\mathcal{L}_{MR}$ and $\mathcal{L}_{CS}$ family, the work [8] and ours are somehow orthogonal. While [8] studies the $absolute$ expressive power of different variants of Linda-like languages (using Turing-completeness as a yard-stick), we study the $relative$ expressive power of different variants of such languages (using modular embedding as a yard-stick).

Finally, this paper extends the exhaustive comparison of the languages in $\mathcal{L}_L$, that was reported in [7].

1.5 Plan of the paper

The remainder of the paper is organised as follows. Section 2 formally defines the syntax of the three classes of concurrent languages considered, while section 3 defines their operational semantics. Section 4 introduces the notion of modular embedding proposed in [15]. Section 5 contains the exhaustive comparison of the expressive power of the languages. The presentation of the propositions establishing the results of the comparisons is preceded by an informal analysis of

General Rule	$\mathcal{L}_L$ Rule
$A ::= C \mid A\,;\,A \mid A \parallel A \mid A + A$	$C ::= tell(t) \mid ask(t) \mid get(t) \mid nask(t)$

$\mathcal{L}_{MR}$ Rules	$\mathcal{L}_{CS}$ Rules
$C ::= (\{M\}, \{M\})$	$C ::= [T]$
$M ::= \lambda \mid +t \mid -t \mid M, M$	$T ::= tell(t) \mid ask(t) \mid get(t) \mid nask(t) \mid T; T$

Fig. 1. Comparative syntax of the languages.

the results from a programming point of view. Figure 4 summarises the results presented in this section. Finally section 6 contains some concluding remarks.

2 The family of coordination languages

2.1 Common syntax and rules

We shall consider a family of languages $\mathcal{L}(\mathcal{X})$, parameterised w.r.t. the set of communication primitives $\mathcal{X}$. The set is in turn a subset of a general set of communication primitives *Slcom*, *Smcom*, or *Stcom* depending on the family under consideration. Assuming this general set, all the languages use sequential, parallel, and choice operators (see "General rule" in figure 1), whose meaning is defined by the usual rules (S), (P), and (C) in figure 2.

2.2 $\mathcal{L}_L$: Linda

The first family of languages is the Linda-like family of languages.

Definition 1. *Define the set of communication primitives Slcom as the set of C's generated by the $\mathcal{L}_L$ rule of figure 1. Moreover, for any subset X of Slcom, define the language $\mathcal{L}_L(\mathcal{X})$ as the set of agents A generated by the general rule of figure 1. The transition rules for these agents are the general ones of figure 2 together with rules (T), (A), (N), (G) of that figure.*

Rule (T) states that an atomic agent $tell(t)$ can be executed in any store σ, and that its execution results in adding the token t to the store σ. (E denotes the empty agent.) Rules (A) and (N) state respectively that the atomic agents $ask(t)$ and $nask(t)$ can be executed in any store containing the token t and not containing t, and that their execution does not modify the current store. Rule (G) also states that an atomic agent $get(t)$ can be executed in any store containing an occurrence of t, but in the resulting store the occurrence of t has been deleted. Note that the symbol $\cup$ actually denotes multiset union.

General rules

$$(S) \quad \frac{\langle A \mid \sigma \rangle \longrightarrow \langle A' \mid \sigma' \rangle}{\langle A \,;\, B \mid \sigma \rangle \longrightarrow \langle A' \,;\, B \mid \sigma' \rangle}$$

$$(P) \quad \frac{\langle A \mid \sigma \rangle \longrightarrow \langle A' \mid \sigma' \rangle}{\langle A \parallel B \mid \sigma \rangle \longrightarrow \langle A' \parallel B \mid \sigma' \rangle}$$
$$\langle B \parallel A \mid \sigma \rangle \longrightarrow \langle B \parallel A' \mid \sigma' \rangle$$

$$(C) \quad \frac{\langle A \mid \sigma \rangle \longrightarrow \langle A' \mid \sigma' \rangle}{\langle A + B \mid \sigma \rangle \longrightarrow \langle A' \mid \sigma' \rangle}$$
$$\langle B + A \mid \sigma \rangle \longrightarrow \langle A' \mid \sigma' \rangle$$

$\mathcal{L}_L$ RULES

$$(T) \quad \langle tell(t) \mid \sigma \rangle \longrightarrow \langle E \mid \sigma \cup \{t\} \rangle$$

$$(A) \quad \langle ask(t) \mid \sigma \cup \{t\} \rangle \longrightarrow \langle E \mid \sigma \cup \{t\} \rangle$$

$$(N) \quad \frac{t \notin \sigma}{\langle nask(t) \mid \sigma \rangle \longrightarrow \langle E \mid \sigma \rangle}$$

$$(G) \quad \langle get(t) \mid \sigma \cup \{t\} \rangle \longrightarrow \langle E \mid \sigma \rangle$$

$\mathcal{L}_{MR}$ RULE

$$(CM) \quad \frac{\sigma = pre^+ \cup \sigma', \; pre^- \cap \sigma = \emptyset,}{\langle (pre, post) \mid \sigma \rangle \longrightarrow \langle E \mid \sigma'' \rangle}$$
$$\sigma'' = (\sigma - post^-) \cup post^+$$

$\mathcal{L}_{CS}$ RULE

$$(CS) \quad \frac{\langle cs \mid \sigma \rangle \longrightarrow^* \langle E \mid \sigma' \rangle}{\langle [cs] \mid \sigma \rangle \longrightarrow \langle E \mid \sigma' \rangle}$$

Fig. 2. Comparative semantics of the languages.

2.3 $\mathcal{L}_{MR}$: Multi-set rewriting

The transition rules (T), (A), (N), and (G) suggest an alternative view of Linda-like communication primitives in terms of which conditions the current store should obey to allow the transitions to occur and which modifications these transitions make on the store.

A natural dual view of communication primitives is then to consider them as the rewriting of pre-conditions into post-conditions. We shall consequently examine, as a second family, languages based on multi-set rewriting. It is here worth noting that this approach has already been taken in [3, 11, 21].

Each communication primitive thus consists of a multi-set of pre-conditions and of a multi-set of post-conditions. Pre- and post-conditions are (possibly empty) multi-sets of positive and negative tuples. Intuitively speaking, the operational effect of a multi-set rewriting $(pre, post)$ is to insert all positive post-conditions and to delete all negative post-conditions from the current dataspace σ, provided that σ contains all positive pre-conditions and does not contain any of the negative pre-conditions. For instance, the operational effect of the multi-set rewriting $(\{+a, -b\}, \{+c, -d\})$ is to add c and delete d from the current dataspace σ provided that σ contains a and does not contain b.

Given a multi-set rewriting $(pre, post)$ we shall denote by pre^+ the multi-set $\{t \mid +t \in pre\}$ and by pre^- the multi-set $\{t \mid -t \in pre\}$. The denotations $post^+$ and $post^-$ are defined analogously.

A multi-set rewriting $(pre, post)$ is *consistent* iff $pre^+ \cap pre^- = \emptyset$. A multi-set rewriting $(pre, post)$ is *valid* if $post^- \subseteq pre^+$, where $\subseteq$ denotes multi-set inclusion.

Definition 2. *Define the set of multi-set communication primitives Smcom as the set of C's engendered by the $\mathcal{L}_{MR}$ rules of figure 1. Given a subset $\mathcal{X}$ of Smcom, define the language $\mathcal{L}_{MR}(\mathcal{X})$ as the set of A's generated by the general rule of figure 1.*

As a result of restricting to consistent and valid multi-set communication primitives, four basic pairs of pre and post-conditions are only possible: $(\{+t\}, \{\})$, $(\{-t\}, \{\})$, $(\{\}, \{+t\})$, $(\{+t\}, \{-t\})$. We shall respectively identify them to $ask(t)$, $nask(t)$, $tell(t)$, and $get(t)$.

For our comparison purposes, given $\mathcal{X}$ a subset of communication primitives of *Slcom*, we shall abuse notations and denote by $\mathcal{L}_{MR}(\mathcal{X})$ the language obtained by restricting multi-set rewriting pairs to component-wise multi-set unions of pairs associated with the communication primitives of $\mathcal{X}$. For instance, if $\mathcal{X} = \{ask, nask\}$, then the language $\mathcal{L}_{MR}(\mathcal{X})$ only involves pairs of the form $(Pre, \{\})$ where Pre may contain positive and negative tokens. Similarly, if $\mathcal{X} = \{tell, get\}$ then $\mathcal{L}_{MR}(\mathcal{X})$ includes only pairs of the form $(Pre, Post)$ where Pre contain positive tokens only provided that each one is associated with one negative counterpart in $Post$ and $Post$ contain negative tokens provided each one is associated to one positive token in Pre as well as positive tokens (without restriction). Note that these notations fully agree with the one introduced in definition 2.

Definition 3. *Define the transition rules for the $\mathcal{L}_{MR}$ family of languages as the general rules of figure 2 together with rule (CM) of that figure.*

Rule (CM) states that a multi-set rewriting $(pre, post)$ can be executed in a store σ if the multi-set pre^+ is included in σ and if no negative pre-condition occurs in σ. If such conditions hold then the execution of the rewriting deletes from σ all the negative post-conditions, and adds to σ all the positive post-conditions.

2.4 $\mathcal{L}_{CS}$: Communication transactions

A natural further refinement is to impose an order on the test of pre-conditions and the evaluation of post-conditions, possibly mixing pre- and post-conditions. We are thus lead to sequences of elementary actions, which we will take, for clarity purposes, in the Linda form instead of the $+t$ and $-t$ of the $\mathcal{L}_{MR}$ family. These sequences will be called *communication transactions*, with the intuition that they are to be executed as a single "all-or-nothing" transaction. They have been employed in Shared-Prolog ([6]) and in PoliS [12]).

Definition 4. *Define the set of communication transactions Stcom as the set of C's engendered by the $\mathcal{L}_{CS}$ rules of figure 1. Moreover, for any subset $\mathcal{X}$ of Stcom, define the language $\mathcal{L}_L(\mathcal{X})$ as the set of agents A generated by the general rule of figure 1. The transition rules for these agents are the general ones of figure 2 together with rule (CS).*

3 Operational semantics

3.1 Observables

Definition 5.

1. *Let Stoken be a denumerable set, the elements of which are subsequently called tokens and are typically represented by the letters t and u. Define the set of stores Sstore as the set of finite multisets with elements from Stoken.*
2. *Let δ^+ and δ^- be two fresh symbols denoting respectively success and failure. Define the set of histories Shist as the set Sstore $\times \{\delta^+, \delta^-\}$.*
3. *Define the operational semantics $\mathcal{O} : Sagent \to \mathcal{P}(Shist)$ as the following function: For any agent A,*

$$\mathcal{O}(A) = \{(\sigma, \delta^+) : \langle A \mid \emptyset \rangle \to^* \langle E \mid \sigma \rangle\}$$
$$\cup$$
$$\{(\sigma, \delta^-) : \langle A \mid \emptyset \rangle \to^* \langle B \mid \sigma \rangle \not\to, B \neq E\}$$

3.2 Normal form

A classical result of concurrency theory is that modelling parallel composition by interleaving, as we do, allows agents to be considered in a normal form. We first define what this actually means, and then state the proposition that agents and their normal forms are equivalent in the sense that they yield the same computations.

Definition 6. *Given a subset $\mathcal{X}$ of Slcom, Smcom, or Stcom, the set Snagent of agents in normal form is defined by the following rule, where N is an agent in normal form and c denotes a communication action of $\mathcal{X}$:*

$$N ::= c \mid c; N \mid N + N.$$

Proposition 1. *For any agent A, there is an agent N in normal form which has the same derivation sequences as A.*

4 Modular embedding

A natural way to compare the expressive power of two languages is to see whether all programs written in one language can be "easily" and "equivalently" translated into the other language, where equivalent is intended in the sense of the same observable behaviour.

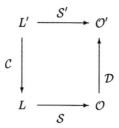

Fig. 3. Basic embedding.

The basic definition of embedding, given by Shapiro [25] is the following. Consider two languages L and L'. Assume given the semantics mappings (*observation criteria*) $S : L \rightarrow \mathcal{O}$ and $S' : L' \rightarrow \mathcal{O}'$, where $\mathcal{O}$ and $\mathcal{O}'$ are some suitable domains. Then L can *embed* L' if there exists a mapping $\mathcal{C}$ (*coder*) from the statements of L' to the statements of L, and a mapping $\mathcal{D}$ (*decoder*) from $\mathcal{O}$ to $\mathcal{O}'$, such that the diagram of figure 3 commutes, namely such that for every statement $A \in L'$: $\mathcal{D}(S(\mathcal{C}(A))) = S'(A)$.

The basic notion of embedding is too weak since, for instance, the above equation is satisfied by any pair of Turing-complete languages. De Boer and Palamidessi hence proposed in [15] to add three constraints on the coder $\mathcal{C}$ and on the decoder $\mathcal{D}$ in order to obtain a notion of *modular* embedding usable for concurrent languages:

1. $\mathcal{D}$ should be defined in an element-wise way w.r.t. $\mathcal{O}$:

$$\forall X \in \mathcal{O}: \; \mathcal{D}(X) = \{\mathcal{D}_{el}(x) \mid x \in X\} \qquad (P_1)$$

   for some appropriate mapping $\mathcal{D}_{el}$;
2. the compiler $\mathcal{C}$ should be defined in a compositional way w.r.t. the sequential, parallel and choice operators (actually, this is only required for the parallel and choice operators in [15]):

$$\begin{aligned}
\mathcal{C}(A \,;\, B) &= \mathcal{C}(A) \,;\, \mathcal{C}(B) \\
\mathcal{C}(A \,\|\, B) &= \mathcal{C}(A) \,\|\, \mathcal{C}(B) \\
\mathcal{C}(A \,+\, B) &= \mathcal{C}(A) \,+\, \mathcal{C}(B)
\end{aligned} \qquad (P_2)$$

3. the embedding should preserve the behaviour of the original processes w.r.t. deadlock, failure and success (*termination invariance*):

$$\forall X \in \mathcal{O}, \forall x \in X: \; tm'(\mathcal{D}_{el}(x)) = tm(x) \qquad (P_3)$$

   where tm and tm' extract the information on termination from the observables of L and L', respectively.

An embedding is then called *modular* if it satisfies properties P_1, P_2, and P_3.

The existence of a modular embedding from L' into L will be denoted by $L' \leq L$. It is easy to see that $\leq$ is a pre-order relation. Moreover if $L' \subseteq L$ then

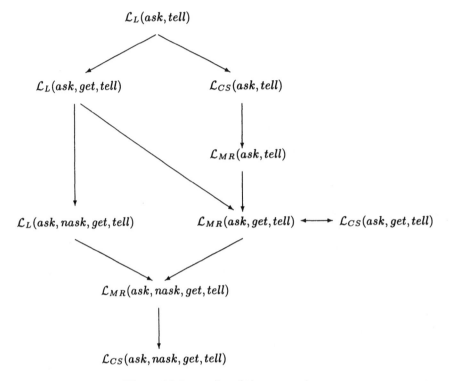

Fig. 4. Main results of the comparisons.

$L' \leq L$ that is, any language embeds all its sublanguages. This property descends immediately from the definition of embedding, by setting C and D equal to the identity function.

5   Comparisons

We now turn to an exhaustive comparison of the relative expressive power of the languages introduced in section 2.

We will consider nine different languages which are obtained by considering three different sets of communication primitives, namely $\mathcal{X} = \{ask, tell\}$, $\mathcal{X} = \{ask, get, tell\}$, and $\mathcal{X} = \{ask, nask, get, tell\}$, for each of the three parameterised languages $\mathcal{L}_L(\mathcal{X})$, $\mathcal{L}_{CS}(\mathcal{X})$, and $\mathcal{L}_{MR}(\mathcal{X})$.

The whole set of separation and equivalence results is summarised in figure 4, where an arrow from a language $\mathcal{L}_1$ to a language $\mathcal{L}_2$ means that $\mathcal{L}_2$ embeds $\mathcal{L}_1$, that is $\mathcal{L}_1 \leq \mathcal{L}_2$. Notice that, thanks to the transitivity of embedding, the figure contains only a minimal amount of arrows. However, apart from these induced relations, no other relation holds. In particular, when there is one arrow from $\mathcal{L}_1$ to $\mathcal{L}_2$ but there is no arrow from $\mathcal{L}_2$ to $\mathcal{L}_1$, then $\mathcal{L}_1$ is strictly less expressive than $\mathcal{L}_2$, that is $\mathcal{L}_1 < \mathcal{L}_2$.

The separation and equivalence results are presented in two steps. Section 5.1 first presents the intuition for these results whereas their formal statements are given in section 5.2.

5.1 Intuitive analysis of the results

Before presenting the proofs of the results illustrated in figure 4, we will try to analyse their intuitive meaning. More precisely, we shall try here to show informally how such formal separation results confirm the intuitive expectations form a programming viewpoint. Of course the intuitive explanation of a separation (or equivalence) result does not formally prove the validity of the result itself. One may indeed argue that even if there is no obvious encoding between the two languages, there may well be a non-trivial encoding that may yield the embedding. The non existence of such embeddings will be formally established by the propositions reported in section 5.2.

Analysis for $\mathcal{X} = \{ask, tell\}$
Let us first consider the case in which $\mathcal{X} = \{ask, tell\}$. It is easy to see that $\mathcal{L}_L(ask, tell)$ does not support a straightforward way of *atomically* testing the simultaneous presence of two resources a and b in the dataspace. Indeed the obvious coding $(ask(a); ask(b))$ will not be executed atomically and may not produce the desired behaviour for instance in: $(ask(a); ask(b); P) + (ask(a); ask(c); Q)$. The language $\mathcal{L}_{CS}(ask, tell)$ instead supports a straightforward way of atomically testing the presence of two resources in the dataspace, via the communication transaction $[ask(a); ask(b)]$, thus intuitively confirming the separation result $\mathcal{L}_L(ask, tell) < \mathcal{L}_{CS}(ask, tell)$.

It is easy to observe that the same kind of test can be naturally expressed also in $\mathcal{L}_{MR}(ask, tell)$ via the rewriting $(\{+a, +b\}, \{...\})$. Moreover the language $\mathcal{L}_{MR}(ask, tell)$ permits to express also tests of the form "if there are at least n copies of a resource a then". For instance the rewriting $(\{+a, +a\}, \{+b\})$ states that if there are at least two copies of resource a then resource b will be added to the dataspace. The same test cannot be easily expressed in $\mathcal{L}_{CS}(ask, tell)$ with $[ask(a); ask(a); tell(b)]$, since the two ask operations may match the same instance of a in the dataspace. The inability of $\mathcal{L}_{CS}(ask, tell)$ to atomically testing the presence of multiple copies of the same resource confirms intuitively the separation result $\mathcal{L}_{CS}(ask, tell) < \mathcal{L}_{MR}(ask, tell)$.

Analysis for $\mathcal{X} = \{ask, get, tell\}$
The addition of the *get* primitive to the set $\mathcal{X}$ gives to each of the former three languages the ability of deleting tuples, hence yielding a non-monotonic evolution of the dataspace. The three separation results $\mathcal{L}_L(ask, tell) < \mathcal{L}_L(ask, get, tell)$, $\mathcal{L}_{MR}(ask, tell) < \mathcal{L}_{MR}(ask, get, tell)$, and $\mathcal{L}_{CS}(ask, tell) < \mathcal{L}_{CS}(ask, get, tell)$ follow such intuition.

The separation result between the basic Linda calculus and the multi-set rewriting calculus continues to hold also after introducing the *get* operation, that is, $\mathcal{L}_L(ask, get, tell) < \mathcal{L}_{MR}(ask, get, tell)$. Indeed the addition of *get* does not still allow $\mathcal{L}_L(ask, get, tell)$ to atomically test the simultaneous presence of two resources a and b in the dataspace.

On the other hand, the introduction of get removes the gap between communication sequences and multi-set rewriting, which have in this case the same expressive power, that is, $\mathcal{L}_{MR}(ask, get, tell) = \mathcal{L}_{CS}(ask, get, tell)$. For instance $\mathcal{L}_{CS}(ask, get, tell)$ can now express tests of the form "if there are at least two copies of resource a then" via the transaction $[get(a); ask(a); tell(a)]$.

Analysis for $\mathcal{X} = \{ask, nask, get, tell\}$
The introduction of the $nask$ primitive into the set $\mathcal{X}$ gives to each language the ability of testing the *absence* of data from the dataspace, and hence to express *if-then-else* conditions of the form "if resource a belongs to the dataspace then do P else do Q". For instance such test can be expressed in $\mathcal{L}_L(ask, nask, get, tell)$ as $(ask(a); P) + (nask(a); Q)$. The additional expressive power given by $nask$ intuitively explains the separations result $\mathcal{L}(ask, get, tell) < \mathcal{L}(ask, nask, get, tell)$, which holds for $\mathcal{L}$ being either $\mathcal{L}_L$, $\mathcal{L}_{MR}$ or $\mathcal{L}_{CS}$.

Even after introducing $nask$, the basic Linda calculus is less expressive of both communication transactions and multi-set rewriting. Indeed $\mathcal{L}_L(ask, nask, get, tell)$ is still not able to atomically test the simultaneous presence of two resources a and b in the dataspace.

The introduction of negative tests instead reverses the relation between $\mathcal{L}_{MR}(ask, nask, get, tell)$ and $\mathcal{L}_{CS}(ask, nask, get, tell)$. Indeed the availability of $nask$ allows $\mathcal{L}_{CS}(ask, nask, get, tell)$ to "count" the number of copies of a resource available in the dataspace. For instance $\mathcal{L}_{CS}(ask, nask, get, tell)$ can express tests of the form "if there are *exactly* two copies of a resource a then do P" via the communication sequence $[get(a); get(a); nask(a); tell(a); tell(a)]; P$ while $\mathcal{L}_{MR}(ask, nask, get, tell)$ can only express test of the form "if there at *least* n copies of resource then". This intuitively explains the last separation result $\mathcal{L}_{MR}(ask, nask, get, tell) < \mathcal{L}_{CS}(ask, nask, get, tell)$.

5.2 Formal results

We now formally state the results of the language comparisons that induce the hierarchy reported in figure 4. To illustrate the proof techniques used we sketch the proof of the first proposition. The other proofs are not included for the lack of space. We first establish some basic relations.

Proposition 2.

i) $\mathcal{L}_L(\mathcal{X}) \leq \mathcal{L}_{MR}(\mathcal{X})$ for any set of communication primitives $\mathcal{X}$
ii) $\mathcal{L}_{MR}(tell, ask, get) \leq \mathcal{L}_{CS}(tell, ask, get)$
iii) $\mathcal{L}_{MR}(tell, ask, nask, get) \leq \mathcal{L}_{CS}(tell, ask, nask, get)$
iv) $\mathcal{L}_{MR}(tell, ask) \not\leq \mathcal{L}_{CS}(tell, ask)$

Proof. i) Immediate by defining the coder as follows:

$$C(tell(t)) = (\{\}, \{+t\}) \qquad C(get(t)) = (\{+t\}, \{-t\})$$
$$C(ask(t)) = (\{+t\}, \{\}) \qquad C(nask(t)) = (\{-t\}, \{\})$$

ii) and iii) Indeed, the non-redundancy of multiple ask queries in $\mathcal{L}_{MR}$ can be reconstructed in $\mathcal{L}_{CS}$ by first getting the tokens and then telling them back. It is thus sufficient to code

$$(\{+g_1, ..., +g_p, +a_1, ..., +a_q, -n_1, ..., -n_r, \}, \{+t_1, ..., +t_s, -g_1, ..., -g_p\}) \text{ into}$$

$$[get(g_1), \cdots, get(g_p), get(a_1), \cdots, get(a_q), tell(a_1), \cdots, tell(a_q),$$
$$nask(n_1), \cdots, nask(n_r), tell(t_1), \cdots, tell(t_s)]$$

iv) By contradiction, assume that there is a coder C. Obviously, for any token t, the computation of $(\{\}, \{+t\})$ succeeds and so should that of $C((\{\}, \{+t\}))$ by P_3. Let us call σ the state resulting from one computation. As $\mathcal{L}_{CS}(tell, ask)$ contains no destructive operations and no negative tests, $C((\{\}, \{+t\}))$; $C((\{\}, \{+t\}))$ has a successful computation resulting in the store $\sigma \cup \sigma$. Now consider $C((\{+t, +t\}, \{\}))$ in its normal form: $(a_1 \; ; \; A_1 + \cdots + a_m \; ; \; A_m)$. Since $(\{\}, \{+t\})$; $(\{\}, \{+t\})$; $(\{+t, +t\}, \{\})$ succeeds, by (P_3), there should exist $i \in [1, m]$ such that $\langle C((\{+t, +t\}, \{\})) \mid \sigma \cup \sigma \rangle \longrightarrow \langle A_i \mid \sigma \cup \sigma \cup \tau \rangle$, for some store τ, Moreover A_i computed from $\sigma \cup \sigma \cup \tau$ should only lead to success and thus, as $\mathcal{L}_{CS}(tell, ask)$ does not contain any destructive operation, A_i started on $\sigma \cup \tau$ has only successful computations. It follows that $\langle C((\{\}, \{+t\})) ; C((\{+t, +t\}, \{\})) \mid \emptyset \rangle \longrightarrow^* \langle C((\{+t, +t\}, \{\})) \mid \sigma \rangle \longrightarrow \langle M_i \mid \sigma \cup \tau \rangle$ is a valid computation prefix for $C((\{\}, \{+t\}))$; $(\{+t, +t\}, \{\}))$ which can only be continued by successful computations. This contradicts by P_3 the fact that $(\{\}, \{+t\})$; $(\{+t, +t\}, \{\})$ has only one failing computation.

It is worth noting that while the $\mathcal{L}_L$ family of languages can be all embedded in the corresponding languages of the $\mathcal{L}_{MR}$ family, the converse does not hold.

Proposition 3.

i) $\mathcal{L}_{MR}(tell, ask) \not\leq \mathcal{L}_L(tell, ask)$
ii) $\mathcal{L}_{MR}(tell, ask, get) \not\leq \mathcal{L}_L(tell, ask, get)$
iii) $\mathcal{L}_{MR}(ask, nask, get, tell) \not\leq \mathcal{L}_L(ask, nask, get, tell)$

We now analyse some embeddings of the $\mathcal{L}_{CS}$ family in the $\mathcal{L}_{MR}$ family.

Proposition 4.

i) $\mathcal{L}_{CS}(tell, ask) \leq \mathcal{L}_{MR}(tell, ask)$
ii) $\mathcal{L}_{CS}(tell, ask, get) \leq \mathcal{L}_{MR}(tell, ask, get)$
iii) $\mathcal{L}_{CS}(tell, ask, get, nask) \not\leq \mathcal{L}_{MR}(tell, ask, get, nask)$

The separation results between members of the family $\mathcal{L}_L$ [7] extend to the members of $\mathcal{L}_{MR}$ and $\mathcal{L}_{CS}$, as shown by the following proposition.

Proposition 5.

i) $\mathcal{L}_L(ask, tell) < \mathcal{L}_L(ask, get, tell) < \mathcal{L}_L(ask, nask, get, tell)$
ii) $\mathcal{L}_{MR}(ask, tell) < \mathcal{L}_{MR}(ask, get, tell) < \mathcal{L}_{MR}(ask, nask, get, tell)$
iii) $\mathcal{L}_{CS}(ask, tell) < \mathcal{L}_{CS}(ask, get, tell) < \mathcal{L}_{CS}(ask, nask, get, tell)$

The following proposition completes the comparisons.

Proposition 6.

$i)$ $\mathcal{L}_L(ask, tell) < \mathcal{L}_{CS}(ask, tell)$
$ii)$ $\mathcal{L}_{CS}(ask, tell)$ and $\mathcal{L}_L(ask, get, tell)$ are incomparable
$iii)$ $\mathcal{L}_{CS}(ask, tell)$ and $\mathcal{L}_L(ask, get, nask, tell)$ are incomparable
$iv)$ $\mathcal{L}_{MR}(ask, tell)$ and $\mathcal{L}_L(ask, get, tell)$ are incomparable
$v)$ $\mathcal{L}_{MR}(ask, tell)$ and $\mathcal{L}_L(ask, nask, get, tell)$ are incomparable
$vi)$ $\mathcal{L}_{MR}(ask, get, tell)$ and $\mathcal{L}_L(ask, nask, get, tell)$ are incomparable

6 Concluding remarks

We have compared the expressive power of three families of coordination models based on shared dataspaces. The first class $\mathcal{L}_L$ relies on Linda's communication primitives, the second class $\mathcal{L}_{MR}$ relies on the more general notion of multiset rewriting, while the third class $\mathcal{L}_{CS}$ features communication transactions that consist of sequences of Linda-like operations to be executed atomically. For each family we have considered three different languages that differ from one another in the set $\mathcal{X}$ of communication primitives used, for $\mathcal{X}$ equal respectively to $\{ask, tell\}$, $\{ask, get, tell\}$ and $\{ask, nask, get, tell\}$.

It is worth mentioning that we have exploited the main proof techniques reported in this paper to perform a wider comparison of the languages, by considering also other sets $\mathcal{X}$ of primitives with $\mathcal{X} \subseteq \{ask, nask, get, tell\}$. Because of lack of space, we reported here only the main comparisons. It is also worth noting that the results presented extend directly to agents containing recursion.

As pointed out in the Introduction, the families $\mathcal{L}_L$, $\mathcal{L}_{MR}$, and $\mathcal{L}_{CS}$ are representative of a substantial amount of coordination languages. We believe that the comparison of the expressive power of different classes of coordination models provides useful insights for both the theory and the practice of coordination-based approaches. The resulting hierarchy highlights the equivalence of different models and indicates which extensions may be worth considering because of their additional expressive power.

References

1. F. Arbab, I. Herman and P. Spilling. An overview of MANIFOLD and its implementation. *Concurrency: practice and experience*, 5(1): 23–70, 1993.
2. J.M. Andreoli and R. Pareschi. Linear Objects: logical processes with builtin inheritance. *New Generation Computing*, 9(3-4):445–473, 1991.
3. J. Banatre and D. LeMetayer. Programming by Multiset Transformation. *Communications of the ACM*, 36(1):98–111, 1991.
4. E. Best, F.S. de Boer and C. Palamidessi. Partial Order and SOS Semantics for Linear Constraint Programs. In [18].
5. M. Bonsangue, J. Kok, and G. Zavattaro. Comparing coordination models based on shared distributed replicated data. To appear in proc. of SAC'99.

6. A. Brogi and P. Ciancarini. The Concurrent Language Shared Prolog. *ACM Transactions on Programming Languages and Systems*, 13(1):99–123, January 1991.
7. A. Brogi and J.-M. Jacquet. On the Expressiveness of Linda-like Concurrent Languages. *Electronic Notes in Theoretical Computer Science*, 1998.
8. N. Busi, R. Gorrieri, and G. Zavattaro. On the Turing Equivalence of Linda Coordination Primitives. *Electronic Notes in Theoretical Computer Science*, 7, 1997.
9. N. Busi, R. Gorrieri, and G. Zavattaro. A Process Algebraic View of Linda Coordination Primitives. *Theoretical Computer Science*, 192(2):167–199, 1998.
10. N. Carriero and D. Gelernter. Linda in Context. *Communications of the ACM*, 32(4):444–458, 1989.
11. N. Carriero, D. Gelernter and L. Zuck. Bauhaus Linda. In P. Ciancarini, O. Nierstrasz and A. Yonezawa (editors) *Object based models and languages for concurrent systems*, LNCS 924, pages 66–76, Springer-Verlag, 1994.
12. P. Ciancarini. Distributed programming with logic tuple spaces. *New Generation Computing*, 12(3):251–284, 1994.
13. P. Ciancarini and C. Hankin (editors). Coordination'96: First International Conference on Coordination Models and Languages. LNCS 1061. Springer-Verlag, 1996.
14. P. Ciancarini and D. Rossi. Jada: coordination and communication for Java agents. In *Second Int. Workshop on mobile object systems*, LNCS 1222, pages 213–228, Springer-Verlag, 1996.
15. F.S. de Boer and C. Palamidessi. Embedding as a Tool for Language Comparison. *Information and Computation*, 108(1):128–157, 1994.
16. R. De Nicola, G. Ferrari and R. Pugliese. KLAIM: a kernel language for agents interaction and mobility. *IEEE Transactions on Software Engineering*, 1998.
17. M. Felleisen. On the Expressive Power of Programming Languages. In N. Jones, editor, *Proc. ESOP'90*, LNCS 432, pages 134–151. Springer-Verlag, 1990.
18. D. Garlan and D. Le Metayer (editors). Coordination'97: Second International Conference on Coordination Models and Languages. LNCS. Springer-Verlag, 1997.
19. D. Gelernter and N. Carriero. Coordination Languages and Their Significance. *Communications of the ACM*, 35(2):97–107, 1992.
20. J.M. Jacquet and K. De Bosschere. On the Semantics of muLog. *Future Generation Computer Systems Journal*:10, pages 93–135, Elsevier, 1994.
21. J.-M. Jacquet and L. Monteiro. Towards Resource Handling in Logic Programming: the PPL Framework and its Semantics. *Computer Languages*, 22(2/3):51–77, 1996.
22. G.A. Papadopolous and F. Arbab. Coordination models and languages. *Advances in Computers*, 48, Academic-Press, 1998.
23. A. Rowstron and A. Wood. BONITA: A set of tuple space primitives for distributed coordination. In *30th Hawaii Int. Conf. on System Sciences*, IEEE Press, Vol. 1, pages 379–388, 1997.
24. V.A. Saraswat. *Concurrent Constraint Programming*. The MIT Press, 1993.
25. E.Y. Shapiro. Embeddings among Concurrent Programming Languages. In W.R. Cleaveland, editor, *Proc. of CONCUR'92*, pages 486–503. Springer-Verlag, 1992.
26. R. Tolksdorf. Coordinating services in open distributed systems with LAURA. In [13], pages 386–402.
27. P. Wegner. Why Interaction Is More Powerful Than Algorithms. *Communications of the ACM*, 1997.
28. G. Zavattaro. On the incomparability of Gamma and Linda. Technical report SEN-R9827, Department of Software Engineering, CWI, 1998.
29. G. Zavattaro. Towards a hierarchy of negative test operators for generative communication. *Electronic Notes in Theoretical Computer Science*, 16(2):83–100, 1998.

Comparing Software Architectures for Coordination Languages

Marcello M. Bonsangue[1], Joost N. Kok[2], and Gianluigi Zavattaro[3]

[1] Centrum voor Wiskunde en Informatica, Amsterdam, The Netherlands
Marcello.Bonsangue@cwi.nl

[2] Leiden Institute of Advanced Computer Science, Leiden University, The Netherlands
joost@cs.leidenuniv.nl

[3] Department of Computer Science, University of Bologna, Italy
zavattar@cs.unibo.it

Abstract. We discuss three software architectures for coordination. All architectures are based on agents. Each agent has a local dataspace that contains shared distributed replicated data. The three architectures differ in the way agents communicate: either through an unordered broadcast, through an atomic broadcast, or through a synchronization among all agents. We first show how to represent both data-driven and control-oriented coordination languages in our model. Then we compare the behavior of the three architectures, under the assumption that the local dataspaces are either sets or multisets.

1 Introduction

A software architecture comprises processing elements, data elements, and rules that characterize the interaction among these components. An essential part of a software architecture is a collection of constraints on processing and data elements that ensure that the system satisfies a set of need requirements [14]. Examples of need requirements are the view processes can have on data and guarantees that certain data is received in the same order by all agents.

When building a software architecture for coordination languages, a designer is confronted with a number of choices, including the view that processes have on data (e.g. data is information, or data is a resource), the kind of coordination to be used (e.g. data-driven or control-oriented), the coordination primitives, and the protocol for implementing a broadcast of data.

We will consider three different classes of software architectures, differing in the broadcast mechanism used. In each architecture there are a number of agents which interact only by broadcasting data to all agents. Each agent consists of an active process together with a local memory used as a data repository.

The processing element of each agent can, besides performing internal computations, executes some coordination operations in order to interact with the other agents. There are operations for inserting data in the local memory (*wrt*), for broadcasting data (*put*), for testing the presence of data in the memory (*rd*), and for the local (*get*) and global (*del*) consumption of data. There are several ways these operations can be implemented: we will consider blocking *rd*, *get*, and *del* operations, and non-blocking *wrt* and *put* operations. Furthermore, the *put* and *del* operations use the broadcast mechanism offered by the architecture.

The three classes of architectures we consider differ in their broadcasting mechanisms. The simplest broadcast mechanism to describe (and hardest to implement in a distributed system) is the synchronous one: when a data value is produced it is inserted immediately in the memory of each agent at the same time. Because there is no observable delay between the production and the receiving of data by all agents, we call this architecture *undelayed*.

In a second architecture, called *globally delayed*, agents communicate through an atomic broadcast: there can be a delay between the production of data and its actual reception by all agents, but all agents are guaranteed to receive the broadcast data value at the same time. We model this global delay using a shared queue of pending messages. When a data value is broadcast, it is inserted in this queue. Eventually it will be removed from the queue and stored in all the memories of the agents at the same time.

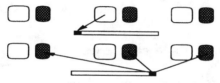

In our third architecture, that we call *locally delayed*, agents use an unordered broadcast, meaning that each agent may receive a broadcast data value at a different moment in time. We model this local delay by associating a queue of pending messages to each agent. When a data value is broadcast, it is inserted in all queues at the same time, but the transfer from each queue to the corresponding dataspace can happen for each agent at a different time.

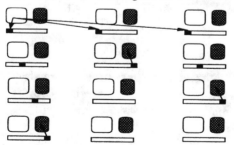

These architectures are parameterized by the structure of the dataspaces, either multisets or sets. In the first case multiplicity of data is significant and hence data is interpreted as a resource. In the second case, multiplicity is insignificant and data is seen as information.

Several coordination languages can be modeled in one or more of these architectures. In this paper we model two simple data-driven coordination languages inspired by Linda [12] and Splice [5], respectively, and a control-oriented coordination language inspired by Manifold [4].

Then we compare the behavior of the three architectures, under the assumption that the local dataspaces are either sets or multisets. We give several equivalence results: informally, we say that two architectures are observationally equivalent if there exists an encoding of one into the other preserving the processing components and such that each step of one architecture can be simulated by the other one up to some unobservable communication steps, and vice-versa. We give also difference results by exhibiting processes that can produce a data value in one architecture but not in the other one. These relationships give useful insights to a designer when building a software architecture. For example it may be interesting to find an equivalent simple model of a distributed system, abstracting from the nature of broadcasting, or, conversely, one might want to implement a simple conceptual model in a distributed architecture.

The structure of the paper is as follows. The next section introduces the definitions common to all three architectures, while the specific description of the architectures is in Section 3. In Section 4 we model simple coordination languages within our architectures. The three architectures are compared in Section 5. In Section 6 we draw some conclusions and discuss related work. In an appendix we give some alternative definitions of the global delete operator.

2   Processing and data elements

Let *Data*, ranged over by $a, b, \ldots$, be a set of *data values*, and define $Msg = Data \cup \{\overline{a} \mid a \in Data\}$, ranged over by $x, y, \ldots$, to be a set of *messages* used by the agents of the architectures for their interactions. The message a denotes the request for insertion of the value a, while $\overline{a}$ represents the request for deletion of a. We use the convention that $\overline{\overline{x}} = x$ for $x \in Msg$. When produced, messages are associated to a sort used by the communication protocol to guarantee a common order in their reception among all agents. We assume the existence of an abstract set *Sorts* of *data sorts*, ranged over by $s, t, \ldots$, and define the set Σ of *broadcastable messages* as follows:

$$\Sigma = \{x{:}s \mid x \in Msg, s \in Sorts\}.$$

Two messages with different sorts (e.g. because broadcast by different agents) may be received by an agent in any order, while two messages with the same sort (e.g. because broadcast by the same process) will be received by any agent in the same order as they were produced.

The behavior of each process is described by a synchronization tree: let *Proc*, ranged over by $P, Q, \ldots$, be the set of all synchronization trees defined by the grammar

$$P ::= 0 \mid \sum_{i \in I} \alpha_i . P_i$$

$$\alpha ::= \tau \mid rd(a) \mid put(a{:}s) \mid wrt(a) \mid del(a{:}s) \mid get(a)$$

where $a \in Data$, $s \in Sorts$ and I is a non-empty (possibly infinite) index set. Informally, τ denotes some internal activity, $rd(a)$ tests for the presence of an occurrence of the value a in the local dataspace without consuming it, $put(a{:}s)$ emits a new instance of the value a that is broadcast to all the agents as the message $a{:}s$, $wrt(a)$ introduces a new instance of value a in the local dataspace, $del(a{:}s)$ broadcasts the message $\overline{a}{:}s$ indicating the request for deletion of one instance of value a, $get(a)$ consumes a local occurrence of value a. The put and del actions associate to data the sorts used during their broadcast.

Following [3,7], we model broadcasting of messages using *queues of pending messages*. A queue q is a partially commuting string defined as a congruence class of finite strings in the monoid $(\Sigma^\star, \cdot, \varepsilon)$ modulo the least congruence such that, for all $x{:}s, y{:}t \in \Sigma$,

$$x{:}s \cdot y{:}t = y{:}t \cdot x{:}s \ \ \text{if} \ s \neq t \,.$$

Commutation of messages of different sorts allows for a compact formalization of several broadcasting mechanisms. We let DQ be the set of all queues of pending messages, and write $\odot$ for the string concatenation $\cdot$ modulo the above congruence. Also, we denote a congruence class containing a single element by the element itself. Hence $x{:}s$ is the congruence class containing the one-element string $x{:}s \in \Sigma$ and ε the congruence class containing the empty string.

When received, messages are stored in *dataspaces*. The set of all dataspaces is denoted by DS and ranged over by d. We will consider two kinds of dataspaces: multisets and sets. In the first case we let $DS = Msg \rightarrow \mathbb{N}$ while in the second case $DS = Msg \rightarrow \{0, 1\}$. For $d \in DS$ and $x \in Msg$ we say $in(d, x) = tt$ if $d(x) > 0$. Also, we define the insertion of $x \in Msg$ into a dataspace $d \in DS$ as follows:

$$d \oplus x = \begin{cases} d[x/d(x) + 1] & \text{if } d(x) + 1 \in cod(d) \text{ and } in(d, \overline{x}) \neq tt \\ d[\overline{x}/d(\overline{x}) - 1] & \text{if } in(d, \overline{x}) = tt \\ d & \text{otherwise} \end{cases}$$

where, for any function $f{:}X \rightarrow Y$ we denote by $cod(f)$ its codomain Y, and, for $x \in X$ and $y \in Y$, we denote by $f[x/y]$ the function mapping x to y and acting as f otherwise. The above operation is defined for both interpretations of a dataspace as set or multiset (the condition on the codomain of the dataspace makes the distinction here), and for adding and removing data values from a dataspace. Informally, a data value a is inserted into a dataspace only if no request for deletion $\overline{a}$ is present. Otherwise a is not inserted and $\overline{a}$ is removed from the dataspace. Conversely, a data value a from a dataspace is removed when the message $\overline{a}$ arrives. In case the message $\overline{a}$ arrives and the value a is not present in the dataspace then $\overline{a}$ is stored into the dataspace.

3 Three software architectures

3.1 The locally delayed architecture

The set $Conf_L$ of possible configurations of the agents in the locally delayed architecture is defined by the grammar

$$C ::= [P, d, q] \mid C \parallel C \,.$$

where $\parallel$ is a commutative and associative parallel composition operator. Here P is a process and $d \in DS$ a local dataspace (together forming an agent), and $q \in DQ$ is a queue containing the messages already produced by some agent in the system but not yet received by (P, d). The dynamical evolution of the agents is specified by a transition relation $\longrightarrow_L$, defined as the least relation in $Conf_L \times (\{\tau\} \cup \Sigma) \times Conf_L$ satisfying the following axioms and rules:

$$(L1) \quad [\tau.P, d, q] \xrightarrow{\tau} [P, d, q]$$

$$(L2) \quad [rd(a).P, d, q] \xrightarrow{\tau} [P, d, q] \qquad \text{if } in(d, a) = tt$$

$$(L3) \quad [put(a{:}s).P, d, q] \xrightarrow{a:s} [P, d, a{:}s \odot q]$$

$$(L4) \quad [wrt(a).P, d, q] \xrightarrow{\tau} [P, d \oplus a, q]$$

$$(L5) \quad [del(a{:}s).P, d, q] \xrightarrow{\overline{a}:s} [P, d, \overline{a}{:}s \odot q] \quad \text{if } in(d, a) = tt$$

$$(L6) \quad [get(a).P, d, q] \xrightarrow{\tau} [P, d \oplus \overline{a}, q] \qquad \text{if } in(d, a) = tt$$

$$(L7) \quad [P, d, q \odot x{:}s] \xrightarrow{\tau} [P, d \oplus x, q]$$

$$(L8) \quad \frac{[\alpha_k.P_k, d, q] \xrightarrow{\ell} [P', d', q'] \quad k \in I}{[\sum_I \alpha_i.P_i, d, q] \xrightarrow{\ell} [P', d', q']} \quad \ell \in \{\tau\} \cup \Sigma$$

$$(L9) \quad \frac{C \xrightarrow{\tau} C'}{[P, d, q] \parallel C \xrightarrow{\tau} [P, d, q] \parallel C'}$$

$$(L10) \quad \frac{C \xrightarrow{x:s} C'}{[P, d, q] \parallel C \xrightarrow{x:s} [P, d, x{:}s \odot q] \parallel C'} \quad x{:}s \in \Sigma$$

The conditions in $(L2)$, $(L5)$, and $(L6)$ say that the rd, del, and get operators are blocking. Rules $(L3)$ and $(L5)$ in combination with $(L10)$ show that the effect of the put and del operations is global to all agents, while that of the rd, wrt, and get operations is local to the agent executing the operations (specified by $(L2)$, $(L3)$, $(L6)$ and $(L9)$). The receiving of a message is specified by $(L7)$.

The labels τ, $a{:}s$ and $\overline{a}{:}s$ in the above specification have been introduced for a structural definition of the transition relation $\longrightarrow_L$. When comparing the architectures we are interested in the reduction steps that the system can execute. To this aim we define a reduction relation $\twoheadrightarrow_L \subseteq Conf_L \times Conf_L$ abstracting from the labels used by the transition relation $\longrightarrow_L$:

$$C \twoheadrightarrow_L C' \text{ if and only if } \exists \ell \in \{\tau\} \cup \Sigma . C \xrightarrow{\ell}_L C'.$$

We define also a weaker reduction relation $\Longrightarrow_L$ as the reflexive and transitive closure of $\twoheadrightarrow_L$, that is $\Longrightarrow_L = (\twoheadrightarrow_L)^*$.

3.2 The globally delayed architecture

The set of configurations of the agents in this architecture is given by

$$Conf_G = \{(A, q) \mid A \in Agents, q \in DQ\},$$

where *Agents* is defined by the grammar:

$$A ::= [P, d] \mid A \parallel A,$$

where $\parallel$ is used here as a commutative and associative parallel composition operator for agents. As usual P is a process and $d \in DS$ is a local dataspace. The difference with the configuration of the previous architecture is that here all agents share the same queue of pending messages.

Observe that $\parallel$ is overloaded because it is used for both agents and configurations; this does not introduce confusion because the operator is usually determined by the context.

The behavior of the agents in the globally delayed architecture is specified by means of the transition relation $\longrightarrow_G$, defined as the least relation in $Conf_G \times (\{\tau\} \cup Msg) \times Conf_G$ satisfying the following axioms and rules:

$$
\begin{array}{ll}
(G1) & [\tau.P, d], q \xrightarrow{\tau} [P, d], q \\[4pt]
(G2) & [rd(a).P, d], q \xrightarrow{\tau} [P, d], q \qquad\qquad \text{if } in(d, a) = tt \\[4pt]
(G3) & [put(a{:}s).P, d], q \xrightarrow{\tau} [P, d], a{:}s \odot q \\[4pt]
(G4) & [wrt(a).P, d], q \xrightarrow{\tau} [P, d \oplus a], q \\[4pt]
(G5) & [del(a{:}s).P, d], q \xrightarrow{\tau} [P, d], \overline{a}{:}s \odot q \qquad \text{if } in(d, a) = tt \\[4pt]
(G6) & [get(a).P, d], q \xrightarrow{\tau} [P, d \oplus \overline{a}], q \qquad\quad \text{if } in(d, a) = tt \\[4pt]
(G7) & [P, d], q \odot x{:}s \xrightarrow{x} [P, d \oplus x], q \\[10pt]
(G8) & \dfrac{[\alpha_k.P_k, d], q \xrightarrow{\ell} [P', d'], q' \quad k \in I}{[\sum_I \alpha_i.P_i, d], q \xrightarrow{\ell} [P', d'], q'} \qquad \ell \in \{\tau\} \cup Msg \\[14pt]
(G9) & \dfrac{A, q \xrightarrow{\tau} A', q'}{([P, d] \parallel A), q \xrightarrow{\tau} ([P, d] \parallel A'), q'} \\[14pt]
(G10) & \dfrac{A, q \xrightarrow{x} A', q'}{([P, d] \parallel A), q \xrightarrow{x} ([P, d \oplus x] \parallel A'), q} \qquad x \in Msg
\end{array}
$$

Here $(G3)$ shows that when a data item is broadcast it is not immediately visible to all agents. The fact that eventually they will receive a message at the same time is modeled by $(G7)$ together with $(G10)$. As in the previous architecture, the *rd*, *del* and *get* operators are blocking ($(G2)$, $(G5)$ and $(G6)$, respectively), the *rd*, *wrt* and *get* operations are local ($(G2)$, $(G5)$ and $(G4)$ together with $(G8)$), and the *put* and *del* operations have a global effect obtained through the broadcasting of a message ($(G3)$ and $(G5)$ together with $(G10)$).

As we have done for the previous architecture, we define a reduction relation $\longrightarrow_G \subseteq Conf_G \times Conf_G$ and its weaker correspondent $\Longrightarrow_G$:

$$
\begin{aligned}
&C \longrightarrow_G C' \text{ if and only if } \exists \ell \in \{\tau\} \cup Msg \,.\, C \xrightarrow{\ell}_G C', \\
&\Longrightarrow_G = (\longrightarrow_G)^*.
\end{aligned}
$$

3.3 The undelayed architecture

The behavior of the agents in the undelayed architecture is specified by the transition relation $\longrightarrow_U$, that is the least relation in $Agents \times (\{\tau\} \cup Msg) \times Agents$ satisfying the following axioms and rules:

$$(U1)\ [\tau.P, d] \xrightarrow{\tau} [P, d]$$

$$(U2)\ [rd(a).P, d] \xrightarrow{\tau} [P, d] \qquad \text{if } in(d, a) = tt$$

$$(U3)\ [put(a{:}s).P, d] \xrightarrow{a} [P, d \oplus a]$$

$$(U4)\ [wrt(a).P, d] \xrightarrow{\tau} [P, d \oplus a]$$

$$(U5)\ [del(a{:}s).P, d] \xrightarrow{\overline{a}} [P, d \oplus \overline{a}] \qquad \text{if } in(d, a) = tt$$

$$(U6)\ [get(a).P, d] \xrightarrow{\tau} [P, d \oplus \overline{a}] \qquad \text{if } in(d, a) = tt$$

$$(U7)\ \frac{[\alpha_k.P_k, d] \xrightarrow{\ell} [P', d'] \quad k \in I}{[\sum_I \alpha_i.P_i, d] \xrightarrow{\ell} [P', d']} \quad \ell \in \{\tau\} \cup Msg$$

$$(U8)\ \frac{A \xrightarrow{\tau} A'}{[P, d] \parallel A \xrightarrow{\tau} [P, d] \parallel A'}$$

$$(U9)\ \frac{A \xrightarrow{x} A'}{[P, d] \parallel A \xrightarrow{x} [P, d \oplus x] \parallel A'} \quad x \in Msg$$

The synchronous behavior of the *put* and *del* operations is modeled by $(U3)$ and $(U5)$ together with $(U9)$. All other operations are local (the remaining axioms together with $(U8)$). As in the previous architectures, the *rd*, *del*, and *get* operations are blocking, while the *put* and the *wrt* operations are not. Observe that in the undelayed architecture sorts do not play any role. Indeed, no queue of pending messages is present and hence sorts could be safely eliminated from the *del* and *put* operations. Nevertheless, they are present for consistency with the previous architectures.

As before, we define a reduction relation $\longrightarrow\!\!\!\!\!\twoheadrightarrow_U \subseteq Agents \times Agents$ and its weaker correspondent $\Longrightarrow_U$:

$$A \longrightarrow\!\!\!\!\!\twoheadrightarrow_U A' \text{ if and only if } \exists \ell \in \{\tau\} \cup Msg . A \xrightarrow{\ell}_U A',$$
$$\Longrightarrow_U = (\longrightarrow\!\!\!\!\!\twoheadrightarrow_U)^*.$$

4 Modeling coordination languages

In this section we give examples about how to model coordination in our architectures.

4.1 A shared data-driven language

We start with a coordination language inspired by one of the abstract models of Linda [12] presented in [11]. It consists of operations acting on a shared dataspace. Processes in parallel can introduce values, test for their presence, and consume them via the following syntax:

$$S ::= end \mid \alpha.S \mid S + S$$
$$\alpha ::= out(a) \mid rd(a) \mid in(a)$$

where a is an element of an abstract set Val of values.

Consider $Data = Val$ and let $Sort = Msg$. We model the above language by means of the undelayed architecture, where we consider the local dataspaces as distributed consistent copies of the same shared dataspace. It is not hard to see that the local dataspaces are kept consistent because we are dealing with a synchronous broadcast, and no local operations like wrt or get are considered. Given a statement S we define its behavior in isolation as the synchronization tree $[S]$. It is given inductively as follows:

$$[end] = 0 \qquad\qquad [out(a).S] = put(a{:}a).[S]$$
$$[rd(a).S] = rd(a).[S] \qquad [in(a).S] = del(a{:}\overline{a}).[S]$$
$$[S_1 + S_2] = [S_1] + [S_2]$$

We could interpret the above language also in the globally delayed architecture using the synchronous del operator as specified in the Appendix. In this case, the way we assign sorts to each message to be broadcasted implies that the order in which data is received is insignificant with respect to the order of its production.

4.2 A distributed data-driven language

Next we model another data-driven coordination language inspired by the abstract model of Splice [5] as presented in [6]. The main difference with the previous language is that the local dataspace of each agent need not to be a consistent copy of a shared one.

Let Val be a countable set of *values*, Var a set of data variables, and Idx a set of *data indexes*. We define the syntax of our distributed data-driven coordination language as follows:

$$\alpha ::= out(\iota, v) \mid rd(\iota, v) \mid in(\iota, v)$$
$$S ::= end \mid \alpha.S \mid S + S$$

where $v \in Val \cup Var$ and $\iota \in Idx$. The language consists of operations for the manipulation of structured data $\langle \iota, v \rangle$, where ι is an index and v a value. Intuitively the coordination primitives are as for the previous language, but *in* acts locally on the store. The index is used to retrieve data, and data variables match with any data item. For example, if $v \in Var$ then $in(\iota, v)$ will consume one of the values with index ι from the local dataspace of the agent executing it. Data is broadcast using a message passing protocol which guarantees that values with the same index are received by any agent in the same order as they where produced. Furthermore, it is required that there is at most one agent producing values with a given index.

The above broadcasting mechanism fits well with those used by the locally and globally delayed architectures. In order to model the language in those architectures, let $Data = Idx \times Val$ and $Sorts = Idx$. Given a statement S we define its behavior in isolation as a synchronization tree $[\![S]\!]$. It is given inductively as follows:

$$
\begin{array}{lll}
[\![end]\!] & = 0 & \\
[\![out(\iota, u).S]\!] & = put(\langle \iota, u \rangle{:}\iota).[\![S]\!] & u \in Val \\
[\![rd(\iota, u).S]\!] & = rd(\langle \iota, u \rangle).[\![S]\!] & u \in Val \\
[\![rd(\iota, v).S]\!] & = \sum_{u \in Val} rd(\langle \iota, u \rangle).[\![S[u/v]]\!] & v \in Var \\
[\![in(\iota, u).S]\!] & = get(\langle \iota, u \rangle).[\![S]\!] & u \in Val \\
[\![in(\iota, v).S]\!] & = \sum_{u \in Val} get(\langle \iota, u \rangle).[\![S[u/v]]\!] & v \in Var \\
[\![S_1 + S_2]\!] & = [\![S_1]\!] + [\![S_2]\!] & \\
\end{array}
$$

where $S[u/v]$ is the statement obtained by replacing all occurrences in S of the variable $v \in Var$ by the value $u \in Val$. The summation used for the rd and in operations denotes the openness of the system to the environment, which has to determine which branch will be chosen.

4.3 A control-oriented language

We conclude this section by modeling a language inspired to the event mechanism of the control-oriented language Manifold [4], of which the operational semantics is given in [3].

Let Evn be a set of events and Pid be a set of process identifiers. We define the syntax of our control-oriented coordination language as follows:

$$
\begin{array}{l}
G ::= ep?S \mid G + G \\
ep ::= (e, p) \mid (*e, *p) \mid (*e, p) \mid (e, *p) \\
S ::= end \mid G \mid raise(e).S \mid post(e).S \\
\end{array}
$$

where $e \in Evn$ and $p \in Pid$. A system consists of several agents with a local store and with a unique process identifier. The behavior of each process is driven by reactions to broadcasted events. Event and process identifiers prefixed by a $*$ are formal parameters to be substituted by actual events and process identifiers, respectively, when a reaction takes place. Raising events means broadcasting them to all agents in the system using a protocol that guarantees that events raised by the same process are received by all agents in the same order as they were raised. Posting events is sending events only to the process itself.

We can use the locally delayed architecture to model the above language. Define $Data = Events \times Pid$ and let $Sort = Pid$. For each $q \in Pid$ and statement G we define the behavior of the agent q executing G as the synchronization tree $[\![G]\!](q)$, defined inductively as follows:

$$
\begin{array}{ll}
[\![(e, p)?S]\!](q) & = get((e, p)).[\![S]\!]_q \\
[\![(*e, *p)?S]\!](q) & = \sum_{e' \in Evn, p' \in Pid} get((e', p')).[\![S[e'/e][p'/p]]\!]_q \\
[\![(*e, p)?S]\!](q) & = \sum_{e' \in Evn} get((e', p)).[\![S[e'/e]]\!]_q \\
[\![(e, *p)?S]\!](q) & = \sum_{p' \in Pid} get((e, p')).[\![S[p'/p]]\!]_q \\
[\![G_1 + G_2]\!](q) & = [\![G_1]\!](q) + [\![G_2]\!](q) \\
\end{array}
$$

and for each statement S and $q \in PId$, $[\![S]\!]_q$ is defined by

$$
\begin{aligned}
[\![end]\!]_q &= 0 & [\![G]\!]_q &= [\![G]\!](q) \\
[\![raise(e).S]\!]_q &= put((e, q){:}q).[\![S]\!]_q & [\![post(e).S]\!]_q &= wrt((e, q)).[\![S]\!]_q \; .
\end{aligned}
$$

Note that events raised by different agents will produce data of different sorts. Hence the order in which data is sent by an agent is preserved.

5 Comparing the architectures

When comparing two architectures we have to deal with two possible kinds of results: either we prove that they are observationally equivalent or that they are observationally different. When proving an equivalence result, we will consider a strong notion of equivalence, and we use no assumptions on the sorts of the broadcast messages. Furthermore we make no assumptions about the initial state of the agents. In this way the equivalence results hold also for weaker notions of observation and for other instances of the sort mechanism. Informally, we say that two architectures are *observationally equivalent* if there exists an encoding of one into the other preserving the processing components, and such that each reduction step of one architecture can be simulated by the other one in zero or more steps, and vice-versa.

On the other hand, when we prove a difference result, we use a weak notion of observation: two architectures are observationally different if there exists an agent executing a process that can produce a data value in one architecture but not in the other one. Sometimes difference results rely on some assumptions about the sorts of the broadcast messages and assumptions about the initial content of the local dataspaces. These assumptions are justified by the protocol used by some broadcast mechanisms for many realistic software architectures. In this way, the difference results we present hold also for stronger notions of observation and for other instances of the sort mechanism.

5.1 Comparison without consuming data

We start by proving that if we consider processes described by synchronization trees without local or global delete operations *get* and *del*, then the above three architectures are all equivalent. Furthermore the equivalences do not depend on the choice between dataspaces as sets or multisets, that is, the multiplicity of data is not important. These results holds because we are dealing with dataspaces that monotonically grow (as no delete operation is permitted).

First we need to introduce some notation. For $A \in Agents$ and $q \in DQ$, we denote by $A \Leftarrow q$ the collection of agents obtained after all values in the queue q have been flushed in all local dataspaces of the agents in A. We define it by induction on the structure of A and q:

$$
\begin{aligned}
[P, d] \Leftarrow \varepsilon &= [P, d] \\
[P, d] \Leftarrow (q \odot x{:}s) &= [P, d \oplus x] \Leftarrow q \\
(A \parallel A) \Leftarrow q &= (A \Leftarrow q) \parallel (A \Leftarrow q) \; .
\end{aligned}
$$

The set DQ of queues can be turned into a meet-semilattice by defining a prefix order as follows: $q_1 \sqsubseteq q_2$ if and only if there exists $q \in DQ$ such that $q_1 \odot q = q_2$ [13]. If every broadcastable message has the same sort then the above order coincides with the usual prefix ordering, while if they have all a different sort then the order coincides with the usual multiset inclusion ordering. For q_1 and q_2 in DQ, we denote by $q_1 \sqcap q_2$ their greatest lower bound.

Next we define an encoding $\mathcal{E}_{LG} \colon Conf_L \to Conf_G$ mapping configurations of the locally delayed architectures into corresponding configurations of the globally delayed architectures:

$$\mathcal{E}_{LG}([P, d, q]) \quad = [P, d], q$$
$$\mathcal{E}_{LG}([P, d, q] \parallel C) = ((([P, d] \Leftarrow q_P) \parallel (A' \Leftarrow q_C)), q \sqcap q'$$

where $A', q' = \mathcal{E}_{LG}(C)$, $(q \sqcap q') \odot q_P = q$, and $(q \sqcap q') \odot q_C = q'$. In other words, we construct a shared queue as the smallest queue among all agents, and flush in the dataspace of each agent the messages that are in its queue but not in the shared one. This encoding is used to prove the following equivalence result.

Theorem 1. *For any configuration $C \in Conf_L$ of the locally delayed architecture with agents containing processes without 'del' and 'get' operators, the following holds:*

1. *for all $C' \in Conf_L$, if $C \longrightarrow_L C'$ then $\mathcal{E}_{LG}(C) \Longrightarrow_G \mathcal{E}_{LG}(C')$,*
2. *for all $C' \in Conf_G$, if $\mathcal{E}_{LG}(C) \longrightarrow_G C'$ then there exists $C'' \in Conf_L$ such that $C \Longrightarrow_L C''$ and $\mathcal{E}_{LG}(C'') = C'$.*

To prove the equivalence between the globally delayed and the undelayed architectures, we define, for $A \in Agents$ and $q \in DQ$ the following encoding:

$$\mathcal{E}_{GU}(A, q) = A \Leftarrow q .$$

Hence we eliminate the shared queue by flushing its pending messages in each local dataspace of A.

Theorem 2. *For any configuration $C \in Conf_G$ of the globally delayed architecture with agents containing processes without 'del' and 'get' operators, the following holds:*

1. *for all $C' \in Conf_G$, if $C \longrightarrow_G C'$ then $\mathcal{E}_{GU}(C) \Longrightarrow_U \mathcal{E}_{GU}(C')$,*
2. *for all $A \in Agents$, if $\mathcal{E}_{GU}(C) \longrightarrow_U A$ then there exists $C' \in Conf_G$ such that $C \Longrightarrow_G C'$ and $\mathcal{E}_{GU}(A) = C'$.*

Finally, we show that in the presence of only *wrt*, *put* and *rd* operators the multiplicity of data is insignificant. We show it only for the locally delayed architecture, but similar results hold also for the other two architectures. For a configuration $C \in Conf_L$ with dataspaces interpreted as multisets, define a flattening function $flat_L$ that returns a configuration obtained by replacing each dataspace d with its associated set $\overline{d}$, where $\overline{d}(x) = 1$ if and only if $d(x) > 0$.

Theorem 3. *Let $C \in Conf_L$ be a configuration of the locally delayed architecture containing agents without 'del' and 'get' operations, and such that each dataspace in C is interpreted as multiset. The following holds:*

1. *for all $C' \in Conf_L$, if $C \twoheadrightarrow_L C'$ then $flat(C) \twoheadrightarrow_L flat(C')$.*
2. *for all $C' \in Conf_L$, if $flat(C) \twoheadrightarrow_L C'$ then $C \twoheadrightarrow_L C''$ with $C' = flat(C'')$.*

5.2 Consuming data, locally

Next we allow agents to contain processes with the local delete operator *get*. First we observe that the equivalence in Theorem 3 does not hold anymore. Consider an agent executing the process

$$P = wrt(a).wrt(a).get(a).get(a).wrt(b).0.$$

If the structure of the dataspace is a set then an agent executing P in any of our three architectures can never produce a b because it blocks at the second $get(a)$. However, if the dataspace is a multiset then the agent will always insert b in its store. Note that the difference holds also if we replace the *wrt* operations in P by *put* operations.

If dataspaces are sets then the locally delayed architecture is different from the globally delayed. Consider the following processes:

$$P = put(a{:}s).put(a{:}s).put(b{:}s).get(c).get(a).get(a).wrt(d).0$$
$$Q = get(b).put(c{:}t).0,$$

where $t \neq s$ (for example because the architecture uses a broadcast mechanism which guarantees that data from the same agent is received by all other agents in the same order as it was produced). Assume P is executed by an agent with a dataspace containing no a and c, while Q is executed by an agent with a dataspace containing no b. Because $t \neq s$, the agent executing P in the locally delayed system may receive c from the agent executing Q before the second a will be stored in its local dataspace. Hence the operation $wrt(d)$ may succeed. This is not the case if the two agents are executed in the globally delayed architecture because when c is broadcast, all agents in the system have already received the value b and hence also the two a's. Because of the set-structure, only one $get(a)$ may now be executed by the process P. The same result holds even if we do not allow for an agent to delete data not produced by itself, since we can replace $get(b)$ by $rd(b)$ in the process Q, and $get(c)$ by $rd(c)$ in the process P.

If dataspaces are multisets then we still have an equivalence between the locally delayed and the globally delayed architectures.

Theorem 4. *If dataspaces are multisets then for any configuration $C \in Conf_L$ of the locally delayed architecture with agents containing processes without the 'del' operator, the following holds:*

1. *for all $C' \in Conf_L$, if $C \twoheadrightarrow_L C'$ then $\mathcal{E}_{LG}(C) \Longrightarrow_G \mathcal{E}_{LG}(C')$,*

2. *for all* $C' \in Conf_G$, *if* $\mathcal{E}_{LG}(C) \longrightarrow_{\!\!\!\!*G} C'$ *then there exists* $C'' \in Conf_L$ *such that* $C \Longrightarrow_L C''$ *and* $\mathcal{E}_{LG}(C'') = C'$.

If dataspaces are sets, then both the locally and the globally delayed architectures are different from the undelayed one, without any assumption on the sorts of the broadcastable messages. Consider the process

$$P = put(a{:}s).put(a{:}t).get(a).get(a).wrt(b).0\,.$$

An agent executing P with a dataspace containing no a in the undelayed architecture cannot produce b, as there is no a present in its dataspace after the execution of the first $get(a)$. This is not the case for the other two architectures, due to the delay in receiving the message $a{:}t$.

Finally, if dataspaces are multisets and agents do not use the asynchronous global delete operator del then the three architectures are all equivalent.

Theorem 5. *If dataspaces are multisets then for any configuration* $C \in Conf_G$ *of the globally delayed architecture with agents containing processes without the 'del' operator the following holds:*

1. *for all* $C' \in Conf_G$, *if* $C \longrightarrow_{\!\!\!\!*G} C'$ *then* $\mathcal{E}_{GU}(C) \Longrightarrow_U \mathcal{E}_{GU}(C')$,
2. *for all* $A \in Agents$, *if* $\mathcal{E}_{GU}(C) \longrightarrow_{\!\!\!\!*U} A$ *then there exists* $C' \in Conf_G$ *such that* $C \Longrightarrow_G C'$ *and* $\mathcal{E}_{GU}(C') = A$.

5.3 Consuming data, globally

Finally we allow agents to contain processes with the asynchronous operator del for the global consumption of data.

Regardless of the interpretation of dataspaces as sets or multisets, the undelayed architecture is different from the other two architectures. Consider the process

$$P = put(a{:}s).del(a{:}t).del(a{:}r).wrt(b)\,, \tag{1}$$

executed by an agent with a dataspace containing no a. In the undelayed architecture this agent cannot produce a b, while in the other two architectures this may happen due to the delay in receiving the first message for the deletion of a.

Also the locally delayed architecture is different from the globally delayed one, regardless of the structure of the dataspaces (set or multiset). Consider the following three processes:

$$P = put(a{:}s).del(a{:}t).put(b{:}t).0$$
$$Q = rd(b).put(c{:}r).0$$
$$R = rd(c).rd(a).wrt(d).0\,,$$

where $t \neq r$. Assume P is executed by an agent with a dataspace containing no a, Q by an agent with a dataspace containing no b, and R by an agent with a dataspace containing no a and c. When c is broadcast in the globally delayed system, the value a has already been stored in all dataspaces, and consumed from them because b is guaranteed to be received after $\overline{a}$. Hence the agent executing R cannot produce d. In the locally delayed architecture, d may be produced by the agent executing R, because c may be stored in its dataspace before b and $\overline{a}$. The above difference remains if we substitute *get* actions for *rd* actions.

6 Conclusions and related work

We have presented three different architectures for coordination languages with primitives for producing data (locally or globally), for consuming data (locally or globally), and for testing the presence of data (locally). We have characterized equivalences and differences among the architectures by pointing out the maximal set of coordination primitives under which the architectures are equivalent. The next table gives an overview of the results in this paper. It is split in two parts, depending on the structure of dataspaces (set or multiset).

	set			multiset		
	$L-G$	$L-U$	$G-U$	$L-G$	$L-U$	$G-U$
rd, put, wrt	$=$	$=$	$=$	$=$	$=$	$=$
rd, put, wrt, get	$\neq$	$\neq$	$\neq$	$=$	$=$	$=$
rd, put, wrt, get, del	$\neq$	$\neq$	$\neq$	$\neq$	$\neq$	$\neq$
rd, put, wrt, get, del_L	$\neq$	$\neq$	$\neq$	$\neq$	$\neq$	$\neq$
rd, put, wrt, get, del_G	$\neq$	$\neq$	$\neq$	$\neq$	$\neq$	$=$

Here L stands for the locally delayed architecture, G for the globally delayed and U for the undelayed one; del_L is the global delete specified in the Appendix by replacing $(L5)$ with $(L5')$, and del_G is the global delete specified in the Appendix by replacing $(G5)$ with $(G5')$ (regardless whether we replace $(L5)$ by $(L5')$).

The result we present here continues the program started by the authors in [7]. In that paper the authors studied a synchronous global delete operator and negative tests for the locally delayed architecture and also for two other architectures based on a shared dataspace. In this paper, we concentrate on operators that are either local or realized via broadcast mechanisms. Moreover, here we separate the description of the software components from the specification of the software architectures. This is a necessary step towards a formal comparison among architectures.

In [1] two possible implementations for the broadcast mechanism of the coordination language LO [2] are presented; the first one corresponds to the broadcast used in our undelayed architecture while the second coincides with that of the locally delayed one. The equivalence between the two implementations is shown by proving that they are both correct implementations of the broadcasting mechanism of LO. We strengthened this equivalence result by presenting a third equivalent broadcast mechanism (the globally delayed one). Furthermore we prove that the equivalence holds because no global consuming operators are considered and because dataspaces have a multiset structure rather than a set structure.

In [9] different implementations of an output operator have been studied in the setting of Linda. In particular, implementations are considered that are similar to our undelayed and globally delayed with the synchronous global delete specified in the Appendix. A formal comparison between the above two implementations is presented in [10] where a simple Linda calculus is proven to be Turing powerful only under the undelayed implementation but not under the globally delayed one. The difference stems from the presence in Linda of operators that permit to test for the absence of data.

We leave for future work the investigation of negative test operators [8, 15] in combination with the locally and the asynchronous delete operators studied in this paper. In [7] some results have already been obtained for negative tests together with globally synchronous delete operators. We also plan to investigate other operators like one that spawns new agents, other forms of consumption operations (like an asynchronous version of the local delete), and also other forms of broadcast, such as the one that preserves the causal dependencies.

References

1. J.-M. Andreoli, L. Leth, R. Pareschi, and B. Thomsen. True Concurrency Semantics for a Linear Logic Programming Language with Broadcast Communication. In *Proc. of TAPSOFT'93*, volume 668 of *LNCS*, pages 182–198, Springer, 1993.

2. J.-M. Andreoli and R. Pareschi. Linear objects: Logical processes with built-in inheritance. *New Generation Computing*, 9(3+4):445–473, 1991.

3. F. Arbab, J.W. de Bakker, M.M. Bonsangue, J.J.M.M. Rutten, A. Scutellá, and G. Zavattaro. A transition system semantics for the control-driven coordination language MANIFOLD. To appear in *Theoretical Computer Science*, 1999.

4. F. Arbab, I. Herman, and P. Spilling. An overview of Manifold and its implementation. *Concurrency: Practice and Experience*, 5(1):23–70, 1993.

5. M. Boasson. Control systems software. In *IEEE Transactions on Automatic Control* 38:7, pages 1094–1107, 1993.

6. M.M. Bonsangue, J.N. Kok, M. Boasson, and E. de Jong. A software architecture for distributed control systems and its transition system semantics. In *Proc. of ACM Symp. on Applied Computing (SAC'98)*, pages 159–168. ACM press, 1998.

7. M.M. Bonsangue, J.N. Kok, and G. Zavattaro. Comparing coordination models based on shared distributed replicated data. In *Proc. of ACM Symp. on Applied Computing (SAC'99)*. ACM press, 1999.

8. A. Brogi and J.-M. Jacquet. On the expressiveness of Linda-like concurrent languages In I. Castellani and C. Palamidessi editors, *Proc. of Express'98*, volume 16(2) of *Electronic Notes in Theoretical Computer Science*, 1998.

9. N. Busi, R. Gorrieri, and G. Zavattaro. Comparing Three Semantics for Linda-like Languages. To appear in *Theoretical Computer Science*, 1999.

10. N. Busi, R. Gorrieri, and G. Zavattaro. On the Expressiveness of Linda Coordination Primitives. To appear in *Information and Computation*, 1999.

11. N. Busi, R. Gorrieri, and G. Zavattaro. A Process Algebraic View of Linda Coordination Primitives. In *Theoretical Computer Science*, 192(2): 167–199, 1998.

12. N. Carriero and D. Gelernter. Linda in context. In *Communications of the ACM* 32:4, pages 444–458, 1989.

13. A. Mazurkiewicz. Trace theory. In W. Brauer et al., editors, *Petri Nets, Applications, and Relationship to other models of Concurrency*, volume 255 of LNCS, pages 279–324, Springer-Verlag, 1987.
14. D.E. Perry and A. L. Wolf. Foundations for the Study of Software Architecture. In *Software Engineering Notes*, ACM SIGSOFT vol. 17:4, pages 40–52, 1992.
15. G. Zavattaro. Towards a Hierarchy for Negative Test Operators for Generative Communication. In I. Castellani and C. Palamidessi editors, *Proc. of Express'98*, volume 16(2) of *Electronic Notes in Theoretical Computer Science*, 1998.

A Alternative global delete operators

The *del* operation we have considered has an asynchronous behavior with respect to both the dataspace of the agent executing it, and also with respect to the dataspaces of all other agents. We could specify a more synchronous behavior of *del* by considering the following rules ($L5'$) and ($G5'$), instead of ($L5$) and ($G5$), respectively.

$$(L5')\ [del(a{:}s).P, d, q] \xrightarrow{\overline{a}{:}s} [P, d \oplus \overline{a}, q]\ \text{if}\ in(d, a) = tt$$
$$(G5')\ [del(a{:}s).P, d], q \xrightarrow{\overline{a}{:}s} [P, d \oplus \overline{a}], q\ \text{if}\ in(d, a) = tt$$

Rule ($L5'$) ensures synchrony with respect to the local dataspace in the locally delayed architecture. For the globally delayed architecture, rule ($G5'$) ensures (with rule ($G10$)) that an instance of a is removed from the local dataspace and also from the space of the other agents (if available) in one atomic step.

If we consider the new rule ($L5'$) for the locally delayed architecture, it is not hard to prove that the three architectures are still different, regardless of the interpretation of the dataspaces as sets or multisets.

More interesting is the analysis of the globally delayed architecture with the new synchronous global delete. Indeed, even if it remains different with respect to the locally delayed architecture (regardless of the use of the rule ($L5$) or ($L5'$)) we obtain an equivalence result.

Theorem 6. *If dataspaces are multisets then for any configuration $C \in Conf_G$ of the globally delayed architecture with a 'del' operator specified by replacing ($G5$) with ($G5'$) the following holds:*

1. *for all $C' \in Conf_G$, if $C \twoheadrightarrow_G C'$ then $\mathcal{E}_{GU}(C) \Longrightarrow_U \mathcal{E}_{GU}(C')$,*
2. *for all $A \in Agents$, if $\mathcal{E}_{GU}(C) \twoheadrightarrow_U A$ then there exists $C' \in Conf_G$ such that $C \Longrightarrow_G C'$ and $\mathcal{E}_{GU}(A) = C'$.*

The same result does not hold if dataspaces are sets. Consider the program

$$P = put(a{:}s_1).put(a{:}s_2).del(a{:}s_3).del(a{:}s_4).wrt(b).$$

If P is executed by an agent with no a in its dataspace then, in the undelayed architecture, it cannot produce b. On the other hand, in the globally delayed architecture, P can produce b due to the delay in receiving the second instance of the datum a.

A Hierarchical Model for Coordination of Concurrent Activities

Carlos Varela and Gul Agha

Department of Computer Science
University of Illinois at Urbana-Champaign, Urbana IL 61801, USA
cvarela@uiuc.edu, agha@cs.uiuc.edu
http://osl.cs.uiuc.edu

Abstract. We describe a hierarchical model for coordination of concurrent activities based on grouping actors into *casts* and coordinating casts by actors that are designated *directors*. The hierarchical model provides a simple, intuitive basis for actor communication and coordination. Casts serve as abstraction units for naming, migration, synchronization and load balancing. *Messengers* are actors used to send messages with special behaviour across casts. Moreover, an implementation of the hierarchical model does not require a reflective run-time architecture. We present the operational semantics for our model and illustrate the model by two sample applications: an atomic multicast protocol and a messenger carrying remote exception-handling code. These applications have been implemented in Java, leveraging the existence of cross-platform, safe virtual machine implementations.

1 Motivation

In order to address the difficulty of developing and maintaining increasingly complex software systems, a number of methodologies to facilitate a separation of design concerns have been proposed. A number of researchers, including the authors, have argued for a separation of code implementing the functionality of software components (the *how*) from code for "non-functional" properties, such as the relation between otherwise independent events at different actors (i.e. the *when*) [3, 15, 38], and the mapping of actors on a particular concurrent architecture (the *where*) [35]. Such separation of concerns results in modular code which allows software developers to reason compositionally and to reuse code implementing functionality, coordination, placement policies, and so forth independently.

We model coordination hierarchically by grouping actors into *casts*. Each cast is coordinated by a single actor called its *director*. We also introduce migrating *messenger* actors to facilitate remote cast-to-cast communication. Casts serve as abstraction units for naming, migration, synchronization and load balancing. Messengers are migrating actors used to send messages (possibly including behaviours) across casts. Our model explicitly represents locality in order to enable an explicit specification of the structure of the information flow between remotely located casts using actor migration.

The hierarchical model is motivated by social organizations, where groups and hierarchical structures allow for effective information flow and coordination of activities. The basic idea is not entirely new. For example, Simon [37] proposed hierarchies as an appropriate model to represent different kinds of complex systems – viz., social, biological and physical systems as well as systems carrying out symbolic computations. This proposal was based on the observation that interactions between components at different levels in a hierarchy are often orders of magnitude smaller than interactions within the sub-components. Simon argues that the near-decomposability property of hierarchic systems also allows for their natural evolution and illustrates this argument with examples drawn from systems such as multi-cellular organisms, social organizations, and astronomical systems.

Regardless of the philosophic merits of Simon's proposition, we believe that a hierarchical organization of actors for coordination is not only fairly intuitive to use but quite natural in many contexts. By using a hierarchical model, we simplify the description of complex systems by repeatedly subdividing them into components and their interactions.

A number of models of coordination require reflective capabilities in the implementation architecture; such reflection is used to support meta-level actors that can intercept and control base-level actors (e.g., see [32, 38, 42, 44]). The need for reflection creates two difficulties. First, it requires a specialized runtime system. Second, it complicates the semantics: correctness of a particular application not only depends on the semantics of application level actors, but also on the semantics of the meta-level architecture.

The hierarchical model proposed in this paper only uses abstractions that are themselves first-class actors. In particular, there is no requirement for meta-level actors which are able to intercept base-level actor messages. The cost of this simplicity results in at least two major disadvantages for the hierarchical model. First, the model does not support the degree of transparency that can be afforded by defining coordination abstractions using reflective architectures. Second, because the hierarchical model is limited to customizing communication, it is not as flexible as a reflective model. However, observe that the actor model represents all coordination through its message-passing semantics; thus customizing communication is far more powerful than it may first appear to be.

Despite these limitations, it is our conjecture that for a large number of applications, the simplicity of the hierarchical model suffices.

The outline of the rest of the paper is as follows. Section 2 briefly discusses research on Actors and other related topics. Section 3 gives an informal overview of the hierarchical model of actor communication and coordination. Section 4 presents the operational semantics of the model based on actor configurations. Section 5 shows two basic but powerful applications of the model: atomic multi-casting and remote exception handling via messengers. Finally, the last section concludes with a discussion including future directions.

2   Related Work

Actors [1, 19] extend sequential objects by encapsulating a thread of control along with procedures and data in the same entity; thus actors provide a unit of abstraction and distribution in concurrency. Actors communicate by asynchronous message passing. Moreover, message delivery is weakly fair – message delivery time is not bounded but messages are guaranteed to be eventually delivered. Unless specific coordination constraints are enforced, messages are received in some arbitrary order which may differ from the sending order. An implementation normally provides for messages to be buffered in a local mailbox and there is no guarantee that the messages will be processed in the same order as the order in which they are received.

The actor model and languages provide a very useful framework for understanding and developing open distributed systems. For example, among others applications, actor systems have been used for enterprise integration [39], real-time programming [36], fault-tolerance [4], and distributed artificial intelligence [13].

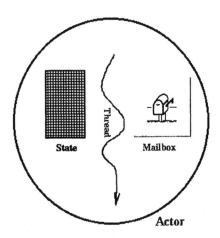

Fig. 1. Actors have their own thread of computation and mailbox

Actors are therefore inherently independent, concurrent and autonomous which enables efficiency in parallel execution [26] and facilitates mobility [5]. However this flexibility comes at a price: given the autonomy of actors and the non-blocking nature of message-passing, coordinating actors is a difficult problem.

ActorSpaces [9] are computationally passive containers of actors. Messages may be sent to one or all members of a group defined by a destination pattern. *Casts* differ from ActorSpaces in that the management of messages coming to a group is handled by a director, which is a computationally active component, and can therefore explicitly support multiple group messaging paradigms. On the other hand, the hierarchical model requires explicit description of how actors are grouped together, since policies such as pattern matching according to particular actor attributes are not directly supported.

Synchronizers [14, 15] are linguistic constructs that allow *declarative* control of coordination activity between multiple actors. Synchronizers allow two kinds of specifications: messages received by an actor may be disabled and, messages sent to different actors in a group may be atomically dispatched. These restrictions are specified using message patterns and may depend on the synchronizer's current state. *Directors* differ from Synchronizers in that directors are not declarative – rather a director is an actor: a director can receive messages and a director may itself be subject to coordination constraints. Coordination of directors not only allows for dynamic reconfigurability of coordination policies but also for a hierarchic composition of constraints.

The hierarchical model is more restrictive in that it requires actors to belong to a single cast at a given time. By contrast, the groups controlled by synchronizers may overlap arbitrarily. However, because the path for messages can be more rigid and the coordination more determinate in the hierarchical organization than in synchronizers, the former has the associated benefit of more predictable performance.

Communication-passing style (CmPS) [21] refers to a semantics in which data communication is always undertaken by migrating the continuation of the task requiring the data to the processor where the data resides. *Messengers* are similar to CmPS continuations in that they improve locality by eliminating coordination communication across machines. However, messengers are migrating first-class entities, or actors. Therefore, messengers can receive messages, change their state, persist over time, and support dynamic message delivery policies. On the other hand, messengers require the underlying run-time system to support actor migration.

Fukuda et al. [16] describe a paradigm for building distributed systems, named `Messengers`. The paradigm has similar motivation as our use of the messenger construct. However unlike Fakuda et al.'s work, we distinguish between actors and messengers (besides our use of hierarchies). Note that in early development of the actor model, Hewitt and his colleagues considered messages to be *unserialized* actors – i.e., messages (unlike serialized actors) could not change their local state (e.g., see [19]).

A number of coordination models and languages [11, 17] use a globally shared tuple space as a means of coordination and communication [10]. A predecessor of Linda, using pattern based data storage and retrieval was the Scientific Community Metaphor [27]. *Sprites*, the Scientific Community's computational agents, share a monotonically increasing knowledge base; on the other hand, Linda allows communication objects (tuples) to be removed from the tuple space. Additional work in this direction includes adding types to tuple spaces for safety, using objects instead of tuples and making tuple spaces first-class entities [20, 25, 31].

In contrast to these approaches, the hierarchical model of actor coordination that we present is based purely on communication which requires the sender to explicitly name the target of a message. Our use of the term coordination is different: following Wegner, we define coordination as *constrained interaction* [43] between actors. Such interaction does not require shared spaces.

The software architecture community has worked on architecture description languages (ADLs) to simplify the development of complex systems. Examples of these languages include Wright [7], Rapide [30] and DCL [8]. In DCL, components and connectors to describe a software architecture can be specified. Components represent the functional level, while connectors are lower-level abstractions which define how an architecture is deployed in a particular execution environment.

Much research and development in industry has focused on open distributed systems; some examples include CORBA [33] and Java-related [18] efforts (e.g., see RMI [22], JavaSpaces [23], JINI [41], and concurrency patterns [28]). Java transforms a heterogeneous network of machines into a homogeneous network of Java virtual machines, while CORBA solves the problems of interactions between heterogeneous environments [2]. While the hierarchical model's concept of actor casts and directors can be implemented using CORBA for coordination of concurrent activities, the concept of messengers is only realizable with approaches such as Java's virtual machine [29] that allow actor behaviours to be safely sent and interpreted across heterogeneous machines.

3   A Hierarchical Model for Coordination

Coordination in the hierarchical model is accomplished by constraining the receipt of messages that are destined for particular actors. An actor can only receive a message when the coordination constraints for such message receipt are satisfied. The coordination constraints are checked for conformance at special actors named *directors*. The group of actors coordinated by a director is defined as a *cast*. *Messengers* are special migrating actors that represent a message from a remote cast.

3.1   Directors and casts

Although the director of a cast plays special roles – such as the "coordinator" of actors internal to the cast, an interface to other casts, a request broker for the service provided by the cast, and so forth – a director has no more "power" than other actors that are in the cast. That is, as far as the run-time system is concerned, a director is just another actor. It is also possible to have completely "uncoordinated" actors, i.e. actors which do not belong to a cast and which therefore have no external constraints on message receipt and processing.

An actor can have at most one director at a given point in time. However, a director may itself belong to a cast and thus be coordinated by another director. This strategy allows for dynamic reconfigurability of coordination constraints, as well as for modular constraint composition. The director-actor relationship forms a set of trees, named the *coordination forest*.

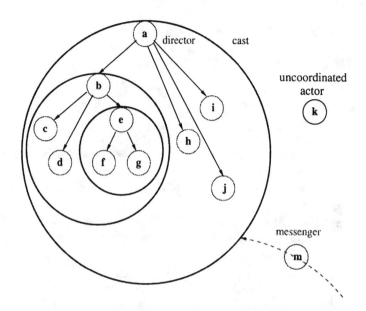

Fig. 2. Coordinated activity with *casts*, *directors* and *messengers*

A message from a **sender** actor is received by a **target** actor only after *approval* by all the directors in the target actor's coordination forest path up to the first common director, if such a director exists, and otherwise, approval is required of all directors in the **target**'s coordination forest path up to the top level.

Figure 2 shows a sample actor configuration. We illustrate valid message paths by describing a few examples based on this sample configuration:

- A message from any actor can go directly to actor a, or to actor k.
- A message from actor f to actor g has to go through their first common director, actor e.
- A message from c to f has to go through directors b and e. However a message from f to c only needs to be approved by b. This is because e is *not* in c's coordination forest path.
- A message from k to b,c,...j has to be approved by a.

3.2 Messengers

A *messenger* is a special actor which migrates with the purpose of carrying a message from a local cast to a remote cast. A messenger may also possibly contain other actor behaviours. For example, messengers may:

- provide more robust message delivery by persisting over temporary failures in the target actor
- attempt message return upon failure in message delivery
- follow mobile actors
- acknowledge message receipt or processing
- handle common exceptions at the target actor's site
- be in charge of networking and naming issues.

4 Semantics based on Actor Configurations

We extend the operational semantics formulated by Agha, Mason, Smith and Talcott [6] in this section to capture the concept of casts and directors. Specifically, we add a δ function which maps actors to directors, and we tag messages to show that they require approval. We also remove the restriction that actor behaviour (λ-abstractions) may not be communicated.

The following two subsections introduce the language used and the reduction rules that define valid transitions between actor configurations.

4.1 A Simple Lambda Based Actor Language

Our actor language is a simple extension of the call-by-value lambda calculus with four primitives for creating and manipulating actors:

newactor(e) creates a new uncoordinated actor with behaviour e and returns its name.

newdirectedactor(e) creates a new actor with behaviour e, directed by the creator, and returns its name.

send(v_0, v_1) creates a new message with receiver v_0 and contents v_1 and puts the message into the message delivery system.

ready(v) signals the end of the current computation and the ability for the actor to receive a new message, with behaviour v.

For more details on this basic actor language, we refer the reader to [6].

4.2 Operational Semantics for Coordinated Configurations

In this subsection, we give the semantics of actor expressions by defining a transition on coordinated open configurations.

We take as given countable sets At (atoms) and X (variables).

Definition (V E M):   The set of *values*, V, the set of *expressions*, E, and the set of *messages*, M, are defined inductively as follows:

$$V = At \cup X \cup \lambda X.E \cup pr(V, V)$$

$$E = V \cup app(E, E) \cup F_n(E^n) \qquad \text{where } F_n(E^n) \text{ is all arity-n primitives.}$$

$$M = <V \Leftarrow V>_X$$

We use variables for actor names. An actor can be either ready to accept a message, written $\text{ready}(v)$, where v is its behaviour, a lambda abstraction; or busy executing an expression, written e. A message from a source actor a targeted to an actor with name v_0, and contents v_1 is written $<v_0 \Leftarrow v_1>_a$.

Let $\mathbf{P}_\omega[X]$ be the set of finite subsets of X, $\mathbf{M}_\omega[M]$ be the set of (finite) multi-sets with elements in M, $X_0 \xrightarrow{t} X_1$ be the set of finite maps from X_0 to X_1, $\text{Dom}(f)$ be the domain of f and $\text{FV}(e)$ be the set of free variables in e. We define actor configurations as follows.

Definition (Actor Configurations (K)): An *actor configuration* with director map, δ, actor map, α, multi-set of messages, μ, receptionists, ρ, and external actors, χ, is written

$$\langle \delta \mid \alpha \mid \mu \rangle_\chi^\rho$$

where $\rho, \chi \in \mathbf{P}_\omega[X]$, $\delta \in X \xrightarrow{t} X$, $\alpha \in X \xrightarrow{t} E$, $\mu \in \mathbf{M}_\omega[M]$, and let $A = \text{Dom}(\alpha)$ and $D = \text{Dom}(\delta)$, then:

(0) $\rho \subseteq A$ and $A \cap \chi = \emptyset$,

(1) if $a \in A$, then $\text{FV}(\alpha(a)) \subseteq A \cup \chi$, and if $<v_0 \Leftarrow v_1>_a \in \mu$ then $\text{FV}(v_i) \subseteq A \cup \chi$ for $i < 2$.

(2) if $a \in D$, and $a_0 = \delta(a)$, $a_1 = \delta(a_0)$, $a_2 = \delta(a_1)$, ..., $a_n = \delta(a_{n-1})$, such that $a_n \notin D$, then $\forall i \in 0..n : (a_i \in A$ and $a_i \neq a)$.

The last rule restricts actor configurations so that (1) all directors in the coordination forest path for an actor belong to the same configuration, and (2) no cycles are allowed in the actor-director relationship.

Definition (Coordination Forest Paths (Δ)): The coordination forest path of an actor a, $\Delta(a)$, in a configuration κ with director map δ, is defined as:

$$\Delta(a) = \begin{cases} \{a\} & \text{if } a \notin \text{Dom}(\delta) \\ \{a\} \cup \Delta(\delta(a)) & \text{otherwise} \end{cases}$$

To describe the internal transitions between configurations other than message receipt, an expression is decomposed into a reduction context filled with a redex. For a formal definition of reduction contexts, expressions with a unique hole, we refer the reader to [6]. Suffice it to say here that R in the following definition, ranges over the set of reduction contexts. The purely functional redexes inherit the operational semantics from the purely functional fragment of our actor language. The actor redexes are: $\text{newactor}(e)$, $\text{newdirectedactor}(e)$, $\text{send}(v_0, v_1)$, and $\text{ready}(v)$.

Definition ($\mapsto$): The single-step transition relation $\mapsto$, on actor configurations is the least relation satisfying the following conditions: [1]

$\langle \mathbf{fun} : a \rangle$

$$e \xrightarrow{\lambda}_{\mathrm{Dom}(\alpha)\cup\{a\}} e' \Rightarrow \langle \delta \mid \alpha\{a \to e\} \mid \mu \rangle^\rho_\chi \mapsto \langle \delta \mid \alpha\{a \to e'\} \mid \mu \rangle^\rho_\chi$$

$\langle \mathbf{newactor} : a, a' \rangle$

$$\langle \delta \mid \alpha\{a \to R[\mathbf{newactor}(e)]\} \mid \mu \rangle^\rho_\chi \mapsto$$

$$\langle \delta \mid \alpha\{a \to R[a'], a' \to e\} \mid \mu \rangle^\rho_\chi \qquad a' \text{ fresh}$$

$\langle \mathbf{newdirectedactor} : a, a' \rangle$

$$\langle \delta \mid \alpha\{a \to R[\mathbf{newdirectedactor}(e)]\} \mid \mu \rangle^\rho_\chi \mapsto$$

$$\langle \delta\{a' \to a\} \mid \alpha\{a \to R[a'], a' \to e\} \mid \mu \rangle^\rho_\chi \qquad a' \text{ fresh}$$

$\langle \mathbf{send} : a, v_0, v_1 \rangle$

$$\langle \delta \mid \alpha\{a \to R[\mathbf{send}(v_0, v_1)]\} \mid \mu \rangle^\rho_\chi \mapsto$$

$$\langle \delta \mid \alpha\{a \to R[\mathbf{nil}]\} \mid \mu, {<}v_0 \Leftarrow v_1{>}_a \rangle^\rho_\chi$$

$\langle \mathbf{redirect} : a, v_0, v_1 \rangle$

$$\langle \delta \mid \alpha \mid \mu, {<}v_0 \Leftarrow v_1{>}_a \rangle^\rho_\chi \mapsto \langle \delta \mid \alpha \mid \mu, {<}\delta(v_0) \Leftarrow \mathbf{msg}(v_0, v_1){>}_a \rangle^\rho_\chi$$

$$\text{if } v_0 \in \mathrm{Dom}(\delta), \delta(v_0) \neq a, \text{ and } v_0 \notin \Delta(a)$$

$\langle \mathbf{receive} : v_0, v_1 \rangle$

$$\langle \delta \mid \alpha\{v_0 \to \mathbf{ready}(v)\} \mid {<}v_0 \Leftarrow v_1{>}_a, \mu \rangle^\rho_\chi \mapsto$$

$$\langle \delta \mid \alpha\{v_0 \to \mathbf{app}(v, v_1)\} \mid \mu \rangle^\rho_\chi$$

$$\text{if } v_0 \notin \mathrm{Dom}(\delta), \text{ or } \delta(v_0) = a, \text{ or } v_0 \in \Delta(a)$$

$\langle \mathbf{out} : v_0, v_1 \rangle$

$$\langle \delta \mid \alpha \mid \mu, {<}v_0 \Leftarrow v_1{>}_a \rangle^\rho_\chi \mapsto \langle \delta \mid \alpha \mid \mu \rangle^{\rho'}_\chi$$

$$\text{if } v_0 \in \chi, \text{ and } \rho' = \rho \cup (\mathrm{FV}(v_1) \cap \mathrm{Dom}(\alpha))$$

$\langle \mathbf{in} : v_0, v_1 \rangle$

$$\langle \delta \mid \alpha \mid \mu \rangle^\rho_\chi \mapsto \langle \delta \mid \alpha \mid \mu, {<}v_0 \Leftarrow v_1{>}_{a'} \rangle^\rho_{\chi \cup (\mathrm{FV}(v_1) - \mathrm{Dom}(\alpha))} \qquad a' \text{ fresh}$$

$$\text{if } v_0 \in \rho, \mathrm{FV}(v_1) \cap \mathrm{Dom}(\alpha) \subseteq \rho$$

The *redirect* and *receive* transition rules ensure that all directors up to the common ancestor between the sender and the target actors (or the highest di-

---

[1] For any function f, $f\{x \to x'\}$ is the function f' such that $\mathrm{Dom}(f') = \mathrm{Dom}(f)\cup \{x\}$, $f'(y)=f(y)$ for $y \neq x$, $y \in \mathrm{Dom}(f)$, and $f'(x)=x'$. $\mathbf{msg}(v_0, v_1)$ is a value expression representing a message with target v_0 and contents v_1.

rector in the target's coordination forest path) get notified and control when to actually send a message to a target actor. Notice the locality of information flow: if two actors belong to the same cast, outside actors and directors, even if in their coordination hierarchy, need not be notified/interrupted. For the configuration sample in Figure 2, a message from c to f, $<f \Leftarrow v>_c$, is redirected to e, $<e \Leftarrow msg(f, v)>_c$, and subsequently to b, $<b \Leftarrow msg(e, msg(f, v))>_c$. After checking coordination constraints, b and e send it to the final target f. Director a is not involved in such internal coordination.

The last two transitions account for the openness of actor configurations. The first transition, *out*, represents a message delivered to an external actor. The second transition, *in*, represents a message coming from an outside system to one of the configuration's receptionists. Notice that this message will be redirected to the root of the receptionist's coordination forest path.

5 Sample Applications

In this section, we illustrate our model by presenting some simple applications of our model: namely, three atomic multicast protocols and an application of messengers to improve locality in remote exception handling.

5.1 Atomic Multicast Protocols

By an atomic multicast protocol, we mean that the receipt of a message by different members of a cast is such that, to an outside actor, the operation can be viewed as a single step. In other words, no other messages are received by any of the actors in the cast until all members of the group have received the message.

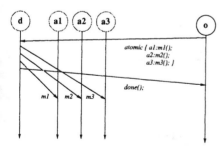

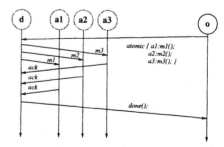

Fig. 3. Atomic multicast   **Fig. 4.** Acknowledged atomic multicast

Figure 3 shows the trace of one possible execution of atomic multicasting. Vertical lines represent local time (increasing in the downward direction) and diagonal lines represent message traversals between actors. Even though the messages are originally directed to actors a1..a3, these actors are in the same cast, and the cast's director can therefore send them atomically (without any inter-leaved messages) to the respective targets. Other messages sent at the same time to these actors are delayed until the atomic multicasting operation is finished. However, because the sending order may be different from the receiving order, this does not guarantee atomicity. A more robust implementation of atomic mul-ticasting is as follows. A director waits for acknowledgement of message receipt by the coordinated actors, before notifying the outside actor of "finalization", as shown in figure 4.

If we wanted to go further and implement *group knowledge* [12] (i.e. everybody in the cast knows that everybody in the cast got the message), we could use a two-phase atomic multicasting protocol. In the first phase, we send the message to every actor in the cast; and in the second phase, we tell every actor in the cast that everybody acknowledged message receipt. Figure 5 shows a sample trace.

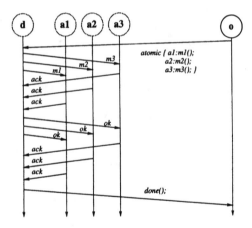

Fig. 5. Global knowledge atomic multicast

We have implemented these three atomic multicast protocols using the Actor Foundry 0.1.9 [34] for Solaris 2.5.1 with UDP plus a reliability transport protocol. Figure 6 shows the timing as measured from the outside actor, when all actors involved in the atomic multicast protocols resided in the same host. We used an empty message (no data) and we averaged the time taken over multiple executions. The results are as expected: time grows linearly with the number of actors, and the slope is doubled with reliability: it takes twice as many messages to do acknowledged atomic multicast than it takes to do basic atomic multicast, and it takes twice as many messages to do global knowledge atomic multicast than to do acknowledged atomic multicast.

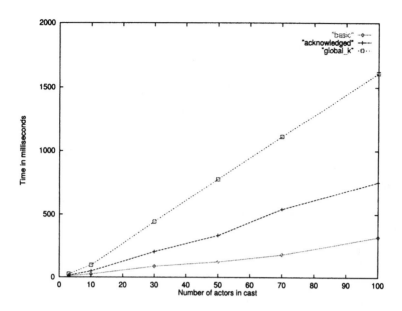

Fig. 6. Performance of different atomic multicast protocols (*in ms.*)

5.2 Remote Exception Handling with a Messenger

In our second example, we use a *messenger* to improve locality in exception handling across remotely located casts.

Suppose we have a sender actor that wants to send a letter to a recipient for processing. Furthermore, let's suppose that sender and recipient are in different hosts as shown in figure 7. If the recipient can't process the letter, an exception would be thrown from the recipient's host to the sender's host. After that, the sender may want to retry sending the letter at a later time.

We could improve locality using messengers by creating a new actor in host A and migrating it to host B with the specific behaviour of sending the original message and handling any associated exceptions that may arise remotely, as shown in figure 8.

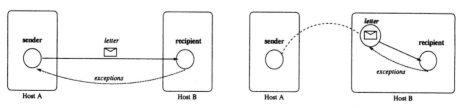

Fig. 7. Passive message across hosts   **Fig. 8.** Messenger across hosts

The algorithm for this example is given in Salsa, a language we're developing that extends Java to support actors and high-level coordination mechanisms. Salsa syntax is Java/C++-like with a few modifications to support actors [40]. In particular, a1:m1->a2:m2 represents sending an asynchronous message m1 to actor a1 with customer a2:m2, meaning that a1 should send another asynchronous message m2 to the acquaintance actor a2 after m1 is processed. The return value of m1 is passed as an argument to a2:m2.

The sender actor embodies the main program. It creates a recipient and a letter and sends the letter with three different exception handling protocols. The first one sends a passive message and ignores failures in the target actor. The second and third invocations use a messenger to handle exceptions at the target host appropriately (with methods retry and failed respectively). The sender also provides a method log in case the messenger ultimately fails to deliver the letter.

```
behaviour Sender {
  Letter letter;
  Recipient recipient;
  public void main(){
    /** Create letter messenger and recipient actor */
    letter = new Letter(self);
    recipient = new Recipient();
    /** Send a letter to a recipient, with possible failure */
    recipient:process(letter);
    /** Send a letter messenger that retries until successful */
    recipient:process(letter) -> letter:retry;
    /** Send a letter messenger with special exception handling */
    recipient:process(letter) -> letter:failed;
  }
  public void log(Recipient recipient){
    System.err:println(recipient + "failed processing the letter." );
  }
}
```

The recipient is an actor that provides a method to process a letter. Once a letter has been processed, it returns null. If the letter needs to be delegated to a third actor, such actor address is returned. If the actor can't temporarily process the letter, the method returns its own address for processing at a later time.

The letter messenger can either:

- retry forever until the letter is successfully processed, or
- retry once after one second and upon a new failure, send an exception message to the original sender to log an error.

```
behaviour Letter extends Messenger {
  Sender sender;
  /** Letter constructor */
  Letter(Sender s){
    sender = s;
  }
  /** Retries sending the letter until successfully processed */
  public void retry(Recipient recipient){
      if (recipient != null)
        recipient:process(self) -> self:retry;
  }
  /** Try once again after a second, else log an error */
  public void failed(Recipient recipient){
      if (recipient != null){
        System.wait(1000);
        recipient:process(self) -> self:failedTwice;
      }
  }
  /** Tell the sender of the letter that it couldn't be processed */
  public void failedTwice(Recipient recipient){
      if (recipient != null)
        sender:log(recipient);
  }
}
```

Notice that by reifying the passive letter into an actor, we're able to handle exceptions much more efficiently at the target actor's remote host.

6 Discussion

Traditional models for coordination of actors require the run-time system to support reflective capabilities in order to constrain certain types of messages from reaching their targets. A typical scenario is that of meta-level actors that are able to intercept message sending, receipt and processing for base-level actors.

The hierarchical model is less demanding of the run-time system in the sense that no special actor architecture is required for coordination of activities. Instead, actors are explicitly grouped in casts, which are in turn, coordinated by directors. These directors do not have more computational or communication capabilities than their coordinated counterparts. However, the model of communication ensures that directors are able to synchronize activities within their respective casts. Inter-cast communication can be performed with traditional asynchronous passive messages, or by using messengers.

A hierarchical structure of coordination may suggest possible bottlenecks at root directors in the coordination forest. However, because communications inside casts need not be coordinated by outside directors, the hierarchical model can be implemented efficiently. For directors above the common ancestor of two communicating actors, communications are internal transitions that need not interrupt outside actors.

Moreover, it is still possible to have actors that do not belong to any casts – such actors incur no unnecessary synchronization overhead at run-time. One strategy for avoiding potential bottlenecks – similar to the current one of replicating Internet domain name servers – is to co-locate directors on multiple nodes. This strategy would provide for limited cast state recovery in the case of failures in the cast's director.

Although the hierarchical model of actor coordination does not provide the sort of transparency and flexibility that reflective models can enable [24, 32, 38, 42, 44], we conjecture that despite its simplicity, it is powerful enough for many applications. The claims in this paper are tentative – further research on techniques for specifying and implementing the linguistic constructs in the hierarchical model is needed. We are currently also exploring the model's applicability to the problem of developing worldwide open distributed systems.

Acknowledgements

We'd like to thank past and present members of the Open Systems Laboratory who aided in this research. In particular, we'd like to express our gratitude to Mark Astley for developing the Actor Foundry and James Waldby for all those *yume* scripts. Thanks also to Reza Ziaei, Prassanna Thati and Nadeem Jamali for useful comments and discussions about this work. Last but not least, we'd like to thank Les Gasser and the anonymous referees for their comments.

References

[1] G. Agha. *Actors: A Model of Concurrent Computation in Distributed Systems*. MIT Press, 1986.

[2] G. Agha, M. Astley, J. Sheikh, and C. Varela. Modular heterogeneous system development: A critical analysis of java. In J. Antonio, editor, *Proceedings of the Seventh Heterogeneous Computing Workshop (HCW '98)*, pages 144–155. IEEE Computer Society, March 1998. http://osl.cs.uiuc.edu/Papers/HCW98.ps.

[3] G. Agha, S. Frølund, W. Kim, R. Panwar, A. Patterson, and D. Sturman. Abstraction and modularity mechanisms for concurrent computing. *IEEE Parallel and Distributed Technology*, May 1993.

[4] G. Agha, S. Frølund, R. Panwar, and D. Sturman. A linguistic framework for dynamic composition of dependability protocols. In *Dependable Computing for Critical Applications III*, pages 345–363. International Federation of Information Processing Societies (IFIP), Elsevier Scienc Publisher, 1993.

[5] G. Agha and N. Jamali. Concurrent programming for distributed artificial intelligence. In G. Weiss, editor, *Multiagent Systems: A Modern Approach to DAI*. MIT Press, 1999. To appear.

[6] G. Agha, I. A. Mason, S. F. Smith, and C. L. Talcott. A foundation for actor computation. *Journal of Functional Programming*, 7:1–72, 1997.

[7] R. Allen and D. Garlan. Formalizing architectural connection. In *International Conference on Software Enginnering*, pages 71–80. IEEE Computer Society, 1994.

[8] M. Astley and G. A. Agha. Customization and composition of distributed objects: Middleware abstractions for policy management. In *Sixth International Symposium on the Foundations of Software Engineering (FSE-6, SIGSOFT '98)*, November 1998.

[9] C. Callsen and G. Agha. Open Heterogeneous Computing in ActorSpace. *Journal of Parallel and Distributed Computing*, pages 289–300, 1994.

[10] N. Carriero and D. Gelernter. *How to Write Parallel Programs*. MIT Press, 1990.

[11] P. Ciancarini and C. Hankin, editors. *First International Conference on Coordination Languages and Models (COORDINATION '96)*, number 1061 in LNCS, Berlin, 1996. Springer-Verlag.

[12] R. Fagin, J. Halpern, Y. Moses, and M. Vardi. *Reasoning about Knowledge*. MIT Press, 1995.

[13] J. Ferber and J. Briot. Design of a concurrent language for distributed artificial intelligence. In *Proceedings of the International Conference on Fifth Generation Computer Systems*, volume 2, pages 755–762. Institute for New Generation Computer Technology, 1988.

[14] S. Frølund. *Coordinating Distributed Objects: An Actor-Based Approach to Synchronization*. MIT Press, 1996.

[15] S. Frølund and G. Agha. A language framework for multi-object coordination. In *Proceedings of ECOOP 1993*. Springer Verlag, 1993. LNCS 707.

[16] M. Fukuda, L. F. Bic, M. B. Dillencourt, and F. Merchant. Intra- and inter-object coordination with messengers. In Ciancarini and Hankin [11].

[17] D. Garlan and D. Le Metayer, editors. *Second International Conference on Coordination Languages and Models (COORDINATION '97)*, number 1282 in LNCS, Berlin, 1997. Springer-Verlag.

[18] J. Gosling, B. Joy, and G. Steele. *The Java Language Specification*. Addison Wesley, 1996.

[19] C. Hewitt. Viewing control structures as patterns of passing messages. *Journal of Artificial Intelligence*, 8-3:323–364, June 1977.

[20] S. Jagannathan. Customization of first-class tuple spaces in a higher-order language. In E.H.L. Arts, J. van Leeuwen, and M. Rem, editors, *PARLE '91, volume 2*, number 506 in LNCS. Springer-Verlag, 1991.

[21] S. Jagannathan. Communication-passing style for coordinated languages. In Garlan and Metayer [17], pages 131–149.

[22] JavaSoft. Remote Method Invocation Specification, 1996. Work in progress. http://www.javasoft.com/products/jdk/rmi/.

[23] JavaSoft. JavaSpaces, 1998. Work in progress. http://www.javasoft.com/products/javaspaces/.

[24] G. Kiczales, J. des Riviéres, and D. G. Bobrow. *The Art of the Metaobject Protocol*. MIT Press, 1991.

[25] T. Kielmann. Designing a coordination model for open systems. In Ciancarini and Hankin [11], pages 267–284.

[26] W. Kim and G. Agha. Efficient Support of Location Transparency in Concurrent Object-Oriented Programming Languages. In *Proceedings of Supercomputing'95*, 1995.

[27] W. A. Kornfeld and C. Hewitt. The scientific community metaphor. *IEEE Transactions on Systems, Man, and Cybernetics*, SMC-11(1), January 1981.

[28] D. Lea. *Concurrent Programming in Java: Design Principles and Patterns*. Addison Wesley, 1997.

[29] T. Lindholm and F. Yellin. *The Java Virtual Machine Specification*. Addison Wesley, 1997.

[30] D. C. Luckham, J. J. Kenney, L. M. Augustin, J. Vera, D. Bryan, and W. Mann. Specification and analysis of system architecture using rapide. *IEEE Transactions on Software Engineering*, 21(4):336–355, 1995. Special Issue on Software Architecture.

[31] S. Matsuoka and S. Kawai. Using tuple space communication in distributed object-oriented languages. In *ACM Conference Proceedings, Object Oriented Programming Languages, Systems and Applications*, pages 276–284, San Diego, CA, 1988.

[32] S. Matsuoka, T. Watanabe, and A. Yonezawa. Hybrid group reflective architecture for object-oriented concurrent reflective programming. In *Proceedings of the European Conference on Object-Oriented Programming*, number 512 in LNCS, pages 231–250, 1991.

[33] Object Management Group. CORBA services: Common object services specification version 2. Technical report, Object Management Group, June 1997. http://www.omg.org/corba/.

[34] Open Systems Lab. The Actor Foundry: A Java-based Actor Programming Environment. Work in Progress. http://osl.cs.uiuc.edu/foundry/.

[35] R. Panwar and G. Agha. A methodology for programming scalable architectures. *Journal of Parallel and Distributed Computing*, 22(3):479–487, September 1994.

[36] S. Ren, G. A. Agha, and M. Saito. A modular approach for programming distributed real-time systems. *Journal of Parallel and Distributed Computing*, 36:4–12, 1996.

[37] H. A. Simon. *The Sciences of the Artificial*, chapter The Architecture of Complexity: Hierarchic Systems. MIT Press, 3rd edition, 1996.

[38] D. C. Sturman and G. Agha. A protocol description language for customizing failure semantics. In *Proceedings of the 13th Symposium on Reliable Distributed Systems*. IEEE Computer Society Press, October 1994.

[39] C. Tomlinson, P. Cannata, G. Meredith, and D. Woelk. The extensible services switch in carnot. *IEEE Parallel and Distributed Technology*, 1(2):16–20, May 1993.

[40] C. Varela and G. Agha. What after Java? From Objects to Actors. *Computer Networks and ISDN Systems: The International J. of Computer Telecommunications and Networking*, 30:573–577, Apr 1998. http://osl.cs.uiuc.edu/Papers/www7/.

[41] J. Waldo. JINI Architecture Overview, 1998. Work in progress. http://www.javasoft.com/products/jini/.

[42] T. Watanabe and A. Yonezawa. An actor-based meta-level architecture for group-wide reflection. In J. W. deBakker, W.P. deRoever, and G. Rozenberg, editors, *Foundations of Object-Oriented Languages*, number 489 in LNCS, pages 405–425. Springer-Verlag, 1990.

[43] P. Wegner. Coordination as constrained interaction. In Ciancarini and Hankin [11], pages 28–33.

[44] A. Yonezawa, editor. *ABCL An Object-Oriented Concurrent System*. MIT Press, Cambridge, Mass., 1990.

A Self–Deploying Election Service for Active Networks*

Christian F. Tschudin

Department of Computer Systems, Uppsala University

Abstract. Active networking aims at minimizing the functionality that is built into a data network: Programmable nodes inside the network enable the deployment of new services at run–time. In a bottom–up approach we presume a network void from any functionality and study the problem of deploying and providing a basic, externally defined and non–trivial distributed service. As a test case we use the robust election of a coordinator. Based on the bully algorithm, we implemented an election service that is fully based on active packets. It deploys itself to every reachable active network segment, continuously scans for newly attached nodes and networks and provides a segment wide election service for all attached nodes. The implementation was carried out in the M0 messenger environment and tested in a worldwide active networks testbed. The complete and self–contained initial 'election service germ' fits in less than 1'200 Bytes and asserts the ubiquitous presence of this service.

Keywords: Active networks, self–deploying service, election protocol, network bootstrap, messengers.

1 Introduction

An active network consists of interconnected nodes which exchange mobile code packets. These packets are executed on arrival, leading to either other "active packets" being sent out and/or some data being stored or modified on the node itself. Based on this minimal functionality, arbitrary new services can be put into operation by sending out active packets that will install service routines on each node. No network-wide services need to be offered by an active network except the submission of active packets to direct neighbor nodes.

In "strong" active networking, every data packet is replaced by a program. "Weakly" active networking also seeks the flexibility offered by mobile code, but adopts a hybrid approach where the network's behavior is modified without replacing the highly optimized lower level protocols. Both, weak and strong active networking is now captured by the more general term of *programmable networks*, which also includes active signaling and extensible proxies.

In this paper we examine the problem of realizing the election of a coordinator in an strongly active network context. Our first goal is to show an election algorithm that works with active packets alone. Secondly, we demonstrate how a node's *local*

---

* Part of this work was done while at the Computer Science Department of the University of Zurich, Switzerland.

coordination primitives can be used to realize a *distributed* coordination service that spans several nodes. Third, we want this mobile code based service to deploy itself, showing robustness in the way it is able to re-elect a new coordinator after a crash, and the adaptability to extend itself as soon as new nodes attach to the network.

The following section describes the elements of an active network in more detail as well as the profile of services that deploy themselves. In section 3 we review Garcia-Molina's classic bully election algorithms and present a simplified version that is better suited for the best-effort nature of active networks. Section 4 describes the implementation of the self-deploying election service. A discussion of this approach and related work is presented in Section 5 before we conclude with Section 6.

2   Active Network Segments and Self-Deploying Services

For the election service to be discussed below, but also in our active network testbed, we use a *network segment* abstraction that resembles an ethernet broadcast network. A segment subsumes point-to-point links in order to provide a uniform network environment: In this case a network will only have two nodes. Active nodes are attached to one or more network segments, leading to a *network of network segments* very similar to the Internet architecture. The main characteristics of the network segment abstraction are:

- unreliable datagram transmission,
- unicast and broadcast transmission,
- simple overlay to "real" networking technologies,
- technology independent addressing format.

Nodes have a *network interface* for each network they are connected to as well as a unicast address for this interface. A special multicast address is defined in order to reach neighbors without having to know their unicast address. Active packets that execute on a node must be able to learn about a node's interfaces as well as the corresponding unicast addresses.

The broadcast facility is an essential and powerful element of the network segment abstraction because it allows the programmer of active packets to discover a network's topology without further support from the active nodes. For this, one has to broadcast a discovery packet into a segment which will execute on all attached nodes. Each executing discovery packet will send back a message, allowing the initial sender to learn the identities and addresses of the reachable neighbors. Doing this recursively by looping over a node's list of interfaces, one can also discover the topology of the full net of segments. Here, the active nodes' persistent storage area is essential in order to leave traces at nodes that have already been visited, otherwise the flooding would never stop.

2.1   A Service Architecture for Active Networks

A service architecture for active networks should be "open" i.e., it should enable the introduction of arbitrary services. The role of an active network node then is to provide the necessary primitives such that new services can be announced and their service access points be published. We assume that the nodes' persistent storage area is used for this.

Because we aim at minimizing built-in network functionality, we do not want the service publication functionality to span beyond a single node. Thus, unlike a tuple space that tries to hide the distributedness of the places where data items can be put into or retrieved from it, we presume that a purely local shared memory abstraction is offered by each node. This provides the basic coordination mechanism on top of which more complex (i.e., distributed) services can be implemented.

One way of introducing a distributed tuple space in this environment is to have active packets announce the tuple space's existence on remote nodes. The announcement consists of a service description that lets potential clients find the service among competing offerings, as well as its methods to invoke the service's primitives. Internal to these methods, active packets are used to do all coordination work with remote nodes as well as accessing the local data structures.

The service architecture for active networks is intrinsically "flat" where all services, regardless of whether they are related to networking (the topology discovery example above), middle-ware (tuple space example) or applications, live in the same space: Active nodes provide a basic, local coordination through the access to the node's persistent storage area, as well as the possibility to send active packets to neighboring nodes. Services also compete against each other i.e., the active network does not provide "the" standard tuple space, but allows for several concurrent implementations to offer the same service.

Linked to this architecture is an economic framework that is essential for an open service environment to work. Resource consumption is monitored and charged to the active packets. The service instances to which the packets belong will have to recover these costs by selling their service. This leads to value chains very much like in the real economy and creates the pressure to minimize consumption of network resources. Competition will eliminate inefficient services and enables to recycle the allocated resources for new usages.

2.2 Self-deploying Services in Active Networks

Active services need not to be manually installed. Instead, they can deploy themselves to potentially all reachable nodes. Our interest is in services that keep control over their own distribution.

Clearly, manually installed services depend on a human operator to configure them and to make sure they are restarted after a computer has shut down. Similarly, active network protocols that are deployed together with an active application (e.g., receiver driven multicasting), lead to dependent services that by design stop as soon as the application does not need their services anymore. In our service architectures, however, we want the elements of the value chain to be as autonomous as possible. Their operation should only dependent on the availability of network resources and the demand for a service. Services for active networks should not have any anchors anymore into specific nodes (network control center) or user applications.

The picture we are using to characterize such services is that of a gas: It can reach into every corner of an active network and make its services available everywhere. Furthermore, it is very hard to eradicate. Active packets differ from molecules in the sense that they can be pro-active. For example, a service can retract from nodes where demand is not sufficient or where competition for resources is too high. A service can also do the opposite if designed to do so i.e., staying at a node with no demand or with scarce resources, although this may require a service-internal mechanism to import the necessary funds. The gas metaphor nicely express the parallelism of (active) network services: Similar to a mix of gases they work in parallel.

A less desired analogy is that gases can form explosive combinations – in the real world of networks we would probably link this to the "feature interaction problem". However, this just expresses the basic hypothesis (and one of the main research topics) of active networking in another way, which is the problem of breaking down programmability barriers without loosing the isolation properties of closed systems.

In the rest of this paper we present such a distributed gas-like service: It combines global self-deployment functionality with a service that is restricted to a local network segment.

3 Election Services

Many algorithms in distributed systems need the service of a coordinator (also called a leader): Mutual exclusion, deadlock detection, replacement of lost tokens are examples for such services. Inside computer networks, the presence of a coordinator is implicitly or explicitly also assumed. Examples are the maintenance of routing tables (default gateway), a directory services (location of the name server) or the coordination of replicated data structures (WEB caches). Instead of manually assigning the node where some coordinator functionality should be placed, we look at a self–configuring system where this node is dynamically determined. The first problem is to choose (elect) a node from equally well suited candidates. The second problem is to assert that a replacement node is found should the coordinator node crash (re-election). The third problem finally is to install the service in all nodes of a network.

In a first part we briefly describe the "bully" election protocol for distributed systems. The adaption of the bully algorithm to the active networks setting and the integration with the (self-)deployment protocol are discussed in sections 3.2 and 3.3, respectively.

3.1 The Bully Election Algorithm

In the following we concentrate on the first (and simpler) version of the two election algorithms that Garcia-Molina presented in [6]. We assume an already configured system where the current leader periodically checks all other nodes. This is done by doing a remote procedure call (RPC) and fetching the remote nodes' state which can be either "normal", "election" or "reorg": Usually, all nodes are in "normal" state.

If the current leader node crashes, some of the subordinate nodes will suspect a failure and will start to elect a new leader. First, they ask around whether there are nodes up and running that have a higher node-identifier than they have themselves. Each node that discovers such a higher-node-identifier neighbor retracts from the race.

The "bulliest" node, however, starts a two-phase-commit protocol (2PC) to assert that all nodes end up with knowing the same new leader.

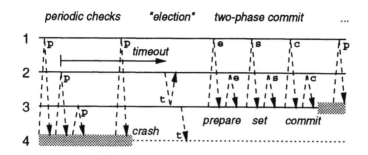

Fig. 1. A trace of Garcia–Molina's election protocol. Node 4 crashes, nodes 2 and 3 find out, node 3 starts a two-phase-commit protocol.

Figure 1 shows the trace of a node crash and reelection in form of a time sequence diagram. Note that all communications between nodes are carried out with remote procedure calls. The following list gives an overview of the RPCs used. We will come back to this list when comparing the active packet types that travel forth and back between the active network nodes. More specifically, we will relate the active packet types to *parts* of these RPCs i.e., either the request or reply message thereof.

p - **Are you normal?** periodically called by the coordinator to signal its presence and to verify the remote node's state.

t - **Are you there?** called in order to find out about (test) the status of a remote node.

e - **Election** called by a potential coordinator to stop a subordinate and to start an election phase (reorganization).

s - **Set new coordinator** called by a potential coordinator to announce the new regime.

c - **Commit** called by the new coordinator to restart the subordinates.

The bully election algorithm handles node failures that occur during an election or reorganization phase by restarting the commit protocol until it succeeds. Note that for a good runtime behavior of Garcia–Molina's protocol we need the timeout values to be randomized or to be dependent on a node's priority. This avoids that all subordinates discover at the same time that the coordinator is not responding anymore.

3.2 A Best-Effort Election Algorithm

Using RPC is convenient if the underlying network software provides such a RPC service, as it detects whether or not a remote node is reachable (if not, the RPC fails). Using RPC in an "empty" active networks context, however, complicates the implementation because of the additional state to maintain (e.g., implementing reliable communications with a datagram network). Also, RPCs can not easily benefit from the available broadcast primitives that we presume. Thus, a first goal is to replace RPC by lower level communication primitives.

Our second goal is to get rid of the two-phase commit protocol which may delay the decision taking for arbitrary long times. Note that the 2PC protocol described above is not sufficient for guaranteeing in all circumstances a correct reply to inquiries about the current coordinator. The underlying reason is the problem of network partitioning, which is why a second, more complicated protocol version was introduced in [6] that uses "process groups". In the context of low-level services that have to deal with network outages and crashed nodes anyway, we think that this degree of perfection is not always required. We therefore relax the service quality and allow that in special circumstance there may be more than one elected coordinator in a set of nodes, but that this conflict will quickly be resolved.

The Light-Weight Election Protocol (LEP) for Active Packets. In the normal state of the light weight election protocol, the coordinator knows all subordinate nodes. A broadcast is used to inform these nodes about the full list of currently reachable nodes. This active update (u) packet prevents that a node timeouts and starts to look around for a new coordinator.

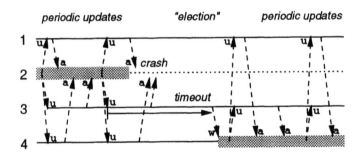

Fig. 2. A trace of the light-weight election protocol: Node 2 crashes, node 3 finds out, node 4 declares itself new leader.

Subordinate nodes have to periodically send alive (a) packets to the coordinator (see the example trace of Figure 2). These packets refresh a "last_visited" entry in the coordinators's data structures. The coordinator can detect nodes that have stopped working by browsing through these values. They are removed from the list (soft-state mechanism) and the new list is sent with the next update broadcast.

In case the coordinator crashes, one or more subordinate nodes will timeout. Because a subordinate can not be sure whether neighbors with higher identifiers also crashed, it sends them a wakeup (w) message. If after a next timeout it still did not receive an update message, it declare itself a coordinator and starts broadcasting update packets.

The update active packet checks the coordinator field of the node it arrived at in order to see whether this node already declared itself a coordinator and whether its identifier is bigger than the one from where the packet came from. If this is the case, it means that there is a more legitimate coordinator around. The update packet then does nothing and relies on the "bullier" coordinator to overwrite the field 'back home'. Otherwise, it overwrites the coordinator field with the new identifier.

The following list summarizes the packet types for the lightweight election protocol:

u - **Update** periodically sent to announce the current coordinator and the list of subordinate nodes. This active packet may overwrite the coordinator variable at the destination node.

w - **Wakeup** sent to other subordinates with higher node id by nodes that suspect that the leader crashed.

a - **Alive** sent by the subordinate nodes in order to refresh (keep-alive) their entry in the coordinator's data structures.

When relating the update, alive and wakeup messages of the LEP to the original bully algorithm, we see that the "are your normal?" RPC corresponds to the update and alive messages. The difference is that we only have a single update (broadcast) message instead of several RPC request messages, and that the alive messages are sent in an asynchronous way instead of the synchronous RPC. The "election" and "commit" RPCs have no equivalent because of the best-effort nature of the LEP. Finally, the "set new coordinator" RPC is covered by the update active packet that may overwrite the destination node's coordinator variable.

Note that the LEP does not impose that the bulliest node always takes over the leader role. In the example of Figure 2 we would presume that nodes 3 and 4 joined the running system *after* node 2 installed itself as coordinator: The coordinator variable of the nodes 3 and 4 would have been set by the first update packet they received. We think that keeping a coordinator in place as long as it does a good job reduces the volatility of the system.

A node that is not coordinator but has the highest identifier in the segment will win a future election should the current coordinator node fail. Usually this happens immediately after a coordinator crash. The following scenario explains why other nodes may "win" the election at the same time and how this is resolved. Consider the case where node 4 arrived into the system just before the crash and that node 3 did not have a chance to learn about the new node. Node 3 would optimistically declare itself new leader, concurrently with node 4. Both would send out update broadcasts. If node 3's broadcast was first, it would "convince" node 1 but fail with node 4. The subsequent broadcast of node 4 will eventually overwrite the coordinator variables in the nodes 1 and 3. Similar cases can be made for lost broadcast packets.

Network partitioning will be treated by the same recovery mechanism i.e., reelection. The network component that is left without coordinator will quickly determine a new one, the other component continues to function with the elected coordinator, the absence of alive packets will drain the coordinator's data structures from nodes that became unreachable. Re-merging of network components will lead to multiple leaders for a short time. The leader with the higher identifier will eventually succeed to overwrite all coordinator variables with its periodic update broadcasts.

3.3 Deployment Protocol

The deployment protocol determines the method by which currently unserved network segments are discovered by the LEP. It also specifies how the light-weight election service installs itself. The interesting part of this is how the code deployment functionality is integrated into the LEP.

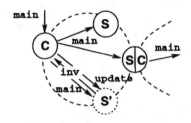

Fig. 3. Deploying the election service: The broadcast and the and on-demand unicast method (main and invite packets).

The LEP service deploys itself by flooding an active network with a main active packet (see figure 3). This active packet contains the complete LEP logic and will be the source of all other LEP packet types introduced above. If a main packet arrives at a node where the LEP service is not already installed, the main packet declares itself coordinator (C) for this segment. Immediately after the initialization on this first node, it broadcasts another main packet in order to reach all neighbors if this segment: The initialization code starts the neighbors in subordinate (S) mode. If a node is also attached to another segment and had no LEP service yet, we install a coordinator for this annex segment from where the flooding continues, but on the other hand still function as a subordinate towards the old segment.

Special attention is needed for nodes that join a segment *after* the LEP service installed itself. They have to be discovered and the LEP service has to extend its reach towards these nodes too. This task is covered by the update packets that are regularly broadcast during the normal LEP operations. If an update packet reaches an uninitialized node, it immediately returns an invite packet that triggers a unicast submission of a main packet towards this newly discovered node (Figure 3).

The flooding of segments eventually terminates as soon as a main active packet encounters a node that already has the LEP service installed: The main packet silently stops execution and does not propagate farther. The presence of the LEP service can be detected by the presence of a trace (footprint) inside the node's common storage area. Potential clients of the LEP service locate the service interface indirectly through a service description that is also put into the storage area. (The reason for this separation is to hide the service's vital internal data structures from malicious clients.)

The overhead of deployment is minimal. No main messenger will be broadcast in segments that already have the LEP service installed. A main messenger that reaches such a segment will immediately stop at the first border node. Nodes that join a network segment *after* service installation will be discovered by the periodic update messengers (which will use the "invite" mechanism to request a main unicast). The initial deployment is a simple wavefront diffusion: It's speed is only limited by propagation delays and code execution latency. Thus, service deployment is in any practical sense "instantaneous" if there are no artificial delays programmed into the deployment code.

4 An Implementation

We successfully implemented the light-weight election protocol (LEP) for active networks in the M0 environment [10]. M0 is a PostScript-like language with a very compact syntax. Active packets are called *messengers* in M0. Each received messenger becomes an independent execution thread that can create new messenger packets and can send them to neighboring M0 nodes. The node's storage area as well as information on the node's interfaces are represented as PostScript *dictionaries*. Some of these dictionaries are writable so messengers can deposit data that will remain there even if the thread terminates. Together with a simple thread synchronization mechanism, these local dictionaries form the only coordination mechanism available to messengers.

The M0 nodes are interconnected via the ANON protocol layer that runs on top of UDP [11]. Each node has its own 128-bits unicast ANON address, a special ANON address is defined for M0 broadcasts. For the deployment experiment we used a configuration of 5 ANON segments with nodes in Japan, the US and Europe (see figure 4).

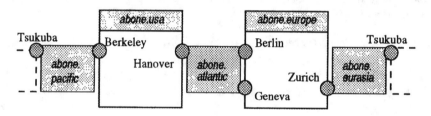

Fig. 4. The network segments of the ANON based "ABONE" as of August 1998.

By carefully choosing short names for variables and procedures, we arrived at a total size of 1168 Bytes for the `main` messenger (this size includes the M0 header but not the "Active Network Encapsulation Protocol" prefix [1] that accounts for an additional 40 to 50 Bytes in the case of ANON).

The `main` messenger contains the full functionality for deployment *and* the LEP service. Furthermore, it implements a code caching scheme in order to reduce the size of the LEP packets that are sent on a repeated basis. Table 1 shows the size of the different messenger types. Note that the size of the `update` sub–messengers depends on the number of reachable nodes in a network segment: Each node accounts for an additional 24 Bytes (16 Bytes for the node's ANON address plus 8 Bytes for the node identifier).

Code Caching Protocol. The `main` messenger installs an instance of the LEP service on each node where no election service is found. This consists of creating the necessary data structures and also includes the definition of subroutines. The goal of this is to download and cache a maximum of code. The subsequent LEP messengers can access these subroutines simply by referring to their names. Thus, sub–messengers mimic simple protocol data units by traveling to a remote host and executing a pre–defined and

Messenger type	Size (Bytes)
main (the "germ")	1168
- update (u)	$88 + n * 24$
- I'm alive (a)	36
- invite	24
- wakeup (w)	24

Table 1. Size of messengers exchanged during LEP operations (n is the number of nodes in the segment).

pre-installed subroutine. This reduces the size of the sub-messengers and at the same time speeds up their execution as the parsing overhead is considerably smaller.

Service Interface. In addition to the data structures and code cache, the main messenger also installs a public service interface and publishes the new service in a special service dictionary. The API essentially consists of the following two procedures:

Get list of neighbors: Procedure that returns a list of <id, network address> pairs of reachable neighbors.

Get current coordinator: Procedure that returns the id of the current coordinator. The network address of the coordinator can be retrieved by looking up the id in the list returned by the first method.

The implementation of these procedures is trivial as they just copy information that is part of the LEP state on this node. This is true for a node in subordinate mode as well as for the coordinator node itself.

Limitations. Several aspects of a robust distributed service were not fully implemented. For example, a problem that can also be found in many other active network environments is the explicit handling of the maximum transfer unit (MTU) offered by the underlying datagram service. First, the current main messenger will not work in networks with a MTU smaller than 1200 Byte because it would be truncated: One would have to add self-fragmentation capabilities to the main messenger (which is not a major problem in M0). Second, the update messenger will be truncated if there are too many nodes in a segment (for example, the limit for an ethernet MTU will be around 60 nodes, for UDP this limit is at 2700 nodes). The solution here is to split the large table and to send several update messengers instead of one. This is also the approach used for the Internet Routing Information Protocol that has to cope with the same problem.

Another incompleteness is the simplified treatment of resource charging in M0. Messengers are supposed to bring their own funds with them which allows them to pay for the consumed node and transmission resources. We did not need to implement this aspect because in our lightly charged testbed the LEP messengers can survive with the default "start money" they receive on reception. In a highly competitive environment, however, they would quickly run out of money. The right way to handle with this issue is to change the API and to request a service fee for each service invocation, enabling the LEP messengers to recover their expenses.

Finally we mention the vulnerability to several malicious attacks. Currently there is no support for clients to identify the service instance they trust. In order to prevent impostors from publishing identically looking service descriptions, we would have to add discriminating information to the service description as well as a cryptographic protocol that allows verification of this data. Another attack is possible if an eavesdropper watches the "footprint" information exchanged at the wire level. Although this data is not accessible to other messengers, a malicious platform could easily grab that information and use it to eradicate the whole distributed service by flooding the net with service specific "killer packets".

5 Discussion

A quite general question about the proposed gas-like service cloud is the problem of steering. As a concrete example consider the problem of terminating such a service after its creator discovers a serious bug. Because the service consists of thousands or millions of small active packets, a central control technique will not work. Moreover, coordinating the reliable termination of a self-deploying distributed service in an unreliable environment is hard because of the danger of network partitioning: If only a single packet is missed and the network regains connectivity just after the cleansing action, the service will instantly re-deploy. A timeout mechanism i.e., letting the LEP service terminate if it did not receive a keep-alive message from some control center, is problematic in case of network partitioning: The network component "on the wrong side of the partitioning" would quickly find itself without election service.

In our implementation we used a second self-deploying service to chase down all service footprints and to disable the LEP service. In order to solve the secondary problem of terminating this self-deploying termination service, we made the termination service persist for a limited amount of time before self-destructing. We consider this to be a temporary solution to the termination problem that will not be satisfactory in the long run as we hope to find security mechanisms that will make such service killings impossible (see the discussion in the limitations section above). More on this topic can be found in [12].

The most viable approach, as we think, is to use an economic framework for answering the termination question. This means that a self-deploying service should *not* be terminable by explicit actions. The main criteria for survival should be whether sufficient clients are around that accept to pay for the service or not and whether the service can make a living with that. Bogus services thus should be phased out by telling the clients about the better version. This is exactly the model used in software distribution today, where for example it is not possible to retract all versions of a WEB browser because of a newly discovered security bug.

5.1 Related Work

Probably the two oldest and at the same time most famous large scale self-deploying "services" are the CHRISTMAS program propagated through e-mail in 1987 and Morris' Internet worm in 1988 [13]. Active networks clearly use the same propagation principle but want to harness the power of network-wide replication.

A notable difference of our approach compared to other active network environments is that we deliberately have no per-packet resource limitations. ANTS [14], for example, uses a time-to-live field that is decremented at every hop – once the packet's counter reaches zero, it is discarded. This mechanism cannot implement a self-deploying service of the sort we presented in this paper, because after a finite number of steps, all packets and its descendents will have been removed.

The "Liquid Software" project [8] also relies on mobile code for dynamically loading service components over the network: It has a nice metaphor that is close to the gas analogy used in this paper.

Several papers have been published last year that discuss the use of mobile agents for collecting information about the state of the network [9, 2]. In these papers little is said about the steering of ants like systems [4]. But it is clear that the general concept of a service that is provided by collection of mobile programs is identical with our approach.

Closer to the Internet and at the application level it is interesting to follow the current WEB caching discussions because of the trend to distribute decision taking and to make protocols leaner. A "self-organizing" WEB cache is presented in [3] where internal network nodes decide for themselves which WEB pages should be cached. A note in [15] refers to the Internet Cache Protocol (ICP) whose 3-way handshake protocol is considered an unacceptable delay source which should be eliminated.

At a more formal level, leader election protocols belong to *self-stabilizing systems* i.e., systems that can regain a consistent state from any possible global starting state. Research has recently gained momentum in this field (see for example the "Comprehensive self-stabilization bibliography" in [7]). Our light-weight election protocol can be useful as a "weakest failure detector" module for agreement protocols and is related to the discussion of relaxing the reliable delivery requirement of agreement protocols (see e.g., the discussion in [5]).

6 Conclusions

In this paper we presented an adaptive distributed election service for active networks. In a first place, this service elects a leader node among neighbors of a network segment with broadcast capability. Based on the "bully" algorithm, it recovers from a crash of the leader node by starting a re-election. This service is also adaptive in a second way, namely by deploying itself to every network segment that becomes (temporarily) reachable from the initial site of deployment.

The novel elements of this approach are that (i) both functionalities are provided by small active packets without central control and (ii) the node-spanning election service is built out of purely local coordination primitives. An implementation in the M0 systems resulted in an initial "service germ" of less than 1200 Bytes.

The gas-like "cloud of active packets" becomes the service instance to which client applications must connect. Local service access points are installed for this purpose.

We envisage a "flat" service space in which the competing service clouds must publish and sell their services side-by-side. Based on the problem of terminating a self-deploying service, the point is made that these services and their clients should arrange in economic value chains without any explicit means to steer their actions from outside. Potentially, such services can run forever.

Acknowledgements

I would like to acknowledge the anonymous reviewers for their helpful comments.

References

1. Alexander, D., Braden, B., Gunter, C., Jackson, A., Keromytis, A., Minden, G. and Wetherall, D.: Active Network Encapsulation Protocol (ANEP), July 1997. http://www.cis.upenn.edu/switchware/ANEP/docs/ANEP.txt
2. Bonabeau, E., Henaux, F., Guérin, S., Snyers, D., Kuntz, P. and Théraulaz, G.: Routing in Telecommunication Networks with "Smart" Ant-Like Agents. In Proc *Second Int. Workshop on Intelligent Agents for Telecommunication Applications* IATA'98, Lectures Notes in AI, Vol 1437, 1998.
3. Bhattacharjee, S., Calvert, K., and Zegura, E.: Self-Organizing Wide-Area Network Caches. In Proc *Infocom'1998, San Francisco, CA,* March 1998.
4. Dorigo, M.: The "Ant Colony Optimization". http://iridia.ulb.ac.be/dorigo/ACO/ACO.html
5. Friedman, R., Keidar, I., Malki, D., Birman, K., and Dolev, D.: Deciding in Partitionable Networks. Technical Report, CS Department, Cornell, Nov. 1995. TR 95-1554.
6. Garcia-Molina, H.: Elections in a Distributed Computing System. IEEE Transactions on Computers, Jan 1982.
7. Herman, T.: Comprehensive Self-Stabilization Bibliography. Working Paper, University of Iowa, Aug. 1998. http://www.cs.uiowa.edu/ftp/selfstab/bibliography
8. Liquid software home page. http://www.cs.arizona.edu/liquid/index.html
9. Minar, N., Kramer, K. and Maess, P.: Cooperating Mobile Agents for Mapping Networks. Proc 1st First Hungarian National Conference on Agent Based Computing, May 1998. http://www.media.mit.edu/~nelson/research/routes-coopagents/
10. Tschudin, C.: The Messenger Environment M0 – a Condensed Description. In Vitek, J. and Tschudin, C. (Eds), *Mobile Object Systems - Towards the Programmable Internet.* LNCS 1222, Springer, April 1997.
11. Tschudin, C.: ANON: A minimal overlay network for active networks experiments. Technical report, CS Department, University of Zurich, Aug. 1998. TR 98-10.
12. Tschudin, C.: Apoptosis - the Programmed Death of Distributed Services. In Vitek, J. and Jensen, C. (Eds), *Secure Internet Programming – Security issues for distributed and mobile objects.* LNCS, Springer, to appear 1999.
13. Spafford, E.: The Internet Worm Program: An Analysis. SIGCOMM, Jan 1989.
14. Wetherall, D., Guttag, J. and Tennenhouse, D.: ANTS: A toolkit for building and dynamically deploying network protocols. In *IEEE OpenArch 98, San Francisco,* April 1998. http://www.tns.lcs.mit.edu/publications/openarch98.html
15. Zhang, L., Michel, S., Nguyen, K. and Rosenstein, A.: Adaptive Web Caching: Towards a New Caching Architecture. 3rd WWW caching workshop, Manchester, England, June 1998.

Mobile Co-ordination: Providing Fault Tolerance in Tuple Space Based Co-ordination Languages

Antony Rowstron

Laboratory for Communication Engineering, Engineering Department,
University of Cambridge, Trumpington Street, Cambridge, UK
aitr2@eng.cam.ac.uk,
http://www-lce.eng.cam.ac.uk/~aitr2

Abstract. In this paper we describe the concept of *mobile co-ordination*, a general purpose approach to overcoming failure of agents when using distributed tuple spaces. We demonstrate why mobile co-ordination is better than using existing techniques such as transactions, how mobile co-ordination can provide extra functionality in the form of *agent wills*, and how the framework to provide this can be implemented in Java and can be used with multiple different tuple space co-ordination languages. Experimental results are presented to show performance gains made when mobile co-ordination is used.

1 Introduction

Early tuple space based languages, such as Linda[1], suffered from poor agent fault tolerance. Since Anderson et al.[2] first proposed the idea of using of transactions in Linda it has become widely adopted, for example in PLinda[3], Paradise[4], JavaSpaces[5] and more recently in TSpaces[6]. In this paper we advocate the use of mobile co-ordination instead of transactions.

A tuple space based system needs two fault tolerance mechanisms, one at the system level for server fault tolerance and one at the user level for application writers to provide fault tolerance at the application layer. In particular at the application layer fault tolerance is required to provide protection against the failure of an agent when the agent has removed one or more tuples from a tuple space that are required by other agents in order for the system as a whole to continue. For example, consider an agent fails whilst performing a series of tuple space operations that together created a higher level co-ordination operation as shown in Figure 1 which shows some Linda operations which increment a shared counter.

$$
\begin{array}{l}
\text{in}(\text{``COUNTER''}_{string}, ?x_{integer}); \\
\text{out}(\text{``COUNTER''}_{string}, ++x);
\end{array}
$$

Fig. 1. A co-ordination operation.

If the agent performing this co-ordination operation was to fail having performed the in then the incremented counter would never be inserted. This would mean that any other agents using this counter would block forever when they next try to read it.

Transactions can be used to overcome this problem, as will be shown later, however, neither the tuple space based co-ordination languages BONITA[7] or WCL[8] developed by the author used transactions, because we considered transactions a poor solution to the problem and at the time we left the problem unaddressed. Here we now address the issue and argue that in many situations resilience to failure provided by transactions is not sufficient. Our proposed solution, mobile co-ordination not only provides the kind of fault tolerance provided by transactions, without altering the underlying semantics, but it also enables the concept of an agent *will* which provides a mechanism for 'tidying' a tuple space up should an agent fail, where a traditional transaction can not be used. Mobile co-ordination is general enough to be applied to many existing tuple space based co-ordination languages that use Java as the host language.

Application fault tolerance is an important problem because the number of tuple space based co-ordination languages for use over the Internet has increased considerably in the last few years, with many companies attempting to create such languages, eg. IBM[6] and Sun[5]. The solution presented in this paper is not only novel in terms of overcoming this problem, but has been extended to introduce the novel concept of agent wills.

In the next section a description of transactions as used in tuple space based co-ordination languages is given, and the short cummings described. In Section 3 we describe the concept of Mobile Co-ordination, using a simple example, and discuss why it provides fault tolerance. In Section 4 the use of agent wills is described. In Section 5 we describe the implementation and discuss the performance issues, and show how, surprisingly, the use of mobile co-ordination is far more efficient than the use of transactions in most cases.

2   Transactions

Transactions have been used for many years in databases and Anderson et al.[2] proposed using this concept in Linda, and this was first done in PLinda and then subsequently in many co-ordination languages. Most implementations provide a similar approach to the transaction implementation. Two new primitives are added to the base tuple space access primitives, which are start and commit primitives.

The start primitive causes the server managing the tuple spaces to retain a copy of all tuples being removed and to hold all tuples being inserted by the agent which performed the start. When the commit command occurs all the tuples being held because the agent removed them are discarded, and any inserted tuples are actually placed into the tuple space and then become visible at that point to the other agents using the tuple space. This way, if the commit is never reached the inserted tuples do not appear in the system and any removed tuples can be replaced. However, any inserted tuples do not appear to other agents until the commit is performed.

The problem with this is that the use of transactions alter the underlying semantics of the co-ordination operations they are placed around. This is shown in Figure 2.

Fragment One	Fragment Two
out($10_{integer}$);	in($10_{integer}$);
in($11_{integer}$);	out($11_{integer}$);

Fig. 2. Example of transaction problems.

The two fragments of pseudo code shown in Figure 2 are assumed to be performed on the same tuple space, and represent a trivial yet important co-ordination construct using tuple spaces. The co-ordination construct is an explicit synchronization between the two fragments. If the start and commit are placed around the co-ordination constructs in Fragment Two then this does not alter the semantics. However, if the start and commit are placed around the co-ordination constructs in Fragment One the two fragments will deadlock. The tuple inserted in Fragment One into the tuple space will not appear until after the tuple inserted in Fragment Two has been read, but this can not occur until after the tuple inserted in Fragment One appear, thus the fragments deadlock.

This altering of the semantics means that the outcome of the co-ordination operations is dependent on whether they are performed inside a transaction or outside a transaction. This is not a desirable side effect, and the primary reason why transactions were not adopted in either BONITA or WCL. It also means that a programmer can not place all the co-ordination operations required in a transaction. For example, consider a program which needs to insert a tuple into a tuple space to signify that the agent is present, and when the agent has finished it removed the tuple. An example of this can be seen in a chat tool a chat client may place the name of the user in a tuple space, so that other users can ask who is currently using the chat tools system. If the agent unexpectedly then this tuple needs to be removed. The problem with a single transaction for this is that the name tuple will never be seen by other agents, until the transaction commits (when it terminates).

To a lesser extent there is another problem, which is how long should a server wait in between the start and deciding that agent has died? Should this be specified by the user? Should it be assumed that the communication layer between the agent and the server has some notion of knowing when the other end has died?

Both these problems are clear if you look at the JavaSpaces[5] specification which describes the behavior of the primitives if performed as part of a transaction or not. Furthermore, the description of the basic primitives include descriptions of how they interact with transactions, and a description of timing flags used with the primitives to control how they interact with transactions. This increases the complexity of the language, and makes it from a simple model into a complex one, with very subtle behavior and interaction possible.

So, transactions alter the semantics of the co-ordination constructs performed within them, and cannot provide the level of fault tolerance required in all applications, due to the fact the tuples do not appear until the transaction commits. We believe the idea of mobile co-ordination overcomes all these problems, and furthermore is in general more efficient and faster.

3   Mobile Co-ordination

Mobile co-ordination involves the movement of co-ordination primitives that make a particular co-ordination operation to the server which stores the tuple space. A co-ordination operation is a high-level co-ordination operation composed of several tuple space access primitives. If the all the co-ordination *primitives* reach the server before any are executed, the entire co-ordination operation will be executed. In other words, this provides a 'all or none' execution of the primitives which make the co-ordination operation. The underlying assumption is that the server is reliable. This provides us with a mechanism to provide fault tolerance at an application level. By moving arbitrary (small) segments of programs containing multiple tuple space access primitives, and by ensuring that the segment is not executed until all the segment and associated state has been transfered to the tuple space server an application can provide fault tolerance.

The aim is to create a framework that supports this, without comprising the simplicity of the tuple space model. At this stage it should be noted that before creating the current implementation many other approaches were considered, including creating some sort of scripting language in which to embed the tuple space primitives. These would have been host language independent but given the current prominence of the Java language for Internet computing it seems acceptable to create a system which works only with that language.

A detailed explanation of how the framework is created in Java is given in Section 5. However, an overview from an application developers perspective is given now. The developer creates a class that contains the tuple space access primitives which they wish to be performed as a single co-ordination operation. In the agent an instance of that class is created, and any necessary information is initialized and stored within the created object. The programmer then simply passes this object to a method associated with the object providing access to the tuple spaces. This manages the moving of the object (its state) and the necessary class files to the tuple space server. The class that contains the mobile co-ordination code must implement an interface *MobileCoordination* which specifies there is a method called `coordination()` in the object. The tuple server server calls this method. The interface also specifies that the method `coordination()` must return an object of the type *Tuple*. This is passed back to the agent. More detail about the implementation is provided in Section 5.

The fault tolerance is provided, because from the server's point of view, it either receives the class file, and the object state in its entirety or it does not receive them at all. If the socket fails before both are received then the server does not (indeed can not) create the object because it catches the exception and terminates the operation. If the server receives all the information correctly it recreates the object and calls the `coordination()` method, thereby performing the mobile co-ordination segment. The tuple that this method returns is passed back to the agent. If the socket has died in between the code starting and ending it does not matter, and the result is 'lost', however, the high-level co-ordination operation will have been executed in its full. Hence it provides either 'all or none' execution of the mobile co-ordination segment.

It should be noted that moving the co-ordination operations to the tuple space server does not alter the semantics, because (currently) the agent thread performing the co-ordination operation is blocked until the result from the migrated code has been returned. This means that it is similar to any other blocking primitive in Linda. It should be noted that it is quite possible to execute the mobile co-ordination operation at the agent, by simply calling the `coordination()` method – however this will not provide the fault tolerance. The reason why the semantics of the tuple space access primitives performed in the mobile co-ordination code is because the system provides 'all or none' execution of the operations *not* atomicity. Other agents are able to interact with and use the tuples that the mobile co-ordination generates. Indeed, the mobile co-ordination section can generate tuples and then subsequently consume them[1]. It is the fact that the tuple space access primitives that compose the co-ordination operation are not atomically executed that allows the semantics not to be altered.

The mobile co-ordination code is expected to handle all exceptions that occur. If an exception is raised which is not handled by the code then an empty tuple is returned to the agent which performed the operation. There are currently no restrictions on the operations that can be performed in the code. However, it makes no sense to perform any I/O operations. Objects can be instantiated within the code once it is executed, however, in order to guarantee the 'all or nothing' approach the class files must be available locally. However, when the object is first migrated, pre-instantiated objects can be transfered.

In order to demonstrate fully how mobile co-ordination performs a simple example is used which is based loosely on the idea of a talk tool. The talk tool does not use a chat server but instead is peer-to-peer, with each talk tool client manipulating the conversation directly in the tuple space. A full example of such a tool using a tuple space language is given in Rowstron[7]. Each client places a tuple in a tuple space with the name of the user in it then it starts to add lines to the conversation and then when finished the tuple containing the users name is removed.

---

[1] At its limit the entire agent could be migrated, however, this is neither necessary nor wanted as it would increase the load at the tuple space server and reduce performance of the system (we discuss this further in Section 7.)

The necessary routines to manage the mobile co-ordination are, in the current implementation, added to the class *TupleSpace*. As well as being able to perform the normal Linda operations (out, in and rd) using the class a number of new methods are added; executeSafe, createWill and cancelWill. It should be noted that executeSafe is not equivalent to an eval operation in Linda.

Figure 3 shows the main program. A very simple centralized tuple space kernel has been used in this example with the Linda style access primitives of in, rd and out. These operations return objects which are instantiations of *Tuple*, and the class *Tuple* provides a method called getField which returns the object stored in the tuple at position specified. Line *2* shows the creation of a tuple space. Lines *5* and *6* create a will for the agent, which will be discussed in the next section. Lines *8* and *9* create an instance of the class InsertLine, which is our high-level co-ordination operation, and insert the necessary values in it. Line *10* causes the object to be migrated to the server, and the result is returned. If the user had wished to execute this locally all they would have done is replace Line *10* with:

```
Tuple t = InsertLine.coordination();.
```

Then Lines *11* and *12* read back the tuple inserted by the mobile co-ordination operation. Finally, in Line *14* the will is canceled, and this will be described later.

```
1  public class TestMobile {
2    TupleSpace gts = new TupleSpace("ts host",8989);
3
4    public TestMobile() {
5      MyWill theWill = new MyWill(gts,"Antony Rowstron");
6      gts.createWill(TheWill);
7      gts.out(new Tuple("Antony Rowstron"));
8      InsertLine mobileCoord = new InsertLine();
9      mobileCoord.insertData(GTS,"Antony","Hello I have joined!");
10     Tuple t = gts.executeSafe(mobileCoord);
11     t = gts.rd(new Template((Integer)t.getField(0),"Antony",
12                     new Formal("java.lang.String")));
13     gts.cancelWill();
14   }
15
16   static public void main(String args[])  new TestMobile();
17 }
```

Fig. 3. Example - Main Class.

Figure 4 shows the high-level co-ordination operation. In Figure 1 in Section 1 the example used is a global counter stored in a tuple space. This is the same idea used to store and manage the conversation in the talk tool. Therefore, the counter tuple is removed, incremented and reinserted, and the necessary line of text is inserted. Lines *4* and *5* allow the object to be set up with the tuple space, and the text for the tuple to be inserted. Lines *7* to *14* provide the method required for *InsertLine* to implement *MobileCoordination*. This removes the counter tuple (line *9*) increments the value and reinserts it (line *11*), then inserts the line we wanted to add (line *12*) and returns a tuple containing the value of the line we inserted (line *13*).

```
1   class InsertLine implements MobileCoordination, Serializable {
2     TupleSpace ts; String name, Text;
3
4     public void insertData(TupleSpace ts, String name, String text) {
5       this.ts = ts; this.name = name; this.text = text; }
6
7     public Tuple coordination() {
8       Tuple count; int cnt;
9       count = ts.in(new Template("C",new Formal("java.lang.Integer")));
10      cnt = ((Integer)count.getField(1)).intValue();
11      ts.out(new Tuple("C",new Integer(cnt+1)));
12      ts.out(new Tuple(new Integer(cnt),name,text));
13      return new Tuple(new Integer(cnt));
14    }
15 }
```

Fig. 4. Example - Mobile Co-ordination Class.

This has shown how the mobile co-ordination works, and has also demonstrated that it is not complicated. It should be noted that the object that is sent to the server is not strictly migrated, it is replicated. A copy of the object and its state remain at the agent.

4   Using mobile co-ordination for Agent Wills

We have already demonstrated how mobile co-ordination can be used to provide the sort of fault tolerance that traditionally is provided by transactions in tuple space based systems. In the above example we are guaranteed not to loose the counter tuple due to agent failure. However, we have not dealt with how the tuple containing the users name can be removed on agent failure (Figure 3, line *7*).

Using mobile co-ordination we have also added the concept of an agent will for an agent. An agent will is a set of tuple space access primitives that are executed when the *tuple space server* managing the tuple spaces decides that an agent owning the will has failed. Currently, a loose interpretation of this is taken, in so far as we allow a will for *every tuple space* (handle) that the agent has. This appears to allow more flexibility than simply allowing one. An agent has the ability to cancel (or execute) a will it has associated with a tuple space explicitly.

In order to demonstrate this consider the example we used in the last Section. In Figure 3 line *5* the 'will object' is instantiated and its internal values are passed to it. Line *6* sets the will in operation. This is achieved by passing it to the tuple space server/manager, which then stores it until required. Finally, line *13* cancels the will. However, it should be noted that it is often the case where the programmer actually wants the will explicitly to be executed (as in this case) to remove the name tuple.

```
1 class MyWill implements MobileCoordination, Serializable {
2   TupleSpace ts; String name;
3
4   public MyWill(TupleSpace ts, String name) {
5     this.ts = ts; this.name = name; }
6
7   public Tuple coordination() {
8     ts.in(new Template(name)); return null; }
9 }
```

Fig. 5. Example - The Will Class.

Any high level co-ordination operation stored in a separate class can be used as an agents' will. There is no difference between a will class an a normal co-ordination operation that is to be performed fault tolerantly. Figure 5 shows the Class used as the will. All it does is remove the tuple containing the users name. It should be noted that it returns a null pointer. It could return a tuple, but given that the connection to the agent has been lost in order for it to be executed there is little point. However, currently it is possible for the agent to request the server to execute the will. When this is done, the result is returned to the user agent. This would be achieved by replacing line *13* in Figure 3 with the line:

```
Tuple tup = gts.executeWill();.
```

It should be noted that if the will was not canceled explicitly then the will would be executed anyway when the agent terminated. This means the need for an explicit execution command may be unnecessary.

To summarize, a will is considered as a high-level co-ordination operation that is only executed if the connection between the agent and the server (in the servers opinion) has failed (or if the agent explicitly asks for it to be executed).

5 Implementation

In this section we present a very brief overview of how the mobile co-ordination system is implemented. The implementation is relatively straight forward and uses the many unique features of Java. In essence, whenever a class is instantiated a *ClassLoader* is used to load the class. At the server end the implementation subclasses the ClassLoader to provide a NetworkClassLoader which gets the class (and the object state) from the agent. Therefore, to load a class the agent provides to the server a socket name and a port number. The agent creates an instance of a serializable class that contains the class file code and the serialized state of the object to be migrated. This is then transfered to the tuple space server. It should be noted that the agent keeps a record of which class files have been passed to the tuple space server, and if the current object is an instantiation of a class whose code has already been passed to the server, then the class file is omitted. This saves on the amount of information passed to the server.

In order for the server to be able to call the necessary methods in the migrated object, the migrated object must implement an interface (currently called *MobileCoordination*). All this specifies is that there should be a method called Coordination() in every object passed.

In order to allow the co-ordination operations in the migrated object to be the same as those used locally, an object which is an instantiation of the TupleSpace class (this holds information about where the tuple space is stored) is able to detect whether it is at the server or at the agent using a hack. This means a TupleSpace object is able to modify its behavior accordingly, if it is at the server then it accesses the data structures directly, and if it is at the agent is passes the instructions through a socket to the tuple space server where they are performed and then the results returned.

6 Performance

Initial thoughts on the mobile co-ordination led us to believe that although the use of mobile co-ordination would provide fault tolerance it would be more expensive (time wise) than using transactions. In the best case it may be possible to piggyback the transaction start and transaction end messages on other messages, therefore requiring no real overhead.

However, it turns out that using mobile co-ordination can be many times more efficient. In general, if more than one tuple read/removal operation is performed then it is more efficient to use mobile co-ordination. In order to demonstrate this, consider a simple program which inserts using (an unordered) out a number tuples each containing a counter and a random number. The code to insert the tuples was written as a high level co-ordination operation which could be performed as a mobile co-ordination operation. The inserted tuples are then read using rd and the random numbers summed. Again, this was created as a mobile co-ordination operation. The agent then executed the mobile co-ordination both remotely (providing fault tolerance) and locally (not providing fault tolerance). Hence we are able to compare the effect (in the absence of faults) of migrating the mobile co-ordination.

Figures 6, 7 and 8 show the results for when between 1 and 200 tuples are inserted, both over a LAN and over a WAN. In the case where the mobile coordination is enabled the size of the class file transferred for the Insert operations is 784 bytes with the object state being a further 187 bytes. For the adding component the class file size is 887 bytes with the object state being a further 176 bytes. Therefore this is approximately 1K to be transferred. The results for a LAN were gathered over a 10 MB/sec Ethernet, using a Pentium Pro 200 MHz PCs running Linux. The WAN results were gathered using an Indy Workstation at York, UK to a Pentium Pro 200 MHz PC Linux running computer at Cambridge.

It should be noted that Figures 6(a) and 8 show the same operation (Insertion over a LAN) however Figure 8 shows the use of an out primitive which provides *out ordering*[2][9]. The provision of *out ordering* means that more messages need to pass between the server and the client. However, the approach taken in the implementation in naive, compared to the kernel described in Rowstron[9]. Therefore, Figure 8 represents the worst case. It should also be noted that Figures 6(a) and 7(a) the insertion time seems to be independent of whether a LAN or a WAN is being used. This is because there are no acknowledgements being returned. Therefore, the time represents the time taken to insert that number of tuples into a socket, which, given the size of the data being sent can probably store it in local buffers.

In all the cases the use of mobility appears to take an almost constant time, regardless of the number of operations performed. This can be explained by considering the time tuple space access can be performed on the server and across the network. On a Pentium Pro 200 MHz PC running Linux it takes approximately $110\mu S$ to read a tuple from a tuple space in the worst case. The time taken to send a message (containing the code and data) over a network, and then for the Java Virtual Machine to unpack and instantiate the class is constant regardless of the number of operations performed. The time difference of performing 1 or 200 tuple space operations is insignificant.

The results show that if more than one single tuple space operation requiring a tuple to be returned is to be performed (eg. not just a single or multiple out primitives), then the mobile co-ordination will provide better performance. In this case, because the add routine read the number of tuples inserted from a tuple in the tuple space and then read that many tuples the mobile co-ordination is always quicker.

This conclusion may seem a little surprising, but if we consider the Maximum Transmission Unit (MTU) for TCP/IP is 1500 bytes[3], and therefore, for sending a 1K packet has much the same effect as sending a 200 byte packet. Given the use of synchronous tuple space access primitives (like in and rd) the agent has to block computation whilst the result tuple is returned. Therefore, the second tuple space access operation can only begin when the first one terminates. In the case of a mobile co-ordination segment, the operations at the server can access the data structure directly, therefore the cost of communication is removed

---

[2] This is where the out primitive is implemented in such a way that it requires an acknowledgment from the server storing the tuple before the next out is performed.
[3] For IPv6 the *minimum* size is 576 bytes.

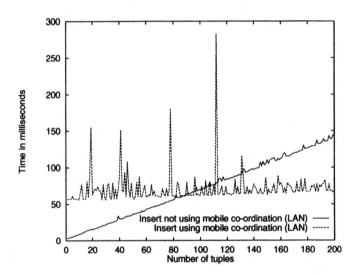

(a) Insert using mobility and not using mobility over a LAN.

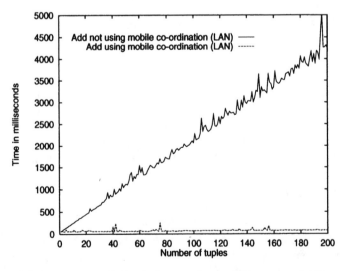

(b) Add using mobility and not using mobility over a LAN.

Fig. 6. The effect of using mobility and not using mobility over a LAN.

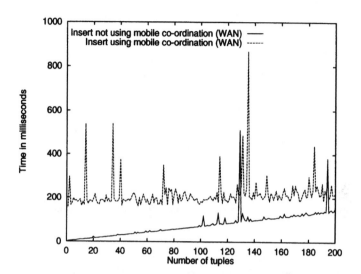

(a) Insert using mobility and not using mobility over a WAN.

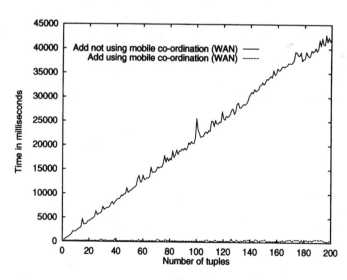

(b) Add using mobility and not using mobility over a WAN.

Fig. 7. The effect of using mobility and not using mobility of a WAN.

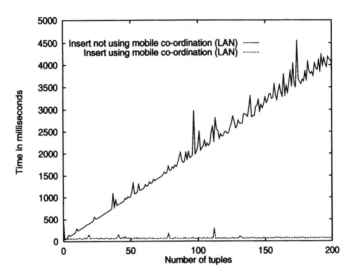

Fig. 8. Insert (with out ordering) using mobility and not using mobility over a LAN.

for the tuple space access. At the tuple space server the time taken to access the data structure is very small compared with the time taken to perform the communication, and therefore multiple tuple space operations can be performed in apparently the same time as a single remote tuple space operation. On a Pentium Pro 200 MHz PC runing Linux it takes approximately $110\mu S$ to read a tuple from a tuple space in the worst case. Therefore, 9 tuple space primitives can be performed in under 1ms. Using the Unix `ping` tool between the machine at Cambridge and the machine used at York provides the following results (for 22 packets); Min time is 11.2 ms, average is 13.7 ms and the max is 24.7 ms. This puts the time to perform nine operations in the full context of expected network latency.

7 Future work

This paper describes the use of mobile co-ordination to provide fault tolerance. The work to date has concentrated on using as single tuple space server. Without doubt multiple servers will have to be used in real implementations. However, transactions have similar problems, and we could make restrictions on tuple spaces which could be accessed within the co-ordination operations migrated. This is an area which we are still considering.

Also, all the performance figures are given from the point of view of the agent. This does not consider extra tuple space server load. Some of this extra load will be offset by reducing the need to construct and deconstruct packets of tuples being sent to the agent. Some control of the amount of CPU time a migrated co-ordination operation can consume needs to be added, otherwise there is the potential for abuse. This is another area still under consideration.

8 Conclusion

In this paper we have demonstrated how the concept of Mobile co-ordination can be used to provide fault tolerance in tuple space based co-ordination languages. Mobile co-ordination provides the same fault tolerance that the use of transactions in many tuple space languages provides, but without the drawback of altering the semantics of the primitives. Also, the same basic technique allows agents to register 'wills' with the tuple space system, that are executed if the agent dies. This has been shown in this paper to extend the fault tolerance support. An example program has been used to demonstrate that the addition of mobile co-ordination does *not* increase the complexity of the language, and therefore, does not extend the load placed on the programmer using it.

The ideas of of mobile co-ordination are applicable to any tuple space based language which uses Java. The demonstration uses a traditional Linda implementation, but the same system has been used with WCL. It can easily be introduced into either TSpaces or JavaSpaces.

It is also interesting that the mobile co-ordination uses the ideas of mobile objects to achieve something that is not feasible without the use of mobile objects (wills).

In the last year the importance of tuple space based co-ordination languages has become very visible with many companies announcing systems which utilize tuple space technology. The need to solve the few remaining drawbacks of such systems has driven this work. The work described here presents a novel approach to providing fault tolerance in one of the best known classes of co-ordination language.

Acknowledgements

I would like to thank Prof. Andy Hopper and the Olivetti and Oracle Research Laboratory for funding me. I would also like to thanks Dr. Alan Wood at York University for allowing access to his computing facilities. I would also like to thank Dr. Stuart Wray for his many long chats on the subject of mobile co-ordination.

References

1. N. Carriero and D. Gelernter. Linda in context. *Communications of the ACM*, 32(4):444–458, 1989.
2. B. Anderson and D. Shasha. Persistent Linda: Linda + Transactions + Query Processing. In *Research Directions in High-Level Parallel Programming Languages*, LNCS 574, 1991.
3. K. Jeong and D. Shasha. Persistent Linda 2: a transaction/checkpointing approach to fault-tolerant linda. In *Proceedings of the 13th Symposium on Fault-Tolerant Distributed Systems*, 1994.
4. Scientific Computing Associates. *Paradise: User's guide and reference manual*. Scientific Computing Associates, 1996.

5. Sun Microsystems. Javaspaces specification. Avaliable from Sun Microsystems WWW Site (http://java.sun.com/products/javaspaces), 1998.
6. P. Wyckoff, S. McLaughry, T. Lehman, and D. Ford. TSpaces. To appear in *IBM Systems Journal*, August, 1998.
7. A. Rowstron. Using asynchronous tuple space access primitives (BONITA primitives) for process co-ordination. In *Coordination 1997*, pages 426–429, 1997.
8. A. Rowstron. WCL: A web co-ordination language. *World Wide Web Journal*, 1998.
9. A. Rowstron. *Bulk primitives in Linda run-time systems*. PhD thesis, Department of Computer Science, University of York, 1997.

A Simple Extension of Java Language for Controllable Transparent Migration and Its Portable Implementation

Tatsurou Sekiguchi[1], Hidehiko Masuhara[2], and Akinori Yonezawa[1]

[1] Department of Information Science, Faculty of Science, University of Tokyo
7-3-1 Hongo, Bunkyo-ku, Tokyo, Japan 113-0033
[2] Department of Graphics and Computer Science, Graduate School of Arts and
Sciences, University of Tokyo
{cocoa,masuhara,yonezawa}@is.s.u-tokyo.ac.jp

Abstract. A scheme has been developed that enables a Java program to be migrated across computers while preserving its execution state, such as the values of local variables and the dynamic extents of try-and-catch blocks. This scheme provides the programmer with flexible control of migration, including transparent migration. It is based on source-code-level transformation. The translator takes as input code a Java program written in a Java language extended with language constructs for migration, and outputs pure Java source code that uses JavaRMI. The translated code can run on any Java interpreter and can be compiled by any just-in-time compiler. We have measured some execution performance for several application programs, and found that the translated programs are only about 20% slower than the original programs. Because migration is completely controlled by using only three language constructs added to the Java language (*go*, *undock* and *migratory*), the programmer can write programs to be migrated easily and succinctly. Our system is available in the public domain.

1 Introduction

Mobile agent systems are a promising infrastructure for distributed systems, in which communication is based on *migration*. Migration is called *transparent* [7] if a migrated program resumes its execution at a destination site with exactly the same execution state as that before migration began. Compared to non-transparent migration, transparent migration is more desirable [3, 5, 7] for writing programs to be migrated and understanding the semantics of migration. The migration transparency of existing mobile systems is, however, not satisfactory.

- Almost all existing mobile systems [9, 10] based on Java do not preserve the calling stack.
- Telescript [17, 18], an early mobile agent system, provides transparent migration, but the unit of migration is restricted to only one object (agent) [6] at a time.

- In the few systems [3, 5, 7, 13] that support transparent migration, the continuation (the complete execution state of the remaining computation) always migrates to the destination, which incurs considerable performance loss, as pointed out by Cejtin et al. [2]

We have extended the Java language by adding three constructs for controlling migration. They are based on our mobile calculus [11] and on mobile languages, such as that developed by Watanabe [16], and allow more flexible control of migration, including transparent migration. We call this flexible migration mechanism *controllable transparent migration*.

With Java, it is difficult to implement a transparent migration mechanism without degrading portability or efficiency for several reasons.

- Consider the case where the runtime system is extended in order to support migration. In this case, we can expect that the execution performance of a migrating program is almost the same as before, and that existing class files can be used for the extended system without recompilation. In return, however, migrating programs are not portable because they can only be executed on a specific interpreter or on the runtime system of a specific just-in-time compiler. This scheme thus does not fit the philosophy of Java, that is, "write once, run anywhere".
- When a migration mechanism is provided as a class library, it offers nearly the same benefits as when a runtime system is extended. Unfortunately, there are several obstacles that are difficult to overcome in this approach. Transparent migration requires transmission of the stack. Dynamic inspection of the stack by Java bytecode itself is forbidden by the *Java security policy*. [1] Therefore, it is difficult to implement transparent migration as a class library.
- In an approach based on source-code-level translation (e.g., Arachne [3]), a Java program is transformed in such a way that the translated Java program can explicitly manage its execution states as Java objects, which enables transparent migration. The major drawback is a slowdown in execution speed due to the code fragments inserted to maintain the information for migration. In a straightforward implementation [3], execution of a transformed program was about twice as slow as that of the original program.

Our migration scheme is based on a source-code-level translation that offers the following features:

portability Programs translated using our scheme require only standard Java and JavaRMI, so a translated program can be run on any Java interpreter and can be compiled by any just-in-time compiler.

efficiency In our scheme, most of the execution state is saved at the time of migration by using an exception-handling mechanism. Therefore, the overhead for ordinary execution is low (about 20% in most cases).

---

[1] A native method can inspect the execution stack at runtime, but the memory layout of objects in the stack heavily depends on the implementation of the runtime system.

accuracy In migration schemes based on source-to-source transformation, it is difficult to simulate exception handling (try-and-catch and throw statements) appropriately. In our scheme, the dynamic extents of the try-and-catch blocks are completely preserved at the time of migration.

Testing of our scheme showed that it can migrate Java programs with a graphical user interface (like migratory applications [1]) between IBM-PC (Pentium / Windows-NT) and Sun workstation (SPARC / Solaris).

The rest of this paper is organized as follows. In Sect. 2, we describe the language constructs we use for migration and explain how the programmer's intention for migration can be described by using the constructs. In Sect. 3 we briefly overview our migration scheme. In the subsequent three sections, we describe our program transformation for transparent migration in detail. In Sect. 7 we discuss the difficulties induced by the source-code-level transformation, and in Sect. 8 we present experimental results showing the execution performance and growth in code size. In Sect. 9, we present photographs in which Java applications are migrated. In Sect. 10, we summarize our scheme and compare it with a related one. We also briefly discuss the need for extending JavaRMI.

2 Java Language Extension

In this section we give a simple example of migration and describe how the programmer specifies migration in source code. The programmer can describe flexible migration by using three language primitives (*go*, *undock* and *migratory*) added to the Java language.

2.1 Starting Migration by Using Go Primitive

Migration takes place by executing a "go" statement. Suppose a method of some object has the following lines of code:

```
System.out.println ("bye!");
go ("//ritsuko:2001/JavaGoExecutor");
System.out.println ("nice to meet you!");
```

The argument of a go statement is the name of a migration server registered in the JavaRMI registry. The migration server is an object that manages migration. When the go statement is executed, the execution state and object are transmitted to the destination host, where the object continues executing just after the go statement. In the above example, "bye!" is displayed on the departure host, and "nice to meet you!" is displayed on the destination host (ritsuko). The migration mechanism in our system is transparent. (1) Even in cases where a go statement appears in a compound statement, such as a for statement, try statement, switch statement, or if statement, the migrated program resumes executing at the destination host. (2) If callee method foo including a go statement is invoked by caller method bar, control returns to method bar on the *destination* host after the method foo returns. This behavior is quite different from that of remote evaluation [14], remote procedure call (RPC) and remote method invocation (RMI). For instance, a migratory Fibonacci method can be written in our language as follows:

```
boolean Moved = false;
public migratory int fib( int n ) {
    if ( n == 0 ) {
        if ( !Moved ) {
            go ("//aki:2001/JavaGoExecutor");
            Moved = true;
        }
        return 1;
    }
    else if ( n == 1 )
        return 1;
    else
        return fib (n-1) + fib (n-2);
}
```

Method fib computes a Fibonacci number by recursively invoking itself. During the computation, fib (and the object executing it) migrates only once (when n is equal to 0), that is, at the point where the execution stack is the deepest. Many systems (e.g., those described in Refs. [9] and [10]) that support mobile computation do not allow the transmission of recursive function invocations. The programmer must therefore write a method and auxiliary class definitions that represent the rest of the computation explicitly. (When we wrote a Fibonacci method in Voyager [10], we had to add extra 35 lines and a class definition representing the execution state.) The keyword migratory at the head of the method above is explained in Sect. 2.3.

2.2 Controlling Transparency by Using Undock Primitive

An undock statement serves as a *marker* that specifies the range of the area to be migrated in the execution stack. It makes it possible to control migration transparency. The brackets of the undock statement restrict the effect of a go statement to the enclosed statements. When the go statement in the undock statement is executed, the rest after the go statement in the undock statement resumes executing at the destination host, while the statements after the undock statement are concurrently executed on the departure host.

```
undock {
    go ("//ritsuko:2001/JavaGoExecutor");
    System.out.println ("nice to meet you!");
}
System.out.println ("bye!");
```

In the above lines of code, only the statements enclosed in the undock brackets are migrated. Therefore, "bye!" is displayed on the departure host, not on the destination host. An undock statement has a dynamic extent similar to a try-and-catch statement. When a go statement is executed in the nested extents of several undock statements, the migrating part is the inside area of the most recently executed undock statement. An area to migrate can be specified by an undock statement in any method defined in any class.

```
o4.d() { ... go(...) ... }
o3.c() { ... o4.d() ... }
o2.b() { ... undock { ... o3.c() ... } ... }
o1.a() { ... o2.b() ... }
```

Fig. 1. Conceptual diagram of a stack.

Figure 1 depicts the migrating areas in a stack where methods a, b, c, and d are called in this order. The stack grows upwards according to a method invocation. The $o.m()$ denotes the invocation of method m of object o. The portions underlined show the migrating areas. The stack frame of the o1.a() is not migrated because the execution of the go statement in method d is in the extent of the undock statement in method b. The stack frames corresponding to the migrating methods are transmitted to the destination host by using the JavaRMI mechanism. In addition to the stack frames, the receiver objects executing the migrating methods are also transmitted. Object o2 executes on both the departure and destination hosts.

2.3 Declaring Method by Using Migratory Primitive

When migration takes place in the extent of a method, the method itself must be declared as such. This is done using the *migratory* primitive. That is, the go statement and the invocation of a migratory method must be written in a migratory method. If they are put in a non-migratory method, they must be enclosed within an undock statement.

3 Overview of Our Transparent Migration

To achieve transparent migration, a method being executed must be suspended, transmitted, and then resumed. In the next three sections we describe our migration scheme based on source-level transformation. In this section we give a brief overview.

The unit of our source-to-source translation is a *method*. A method is transformed in such a way that the translated method can explicitly manage its execution state as Java objects. The migratory modifier of a method is used to determine if the method is to be transformed for migration. Migratory declarations make source-level translation easier. The system proposed by Fünfrocken [5] is also based on source-to-source translation, but it requires the fixed-point iteration of a call-graph to determine the set of methods that should be translated because it lacks this kind of declaration.

3.1 Saving the Execution State

The execution state of each method consists of the execution point from which the method resumes and the values of all local variables. A method is transformed in such a way that (1) all the variable declarations are elevated and moved to the head of the method and (2) it captures NotifyMigration exceptions. The current execution point is continuously saved to a newly introduced special variable during ordinary execution of the method. When migration takes place, an exception is raised and captured by the method. This causes the method to store the values of all local variables into a state object. The method then propagates the exception to the caller. A state object is defined for each method, and all the state objects created during the state-saving process are connected as a chain. The details of this state-saving will be described in Sect. 5.

3.2 Transmitting the Execution State

Eventually, the exception is either captured by an undock statement or it reaches the bottom of the stack. Then, the chained state objects are serialized and transmitted to the destination host by using JavaRMI. The receiver objects executing the migrating methods are also transmitted.

3.3 Restoring the Execution State

The execution state is recovered from the chain of state objects. A method is transformed so that (1) it takes the corresponding state object as an extra parameter and (2) it can resume its execution from any statement in its body, as will be described in Sect. 4. When a method m was being suspended by calling another method m' at the time of migration that was caused by calling m', a code fragment is inserted so that m' is called before resuming the execution of m. The value of each local variable is properly restored before executing the body of the method, as described in Sect. 5. The state of the execution stack (and the dynamic extents of the try-and-catch statements) is reconstructed at the destination host by calling the method at the bottom of the stack with the corresponding state object as the extra argument. This reconstruction is described in Sect. 6.

4 Resuming a Method

To enable a migrated method to resume execution, a mechanism that enables execution to jump to any program point is needed. In other words, a way to resume *control* is needed.

Migration in the C language by using source-code translation [3] exploits a simple jump mechanism: goto statements. Java, however, does not have goto statements. Its break and continue statements permit only escaping from a block statement, there is no way to jump into a compound statement. Our scheme implements the jump facility with low overhead by using switch-case statements and the unfolding technique. This facility is based on transforming a method into a form in which the method can be resumed from any program point. Doing this requires two preprocessings.

4.1 Preprocessings

Splitting an Expression with Side-Effects. Resuming execution of a statement needs special care that contains side effects. Consider the following assignment statement (where foo is a migratory method):

```
y = a[x++] + foo(x) + b[x++];
```

If the method containing this statement is to be resumed immediately after method foo is invoked, we must know the values of a[x++] + foo(x) before migration and assigns the sum and b[x++] to variable y after migration. Although these intermediate values do not appear as local variables in the method, they must be captured and restored after migration. To handle these intermediate values, a statement including side effects is decomposed into a sequence of atomic operations. The above statement is decomposed as follows.

```
tmp3 = a; tmp4 = x++;
tmp5 = tmp3[tmp4];
tmp6 = foo(x);
tmp7 = b; tmp8 = x++;
tmp9 = tmp7[tmp8];
y = tmp5 + tmp6 + tmp9;
```

New variables (tmp3,...,tmp9) are generated to keep track of the intermediate values. This transformation guarantees that we can avoid resumption from within an expression. This does not seem to be the case in Fünfrocken's scheme [5].

Elevating Variable Declarations. Next, we identify all the local variables (including the intermediate variables introduced in the first preprocessing) in the method, elevate the variable declarations, and move them to the head of the method. Unlike the C language, Java allows variable declarations to be placed almost anywhere in a method. Because the statements in a method may be reordered or duplicated during the subsequent transformations, elevating the variable declarations avoids the difficulties of code reordering and duplication. If we duplicated a block of statements including a variable declaration, the resulting code fragment would contain two declarations for the same variable. Elevating avoids this. When a variable is declared with its initial value, we elevate only its declaration and leave the assignment of the initial value at the original program position.

4.2 Jump Facility

Our scheme enables execution to jump to any top-level statement in the method. A top-level statement is one that is not enclosed in an other statement, such as a if statement or a for statement. Note that the goto facility of the C language can be simulated in Java, but only at the top-level. Consider the following Java code fragment.

```
TopLevel: for( ;; ) switch (EntryPoint) {
    case 0:
        ...
    case 1:
        ...
    case 2:
        ...
}
```

Each case statement can be considered a label used as a destination of a goto statement. An occurrence of goto n; is encoded as {EntryPoint = n; continue TopLevel;}. By following this approach, a method in which every statement appears at the top level can be transformed into a resumable form. Consider the following method.

```
void bar() {
    foo(); // migratory method invocation
    System.out.println("after foo");
}
```

To resume this method after invoking foo, we make the following transformation by adding a switch statement, assuming variable EntryPoint is set to 1.

```
void bar() {
  TopLevel: for( ;; ) switch (EntryPoint) {
    case 0:
        foo(); // migratory method invocation
    case 1:
        System.out.println("after foo");
        return;
    }
}
```

In our migration scheme, a method does not have to be resumable from every statement because a method is resumed only immediately after a migratory method is invoked. The reason for this will be explained in Sect. 6.

4.3 Unfolding Technique

To enable execution to be resumed in the middle of a compound statement, such as if statements and for statements, (1) the sub-statements after the resumption point and (2) the subsequent statements that should be executed until control reaches the top level are duplicated at the top level. By representing a compound statement as a while construct, we illustrate the necessary transformation below. Consider the following code fragment.

```
while(C1) {
    while(C2) {
        A;
        foo(); // migratory method invocation;
        B;
    }
}
return;
```

A and B are arbitrary non-migratory statements, and C1 and C2 are arbitrary non-migratory expressions. By unfolding the loops, we translate this code fragment into the following code fragment.

```
label1:
    while(C1) {
        while(C2) {
            A;
            foo(); // migratory method invocation;
            B;
        }
    }
    return;
label2:
    while(C2) {
        A;
        foo(); // migratory method invocation;
        B;
    }
    goto label1;
label3:
    B;
    goto label2;
```

(This unfolding duplicates the contents of the inner loop at the top level.) The resumption point is at label3 when method foo is called at the time of migration. All the labels are at the top level so they can be implemented by top-level jumps. By jumping to label3, execution is apparently resumed immediately after foo(). As illustrated above, if we have top-level jumps, a method is resumable from any point by using unfolding.

The size of a transformed method increases in proportion to $O(n^2)$, where n is the maximum depth of the loops, because the body of a loop with a depth of n is unfolded n times.

Because labels must be at the top level, a try block cannot bridge several labels. If a loop appears in a try block, the block is duplicated so that it does not bridge labels. In our current implementation, to reduce the size of a transformed method, an optimization is performed such that the bodies of the catch blocks are shared among the duplicated try-and-catch statements.

5 Saving and Restoring Local Variable Values

Saving and restoring the values of local variables in a method play an important role in implementing migration. In this section, we first touch upon a related study in which migration is implemented by source-code translation and then describe our scheme.

5.1 The Arachne Scheme

In the Arachne scheme [3], migration in the C language is based on source-code translation. A native stack frame is not used to save the values of local variables; instead a stack is managed at the user-program level. A special object representing a stack frame is allocated for every function invocation. Each access to a local variable is replaced with the corresponding field access to the special object. A stack is transmitted to a remote site by transmitting these special objects. Unfortunately, applying the Arachne migration scheme to Java causes a considerable performance loss, as discussed in Sect. 8.

5.2 Our Scheme

Our scheme for saving the values of local variables is as follows. The body of each migratory method is enclosed by a try statement to capture a special exception, NotifyMigration, that is signaled by the occurrence of migration. When the method actually captures the exception, the values of all local variables are stored into a new state object, and the exception is raised again. This procedure repeats until the exception reaches the bottom of the stack or is captured by an undock statement.

For each method, a class for the state object is defined. The instance variables of the class record (1) the values of all the local variables, including EntryPoint, (2) a reference to the receiver object of the method (i.e., the value of this), and (3) the state object of the sub-method invoked by this method on resumption. Every state class inherits a common base class, so that state objects can constitute a chain.

When restoring the values of local variables, a state object containing the values is applied to the method as an extra argument. The values of the local variables are set to those stored in the object at the head of the method. For ordinary method invocation, the null value is passed to the extra argument.

Putting saving and restoring together, the transformation of a method looks like the following.

```
void foo() {                          void foo(State_X_foo State) {
    int x = 0;                            int x;
    ... the body of a method ...          if ( State == null )
}                                             x = 0;
                                          else
                                              x = State.x;
                          ⇒               try {
                                              ... the body of a method ...
                                          } catch (NotifyMigration e) {
                                              State = new State_X_foo(this);
                                              State.x = x;
                                              e.Append(State);
                                              throw e;
                                          }
                                      }
```

In the code on the righthand side, State_X_foo is the name of a state object. A state object is defined for each method and contains all the local variables of that method. Exception e maintains the chain of state objects. A state object is appended to the chain by executing e.Append(State). The chain of state objects is transmitted to a destination site by using the JavaRMI mechanism. At the destination, the execution state is reconstructed based on the chain of state objects, and execution resumes there.

6 Reconstructing Stack of Method Invocations

A method is resumed by using a combination of the techniques described in the previous two sections. Resuming a *call stack* of method invocations, however, requires a different technique because the dynamic extents of try-and-catch blocks spanning method invocations must be reconstructed. If these dynamic extents are not preserved, the semantics of throwing an exception is violated. The call stack of method invocations is reconstructed by calling each method in the stack with its own state object as the extra argument in the order that the methods were invoked before migration. Suppose method m' was called by method m, and migration takes place. We need to insert a code fragment that executes the rest of m' at the resumption point in method m. When method m is called with its state object, m resumes m' and after returning from m', the rest of m is executed. To implement such a behavior, method bar from Sect. 4.2 is translated as follows.

```
void bar(State_X_bar State) {
  TopLevel: for( ;; ) switch (EntryPoint) {
    case 0:
        EntryPoint = 1;
        foo (null); // migratory method invocation
    case 1:
        if ( State != null ) {
            foo ((State_X_foo)State.Child);
            State = null;
```

```
        }
        System.out.println("after foo");
        return;
    }
}
```

State_X_bar and State_X_foo are the names of the state classes defined for methods bar and foo, respectively. Suppose that a migration takes place when method foo is being called. On restart, a state object is passed to the corresponding method bar (the state object is referred to by variable State in the above code fragment). The state object shows that the value of EntryPoint has been set to 1. Therefore, control is transferred to case 1. Then, method foo is invoked with State.Child, where State.Child refers to the state object of the callee of this method, namely the state object of method foo.

7 Limitations due to Source-Level Translation

There are limitations in the current implementation of our migration scheme. Most of the limitations are essentially due to source-level translation. Therefore, similar limitations apply to other migration schemes based on source-level translation.

There are three areas in a program from which a go statement and a migratory method cannot be called, meaning that migration cannot take place.

- in a class initializer (a static initializer)
- in an instance initializer, and
- in a constructor

It is difficult to resume in a class or instance initializer because it is difficult for a user program to reconstruct the effects of executing these initializers. They are invoked by the runtime system when a class is loaded or an object is created. A constructor is also invoked by the runtime system, so it cannot be resumed. To allow invoking a migratory method from these areas, we must simulate the effects of these initializers and a constructor by combining other language constructs.

Another limitation is that locking cannot be preserved on migration. If a lock has been acquired by a synchronized statement or a synchronized method, it is released at the time of migration by the exception notifying migration. Although the locked state of an object is correctly recovered after migration, the state of the threads that were waiting on the migrating object cannot be preserved because the exception used in our migration scheme releases the object lock. The locked state is thus temporarily lost on migration.

8 Performance

To evaluate the overheads imposed by our translation scheme, we carried out benchmark testing by executing several Java application programs. The execution performance of programs transformed by our scheme was compared with

program	elapsed time(ms)			byte code size(bytes)		
	original	transformed	growth	original	transformed	growth
fib(25)	290	821	+183%	1274	3563	2.80
qsort(200000)	7691	9794	+27.3%	2765	5035	1.82
nqueen(11)	17816	20580	+15.5%	1647	2387	1.45
Richards	4777	4783	+0.125%	10868	25482	2.34
DeltaBlue	25881	28047	+8.37%	28257	50983	1.80

(JDK 1.1.7a, AMD-k6 200MHz)

Table 1. Execution performance and growth in byte code size of programs transformed by our scheme.

that of the original programs. Migration does *not* take place during the execution of the benchmark programs. The results are shown in Table 1. The overheads with the Fibonacci method is rather high because the body of Fibonacci is very small. Most of the overhead is due to extra control transfers induced by the unfolding. When the body of a method is very small, the overhead of code insertion is tend to be high. For the quick sort and N-queen applications, the elapsed times were approximately 20% higher than those of the original applications. Richards is a medium-scale benchmark program simulating the task dispatcher in an operating system. DeltaBlue [4] is a medium-scale constraint solver benchmark program (about 1000 lines in the case of Java). Java versions of Richards and DeltaBlue are available with the source code from Sun Microsystems Laboratories [15]. (Richards has seven variants. We used the one called "richards_gibbons".)

The growth in code size due to program transformation is also shown in Table 1. The growth rate was less than twice except for the Fibonacci method and Richards, but even in these cases it was less than 3 times. In general, the code size grows in proportion to the square of the depth of the loops.

	elapsed time(ms)
original quicksort	7691
Arachne-style quicksort	16300
cost of field selection	5825
cost of state object allocation	2784

(JDK 1.1.7a, AMD-k6 200MHz)

Table 2. Performance of Arachne scheme.

For comparison, we applied the Arachne scheme to Java and measured the execution performance. As shown in Table 2, the direct adoption of the Arachne scheme to Java causes a considerable performance loss. The elapsed time for executing a method transformed by using the Arachne scheme was about twice that of the original method. The overheads can be roughly divided into two parts. The first and major overhead is the cost of field selection. The second is the cost of allocating state objects at the head of the method.

Fig. 2. Applications migrating from one computer to another.

9 Sample Mobile Applications

The two photographs in Fig. 2 show three applications migrating between two computers. The applications are the graph layout program included in JDK as a demo application, the tower of Hanoi, and quick sorting. The latter two applications are written using conventional recursive functions. We used two hosts, and the applications migrated from one to the other at different times. Each application had a window (an instance of java.awt.Frame class). Because a window is serializable, it can be transmitted to a remote host by using JavaRMI. When a visible window is transmitted to a remote host by using JavaRMI, the window still remains at the departure host and the moved window is not mapped on the display of the destination host automatically. Therefore, when an application migrates, the window remaining at the departure host must be explicitly deleted, and the window at the destination host must be explicitly mapped. This behavior is simply implemented by using go and undock. The code fragment that deletes the window at the departure host is as follows.

```
undock {
    ... the body of an application ...
}
dispose();
```

When an application migrates, the control at the departure host exits the undock statement shown above. The code fragment that maps the window at the destination host is as follows.

```
go (destination);
show();
```

If migration succeeds, show() is executed at the destination.

In the left picture of Fig. 2, all the applications are running on the host whose monitor is shown on the left. In the right picture, Hanoi and quick sorting have migrated to the right host.

10 Conclusion

We have developed language constructs for describing controllable transparent migration and its portable and efficient implementation based on Java source-code-level transformation. The translated code can run on any Java interpreter and be compiled by any just-in-time compiler. Nevertheless, it usually runs only about 20% slower than the original code. The transformation algorithm (1) translates the method into a form that makes it restartable from any of its statements, (2) inserts code for saving and restoring the values of local variables, and (3) inserts code for reconstructing the calling stack and the dynamic extents of the try-and-catch statements. The translator is written in Standard ML and is available in the public domain [12].

Transference of *several* threads at a time is not supported in our current migration scheme, but we believe that it can be added by simply extending the scheme.

Although our scheme and Fünfrocken's [5] were developed independently, both are based on Java source-code translation and use exception handling to transmit the execution stack. An important difference between them is in the way that method execution is resumed. In Fünfrocken's scheme, a so-called *artificial* program counter is used to skip the code fragments that have been already executed. An additional code fragment that checks whether the current statement should be skipped is inserted for each statement. (Successive statements can be grouped if they do not include migratory method invocations.) Our scheme does not need such checking, but in some cases, a compound statement needs to be unfolded. In saving a state, Fünfrocken's scheme inserts additional code that records the values of local variables into the state object for each migratory *method invocation*. In contrast, additional code is inserted for each *method* in our scheme because all variable declarations are moved to the head of the method. Fünfrocken's scheme performs fixed-point iteration of a call-graph to find the set of migratory methods. Our scheme does not need such an iteration because a migratory method is declared as such. The difference in performance cannot be directly compared because Fünfrocken did not report execution performance. He did report the growth in code size due to source-code transformation. The growth factor was about 3.65 to 4.7 times compared to the original programs. In our scheme, the growth factor is about 1.45 to 2.8 times.

From our experience in writing mobile applications with graphical user interfaces, we feel that the JavaRMI mechanism needs to be extended for transmitting graphical user interfaces. When a visible window is transmitted to a remote host by using JavaRMI, the window remains at the departure host and the moved window is not mapped on the display of the destination host automatically.

Therefore, when an application migrates, the window remaining at the departure host is explicitly deleted, and the window at the destination host is explicitly mapped. The applications we wrote had only one window; if applications with several windows were written, this code insertion would be cumbersome. Therefore, we need a mechanism that specified methods are automatically invoked before and after migration, analogous to that of the :before and :after methods in the common lisp object system (CLOS) [8]. Such a mechanism would be useful for any resource that needs initialization and finalization, not for only graphical user interfaces.

References

1. Krishna A. Bharat and Luca Cardelli. Migratory Applications. In *Proceedings of the 8th Annual ACM Symposium on User Interface Software and Technology*, 1995.
2. Henry Cejtin, Suresh Jagannathan, and Richard Kelsey. Higher-Order Distributed Objects. In *ACM Transactions on Programming Languages and Systems*, volume 17(5), pages 704–739, 1995.
3. Bozhidar Dimitrov and Vernon Rego. Arachne: A Portable Threads System Supporting Migrant Threads on Heterogeneous Network Farms. In *Proceedings of IEEE Parallel and Distributed Systems*, volume 9(5), pages 459–469, 1998.
4. Bjorn N. Freeman-Benson, John Maloney, and Alan Borning. An Incremental Constraint Solver. In *CACM*, volume 33(1), pages 54–63, 1990.
5. Stefan Fünfrocken. Transparent Migration of Java-Based Mobile Agents. In *MA'98 Mobile Agents*, 1477, *Lecture Notes in Computer Science*, pages 26–37, 1998.
6. General Magic Inc. *Telescript Programming Guide*. Version 1.0 alpha 2, 1996.
7. Robert S. Gray. Agent Tcl: A Transportable Agent System. In *Proceedings of the CIKM Workshop on Intelligent Information Agents*, 1995.
8. Guy Steele Jr. *Common LISP: The Language*. Digital Press, 1984.
9. Danny B. Lange and Daniel T. Chang. IBM Aglets Workbench: A White Paper, 1996. IBM Corporation.
10. Voyager core package technical overview, 1997. ObjectSpace Inc.
11. Tatsurou Sekiguchi and Akinori Yonezawa. A Calculus with Code Mobility. In *Proceedings of Second IFIP International Conference on Formal Methods for Open Object-based Distributed Systems*, pages 21–36. Chapman & Hall, 1997.
12. Tatsurou Sekiguchi. JavaGo, 1998. http://web.yl.is.s.u-tokyo.ac.jp/amo/.
13. Kazuyuki Shudo. Thread Migration on Java Environment. Master's Thesis, University of Waseda, 1997.
14. James W. Stamos and David K. Gifford. Remote Evaluation. In *ACM Transactions on Programming Languages and Systems*, volume 12(4), pages 537–565, 1990.
15. Sun Microsystems Laboratories. Benchmarking Java with Richards and DeltaBlue. http://www.sunlabs.com/people/mario/java_benchmarking/index.html.
16. Takuo Watanabe. Mobile Code Description using Partial Continuations: Definition and Operational Semantics. In *Proceedings of WOOC*, 1997.
17. James E. White. Telescript Technology: An Introduction to the Language, 1995. General Magic white paper.
18. James E. White. Mobile Agents. In Jeffrey Bradshaw, editor, *Software Agents*. The MIT Press, 1996.

Coordination Among Mobile Objects

Luigia Petre and Kaisa Sere

Turku Centre for Computer Science (TUCS) and Åbo Akademi University,
FIN-20520, Turku, Finland.
{Luigia.Petre, Kaisa.Sere}@abo.fi

Abstract. When designing distributed object-based systems one is often faced with the problem of modelling the *movement* of objects from site to site in a distributed network. In order to model such an activity, some supervising or *coordination* mechanisms are needed, to insure correctness of both movement and communication in the network. In this paper we propose distributed object-based action systems as a basis for (coordinated) mobile computing. In order to model mobility and coordination we extend the action systems and OO-action systems formalisms with so called *mobile objects* and *coordinator objects*. The mobile objects move in some domain whereas the coordinator objects control the actions of the mobile objects within their respective domains. We show the applicability of the proposed framework with a small though nontrivial example.

1 Introduction

Action systems [4] and OO-action systems [7], their object-oriented extension, have proven their worth in the design of parallel and distributed systems [5, 7]. In the design of distributed object-based systems one is often faced with the problem of modelling the movement of objects from site to site in a distributed network. In describing mobility, the coordination mechanisms play an essential role, insuring the correct functionality of the system. In this paper we propose distributed object-based action systems [8] as a basis for (coordinated) mobile computing.

Recently, several languages and models for coordinating the work of independent agents have been proposed in the literature [14, 17]. Linda [11] and Manifold [3] are examples of languages dedicated for coordination. LLinda [16] is a Linda-based coordination language extended with localities. We focus on languages where one can describe both coordination and computation aspects of a system. For Gamma programs [6], for instance, a coordination construct called scheduler is introduced [13], with a separate framework to reason about them. MobileUNITY [21] is a recent extension of UNITY [12] towards mobility. One of the main novelties of MobileUNITY is the facility to coordinate mobility. In our earlier work [18] we have shown how coordination can be modelled within an existing formal framework, action systems, where both computation and coordination aspects are treated equally and uniformly without introducing new language constructs. One of the goals in this paper is to show how these concepts carry over to the coordination of objects and mobility within OO-action systems. OO-action systems model classes and instances of classes, i.e. objects, are created at run time. The objects themselves are typically *active* having a local state and autonomous actions. Communication between objects takes place via method invocations. An OO-action system thus models a set of distributed objects [8].

In order to model mobility and coordination we extend the OO-action systems formalism with special classes. One of the new forms of classes will stress the *location* and *movement*; the instances of these classes are called *mobile objects*. A mobile object is the unit of mobility. It has a state of its own which it carries with it when moving from location to location. The range of values of the location models the domain in which the mobile object moves. As this set of values can be very large, it is divided into smaller sets, called cells, which form a partition of the initial domain. Every cell is managed by a *coordinator object*, produced by a *coordinator* class. The coordinator object is responsible for scheduling events and supervising the mobile objects within its cell. This is done in such a way that the mobile object is not aware of the coordination taken place.

The first model incorporating active objects was the actor model [19, 1]. Recently, several formalisms and languages that offer active objects have also been proposed, e.g. Java, POOL [2], and Oblique [9], which supports distributed object-oriented computation and allows mobile objects much the same way as our formalism. Oblique is, however, intended as a programming language whereas we consider OO-action systems more to be a specification language containing constructs that are not directly implementable. A somewhat similar view on objects as taken here is defined for the DisCo specification language [20], an action system related language. For DisCo, they do not, however, consider mobility nor do they support the idea of separating coordination and computation. More formal frameworks to model and reason about mobility are the π-calculus [22], Mobile Ambients calculus [10], MobileUNITY [21], and COMMUNITY [24]. The first two are event-based formalisms whereas the latter two are state-based like action systems. MobileUNITY uses temporal logic as its formal basis. The semantics of COMMUNITY is based on category theory.

Action systems as well as OO-action systems are defined using the predicate transformer semantic [15] and the refinement calculus [5]. Therefore there is a notion of *refinement* for OO-action systems within the refinement calculus [7] for reasoning about distributed objects. Even though the connection with the refinement calculus is out of the scope of the present paper, all the constructs we develop are such that they fit into the refinement calculus framework. The refinement calculus provides us thus a solid mathematical foundation to work on. For example, distributed mobility classes can be stepwise developed from ordinary classes to their implementation, decentralised coordinators can be derived from centralised coordinators, and coordinators can be stepwise brought about [18]. The correctness of every step can be verified within the refinement calculus or performed by appealing to pre-proven transformation rules.

We proceed as follows. In section 2 we give an overview of distributed OO-action systems. In section 3 we show how to specify movement and introduce the notion of a mobile object; we also consider a first approach of the example we will use throughout the paper. In section 4 we treat the notion of coordination in OO-action systems. Thereafter we develop a method of coordination in mobile environments and apply it on the example. We conclude in section 5 with some final remarks.

2 Distributed OO-action systems

In this section we present the OO-action systems formalism, focusing on distribution. An OO-action system consists of a finite set of classes, each class specifying the behaviour of objects that are dynamically created and executed in parallel. We first present the specification language for classes and objects. Then we describe the OO-action systems approach and its suitability for distribution.

We will consider a fixed set *Attr* of attributes (variables) and assume that each attribute is associated with a nonempty set of *values*. We consider the following language of *statements* defined by the grammar

$$S ::= abort \mid skip \mid x := v \mid p \mid \text{if } b \text{ then } S \text{ else } S \text{ fi} \mid S ; S .$$

Here x is a list of attributes, v a list of values (possibly resulting from the evaluation of a list of expressions), b is a predicate and p a procedure name. Intuitively, '*abort*' is the statement which always deadlocks, '*skip*' is the stuttering statement, '$x := v$' is a multiple assignment, 'p' is a procedure call, '$S_1 ; S_2$' is the sequential composition of two statements 'S_1' and 'S_2' and 'if b then S_1 else S_2 fi ' is the conditional composition of two statements 'S_1' and 'S_2'. A procedure declaration $p = P$ consists of a header p and of a body P. The semantics for this set of statements is well-defined via the weakest precondition *wp* predicate transformer [15].

Let further *CName* be a fixed set of class names and *OName* a set of valid names for objects. We will also consider a fixed set of object variables *OVar* assumed to be disjoint from *Attr*. The only valid values for object variables are the names for objects in *OName*. We extend the grammar above:

$$S ::= ... \mid n := o \mid new(c) \mid n := new(c) \mid n.m .$$

Here n is an object variable, o is an object name (possibly resulting from the evaluation of an expression), c is a class name and m is a method name. The statement '$n := o$' stores the object name o into the object variable n, '$n.m$' is a call of the method m of the object the name of which is stored in the object variable n. Note that method calls are usually prefixed by an object variable. If such a prefix is missing, the called method should be declared in the calling object. There are two object constructors '$new(c)$' and '$n := new(c)$'. The latter assigns the name of the newly created instance of the class c to the object variable n. The semantics for this extended set is defined within predicate transformers via a translation to the action systems formalism [7].

We further enrich our language by defining a grammar of *actions*:

$$A ::= b \rightarrow S \mid x :\in V \mid \|_I A_i .$$

Here b is a predicate and I an index set ranged over by i. The action '$b \to S$' is a guarded statement that is executed only when the *guard* 'b' evaluates to *true*, i.e., when the action '$b \to S$' is *enabled*. The action '$\|_I A_i$' is the nondeterministic choice among actions 'A_i' for $i \in I$. Given a nonempty set V of values and an attribute x, we denote by '$x :\in V$' an abbreviation for the nondeterministic assignment '$\|_{v \in V} true \to x := v$'. The semantics for actions is also defined using the weakest precondition predicate transformer in a standard way [5].

Compared to the original language of OO-action systems [7] the above language with two syntactic categories, statements and actions, is slightly restricted. This restriction is done as we do not want to present the formal semantics of the language which would be needed for some of the more advanced constructs. This form of the language is, however, enough for our purposes in this paper.

A *class* is a pair $\langle c, C \rangle$, where $c \in CName$ is the *name* of the class and C is its *body*, that is, a collection of data (attributes and object variables), services (procedures and methods) and behaviour (a set of actions to be executed in object instances of the class):

$$
C = \|[\begin{array}{ll}
\textbf{attr} & x := x_0 \\
\textbf{obj} & n := n_0 \\
\textbf{meth} & m_1 = M_1 ; \cdots ; m_h = M_h \\
\textbf{proc} & p_1 = P_1 ; \cdots ; p_k = P_k \\
\textbf{do } A \textbf{ od}
\end{array}
\tag{1}
$$
$$]\|$$

The class body consists of an action $A = \|_I A_i$ of the above grammar and of four declaration sections. The first declaration is for the *local attributes* in the list x, that describe variables that are local to an object instance of the class; this means they can only be used by the instance itself. The variables are initialized to the values x_0.

The list n of *object variables* describes a special kind of variables local to an object instance of the class. They contain names of objects and are used for calling methods of other objects. The object variables are initialized to the values n_0. We assume that the lists x and n are pairwise disjoint.

A *method* $m_i = M_i$ describes a procedure of an object instance of the class. They can be called by actions of the object itself or by actions of another object instance of possibly another class. A method consists of an header 'm' and a body 'M'. The latter is a statement of the above grammar.

A *procedure* $p_i = P_i$ describes a procedure that is local to the object instances of the class. It can be called only by actions of the object itself. Like a method, it consists of an header 'p' and a statement forming the body 'P'.

The *action* specified in the **do** ... **od** loop of a class is a description of the autonomous behaviour that an object instance of this class has at run time. An action can refer to the object variables and to the local attributes declared within the class itself. It can contain procedure calls only to procedures declared in the class and method calls of the form $n.m$ to methods declared in another class or itself. Calls to methods of other objects are possible *only* if the calling object has a reference, i.e. an object variable, to the called object; this models the encapsulation mechanism.

An *OO-action system OO* consists of a finite set of classes

$$OO = \{\langle c_1, C_1 \rangle, ..., \langle c_n, C_n \rangle\} \tag{2}$$

such that actions in each C_i or bodies of methods and procedures declared in each C_i do not contain *new* statements referring to class names not used by classes in OO.

There are some classes in OO, marked with an asterisk $*$. Execution starts by the creation of one object instance of each of these classes. Every object has a local state. An object, when created, chooses enabled actions and executes them. If there is more than one enabled action at any given state, say A_1, A_2, A_3, the choice between them is nondeterministic, i.e. $A_1 \parallel A_2 \parallel A_3$. There is no notion of fairness in this model. Hence, unlike in e.g. Unity [12], the actual execution of any single action cannot be guaranteed. Actions are taken to be *atomic*. Because of this, actions within an object operating on disjoint sets of attributes and object variables can be executed in parallel. They can also create other objects. Moreover, enabled actions of different objects can be executed in parallel as they are operating on disjoint sets of attributes.

Objects interact by executing methods of other objects. The meaning of a call on a method is determined by the *substitution principle*: Let A be an action in an object o_1 calling a method m in some object o_2. Upon the call, the body of the method is substituted for each method call. Hence, the action A becomes $A[o_2.M/n.m]$ where n is the object variable in o_1 containing the reference to o_2 and M is the body of the method m in the object o_2. The action A is then executed jointly by the objects o_1 and o_2 in an atomic fashion. Joint actions between more than two objects are modeled similarly. Here we assumed that the method m is parameterless. For a similar principle including parameters, the reader is refered elsewhere [18].

Computationally, an OO-action system is a parallel composition of many objects, each of them representing an instance of a class [7]. As decribed above, we can have parallel activity within an object as well as between different objects. Initially, only the objects generated from the classes marked with an asterisk are active, i.e. their actions are potentially enabled. These actions might make other objects active by executing a *new* statement.

Let us assume that we have a network of nodes which model some processes and edges which model the communication links between the processes. Assume further that each object in an OO-action system is associated with one of the processes and that the processes execute the enabled actions nondeterministically respecting the atomicity requirement. Due to this requirement, two actions cannot interfere with each others execution. The joint execution of an action by two or more objects naturally requires a communication link between the processes via which the method calls are carried through. Hence, an OO-action system models a distributed object-based system [8].

3 Specifying movement

We argued above that a set of objects constitutes a distributed system provided that the different objects are associated with and executed by some nodes in a network of processes. In this section we introduce the notion of a *mobile object* in our framework and describe how to model a system where objects *move* from node to node in a network.

The systems we want to model usually consist of an arbitrary number of agents which can move freely in some domain and, in the same time, do whatever computation they desire. Besides, at every moment these agents might want to communicate with other agents. Comparing the situation with distributed systems above, we should note the main difference: *the objects are moving* and their behaviour can vary from location to location. Depending on their current location they can or cannot communicate, i.e., invoke method calls, with other objects. Otherwise, they behave as normal distributed objects. Hence, they carry their local state with them. Moreover, when an object moves from one location to another in its domain, it becomes active in the new location and ceases to exist in the original location.

Let *OLoc* denote the domain of mobility. We extend our language with two new statements:

$$S :: = \ldots \mid move(OList, Lexp) \mid l := move(OList, Lexp) \qquad (3)$$

Here *Lexp* is an expression yielding as result a location within the domain *OLoc* and *OList* is a list of object names ($\subseteq$ *OName*). The *move*(*OList*, *Lexp*) statement evaluates the expression *Lexp* with the subsequent movement of the objects in *OList* to this location. The statement $l := move(OList, Lexp)$ stores the value of the evaluation ($\in$ *OLoc*) in a special attribute l. The predicate

$$at(OList, Lexp)$$

is used to check whether the objects in *OList* are at a certain location obtained by the evaluation of *Lexp*. When the list *OList* is missing, the issuing object is the target of the movement or of the predicate evaluation. Now we can make the following definition:

Def. 1 *A* mobility class $\langle mc, \mathcal{MC} \rangle$, *is a class of the form (1) with an additional declaration:* **loc** $l{:}R$. *The attribute l is local and the actions, the bodies of methods, and the bodies of procedures contain statements in the extended language (3). A* mobile object *is an instance of this class.*

The *location attribute* l describes a special kind of variable local to a mobile object. It stores values of locations, representing the position of the object. The type R ($\subseteq$ *OLoc*) of the location attribute is obligatory and denotes the domain in which the mobile object moves. The location attribute can be initialised to some value denoting the initial location of the object. The domain *OLoc* of mobility is to be understood as a powerfull specification abstraction for the possible values a location can take. It can thus model sites in a network, roads, maps or aircraft trajectories. A similar abstraction is also made in MobileUNITY [23].

Changes in the values of the location attribute as well as executing *move* statements model the *movement* of object(s) to another position in their domain. The predicate $at(OList, l)$ can be used in guards and other boolean expressions to determine whether the current location of the object(s) is l. When this predicate is used as part of a guard, we call the guard a *location guard*.

The mobility class of Def. 1 is a class in the sense of (1), because the location attribute is merely a new kind of local attribute and the new statements can be understood as assignments to this attribute. Thus, we have extended our language by showing that the concept of a mobile object can be embedded into our framework for distributed objects.

We are now in a position to make the following definition:

Def. 2 *A* mobile-oriented action system *is a finite set of classes*

$$\mathcal{MO} = \{\langle c_i, C_i \rangle_{i \in \{1,...,n\}}, \langle mc_j, \mathcal{MC}_j \rangle_{j \in \{1,...,s\}}\} \tag{4}$$

where every $\langle c_i, C_i \rangle$ *is a class in the sense of (1) and every* $\langle mc_j, \mathcal{MC}_j \rangle$ *is a mobility class.*

Observe that $\mathcal{MO}$ is an object-oriented action system in the sense of (2).

Mobile objects cannot communicate, i.e., invoke method calls, with other objects unless they are in a certain vicinity. Hence, the reciprocal visibility of two objects, at least one of them being mobile, needs to be guarded by a location guard. Unless this guard is true, the two objects are reciprocal invisible, even though they have references to each other via the object variables. When the location guard becomes true the communication via method calls can take place. The domain defined by the location guard can be seen as the *proximity* of the object, where communication can take place. This mechanism resembles MobileUNITY's transient variable sharing and transient action synchronisation [21] in that the communication and the visibility of two entities is possible only in the proximity of the mobile entity. Action syncronisation is here modeled by method calls: when an action calls a method in another object, the two objects get synchronised. In a similar manner we can of course synchronise more than two objects. Mobile objects as defined in this paper do not share variables. However, in the general OO-action systems framework the view of objects sharing attributes is supported [7] and hence, our model of mobility extends to this.

An example: a luggage distribution system As an example of how to model mobile objects within OO-action systems, we consider a luggage distribution example where the task is to model the luggage transport and delivery in an airport station.

On a given trajectory, one/many *carts* are moving forward or just wait for some service to be done for them. Carts are given pieces of luggage, here called *bags*, by some stations on the trajectory, called *loaders*. The task of the carts is to transport the bags to some destination on the trajectory, where another station (the *unloader*) takes the bags from the carts. After this, the unloaders give the carts a new destination to a loader. The cart is restricted to carry only one or zero bags at a time. The trajectory is circular and there are as many loaders and unloaders as needed. The cart moves itself as long as it has not reached its destination and, when reaching the destination, the loading or unloading can be performed. We focus on modelling the movement of one cart; a system dealing with many carts is left for the next section.

The example is modelled by the following mobile-oriented action system[1]:

$$\{\langle Chief, ch\rangle^*, \langle Device, dev\rangle, \langle Cart, cart\rangle\}$$

Our system contains three classes. The *Chief* class, which starts the execution, is responsible for creating the mobile object in the system, the *cart*, and also for creating as many loaders and unloaders as needed. This need is considered here an internal policy of the system, which we have modelled by the attributes *ld_need*, *uld_need*.

$$ch = \lfloor\!\lceil \quad \textbf{attr} \quad cart\_need, ld\_need, uld\_need := T, T, T$$
$$\textbf{obj} \quad ld, uld:Device; cart:Cart$$
$$\textbf{do} \quad ld\_need, uld\_need :\in \{T, F\}$$
$$\| \quad ld\_need \rightarrow ld := new(Device) \; ; \; ld.SetType(Loader)$$
$$\| \quad uld\_need \rightarrow uld := new(Device) \; ; \; uld.SetType(Unloader)$$
$$\| \quad cart\_need \rightarrow cart := new(Cart) \; ; \; cart\_need := F;$$
$$cart.SetCanMove(T)$$
$$\textbf{od}$$
$$\rceil\!\rfloor$$

Since the loader and the unloader are similar concepts, we model them by one class, called *Device*, whose *type* attribute can have two values: *Loader* or *Unloader*. When the *Chief* creates devices, it calls the method *SetType* to properly set this attribute.

$$dev = \lfloor\!\lceil \quad \textbf{attr} \quad loc:integer \; ; \; cargo:queue\ of\ integer \; ; \; type:\{Loader, Unloader\}$$
$$\textbf{proc} \quad Destination(val\ bag:integer, res\ dest:Device \times integer);$$
$$NextLoader(val\ ld:Device, res\ dest:Device \times integer)$$
$$\textbf{meth} \quad Load(res\ bagid:integer, dest:Unloader, destloc:integer)$$
$$= (\quad \textbf{if } cargo \neq \emptyset \textbf{ then}$$
$$cargo, bagid := cargo.tail, cargo.head;$$
$$Destination(bagid, (dest, destloc))$$
$$\textbf{else } NextLoader((dest, destloc))$$
$$\textbf{fi });$$
$$Unload(valres\ bagid:integer, res\ dest:Unloader, destloc:integer)$$
$$= (NextLoader((dest, destloc)) \; ; \; cargo, bagid := cargo \bullet bagid, 0);$$
$$SetType(val\ newtype:\{Loader, Unloader\}) = (type := newtype)$$
$$\rceil\!\rfloor$$

The device has a *loc* attribute, which models the location of the device. However, it is not modified, because the stations are not supposed to move. Hence it is not specified as location in the sense of Def. 1. Still, the position is important for the system, because it represents part of the destination for carts, modelling the address of the station. The *cargo* attribute stands for the set of bags to be loaded into carts, for loaders, or for the bags which are taken from the carts, for unloaders. The methods *Load* and *Unload* are used respectively by the loader

---

[1] For simplicity, we show the types of attributes and object variables only for those entities with no specified initial value. When an initial value is specified, the type of the respective entity can be easily deduced from it. For convenience also, we allow initial values to be returned by some initialisation procedures, specified in the procedure declaration. Entities with no specified initial value get arbitrary initial values in their domains. For procedures with no special significance to our example we do not specify their bodies.

and unloader. The procedures *NextLoader* and *Destination* are used internally in these methods. There is no autonomous activity within a device.

The cart is our mobile object and its corresponding class, $\langle Cart, cart\rangle$, stands for the mobility class in our mobile system. Its *location* is changed by the cart itself as it moves forward. Incrementing the location attribute value is treated modulo the length of the circular trajectory. Therefore the type of the *loc* attribute is an interval of integers $[0, ..., length - 1]$. The constant *length* represents the length of the trajectory. When the cart is created, its location is 0. Then, the cart keeps moving stepwise. The chief makes the cart to move using the method *SetCanMove* of the cart. As a result, the cart will all the time be able to move as the *canmove* attribute remains *true*. Thus, upon reaching its destination it can either stop for service or continue moving, as at this point both actions are enabled.

$$
\begin{aligned}
cart = \ \| [\quad &\textbf{loc} \quad loc{:}[0, ..., length - 1] \ ; \ loc := 0 \\
&\textbf{attr} \quad bagid, destloc, canmove := 0, InitDest().snd, F; \\
&\textbf{obj} \quad dest{:}Device \ ; \quad dest := InitDest().fst \\
&\textbf{proc} \quad InitDest(res \ dest{:}Device \times integer); \\
&\textbf{meth} \quad SetCanMove(val \ can{:}boolean) = (canmove := can) \\
&\textbf{do} \quad canmove \to loc := move(loc + 1) \\
&\qquad \| \ at(destloc) \land bagid \neq 0 \to dest.Unload(bagid, dest, destloc) \\
&\qquad \| \ at(destloc) \land bagid = 0 \to dest.Load(bagid, dest, destloc) \\
&\textbf{od} \\
\ ] &
\end{aligned}
$$

The cart needs to know both the identity *dest* and the location *destloc* of its destination. This is because, on one hand, when it reaches the destination, it makes a method call to the device, *dest.Load* or *dest.Unload*, in order to be served, and, on the other hand, it moves as long as it has not reached its destination. Initial values to these attributes are given by the procedure *InitDest(...)*, which chooses an arbitrary loader in the system and assigns its identity to *dest* and its address to *destloc*. The cart carries a bag if the attribute *bagid* is not zero.

The services to be performed for the cart are specified in the device's methods *Load* and *Unload*. If the cart arrives at a loader station that has no bag to give to it, the station serves the cart by delivering a new destination. If the loader has bags to deliver, it modifies the *bagid* attribute of the cart, as well as its destination. If the cart arrives at an unloader station, this one takes over the bag from the cart and gives the cart a new destination.

It is important to notice the communication strategy between our objects. The cart cannot communicate with loaders and unloaders unless it is close to them, i.e., when the location guards $at(destloc) \land bagid = 0$ or $at(destloc) \land bagid \neq 0$ hold.

4 Coordinators

The mobile-oriented action systems described so far have a nondeterministic model of execution. This is the most general paradigm one can assume at the specification level. The coordination pattern we are considering here is essentially that of restricting the nondeterminism in a regulated manner.

Coordination and object-orientation The underlying execution model for OO-action systems is 'very' nondeterministic. The scheduling of certain actions for execution cannot hence be guaranteed. However, when specifying coordinators we want to enforce the execution of specific coordinator actions. The notion of coordination was previously defined in terms of prioritizing composition for action systems [18] where the coordinator having higher priority can interrupt the computation of the system it is coordinating. Here we define a similar simple yet powerful composition operator on actions, objects, and classes suitable for object-oriented systems.

Consider two actions $A = a \to S$ and $B = b \to T$. Their *prioritizing composition* $A \parallel B$ is defined as

$$A \parallel B \mathbin{\widehat{=}} (a \to S) \mathbin{[\![} (\neg a \wedge b \to T) \tag{5}$$

We say that the action A *coordinates* the action B. Essentially, action A has a higher priority than action B so that A is executed if it is enabled, while B is potentially executed only when A is not enabled. With the above definition we have extended our language of actions:

$$A ::= \ldots \mid A \parallel A.$$

Let us lift coordination of actions to act on objects. In order for an object o_1 to influence another object o_2 the former needs a reference to the latter via an object variable, say n. Then o_1 can call the methods of o_2. Assume that some action A in o_1 calls some method $m = M$ of o_2. When A is executed, it will be executed jointly with the two involved objects as A becomes $A[o_2.M/n.m]$ following the substitution principle. For o_1 to have influence on o_2 and enforce the execution of A we want A to coordinate the actions in o_2. Hence, we have the following definition:

Def. 3 *Let $o_1, o_2 \in OName$ be two objects. We say that object o_1 coordinates object o_2, denoted by $o_1 \parallel o_2$, if o_1 has a reference to o_2 via some object variable and the actions in o_1 coordinate the actions in o_2. We call o_1 the coordinator object and o_2 the* coordinated *object.*

Hence, according to the above definition, $o_1 \parallel o_2$ implies that every action in o_1 coordinates every action in o_2 whenever o_1 has a reference to o_2. We now lift the above definition for classes and consider a distributed object-based system as described in section 2. We give the following definition:

Def. 4 *Class $\langle c_1, C_1 \rangle$ coordinates class $\langle c_2, C_2 \rangle$, denoted by $\langle c_1, C_1 \rangle \parallel \langle c_2, C_2 \rangle$, if every object instance of c_1 is the coordinator for every object instance of c_2. We call c_1 the coordinator class and c_2 the* coordinated *class.*

As OO-action systems is a class-based formalism, we use this definition when specifying systems in practice. Hence, we associate priorities to classes of objects rather than to single objects.

Let us analyse the definition more closely. Let A be an action in some object instance o_1 of c_1 and B and C the actions of object instances o_{2_1} and o_{2_2} of c_2, respectively. Because these objects are part of an OO-action system, their underlying model of execution is $A \mathbin{[\![} B \mathbin{[\![} C$ where the scheduling is nondeterministic. However, following Def. 4, it is interpreted as $A \parallel (B \mathbin{[\![} C)$ giving a higher priority to the action generated by c_1 than to those generated by c_2. Hence, we have that $o_1 \,/\!/\, o_{2_1}$ and $o_1 \,/\!/\, o_{2_2}$. Further, from Def. 3 we have that the object o_1 coordinates the other objects if and only if o_1 has a reference to either o_{2_1} and o_{2_2}. Assume that o_1 has a reference to o_{2_1} but not to o_{2_2}, i.e., the action A calls a method in object o_{2_1}. Then, following Def. 3, the object o_1 coordinates the object o_{2_1} only, and for the actions A, B and C we obtain the model of execution described by $(A \,/\!/\, B) \,\|\, C$. Based on this observation, we have the following lemma:

Lemma 1 *Let $\langle c_1, C_1 \rangle \,/\!/\, \langle c_1, C_2 \rangle$. Then an object instance of c_1 is a coordinator for an object instance of c_2 if the former has a reference to the object instance of c_2.*

Hence, the coordinator object needs to have a reference to the coordinated object. The idea behind our approach is to split the computation and coordination aspects of objects such that the coordinated object never makes references to its coordinator (even though this is not enforced by the formalism). This implies that the coordinated object is not aware of the presence of the coordinator.

Our model of coordination for OO-action systems incorporates a *referenced object*-approach. This means that when a class coordinates another class, the actions of the instances of the former act with priority over all the actions of all referenced instances of the latter class. The objects that are not referenced can execute their actions independently of those of either class. Informally, we could say that the coordinator acts only over those objects it 'knows' about. This set of known objects for a specific object can vary during the execution. Hence, we actually have modelled a system with dynamic priorities.

Coordination in mobile environments Let us now turn back to mobility classes and consider how to coordinate mobile objects where the dynamic set of known objects is a reality and it is not meaningfull for a coordinator to 'see everywhere'. Hence, a coordinator can only know objects within a certain neighbourhood.

We start by stating a format for the coordinator class which focuses the range of mobility.

Def. 5 *Let $\langle mc, MC \rangle$ be a mobility class. Let R be the type of the location attribute in MC and let $R = R_1 \cup R_2 \cup ... \cup R_q$ be a partition for R. A coordinator class $\langle cc, CC \rangle$ for $\langle mc, MC \rangle$ is a class in the sense of (1), with an additional declaration* **cell** *$c{:}R$ and a special method SetR, where c is a constant local attribute, that can be used in the actions and bodies of methods and procedures. The latter ones contain statements in the extended language (3). The class has exactly q instances, called coordinator objects; the type of the* cell *attribute of the j:th object instance is $R_j, j \in \{1, ..., q\}$ set by the method $SetR(R_j)$ at construction.*

The *cell* attribute is interpreted as a local constant describing the visibility domain for the coordinator. It has as type the type of the location attribute in the mobility class it is coordinating. However, every coordinator object has an element of the partition as the type for the *cell* attribute as given by the implicit subtyping. When a coordinator object is created, the *cell* attribute is initialised to the respective element of the partition via a call to the method *SetR*. We assume this attribute to be unchanged during the lifetime of the object. The list n contains references to the coordinated objects, and possibly other needed references. The fact that the number of object instances of the coordinator class is limited to q should be interpreted as a constraint applied to the class constructor: it can be called only q times after which it becomes disabled.

The coordinator class in Def. 5 is a class in the sense given by (1), so we have integrated the concept of a coordinator within our framework. Every coordinator class is associated with a single mobility class. We have the following definition:

Def. 6 *A* mobile-coordinated action system *consists of a finite set of classes*

$$\mathcal{MCO} = \{\langle c_i, C_i \rangle_{i \in \{1,\ldots,n\}}, \langle mc_j, \mathcal{MC}_j \rangle_{j \in \{1,\ldots,m\}}, \langle cc_j, \mathcal{CC}_j \rangle_{j \in \{1,\ldots,s\}}\}$$

where $s \leq m$ *and where* $\langle cc_j, \mathcal{CC}_j \rangle \parallel \langle mc_j, \mathcal{MC}_j \rangle, \forall j \in \{1,\ldots,s\}$. $\langle c_i, C_i \rangle$ *is a class in the sense of (1),* $\langle mc_j, \mathcal{MC}_j \rangle$ *is a mobility class, and* $\langle cc_j, \mathcal{CC}_j \rangle$ *is a coordinator class. Every coordinator class coordinates a certain mobility class denoted by the* where-*clause. We usually denote* $\mathcal{MCO}$ *by*

$$\{\langle c_i, C_i \rangle_{i \in \{1,\ldots,n\}}, \langle mc_i, \mathcal{MC}_i \rangle_{i \in \{s+1,\ldots,m\}}\} \cup \{\langle cc_j, \mathcal{CC}_j \rangle \parallel \langle mc_j, \mathcal{MC}_j \rangle\}_{j \in \{1,\ldots,s\}}$$

Such a system is a more deterministic OO-action system than those defined by (2) and (4) in that of enforcing coordinator's actions to always execute with priority over the respective mobility class's actions.

We want to stress the importance of Lemma 1 in the mobile-coordinated framework. One coordinator object will execute its actions with priority only over those mobile objects it has a reference to, which are the objects that are in its vicinity or visibility domain or *cell*. As the mobile objects are moving all the time, the set of referenced mobile objects will vary dynamically providing us with a natural and intuitive model.

The luggage distribution example Let us return to the example. Our system of luggage distribution, which now manages more than one cart, is described by the following system

$$\{\langle Chief, ch \rangle^*, \langle Device, dev \rangle\} \cup \{\langle Coord, coord \rangle \parallel \langle Cart, cart \rangle\}.$$

We have many carts, instances of class *Cart*, that are moving on the given circular trajectory. They need to be coordinated in order for them not to cause collisions with each other. Therefore a new class, the *Coord* class, is added to our system. Thus we have one mobility class, *Cart* and its corresponding coordinator class, *Coord*. Let us first consider the coordinator *Coord*.

$$
\begin{aligned}
coord = \; \| \quad &\textbf{cell} \quad seg\text{:}integer \\
&\textbf{attr} \quad status := T \\
&\textbf{obj} \quad crt\_cart\text{:}Cart, next\text{:}Coord \\
&\textbf{meth} \quad SetSeg(val\ newseg\text{:}integer); \\
&\qquad\quad GetStatus(resl\ status\text{:}boolean); \\
&\qquad\quad SetStatus(val\ status\text{:}boolean); \\
&\qquad\quad SetCart(val\ newcart\text{:}Cart); \\
&\qquad\quad SetNext(val\ newcoord\text{:}Coord) \\
&\textbf{do} \ \ldots \ \textbf{od} \\
\|
\end{aligned}
$$

The domain on which the carts are moving is given by the trajectory whose type is $[0, length - 1]$. We split the trajectory into $length$ div 10 segments, which stand for the cells, each segment having ten units. Therefore, the length of the trajectory, modeled by the integer constant $length$, is to be divisible by 10. Moreover, the segments are numbered from 1 to $length$ div 10.

The seg attribute of the $Coord$ class models the segment a coordinator object manages. When a coordinator object is created, the attribute seg is set to a number between 1 and $length$ div 10, using the method $SetSeg$. The attribute $status$ reflects the status of the segment, being $true$ if there is no cart on the segment. Initially all segments are free. For accessing this attribute the methods $GetStatus$ and $SetStatus$ are available in the coordinator class. A coordinator object has two object variables: one to the current cart it supervises, if any, and the second to the coordinator object responsible for the next segment along the trajectory. The latter reference is needed in order for the handoff to be performed when a cart leaves a segment and enters the next one. These object variables are modified by the methods $SetCart$ and $SetNext$.

Below we consider the other three classes in the system. The action of $Coord$ above is explained later. The responsibilities of the chief are (1) to create loaders and unloaders in a nondeterministic fashion, (2) to create and initialise the coordinators, and (3) to create carts.

```
ch = |[ attr  cart_need, ld_need, uld_need, newcarts := T, T, T, F
         obj   cart:Cart, ld, uld:Device
               coord_id:array[1..length div 10] of Coord;
               coord_id := Initially()
         proc  SetNewCarts(val new:boolean) = (newcarts := new);
               Initially() = ([coord_id[i] := new(Coord) ; coord_id[i].SetSeg(i)];
                                          for i ∈ {1, ... , length div 10}
                             [coord_id[i].SetNext(coord_id[i + 1])];
                                          for i ∈ {1, ... , (length div 10) - 1}
                             coord_id[length div 10].SetNext(coord_id[1])
         do    cart_need, ld_need, uld_need :∈ {T, F}
               ‖ ld_need → ld := new(Device) ; ld.SetType(Loader)
               ‖ uld_need → uld := new(Device) ; uld.SetType(Unloader)
               ‖ cart_need ∧ ¬newcarts → cart := new(Cart) ; SetNewCarts(T);
               ‖ newcarts ∧ coord_id[1].GetStatus() → (coord_id[1].SetStatus(F);
                   coord_id[1].SetCart(cart) ; cart.SetCanMove(T) ; SetNewCarts(F));
         od
     ]|
```

The creation and initialisation of the coordinators is done using the procedure '$Initially()$' in $Chief$: $length$ div 10 objects of the class $Coord$ are created corresponding to the $length$ div 10 segments of the trajectory and then the coordinators are linked in a circular list. The object variables $coord\_id[1], ...,$ $coord\_id[length\ div\ 10]$ are used as references to them. The **for** clause stands for the sequential repetition of the statement in square brakets, as many times as the predicate after **for** states.

The creation of carts is conditioned by the need of carts in the system ($cart\_need = T$) and by the availability of the chief to create a new cart

($newcarts = F$). The latter attribute is modified by the procedure *SetNewCarts*. A reference to a newly created cart is communicated to the coordinator of the first segment when its segment is free. Therefore, if the system needs carts and the chief is willing to create one, a new cart is generated. When the coordinator of the first segment is free, the cart is given permission to move and the coordinator is set to 'having a cart on its segment'. Observe that now the cart is allowed to move only after the coordinator takes over its supervision.

The *Device* class is as before. The *Cart* class is also as before except for a new method to be used by the coordinator: *EnterNewSeg*. By calling this method the coordinator checks whether the cart will leave its current segment:

$$EnterNewSeg(res\ ens{:}boolean) = (ens := ((loc + 1)\ mod\ 10 \leq loc\ mod\ 10 - 1))$$

Observe this small modification of the mobility class. Essentially the coordinator acts as a wrapper for the coordinated class, by adding to it only a service it will use. The coordination of the cart is specified by an action in *Coord*:

$$crt\_cart \neq null \wedge crt\_cart.EnterNewSeg() \rightarrow$$
$$\text{if } next.GetStatus \text{ then } crt\_cart.SetCanMove(T);$$
$$next.SetStatus(F)\ ;\ next.SetCart(crt\_cart);$$
$$self.SetStatus(T)\ ;\ self.SetCart(null)$$
$$\text{else } crt\_cart.SetCanMove(F)$$
$$\text{fi}$$

Thus, if the coordinator has a cart to supervise ($crt\_cart \neq null$) and the cart is ready to enter a new segment, the coordinator checks the status of its next neighbour. Only if the next coordinator is free ($next.GetStatus$), the cart is allowed to continue its movement, otherwise it has to wait. At the handoff moment the next coordinator gets hold of a reference to the entering object and becomes occupied with the cart coming from its predecessor, while the previous coordinator becomes free. Hence, the coordinator knows about at most one mobile object at a time. Observe that the above action is a joint action by three objects, two coordinator objects and a mobile object. As the action has a higher priority than the actions of the mobile object, the movement can be controlled without delay, via a call to *SetCanMove*. Hence, if simultaneously both this action and the movement action in the cart are enabled, the former will be selected and, as a consequence, the latter might become disabled. The cart can still miss its destination though.

This small example gives an intuitive reason for justifying the need of coordination in mobile systems. The basic computation of a mobile object is specified independently of the aspects related to the environment of mobility. No matter where they are, the mobile objects should perform correctly their operations, like loading/unloading/moving for our example, or communicating with other mobile objects etc. For this reason we need a certain infrastructure that 'knows' about the domain of moving and can assist the mobile objects. This infrastructure is represented by the coordinators.

5   Concluding remarks

In this paper we have defined the concepts needed to model coordination and mobility within the object-based OO-action systems formalism. Coordination can be *data-driven* like in Linda [11] or *control-driven* like in Manifold [3]. Action systems support both views to coordination [18]. We focused on control-driven coordination here, but the ideas carry over to data-driven coordination, too. Our approach to mobility is very abstract leaving space for a designer to specialise the concepts to many different environments.

We exemplified the defined concepts with a small yet nontrivial example also specified in MobileUNITY [23] as well as in COMMUNITY [24], neither of which supports object-orientation. In the former approach a centralised set of coordination rules is given in an interactions section that all participants of the system must obey. We obtain this case when we have only one cell and hence only one coordinator ($q=1$). However, in our approach the coordination is decentralised among sets of coordinators supporting the idea of distribution. Category theory based COMMUNITY uses morphisms to model coordination. Sets of actions from interacting entities are put in a specific relation, corresponding to the type of interaction between entities: inhibition, synchronisation and communication. All these interaction types are possible in our approach, too. The inhibition and synchronisation are modeled by the coordination while the communication is done via method calls.

By defining both mobility and coordination classes we also obtained a modularity advantage, by separately developing the computation and coordination aspects of a system. The new types of classes are also classes in the original sense of OO-action systems. Therefore within the architecture of an OO-action systems specification using this extended framework we have classes that model active (distributed) objects, others that model mobile objects, and separately classes modelling coordinator objects all within a single framework.

Finally, we want to stress the fact that in this paper we defined the concepts needed to specify mobile object-oriented systems. The approach comes with a formal framework, the refinement calculus that was not discusses here, to formally derive systems from their high level abstract specifications to detailed implementations. Besides refining certain types of classes and their relationships with each other, we can also further refine the communiaction structure, e.g. to include broadcasting. Moreover, as our approach is object-oriented we can reuse our classes in a convenient manner, a feature also supported by the refinement calculus. The details of these concepts within mobile-coordinated action systems, as well as more dynamic properties for the coordinators are left for future research.

Acknowledgments. The work of Kaisa Sere is supported by the Academy of Finland.

References

1. G. Agha. *Actors: A Model of Concurrent Computation in Distributed Systems.* MIT Press, Los Alamos, California, 1986.
2. P. America, J. W. de Bakker, J.N. Kok, and J.J.M.M. Rutten. Operational semantics of a parallel object-oriented language. In *Proc. 13th ACM Symposium on Principles of Programming Languages*, pages 194–208, 1986.

3. F. Arbab. The IWIM Model for coordination of concurrent activities. In [14].
4. R. J. R. Back and R. Kurki-Suonio. Decentralization of process nets with centralized control. In *Proc. of the 2nd ACM SIGACT-SIGOPS Symp. on Principles of Distributed Computing*, pages 131–142, 1983.
5. R. J. R. Back and K. Sere. Stepwise refinement of action systems. *Structured Programming*, 12:17-30, 1991.
6. J.-P. Banâtre and D. Le Métayer. Programming by multiset transformation. *Communications of the ACM*, 36(1):98–111, January 1993.
7. M. M. Bonsangue, J. N. Kok, and K. Sere. An approach to object-orientation in action systems. In *Mathematics of Program Construction (MPC'98)*, Marstrand, Sweden, June 1998. *Lecture Notes in Computer Science* 1422, Springer–Verlag.
8. M. M. Bonsangue, J. N. Kok, and K. Sere. Developing Object-based Distributed Systems. In *Proceedings of IFIP TC6/WG6 Third International Conference on Formal Methods for Open Object-Based Distributed Systems (FMOODS'99)*, Florence, Italy, February 1999.
9. L. Cardelli. A language with distributed scope. *Computing Systems* 8(1):27–29, 1995.
10. L. Cardelli and A. D. Gordon. Mobile Ambients. In Maurice Nivat (Ed.) *Foundations of Software Science and Computational Structures* , VOL. 1378 of *Lecture Notes in Computer Science*, 140-155. Springer–Verlag, 1998.
11. N. Carriero and D. Gelernter. Coordination languages and their significance. *Communications of the ACM*, 35(2):97–107, February 1992.
12. K. Chandy and J. Misra. *Parallel Program Design: A Foundation*. Addison–Wesley, 1988.
13. M. Chaudron and E. de Jong. Towards a Compositional Method for Coordinating Gamma Programs. In [14].
14. P. Ciancarini and C. Hankin, editors. *Coordination'96: Coordination Languages and Models*, VOL. 1061 of *Lecture Notes in Computer Science*. Springer–Verlag, 1996.
15. E. W. Dijkstra. *A Discipline of Programming*. Prentice–Hall International, 1976.
16. R. De Nicola, G. L. Ferrari, and R. Pugliese. Coordinating Mobile Agents via Blackboards and Access Rights. In [17].
17. D. Garlan and D. Le Métayer, editors. *Coordination'97: Coordination Languages and Models*, volume 1282 of *Lecture Notes in Computer Science*. Springer–Verlag, 1997.
18. E. Hedman, J. N. Kok, and K. Sere. Coordinating Action Systems. In [17].
19. C. Hewitt. Viewing control structures as patterns of passing messages. *Artificial Intelligence* 8(3), 1997.
20. H.-H. Järvinen and R. Kurki-Suonio. DisCo specification language: marriage of actions and objects. In *Proc. of the 11th International Conference on Distributed Computing Systems*, IEEE Computer Society Press, pages 142-151, 1991.
21. P. J. McCann and G.-C. Roman. Compositional programming abstractions for mobile computing. *IEEE Transactions on Software Engineering* VOL. 24, No. 2, pp. 97–110, February 1998.
22. R. Milner, J. Parrow, and D.J. Walker. A calculus of mobile processes. *Information and Computation 100* No. 1, pages 1–40, 1992.
23. G.-C. Roman, P. J. McCann, and J. Y. Plun. Mobile UNITY: Reasoning and Specification in Mobile Computing. In *ACM TOSEM*, VOL. 6, No. 3, pp 250-282, July 1997.
24. M. Wermelinger and J. L. Fiadeiro. Connectors for Mobile Programs. In *IEEE Transactions on Software Engineering*, VOL. 24, No 5, pp. 331-341, May 1998.

Simulation of Conference Management Using an Event-Driven Coordination Language

Adriano Scutellà

CWI
P.O. Box 94079, 1090 GB Amsterdam, The Netherlands
email: adriano@cwi.nl

Abstract. We propose a simulation solution of a case study in coordination using **MANIFOLD**. The case study regards "peer reviewing and evaluation of submissions to scientific conferences." The solution simulates the flow of activities to for such a case study. The architecture of the application can be used to implement a real application.

1 Introduction

The objective of this paper is to present a solution to a case study in coordination [CG92,MC94,Coo96,Coo97] using a pure control-based coordination language, namely **MANIFOLD** [Arb95,Arb96a,Arb96b].

With respect to the case study an architectural design and a simulation of the activities are presented. The case study regards peer reviews and evaluation of submissions to a scientific conference [CNT98]. It is introduced in Section 2. In this case study, we find both machine-machine and machine-human being interactions. The application we developed simulates the evolution of those activities needed to accomplish the goal of peer reviewing and evaluation of submissions to a confererence.

The IWIM model [Arb95,Arb96a] is the coordination paradigm on which **MANIFOLD** is based, it fits quite nicely within the nature of the problem we have to treat. Before we present the details of our solution in section 4, we briefly introduce **MANIFOLD** in section 3. We conclude the paper with some remarks (Section 5) and some planning for future work (Section 6).

2 A case study in coordination: Conference Management on the Internet

The specification of the case study appears in an electronic note [CNT98]. The purpose of this note is: *"to informally specify a case study in coordination describing a real world problem."* The case study concerns *"peer review and evaluation of submissions to scientific conferences."* The problem is about managing the dependencies of activities (the workflow as it is named in [CNT98, p. 3]) necessary to prepare the program and produce the proceedings of a scientific conference.

The idea to study this problem comes from the observation that there are already available procedures for electronic submission, collection of Referee reports, and PC meeting support based on Internet communication mechanisms, namely e-mail or WWW see for instance [Sas96,MC96,Tol98].

Implicit in the specification is the aim to automate those tasks that are boring, long or repetitive.

2.1 Specification of the problem

We recall here the original specification and requirements a solution has to satisfy. For the sake of brevity we condensed it but we have not left out any importatnt detail.

Agents and Roles. The system to be specified includes several agents. The authors of the note say the term *agent* is to be taken as primitive: an agent is an entity which can act autonomously.

Some agents are roles: They represent human users which can perform some operations. There are the following roles involved in the case study: Author (submitter of a paper[1]); PC Chair; PC Member; Reviewer; Editor of proceedings.

Any of the roles above may overlap: for instance, an author can also be a PC Member or a Referee. We may admit that each role has a unique identity, so that it is possible to refer to the same person by identifying the various roles played, as precised in [CNT98].

The involved entities communicate using electronic mail or a WEB browser.

Dynamics. In [CNT98, p. 3] we read that: *"the dynamics of the workflow to be enacted is specified by defining a number of tasks"* and: *"the order of listing does not impose any sequentiality, apart from the necessary one when a task has to complete its output before some other task can start."* Here follows a list for these tasks.

1. **SUBMISSION OF PAPERS.**
   A submission form is available from the conference site. Authors submit papers (either on-line, by WWW, or off-line, by e-mail), to the conference site.
   A submission consists of: (1) the submission form, (2) an ASCII file containing title and abstract, (3) the URL of a file containing the paper in the format declared in the submission form.
   If a submission does not conform to the above requirements, it is not accepted and its sender is invited to resubmit. Otherwise a submission is stored at the conference site and its corresponding author gets an acknowledgement.

2. **BIDDING FOR PAPERS.** Each PC Member examines the list of submissions and selects a subset of papers to review. The PC Chair can alter each subset to balance the load among PC Members.

3. **DISTRIBUTION OF THE PAPERS TO REFEREES.** After the deadline for submissions has expired, papers selected by PC Members will be distributed to them. Papers will be reviewed with the help of Referees.

4. **COLLECTION OF THE REPORTS.** Referees must fill in a form to deliver their reports that will be collected for further use.

5. **PREPARATION OF STATISTICS.** An agent scans all reports and fills up a table in a standard spreadsheet to generate statistics and an initial proposal for ranking all papers to be used during the PC meeting.

---

[1] If the paper is co-authored the corresponding author is who (first) submitted the paper.

6. **PC MEETING.** During this phase PC Members meet to decide on submitted papers. Each PC Member needs to access all data pertaining the submission and evaluation reports, decide on acceptance status and record such a decision.

7. **COMMUNICATION OF RESULTS.** Once the list of accepted papers is formed, results and Referee reports are communicated to the authors.

8. **SUBMITTING CAMERA READY COPY.** Authors submit camera ready versions, compliance with camera ready standars is checked and late authors are warned.

9. **PREPARING THE PROCEEDINGS.** Camera ready versions are collected, the editor prepares a preface. A draft of the proceedings is prepared. The editor and the PC Chairs are informed when the proceedings are done.

That concludes the description of the problem together with some requirement the solution should satisfy.

The authors suggest that the interest could focus on one or more of the subsequent points: (1) *formal specification*, (2) *model/language comparison*, (3) *coordination ontologies*, (4) *architectural design*, (5) *animation/simulation*, (6) *implementation*.

The principal requirement for this case study is to automate as much as possible the above phases. We address the problem using a coordination language for simulation and with an eye towards a prototype implementation of a program. We will also see that the approach leads naturally to an architectural design of the software structure for the system.

3 An overview of MANIFOLD

This section provides a necessarily brief introduction to **MANIFOLD** [Arb95,Arb96b], one realization of the IWIM model of coordination [Arb95,Arb96a] which we do not describe because of the correspondence between **MANIFOLD** constructs and IWIM concepts.

3.1 The language MANIFOLD

MANIFOLD is a strongly-typed, block-structured, event-driven coordination language [Arb95] based on a concrete model in the IWIM family where each of the basic concepts of process, event, port, and channel in IWIM corresponds to an explicit language construct. All communication is asynchronous in **MANIFOLD** and the separation of computation and communication concerns is strongly enforced.

Processes. In **MANIFOLD**, the atomic workers of the IWIM model are called atomic processes.

Atomic processes can only produce and consume data units through their ports, generate and receive events, and compute. In this way, the desired separation of computation and coordination is achieved.

Coordination processes are written in **MANIFOLD** and are called *manifolds*. The header of a manifold defines its name, number and types of its parameters, names of its input and output ports and their attributes. The body of a manifold is a bloc consisting of a finite number of states. Each state has a label and a body. The label of a state defines the condition under which a transition to that state is possible: It is an expression defined in terms of event occurrences that can be matched by incoming event occurrences (see Section 4.1 *et segg*).

A manifold process, coordinating the activity of some atomic processes, may itself be considered as an atomic process by another manifold process, giving rise to a sophisticated hierachy of coordinators.

Streams. In **MANIFOLD**, the asynchronous IWIM channels are called streams. A stream is a communication link that transports a sequence of bits, grouped into (variable length) units. It represents a reliable, unbounded and directed flow of information from its *source* to its *sink*. The constructor of a stream between two processes is, in general, a third process. Once a stream is established between a producer process and a consumer process, it operates autonomously and transfers the units from its source to its sink. The sink of a stream requiring a unit is suspended only if no units are available in the stream. The suspended sink is resumed as soon as the next unit becomes available for its consumption.

There are four basic stream types designated as BB, BK, KB, and KK (corresponding to the four basic asynchronous channel types in IWIM), each type of stream behaves according to a slightly different protocol. See [Arb96b] for details.

Events and State Transitions. In **MANIFOLD**, a process that has *raised* an event continues with its processing, while the resulting event occurrence propagates through the environment independently.

Any *observer* process that is interested in an event occurrence will automatically receive it in its *event memory*. Observed events can be examined and reacted on by a process at its own leisure. In reaction to event occurrences, the observer process can make a transition from one state to another.

The only control structure in the **MANIFOLD** language is the event-driven state transition mechanism [2]. Upon transition to a state, all instructions specified in its body are performed in some non-deterministic order. Then, the state becomes *preemptable*: If conditions for transition to another state are satisfied, the current state is preempted[3] and a transition to a new state takes place. The most important instructions in a state body are: (1) creation and activation of processes, (2) generation of event occurrences and (3) connection of streams to ports of various processes.

Ports. A *port* is a opening at the boundary of a process, through which the information produced and consumed by the process is exchanged. Information either flows into a process trough an *input* port or it flows out of the process trough an *output* port. Information is quantized in discrete bundles called units. A *unit* is a packet containing an arbitrary number of bits.

Ports through which units flow into a process are called the *input* ports of the process. Similarly, ports through which units flow out of a process are called the *output* ports of the process. The standard ports input, output, and error are always defined for all process instances in **MANIFOLD**.

---

[2] More familiar control structures, such as the sequential flow of control, conditional constructs and loop constructs can be built out of this event mechanism, and are also available in the language as convenience features [Arb96b].

[3] Meaning that all streams that have been constructed are preempted.

The ports of a process are its only interface to the topology of the communication network of an application. Generally, this topology is changed dynamically by some manifold instances, without the direct involvement of the affected processes.

4 Description of the application

In [ACH98] the authors address a number of issues to be kept in mind when developing coordination applications:

1. What is to be accomplished by coordination?
2. What is being coordinated?
3. What are the media for coordination?
4. What are the protocols and rules for coordination?

This section illustrates the design decisions that lead to the development of the application keeping in mind above questions. The approach followed has been advocated in [PA98a]. This approach structures the application into a hierarchy of processes distinguished in coordinator and coordinated processes.

A process serves the only purpose to model and simulate the external behaviour of entities specified in Section 2. Processes exchange data between them through channels: data are, for instance, a submission form or a paper to be submitted. A process, by itself, is seen as a black-box capable of consuming and producing data units through its named ports. In addition to data exchange, a process raises and reacts to a set of interesting events that will drive its evolution.

The requirements in [CNT98] specify the *coordination objective* to be the management of the activities necessary to reviews papers submitted to a conference with the aim to automate these activities. Once established the objective, let us turn to the question: "*What is being coordinated?*" At first, one is tempted to answer that what is being coordinated are the processes mentioned above. Indeed, they are being coordinated, but with respect to what? Remember: The aim is to automate as much as possible all those activities that can be automated. We cannot hope to fully automate the meetings of the Program Committee, because these meetings must be held by humans, though we may attempt to make the paper review and selection process more efficient [Nie97]. What we can hope to automate and coordinate, as requested in the specification, is the workflow. In this respect the process of submission of papers (listed as point 1 in the dynamics for the problem) is a sequence of more elementary activities [4] that can be automated; the distribution of papers to Referees (point 3 of the specification) consists in another bunch of activities that can be automated. Coordinating the dynamics means to make sure that the workflow is enacted as prescribed.

As *means* for coordination we use the event based method of **MANIFOLD**, the flow of information is enacted using point-to-point channels.

Regarding *protocols and rules* we realize that for this case, most of the coordination will consist in "forcing" the processes to execute some of the activities in a prescribed order, determined by the reaction to the events the processes received: this kind of coordination is a sort of *synchronization* between the various phases. Indeed, let us consider a PC Member and let us consider the bidding related activity. A PC Member should do the bidding and, *after*, receive some bunch of papers to review. Note that

---

[4] Together they form the *macroactivity* of submission.

what we just said is not exactly what the specification prescribes. Indeed, the specification says that the paper is supposed to stay in some store where it will be retrieved by: "*an agent that sends by e-mail another agent to each PC Member which, when run on the PC member's local system, fetches from a given URL all the papers assigned to that member for refereeing.*"[CNT98, p. 3] Notice that this suggests already an implementation, in fact, it sounds like a design rather than a requirements specification. There is no inherent reason why an agent should send another agent to accomplish some particular task. The point is that the PC Members are notified of the papers assigned to them, and they retrieve them. There can be many ways to retrieve the papers (see section 5.2). The requirements should only impose automatization as much as possible. The same kind of remarks apply to other phases (4 and 5) of the dynamics.

We profit of the disgression to say that, while elaborating the case study, we added some extensions that do not alter the original workflow but require some special treatment. These extensions do constitute an important part in the coordination activity and are features that influence the way the workflow is enacted. Actually the majority of extensions should be called *exceptions* since they deviate from what can be considered the normal behaviour.

Pictures for processes are represented in Figure 1. Each process has ports depicted as small rectangular boxes labeled with their names (in this case only *input* and *output*), Each process has an outgoing arrow representing the events that process can raise, and it has an incoming arrow with the list of incoming events.

In addition to the liberty of extending the case study it is also possible to simplify something: A simplification we adopt is that the actual flow of complex data structures may be represented by a single piece of information, a (symbolic) constant will represent a form, another a paper and so on. Our concern being simulation one may recognize that this is not a major departure.

In the remaining part of this section we describe the application. We use the IWIM model of coordination to establish a conceptual architecture. This model helps us in the design of the application since it defines also a structure for the application itself. The conceptual model, together with the description of the processes in isolation will be used in the framework proposed in [PA98a] to have a finite product. The general framework advocated in [PA98a] consists of three levels: (i) the top level defines graphically the interrelationships (and behaviour) of the processes; (ii) the middle level consists in a verbal (semi-formal) description of the states that define each process and how it reacts when receiving some event; (iii) the third level is the implementation of the scenario outlined with the use of the conceptual model and points (i) and (ii).

For the interested reader level (i) can be better exploited using the environment presented in [BA96] that translates the visual description to **MANIFOLD** code.

4.1 Design of the application

The structure of the application is hierarchical. We isolate, firstly, various processes being part of the application.

Another process simulates the site of the conference, let us call it *datastore*[5]. Figure 1 depicts these processes.

---

[5] The name 'datastore' has been chosen because it suggests that all material (submission forms, submitted papers) will be stored and retrieved later for further use by other processes.

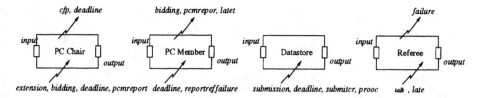

Fig. 1. Processes of the application

The coordination dependency. The basic idea leading to the hierarchy of coordinator and coordinated processes is inspired by the specification and also by common sense. It seems reasonable that a PC Chair has more coordination responsabilities than a PC Member (who may have to coordinate only the Referees choosen to help him). In section 5 we will discuss some variant to the coordination scheme we present and we will see, anyhow, that no major changes will result to the overall architecture and behaviours of the application. Referees have nothing to coordinate since their job is to produce a review for each paper received, also an author has no entity to coordinate.

We devised the hierarchy of processes we have been talking about concurrently with the specification of the processes. The picture in Figure 2 shows this hierarchy.

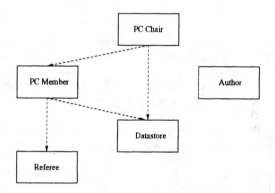

Fig. 2. The Hierarchy of Processes

The dotted arrows show the coordination dependency. We point out explicitly that generally every coordinator knows *only* the processes pointed out by the arrows. Therefore the PC Chair does not know, in principle, the identity (or even the existence) of any Referee or author process.

In the figure authors are stand alone processes, but this does not imply that they are not coordinated. The idea is that authors are not really part of the system that manages the conference. They are actors that participate to the game [6], from the point of view of authors the conference management system is open.

The dependency we talk about here, though informal, is based on the permanent knowledge a coordinator has; in practice (see Section 5.2).

---

[6] One may argue that being late submitters may alter the prescribed activity, but this is not the case since these are exceptions and handled, as such, in special cases.

Author and Referee processes. For the sake of brevity we omit a detailed description of Authors and Referees. The interested reader can find their description, as well as the **MANIFOLD** code for the application in an expanded version of this paper [Scu98].

Basically an author receives an index that denotes its unique address. The Author waits for the call for papers and decides whether to submit one or more papers to the conference. A submission is represented by a tuple S = <AI, FORM, TITLE, ABSTRACT, PAPER> carrying the identity of the author AI, the form FORM, the title TITLE, abstract ABSTRACT and the paper PAPER. Later ifthe Author receives an acceptance advice (an event) the camera ready copy is prepared and sent, upon detection of the camera ready request.

A Referee does not have much work to do if not for receiving some papers and reviewing them.

It may happen that the Referee has produced a review that is quite in conflict with the review of another Referee for the same paper: the PC may decide to let the two Referees talk to each other so that they reach an agreement. It is also possible that the reviewer fails to produce a report (so that it has to be replaced). We take into account all these extensions in the application.

For brevity we omit any description of the Editor.

Datastore: Level(ii). Each state will carry a label: It is the matching expression for event occurrences.

State: begin. In this state datastore ds just executes some initializations.

State: submission. On reception of the event **submission** (from some author a) ds sets up a stream a -> ds so to receive the submission tuple S^7. Once the submission has been received, a conformance check is done. If the submission is done properly it will be stored and a confirmation sent. If the submission has some fault the author is invited to resubmit by sending a negative acknowledegement.

State: deadline. All stored submissions will be distributed to all PC Members.

State: submitcr. On reception of the event **submitcr** datastore will set to receive and store the camera-ready copy from some author.

State: dsextension. The datastore prepares to receive and store a late submission.

State: deliverext. The datastore delivers late submissions data.

State: proceedings. Upon reception of the event **proceedings** (from PC Chair) the list of proceedings is sent to the editor.

PC Chair: Level(ii). The PC Chair has a lot of internal activities to do: select or alter the load of papers for each PC Member, decide for extension requests, etc. Other activities may or may not be modelled, in this area fall, for instance, activities like evaluation meetings. We point out explicitly that most activities involving the PC-Chair as a role cannot be automated and not even simulated unless a particular policy is choosen.

State: begin. Authors a, PC Members m, are created and activated, each of them receives a unique index. An instance of datastore (named ds) is created and activated. After this preparation the event **startconference** is posted.

---

[7] This is possible since any event raised carries its event source that is therefore -*only* in that state- known by the handler (ds, in this case).

State: startconference. The event cfp is broadcasted. An alarm process is activated: it will signal when the deadline occurs posting the event deadline.

State: extension. If an author a asks for an extension this may or may not be accepted.

If it is accepted then an event dsextension is raised so that ds will prepare to receive the late submission. A stream a -> ds is created to transmit the submission data from the requesting author to the datastore ds. Another stream ds -> a is needed for confirmation of submission by ds.

If the extension is rejected the author is informed setting a stream Chair -> a to carry the negative information.

State: deadline. The distribution of the papers to the Referee is perfomed, by setting up as many streams (ds -> m) as many PC Members m have been created. The PC Chair will retrieve all submissions data. The event deadline is raised to inform that the deadline has occurred.

A suitable manner (or subprocess) will take care of distributing late submitted papers.

State: bidding. On reception of the event bidding from some PC Member m, the PC Chair may or may not agree with the choices made by the PC Member. A suitable manner is invoked that will decide on the load balance for each Referee[8]. An alarm is activated (to post the event evaluation) that signals it is time for the PC to have a meeting.

State: pcmreport. Detection of the event pcmreport signals that a PC Member m wants to deliver its reviews. They will be stored by PC Chair for further use.

State: evaluation. In this state the meeting is held and decisions are taken. The event accept is posted (so that the PC Chair will communicate the results to the authors). A manner will take care of communicating the results to all authors.

An alarm is activated to post the event proceedings.

State: proceedings. Camera ready copies stored by the datastore ds are forwarded to the editor of the proceedings.

PC Member: Level(ii).

State: begin. In this state some preparation is made and an index, MI, is received analogously to author processes.

State: deadline. On detection of the event deadline submitted papers are retrieved and PC Member selects the ones to be reviewed, then it raises the event bidding and prepares to create and use Referees posting the event spawnreferee.

State: spawnrefeee. Referees are created, activated and papers are sent to them.. An alarm is activated so that PC Member can warn late Referees.

State: reportref. A Referee signals its report is ready. Some bookkeeping is made to collect and order all reports. PC Member raises the event pcmreport for PC Chair to know reports and reviews are ready.

State: failure. A Referee r failed. PC Member sets a stream r -> m to get the paper r cannot review. Another Referee has to be created for handling the paper.

5 Discussion

There are various points that can be discussed regarding both the problem and the specific solution we are presenting.

---

[8] This is one of the activity that can be only partially automated.

5.1 Some remarks on the problem object of study

This problem has been proposed in [CNT98] as a case study on applicability of coordination models and languages to a general class of problems known under the names of *groupware, workflow, electronic commerce, business process reengineering*, in particular the authors proposed it as a *workflow* case study. All these kinds of activities are, more and more often, done in conjunction with computer-based cooperative environments such as electronic-mail services or teleconferencing, eventually using the technology offered by the WWW.

The proposed case study presents some interesting issues, hierarchies and distribution, that can be studied in order to grasp some recurrent patterns, schemes, paradigms of coordination that could form a set of techniques to be used in similar, or even completely different, problems with the same structure, as proposed in [MC94]. Howewer, as far as workflow is concerned we believe that the problem does not fit in a typical workflow scenario: in an organization, workflow is intended as a sort of more or less continuos 'flow' of information to and from different places. In the present problem there is not much continous flow of information: all communications are generally one-shot (communications that take place once and for all): for instance, an author submits forms and papers all at once and, if everything is compiled correctly, the submission activity is finished; a Referee receives the paper to review (one shot) and later produces a review for that paper (one shot). Anyway, if we want to attain to the specification, we can then understand that, essentially, the authors suggest indirectly that the purpose to be achieved is that of synchronizing the various phases as described in points 1 to 9 of the dynamics.

As far as we take the point of view that *"coordination is the management of activities"* [MC94] then this problem is an instance of a general class of problems where scheduling of activities and orchestration of the communication have the prominent role. Simulations show (but there was no need for simulation to get it), there are some macroactivities that can be localized: The first consists of the communications established between the authors and the PC Chair or conference site in order to submit papers. A second bunch of communication activities goes on when it is time to (bid and) distribute the papers. After the meetings of the PC, we see some communication going on between PC Chair and authors (communication of results). An activity similar to that of submission happens when authors have to submit a camera ready copy. Finally the camera ready copies will be sent to the editor of proceedings. These *macroactivities* are to happen essentially in sequence, even if in order to speed up the whole process, some of them may overlap (it has been suggested in [Nie97] that bidding could happen concurrently with submissions so that also the distribution process can start before the deadline). This sequentiality is inherent to the problem at hand.

A first coordination scheme that is possible to identify here is the *producer/consumer* relationship, that is, a situation where one activity produces something that is used by another activity. In information systems the producer/consumer relationship occurs when one person or a computer program in one organization uses information produced by some other entity. As it is pointed out in [MC94] producer/consumer relationships lead to some kinds of dependencies that we see appearing, in various forms, also in the problem which is the object of our study, that is: (1) prerequisite constraints and (2) transfer (of information). Prerequisite constraints is quite common as dependency relation when a producer activity has to be completed before the consumer activity may take place. In this case we have that submissions have to take place before biddings and distributions; the evaluation meetings have to be held after the reviews have been produced and so on. The actual schedule of the activities is summarized in Figure 3.

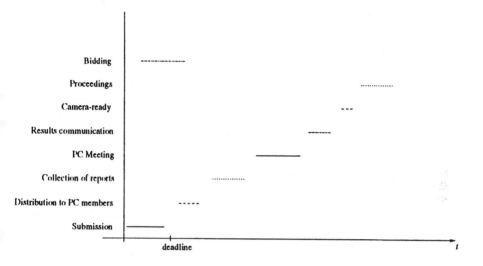

Fig. 3. Scheduling of the activities workflow

We pictured the activity of *bidding* on top of the diagram because, even if nowadays bidding seems to be a growing practice practice, it is not yet widely used. Indeed we did not take into account bidding as an overlapping activity, but as something that happens after all submissions have been completed. Notice that only after completion of submissions can a PC Member be capable to fully bid, since only then will he be able to know all papers that have been submitted. Notice also that a PC Chair, as role, may decide on the alteration of the load of work for each PC Member only after he knows (1) all members' biddings, (2) all papers that have been submitted.

In connection with the prerequisite contraints there is also the management of the "transfer" from the producer activity to the consumer activity. In our case, we transfer information and therefore we talk about communication: this is a crucial point, at least for this problem. Management of the communication between the various processes (activities) and entities involved is the principal coordination activity. Note how the blocking input/output constructs of **MANIFOLD**, the possibility of directing the flow of information passing trough a stream and the anonymous communication mechanism, provide the means to manage communication in a very powerful, expressive and secure way. The overlapping we were suggesting between the submission activity and the bidding and distribution activity is a way to control the timing (so to optimize it) and has been already studied in different contexts [Sch82,Sch86].

The scheduling becomes a bit more elaborated, if we take into account some extension as we did, for each component of the system but still the various phases have the same time overlap. With these extensions the case study becomes a bit more complicated from the point of view of coordination: there are more decisions to be taken by each coordinator but still retains its natural classification of a case study in coordination where the main paradigms are producer/consumer relationships and transfer of information.

To summarize, the problem we are studying presents some interesting coordination aspects, classified under the paradigms of producer/consumer, comunication and coordination hierarchies, even if it cannot be presented as a proper workflow problem. Studying different solutions to the problem may help to recognize some other hidden coordination aspects, it may help also to estimate and compare the cost of the coordination effort. With regards to different solutions we discuss, in the following section, a slightly different architecture and division of tasks between the various entities.

5.2 A comparison between various approaches

We already described what is the conceptual architecture underlying this solution and, in fact, we committed ourselves to some design decisions that in a way would produce a natural architecture for the application.

Different behaviour of the system agents. Consider a PC Chair. It is the entity that supervises most of the activities of various processes. As it stands, the process modelling the behaviour of the PC Chair does a lot that the real Chair has to do but that can be automated, in principle, if we accept that most of the activities can undergo a disciplined policy.

An example of regulation is the bidding and distribution of papers: after the deadline for submissions is expired, the actual distribution of papers among the various PC Members and Referees is perfomed. There are various ways to distribute the papers; here is a list that by no means intends to be exhaustive: (1)The PC scans all papers and distributes them according to personal taste. (2)There can be an automatic matching according to keywords. (3)Titles and abstracts may be broadcast, then a bidding mechanism can be implemented. (4)The PC Chair decides to distribute the papers based on the expertise of the various PC Members.

With the exception of items 1 and 4 above, all of the solutions proposed can be automated and therefore transferred, as activities, to the datastore process (simulating the behaviour of the site), so that the PC Chair does not have to bother himself (as human) with distribution, bidding and related phases of the reviewing process. Of course, only the PC Chair may decide on late submissions and together with the PC Members decide on the evaluation and acceptance phases.

There are no major changes involved when we assume an automatization of the bidding and distribution mechanisms. They are handled by the process module PCCHAIR under the states labeled **deadline** and **bidding**. The pieces of code relative to these states may be happily passed to the coordinator module datastore that will do the very same job of the PC Chair module, with less coordination effort done by the PC Chair and more coordination effort done by the datastore. In case of automatization the PC Chair can coordinate very few activities: extension requests, meetings.

For implementation reasons the coordination dependency is as Figure 4.

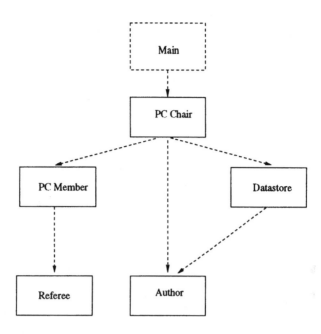

Fig. 4. The Hierarchy of Processes

The changes implied by this architecture concern the activity of creation of processes: the process Main creates a PCCHAIR that, in turn, creates datastore, PC Members and Author processes. This implementation has been adopted for reasons which are independent from the conceptual architecture and the two architectures are equivalent.

The dataflow still remains the same whatever solution we adopt. The effort to minimize the activity of human beings (by automatic means) and make it more efficient is to be done at the level of problem analysys not of some eventual solution. Analysts should individuate what are the activities that can be automated (and we indicated a few), they should find solutions on how they can be automated and seek for the most promising coordination patterns so that the effort is minimal.

5.3 Control driven coordination versus Shared dataspace coordination

Coordination models and languages are commonly classified as either *data-oriented* or *control-oriented* [ACH98]. The majority of coordination models and systems can be viewed as part of data-oriented approaches to coordination, and are based on the notion of shared dataspace. Linda and its derivatives [CG92,Coo96,Coo97] are representative of this class.

A discussion on the impact that the use of a specific coordination model and language has on the architectural design and the program structure appears in [Arb97]. A shared data space may or may not be the natural solution for some problems. We are not aware of concrete solutions that use a model or language based on a shared data space. A very elementary solution may be represented in figure 5.

All processes put data into the shared dataspace and retrieve data from it. Now, even if safety may be guaranteed by avoiding that some process (accidentally) retrieves

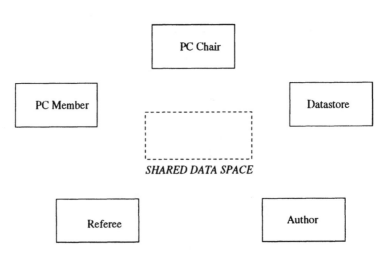

Fig. 5. A shared data space solution

some data that have to be kept secret, the nature of the shared data space is that of being public; safe delivery of data has to rely on the assumption that the processes do pick up only data that pertinent to them. To forbid a process to get data not pertinent to its activity some filter has to be supplied. A solution to the multiple access could be to use the notion of multiset (like in Bauhaus Linda [CGZ94]).

With respect to the coordination effort notice that for each one shot communication necessary in the IWIM-like approach here two shots are necessary: Consider, again, a submission the author has to put data in the shared space (first shot) and then they have to be retrieved by the interested process (second shot).

With only the possibility of one shared data space we actually see no way to implement hierachies of coordinators, as we did.

6   Concluding remarks

In this paper a simulation for the case study proposed in [CNT98] has been presented. The general framework advocated in [PA98a] together with the intuitive coordination dependencies helped to design the application. Other topics

addressed in this paper are the design architecture and the structure of an application that simulates the management of activities (coordination) and the data-flow between involved entitities.

Some variants to this architecture have been discussed, including a sketch of the architecture that a solution based on shared data space could have.

Simulations have been conducted on a Sun Sparc Station 4 with a number of authors varying from 5 to 100, and a number of PC Members varying from 2 to 15, all yielding the same kind of behaviours divided in the phases evidenced in Figure 3.

We outlined that some of the activity concerned with each phase can be automated so to reduce the effort made by humans in order to manage the activities involved which is the only aim of the case study.

The same architecture proposed here could be used as architecture for a real application to manage the conference activities. With respect to the simulation we look forward to another kind of simulation, stemming from the animation of the formal semantics of **MANIFOLD** [ABBRSZ98]: with this alternative it should be possible to prove some property about the application and the problem. The author is involved in a program to study the applicability of the model-checker SPIN [Hol91] to **MANIFOLD** applications [FS99] and this problem could be a good test-bench.

The coordination paradigm enforced by the IWIM model has been of importance in devising the design of the application thanks to the fact that any concept of the model has a corresponding construct in the language **MANIFOLD**. This shows that a good programming paradigm may help also in minimizing the effort of developing coordination programs. When writing the application we sometimes encountered the need for events to carry information (for instance units or references to processes, ports and so on, also in a parametric way). When a (process) Referee fails we saw that the event failure is raised, then a connection has to be established to retrieve the paper by the PC Member coordinator of the Referee. An event that would carry the paper (reference) would simplify the job

Acknowledgements. We thank Kees Everaars and Alan Fagot for reading drafts of this document. Giuseppe Manco and Eric Monfroy have been suggesting many ways of improving both the presentation and the application. Thanks also to Freek Burger and Kees Blom for the help they gave when we have been writing the **MANIFOLD** code for this case study. Jan Rutten suggested the Referee conflict extension.

This work has been supported by SION project n. 612-33-007 CoLa and by the ESPRI Working Group COORDINA.

References

[Arb95]   F. Arbab. "Coordination of massively concurrent activities." Technical Report CS-R9565, Centrum voor Wiskunde en Informatica, Amsterdam, 1995. Available on-line at http://www.cwi.nl/ftp/CWIreports/IS/CS-R9565.ps.Z.

[Arb96a]   F. Arbab. The IWIM model for coordination of concurrent activities. In [Coo96], pages 34–56.

[Arb96b]   F. Arbab. Manifold version 2: Language reference manual. Technical report, Centrum voor Wiskunde en Informatica, Amsterdam, The Netherlands, 1996. Available on-line at http://www.cwi.nl/ftp/manifold/refman.ps.Z.

[Arb97]   F. Arbab. "The influence of coordination on program structure" *Prooceedings of the 30th Hawaii International Conference on System sciences,* 1997.

[ABBRSZ98] F. Arbab, J. de Bakker,M.Bonsangue,J.Rutten, A.Scutellà, G.Zavattaro. *A transition system semantics for the control-driven language MANIFOLD.* To appear in *theoretical Computer Science,* 1999.

[ACH98]   F. Arbab, P. Ciancarini, and C. Hankin. "Coordination languages for parallel programming." *Parallel Computing,* special issue on Coordination, 1998.

[BA96]   P. Bouvry and F. Arbab. "Visifold: A visual environment for a coordination language." In [Coo96], pp.: 403–406.

[CG92]   N. Carriero and D. Gelernter. "Coordination Languages and their significance." *Communications of the ACM,* 35(2):97–107, 1992.

[CGZ94]   N. Carriero, D. Gelernter and L. Zuck. "Bauhaus Linda". In: *Object-based Models and Languages for Concurrent Systems*, LNCS 924, Springer-verlag, Berlin, pp.: 66-76.

[Coo96]   P. Ciancarini and C. Hankin, editors. *Coordination Languages and Models, Proceedings of the 1st international conference COORDINATION'96*, LNCS, 1061, Berlin Springer-Verlag, 1996.

[Coo97]   D. Garlan and D. Le Métayer, editors. *Coordination Languages and Models, Proceedings of the 2nd international conference COORDINATION'97* LNCS, 1252, Berlin, Springer-Verlag, 1997.

[CNT98]   P. Ciancarini, O. Niestratz, and R. Tolksdorf. A case study in coordination: Conference Management trough the Internet. Electronic note.

[FS99]   A. Fagot, A.Scutellà. *A preliminary study of state reachability of* **MANIFOLD** *applications (extended abstract)*. Available on line at: `http://www.cwi.nl/ adriano/maniprom.ps` or at: `http://www.cwi.nl/ fagot/maniprom.ps` .

[Hol91]   G .Holzmann. *Design and Validation of Computer Protocols* Prentice Hall, Englewood Cliffs, New Jersey, USA, pp.: VII-500, 1991.

[MC94]   T.W. Malone and K. Crowston. "The Interdisciplinary Study of Coordination." *ACM Computing Surveys*, Vol. 26, No.1, March 1994, pp.: 87-119.

[MC96]   G. Mathews and B. Jacobs. Electronic Management of the Peer Review Process. *Computer Networks and ISDN Systems*, 28(7-11):1523, November 1996.

[Nie97]   O. Niestrastz. Identify the champion. Available on-line at`http://www.iam.unibe.ch/oscar/PDF/champion.fm.ps`, 1997.

[PA97]   G. Papadopoulos and F. Arbab. "Control-based coordination of human and other activities in cooperative information systems." In [Coo97], pages 422–425.

[PA98a]   G. A. Papadopoulos and F. Arbab. "Modelling Activities in Information Systems Using the Coordination Language **MANIFOLD**" *Thirteenth ACM Symposium on Applied Computing (SAC'98)*, Atlanta, Georgia, USA, 1998, ACM Press (to appear).

[Sas96]   V. Sassone. Management of electronic submission, refereeing, and PC meeting. (Manual of a WWW system), Nov. 1996.

[Sch82]   *Japanese Manufacturing Techniques*. Free Press. New York, 1982.

[Sch86]   *World Class Manufacturing*. Free Press, New York, 1986

[Scu98]   A. Scutellà. *Simulation of a conference Management System using* **MANIFOLD**. In preparation.

[Tol98]   R. Tolksdorf. Conference reviewing. Available on-line at: `grunge.cs.tu-berlin.de/ tolk/reviewing.html`, 1998.

Internet-Based Coordination Environments and Document-Based Applications: A Case Study

Davide Rossi and Fabio Vitali

Dipartimento di Scienze dell'Informazione, University of Bologna - Italy
{Davide.Rossi, Fabio.Vitali}@CS.UniBO.IT

Abstract. In this paper we discuss a solution to the conference management problem, a case study in designing a groupware application distributed over the WWW. The case study requires supporting the coordination of activities of people engaged in reviewing and selecting papers submitted for a scientific conference. We discuss why such an application is interesting and describe how we designed its software architecture. The architecture we suggest implements what we call an *active Web*, because it includes agents able to use services offered by WWW infrastructures. A special kind of agents are *active documents*, which are documents that carry both some content and some code able to manipulate such a content. Users, agents, and active documents can interoperate using a set of basic services for communication and synchronization. The active Web implementation we describe here is based on coordination technology integrated with Java.

1 Introduction

The World Wide Web is now the most popular platform to access Internet services, so it has the potential to become the standard infrastructure to build integrated applications. In fact, most application domains are turning to the World Wide Web as the environment of choice for building innovative applications leveraging on the open standards, their diffusion, and the programmable nature of the available services. For instance, there is a growing interest in document management systems based on the World Wide Web infrastructure. These applications typically exploit *multiagent* technologies, meaning that they are highly concurrent, distributed, and often based on mobile code [MD97]. We expect that document-centric applications will exploit the forthcoming XML technology, which allows to define *active documents*, that is messages which refer not only to content but also to code for manipulating such content [CV99].

However, the World Wide Web in its current state does not provide enough support for document-centric applications based on agent-oriented programming, like groupware or workflow, which require sophisticated agent coordination.

In fact, most WWW applications are either server-centric (interfacing applications via CGI to a mainframe-like central server machine), client-centric (applets providing application services to users without a real distribution concept), or not integrated at all with the Web (applications whose user interface is implemented by applets or plug-ins connecting with some proprietary protocol to a proprietary server). All these approaches do not really satisfy the idea of an active Web based on some structured configuration of (autonomous) agents: they are either not really distributed, or not integrated with the Web.

The PageSpace architecture [CTV+98] provides a reference framework for overcoming these limitations, establishing an original design paradigm for Web-based applications that are composed of autonomous agents performing their duties regardless of their physical positions. In this paper we demonstrate the flexibility of PageSpace by describing a case study where this architecture has been fruitfully used.

The paper is structured as follows:

In Sect. 2 we describe a case study in document-centric groupware over the Internet: the management of a scientific conference. In Sect. 3 we discuss the issues arising when creating distributed, interactive applications on the WWW. In Sect. 4 we illustrate the PageSpace, a reference architecture for agent based interactive applications over the WWW. In Sect. 5 we discuss how we exploited PageSpace to design a conference management system. In Sect. 6 we conclude the paper and present some considerations on how to extend our approach to active documents.

2   The case study

The purpose of this section is to informally specify a case study that concerns the peer review and the evaluation of submissions to scientific conferences exploiting the Internet as the infrastructure for communication and cooperation. More precisely, we intend to specify a system for supporting all the activities which typically have to be performed by a number of people widely distributed all over the world to submit, select, and prepare the set of papers which will be published in the proceedings of a scientific conference. The goal is to build the final version of conference proceedings, including the list of accepted papers.

Following the idea that *"coordination is the management of dependencies"* [MC94], conference workflow management is concerned with managing the dependencies of activities (the workflow) necessary to produce the proceedings of a scientific conference (and of course the list of authors invited to present their papers).

Most scientific communities have established policies and mechanisms implementing some kind of conference management aiming at minimizing the organizational efforts but keeping high the quality of papers being accepted and the fairness of the selection process. It is a usual choice that a *program committee* is established to take decisions about which papers are accepted and which are rejected. Authors interested in presenting their work submit papers to such a committee for review.

Within the committee, a group decision has to be taken according to some fair policy. The decision is usually reached by reaching a consensus or voting or ranking submissions with the help of several reviewers who help the PC members in evaluating each paper.

We believe that the proposed case study includes interesting coordination issues to study. It involves a set of coordination activities and requires coordination as a workflow itself. The case study can serve as an example of a real life application with prominent coordination aspects. The case study is sufficiently familiar to many scientists, who normally participate to conferences as either authors, reviewers, PC members, or PC chairs. The case study is also a simple instance of a general class of problems, in which a composite document has to be produced as the result of a workflow of activities by several people.

Interestingly, this case study is inspired by some already available systems for electronic submission, collection of referee reports, and PC meeting support based on Internet communication mechanisms, namely e-mail or WWW. In fact, there currently exist some conference management systems that use either the WWW or e-mail to perform most communication acts. Ideally, PC chairs, PC members and reviewers have a reliable Internet connection, and work in such an environment using a browser. However, scientists usually travel a lot. Moreover, most of the tasks to be performed are boring, long, and repetitive – e.g. fetching the papers, or filling referee report forms – and are better performed off-line.

We are interested in solutions coordinating both communication media, that is, e-mail and WWW, in order to support both asynchronous and synchronous coordination.

2.1 Agents and Roles

The system we intend to specify includes several agents. We take the term *agent* as primitive; intuitively, an agent is an entity which can act autonomously; an agent can send/receive messages according to some well known protocol (non necessarily reliable): e.g. snail mail, e-mail, HTTP, or others.

All agents have unique identities; for simplicity, we define these identities as unique URLs. For instance, an agent is the conference site and is named url.of.conference. Another agent can communicate with the conference site using different protocols:

- http://url.of.conference
- mailto://url.of.conference

Some agents perform *roles*, since they represent human users which can perform some operations. The following roles are involved in the case study:

- author (submitter of a paper); if the paper is co-authored, the corresponding author is the author who actually submitted the paper;
- PC chair;
- PC member;

- reviewer;
- editor of proceedings.

Each role can be represented by several agents, which differ in their URLs. For instance, a typical conference could have a hundred or more authors, two PC chairs, twenty PC members, scores of reviewers, and one editor of proceedings.

The operations that each role can perform are those described in the next subsection.

2.2 Dynamics of the case study

We will specify the dynamics of the workflow to be enacted defining a number of tasks which the conference management system has to support. The tasks are listed below in some arbitrary order.

1. **SUBMISSION OF PAPERS**.
   A submission form, including basic information on the submission like authors, affiliations, paper title, corresponding author, format of the paper being submitted, is available on request from the conference site (authors can ask such a form to the conference site agent). Authors submit papers to the conference site.
   A submission may consist of the submission form appropriately filled, an ASCII file containing title and abstract and the paper (or its URL) in the format declared in the submission form (e.g. in PostScript).
   If a submission does not conform to the above requirements, it is not accepted and its sender is invited to resubmit. If a submission conforms it is stored in the conference site and its corresponding author gets an acknowledgement.
2. **BIDDING FOR PAPERS**.
   Each PC member examines the list of submissions and selects a subset of "interesting" papers to review. The PC chair can alter each subset to balance the review load among PC members.
3. **DISTRIBUTION OF THE PAPERS TO THE REFEREES**.
   After the deadline for submissions is expired, an agent sends by email a message to each PC member to fetch the papers assigned to that member and start the refereeing. The message could even be "active", in that it would autonomously contact the site at the URL given, fetch the papers, and on request generate the forms for reviews to be submitted back to the conference site.
   Unauthorized access to all submitted papers has to be prevented, so that the list of the submissions – not to mention the papers – remains confidential.
4. **COLLECTION OF THE REPORTS**. A WWW form is provided for online input of referee reports into the conference site. Also, forms can be obtained by sending an email message to the conference site, and forms filled offline can be submitted directly by email.
   In this and in the following phases there are some security and authentication issues at stake. The confidentiality of information has to be ensured by using

passwords to allow access only to PC members, and by using a unique address for each PC member to which all communication is directed.

This phase is managed by an agent that answers to requests of forms and collects the incoming reports. The agent generates a file for each submitted paper in which it collects the relative reports.

5. **PREPARATION OF STATISTICS** An agent scans all paper reports and fills up a table in a standard spreadsheet to generate statistics and an initial proposal for ranking all papers to be used during the PC meeting.

6. **PC MEETING.** During this phase all PC member needs to be able to:
   - access the list, the abstracts, and the files of the submissions;
   - access the referee reports collected so far for specific papers;
   - access the logs of comments on specific papers;
   - access the ranking table of all submissions;
   - read or write comments about a paper on a log file reserved for such task;
   - finally, decide on acceptance status and record the decision.

   All this is provided via (password protected) links from a WWW page to appropriate (active) elements. In addition, all the features are also available by email by sending messages with suitable subjects to the mail server agent. The situation gets more complex if PC members are allowed to submit papers. In this case one must deny them information about their own submissions, and, possibly, also the possibility of inferring such information.

7. **COMMUNICATION OF RESULTS.** Once the list of accepted papers is formed, an agent takes care of communicating the results and the referee reports to the authors. Other agents generate a list of the abstracts of the accepted papers (for instance, in HTML), extract a list of sub-referees for the referee reports, and prepare a synopsis of the result for the PC Chair.

8. **SUBMITTING CAMERA READY**
   Authors of accepted papers submit camera ready versions. An agent controls compliance with the standards for camera ready submissions and issues reminders to authors that are late in re-submitting.

9. **PREPARING THE PROCEEDINGS**
   An agent collects all the camera ready papers, asks and waits for a preface from the editor of proceedings, and finally prepares a draft of the proceedings. The editor and the PC chairs are informed by e-mail when the proceedings are done.

2.3 "Solving" the case study

This case study has been inspired by the personal experience of the authors of [CNT98] as PC members and especially by ideas described in [Sas96,MJ96,Nie97,Tol98]. In fact, there are already a number of Web-based conference management systems which are being used for supporting peer review. In our experience the most robust and rich in features are the systems supporting the WWW and the AAAI conferences. Information on these systems is scarce; our description of informal requirements above is an attempt to summarize some existing systems. Interestingly all the systems we have examined support different conference organizational models. For instance, there are systems supporting conferences organized as a set of workshops; there are systems were papers are classified by authors according to some keyword systems, and then they are automatically assigned to PC members after they have selected a set of keywords representing their "reviewing ability".

Most interestingly, only the simplest systems assume a centralized repository of papers and reviews. The system used for the WWW conference instead allows the authors to submit *only the URL* of their paper, that is then directly accessed by reviewers only when necessary.

Here we are interested in "solving" this case study describing an agent-based software architecture of a conference management system.

3　Designing an active Web

The World Wide Web was born as a hypertext document browsing system. The components of this system are servers, clients, and documents. The interactions among these components are driven by the HTTP protocol and the CGI-BIN mechanism. HTTP is a simple interaction protocol used by clients in order to retrieve documents stored on a disk under the control of an HTTP server. Usually documents are stored as files on the server's disk. However, documents can also be created on-the-fly: with CGI-BIN a client requests a document as the output of a process run by the server at the client's request. Things are really as easy as that but this simple mechanism can be used in a "tricky" way in order to implement more complex forms of interaction among documents, clients, and servers.

According to its original design, the only activity that can be dynamically triggered in the World Wide Web is associated to the CGI-BIN mechanism. Soon users demanded more interaction than just browsing documents and this brought to the development of a family of languages to embed code within an HTML document and have it executed by the user's browser. These languages (or even architectures to transfer executable code, as in the case of Microsoft's ActiveX) are very different in capabilities and target; some in fact are scripting languages intended to interact heavily with the document itself (as in the case of JavaScript), some are complex and full-fledged languages that have little interaction with the document (as in the case of Java).

Nevertheless, these technologies give us the ability to "activate" two key components of the WWW architecture, that is, servers and clients. However, we still lack techniques and protocols to allow these components to interoperate. Usually, in fact, current projects aiming at the exploitation of the WWW as an active distributed platform locate computing components just on one side (either at the server or at the clients). Our approach is different because we redefine the coordination capabilities of WWW middleware in which the activity takes place.

4   The WWW as an agent world

An *active Web* is a system including some notion of agent performing some activity. The activities can take place at the client, at the server, at the middleware level, at the gateway with another active software system (e.g. an external database, decision support system or expert system) or even at the user level. An active Web includes several *agents*, with a well-defined behavior. Each component of an active Web is seen as an autonomous agent in a world offering coordination services to agents: thus, an agent is not just capable of computations but it should also be able to interact (in possibly complex ways) with other agents.

The interaction among agents is usually accomplished using client/server architectures (as in any RPC-based system, such as CORBA). However, sometimes the client-server framework misses its main goals (that is, modular design and simple interaction behavior) when the interactions among the components change in time and the client/server relationship can be reversed, or when the designer needs decoupling among components (that is something we really need when we have to deal with a world-wide distributed system including heterogeneous networks).

A solution to this problem consists in designing the distributed application as an agent world in which agents are spatially scattered and act autonomously: this schema fits quite well into the distributed objects model. In our coordination-based approach agents perform sequences of actions which are either method invocations or message deliveries. Synchronization actions (e.g. starting, blocking, unblocking, and terminating an activity) are the remaining mechanisms in object invocation. More precisely, we distinguish between *agent computation*, that is what concerns the internal behavior of an agent, and *agent coordination*, that is what concerns the relationship between an agent and its environment: synchronization, communication, and service provision and usage.

Coordination models separate coordination from computation, not as independent or dual concepts, but as orthogonal ones: they are two dimensions both necessary to design agent worlds. A coordination language should thus combine two programming models: one for coordination (the inter–agent actions) and one for computation (the intra–agent actions). The most known example of coordination models is the Tuple Space as available in Linda, which has been implemented on several hardware architectures and combined with different programming languages.

Linda can be seen as a sort of assembly coordination language in two ways. First and foremost, it offers very simple coordinables, i.e., active and passive tuples, which represent agents and messages, respectively; furthermore, it offers a unique coordination medium, the Tuple Space, in which all tuples reside, and a small number of coordination primitives. Secondly, Linda is a sort of coordination assembly because it can be used to implement higher level coordination languages. For instance, we have used it to implement Jada, a library which adds coordination primitives to Java [CR97].

4.1 The PageSpace

PageSpace is a reference architecture for multiagent applications built on top of
the WWW [CTV+98]. PageSpace applications consist of a number of distributed
agents to be coordinated to accomplish some cooperative task.

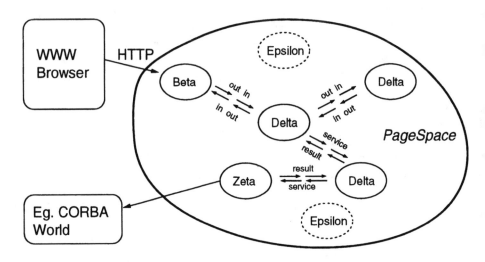

Fig. 1. The PageSpace reference architecture

PageSpace includes a number of agent types, depicted in Fig.1.

- *Alpha* agents, or *user-agents*, are user interface agents. Alpha agents consists
  of applets, scripts, and HTML pages.
- *Beta* agents, or *avatars*, are a persistent representation of users on the PageS-
  pace. They allow the users to access the application agents on the PageSpace,
  provide the user with the required Alpha, and collect the messages addressed
  to the Alpha agent or the user in their absence.
- *Delta* agents, or *application agents*, perform the computations of the application. They offer services by interacting with the shared data. Some delta
  agents have to interact with the user, and therefore must be able to produce
  an interface, usually in the form of an Alpha agent that is then downloaded
  to the client. Others do not directly interact with the user, and just offer
  services to other application agents.
- The *Gamma* space is a coordination environment used for the specific implementation of a PageSpace. In this paper we will use Jada [CR97].
- *Zeta* agents, or *gateway agents*, allow a PageSpace to interact with external
  environments such as other coordination environments or distributed applications residing outside the PageSpace.

Every browser includes at least one user-agent, which is connected and interacts directly with an avatar, running on a PageSpace server. A set of Delta

agents implement the coordination mechanisms necessary to an active Web application. Gateway agents provide access to external services, like e-mail or a CORBA ORB.

4.2 Coordination mechanisms for agents

In [CR97] we introduced Jada, a Java-Linda combination. Jada was a first experiment in combining Java with a coordination model, and provides some basic coordination mechanisms. Here we describe an enhanced version of the original Jada: MJada.

MJada adds to Jada the support for coordination among (possibly mobile) agents. The MJada coordination medium is the tuple space, introduced in Linda [CarGel92]. However, Linda uses only one tuple space, although it can be physically distributed. On the contrary, MJada supports *multiple nested tuple spaces*, which form a hierarchical coordination structure based on the TupleSpace object. Hence a TupleSpace offers some "navigation" methods that allow a thread or an agent to navigate the coordination structure, expressing itineraries as sequences of names similar to UNIX file system names. Names are expressed by paths, so both "/space" and "/chapter/section" are valid names. A TupleSpace object can be created with

```
TupleSpace tuple_space = new TupleSpace();
```

An agent can connect a tuple space with the join() method. For instance, after the following statement

```
tuple_space.join("space1");
```

all operations on tuple_space will be relative to the tuple space called *space1*.

The join() method can be used to navigate through the tuple space as if it was a file system: absolute and relative paths are accepted, the name ".." refers to the encompassing tuple space, and name items can be combined (as in, for instance, "space2/space3"). For flexibility, additional methods are provided to move to the encompassing tuple space, leave(), or to the root tuple space, leaveAll().

A tuple is represented by the Tuple class and contains a set of Java objects. We can create a tuple with standard Java constructors as in the following:

```
Tuple tuple = new Tuple("Hello!", new Integer(1));
```

Tuples can be inserted into a tuple space with the out() method.

```
tuple_space.out(tuple);
```

Tuples can be read or withdrawn from a space using the following methods

```
- Result read(Tuple formal)
- Result in(Tuple formal)
```

Tuples are retrieved from a tuple space using an associative mechanism: when an agent calls the in method it has to pass it a tuple that is used as a matching pattern. The in method returns a tuple (if any) that matches the given pattern. The same applies for the read method, with the exception that a tuple that is read is not removed from the tuple space.

Two tuples match if they include the same number of items and each item of the first tuple matches the corresponding item of the second tuple.

In order to have flexible matching operations we rely on the concepts of *formal* and *actual* tuple items: since a *formal item* is an instance of the Class class (the meta-class used in Java), all actual items of the specified class satisfy the matching.

For instance, the following is a template tuple with an actual field of class String and a formal field of class Class that matches all actual items of class Integer.

```
Tuple template = new Tuple("Hello!", Integer.class);
```

This tuple matches both:

```
Tuple alpha = new Tuple("Hello!", new Integer(3));
Tuple beta = new Tuple("Hello!", new Integer(7));
```

Differently from Linda, disruptive MJada operations do not return a result tuple, but a placeholder for that tuple represented by the Result class. The placeholder can then be used to test result availability, to fetch a result or to kill the request. Trying to fetch a tuple that is not available will block the calling thread, resulting in the same coordination mechanism used in Linda.

Tuple spaces in MJada can either be "local", i.e., shared among concurrent threads running in the same Java Virtual Machine, or "remote", i.e., running on a (possibly) remote host and accessed via an ad-hoc proxy class in a way that is similar to the one used by RMI.

The main feature of MJada to support mobile agents coordination is the ability of transparently abort and re-send a request for a pending in or read operation among migrations. Thus, if an agent performs:

```
Result result=remote_tuple_space.In(my_tuple);
```

and the requested tuple is not available at call time, it can migrate to another place and the result object will still refer to a valid in operation performed on the remote tuple space.

MJada provides also multiple-result operations that allow one to read or withdrawn all tuples that match a given template.

```
- Enumeration readAll(Tuple formal)
- Enumeration inAll(Tuple formal)
```

Result tuples can then be fetched using Java enumerations. Linda does not have a similar operation.

In addition to the previous basic tuple operations Jada introduces a new coordinative computing framework based on tuple *collections*. A tuple collection, represented by the `TupleCollection` class, defines a sequence of tuples having the same signature. In order to build a tuple collection we write

```
TupleSpace space = new TupleSpace(); Tuple pattern = new
Tuple(String.class, Integer.class); TupleCollection tc = new
TupleCollection(space, pattern);
```

where `space` is the tuple space where collected tuples reside and `pattern` is a tuple which define the tuples' signature. Tuples can be inserted in a collection using the `add()` method

```
tc.add(new Tuple("Hello!", new Integer(1)));
```

If the specified tuple has a signature different from the collected one, an exception is thrown. The main feature of collections is that tuples can be read or withdrawn in the same order they were inserted.

Tuple collections capture a recurrent pattern of coordinative programming, the consuming of a sequence of tuples, and noticeably simplify the source code.

MJada has been used to implement an instance of PageSpace called MUD-Web.

5 Designing a conference management system

PageSpace is a reference architecture, independent from a specific coordination model or language. MUDWeb is an actual software architecture we designed instantiating PageSpace using MJada. MUDWeb takes its name from MUDs. A MUD (Multi User Dungeon) is a cooperative interactive environment shared by several people to socialize and interact; MUDs have been proposed as enabling technologies for some kinds of groupware applications [D+97,DHW98]. A MUD usually represents the infrastructure of a role-playing game (hence the name) where human and robot players interact, visit dark and magical places, fight monsters or other players, and seek treasures. More generally, a MUD is an abstract platform that creates shared virtual realities. Thus, a MUD is a very powerful abstraction to describe a general platform for cooperative work (possibly on the WWW), that provides a general framework for users to interact with each other, and with resources such as documents.

The MUDs, generally, are based on the concepts of *rooms*, *items* and *players* (or *users*). The whole virtual space inside a MUD is partitioned in rooms. Each room can contain several users and items. Each user can move from a room to another one can can interact only with the items in its same room: use can use them, get them and so on. ¿From this point of view objects are passive entities that are "activated" by the users. Also interactions among users can take place only if the users are in the same room (note that in this context the world room does not necessarily mean a closed place: a room in a MUD might virtually represent a cave in a dungeon or a garden around an enchanted castle; a room is a partition of the virtual space in which interactions take place).

As we pointed out, when wandering inside a MUD we might meet robot players. As the name suggests the robot player behave just like other users but there is no human counterpart behind it: the actions of the robot player are driven by (possibly A.I. based) programs. We can think of a robot player as a synthetic user or as an active item. We'll show later that these two concepts can lead to very different implementations.

Mapping a MUD in a system based on multiple tuple spaces like MJada is quite straightforward: we can use a tuple space for each room; an item contained in a room is a tuple stored in the tuple space representing the room; each user is an agent that can freely move around rooms.

Robot players are synthetic users, i.e., programs that access the MUD using the MJada primitives. We can use robot players to provide simple services to other users (in fact we will often refer to robot player as to server agents). By interacting with a server agent, the users can activate a service and, eventually, gather its output. Since the relationship among agents in MJada takes place by exchanging tuples, the same protocol is used to activate the services of the server agents.

From a software architecture point of view MUDWeb consists of a number of services which agents can use according to a number of protocols based on tuple exchanges. MUDWeb includes several rooms which correspond to tuple spaces including some basic server agent. The whole architecture is implemented by a server organized as nested tuple spaces. Fig.2 shows the software architecture of MUDWeb.

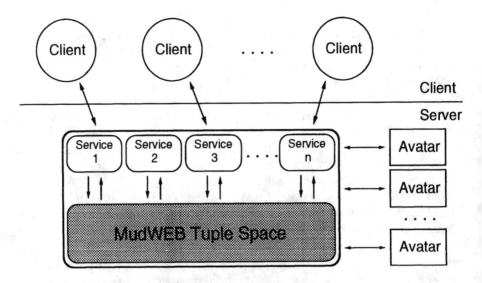

Fig. 2. A MUD-like active Web

Services wait for command tuples and perform services based on their content. Services are generally simple, specialized agents that react to a limited list of commands. The functionalities of an application are thus implemented by a number of services cooperating together. Clients are user interfaces using some role-specific HTML page or Java applet.

An agent server supports three kinds of agents: the *avatars*, the *services*, and the *mudshell*. The avatar is the persistent representation of a human user. The avatar interacts with the user interface displayed within a WWW browser, and it accepts commands and returns data in a variety of methods, including e-mail messages. Services are the PageSpace's Delta or application agents, i.e., they are the modules on the shared space that provide the actual computations of the distributed application. The MUDShell is the client of the MUDWeb application, and is the interface framework where the interaction with the user takes place: the MUDShell provides primitives for moving from one available shared space to another, and it allows the user to interact with the services by providing a MUD-like text box for direct commands, and by displaying the most common ones on additional buttons. Furthermore they allow avatars to display their interfaces just like the other services.

5.1 A conference management system

MUDWeb can be used not just to implement interactive games, but also for supporting a complex workflow. We have used it to design and implement a workflow system supporting the management of a scientific conference. Although there are probably more direct ways to implement workflow support for a conference, we found it interesting that such a seemingly remote metaphor, the MUDWeb, could be fruitfully used for this purpose. Our system, named *ConfManager*, has the goal to simplify the management of the review of papers submitted to a scientific conference.

Submitted papers are stored in rooms; authors, reviewers, and program committee members are represented by avatars which support both synchronous (online) and asynchronous (e-mail) communication interactions.

ConfManager includes the following rooms:

- SubmittedPaper Every paper is stored in a room of this type, that is dynamically created when the paper is submitted. The room will also store the reviews when they will be ready.
- ReviewRoom is used by reviewers to store their reviews before they are finalized.
- SelectRoom is a room accessible to the program committee members only; it stores the scores assigned to papers.
- Papers is a room reserved to the conference organizers: it contains managing data like the full list of submitted papers and the address data of authors.

The workflow related to the management of a conference is implemented by the interaction of the agents and the services. Each service activates whenever

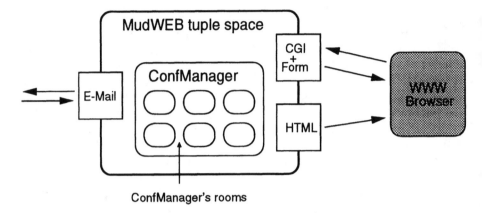

Fig. 3. Conference management mapped onto MudWeb

there are in the room it controls the items it needs to perform its activities. *ConfManager* offers in each room some specific services:

- **Services for authors of papers**: When a paper arrives it is stored in a room created on purpose, also including an avatar representing the corresponding author. The avatar can answer simple questions on the status of the submission.
- **Services for reviewers**: Each *SubmittedPaper* room, created to store a submitted paper, can also store reviews for the paper. User input is handled by some HTML forms and a few CGI scripts. The CGI scripts generate a review form and generate a tuple for each review. The tuple is stored in the same room containing the paper being reviewed until it is "confirmed"; after the confirmation the tuple is moved in the selectRoom.
- **Services for PC members**: PC members can act like both reviewers and authors. The service *Services.Selector* that can be activated in the *SelectRoom* room allows a PC member to choose what kind of interaction he is interested in.

All the tasks mentioned in section 2.2 are supported and available to the appropriate users. All of them are implemented by services that can either be activated by the users or by other agents.

All services come in two flavors, synchronous and asynchronous. For instance, the service *Services.Announcer* accepts reviews coming by e-mail, checking that they refer to the paper stored in the same room. The service *Services.Submitter* is similar to the preceding one, but supports on line user interaction.

Asynchronous services rely upon *avatars*, which have to be programmed to perform the necessary tasks. The (server-side) avatar acts as an e-mail client of an e-mail server; it controls the user mailbox and processes the messages it contains.

6 Conclusions and Future Work

We have presented a case study in document-centric groupware. We have sketched a solution using PageSpace, an agent-based reference architecture used to design an actual software architecture based on the MUD metaphor.

The case study we have exposed can be used to compare modern object oriented middleware infrastructures: for instance, we are developing a conference management system based on Lotus Notes. Another issue we are exploring is security, that is especially important for multiuser applications.

As we pointed out before MUD's robot players can be seen as synthetic users or as active items.

As of now we pursued only the first approach. It is however evident that there are classes of applications in which the documents we have to deal with can be "active"; i.e. are subject to auto-modifications.

A document that represents a stock exchange's stock, for example, should periodically update its own value. A document that represent a contract should change its own state (and maybe it should also warn some users) when its expiration date is reached. We usually refer to this class of documents as *active documents*. In a MUD, the mapping of active documents into synthetic players is not natural and often not even correct: players and active documents are different concepts. It seems evident that active documents should be mapped into active items. The problem we face, using this approach, is that we need a standard framework that enable us to represent both the contents of the document and its semantic.

XML [BPS97] is an extensible document markup language that provides a unified framework for describing orthogonally a document structure, its rendering, and its semantics. Introducing a technique that we call "displets" [CV99], our workgroup has integrated XML with Java, thus we can use a Turing-equivalent language for manipulating XML documents. The purpose of displets is to have active documents that are able to render themselves: we are planning to re-use the same concepts that are at the base of the displets to implement some more general-purpose kind of active documents.

The integration of this kind of active documents into the active items of a MUD environment based on MJada is very easy and opens new and interesting opportunities to design an active document management system based on the MUD metaphor, the PageSpace architecture and the MJada technology. We are currently engaged on this work.

Acknowledgments. PageSpace has been supported by the EU as ESPRIT Open LTR project #20179 as a joint research with people in TU Berlin. The case study requirements have been defined together by P. Ciancarini (Univ. of Bologna, Italy), R. Tolksdorf (TU Berlin, Germany) and O. Nierstrasz (Univ. of Berne, Switzerland), with partial support from EU WG "Coordina" project. The author wish to thank Paolo Ciancarini who has been the coordinator of the project of which this work is part of.

References

[BPS97]   T. Bray and J. Paoli and C. Sperberg-McQueen. Extensible Markup Language (XML). *The World Wide Web Journal*, 2(4), 1997.

[CarGel92] N. Carriero and D. Gelernter. Coordination Languages and Their Significance *Communications of the ACM*, 35(2), 1992.

[CNT98]   P. Ciancarini and O. Niestrasz and R. Tolksdorf.   A case study in coordination: Conference Management on the Internet. ftp://cs.unibo.it/pub/cianca/coordina.ps.gz

[CR97]   P. Ciancarini and D. Rossi. Jada: Coordination and Communication for Java agents. In J. Vitek and C. Tschudin, editors, *Mobile Object Systems: Towards the Programmable Internet*, volume 1222 of *Lecture Notes in Computer Science*, pages 213–228. Springer-Verlag, Berlin, 1997.

[CTV+98]   P. Ciancarini, R. Tolksdorf, F. Vitali, D. Rossi, and A. Knoche. Coordinating Multiagent Applications on the WWW: a Reference Architecture. *IEEE Transactions on Software Engineering*, 24(5):362–375, 1998.

[CV99]   P. Ciancarini and F. Vitali. Managing complex documents over the WWW: a case study for XML. *IEEE Transactions on Knowledge and Data Engineering*, 11(1):(to appear), January 1999.

[D+97]   T. Das et al. Developing Social Virtual Worlds using NetEffect. In *Proc. 6th IEEE Workshops on Enabling Technologies: Infrastructure for Collaborative Enterprises (WETICE)*, pages 148–154, Boston, June 1997. IEEE Computer Society Press.

[DHW98]   J. Doppke, D. Heimbigner, and A. Wolf. Software Process Modeling and Execution within Virtual Environments. *ACM Transactions on Software Engineering and Methodology*, 7(1):1–40, January 1998.

[GHJV95]   E. Gamma and R. Helm and R. Johnson and J. Vlissides. Design Patterns Addison-Wesley, 1995

[MC94]   T. Malone and K. Crowstone. The Interdisciplinary Study of Coordination. *ACM Computing Surveys*, 26(1):87–119, 1994.

[MD97]   J. Munson and P. Dewan. Sync: a Java Framework for Mobile Collaborative Applications. *IEEE Computer*, 30(6):59–66, 1997.

[MJ96]   G. Mathews and Barry Jacobs. Electronic Management of the Peer Review Process. *Computer Networks and ISDN Systems*, 28(7-11):1523, November 1996.

[Nie97]   O. Niestrasz. Identify the champion. www.iam.unibe.ch/oscar/PDF/champion.fm.ps, 1997.

[Sas96]   V. Sassone. Management of electronic submission, refereeing, and pc meeting. (Manual of a WWW system), Nov. 1996.

[Tol98]   R. Tolksdorf. Conference reviewing. grunge.cs.tu-berlin.de/~tolk/reviewing.html, 1998.

Coordination of a Parallel Proposition Solver

C.T.H. Everaars and B. Lisser
email: Kees.Everaars@cwi.nl and Bert.Lisser@cwi.nl

CWI, P.O. Box 94079, 1090 GB Amsterdam, The Netherlands, Telefax 020-5924199
(+31 20 5924199)

Abstract. In this paper we describe an experiment in which **MANIFOLD** is used to coordinate the interprocess communication in a parallelized proposition solver. **MANIFOLD** is very well suited for applications involving dynamic process creation and dynamically changing (ir)regular communication patterns among sets of independent concurrent cooperating processes. The idea in this case study is simple. The proposition solver consists of a fixed numbers of separate processing units which communicate with each other such that the output of one serves as the input for the other. Because one of the processing units performs a computation intensive job, we introduce a master/worker protocol to divide its computations. We show that this protocol implemented in **MANIFOLD** adds another hierarchic layer to the application but leaves the previous layers intact. This modularity of **MANIFOLD** offers the possibility to introduce concurrency step by step. We also verify the implementation of the proposition solver using a simple family of assertions and give some performance results.

1 Introduction

Correctness assertions, about e.g., the safety of railway platforms, the working of embedded systems, or computer programs are frequently formulated as statements in propositional logic [1]. Such a proposition, formulated in some specification language, can then form the input for a proposition solver that tests the correctness of the assertion. In general, we can see a proposition solver as a system that solves equations such as $p(x) = true$, where x stands for the free boolean variables in proposition p. The satisfiability of the proposition p is checked and a solution of the equation is computed, provided that p is satisfiable. In [2] we can find a description of a library containing formal specifications of components that can be used as building blocks for a generic solver tool for logical propositions.

In this paper we describe how the actual implementation of the solver components are used in cooperation with each other to build a real working parallel proposition solver. The different components of the solver were implemented (in C) by a group of researchers in the department of Software Engineering at CWI (Centrum voor Wiskunde en Informatica) in the Netherlands in cooperation with the Dutch Railways for checking railway safety systems [1]. Finishing the implementation (and debugging) of the individual components, they looked for an efficient interprocess communication tool that could take care of the necessary communication channels between the different components. There are many different languages and programming tools available that can be used to implement this kind of communication, each representing a different approach to communication. Normally, languages like Compositional C++, High Performance Fortran, Fortran M, Concurrent C(++) or tools like MPI, PVM, and PARMACS are used (see [3] for some critical notes on these languages and tools). There is, however, a promising novel approach: the application of *coordination* languages [4–6]. In this paper we describe how the coordination language **MANIFOLD** is used for the interprocess communication between the different components of this proposition solver. **MANIFOLD** is a coordination language developed at the CWI in the Netherlands. It is very well suited for applications involving dynamic process creation and dynamically changing (ir)regular communication patterns among sets of independent concurrent cooperating processes [7,8]. Programming in **MANIFOLD** is a game of dynamically creating process instances and (re)connecting the ports of some processes via streams (asynchronous channels), in reaction to observed event occurrences. This style reflects the way one programmer might discuss his interprocess communication application with another programmer on telephone (let process a connect process b with process c so that c can get its input; when process b receives event e, broadcast by process c, react to that by doing this and that; etc.). As in this telephone call, processes in **MANIFOLD** do not explicitly send to or receive messages from other processes. Processes in **MANIFOLD** are treated as black-box workers that can only read or write through the openings (called ports) in their own bounding walls. It is always a third party - a coordinator process called a manager - that is responsible for setting up the communication channel (in **MANIFOLD** called a stream) between the output port of one process and the input port of another process, so that data can flow through it. This setting up of the communication links from the *outside* is very typical for **MANIFOLD** and has several advantages. An important advantage is that it results in a clear separation between the modules responsible for computation and the modules responsible for coordination, and thus strengthens the modularity and enhances the re-usability of both types of modules (see [3,8,9]). The **MANIFOLD** system runs on multiple platforms and consists of a compiler (**MC**), a linker (**MLINK**), a run-time configurator (**CONFIG**), a run-time system library, a number of utility programs, and libraries of built-in and predefined processes of general interest. Presently, it runs on IBM RS60000 AIX, IBM SP1/2, Solaris, Linux, Cray, and SGI IRIX.

In this paper our primary goal is to illustrate **MANIFOLD** in a real case study, thus showing its core concept of *"coordination from the outside"*. The rest of this paper is organized as follows [1]. In section 2 we give a formal description

---

[1] In an extended version of this paper we also give a brief introduction to the **MANIFOLD** language by discussing a parallel/distributed "toy" application. It is located at http://www.cwi.nl/farhad/manifold.html.

of the proposition solver, its different functional units, and the communication scheme that must be set up. Because **MANIFOLD** allows direct point to point communication between processes (agents) there is a natural $1-1$ mapping from the desired communication scheme onto the **MANIFOLD** coordination modules [2]. This mapping is described in section 3. Because one of the functional units is responsible for the heavy computational work in the proposition solver, we apply a coarse-grain restructuring on that functional unit to exploit parallelism. This adds another hierarchic layer to the application which we describe in section 4. In section 5, we test the proposition solver with a family of assertions and give some performance results. Finally, the conclusion of the paper is in section 6.

2 A Formal Description of the Proposition Solver

In this section we describe the solver components we use to build a parallel proposition solver that solves closed quantified propositions. For a full description of the components we refer to the formal specifications in [2] and for an elementary introduction literature on logic we refer to [10]. The task of solving closed quantified propositions can be divided in four transformations which will be done sequentially in such a way that the output of one transformation serves as input for the next transformation.

The sequence of transformations a proposition has to go through in succession is as follows (for details we again refer to [2]):

- **PRENEX** [3] is the component that transforms a proposition to a prenex normal form (i.e., a quantifier free proposition preceded by a row of quantifiers).
- **CNF** (Conjunctive Normal Form) is the component that transforms a proposition in the prenex normal form to a quantified conjunctive normal form (i.e., a conjunctive normal form preceded by a row of quantifiers). This is done in the following way. First the proposition in the prenex normal form is split by a separate splitting component named **SPLIT** in a quantifier free part and a list of quantifiers. The quantifier free part is transformed by a separate component named **CNFHH** (Conjunctive Normal Form Heer-Hugo) to an existential conjunctive normal form (i.e., a conjunctive normal form preceded by a row of existential quantifiers). This output and the list of quantifiers are joined together by a component named **JOIN**, which results in a quantified conjunctive normal form.

---

[2] This is in contrast to the model of ToolBus[12] we once used to implement our communication scheme. There, we were forced to adapt our desired communication scheme because only interprocess communication via a central manager process was allowed. Also, ToolBus does not support thread-level parallelism, which is necessary in our application, and it imposes many unnecessary data format conversions on every communication. These observations lead us to look into using **MANIFOLD**.

[3] From here on in this paper we use small letters for processes and software components and capital letters for transformations and manifolds.

- **UQE** (Universal Quantifier Eliminator) is the component that transforms quantified conjunctive normal forms to existential conjunctive normal forms. This transformation is done by the rule

$$\forall x. \exists y. \phi(x, y) = \exists y_1. \phi(\mathit{false}, y_1) \wedge \exists y_2. \phi(\mathit{true}, y_2) = \exists y_1, y_2. (\phi(\mathit{false}, y_1) \wedge \phi(\mathit{true}, y_2))$$

  and is the most computation intensive part of the proposition solver.
- **HH** (HeerHugo) is the component that simplifies existential conjunctive normal forms. Heerhugo has been developed at the University of Utrecht and CWI for checking railway safety systems [11].

3   The Coordination in the Proposition Solver

The communication patterns in the proposition solver as given in section 2 in fact describe a pipeline model. It is a sequence of functional units ("stages") which performs a task in several steps. Each functional unit takes its input and produces output, where the output of one serves as the input for next stage. This arrangement allows all the stages to work in parallel, thus giving greater throughput than if each input had to pass through the whole pipeline before the next input could enter. We can visualize such a system as a set of nodes that are connected by streams in which data flows in one direction.

Each functional unit as described in section 2 has been implemented as a separate software component written in C. The generic data type used in the implementation to store a proposition, is a tree structure and is called a term. In the software components all kinds of operations are done on these terms, e.g., composing and decomposing terms, reading and writing terms, etc. For this we use the primitives defined in the term library of ToolBus [12]. This is just a collection of some specialized string manipulation functions that are independent of the model and facilities of ToolBus as an interprocess communication package.

Because the terms we communicate among the software components are very big (sometimes more than 7 megabytes) it is obvious that we want the interprocess communication in shared memory. This way it is sufficient to transport the pointer to a term from one software component to another. As already stated, transporting data in **MANIFOLD** is special. In **MANIFOLD** processes do not read and write *directly* from and to other processes, but they read and write from and to their own ports. It is a third party (a coordinator) that sets up, from the *outside*, the connections between them. For the manifolds written in C (also called atomic processes) we do this reading and writing to and from ports using, respectively, the functions `AP_PortRemoveUnit` and `AP_PortPlaceUnit` from the atomic process interface library. This is a standard **MANIFOLD** library with many C functions, which allows access to the **MANIFOLD** world. Besides the standard ports named `input`, `output`, and `error` we also have ports with user defined names, as we will see.

In the actual implementation of the proposition solver we need two additional software components; one for reading the assertion we want to verify (i.e., a term) and another for writing the truth value of the assertion to the screen. These are named, respectively, **rd** and **pr** (Print Result). Below, we enumerate the different software components, describe them using **MANIFOLD** terminology, and show the stream connections between them in figure 1.

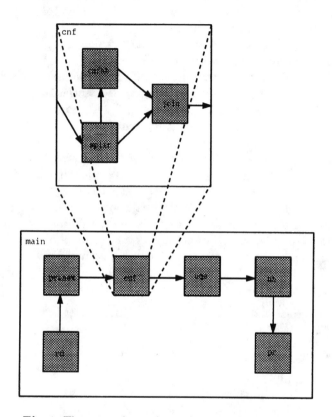

Fig. 1. The network topology of the proposition solver

- **rd** reads a term representing a quantified closed proposition from a file and writes a pointer to this term to its own output port.
- **prenex** reads a term pointer to a quantified closed proposition from its input port, transforms the term to its prenex normal form, and writes a pointer to this result to its own output port.
- **cnf** reads a pointer to a term in prenex normal form, transforms the term to its quantified conjunctive normal form, and writes a pointer to this result to its own output port. **cnf** does not do the work by itself but behaves as a manager that delegates the work to others. The workers coordinated by **cnf** are:
    - **split** reads from its input port a pointer to a term in prenex normal form (this is the same pointer read by **cnf** from its input port), splits

the term into a quantifier-free part and a list of quantifiers, the pointers to which are written to two user-defined output port **qfprop** (Quantifier-Free PROPosition) and **qvarlist** (Quantifier VARiable LIST), respectively.

- **cnfhh** reads a pointer to a quantifier-free proposition, transforms the term to an existential conjunctive normal form, and writes a pointer to this result to its own output port.
- **join** reads from a user defined input port named **qvarlist**, a pointer to a term representing a list of free quantifiers, reads from another user defined input port named **ecnf1** (Existential Conjunctive Normal Form 1) a pointer to a term representing an existential conjunctive normal form, joins these terms together to obtain a term representing a quantified conjunctive normal form, and writes a pointer to this result to its own output port.

- **uqe** reads a pointer to a term in quantified conjunctive normal form from its input port, transforms it to its existential conjunctive normal form, and writes a pointer to this result to its own output port.
- **hh** reads a pointer to a term in existential conjunctive normal form from its input port, transforms it to a simpler existential conjunctive normal form, and writes a pointer to this result to its own output port.
- **pr** reads a pointer to a term in existential conjunctive normal form, evaluates the value of this term and prints its value, which can be "true", "false" or "I don't know" to the screen.

The **MANIFOLD** source code of the proposition solver is very simple and is shown below.

```
1  //pragma include "hugo4.ato.h"
2
3  #include "MBL.h"
4
5  #include "rdid.h"
6
7  manner init_tb atomic.
8
9  manifold RD(port in filename) atomic {internal.}.
10
11 manifold PRENEX() atomic {internal.}.
12
13 manifold SPLIT()
14    port out qfprop.
15    port out qvarlist.
16    atomic {internal.}.
17
18 manifold CNFHH() atomic {internal.}.
19
20 manifold JOIN()
21    port in qvarlist.
22    port in ecnf1.
23    atomic {internal.}.
24
25 manifold UQE() atomic {internal.}.
26
27 manifold HH() atomic {internal.}.
28
29 manifold PR() atomic {internal.}.
30
31 /****************************************************/
32 manifold CNF()
33 {
34    process split is SPLIT.
35    process cnfhh is CNFHH.
36    process join is JOIN.
37    begin:
38       {
39          MES("begin"),
40          activate(split, cnfhh, join),
```

```
41          input -> split,
42                  split.qfprop -> cnfhh -> join.ecnf1,
43                  split.qvarlist -> join.qvarlist,
44          join -> output
45      ).
46
47   end: MES("end").
48
49  )
50  /****************************************************/
51  manifold Main(process arg)
52  (
53      process rd is RD(tuplepick(arg, 2)).
54      process prenex is PRENEX.
55      process cnf is CNF.
56      process uqe is UQE.
57      process hh is HH.
58      process pr is PR.
59
60      begin:
61          (
62              MES("begin"),
63              init_tb,
64              activate(rd, prenex, cnf, uqe, hh, pr),
65              rd -> prenex -> cnf -> uqe -> hh -> pr
66          ).
67
68      end: MES("end").
69  )
```

The source code is in principle no more than the declarations of the different software components with their ports and the specification of the connections among them at each of the hierarchic layers. We now walk through the code.

With the pragma on line 1 we can verify the prototyping of the manifolds written in C with the declarations given for them in manifold source files. A mismatch will result in a syntax error issued by the C compiler.

On lines 3 and 5 we include some .h files for predefined processes and sub-programs used in this source code.

Line 7 is the declaration for a subprogram written in C (denoted by the keyword atomic). It is used for initializing the term library of ToolBus [12].

Hereafter we see the declarations of eight manifolds implemented as atomic processes written in C (lines 9, 11, 13, 18, 20, 25, 27, and 29) and two manifolds written in the manifold language (lines 32 and 51). The Main manifold (line 51) and the RD (line 9) are the only manifolds in the source file that have arguments. The argument of Main is used to pass the filename, containing the proposition(s) we want to verify, from the Unix command line into the **MANIFOLD** world. The way we do that in **MANIFOLD** is analogous to the way we do such things in ANSI C. The argument in the RD manifold is meant to pass a filename to the underlying C function so that it can open this file and read a proposition from it.

All the manifolds in this source code have only the standard set of ports (input, output and error) except the SPLIT and JOIN manifolds. These two, as explained earlier, have additional user-defined ports. SPLIT has two additional *output* ports named qfprop and qvarlist (lines 14 and 15) and JOIN has two additional *input* ports named qvarlist and ecnf1 (lines 21 and 22).

The CNF manifold written in the **MANIFOLD** language is a manager that coordinates the three worker manifolds SPLIT, CNFHH, and JOIN. The workers are created in the global declaration part of CNF (lines 34-36). In the begin state of CNF we print a message to the screen to indicate that we are in the begin state (line 39), we activate process instances (line 40), and set up the desired connections (lines 41-44) as shown in figure 1. In **MANIFOLD** we use the notation $p.i$ to refer to port i of the process instance p. Furthermore, $p \rightarrow q$ means the same as $p.output \rightarrow q.input$ and to refer to the standard ports of a process instance from inside the process itself, we use the words input, output, and error. Thus line 41 means: connect the standard input port of (an instance of) CNF to (the input port of) split and line 42 means connect the qfprop output port of split to (the standard input port of) cnfhh and (the standard output port of) cnfhh to the ecnf1 input port of join.

We also have added an **end** state in the CNF manifold (line 47). We switch to this state when all the connections between the different process instances in the **begin** state are broken (each at least on one side).

Note that CNF is a real manager. He delegates his input to others (line 41: input ->) and presents their output as coming from himself (line 44: -> output).

In the Main manifold, we create in its declaration part the process instances we need and we also have a **begin** and an **end** state. The actual argument used in the creation of process rd (line 53) is a filename that contains the proposition to be verified by the proposition solver. This filename is picked out (with the predefined process tuplepick) as the second argument in a list of arguments that has been typed in on the Unix command line. This list of arguments is know in Main via the argument arg (line 51).

In the **begin** state, Main prints a message (line 62), initializes the term library (line 63), activates the process instances (line 64) and sets up the connections among them as shown in figure 1.

A call to a makefile creates the executable for this **MANIFOLD** application which is named hugo. When we type in hugo x on the command line, where x is a filename that contains a proposition then the proposition solver calculates its truth value.

This coordination protocol is all that is needed for this application and the application runs fine as long as we wait and feed it a new proposition only after the previous one has been handled. As soon as we allow more than one term in the pipeline, the proposition solver crashes with a fatal signal caused by a bad memory reference. Indeed, there is nothing wrong with our protocol, nor with the solver components, per se. The problem is in the term library used in this application. This term library is a collection of string manipulating functions that was originally developed as a component of ToolBus [12]. These functions (and ToolBus) were developed without any regards for threads, i.e., they were not implemented in a "thread friendly" style. Essentially, to be "thread friendly", functions must be reentrant and generally avoid references to global variables, except through fine-grain locks. Such functions can be used in multi-threaded applications, and especially on proper multi-processor platforms, this can significantly improve performance. There are two alternatives for rectifying this problem: (1) make the functions reentrant and introduce the necessary fine-grain locking to make the term library thread-safe; and (2) introduce a coarse-grain lock to regulate the access to the entire library. Both alternatives are semantically correct and avoid the crash. The first involves a good deal of rewriting of the library functions. The second is easier to implement, but because the library is heavily used in this application, it inhibits performance improvements (on multiprocessor platforms) by sequentializing term manipulation at the overly-coarse level of library access. Because using the ToolBus term library in this application suffers from some additional serious drawbacks (many redundant format conversions, inefficient memory utilization, slow garbage collection, and problems with handling big terms) it was decided to replace the library with a new one. However, we use the second alternative here as interim solution, and focus on other coordination issues in this application. This leads to next issue.

The **UQE** transformation performs a computation intensive simplification on a list of terms. In principle, we can cut this list into a number of pieces and perform the simplification transformation on each of the sub-lists. When we take care that the transformations on the sub-lists are carried out in separate worker processes, then they can run in parallel, as separate threads executing on different processors on multi-processor hardware. In the next section, we describe this restructuring of the **UQE** transformation using a master/worker protocol implemented in **MANIFOLD**.

4 Restructuring the UQE Transformation

The introduction of the master/worker protocol in the **UQE** transformation adds another hierarchic layer to the application but leaves, as we can see in figure 2, the previous layers intact. New in this figure are the manifold M_UQE, in which the master/worker protocol is implemented, and another manifold named WORKER, which performs a simplification transformation on a sub-list. We show the **MANIFOLD** program for this new structure below.

```
1  //pragma include "hugo6.ato.h"
2
3  #include "MBL.h"
4
5  #include "rdid.h"
6
7  #define NPART 5
8
9  #define IDLE terminated(void)
10
11 manner init_tb atomic.
12
13 manifold RD(port in filename) atomic (internal.).
14
15 manifold PRENEX() atomic (internal.).
16
17 manifold SPLIT()
18   port out qfprop.
19   port out qvarlist.
20   atomic (internal.).
21
22 manifold CNFHH() atomic (internal.).
23
24 manifold JOIN()
25   port in qvarlist.
26   port in ecnf1.
27   atomic (internal.).
28
29 event divide, mission_accomplished, goon_uqe.
30
31 manifold UQE(port in npart)
32   port out workers.
33   atomic (internal. event divide, mission_accomplished, goon_uqe.).
34
35 manifold WORKER(event ready) atomic (internal.).
36
37 manifold HH() atomic (internal.).
38
39 manifold PR() atomic (internal.).
```

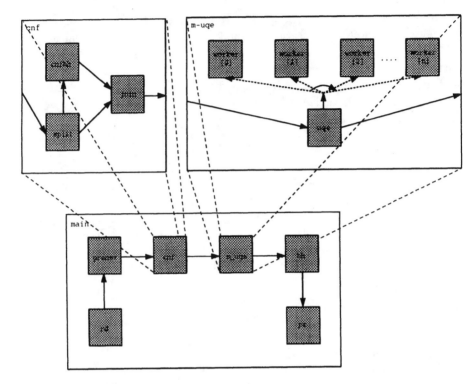

Fig. 2. The new network topology of the proposition solver

```
40
41  /*****************************************************/
42  manifold M_UQE()
43  (
44     event wait, ready.
45
46     process uqe is UQE(NPART).
47
48     priority wait > ready.
49
50     auto process i is variable.
51
52     auto process count is variable(0).
53
54     auto process worker is variable[NPART].
55
56  begin:
57     for i = 0 while i < NPART step i = i + 1 do
58        worker.input[i] = &WORKER(ready);
59     (
60        MES("begin"), activate(uqe), getunit(input) -> uqe, IDLE
61     ).
62
63  divide:
64     (
65        save *.
66        begin:
67           MES("divide");
68           for i = 0 while i < NPART step i = i + 1 do
69           (
70              getunit(uqe.workers) -> $worker.output[i],
71              MES("job to worker", i)
72           );
73           post(wait).
74     ).
75
76  wait:
77     (MES("wait"), preemptall, IDLE).
78
```

```
79  ready.*:
80    (MES("ready"), count = count + 1);
81    EMES(count);
82    if (count == NPART) then (
83      count = 0, raise(goon_uqe),
84      post(wait),
85      MES("goon_uqe has been raised and wait has been posted")
86    ) else (
87      post(wait),
88      MES("wait has been posted")
89    ).
90
91  mission_accomplished:
92    MES("mission_accomplished");
93    for i = 0 while i < NPART step i = i + 1 do
94      deactivate($worker.output[i]).
95
96  end:
97    (MES("end"), output = uqe.output).
98
99  )
100
101 /*****************************************************/
102 manifold CNF()
103 (
104   process split is SPLIT.
105   process cnfhh is CNFHH.
106   process join is JOIN.
107   begin:
108     (
109       MES("begin"),
110       activate(split, cnthh, join),
111       input -> split,
112                split.qfprop -> cnfhh -> join.ecni1,
113                split.qvarlist -> join.qvarlist,
114       join -> output
115     ).
116
117   end: MES("end").
118
119 )
120 /*****************************************************/
121 manifold Main(process arg)
122 (
123   process rd is RD(tuplepick(arg, 2)).
124   process prenex is PRENEX.
125   process cnf is CNF.
126   process m_uqe is M_UQE.
127   process hh is HH.
128   process pr is PR.
129
130   begin:
131     (
132       MES("begin"),
133       init_tb,
134       activate(rd, prenex, cnf, m_uqe, hh, pr),
135       rd -> prenex -> cnf -> m_uqe -> hh -> pr
136     ).
137
138   end: MES("end").
139 )
```

The UQE manifold is slightly different than its previous version presented earlier. It now has a parameter (line 31) that indicates in how many pieces the list is be cut, it has a user-defined port named workers (line 32) and it can raise and receive events (line 33). On the other hand, the structure of the manifolds CNF (line 102) and Main (line 121) has not changed except that now M_UQE is used in the pipeline of Main (line 134). Below, we give separate descriptions of the new manifolds. These descriptions also explain how they cooperate with each other according a master/worker protocol.

The new UQE manifold is still implemented in C (line 31) but it now behaves as follows:

1. Read a term pointer from the input port.
2. Do some computational work, but when a list of terms must be simplified, don't do it yourself. Instead raise the event divide (this is done by an AP_Raise call in the C code of UQE) to signal a coordinator (this will be the

manifold M_UQE) to delegate some work (we see later how this event will be handled by M_UQE).

3. Divide the list of terms in NPART pieces (which is set to 5 on line 7) and write the pointers to the sub-lists to the user-defined output port workers (line 32).

4. Wait until the delegated work is done. This will be noticed by receiving the goon_uqe event in the event memory, which is raised by the coordinator M_UQE (line 83).

5. Merge the sub-lists of terms into one big list.

6. Repeat steps 2, 3, 4, and 5 as many times as needed. When UQE is done with all its work, it raises the event mission_accomplished (by an AP_Raise call in the C code) to signal the coordinator M_UQE that it is done.

The WORKER manifold is implemented in C (line 35) and it behaves as follows:

1. Read a pointer to a sub-list of terms from the input port.

2. Perform the simplification on the sub-list.

3. Raise (by a call to AP_Raise in the C code) the event received as a parameter (line 35) when the simplification transformation on the sub-list is done.

4. Repeat steps 1, 2, and 3 until deactivated by M_UQE (line 94).

The M_UQE manifold is implemented in the **MANIFOLD** language (line 42) and behaves as follows.

In its begin state, NPART workers are created (line 58) whose references (denoted by &) are stored in an array named worker (line 54). Further, we activate in this state the already created uqe (respectively on lines 60 and 46) and take out a unit from the input port, representing a term pointer so that uqe can consume it (line 60). We remark here that the only reason why we store the process references in an array is to use it in a "for loop" and other syntactic constructs of the **MANIFOLD** language. With the dereference operator (denoted by $) we can always make a handle back to the process instance as shown on line 70.

Sooner or later, UQE raises the divide event (see step 2 in the description of the UQE manifold) which causes a state switch to the divide state (line 63). In that state, the pointers to the sub-lists are transported to the workers (line 70) so that they can do their simplification transformations in parallel. When the workers are ready, they raise the ready event (see step 3 in the WORKER manifold). These events are counted in the ready state (line 79). When there are NPART ready events counted (line 82) all workers are done simplifying their sub-lists. In this way, we create a synchronization point in the application. After this rendez-vous of workers, the event goon_uqe is raised (line 83) to signal UQE to merge (in shared memory) the sub-lists into one big list (step 5 in the UQE manifold). Thereafter, the wait event is posted (line 84) which causes a state switch to that state (line 76). There, two things can happen: either another divide event is received, in which case the sequence of actions just described starts again, or the mission_accomplished event is received, in which case we deactivate the workers (line 94).

Note that in the M_UQE module (in principle this counts for every manager module) we only discuss coordination issues. In this sense, it forms an isolated piece of code that we can consider as the realization of a cooperation model (in this case a master/worker model). Therefore, it is irrelevant what it coordinates. Our M_UQE manifold can just as happily orchestrate the cooperation of any pair of processes that have the same input/output and event behavior as UQE and WORKER do, regardless of what computation they perform (see also [13] for this phenomena).

5 Some Experiments

In this section we describe a family of test assertions and show how we transform them into a family of closed quantified propositions. We also give the general format of these propositions, verify them, and give some performance results.

5.1 The Test Assertion

To verify the implementation of the proposition solver we use the following family of assertions which are parameterized by n.

Each bit string of length n is a standard binary representation of an integer between 0 and $2^n - 1$.

The formal definition of this assertions is as follows:

$$\forall b \in B_n. \ (\exists k \in N : 0 \leq k < 2^n). \ b = r_n(k)$$

where B_n is the set of possible bit strings of length n and $r_n : N \mapsto B_n$ is the standard representation of the integers on a bit string of length n.
We can transform each of these assertions to a closed quantified proposition. For convenience we take $n = 2$. The predicate $0 \leq k < 2^2$ is equivalent to the logical formula

$$k = 0 \vee k = 1 \vee k = 2 \vee k = 3.$$

Let $[x_0 x_1]$ be a bit string of length 2. The transformation of this formula to the bit string format is now as follows:

$$[x_1 x_0] = [00] \vee [x_1 x_0] = [01] \vee [x_1 x_0] = [10] \vee [x_1 x_0] = [11].$$

If we work it out, this is equal to

$$x_1 = 0 \wedge x_0 = 0 \vee x_1 = 0 \wedge x_0 = 1 \vee x_1 = 1 \wedge x_0 = 0 \vee x_1 = 1 \wedge x_0 = 1.$$

The assertion ($n{=}2$) is that for all $[x_1 \ x_0] \in \{ [00], [01], [10], [11] \}$ this formula must be equal to *true*. The last step is the transformation of this assertion to a closed quantified proposition. Let 1 represent *true* and 0 represent *false*, then the formula "$x_1 = 1$" becomes "$x_1 = true$" which is the same as the proposition "x_1", and

the formula "$x_1 = 0$" becomes "$x_1 = false$" which is the same as the proposition "$\neg x_1$".

With similar results for x_0 instead of x_1, the assertion ($n=2$) becomes the following closed quantified proposition:

$$\forall x_1.\forall x_0. \; (\neg x_1 \wedge \neg x_0 \vee x_1 \wedge \neg x_0 \vee \neg x_1 \wedge x_0 \vee x_1 \wedge x_0).$$

5.2 The General Format of the Test Assertions

The general format of the test assertions $\phi(n)$ is as follows:

$$\forall x. \bigvee_{i=0}^{2^n-1} \bigwedge_{j=0}^{n-1} \neg_j^i \, x$$

where $\forall x$ stands for the row

$$\forall x_{n-1} \ldots \forall x_0$$

and

$$\neg_j^i \, x = x_j \quad \text{if } bit_j(i) = 1$$
$$\neg x_j \text{ if } bit_j(i) = 0.$$

$bit_j(i)$ returns the value of the jth bit of the binary representation of i on a bit string of length n. $\bigvee$ and $\bigwedge$ are, respectively, the generalized $\vee$ and $\wedge$ operators. It is evident that the result of the evaluation of $\phi(n)$ must be $true$.

5.3 Verification and Performance Results

We have verified the family of assertions for $n = 1$ up to 10. They all evaluate to "true". We did these experiments on SGI 16 processor machine of which only 5 processors were available for general use (that is why we set NPART to 5, line 7). The results of our performance measurements for the two cases (i.e., with and without the master/worker protocol) are summarized in table 1.

Note that the approach with the master/worker protocol does not improve the performance of the application. This is no surprise when we recall that we only added a hierarchic coordination layer to the application without the possibility to exploit its performance advantage through parallelism. Due to the coarse-grain lock for the thread-unsafe term library, in fact nothing is done in parallel. With a new thread-safe library we expect other results. For instance, we remark here that MANIFOLD has been successfully used to implement a parallel version of a semi-coarsened multi-grid Euler solver algorithm, using a similar master/worker protocol as the one described here. In that case, all programs were thread-safe, and the performance was improved from almost 9 to over 2 hours on a 4 processor machine [14].

n	approach I	approach II
1	4.926	7.059
2	3.729	6.732
3	3.969	6.536
4	3.865	7.364
5	4.397	10.419
6	5.453	11.993
7	8.738	17.546
8	22.227	40.578
9	81.109	124.262
10	372.855	465.731

Table 1. Elapsed time (in seconds) for the 10 assertions for the two approaches (approaches I and II are, the pipeline model without and with the master/worker protocol respectively).

6   Conclusions

Our experiment using **MANIFOLD** to coordinate the interprocess communication in a proposition solver indicates that this coordination language is well suited for this kind of task. The highly modular structure of both **MANIFOLD** programs in our case study and the ability to use the separately developed functional units is remarkable.

The property of **MANIFOLD** that enables such high degree of modularity is inherited from its underlying IWIM (*Idealized Worker Idealized Manager*) model in which communication is set up from the *outside*. The core relevant concept in the IWIM model of communication is isolation of computation responsibilities from communication and coordination concerns, into separate pure computation modules (as the functional units in the proposition solver written in C) and pure coordination modules (as Main, CNF and M_UQE).

The modularity of **MANIFOLD** also offers the possibility to introduce concurrency step by step. We can therefore proceed as follows. We initially plug a block of code as a monolithic computing process into a concurrent structure (as we did with UQE) to obtain a running parallel/distributed application. As more experience is gained through running the new application, computation bottlenecks may be identified (UQE). This may lead to replacing some such monolithic blocks of code with more **MANIFOLD** modules (M_UQE) that coordinate the activity of smaller blocks of computation code (WORKER), in a new concurrent sub-structure.

Another important advantage of **MANIFOLD** is that it makes no distinction (from the language point of view) between distributed and parallel environments: the same **MANIFOLD** code can run in both (see our WWW pages) .

All these features make **MANIFOLD** a suitable framework for construction of modular software on parallel and/or distributed platforms.

Acknowledgments

We thank Farhad Arbab for his suggestions to improve this paper and Freek Burger for his programming advice.

References

1. J.F. Groote, J.W.C. Koorn, and S.F.M van Vlijmen. The safety guaranteeing system at station hoorn-kersenboogerd (extended abstract). In *Proc. 10th Annual Conference on Computer Assurance (COMPASS '95)*, pages 57–68, 1995.

2. B. Lisser and J.v. Wamel. Specification of components in a proposition solver. In J.v. Wamel J.F. Groote, B. Luttik, editor, *Proc. 3th International Conference on Formal Methods for Industrial Systems*, pages 271–298. CWI, 1998.

3. F. Arbab. The influence of coordination on program structure. In *Proceedings of the 30th Hawaii International Conference on System Sciences*. IEEE, January 1997.

4. D. Gelernter and N. Carriero. Coordination languages and their significance. *Communication of the ACM*, 35(2):97–107, February 1992.

5. F. Arbab, P. Ciancarini, and C. Hankin. Coordination languages for parallel programming. *Parallel Computing*, 24(7):989–1004, July 1998. special issue on Coordination languages for parallel programming.

6. G.A. Papadopoulos and F. Arbab. *Coordination Models and Languages*, volume 46 of *Advances in Computers*. Academic Press, 1998.

7. F. Arbab. Coordination of massively concurrent activities. Technical Report CS–R9565, Centrum voor Wiskunde en Informatica, Kruislaan 413, 1098 SJ Amsterdam, The Netherlands, November 1995. Available on-line http://www.cwi.nl/ftp/CWIreports/IS/CS-R9565.ps.Z.

8. F. Arbab. The IWIM model for coordination of concurrent activities. In Paolo Ciancarini and Chris Hankin, editors, *Coordination Languages and Models*, volume 1061 of *Lecture Notes in Computer Science*, pages 34–56. Springer-Verlag, April 1996.

9. F. Arbab, C.L. Blom, F.J. Burger, and C.T.H. Everaars. Reusable coordinator modules for massively concurrent applications. *Software: Practice and Experience*, 28(7):703–735, June 1998. Extended version.

10. A. Nerode and R. Shore. *Logic for Applications*. Texts and Monographs in Computer Science. Springer-Verlag-Hall, 1993.

11. J.F. Groote. The propositional formula checker HeerHugo. Technical report, CWI, 1997. Unpublished note.

12. Jan Aldert Bergstra and Paul Klint. The ToolBus coordination architecture. In P. Ciancarani and C. Hankin, editors, *Coordination Language and Models*, number 1061 in LNCS. Springer Verlag, 1996.

13. F. Arbab, C.L. Blom, F.J. Burger, and C.T.H. Everaars. Reusable coordinator modules for massively concurrent applications. In L. Bouge, P. Fraigniaud, A. Mignotte, and Y. Robert, editors, *Proceedings of Euro-Par '96*, volume 1123 of *Lecture Notes in Computer Science*, pages 664–677. Springer-Verlag, August 1996.

14. C.T.H. Everaars and B. Koren. Using coordination to parallelize sparse-grid methods for 3D CFD problems. *Parallel Computing*, 24(7):1081–1106, July 1998. special issue on Coordination languages for parallel programming.

CLAM: Composition Language for Autonomous Megamodules

Neal Sample, Dorothea Beringer, Laurence Melloul, Gio Wiederhold

Computer Science Department
Stanford University, Stanford CA 94305
{Nsample, Beringer, Melloul, Gio}@cs.stanford.edu

Abstract. Advances in computer networks that support the invocation of remote services in heterogeneous environments enable new levels of software composition. In order to manage composition at such a high level we envision a need for purely compositional languages. We introduce the CLAM composition language, a megaprogramming language. By breaking up the traditional CALL statement the CLAM language focuses on the asynchronous composition of large-scale, autonomous modules. Furthermore the language has the capability to support various optimizations that are specific to software composition.

1 Introduction

Component software revolutionizes the traditional, programmatic method of building software by introducing a new paradigm in which software is created by leveraging a market of reliable and secure software components [1]. While the component model of software engineering has been promoted for several years [2], it is only in the past few years that infrastructure technology enabling such composition has become stable and sufficiently widespread to encourage serious adoption of the model.

Distributed component software relies on protocols such as DCE [3], CORBA [4], DCOM [1] and Java RMI [4]. Using these protocols, a core software service can be made available to many clients. In order to use these software services, a client program must conform to the Application Program Interface (API) of the desired distribution protocol. However, different servers use different distribution protocols and they do not effectively interoperate. In order to use a distributed software service for composition in the large, a client programmer must be familiar with heterogeneous distributed systems, client-server programming, large-scale software engineering, as well as the application domain. While this is not unrealistic for modest programs composed of small-scale components such as ActiveX controls or JavaBeans [4], as components and assemblies scale upwards, and as more not-technically skilled domain experts would like to make use of distributed components and compose them, this becomes an increasingly unrealistic expectation for most practitioners.

In the CHAIMS (Composing High-level Access Interfaces for Multi-site Software) project, we are attempting to alleviate the knowledge requirements for composition by distinguishing between composition, computation, and distribution. We intend to free the compositional expert from any knowledge of distributed systems and computational programming. At the same time, we recognize that the compositional expert needs more control over the execution and timing of remote method calls as remote server software scales in size. Furthermore, the ability to integrate components that are only accessible by differing distribution protocols is necessary.

With this in mind, we introduce a programming language, CLAM, that is designed for the composition of large-scale modules or services, which we refer to as *megamodules*. A client program that composes various megamodules is known as a *megaprogram*. Megamodules will often be written in different languages, reside on different machines, and be integrated into different distribution systems. Some system is required to bridge the differences in architectures, languages, and distribution systems. We believe that the CPAM (CHAIMS Protocols for Autonomous Megamodules) component of the CHAIMS project adequately addresses those major differences at the runtime level. The support provided by CPAM presents a unique opportunity to investigate a language that strictly addresses composition, without worrying about the aforementioned differences in architectures, module implementation languages, and distribution systems.

We highlight the difference between *coordination* and *composition*. Coordination languages have been studied and used for years, and including languages like SAIL, Ada, and Jovial. Coordination is closely related to *synchronization, proper ordering,* and *timing*. Composition is concerned with the act of *combining* part or elements into a whole. Appropriate composition of autonomous services is an important step that must be taken before specific coordination events occur.

2 CLAM in a Sea of Languages

2.1 Objectives

The structure of the CLAM language is motivated by the features a megaprogramming language should support. A language intended for a large-scale environment should implicitly take advantage of parallelism rather than assume sequential execution. We also expect a megaprogramming language to support compile-time as well as run-time optimization. The control structure within the language should reflect the simple elegance achievable when *composition only* is the goal, rather than the traditional composition coupled with computation. Finally, we assume that the environment in which a general megaprogramming language operates is heterogeneous, and therefore the run-time architecture for such a language must bridge competing distribution protocols. Language specific requirements should not impose further limitations on that runtime system.

2.2 Other Approaches

With base-level runtime support for heterogeneous module interoperability provided by a system like CPAM, the focus of the language may turn to module composition. There are myriad languages designed for computation, some of which have support for coordination as well. Such languages and language extensions include FX, Orca, and Opus. These languages were not designed to be *purely* (or seemingly even "primarily") *compositional* languages, however. As such, each of these more "traditional" languages suffers from deficiencies when used for composition. FX requires that all modules are written to conform to the FX language, including data representations. FX codes are also static compositions, and do not have the dynamism expected in an online system [9]. *Static* compositions cannot change or adapt to varying runtime conditions. Orca has its own distinct runtime support for use with its composition primitives, thus radically limits the potential for use of legacy codes in a composed program. The Opus extensions to HPF take a data-centric view that requires a programmer to have intimate knowledge of all data in a process, including typing and semantic meaning, to set up a megaprogram [9, 10].

Developing languages that have some unique features that make them particularly suited to specific domains is not new. LISP was developed to be good at processing lists and has seen widespread application (especially in AI) where that ability is critical. Fortran was designed with significant support for scientific computation and was well suited to that domain, even before additional features such as dynamic allocation of memory were added. CLAM is unique in that its problem domain is *composition*. CLAM does not limit its application potential by focusing on specific implementation schemes. List processing, scientific computing, database access and updating, and all other work on user data is left to the megamodules. CLAM only composes those megamodules and does not restrict itself in ways that any particular megamodule's implementation language necessarily must do.

2.3 MANIFOLD

Like CLAM, the MANIFOLD language is an attempt at a compositional language [11]. MANIFOLD has a control-driven semantic (via "events") which makes it quite different from the data-centric approaches mentioned in 2.2. The MANIFOLD language has the following building blocks: *processes, ports, streams,* and *events* [12]. Processes are black box views of objects that perform useful work. Ports are access points to processes. Data is passed into and out of ports. Streams are the means to interconnect processes and ports. Events are independent of streams, and convey information through a different mechanism.

MANIFOLD assembles processes using the Ideal Worker Ideal Manager (IWIM) model [12]. In IWIM, compositional codes (known as "managers") select appropriate processes ("workers," in IWIM), even online (at runtime), for a given problem. The processes selected by a manager are workers for that manager. Nesting is possible in the IWIM model, so that one manager's worker may manage workers below it.

IWIM can be viewed like a contractor relationship: a general contractor may hire subcontractors to perform a certain job, and the subcontractors in turn may have additional subcontractors. The general contractor is not concerned with additional layers of contractors/workers, only that the original subcontractor completes the assigned task. MANIFOLD and CLAM both follow this model.

CLAM does not use a black box object view of service providers like MANIFOLD. CLAM treats objects that provide services as entities with exposed methods. These methods can be accessed in a traditional way: invoked with input parameters and with available return values. This can be done in MANIFOLD as well. CLAM, however, extends this simple notion of composition and task atomicity by decomposing the traditional CALL statement, as described in 3.1 and 3.2. In this way, CLAM allows for increased control over scheduling, and allows for runtime inspection of processes. With similar composition features to MANIFOLD, coupled with further CALL statement decomposition, CLAM achieves greater levels of expressiveness. This is especially apparent in 3.2, where we examine optimization opportunities available when the traditional CALL statement is extended with additional functionality.

All MANIFOLD programs can be expressed in CLAM, but the reverse is not true. Because of the special scheduling primitives available in CLAM, more control over process scheduling is possible. Absent these scheduling primitives, and without extensions in CLAM to reuse input parameters to remote invocations, CLAM would be very similar to MANIFOLD.

2.4 A CLAM Language Program

CLAM is not "polluted" with computation and runtime issues because it attempts to be a composition only language. CLAM provides a clean and simple way to achieve the composition painfully achieved within other languages. CLAM has been used to generate working megaprograms compiled with CPAM runtime support. One such megaprogram that frequently appears in the CHAIMS literature finds the least expensive route for transporting goods between two cities [8, 13]. This transportation megaprogram composes five megamodules to achieve this goal.

The following fragment is from an actual transportation megaprogram, for sake of space, some elements have been omitted:

```
// Fragments from megaprogram for finding the cheapest
// route for transporting certain goods between cities

// bind to the megamodules
best_handle        = SETUP ("PickBest")
route_handle       = SETUP ("RouteInfo")
cost_handle        = SETUP ("AirGround")
io_handle          = SETUP ("InputOutput")
best_handle.SETPARAM (criterion = "cost")


// get information from the user about the goods to be
// transported (start and end time, size and weight)
```

```
// and the two desired cities
input_cities_handle = io_handle.INVOKE ("input_cities")
input_goods_handle  = io_handle.INVOKE ("info_goods")
WHILE (input_cities_handle.EXAMINE() != DONE) {}
(mycities = cities) = input_cities_handle.EXTRACT()

// terminate call to "input_cities" within InputOutput
input_cities_handle.TERMINATE()

// get all routes between the two cities
route_handle = route_handle.INVOKE("AllRoutes",
  Pair_of_Cities = cities)

...


//terminate all invocations with "InputOutput" module
io_handle.TERMINATE()
```

3 CLAM Language Semantics

3.1 Parallelism

The compositional programming language CLAM will be used to schedule and organize megamodules. Since remote megamodules can all operate in parallel, the megaprogramming language coordinating these megamodules should be as asynchronous as possible, thus mirroring the everyday world where tasks are often done in parallel. This is particularly important for large-scale megamodules in which each invocation can be expected to be both long running and resource intensive. Synchronous invocation works well for small-scale services. However, as remote services increase in size and power, it is increasingly important that the client has the ability to decide when it wishes to start a specific invocation. In addition, the client must have control returned immediately after starting an invocation so that it can initiate new invocations. When the client needs the results from a particular invocation, it can wait for that invocation, thus synchronizing only when necessary.

In traditional programming languages the primitive to invoke a particular routine, which we refer to as the CALL statement, typically assumes synchrony in execution, forcing possibly parallel tasks into a sequential order or requiring parallelism at the client side. By breaking up the CALL statement into several primitives, we get the asynchrony necessary to support parallel invocation of remote methods out of a sequential client. There is also another reason for breaking up the CALL statement. The CALL statement performs many functions: handling the binding to a remote server, setting local parameters, invoking the desired method, and retrieving the results. For large-scale composition, thinking of the CALL statement as an atomic primitive may make the system unwieldy [5]. Therefore, subdividing the CALL statement into several primitives also gives the megaprogrammer more control over the timing and the execution of the various functions of a CALL statement.

To harness the potential parallelism within a megaprogram, we decompose the traditional CALL statement into the following primitives:

- SETUP

The purpose of the SETUP call is to establish communication with a designated megamodule. SETUP can mean different things depending on the runtime system supporting CLAM. When compiled to CPAM within the CHAIMS system, SETUP primarily establishes communications to megamodules using whatever location scheme is appropriate (e.g. CORBA). Using CLAM with a runtime system like MARS [7], SETUP would likely start a server, rather than simply establish communication to a static one. The SETUP primitive is necessary to direct the runtime client to server/megamodule information at known at compile time (e.g., information taken from the repository we discuss below).

The SETUP calls from the sample CLAM program introduce CLAM handles, e.g.:

```
best_handle  = SETUP ("PickBest")
```

The call to SETUP returns a handle to the megamodule requested, without regard to the locations or implementation of the megamodule. Messy details such as network location and transportation protocols, unimportant to the module composer, are not used in the language, but briefly introduced in 4.1 for the interested reader.

- SETPARAM

The SETPARAM call is used to establish parameters referred to in any method of any particular megamodule that has already been "SETUP." It can also be used to set global variables within a megamodule, i.e. variables used by multiple methods within a single megamodule. If no parameters are set by SETPARAM, the assumption is that the megamodule has suitable default values for an invocation, or the corresponding INVOKE call has all necessary parameters. Many remote procedure calls to major services include various environment variables that are repeated with every invocation. CLAM eliminates that overhead with SETPARAM.

SETPARAM is called using the megamodule handle returned from a SETUP. Again, we see this in the sample program:

```
best_handle.SETPARAM (criterion = "cost")
```

Here, SETPARAM is used to set a global value for criterion. Whenever criterion is required in any method within a particular megamodule, the value set by SETPARAM may be used for free, or overridden for a particular invocation.

- **GETPARAM**

The GETPARAM call can return the value, type, and descriptive name of any parameter of any method of a particular megamodule. It can also return any value of that megamodule's global variables. GETPARAM can be done immediately following SETUP to examine initial and/or default values within a megamodule. It can also be done after a method invocation to inspect changes to global variables, if needed. All parameters have at least a global setting.

- **INVOKE**

The INVOKE call starts the execution of a specified method. Any parameters passed to a method with a call to INVOKE take precedence over parameters already set using SETPARAM. Execution of a specific method returns an "invocation handle." This handle can be used to examine a specific instance of an invocation, and to terminate it as well. We see invocation handles returned in the sample code from 2.4:

```
input_cities_handle = io_handle.INVOKE ("input_cities")
input_goods_handle  = io_handle.INVOKE ("info_goods")

route_handle = route_handle.INVOKE("AllRoutes",
  Pair_of_Cities = cities)
```

With this expressiveness, megaprograms can request multiple instances of the same method from a single megamodule. Single instances can also be terminated with handles. Also, there is no synchronous invocation, so we see the above pairs of modules starting concurrently.

- **EXTRACT**

The EXTRACT call collects the results of an invocation. A subset of all parameters returned by an invocation can be extracted. Extraction can occur at any point, including partial extractions or extractions of incomplete data. It is up to the megaprogrammer to understand when and if partial extraction is meaningful (we will discuss how another primitive, EXAMINE, reveals that the invocation is DONE or NOT_DONE).

Extraction of data is shown in the transportation code. Note, the return value is not another handle type, but a storage location for the return data:

```
(mycities = cities) = input_cities_handle.EXTRACT()
```

- **TERMINATE**

The TERMINATE call kills either a running invocation or a connection from a megaprogram to a specific megamodule. Terminating a connection to a megamodule necessarily kills all running invocations within that megamodule initiated by the client issuing the TERMINATE. Invocations belonging to other megaprograms accessing the same megamodule are unaffected, of course. Termination of a specific method from a single client does not invalidate values set by SETPARAM.

Calls of the two possible termination types are shown in 2.4:

```
input_cities_handle.TERMINATE()  //acts on an invocation
io_handle.TERMINATE()            //acts on a module
```

The first TERMINATE shown above acts on a single method invocation. The second type of TERMINATE show above ends all invocations within a particular megamodule.

With this breakdown of the method CALL process, CLAM can take advantage of implicit and explicit parallelism. If we assume that all traditional CALL statements are *asynchronous*, some parallelism can be achieved without the decomposition found in CLAM. However, some decomposition is implicit in asynchrony as callbacks are required to retrieve data from invocations. Also, traditional asynchronous CALL statements do not yield the scheduling benefits from the primitives in 3.2. Nor do they allow for SETPARAM type operations.

3.2 Novel Optimization Opportunities

As components increase in size, the ability to schedule and plan for the execution of remote services becomes more critical. Traditional optimization methods have focused, quite successfully, on compile-time optimization. The CLAM language coupled with the CPAM (or another suitable) architecture has the potential to support both run-time and compile-time optimization, thus conforming to the dynamic nature of a distributed environment. Here we extend the work done on dynamic query optimization for databases into software engineering [6].

There are both compile-time and runtime optimizations possible with CLAM. The compile-time optimizations depend of the specific support system, so we focus on runtime optimizations with CLAM. There are four main runtime optimizations we focus on here: simple selection of appropriate megamodules, optimizing setup parameters, scheduling parallel megamodules based on cost functions, and partial extractions.

ESTIMATE for Module Selection. In a widely distributed environment, the availability of megamodules and the allocation of resources they need is beyond the control of the megaprogrammer. Furthermore, several megamodules might exist that offer the same functions. Therefore a client must be able to check the availability of megamodule services and get performance estimates from megamodules prior to the invocation of their services. This needs to be done at run-time, as the compile-time estimation may change by the time the megaprogram is executed. Traditional CALL statements do not consider the notion of execution cost estimates. As such estimates become increasingly important to both module users and providers, explicit language support becomes essential.

The following primitive is added to CLAM to help composers take advantage of runtime selection:

- ESTIMATE

The ESTIMATE call returns an estimation of the would-be cost of a specific method invocation. CLAM recognizes three metrics for estimation: invocation fee, invocation time, and invocation data volume. It is up to the megaprogrammer to use this data in a meaningful way. With the information returned from ESTIMATE, megaprograms can schedule invocations from specific service providers based on costs of their services.

An example of using values from ESTIMATE to steer execution (note, INVEX is short for "invoke and extract," and shown in 3.3):

```
cost1 = method1_handle.ESTIMATE()
cost2 = mathod2_handle.ESTIMATE()
IF (cost1 < cost2) THEN result = method1_handle.INVEX()
ELSE result = method2_handle.INVEX()
```

ESTIMATE provides the CLAM language programmer more scheduling ability than MANIFOLD. This makes ESTIMATE a useful language addition for scheduling, without limiting CLAM in other ways.

By using the ESTIMATE primitive, megaprogram users (or compiled megaprograms) can make online choices about particular megamodules to use. These decisions may be based on factors important during that particular megaprogram invocation. In some instances, importance may lie with the cost of the solution, the time necessary to deliver an acceptable solution, or the data volume returned from a particular query.

Parallel Scheduling. It can be difficult at compile time to appropriately schedule distributed services to optimize performance. Even with compile time estimates of module execution times/costs, actual runtime performance may differ significantly. To combat the problem of compile time naiveté, we include a runtime process examination primitive in CLAM.

- EXAMINE

The EXAMINE call is used to determine the state of an invocation. EXAMINE returns an enumerated status to the megaprogram. It can return DONE, PARTIAL, NOT_DONE, and ERROR. The examination of a method before invocation cannot be done, as EXAMINE operates on an invocation handle. Recent discussions about the extension of CLAM indicate that an important addition to EXAMINE would be an indicator of the degree of completion: a value, usable by a megaprogrammer, whose meaning is not enforced by the language. Such an additional return value could be used to indicate the level of progress of an invocation (or anything else of interest), but is not specifically required from megamodules.

EXAMINE is used in the transportation example in 2.4 to synchronize the megaprogram after section of parallel code:

```
WHILE (input_cities_handle.EXAMINE() != DONE) {}
```

EXAMINE may be called with the name of a result value as a parameter, to retrieve information about a specific parameter.

Compile time scheduling can be done in many cases. With EXAMINE, distributed services can be scheduled based on much more accurate runtime information from. Megaprogrammers have language level scheduling ability with CLAM. This is not found in other languages like MANIFOLD.

Progressive Extractions. The EXAMINE primitive allows for online process steering. Speculative scheduling may be done based on estimated times of completion returned from EXAMINE. Advanced scheduling and steering can be achieved as well. Recall that EXAMINE has a second parameter, the meaning of which is defined by the megaprogrammer (and detailed in the repository). A call to EXAMINE may return "PARTIAL" in the first field and "70%" in this second field, indicating a 70% confidence in the result at that point of the invocation. If some level of confidence less than 100% is acceptable for a particular problem, then early extraction based on an EXAMINE statement can save megaprogram users on potentially many fronts, including process time and cost.

Optimizing Setup Parameters. The megaprogrammer may also wish to dynamically check the performance of various megamodules by optimizing various setup parameters, e.g., search parameters or simulation parameters. These parameters may influence the speed and quality of the results, and the megaprogrammer may need to try several settings and retrieve overview results before deciding on the final parameter settings. This is best done during run-time execution. This type of language support is also included in the CLAM specification.

The SETPARAM primitive makes perturbation of input sets easy. By inspecting megamodule progress using EXAMINE (shown in 3.2), users can perform online tests of invocation status. When "tweaking" input parameters to expensive (in terms of fee, time, etc.) processes, partial extraction of data (3.2) and early termination may yield great cost savings. With certain classes of problems, particular setup parameters may not converge on a solution. Using EXAMINE with partial extractions can save users significant costs by *not* computing unacceptable solutions. With many languages, users must wait until a process is complete before testing the viability of the results. There are no primitives for interim process examination.

3.3 Simplicity in Control Flow

CLAM was designed with module composition in mind, and appears to have a very limited set of primitives for megaprogrammers to work with. In reality, the CLAM primitives are a sufficient set tailored specifically to megamodule composition, with little regard for providing functionality beyond composition. Even complex comparisons and altering control flows based on megamodule output require helper modules to analyze and reason about user data.

CLAM strives to remain a language solely for *composition* and not for *computation*. As such, the use of simple CLAM data types for activities other than control flow are quite restricted. Megaprogrammers can assign to a limited set of simple data types (mentioned in 4.2), and make comparisons, but little else. Because of this, the language is very elegant.

Control flow is achieved through the use of simple IF and WHILE constructs. Both are used with boolean expressions composed of comparisons among simple data types. The WHILE loop has the following form:

```
WHILE (Boolean Expression) Statement_list
```

The WHILE is a control mechanism used before making invocations that depend on termination of previous event(s). There are many forms of loops available in different languages, but only the simple WHILE in CLAM. Other loop types, such as DO...WHILE and DO...UNTIL can be constructed from the simple WHILE loop.

The IF statement is a control mechanism used before making invocations which depend on the value of previous result(s) or meta-information like performance data. The IF statement has the following form:

```
IF (Boolean Expression) THEN Statement_list
[ELSE Statement_list]
```

Boolean expressions take many forms. The simplest boolean expression is a single boolean variable. Equality tests between integers, strings, and booleans also yield boolean results (a == b). Also, comparison tests may be done for integers and reals (a<b, a>b, a<=b, a>=b).

By using the IF and WHILE statements, megaprogrammers can write programs in CLAM that have conditional execution paths. These paths may change based on multiple factors including module availability (at setup time), estimations of invocation costs (before potential execution), and progress of particular megamodules (during execution). The sample megaprogram shows the use of a WHILE statement with a megaprogram, and the example for optimization shows the use of an IF statement.

There are two shortcut primitives in CLAM: INVEX (for INVOKE-EXAMINE-EXTRACT) and EXWDONE (for EXTRACT when DONE). These two shortcuts are useful for synchronizing parallel executions, and stalling pipelined megaprograms until critical results become available.

- INVEX

The INVEX call starts the execution of a specified method the same way the INVOKE primitive does. However, INVEX does not return until it collects the results of the invocation. There is currently no possibility to EXAMINE or TERMINATE an INVEX call, though this is still under investigation (there is no reason to EXAMINE or TERMINATE, except in case of error). The INVEX shortcut, operating similarly to the traditional call statement, blocks until method execution is complete and results have been collected. This can be an important short cut when strict synchronicity is desired, or for short methods of helper modules.

- EXWDONE

The EXWDONE call waits until all desired results from a particular invocation are available and then collects those results. There is a clear relationship between EXWDONE and INVEX; INVEX is equivalent to INVOKE immediately followed by EXWDONE. As such, EXWDONE facilitates the addition of instructions between an INVOKE and a corresponding EXTRACT from a single invocation, with the same possibility for synchronization as INVEX.

4 Implementing CLAM

The complete CHAIMS system is based on three main components: CLAM (the language), the CHAIMS compiler, and CPAM (for runtime support). It is a working implementation of the CLAM language. Because a compiler and system supporting the current version of CLAM was developed parallel to CPAM, they coexist naturally. However, the CLAM language is not restricted to use with CPAM and the CHAIMS system. CPAM provides runtime support for myriad communication protocols to CLAM, but is not critical to the language.

As a language, CLAM can compile to alternate runtime systems, such as MARS (Multidisciplinary Application Runtime System), recently developed at the University of Wyoming [7]. MARS, like CPAM, is a self-contained runtime system capable of exchanging data between heterogeneous autonomous megamodules. As such, CLAM is truly an independent part of CHAIMS, with unique language features specifically appropriate for compositional programming.

4.1 CLAM Repository

To keep implementation details away from the language, there must be a clear mapping of names between the megaprogram and information needed by the runtime system. For instance, in the sample megaprogram presented, there are many hidden issues even within the single statement:

```
route_handle = SETUP ("RouteInfo")
```

"RouteInfo" is a megamodule that the megaprogrammer wishes to use, but where is it located on the network? What protocols does it communicate with? What are its available invocation methods? The first two issues, location and communication protocols are of no real concern to the megaprogrammer, but there must be a way for the module specified in the CLAM language statements to be located by the runtime system. The third issue, available methods, is more important to the programmer. He must be able to know about methods of megamodules.

To resolve these three issues (locations, protocol, methods), there is a repository where megamodules are registered. The repository provides critical information to the runtime system about location and protocol to the compiler, and provides method information to the megaprogrammer.

The entry in the repository for the megamodule "RouteInfo" shown in the sample megaprogram has the following information:

```
MODULE "RouteInfoMM" CORBA ORBIX sole.stanford.edu
"RouteInfoModule"
```

This repository entry, typical for a CORBA megamodule, consists of the tag "MODULE," the module name, the tag "CORBA," the object request broker type ("ORBIX" here), the hostname, and the service. This information is important to the runtime system, but not to the megaprogrammer. The methods available to the megaprogrammer and the parameters used also appear in the repository:

```
METHOD RouteInfoMM.GetRoutes (IN CityPair, RES Routes)
   /* gets all routes between 2 cities */
PARAM RouteInfoMM.CityPair     OPAQUE
   /*data containing a city pair    */
PARAM RouteInfoMM.Routes       OPAQUE
   /*data containing routes         */
```

The method and parameter entries in the repository allow for type checking within the megaprogram. The use of any full-featured standard repository system would be appropriate <<>>>(e.g., from CORBA or X500 realms)<<>>. There is no intrinsic contribution to this project from our particular repository system; it must simply be available, in some form, to the megaprogrammer and to the client program.

4.2 CLAM Data Types

There are six data types in CLAM:

- opaque
- integer
- string
- Boolean
- real
- datetime

The first type, *opaque*, is a complex type. Elements of type opaque are exclusively used as user data (i.e. megamodule data) and are not modifiable with CLAM language statements. Opaque data is transferred between megamodules but never processed in the megaprogram. That data generally cannot be directly examined by a program written in a compositional language without violating the notion of being composition only. Opaque data follows the concepts also found in other compositional languages like MANIFOLD.

The other five types are simple CLAM types. Data of simple type is primarily used for control, and it can be received from megamodules with the primitive EXAMINE (the time parameter of type datetime, data volume of type integer, and fee of type real) and the primitive EXTRACT. EXTRACT allows programs to have special methods in megamodules that take opaque types as input and have simple CLAM types as results. Though CLAM does not provide any arithmetic on complex types, it provides comparisons for simple types.

There are no classes or amalgamated data types in CLAM. This makes sense since CLAM aims to be a purely compositional language. There are no complex calculations or comparisons in the megaprogram, nor are there large data structures within the megaprogram itself that are queried or updated within the megaprogram. Literals may be assigned to the five simple types but, true to its compositional nature, there are no other (non-comparison) operators in CLAM (such as an integer increment operator).

By restricting the data type set in this way, the CLAM language remains elegant. If control decisions are to be made using CLAM data types (perhaps from a call to EXAMINE), they can be done within the megaprogram or by invoking methods of helper modules, e.g. for cost-functions. If decisions must be made about opaque user data, rather than extend CLAM to handle all possible data representations for an arbitrary megamodule, the decision is also pushed to a helper megamodule. This helper module will be able to inspect data, and pass back control information as a CLAM type.

5 Conclusions

The CHAIMS project investigates a new programming paradigm: compositional programming. As increasing numbers of autonomous codes become available to megaprogrammers, the importance of the composition process rises as well. CLAM, developed within the CHAIMS project, is an important piece of the investigation of compositional programming, and represents a purely compositional language.

Does CLAM take advantage of the opportunities presented within a programming paradigm shifting towards composition? We believe it does. Breaking down the traditional CALL statement as CLAM does provides new opportunities for parallelism within megaprograms. Such parallelism, intrinsically important because of the nature of autonomous megamodules, is not achievable with standard languages not designed for composition. CLAM provides a tool to harness the asynchrony necessarily present when dealing with independent information suppliers.

CLAM is simultaneously suited to take advantage of novel optimization opportunities. Simple compile-time optimizations are possible with CLAM, but the possible runtime optimizations will likely prove to be much more significant. As a language, CLAM delivers explicit language support for runtime optimizations. The inclusion of cost estimation methods allows easy online examination of invocation costs. That language-level support means that CLAM can easily handle runtime optimizations not possible in current language approaches based on the traditional CALL routine.

A new composition language should not place increased language restrictions on heterogeneity. Differences in communication protocols should not affect the megaprogrammer. The composition language of choice should not be fundamentally tied to any specific protocol. As mentioned before, the CLAM language does not distinguish between the different protocols at a semantic level. Any need to separate features is done at the level of the compiler or support system. Furthermore, by not committing itself to computations on user data, CLAM is not restricted in its ability to pass data between arbitrary megamodules. The opaque data type in CLAM can handle whatever objects are returned by a megamodule, without restriction.

The compositional programming paradigm represents a next level of abstraction in programming. Machine code can be mapped to assembly language instructions. Assembly can be generated by high level programming languages. High level languages enhance a programmer's ability to generate increasingly complex sets of assembly language code, without adding new assembly language instructions or changing their meaning. High level programming languages are a powerful means to abstract away the tedious details of the assembly language and machine code below them. Composition languages are to high level programming languages what those languages were to assembly and machine code. They enable programmers to use megamodules written in high level languages as a useful construct who's implementation details are not of great concern (like assembly language is to the high level language). CLAM is a step toward this next level of programming.

The CHAIMS project is supported by DARPA order D884 under the ISO EDCS program, with the Rome Laboratories being the managing agent, and also by Siemens Corporate Research, Princeton, NJ. We also thank the referees of COORD'99 for their valuable input, and the various Master's and Ph.D. students that have contributed to the CHAIMS project.

References

1. W. Tracz: "Confessions of a Used Program Salesman"; Addison-Wesley, 1995
2. P. Naur and B. Randell, eds.: "Software Engineering"; Proc. of the NATO Science Committee, Garmisch, Germany, October 7-11, 1968. Proceedings published January 1969
3. W. Rosenberry, D. Kenney and G. Fisher: "Understanding DCE"; O'Reilly, 1994
4. C. Szyperski, "Component Software: Beyond Object-Oriented Programming", Addison-Wesley and ACM-Press New York, 1997
5. G. Wiederhold, P. Wegner, and S. Ceri: "Towards Megaprogramming: A Paradigm for Component-Based Programming"; Communications of the ACM, 1992(11): p.89-99
6. G. Grafe and K. Karen: "Dynamic Query Evaluation Plans"; In James Clifford, Bruce Lindsay, and David Maier, eds., Proceedings of the 1989 ACM SIGMOD International Conference on Management of Data, Portland, Oregon, June 1989
7. N. Sample and M. Haines: "MARS: Runtime Support for Coordinated Applications"; Proceedings of the 1999 ACM Symposium on Applied Computing, San Antonio, Texas, Feb-Mar 1999.
8. C. Tornabene, D. Beringer, P. Jain and G. Wiederhold: "Composition on a Higher Level: CHAIMS," unpublished, Dept. of Computer Science, Stanford University.
9. H. Bal and M. Haines: "Approaches for Integrating Task and Data Parallelism," Technical Report IR-415, Vrije Universiteit, Amsterdam, December 1996.

10. M. Haines and P. Mehrotra: "Exploiting Parallelism in Multidisciplinary Applications Using Opus," Proceedings of the Seventh SIAM Conference on Parallel Processing for Scientific Computing, San Francisco, CA, February 1995.

11. F. Arbab, I. Herman, and P. Spilling: "An Overview of MANIFOLD and its Implementation," *Concurrency: Practice and Experience*, Volume 5, issue 1, 1993.

12. G. Papadopoulos and F. Arbab: "Modeling Electronic Commerce Activities Using Control Driven Coordination," Ninth International Workshop on Database And Expert Systems Applications (DEXA 98): Coordination Technologies for Information Systems, Vienna, August 1998.

13. D. Beringer, C. Tornabene, P. Jain, and G. Wiederhold: "A Language and System for Composing Autonomous, Heterogeneous and Distributed Megamodules," DEXA 98: Large-Scale Software Composition, Vienna, August 1998.

Modeling Resources for Activity Coordination and Scheduling

Rodion M. Podorozhny , Barbara Staudt Lerner and Leon J. Osterweil

University of Massachusetts, Amherst MA 01003, USA

Abstract. Precise specification of resources is important in activity and agent coordination. As the scarcity or abundance of resources can make a considerable difference in how to best coordinate the tasks and actions. That being the case, we propose the use of a resource model. We observe that past work on resource modeling does not meet our needs, as the models tend to be either too informal (as in management resource modeling) to support definitive analysis, or too narrow in scope (as in the case of operating system resource modeling) to support specification of the diverse tasks we have in mind.

In this paper we introduce a general approach and some key concepts in a resource modeling and management system that we have developed.

We also describe two experiences we have had in applying our resource system. In one case we have added resource specifications to a process program. In another case we used resource specifications to augment a multiagent scheduling system. In both cases, the result was far greater clarity and precision in the process and agent coordination specifications, and validation of the effectiveness of our resource modeling and management approaches.

Keywords

Resource modeling, resource management, process programming, planning, agent coordination

1 Introduction

Resources are essential to the performance of any task. Indeed, it is not unreasonable to adopt as a working definition that a resource is any entity or agent that is needed in order to perform a task, but for which there is only a limited supply available. That being the case, it is reasonable that specifications of needed resources be present in specifications of the way in which tasks are to be done, and in attempts to automate support for such tasks.

The need for the specification of resources has been realized by other communities. Resource specifications are important in operating systems, where contention for resources can lead to such dangerous situations as deadlock and starvation. Thus, operating systems incorporate models of key resources, keep track of resource utilization and analyze utilization to either recognize or avoid such pathologies as deadlocks. Resource specifications are important in management as well, where they are critical to the effective scheduling of tasks to individuals and granting of access to, and utilization of, scarce resources to support the execution of tasks.

More recently workflow, software process, and activity coordination research has reconfirmed the importance of resource specification. One key goal of systems that support the modeling and execution of processes is to expedite the performance of complex tasks. Early systems in this area have focused particularly strongly on the structure of these tasks. Analysis of task structures has been shown to be useful in indicating possible parallelization of activities, for example. But it has become increasingly clear that such analyses are handicapped if they are not supplemented by consideration of resources.

Thus, for example, a simple structural analysis of a process specification may seem to indicate that two tasks may be parallelizable. But if both require access to a single resource that cannot be shared, then parallelization of the tasks is impossible. As another example, a project is likely to benefit if the most experienced or competent performers are assigned to the most critical tasks. Only analysis and evaluation of available human resources can help here.

These realizations have sparked an interest in resource modeling, specification, and analysis by the community of researchers working on process, workflow and activity coordination technology. Study of the existing literature in the area of resource specification indicates that the existing work is insufficient to meet the needs of these newer areas. Management resource modeling is too informal to support the needs of workflow and process. Models in this area are largely intended to support humans who are expected to make judgments about resource allocation that may be mostly intuitive. Operating system resource modeling is, in contrast, quite rigorous and precise. The rigor and precision of models in this area is necessary as they are used to support automated analyses and reasoning. The resources about which such reasoning is carried out are, however, rather limited in scope and nature. Generally operating systems reason about hardware resources such as storage devices and blocks of central memory.

Resource models for use in workflow, process, and activity coordination are intended to support automated reasoning and analysis about the full spectrum of resources that may be needed in any activity to be modeled. As the span of applicability of these systems is very broad, they seem to require at least the breadth and diversity of scope that characterize management resource models. But as the goals of such systems include the ability to reason definitively about such issues as deadlock, and optimal allocation, the rigor and precision that characterizes operating system resource modeling also seems necessary here.

In this paper we describe early experiences with such a system. Our resource specification and modeling system is designed to support the representation of an unusually broad spectrum of resource types with precision and rigor that seems sufficient to support powerful reasoning and inference.

2 Overview

Our resource management system is intended to be a component that should be useful and usable in a variety of larger systems that may, for example, support processes execution, carry out reasoning about real-time systems, or perform multiagent planning. Since we believe that the need for powerful and precise resource management is widespread we have designed this component to support the modeling of a wide range of types of resources, from physical entities such as robots, to electronic entities such as programs or data artifacts, and to human entities. The resource management component similarly does not prescribe specific protocols about how resources should be used, but rather leaves the definition of those protocols to the external system with which it is to be integrated. In this section, we present an overview of our resource management component, introducing some key terminology. A detailed and rigorous presentation of our resource management system cannot be presented here due to space limitations. This is the subject of a separate, companion paper that is to appear shortly.

A **resource model** is a model of those entities of an environment that may be required, but for which an unlimited supply cannot be assumed. The resource model is organized as a collection of resource instances, resource classes, and relations among them.

A **resource instance** is a representation of a unique entity from the physical environment, such as a specific person, printer, or document. Each resource instance is described using a set of typed attribute-value pairs. There are predefined attributes required of all resources, such as a name and description, as well as user-defined attributes that are specific to the various types of resources. The attribute values of a resource serve to identify the resource and distinguish it from other similar resources. For example, a printer might have an attribute indicating whether it produces color or black output, but that attribute would not be required of resources that are not printers.

A **resource class** represents a set of resources (other classes and/or instances) that have some common attributes. The resource classes in a resource model form a singly-rooted DAG. The root of the DAG is the predefined resource class named Resource. Each child class inherits all the attributes of its parent, but presumably adds in some additional attributes.

There are two kinds of resource classes: schedulable and unschedulable. A **schedulable resource class** is a collection of resources, each of which can be allocated to a task. These instances are generally sufficiently similar that they are often substitutable for each other. For example, Laser-Printer might be a schedulable resource class, as laser printers generally offer the same sorts of printing capabilities. Thus, a **schedulable resource class** can be viewed as a conceptual generalization that groups a number of resources with very similar capabilities and performance characteristics.

An **unschedulable resource class** is more abstract and is intended more as an organizational convenience when defining the resource model. For example, the distinguished root Resource is not schedulable, and the class Hardware is generally not likely to be schedulable either.

A resource model also contains three relations that connect the resource classes and instances in the model: the **IS-A** relation, the **Requires** relation, and the **Whole-Part** relation.

The **IS-A relation** is the relation that defines pairs of classes (or class-instance pairs) that share sets of attributes. In particular, the attributes of the parent in the **IS-A relation** are all inherited by the child in the relation.

The **Requires** relation connects one resource instance or resource class to another to indicate that some particular resource class, or instance, is always required in order for the first to be useful. For instance, a particular piece of software might require a computer with a particular operating system or with some minimum memory requirements. Use of this relation dictates that these dependency requirements are universally true, independent of any particular application in which the related resources are used.

A **Whole–Part** relation connects resources that may at times need to be considered part of an aggregate resource in addition to being considered as individual resources. For example, individual developers are separate resources, but may also at times need to be considered to be part of a development team.

We have taken resource models represented as just described and built around them a resource management system. The purpose of this system is to support applications that need to allocate resources and keep track of current allocation status. This system defines four primary operations on the resource model:

- **Identification**, which identifies specific resource instances that can satisfy specific stated requirements. Requirements can be expressed either as a specific resource name (which could be a class or instance name), or by queries over the attribute values of the resource class that is required.
- **Reservation**, which reserves a specific resource instance (generally one that has previously been identified) for a specific duration of time.
- **Acquisition**, which locks a resource instance for use in a specific activity. The resource instance is generally one that has been previously reserved or one identified with a resource specification.
- **Release**, which frees a reserved or acquired resource instance so that it can be used by other activities.

Reservation and acquisition do not necessarily require exclusive use of a resource instance. Instead, they can specify the quantity or fractional usage of a resource instance that they will require. For example, a person might be required to work on a specific assignment for 10 hours/week for 4 weeks. The remaining capacity can be allocated to other activities that request it.

3   Experiences with our approach

We have gained experience with our resource manager by integrating it into two different systems. The first is Little-JIL, a visual process programming language. The second is MASS, a multi-agent planning system. In this section, we describe how the resource manager meets resource management needs in these two application domains.

3.1 Integration with Little-JIL

In Little-JIL ([8], [17]), a process is represented as a hierarchical decomposition of steps. Attached to each step is a list of resources that are required to carry out that step. Typical resources in Little-JIL include execution agents (human, software, robots, for example), physical resources (printers, computers, specialized hardware, for example), licensed software (compilers, design tools, word processors, for example), and access permissions for data (documents or portions thereof, for example).

In Little-JIL, each step has an execution agent. From Little-JIL's perspective, the execution agent is distinguished from the other resources by virtue of the fact that it is the entity with which the Little-JIL interpreter communicates to assign tasks and get results. From the resource manager's perspective, however, an execution agent is simply a resource.

Little-JIL assumes that a resource model describing all available resources is defined outside of the process. The resource specifications attached to steps enable the identification, acquisition, and release of resource instances that meet the needs of the step. This binding between specific resource instances managed by our resource manager and specific step instantiations in a Little-JIL process being executed is done dynamically as follows.

The resource declarations attached to each step identify the name of a resource class or instance and, optionally, a query defined in terms of the attribute values of the desired instance.[1] When a step is first considered for execution, all resources required by the step are *identified*. If the resource manager cannot find a matching resource in the resource model, an exception is thrown indicating this and control flows to an exception handler defined for the Little-JIL program. Assuming the necessary resources exist in the model, the execution agent resource is *acquired* and Little-JIL assigns to it responsibility for executing the step to which it is bound. The execution agent may have several steps assigned to it and therefore might not actually start the step for some time (minutes or even weeks, depending on the nature of the process). In order to not tie up the resources for an unnecessarily long period of time, the Little-JIL interpreter does not actually *acquire* the rest of the resources required for the step until the agent indicates that it is starting the step. At that point, it is possible that the necessary resources are being used elsewhere. In this case, the resource manager indicates its inability to acquire the resources and Little-JIL throws an exception that again is handled by a handler designed to deal with exceptions of this sort. Resources may be passed to substeps when those substeps are ready for execution. When the step (and all its substeps) have completed, Little-JIL *releases* the resources that were acquired for execution of that step.

A Static Resource Model Figure 1 shows a resource model used within a simple Little-JIL process that specifies the coordination of a team of people

---

[1] Currently these queries are written in Java, but ultimately we expect to provide a query language that will allow in-place resource specifications directly in the process definition.

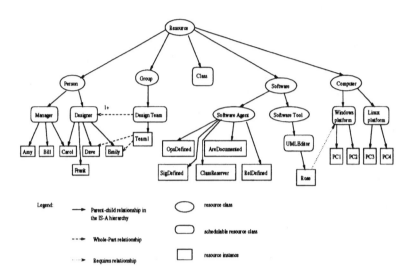

Fig. 1. Resource Model used in a Little-JIL Design Process

who are carrying out an object oriented design activity. This model defines six unschedulable resource classes used to organize the model: Person, Group (of people), Software, Software Agent, Software Tool, and Computer. Person is subdivided into two schedulable classes: Manager and Designer. There are three instances beneath Manager: Amy, Bill, and Carol. There are four designer instances: Carol, Frank, Dave, and Emily. Carol apparently has both managerial and design expertise and thus can serve in either role. The figure shows only the names of the resources, but not their other attributes. The attributes associated with Person include such things as Salary and Years of Experience. The Designer class might add additional attributes such as Domains of Expertise.

Most of the edges in the resource model represent IS-A relations. There is a Requires relation between Rose, an instance of UMLEditor, and the schedulable resource class that represents PCs running Windows. This indicates that any step that uses Rose also requires a PC running Windows. Because the Requires edge exists, a step that uses Rose does not need to declare its need of a Windows PC explicitly.

This example also illustrates an important interplay between the different types of relations. Were it not for the Requires relation just mentioned, it might be reasonable to treat Computer as a schedulable resource class having four instances. But the need to indicate the dependence of the Rose software resource on a particular kind of platform creates a need for the schedulable resource class Windows-Platform as a subclass of Computer, which at that point is most reasonably considered to be an unschedulable class.

The alternative of having the four computer platform instances all be children of the Computer unschedulable resource class requires that the operating system simply be an attribute attached to the instances. There are several reasons not to do that, however. First, if we had done that, it would not be possible to specify in the resource model that Rose required a computer running Windows without binding it to specific computers, which is overly restrictive. If we choose not to represent the requires relation in the model, the process programmer would be forced to add the Windows computer as a resource at each step that specified Rose. Furthermore, if we had another UMLEditor that ran on Linux, the resource specification would become more complicated in order to ensure that compatible software licenses and computing platforms were available when the step began.

The resource model also includes a Whole-Part relation between the Design Team class and the Designer class, indicating each design team contains one or more designers. The Team1 instance is therefore required to have one or more designers as parts. In this case, it has two members, Dave and Emily. It is possible that the initial resource model might not include any specific teams. The teams could be created during process execution, creating both the Team instances as well as the Whole-Part edges identifying the team members. In the figure, we have shown the team composition, which may have been created statically before execution of the process, or may be thought of as a snapshot of the resource model after the relation has been created dynamically.

Figure 1 also shows two types of software: software agents and software tools. A software agent is a piece of software that can be assigned the responsibility of performing a step of the process, whereas a software tool is a licensed tool that a user requires in order to complete a step. Thus, the software agents are resources required directly by the Little-JIL process, while software tools are resources required by the human agent carrying out a process step.

The remaining resource class is named Class. This class represents a data artifact, namely the collection of the designs of the various individual classes that are created as the products of the activity of designing the particular application system that is being specified by this process. These application classes are represented as resources instances, and represented in our resource model, in order to support coordination of the activities of the designers of the application. Specifically, as the design of the application proceeds, individual classes of the design being created will have to be acquired as resources for various substeps of the individual process steps, in order to make them available to the individual designers who are the execution agents of those steps. In this way, the resource manager can prevent multiple designers from working on the design of the same class. Different processes could, of course, allow designers to work on the same class design collaboratively, or even require that different designers must work on the same class collaboratively. Our resource modeling and management capability can be used to support all of these situations. It should be noted that the resource model shows no resource instances as children because this example assumes that the various instances are to be created dynamically and the design process has not yet progressed to the point of creating any of them.

Dynamic Interaction between a Little-JIL Process and the Resource Manager The process that used this resource model was a simple multi-user

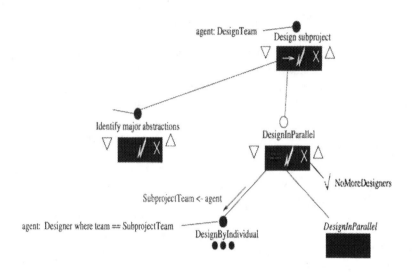

Fig. 2. A Little-JIL Process with Resource Declarations

design process built on top of the Booch Object Oriented Design methodology ([1], [13]) as shown in Figure 2. In this process, a design team is given a design task. They perform some initial design activities as a team and then subdivide the assignment into individual design assignments. The design activity follows the four step Booch methodology of 1) identifying abstractions, 2) identifying the semantics of the abstractions, 3) identifying the relationships between abstractions, and 4) implementing the abstractions. Each of these steps is carried out by a human (or team of humans), but some substeps are used to check postconditions on completion of some of these steps, and these substeps may have software systems as their execution agents. For example, the AreDocumented substep (Figure 1) is invoked after identifying the abstractions to check that some documentation exists for each named abstraction. This substep is to have a software system as its execution agent.

Some comments on this example seem to be in order. First, we note that software systems often have a distinctive nature in the resource model as these systems are often available in sufficient abundance that scheduling of them is not required. Such is the case in this example, and that explains why requests for them are not shown in this Little-JIL process program. The software systems required here are not licensed software, there is no contention for them, no need to schedule them, and thus they do not need to be part of the resource model.

It is also worth noting that in this example we see a case where a specific resource instance is specified as the required execution agent for a step. It is more usual for a specification to name a resource class. In cases where specific resource instances are specified, these resource instances may be introduced into (or even created for) the model to support the specific process. In such cases, these software agents are not the types of general reusable, contended-for resources we normally expect to find in a resource model. They exist simply because the

Little-JIL interpreter requires that all agents be treated as resources. Because of this we found that it was sometimes necessary to customize a resource model to support a specific Little-JIL process. Our experience was that such customizations turned out to be simple to do, and did not seem to have any noticeable effect on the operation of the resource manager.

The Whole-Part relation between a team and its members is critical in expressing the notion of team and individual responsibilities commonly found within organizations. The design team as a whole is responsible for an entire subproject. As a team they meet to decompose the subproject into major abstractions that can be further designed in (relative) isolation by individual designers. This is represented in the process by specifying a `Design Team` to be the agent for the `Design Subproject` step. At this point the resource manager is asked to acquire all team members for the design activity. Once this has been done, the entire team is inherited as the agent for the `Identify Major Abstractions` step. Once this step is complete, the `Design In Parallel` step is invoked. As the first substep of `Design In Parallel`, the `Design By Individual` step is invoked, and this step requires as an execution agent a `Designer` who is a member of the `Design Team`. The purpose of this step is to give an individual assignment to an individual member of the team.[2] Since the design team members have already been acquired by a parent step, they are not re-acquired here. Instead, their assignments are simply refined to the more specialized tasks at hand. This is done by making the members of the design team be the entire resource model that is available for reservation and allocation to this step. The Whole-Part relation is essential to guiding the resource manager in doing this.

The design process demonstrates another feature that we have found to be a particularly effective use of a resource model to support the definition of reusable processes. The motivation behind separating a resource model from the process is to allow a single process to be reused effectively across a range of resource availability scenarios. The process specifies the essential resource requirements using specifications, while the specific instances are bound dynamically based upon what is available in the environment. In addition to supporting substitutable resources, this also allows us to specify a process in which activities can be performed in parallel if sufficient resources exist but need to be done sequentially if there are insufficient resources. This has led to a common Little-JIL idiom of resource-bounded parallelism as exemplified by the `Design In Parallel` step. Resource-bounded parallelism allows multiple instantiations of a step to be performed in parallel, with each step getting new resources. When all the available resources have been allocated, a newly instantiated step's request for resources will be denied, an exception will be thrown, and no more parallel instantiations will be created. We have also found resource-bounded recursion to be a useful idiom, although it does not occur in this example.

In addition to the interaction between the resource manager and the Little-JIL interpreter, the agents themselves can communicate directly with the re-

---

[2] Note that we have elided many details in order to focus on the essential resource management issues of interest here.

source manager when the default identification/acquisition/release semantics provided by the interpreter are insufficient. For example, an agent, rather than the process program, might be in the best position to select which specific resources to acquire, or might want to release resources in some substep rather than waiting for the entire step to complete. This is particularly true for the management of human resources, where one would almost certainly want a human manager to make such decisions as which people should perform which specific assignments. The entire functionality of the resource manager is thus available to agents to refine the use of resources within a process. For example, a GUI tool might allow the human designer to select which classes the designer wants to work on, acquiring those classes for the designer and thereby preventing other designers from working on the same classes simultaneously. Other processes might provide other mechanisms for doing this binding, such as having a human manager specify all class-designer assignments.

3.2 Integration with a Multi-Agent Planning System

The second resource sensitive system that was used to evaluate the resource manager is MASS [14], a multi-agent planning system. The resource manager was used in an application of MASS to the task of housekeeping. Although the MASS computational model is significantly different from that of Little-JIL, the resource manager was still found to be useful.

In MASS, as in Little-JIL, a process is considered to be a collection of steps, each of which is executed by an execution agent. But in MASS, unlike Little-JIL, the set of execution agents is established at the beginning of the process, when the set of steps is also established, but rather than having a step interpreter bind execution agents to steps, the agents identify the steps themselves and bind them as their tasks. Thus, the execution agents do not need to be represented using schedulable resource classes. They are regarded as being fixed from the outset. As a result, they are not depicted in our resource model.

The collection of resources that the agents need is also fixed from the outset. While their availability cannot be assured at any time, their existence is never in doubt. Thus, the use of the Identify method of our resource manager was not needed. In MASS agents acquire resources when they need them, release them when they are done, and react appropriately if they are not available when the agent wants them.

We now briefly outline an example of the use of the resource manager for a specific application of MASS. In this example, the agents are a dishwasher, a washing machine, a vacuum cleaner, an air conditioner, and a heater. The resource model for this example is shown in Figure 3.

While the MASS system does not require the use of many capabilities offered by the resource management system, it did require augmenting the resource management system by adding a rather different type of resource, namely consumable resources. Consumable resources are those that have a limited capacity, but may be shared by different agents up to that capacity level. The resource may either be exhausted through use, or may be regenerated either instantaneously or over

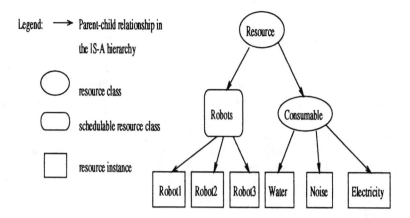

Fig. 3. Resource Model for the Housekeeping Task

time. In our example there are three consumable resources: water, allowed noise, and electricity. All are instantaneously regenerated when released by an agent. In the example, depending on the capacity of the water flow, it might or might not be possible to operate the dishwasher and washing machine at the same time. Similarly, this application limits the amount of noise that can be produced at one time. It is possible that an agent will not be able to execute at a particular time because it would raise the noise volume above the desired threshold.

We were able to model consumable resources by adding a capacity attribute. For example, the capacity of water might be expressed in gallons per minute. When an agent acquires a resource, it indicates how much capacity it needs. If there is sufficient capacity remaining, it is given to that agent. Otherwise, an exception is thrown so the agent can decide whether to wait or to work with a lower capacity. When the agent is done with the resource, it releases the capacity it was using.

This particular resource model is an approximation of the resource environment. A more complete representation would have also modeled the access points, such as faucets or electrical outlets, as resources that were contended for. This model also assumes a constant capacity for the resources. Some consumable resources are more accurately represented as resources whose capacity decreases until an agent replenishes the resource. An example of this would be paper for a printer or gasoline for a car.

The following is an informal description of a typical task that MASS can solve. Let us assume it is 16:00 now. In a two hour period the following goals have to be accomplished to prepare for the arrival of guests:

- The dishes have to be cleaned
- The tablecloth has to be washed
- The floors need to be cleaned
- Room temperature needs to be at 68 degrees when the guests arrive

Constraints:

- The noise level should be low between 17:00 and 17:30 so the baby can nap.

The MASS system orchestrates activities performed by the agents taking into account resource and environmental constraints. Every agent produces its own local schedule. An agent informs other agents of its schedule and conducts negotiation if there are any conflicts over resources. Resource conflicts can occur if the agents, as a group, intend to use more capacity of a particular resource during a particular time period than is available in the environment. In the case of contention for a resource, agents negotiate the use of the resource and decide which one of them is going to get access to the resource during this time. Once the decision is made the local schedules of the agents involved are correspondingly updated to exclude the contention.

This example, combined with the Little-JIL example, demonstrates the flexibility provided by the resource manager. The types of resources modeled and the ways in which the resources are used are quite different in the two cases. Even so, the resource manager was able to address all these concerns and operate effectively in these very different environments.

4 Related work and other Approaches

High adaptability to new environments, the use of a predefined, yet extensible, resource class abstraction (i.e. through the use of our IS-A hierarchy) and ease of integration are some key characteristics that differentiate our work from previous approaches to resource modeling in resource sensitive systems.

Other resource modeling and specification work has been done in such resource sensitive application areas as software process, operating systems, artificial intelligence planning and management. The approaches in these areas have some similarities to our own work, as they concern themselves with such similar problems as the coordination of activities that can span long time periods.

4.1 Related work in software process

There have been a number of software process modeling and programming languages and systems that have addressed the need to model and manage resources. Among the most ambitious and comprehensive have been APEL [9], and MVP-L [11], both of which have attempted to incorporate general resource models and to use resource managers to facilitate process execution. We believe that these systems do not support resource modeling with sufficient rigor, precision, and generality. There are a number of other languages that provide for the explicit modeling of different sorts of resources that seem to fit nicely into our larger resource modeling capability. Merlin [5], for example, provides rules for associating tools and roles (or specific users) with a work context (which may be likened to a Little-JIL step). Some others that offer similar limited capabilities are ALF [4], Statemate [7], and ProcessWeaver [2]. In all of these cases, however, the sorts of resources that are modeled are rather limited in scope.

4.2   Related work in operating systems

The problem of scheduling resources has been extensively studied in the field
of operating systems ([3], Chapter 6.4). The most common resources in this
problem domain include peripheral devices and parts of code or data that require
exclusive access. The differences between the needs of resource management in
operating systems and software engineering (or artificial intelligence) arise from
the fact that operating system resources:

- are generally all resource instances, and hence there is little need for resource
  hierarchies.
- are used for much shorter periods of time (hence, more elaborate notions of
  availability are not usually needed).
- are generally far less varied (e.g. Humans are not considered to be resources
  in operating systems)

As a result operating systems resource management systems are of only limited applicability to our needs.

4.3   Related work in AI planning systems

Probably, the closest resource modeling approach to ours is suggested in the **DI-
TOPS/OZONE** system. **OZONE** is a toolkit for configuring constraint-based
scheduling systems [12]. **DITOPS** is an advanced tool for generation, analysis
and revision of crisis-action schedules that was developed using the **OZONE**
ontology. The closeness is evidenced by the fact that **OZONE** also incorporates
a definition of a resource, contains an extensive predefined set of resource attributes, uses resource hierarchies, offers similar operations on resources, and also
resource aggregate querying. We believe that our resource modeling approach
places a greater emphasis on human resources in the predefined attributes and
allows for an implementation that is easier to adapt to different environments.

The Cypress integrated planning environment is another example of a resource-
aware AI planning system. It integrates several separately developed systems
(the SIPE-2 planning execution [16], PRS-CL, etc.) The ACT formalism [10]
used for proactive control specification in the Cypress system has a construct
for resource requirements specification. It allows the specification of only a particular resource instance. The resource model does not allow for resource hierarchies and the set of predefined resource attributes is rigid and biased towards
the problem domain (transportation tasks).

4.4   Related work in management

An example of a resource modeling approach in a management system is presented in the Toronto Virtual Enterprise (**TOVE**) project [6]. This approach suggests a set of predefined resource properties, a taxonomy based on the properties[3]

---

[3] Properties include Divisibility (this property can take two values - Consumable or
Reusable), Quantity, Component (part-of relationship), Source

and a set of predicates that relate the state with the resource required by the activity [4]. The predicates have a rough correspondence to some methods of our resource manager. It is very likely that our resource manager would satisfy the functionality requirements for a resource management system necessitated by the activity ontology suggested in the **TOVE** project.

4.5 Related work in other distributed software systems

The **Jini** distributed software system [15], which is currently being developed by Sun Microsystems, seems to employ a resource modeling approach that seems somewhat similar to ours. The **Jini** system is a distributed system based on the idea of federating groups of users and the resources required by those users. The overall goal of the system is to turn a network into a flexible, easily administered tool on which resources can be found by human and computational clients. One of the end goals of the **Jini** system is to provide users easy access to resources. **Jini** boasts the capability for modeling humans as resources, allows for resource hierarchies, provides ways to query a resource repository using a resource template that is very similar to resource queries in our suggested approach. Because information about **Jini** is limited it is difficult to say what kind of a resource model is used. It is also difficult to see how easily **Jini's** resource model can be adapted to new environments.

5   Evaluation and Future Work

These two applications of the resource system confirmed that the features of the system we have developed are of substantial value, and that the approaches we are taking seem appropriate. Our experiences have resulted in the creation and modification of our initial notions and decisions.

For example, the `Whole-Part` relation was incorporated into the resource modeling capability after the need became apparent in trying to address the problem of programming the design of software by teams.

In addition, the MASS example showed the need to treat acquisition and release of consumable and replenishable resources differently from reusable ones. The IS-A hierarchy of the resource model was modified to include the Consumable class and an attribute describing this property for every resource instance was introduced. In addition to that, the semantics of acquisition and release of a consumable resource was modified to decrease the capacity of a consumable resource after it was used by a consumer (e.g. dishwasher for water resource), increase it after it was used by a producer (e.g. pump for water resource) and allow several agents to use the same consumable resource for the same period of time if there is enough capacity.

Predicates include: *use(state,activity)*, *consume(state,activity)*, *release(state,activity)*, *produce(state,activity)*, *quantity(state,resource,amount)*

Our experiences have encouraged us to continue to develop our resource model and resource management system further. Next we plan to introduce features that would ease definition of the resource model and resource requirements. The process of definition of the resource model can be facilitated by a resource specification language and a GUI. The resource specification language would also enforce rigor in definition of resources. The GUI to support definition of a resource model would provide a user-friendly way to change or modify the resource model. A resource requirement specification language would allow a non-programmer to specify the requirements (currently the queries are specified in Java). We believe that this language should be orthogonal to the activity specification language so that it would be able to enhance an arbitrary resource sensitive activity specification.

Finally, we are completing work on more complete, precise, and rigorous specifications of the resource modeling formalism and the resource manager.

6 Acknowledgments

We wish to thank Stan Sutton, Eric McCall, Sandy Wise and the members of the Software Process team of the University of Massachusetts Laboratory for Advanced Software Engineering Research (LASER) for their many helpful comments and suggestions, and for their assistance with the Little-JIL evaluation. We would also like to thank Regis Vincent for his assistance with the MASS evaluation. Finally, we acknowledge the support of the Defense Advanced Research Projects Agency, and Rome Laboratories for their support of this research under grant F30602-94-C-0137 and F30602-97-2-0032.

References

1. G. Booch. *Object-Oriented Design with Applications*. The Benjamin/Commings Publishing Company, Inc., 1994.
2. C.Fernström. PROCESS WEAVER: Adding process support to UNIX. In *The Second International Conference on the Software Process*, pages 12–26, 1993.
3. H. M. Deitel. *An Introduction to Operating Systems*. Addison-Wesley, Reading, Massachusetts, 1984.
4. G.Canals, N.Boudjlida, J.-C.Derniame, C.Godart, and J.Lonchamp. ALF: A framework for building process-centered software engineering environments. In A. Finkelstein, J. Kramer, and B. Nuseibeh, editors, *Software Process Modelling and Technology*, pages 153–185. Research Studies Press, Ltd., Taunton, Somerset, England, 1994.
5. G.Junkermann, B.Peuschel, W.Schäfer, and S.Wolf. MERLIN: Supporting cooperation in software development through a knowledge-based environment. In A. Finkelstein, J. Kramer, and B. Nuseibeh, editors, *Software Process Modelling and Technology*, pages 103–129. Research Studies Press, Ltd., Taunton, Somerset, England, 1994.
6. M. Gruninger and M. S. Fox. An Activity Ontology for Enterprise Modelling. Submitted to AAAI-94, Dept. of Industrial Engineering, University of Toronto, 1994.

7. D. Harel, H. Lachover, A. Naamad, A. Pnueli, M.Politi, R. Sherman, A. Shtull-Trauring, and M. Trakhtenbrot. STATEMATE: A working environment for the development of complex reactive systems. *IEEE Trans. on Software Engineering*, 16(4):403–414, April 1990.

8. D. Jensen, Y. Dong, B. S. Lerner, E. K. McCall, L. J. Osterweil, J. Stanley M. Sutton, and A. Wise. Coordinating agent activities in knowledge discovery processes. In *Proceedings of the International Joint Conference on Work Activies, Coordination, and Collaboration (WACC '99)*, San Francisco, February 1999.

9. J.Estublier, S.Dami, and A.Amiour. APEL: A graphical yet executable formalism for process modelling. In *Automated Software Engineering*, March 1997.

10. K. L. Myers and D. E. Wilkins. The Act Formalism. Working document: Version 2.2, SRI International, Artificial Intelligence Center, September 25 1997. http://www.ai.sri.com/ act/act-spec.ps.

11. H. Rombach and M.Verlage. How to assess a software process modeling formalism from a project member's point of view. In *The Second International Conference on the Software Process*, pages 147–159, 1993.

12. S. F. Smith and M. A. Becker. An Ontology for Constructing Scheduling Systems. In *Working Notes from 1997 AAAI Spring Symposium on Ontological Engineering*, Stanford, CA, March 1997.

13. X. Song and L. J. Osterweil. Engineering Software Design Processes to Guide Process Execution. *IEEE Transactions on Software Engineering*, 24(9):759–775, 1998.

14. R. Vincent, B. Horling, T. Wagner, and V. Lesser. Survivability Simulator for Multi-Agent Adaptive Coordination. *Proceedings of International Conference on Web-Based Modeling and Simulation*, 30(1):114–119, 1998.

15. J. Waldo. *Jini Architecture Overview*. Sun Microsystems, Inc., 901 San Antonio Road, Palo Alto, CA 94303, 1998. http://www.javasoft.com/products/jini/index.html.

16. D. E. Wilkins. *Using the SIPE-2 Planning System: A Manual for Version 4-17*. SRI International Artificial Intelligence Center, Menlo Park, CA, October 1997.

17. A. Wise. Little-JIL 1.0 Language Report. Technical report 98-24, Department of Computer Science, University of Massachusetts at Amherst, 1998.

Static Analysis of Real-Time Component-Based Systems Configurations*

Candida Attanasio, Flavio Corradini, and Paola Inverardi

Dipartimento di Matematica Pura ed Applicata
Università dell'Aquila
Via Vetoio, Loc. Coppito, L'Aquila, Italy
fax +390862433180
{flavio,inverard}@univaq.it

Abstract. Nowadays, more and more often, complex systems are built by assembling together different system components. This technology also affects the construction of heterogeneous and/or hybrid systems where components can represent hardware sensors, software controllers, etc. Moreover the resulting system is normally distributed. These systems have often real-time constraints/requirements and each component is characterized by its own speed determined by its local clock. In this paper we present a framework in which it is possible to specify and statically analyze the architecture of a system as a network of (parallel) components, each one with its own local clock. Then configuring the system means to formally define how to get the global clock out of the local clocks. This allows us, besides the usual behavioral and timing analysis, to, for example, verify if, and how changing the local speed of a component can affect the global performance of the system.

1 Introduction

Heterogeneous and hybrid systems are built by assembling together different system components like hardware sensors, software controllers, etc. Besides the traditional field of *control systems* [12, 2, 19], the need of assembling together heterogeneous components is more and more frequent due to the widespread diffusion of information technology in any application field, from multimedia applications to telecommunication systems. These systems have often real-time constraints/requirements and each component is characterized by its own speed determined by its local clock. This means that at each tick of its clock the component can perform an action. In our view, configuring a system out of such components means to decide two things, how the components are *connected* together in a given architecture and, with respect to time how to determine a global clock of the system in terms of the various local clocks. To a certain extent the latter consists in adjusting the local clocks to suitably relate each other. In

---

* This work has been partially funded by CNR, Progetto:Metodologie, e strumenti di analisi, verifica e validazione per sistemi software affidabili

physical terms this can be seen as deciding the starting time of each component. In the literature, much attention has been given to the the first configuration step, both at the architectural level and at the specification level [20, 15, 17, 4, 18], and to modeling time in various formalisms [7, 14, 21, 19, 9, 13]. In this paper we present a framework in which it is possible to specify the architecture of a system as a network of (parallel) components, each one with its own local clock. Thus, the configuration of the behavioral part is achieved by putting the components in parallel and let them communicate upon synchronization, similarly to [18]. The configuration of the clocks means to formally define the global clock out of the local clocks. This is done by modeling the clocks as higher order terms in a given signature, and by relating each other through a *unification* process [16], which allows a common clock to be defined. Then, if there exists a unifier, all the local clocks will be expressed as suitable linear functions of the global one. Due to the properties of the unification process, i.e. the existence of a unique most general unifier, this clock configuration step is *optimal* that is, it is the best way to relate the local clocks so that the maximum number of synchronizations in the system can happen. The ability of modeling the clock configuration step allows us, besides the usual behavioral and timing analysis, to statically analyze the systems with respect to different configurations. For example, we can verify if, and how, changing the local speed (i.e. the local clock) of a component can affect the global performance of the system. That is the amount of synchronizations in the system increases or decreases. We apply our analysis framework to two different classical examples, "The Mine Pump" and the "The Lip Synchronization Problem". The paper is organized as follows: Section 2, introduces the language of components, and its operational semantics. The language is CCS-like [20]. It is worth noticing that our approach is highly independent from the language chosen to model the behavioral aspects of components. Our choice has been mainly motivated by the simplicity and by the diffusive familiarity this class of languages exhibit. Section 3, presents our first case study used to illustrate the approach. It is a well known and studied example in the literature of which several different specifications exist [19]. Section 4 presents the second case study, i.e. a formalization of the lip synchronization problem. Section 5 shows how we can analyze the system at configuration level, that is how we can compare the behavior of different configurations obtained by considering the same components but with different speed. Section 6 discusses related works, and Section 7 presents conclusions and future works.

2 The Language and Its Transitional Semantics

The language we consider in this paper is deliberately simple. We consider Nets of Automata, a CCS-like language where parallelism can only appear at the top level. This language is close to the language presented in [18].

Similarly to [20], we assume a set of actions A (ranged over by α) from which we obtain the set of co-actions $\bar{A} = \{\bar{\alpha} \mid \alpha \in A\}$ useful to model process synchronizations. We use Act (ranged over by $a, b, \ldots$) to denote $A \cup \bar{A}$, the set of visible actions. The invisible action, useful to model internal activities of process executions, is denoted by $\tau \notin Act$ and we use Act_τ (ranged over by μ) to denote the set of all actions $Act \cup \{\tau\}$. Process *variables*, used for recursive definitions, are ranged over by x. **N** (ranged over by n, m, ...) denotes the set of natural numbers, while N, M, ... denote variables over **N**.

We start by defining regular processes or $\mathcal{RP}$ [20] which specify finite, nondeterministic automata familiar from the theory of regular languages. The set of regular processes, $\mathcal{RP}$ (ranged over by p, q, ...), over Act_τ and V, is the set of closed (i.e., without free variables) generated by the following grammar:

$$ p ::= nil \ \Big| \ \mu.p \ \Big| \ p + p \ \Big| \ x \ \Big| \ \text{rec } x.\,p \ . $$

Process *nil* denotes a terminated process. By prefixing a term p with an action μ, we get a process term $\mu.p$ which can perform an action μ and then behaves like p. $p_1 + p_2$ denotes the non deterministic composition of p_1 and p_2, while rec $x.\,p$ is used for recursive definitions.

A distributed, interacting process, or $\mathcal{IP}$ term, is a (finite) parallel combination of regular processes equipped with their own local clocks, or a term restricted by an action, or a term relabeled according to a function $\Phi : Act_\tau \longrightarrow Act_\tau$ that preserves co-actions and leaves τ fixed.

Definition 1. (*Interacting Processes*) The set $\mathcal{IP}$ (ranged over by P, Q, ...) of interacting processes is the least one satisfying the following grammar:

$$ P ::= \ <p, \lambda^N x.t^m(x)> \ \Big| \ P|Q \ \Big| \ P\backslash\{a\} \ \Big| \ P[\Phi] $$

where $p \in \mathcal{RP}$, $a \in Act$, $m \in \mathbf{N}$, N is a degree variable and t is a first order term on a certain signature Σ.

We model local clocks with a restricted form of the so called "iterative terms" defined in [16]. Iterative terms are higher order terms that finitely represent infinite sequences of first order terms. Thus they seem natural candidates to model time in a discrete way (it can be thought as an infinite sequence of finite objects) and time passing.

Here we concentrate on the subclass of iterative terms of the form $\lambda^N x.t^m(x)$, where m is a natural number and N is a variable over natural numbers. For instance, a term like $\lambda^N x.t^2(x)$ denotes the sequence $\{x, t^2(x), t^4(x), t^6(x), ...\}$. This sequence can be thought as the time instants (ticks) where a process is active and hence can perform an action. It is obtained by letting $N \in \{1, 2, ..., \omega\}$; $N = 0$ generates x, $N = 1$ generates $t^2(x)$, $N = 2$ generates $t^4(x)$, ... For this reason N is called degree variable. We can think of x as the starting time and of $t^i(x)$ as the $i-$th tic of the local clock (t is a first order term on a certain signature Σ). By varying on the degree variable and assuming different expressions in the body of λ iterative term, we can have a different scale of the time and hence different local clocks (different speeds). For instance term $\lambda^L x.t^3(x)$ denotes $\{x, t^3(x), t^6(x), t^9(x), ...\}$ and is always obtained by letting $L \in \{1, 2, ..., \omega\}$.

$\lambda^N x.t^2(x)$ and $\lambda^L x.t^3(x)$ with N and L different variables denote the temporal scales of two systems evolving independently according to their own relative speed. The intuition here is that each λ iterative term represents an infinite sequence of elements, thus modeling the time sequence.

We can now analyze how a global system behaves when a component is scheduled to be executed on a slower or faster architecture. This amounts at comparing two different configurations where the same component has a slower, respectively faster, local clock. This can be done by considering local clocks with different temporal scales; for instance a system with local clock $\lambda^N x.t^2(x)$ is faster than the one with local clock $\lambda^L x.t^3(x)$ because from the starting time (x) to a common time $(t^6(x))$ the former local clock has four ticks $(\{x, t^2(x), t^4(x), t^6(x)\})$ and hence the system is able to perform four actions, while the latter has only three $(\{x, t^3(x), t^6(x)\})$. Common times are interesting to study possible system synchronizations. In order to synchronize two processes must be able to perform communicating actions at the same time. Thus two processes running with speed detected by $\lambda^N x.t^2(x)$ and $\lambda^L x.t^3(x)$ respectively, may synchronize (if they can perform communicating actions) at times $(\{t^6(x), t^{12}(x), t^{18}(x), ...\})$.

A natural question is whether or not is it always possible to find these common times, i.e. times where process components possibly synchronize. To this respect we exploit a theorem from the theory of iterative terms. It states that the problem of determining whether for any pair of iterative terms there exists an (infinite) sequence of common terms or not is decidable. In case it exists the theorem also gives the maximum sequence of common terms (which, intuitively, correspond to the maximum sequence of times where processes can synchronize). In the class of iterative terms we are considering it is always possible to find the maximum sequence of common terms. The theorem gives the most general unifier among terms. The most general unifier relates the degree variables of the iterative terms with a fresh variable degree which generate the maximum sequence of common terms. For instance, the two terms $\lambda^N x.t^2(x)$ and $\lambda^L x.t^3(x)$ initially independent unify for $L = 2Q$ and $N = 3Q$ with Q a fresh name. Thus we could also consider iterative terms $\lambda^{3Q} x.t^2(x)$ and $\lambda^{2Q} x.t^3(x)$ to generate the sequence $\{x, t^6(x), t^{12}(x), t^{18}(x), ...\}$

The notion of most general unifier is exploited in this paper to detect the least common time (after the starting one) of a given set of iterative terms representing local clocks of parallel processes. This time is the least time where all processes in the net can do something. The iterative terms then behave "periodically" with respect to this least time. In the period between the starting time, i.e. the degree variable is $= 0$, and the least time, each iterative term can generate different terms. For instance $\lambda^N x.t^2(x)$ generates $\{x, t^2(x), t^4(x), t^6(x)\}$ while $\lambda^L x.t^3(x)$ generates $\{x, t^3(x), t^6(x)\}$, where $t^6(x)$ is the least time . These terms can be ordered in a standard way: $x < t^2(x) < t^3(x) < t^4(x) < t^6(x)$. This ordered sequence gives the finest discretization of the time for the two components. At each time of the sequence one of them can perform an action. Being finite, this sequence can be put in bijection with a finite segment of the natural numbers. We can build a matrix of n entries and m columns where n corresponds to the length of the finest sequence from the starting time to the one preceding the least common time and m is the number of parallel regular processes in an interactive term. In our example we have four entries, one for each element of set $\{x, t^2(x), t^3(x), t^4(x)\}$ and two columns, one for each component.

This matrix indicates which processes are active at a given time, and hence also which processes may engage in a synchronization. To build the matrix, consider the finest (ordered) sequence of terms until the common one and take a term t in the sequence. We put an X at the entry corresponding to t and column corresponding to the process p if the local clock associated with p has term t in its sequence. We denote with p also every p-derivative, that is every state that p reaches during a computation (or, more formally, every state p' such that $p \to^* p'$, where $\to^*$ is the reflexive and transitive closure of the transitional semantics in Table 2). For this reason, a process p and every derivative p' of p are indexed by a common name. We will write $(p)_i$ and $(p')_i$, where index i can be a natural number or the name of p itself. In this latter case, if clear from the context, we will often omit the index.

The matrix corresponding to interactive process

$$P = <p_1, \lambda^N x.t^2(x)> \mid <p_2, \lambda^M x.t^3(x)>$$

with p_1 and p_2 two regular processes is given in Fig. 1.

Table 1. A Matrix for P

	p_1	p_2
x	X	X
$t^2(x)$	X	
$t^3(x)$		X
$t^4(x)$	X	

With abuse of notation, in the rest of this paper, we identify the entries of the matrix with indexes of the matrix itself, i.e. the natural numbers from 0 to $n-1$. We write $\#M$ to denote the number of entries of matrix M.

Once matrix M is defined, the next step is to show how an interactive process evolves.

The transitional semantics of a $\mathcal{IP}$ process term, is given in terms of labelled transition systems[1] where the states are processes enriched by a local execution

---

[1] A *labelled transition system* is a triple $\langle S, L, T \rangle$, where S is the set of *states*, L is the set of *labels* and $T = \{\xrightarrow{l} \subseteq S \times S \mid l \in L\}$ is the *transition relation*. As usual, we will write $s \xrightarrow{l} s'$ instead of $\langle s, s' \rangle \in \xrightarrow{l}$.

time which record the local view of the elapsing of time together with the value of the global clock (corresponding to the maximum of local views). Formally, we introduce *extended processes*, obtained by equipping each sequential component of a process with a local execution time. This is done, syntactically, via a *local execution time prefixing* operator, $n \Rightarrow \_$. The set $\mathcal{D}$ (ranged over by d, d' ...) of extended processes is the set of terms generated by this grammar.

$$d ::= n \Rightarrow (p)_i \mid d|d' \mid d\backslash\{\alpha\} \mid d[\varPhi].$$

where $p \in \mathcal{RP}$, $n \in \mathbf{N}$ is the local execution time and i (a natural number or a process name) is the name of the process such that p is a derivative of.

A *timed process* (or *state*) $d \triangleright n$ is an extended process d, equipped with a global clock n. The global clock represents the global observation time for the execution. Here, we require that $n \geq maxclock(d)$, where $maxclock(d)$ gives the maximum of clock values m occurring in subterms of d of the form $m \Rightarrow p$. We use $\mathcal{S}$ (ranged over by s, $s',\ldots$) to denote the set of timed processes.

A timed action is a pair (μ, n) where $\mu \in Act_\tau$ and $n \in \mathbf{N}^+$. Intuitively, a label $\mu@n$ means that action μ has been completed exactly n time units after the computation began. Thus we are considering an *absolute* time. As usual, the transition relations are given through a set of inference rules, as listed in Table 2. The transition relation is of the form $s \xrightarrow{\mu@n}_M s'$ meaning that state s becomes state s' by performing an action μ at time n.

Let us comment the rules in Table 2. First of all we remark that the rules implement the so-called *maximal progress*, where a process can delay the execution of visible actions provided that it cannot perform invisible actions (synchronizations) earlier. Thus, the rule for action prefixing Act states that a process $(m \Rightarrow (a.p)_i) \triangleright n$, i.e., a process $a.p$ with identification tag i, local execution time m and global clock n, can perform an action a at any time n' such that (i) n' is greater than the local and global views of the time and (ii) process i is allowed to perform an action in the current period of time, $M[n' \bmod \#M, i] = X$. The local execution time of the target state is $n' + 1$ to avoid the execution of multiple actions at the same time by the same component. The execution of invisible actions, instead, cannot be delayed, they have to be performed as soon as they can. This is what rule $Urgency$ says. Clearly, this rule is strictly related to $Synch$.

Rule Sum_1 says that in a nondeterministic composition a component can perform an action at time n' if the other ones cannot perform invisible actions earlier. Rule Par_1 is similar. Rules Res, Rel and Rel for restriction, relabeling and recursive definitions are as usual. Rule $Synch$ deserves more explanation. The basic idea behind this rule is that synchronizations cannot be delayed. They must be performed as soon as they can. In other words, two processes can synchronize when they perform complementary actions at the same time; if one of the two is able to execute such an action before the other, then a form of *busy-waiting* is allowed. This permits to model a situation in which a faster process can wait for a slower partner. However, when both partners are ready to

Table 2. The Structural Rules for the Operational Semantics: symmetric rules omitted.

$$Act \frac{n' \geq max\{m,n\} \text{ and } M[n' \bmod \#M, i] = X}{(m \Rightarrow (a.p)_i) \rhd n \xrightarrow[M]{a@n'} (n'+1 \Rightarrow (p)_i) \rhd n'}$$

$$Urgency \frac{n' = min\{k \mid k \geq max\{t,n\} \text{ and } M[m \bmod \#M, i] = X\}}{(m \Rightarrow (\tau.p)_i) \rhd n \xrightarrow[M]{\tau@n'} (n'+1 \Rightarrow (p)_i) \rhd n'}$$

$$Sum_1 \frac{(m \Rightarrow (p)_i) \rhd n \xrightarrow[M]{\mu@n'} d \rhd n' \text{ and } \neg((m \Rightarrow (q)_i) \rhd n \xrightarrow[M]{\tau@n''} \text{ and } n'' < n')}{(m \Rightarrow (p+q)_i) \rhd n \xrightarrow[M]{\mu@n'} d \rhd n'}$$

$$Rec \frac{(m \Rightarrow (p[\text{rec } v.\, p/x])_i) \rhd m \xrightarrow[M]{\mu@n'} d \rhd n'}{(m \Rightarrow (\text{rec } x.\, p)_i) \rhd m \xrightarrow[M]{\mu@n'} d \rhd n'}$$

$$Par_1 \frac{d_1 \rhd m \xrightarrow[M]{\mu@n} d_1' \rhd n \text{ and } \neg(d_2 \rhd m \xrightarrow[M]{\tau@n'} \text{ and } n' < n)}{(d_1 \mid d_2) \rhd m \xrightarrow[M]{\mu@n} (d_1' \mid d_2) \rhd n}$$

$$Synch \frac{d_1 \rhd m \xrightarrow[M]{a@n} d_1' \rhd n, \; d_2 \rhd m \xrightarrow[M]{\bar{a}@n} d_2' \rhd n \text{ and } \neg((d_1|d_2) \rhd m \xrightarrow[M]{\tau@n'} \text{ and } n' < n)}{(d_1 \mid d_2) \rhd m \xrightarrow[M]{\tau@n} (d_1'|d_2') \rhd n}$$

$$Res \frac{d \rhd m \xrightarrow[M]{\mu@n} d' \rhd n, \; \mu \notin \{a, \bar{a}\}}{d\backslash\{a\} \rhd m \xrightarrow[M]{\mu@n} d'\backslash\{a\} \rhd n} \qquad Rel \frac{d \rhd m \xrightarrow[M]{\mu@n} d' \rhd n}{d[\Phi] \rhd m \xrightarrow[M]{\Phi(\mu)@n} d'[\Phi] \rhd n}$$

synchronize, the handshaking immediately occurs. We would like to note that this treatment between visible actions (lazy) and invisible actions (urgent) is only apparently different. Invisible actions denote synchronizations between two parallel components of the same process ("internal" synchronizations), while visible actions model synchronizations with the external environment ("external" synchronizations). Thus delayed executions of visible actions models a situation in which the process responsible for their execution is faster with respect to an hypothetic external slower partner.

It is worth of noting that the time grows unboundedly during a process execution; indeed, it features as an absolute time. As a consequence of this fact, our transition systems are, in general, infinite states transitions systems. A finite characterization of the transitional semantics given in Table 2, can be obtained as in [3]. There, the time features as a relative time (relative to the period fixed by the local clocks). The finiteness of the transition systems associated with $\mathcal{IP}$ processes can be useful for automatic verification.

In the rest of this paper we apply our framework on a couple of classical examples: "The Mine Pump" taken from [19] and "The Lip Synchronization Problem" taken from [5].

3   The Mine Pump

Water percolating into a mine is collected in a sump to be pumped out of the mine. The water level sensors, Sensor D and Sensor E, detect when water is above a high and a low level respectively. A pump controller switches the pump on when the water reaches the high water level and off when it goes below the low water level. An operator must be informed of any level becoming critical so that the mine must be evacuated. If, due to a failure of the pump, the water cannot be pumped out, the mine must be evacuated. Another sensor, Sensor A, is in the mine to monitor the methane levels. The mine must be evacuated in case of critical levels. To avoid the risk of explosion, the pump must be operated only when the methane level is below a critical level.

Let us describe the intended behavior of the sensors. $SensorD$ performs an internal action τ when the level of water is not high while it performs an action HighWater (hw) when the water must be pumped out. When the level of the water is too high the mine must be evacuated. In such a case $SensorD$ performs an action DangerWater (dw). $SensorE$ is similar. When the level of water is fine it performs an action τ while if the water is below a LowWater it performs an action lw. $SensorA$ detects a dangerous methane level and, in this case, it performs an action dm. If the methane level is not dangerous, it performs either an action b or an action τ depending on whether the external environment is interested in the methane level or not, respectively.

$$SensorD \equiv \text{rec } x.\,(\tau.x\ +\ hw.x\ +\ dw.x)$$
$$SensorE \equiv \text{rec } x.\,(\tau.x\ +\ lw.x)$$
$$SensorA \equiv \text{rec } x.\,(\tau.x\ +\ b.x\ +\ dm.x)$$

The pump receives *on* or *off* commands from the pump controller when the water must be pumped out or not respectively.

$$Pump \equiv \text{rec } x.\,(\overline{on}.x\ +\ \overline{off}.x)$$

The pump controller is the parallel composition of controllers: $ContrA$, $ContrE$ and $ContrD$. $ContrA$ receives signals by $SensorA$, $ContrE$ by $SensorE$ and $ContrD$ by $SensorA$.

$$Controller \equiv ContrA \mid ContrE \mid ContrD.$$

When $ContrA$ receives a DangerMethane (it communicates with $SensorA$ by performing an action $\overline{dm}$) message it switches off the pump because there could be risk of explosion; the pump must not be operated if the methane level is critical. Then $ContrA$ informs the environment that the mine must be evacuated.

When $ContrE$ receives a LowWater (it communicates with $SensorE$ by performing an action $\overline{lw}$) it simply switches off the pump.

$ContrD$ behaves differently in case it receives a DangerWater or a HighWater. In the former case it informs the environment that the mine must be evacuated. In the latter case it controls if the methane level is dangerous or not. In the former case it switches off the pump (in case it is pumping out water) to avoid risk of explosion and informs the environment that the mine must be evacuated, in the latter case it switches on the pump.

$$ContrA \equiv rec\ x.\ \overline{dm}.off.evacuate.x$$
$$ContrE \equiv rec\ x.\ \overline{lw}.off.x$$
$$ContrD \equiv rec\ x.\ \overline{dw}.evacuate.x\ +\ rec\ x.\ \overline{hw}.(\overline{dm}.off.evacuate.x\ +\ \overline{b}.on.x)$$

The whole system is the parallel composition of the sensors, the pump and the pump controller. In our initial configuration, $System_1$, we assume that $SensorA$, $SensorE$ and the $Pump$ are the faster devices. These are faster than $SensorE$ which in turn is faster then the three controllers.

$$
\begin{aligned}
System_1 \equiv (&< SensorD, \lambda^N x.t^3(x) > \ | \\
&< SensorA, \lambda^S x.t^2(x) > \ | \\
&< SensorE, \lambda^M x.t^3(x) > \ | \\
&< ContrA, \lambda^R x.t^4(x) > \ | \\
&< ContrE, \lambda^R x.t^4(x) > \ | \\
&< ContrD, \lambda^R x.t^4(x) > \ | \\
&< Pump, \lambda^P x.t^2(x) >)\backslash A
\end{aligned}
$$

where $A = \{b, dm, dw, lw, hw, on, off\}$. The matrix associated with $System_1$ is shown in Table 3. The least common time is t^{12} (remember that it is the first time, after the starting time x, in the sequence generated by the most general unifier, that is the first time at which *all* components can perform an action). The finest sequence is

$$\{x, t^2(x), t^3(x), t^4(x), t^6(x), t^8(x), t^9(x), t^{10}(x)\}.$$

These times are denoted by the fragment of natural numbers $\{0, 1, 2, 3, 4, 5, 6, 7\}$. We recall that these are all the (local relative) times at which some component can perform an action.

4   The Lip Synchronization Problem

A number of specifications of the lip synchronization algorithm, allowing for both automatic and semi-automatic verification, can be found in the literature. Here, we provide a high level description of the problem concentrating on structural properties related to the (possible) interactions among components. For a deep study of the temporal aspects see [6].

Two data sources, a sound source and a video source, generate a pair of data streams. These streams are received at a presentation device. The problem is to ensure that play out the two streams at the presentation device is acceptably synchronized. Sound and video sources, sound and video managers, a controller and a presentation device are the system components. When a sound packet arrives at the presentation device a *savail* signal is passed to the sound manager. When appropriate the sound manager returns a *spres(ent)* to the presentation

Table 3. A Matrix for $System_1$

SensA	SensD	SensE	ContrD	ContrE	ContrA	Pump
X	X	X	X	X	X	X
X						X
	X	X				
X			X	X	X	X
X	X	X				X
X			X	X	X	X
	X	X				
X						X

device indicating that the packet can be presented. The video manager has a corresponding behavior. The controller contains the body of the lip synchronization algorithm. It receives *sready* (respectively *vready*) from the sound (respectively video) manager, indicating that a sound (respectively video) packet is ready to be played. The controller then evaluates if it is appropriate or not to play the particular packed (synchronizations on channels α and β respectively). It either returns an *sok* (respectively *vok*) or, if an acceptable synchronization is not recoverable, it signals an error (on channel e_2) which will then be delivered to the presentation device (on channel e_1).

Let us first describe the behavior of the sound and video sources:

$$Sound \equiv \text{rec } x. \, sstream.x$$
$$Video \equiv \text{rec } x. \, vstream.x \, .$$

The presentation device is the parallel composition of a sound presentation device and a video one

$$PresDev \equiv PresDevS \mid PresDevV$$

where

$$PresDevS \equiv \text{rec } x. \, \overline{sstream}.savail.(\overline{spres}.splay.x \, + \, \overline{e}_1.error.x)$$
$$PresDevV \equiv \text{rec } x. \, \overline{vstream}.vavail.(\overline{vpres}.vplay.x \, + \, \overline{e}_1.error.x) \, .$$

The Controller is defined by

$$Controller \equiv ControllerS \mid ControllerV$$

where

$$ControllerV \equiv rec\ x.\ \overline{vready}(\alpha.vok.x\ +\ \beta.e_2.x)$$
$$ControllerS \equiv rec\ x.\ \overline{sready}(\overline{\alpha}.sok.x\ +\ \overline{\beta}.e_2.x)\ .$$

Finally, the sound and video manager have the following behavior:

$$SoundManager \equiv rec\ x.\ \overline{savail}.sready.(\overline{sok}.spres.x\ +\ \overline{e}_2.e_1.x)$$
$$VideoManager \equiv rec\ x.\ \overline{vavail}.vready.(\overline{vok}.vpres.x\ +\ \overline{e}_2.e_1.x)\ .$$

The whole system describing the lip synchronization problem, is the parallel composition of the Sound and Video sources, presentation devices, controllers and sound, video managers. A possible (actually particularly favorable, as we will see later on) association of local clocks to the lip parallel components is

$$
\begin{aligned}
Lip_1 \equiv (&< Sound, \lambda^N x.t^2(x) >\ \mid \\
&< Video, \lambda^S x.t^4(x) >\ \mid \\
&< SoundManager, \lambda^M x.t^3(x) >\ \mid \\
&< VideoManager, \lambda^Q x.t^3(x) >\ \mid \\
&< ControllerS, \lambda^R x.t^2(x) >\ \mid \\
&< ControllerV, \lambda^R x.t^2(x) >\ \mid \\
&< PresDevS, \lambda^P x.t^2(x) >\ \mid \\
&< PresDevV, \lambda^T x.t^2(x) >) \backslash B
\end{aligned}
$$

where $B = \{sstream, savail, sready, sok, spres, vstream, vavail, vready, vok, vpres, \alpha, \beta, e_1, e_2\}$.

The matrix associated with Lip_1 is shown in Table 4. The least common time is t^{12}. The finest sequence is $\{x, t^2(x), t^3(x), t^4(x), t^6(x), t^8(x), t^9(x), t^{10}(x)\}$ and SMn, VMn, CoS, CoV, PDvS, PDvV stand for SoundManager, videoManager, ControllerS, ControllerV, PresDevS, PresDevV, respectively.

5 Analyzing System Behaviors

In this section we show how our model can be fruitfully used to analyze system properties. We are particularly interested in proving properties related to the interaction capabilities of the system components. These may influence both the system performance and its functionality. This is because parallel components can only synchronize at given time instances (detected by the local clocks). Hence, some synchronizations might not happen. Note that in the case of the Mine Pump System and the Lip one, every action will eventually be performed. This is mainly the reason why our systems are deadlock-free.[2]

---

[2] It is worth of noting that our timed process algebra do not have processes which may cause the stop of the passage of time, the "time stop" phenomenon, as in TCCS

Table 4. A Matrix for Lip_1

Sound	Video	SMn	VMn	CoS	CoV	PDvS	PDvV
X	X	X	X	X	X	X	X
X				X	X	X	X
		X	X				
X	X			X	X	X	X
X		X	X	X	X	X	X
X	X			X	X	X	X
		X	X				
X				X	X	X	X

To show that synchronizations in a parallel system may influence the system performance, we first show what happens in the sub-class of concurrent but non communicating systems, and then what happens when synchronization is allowed.

Consider a simple concurrent but not communicating system such as the high level water sensor in parallel with the methane level sensor:

$$< SensorD, \lambda^R x.t^4(x) > \; | \; < SensorA, \lambda^R x.t^4(x) > .$$

If we make the temporal scale finer, then the performance of such systems always increases. In the case of sensors, this means that more checks are made in the same interval of time and, hence, also that the danger level methane and the high level water are eventually detected sooner.

This property, however, is not always desirable. Consider, for instance, the system composed by the video presentation device and the sound presentation device

$$< PresDevS, \lambda^P x.t^2(x) > \; | \; < PresDevV, \lambda^P x.t^2(x) >$$

(see [21]). Processes with time stops may cause the deadlock of all processes which are in parallel composition or in alternative composition with the process itself.

Thus, the Mine Pump System and the Lip one, are deadlock-free in usual sense; i.e., they never reach states where no action can be performed. In other words, they are deadlock-free according to the standard untimed operational semantics.

Also in this case a finer temporal scale always means observing actions before thus increasing system performance. But this is a case where the two components must proceed together (at the same speed) because it is critical that a sound stream is played out within a reasonable interval of time after/before the video stream is played out.

In presence of synchronization, instead, it is not always the case that faster components imply faster systems. Consider

$$((0 \Rightarrow SensorD \mid 0 \Rightarrow SensorA \mid 0 \Rightarrow SensorE \mid 0 \Rightarrow ContrD \mid 0 \Rightarrow ContrA \mid$$
$$0 \Rightarrow ContrE \mid 0 \Rightarrow Pump)\backslash A) \triangleright 0,$$

the initial state of $System_1$.

The first time the Pump can be switched on in $System_1$, due to a HighWater level, is $t^8(x)$. This is a case in which the Pump works faster than the Controllers. If we consider another configuration

$$
\begin{aligned}
System_2 \equiv (&< SensorD, \lambda^N x.t^3(x) > \mid \\
&< SensorA, \lambda^S x.t^2(x) > \mid \\
&< SensorE, \lambda^M x.t^3(x) > \mid \\
&< ContrA, \lambda^R x.t^4(x) > \mid \\
&< ContrE, \lambda^R x.t^4(x) > \mid \\
&< ContrD, \lambda^R x.t^4(x) > \mid \\
&< Pump, \lambda^P x.t^5(x) >)\backslash A,
\end{aligned}
$$

we have a Mine Pump System in which the Pump is slower than the Controllers. As a result of this fact, we get a matrix with 44 entries and the first time the Pump can be switched on due to a HighWater level, is time $t^{20}(x)$.

As already said before, however, not always faster components imply a better performance of the global system. Consider a new configuration $System_3$ obtained from $System_1$ by replacing the local clocks of the Controllers with $\lambda^R x.t^3(x)$. In $System_1$, the least time an *evacuate* action (due to a danger level of methane) can be observed by the external operator is $t^8(x)$. In $System_3$, instead, an *evacuate* can only be observed at time $t^9(x)$, although the Controllers are faster than the ones in $System_1$.

Regarding the lip synchronization problem we can exploit an assignment of speeds to the parallel components where sound and video streams are played out together and hence "well-synchronized". This is the case, for instance, of the local clocks associated with the components in Lip_1. On the other hand, there are assignments of local clocks which lead the system to unwanted behaviors because, for instance, sound and video streams are played out at different time instances. For an evidence of this fact consider system Lip_2 defined by:

$$Lip_2 \equiv (< Sound, \lambda^N x.t^2(x) > \mid$$
$$< Video, \lambda^S x.t^4(x) > \mid$$
$$< SoundManager, \lambda^M x.t^3(x) > \mid$$
$$< VideoManager, \lambda^Q x.t^2(x) > \mid$$
$$< ControllerS, \lambda^R x.t^2(x) > \mid$$
$$< ControllerV, \lambda^R x.t^2(x) > \mid$$
$$< PresDevS, \lambda^P x.t^2(x) > \mid$$
$$< PresDevV, \lambda^T x.t^2(x) >) \backslash B$$

which simply differ by Lip_1 because of a faster $VideoManager$. Lip_2 plays out a video stream at $t^{36}(x)$ while the corresponding sound stream at time $t^{46}(x)$.

Others interesting properties related to our systems can be analyzed by mapping our abstract interpretation of time and time passing into the common notion of time. This can be done by associating the common t, appearing within local clocks, with a fixed duration. Then, every $t^m(x)$ (for $m \in \mathbf{N}$) denotes a real time for an external observer. If n denotes the number of entries of the actual matrix, the real time associated with $t^m(x)$ can be calculated by $m \bmod n$ (the actual entry of the matrix or, in other words, the relative time) and by $m \ div \ n$ (how many times the entry of the matrix reaches n and, hence, a new slot of observation is taken into account). Then, regarding to the mine pump system, we can, analogously to what presented in /citeACI99 answer to safety requirements such as: Can the pump be switched on in one hour? After how many time units ControllerA switches off the pump after receiving a DangerMethane command by SensorA? Can the external environment be informed in one hour if the mine must be evacuated? When the controller receives a DangerWater which is the least time the environment is informed that the mine must be evacuated? Are there actions which will never be performed? Is our system deadlock-free? And, eventually, which is the least time it will reach a deadlock state?

These questions may have different answers depending on the local clocks chosen to specify the speed of the parallel components, that is depending on the considered configuration. Note that most of these questions can be answered statically, that is by just looking at the matrix, once the unification process has been performed. This is a relevant difference with other approaches to the description of the Mine Pump case study, as reported in [2].

6   Related Works

The main aim of this work is concerned with the static analysis of behavioral aspects of systems obtained by assembling together components running at (possibly) different speed. This is the reason why we consider system activities as instantaneous events (by abstracting from their duration) while concentrating on the relative speed of the system components.

The relative speed between components, indeed, directly influence the interaction capabilities of the system components which, in turn, may influence the system performance. The system description language we consider implements several ideas from classic timed process description languages. The view of system activities as instantaneous events is taken from [21] (and related works, see references therein), while the idea of using local clocks is taken from [7, 14, 10].

We also have some technical similarities with *Timed CSP* [22], though Reed and Roscoe mainly concentrate on denotational semantics based on timed *traces* in the sense of Hoare. In *TCSP*, actions are atomic and time passes between them. However, the delay between the execution of the actions by a system component is fixed and equal for every action. Though not explicit present in our approach, we can also think of a similar notion of duration. Indeed, we can smoothly assume that every tic in a period of time (every entry of the matrix describing the elapsing of time) takes a certain fixed time. Moreover, in *TCSP*, the actions are observed in two different ways: a denotes the communication of action a at any time while $â$ denotes the communication of action a at the moment it becomes available. The former actions correspond, in our setting, to delayed actions while the latter ones are the urgent actions (those performed witout any delay).

The main difference with these works is that we can model different speed for different system components. This is not possible neither in [21, 22], where the existence of a unique global clock is made explicit (and based upon the fact that all system components must synchronize), nor in [7, 14, 10], where the local clocks are assumed to elapse in the same way (by making the system components running at the same speed).

Moreover, our aim is to carry on a static analysis of the system which should permit the evaluation of the synchronization potentiality of a component-based system at configuration time. Depending on the analysis results it should be possible to *adjust* the local speed of the components or change the behavioral system configuration. Clocks, in fact, are not involved in the semantics of the operations, the only link in between the time and the behavioral operations is due to the definition of time passing.

This aspect differentiate our approach from others. For example, the notion of local clocks and a calculus for synchronizing local clocks, is also presented in the language SIGNAL [1, 11]. There, a clock is associated with a signal and clocks can be of different frequencies. The calculus of clocks at compilation time allows the construction of a forest of clocks associated with the program, the primitive operators of the calculus explicitly take the clocks into account and might require two signals to exhibit the same clocks. Although the notion of local clocks and of their calculus might resemble our approach, the use of these notions in the two approaches is different. The principal purpose of the clock calculus is to detect potential inconsistencies and contradictions as well as to give a synthetic representation of the global synchronization capability of the program starting from the local synchronization capabilities. Whereas our approach focuses on the configuration phase and on the possibility of statically analyze the performance of a configuration with respect to the relative speed of its components, in a relatively simple way.

7 Conclusions and Future Work

In this paper we have presented a new approach to model configurations of real-time components, each one characterized by its own local clock/speed.

We model a configuration as a network of parallel components, components are described in a simple regular process algebra while clocks are represented as simple iterative λ terms, i.e. terms which finitely represent infinite sequences of first order terms. Thus we model different times (clocks) with different sequences of terms, common subsequences of terms (modulo ordinary unification) among different sequences show that the various clock synchronize on those time units. Thus the sequence of time units obtained by taking all the terms that are in common among the various local sequences, represent the possible global synchronization times of the system.

The system configuration can evolve according to an operational semantics, which can be considered quite standard except for the treatment of the local clocks, that is each component can perform an action according to its own clock but synchronizations among different components can happen only if the components perform complementary actions at the same time. Thus at configuration time a sort of *tuning* of the local clocks is performed, in order to identify the best way to relate the clocks each other in order to maximize the system synchronizations. We have defined this tuning operation as the unification of the λ iterative terms that represent the local clocks. In this way all the local clocks will be expressed in terms of a unique (faster) clock, which we assume as the global clock. At each tick of the global clock some action can happen. The property of the unifier to be most general, allows us to obtain that this time configuration step is *optimal*, that is it maximizes the synchronization capabilities of the system.

Due to the fact that clocks are discrete and have a finite period, we can finitely model the time with a matrix which describes the timing behavior of each component in between two time instants of the common sequence. This basically describes component potentiality to perform an action between two instants in which all the components in the system can perform an action.

As we have shown in the example this modeling allows us to statically reason more effectively on real-time component-based systems both in term of real-time properties and of global performance of the system.

The λ iterative terms we used in this paper were very simple and did not show the λ iterative terms potentiality. We expect to better exploit the λ iterative terms expressive power in modeling, besides time, other quality parameters of heterogeneous system components, like for example frequency or capacity. Future works are in the direction of applying our approach to different kind of systems for which some kind of tuning of quality parameters should be done at configuration time.

References

1. Amagbegnon,T.P., Besnard,L., Le Guernic,P.: Implementation of the data-flow Synchronous Language Signal. Proc. ACM Symposium on Programming Languages design and ImplementationACM (1995) 163-173.

2. *Formal Methods for Industrial Applications.* Abrial,J-R., Börger,E., Landmaack,H. Eds., Springer Verlag (1996).
3. Attanasio,C., Corradini,F., Inverardi,P.: Yet Another Real-Time Specification for the Steam Boiler: Local Clocks to Statically Measure Systems Performance, Proc. of Fase'99, LNCS, Springer-Verlag (1999), to appear.
4. Allen,R., Garlan,D.: A Formal Basis for Architectural Connection. ACM Transactions on Software Engineering and Methodology, 6(3) (1997) 213-249.
5. Blair,G.S., Blair,L., Bowman,H., Chetwynd,A.: Formal Specification in Distributed Multimedia Systems. University College London Press (1997).
6. Bowman,H., Faconti,G., Katoen,J-P., Latella,D., Massink,M.: Automatic Verification of a Lip Synchronization Algorithm Using UPPAAL. In FMICS'98 (1998).
7. Aceto,L., Murphy,D.: Timing and Causality in Process Algebra. Acta Informatica 33(4) (1996), 317-350.
8. Cleaveland,R., Parrow,J., Steffen,B.: The concurrency workbench: A semantics-based tool for the verification of concurrent systems. In ACM Transaction on Programming Languages and Systems 15 (1993).
9. Coen-Porisini,A., Ghezzi,C., Kemmere,R.A.: Specification of Realtime Systems Using ASTRAL. In IEEE Transaction on Software Engineering 23 (9) (1997).
10. Corradini,F.,: On Performance Congruences for Process Algebras. Information and Computation 145 (1998), 191-230.
11. Project EP-ATR. Rapport d'activite' scientifique 1997. IRISA, INRIA-Rennes (1997).
12. Friesen,V., Jähnichen,S., Weber,M.: Specification of Software Controlling a Discrete-Continuos Environment. ACM Proceedings ICSE97 (1997), 315-325.
13. Ghezzi,C., Mandrioli,D., Morzenti,A.: TRIO: A Logic Language for Executable Specifications of Real-Time Systems. Journal Systems and Software, 25 (2) (1994).
14. Gorrieri,R., Roccetti,M., Stancampiano,E.: A Theory of Processes with Durational Actions. *Theoretical Computer Science* 140(1) (1995), 73-94.
15. Hoare,C.A.R.: *Communicating Sequential Processes.* Prentice-Hall, Englewood Cliffs, New Jersey (1985).
16. Intrigila,B., Inverardi,P., Venturini Zilli,M.: A Comprehensive Setting for Matching and Unification over Iterative Terms. Submitted to *Fundamenta Informaticae.*
17. Inverardi,P., Wolf,A.L.: Formal Specification and Analysis of Software Architectures using the Chemical Abstract Machine Model. *IEEE Transactions on Software Engineering,* 21(4) (1995), 373-386.
18. Kramer,J., Magee,J.: Exposing the skeleton in the coordination closet. Proc. of Coordination'97, LNCS 1282, Springer-Verlag (1997), 18-31.
19. *Real-Time Systems Specification, Verification and Analysis.* Mathai,J. Ed., Prentice Hall Internation Series in Computer Science (1996).
20. Milner,R.: *Communication and concurrency.* International series on computer science, Prentice Hall International (1989).
21. Moller,F., Tofts,C.: A Temporal Calculus of Communicating Systems. Proc. of CONCUR'90, LNCS 459, Springer-Verlag (1990), 401-415.
22. Reed,G.M., Roscoe,A.W.: A timed model for communicating sequential processes. *Theoretical Computer Science* 58, pp. 249-261, 1988.

Acme-Based Software Architecture Interchange*

David Garlan and Zhenyu Wang

School of Computer Science
Carnegie Mellon University
Pittsburgh, PA 15213, USA
garlan@cs.cmu.edu, zwang@cs.cmu.edu

Abstract. An important issue for the specification and design of software architectures is how to combine the analysis capabilities of multiple architectural definition languages (ADLs) and their supporting toolsets. In this paper, we describe our experience of integrating three ADLs: Wright, Rapide, and Aesop. We discovered that it is possible to achieve interoperability in ADL tools for a non-trivial subset of the systems describable by these languages, even though the languages have different views about architectural structure and semantics. To carry out the integration we used the Acme architectural interchange language and its supporting tools.

1   Introduction

An increasingly important problem for complex software systems is the ability to specify and analyze their architectures. At an architectural level of design, one typically identifies the key computational entities and their interactions. These high-level descriptions are then used to understand key system properties such as performance (latencies, throughputs, bottlenecks), reliability, modifiability, etc.

Unfortunately, current practice relies on little more than informal diagrams and notations to support this activity. This imprecision in defining architectures limits the ability to carry out useful analyses, and even to communicate with others effectively. In response, a number of formal architectural description languages (ADLs) have been developed [MT97]. Typically, each of these ADLs supports the description of architectural *structure* together with some form of associated *semantics*. The particular semantics usually determines what kinds of useful analyses can be carried out on systems described in that ADL.

To take a few examples, Rapide [LAK+95] provides semantics based on posets, and supports analyses based on (among other things) animation and simulation. Wright [AG97] provides semantics based on CSP, and supports static

---

* Research sponsored by the Defense Advanced Research Projects Agency, and Rome Laboratory, Air Force Materiel Command, USAF, under agreement number F30602-97-2-0031, and by the National Science Foundation under Grant No. CCR-9357792. The U.S. Government is authorized to reproduce and distribute reprints for Governmental purposes notwithstanding any copyright annotation thereon.

analyses of deadlock freedom, and interaction consistency. Darwin [MDEK95] provides semantics based on the Pi Calculus, and supports description of dynamically reconfigurable distributed systems.

For any particular system, it may be that the desired analyses are completely covered by those supported by a single ADL. However, in general it is useful to exploit capabilities of multiple ADLs. Unfortunately, each of the current ADLs stands in isolation, making it difficult to do this.

One proposal to help ameliorate the situation is to use a common *architectural interchange language* for exchanging architectural descriptions between various ADLs.[1] Specifically, a notation called Acme, has been proposed as a candidate interchange language [GMW97]. Acme provides a simple, generic vocabulary for describing architectural structures as hierarchical graphs of components and connectors. In addition, Acme has a flexible annotation mechanism that permits each ADL to encode non-structural information (such as types, signatures, protocols, performance and reliability estimates, etc.).

To the extent that different ADLs share an interpretation of the Acme encoding, they can communicate. However, even when they do not, it may be possible to massage the Acme representation to make a given description accessible by other ADLs.

In order for such a scheme to work, however, two assumptions must hold. First, it must be possible to translate sufficient semantic content of an architectural description from one ADL to another. Otherwise, it will not be possible to exploit the analysis capabilities of each. Second, the use of Acme must provide advantages over pairwise translation (i.e., direct ADL-to-ADL). Otherwise, there would be no reason to go through an *intermediate* form.

In this paper we present a case study that sheds light on these two assumptions. Specifically, we describe our experience using Acme to integrate three ADLs: Wright, Rapide and Aesop. With respect to semantic translation issues, we will focus primarily on Wright and Rapide, since these were the most problematic. As we will illustrate, it is possible to map a substantial subset of Wright descriptions into Rapide, even though the two languages have somewhat different views about architectural structure and the semantics of architectural behavior. We also briefly consider the cost effectiveness in using Acme to carry out the translation.

2 Wright, Rapide, and Aesop

Before describing our approach to integration, we first briefly describe the three ADLs that we attempted to integrate.

Wright

Wright models system structures using the abstractions of components, connectors, ports, roles and configurations [AG97, All97]. *Components* represent

---

[1] Here and elsewhere, when we refer to an ADL we will mean that ADL *and* its associated toolset.

processing elements and *connectors* describe interactions between them. Each component and connector has an associated specification described using a variant of CSP. These specifications describe the abstract behavior of the element in terms of the events that it can engage in. Additionally, both components and connectors have interfaces. Component interfaces are called *ports*, while connector interfaces are called *roles*. These interfaces are described by protocol specifications (also in CSP). System descriptions, called *configurations* are defined by attaching roles of connectors to ports of components.

Wright provides a number of useful static analyses of architectural descriptions [All97], including:

- Port-component consistency: checks whether a port protocol is a valid projection of the component's internal behavior.
- Port-role compatibility: checks whether a port's behavior meets the requirements imposed by a connector to which it is attached.
- Connector deadlock-freedom: checks whether a connector represents an interaction that cannot deadlock.
- Attachment completeness: checks that any unattached port or role makes no assumptions about the behavior of its environment.

These checks (and others) are carried out by the Wright toolset using FDR [FDR92], a commercial model-checker for CSP.

Rapide

Rapide also describes an architecture as a composition of components [LAK+95]. Each component (called a *module*) has a set of *interfaces* that describe patterns of events that can take place. Component behavior is specified in terms of the way outgoing events are produced in response to incoming events.

Rapide provides a fixed form of connection: essentially, a connector indicates how output events produced at one interface appear as input events at other interfaces. Rapide also provides a bundling facility for connectors, called services.

Rapide's primary form of analysis is based on tool-supported examination of system runtime behavior. Thus Rapide can function as a kind of architecture simulation language: sets of traces (technically, *posets*) can be examined for satisfaction of desirable ordering relations. Additionally, Rapide provides runtime animation capabilities with its "Raptor" tools.

2.1 Aesop

Aesop provides a toolkit for describing and enforcing architectural *styles* [GAO94]. An architectural style is a set of component and connector types, together with rules for how they can be legally combined. For example, a Pipe-Filter style might describe a filter component type and a pipe connector type, together with rules that indicate how pipes must connect output ports of one filter to input ports of another. Or, a client-server style might describe client and server component types and a client-server connector type, with rules that govern how many clients can communicate with a given server, and whether servers can communicate directly with other servers.

Aesop includes a graphical editor that can be specialized with visualizations appropriate to different styles. It also serves as a harness for analysis tools that can be invoked on architectural descriptions.

Viewed as an ADL, Aesop represents architectures as a system of objects. It uses an object-oriented language for describing both the types of components and connectors in a style as well as the semantic "behavior" of architectural instances.

3 Integration Scheme

The three ADLs described above have complementary capabilities. With its graphical editing capabilities, and support for domain-specific architectural design (using styles), Aesop is a good front end for architectural design. To carry out deeper semantic analyses on these designs, Wright provides capabilities for statically checking the consistency and completeness of the design. With its support for simulation, runtime analysis and animation, Rapide provides other important capabilities for evaluating an architectural description.

Clearly it would be beneficial to harness all three in a single environment. However, a number of difficulties present themselves. First, each ADL has a somewhat different view of the structure of architectures. Second, and more importantly, there are some significant differences in the way the languages specify architectural properties, such as abstract behavior. How can one bridge these mismatches?

In an attempt to answer this question we created a prototype environment in which all three ADLs were integrated using Acme as an interchange language, together with several Acme-based architectural transformation tools that we developed to handle the mismatch problems.

Acme

As noted earlier, Acme provides a simple structural framework for representing architectures, together with a liberal annotation mechanism [GMW97]. Acme does not impose any semantic interpretation of an architectural description, but simply provides a syntactic structure on which to hang semantic descriptions, which can then be interpreted by tools. The Acme language is a simple textual notation, designed for ease of tool manipulation.

An architectural design is shared among several ADLs by first translating the design into an Acme representation (see Figure 1). This representation can then be read by other ADLs that understand Acme, or it can be manipulated by tools that operate on Acme directly. Acme comes with a rich library for parsing, unparsing, and manipulating the representations, together with a growing corpus of tools for performing graphical layout, Web generation, and analysis.

Using Acme

To integrate the three ADLs we used the integration scheme illustrated in Figure 2. In this ensemble Aesop acts a graphical editor, exploiting its visualization and style-enforcement capabilities. Aesop descriptions are initially annotated with Wright specification fragments.[2] To carry out *static analyses* on these designs we translate Aesop into Acme, and then to native Wright, on which Wright's analysis tools can be invoked. To carry out *dynamic analyses* we use an intermediary tool that transforms Acme with Wright annotations into Acme with Rapide annotations. This transformed description can then be mapped into native Rapide on which Rapide's behavior analyzer and animator can be invoked.

In this scheme Acme plays the role of an intermediary representation, that can be operated on by the various translation tools. While Acme provides neutral ground through which ADL translation can take place, clearly it does not make the differences between different ADLs disappear. In particular, although Wright, Aesop, and Acme are quite similar in their treatment of structure, there are significant differences between Wright and Rapide both structurally and semantically.

With respect to architectural structure, the most significant difference is that Wright permits the definition of new kinds of connectors (and their semantics), while Rapide provides a fixed set. Another key difference is that Rapide permits the creation of new architectural elements at runtime, while Wright describes only static architectures.

With respect to semantics, both Wright and Rapide describe the behavior of architectures in terms of patterns of events. However, there are three significant differences. First, Wright's behavior definitions are functional (with heavy reliance on recursion), whereas Rapide's are largely imperative. Second, Rapide imposes some restrictions on the use of nested parallelism in its descriptions, whereas Wright does not. Third, non-determinism can be made explicit in Wright

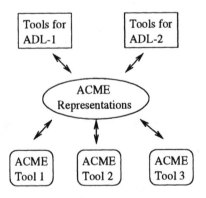

Fig. 1. Acme-based Integration

---

[2] Alternatively, as we illustrate later, the user can start with a Wright specifications, which can be imported into Aesop (via Acme) for graphical viewing.

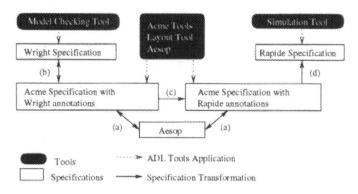

Fig. 2. Integration of Aesop, Wright, and Rapide

specifications (using the CSP's internal choice operator), while it is implicit in Rapide.

In the next section we briefly describe how we handle these and other problems.

4 Integration Details

As illustrated in Figure 2, there are four key translations that contribute to the overall integration (labeled (a) – (d)).

(a) Aesop ↔ Acme

Translation between Acme and Aesop is relatively straightforward because Aesop and Acme have a similar notion of structure. In particular, in Aesop connectors are first class entities, which map well to Acme connectors. In the reverse direction Acme components and connectors can be mapped to components and connectors in the "generic" Aesop style. Further, Aesop permits arbitrary properties to be associated with architectural objects, providing a natural home for Acme property lists. (Although we don't have space to discuss it here, styles in Aesop are easily represented using the "families" of Acme.)

(b) Wright ↔ Acme$_{Wright}$

The translation from Wright to Acme consists of mapping Wright's components and connectors to Acme's, and then adding properties to those elements that correspond to the Wright behavior descriptions. That is, each component and connector is annotated with a property that specifies its Wright behavior. Since Wright and Acme have a similar view of structure this step is likewise straightforward.

(c) Acme$_{Wright}$ → Acme$_{Wright+Rapide}$

In this step the properties that characterize Wright behavior are transformed to create additional properties that characterize Rapide behavior. To do this we must find a way to create Rapide module code fragments from the Wright "process" annotations stored in the Acme representation.

Wright processes are defined using a subset of CSP that includes operators for event sequencing (→), external choice (), internal choice (⊓), and parallel composition (‖).[3] In addition, unlike CSP, Wright distinguishes between initiated and observed events: the former is indicated with an overbar.

Figure 3 shows how each of these constructs is mapped into a Rapide specification. Most of the translations are straightforward: Wright initiated events correspond to Rapide output events, while observed events correspond to Rapide input events. Top-level parallelism can be translated directly to the "parallel" construct of Rapide. Guarded external choice simply becomes the Rapide event-trigger case statement.

Map $(\overline{e} \to P)$ = e(); Map(P);

Map$(e \to P)$ = await e(); Map(P);

Map $(P_1 \| \cdots \| P_n)$ =
    parallel
        Map(P_1)
        ‖
        . . .
        ‖
        Map(P_n)
    end parallel;

Map $(e_1 \to P_1 \cdots e_n \to P_n)$ =
    await
        $e_1 \Rightarrow Map(P_1); \ldots; e_n \Rightarrow Map(P_n)$;
    end await;

Map $(P_1 \sqcap \cdots \sqcap P_n)$ =
    $\tau()$;
    await
        $\tau() \Rightarrow Map(P_1); \ldots; \tau() \Rightarrow Map(P_n)$;
    end await;
    where τ is defined as an internal event of the module

Fig. 3. Acme$_{Wright}$ to Acme$_{Wright+Rapide}$

---

[3] Space does not permit a detailed description of these operators: however, a detailed understanding is not necessary to understand the main ideas of the paper.

The only three non-obvious parts are the handling of non-determinism, nested parallelism, and recursion.

To handle non-determinism that arises from an internal choice in CSP ($\sqcap$) we introduce a local Rapide event τ (invisible to other modules) that serves as a guard for each of the processes in the choice. Since multiple choices with the same event guard in Rapide is treated as non-deterministic choice, we achieve the desired effect.

To handle nested parallelism we could have used CSP's algebraic operators to eliminate parallelism before performing the translation. However, as it turns out, nested parallelism is rarely used in Wright, and so instead we constrain our translation to apply only to Wright descriptions that don't use this feature. (Use of nested parallelism can be easily checked for, and a warning can be issued to the user, who can perform the transformation by hand if desired.)

To handle recursion in CSP processes, we first map CSP processes into a state machine and then generate Rapide code to simulate this state machine. This is accomplished by assigning a state number to each process and defining a Rapide variable that records the current state of execution. When one process (recursively) transitions another process, the translation arranges for the state variable to change correspondingly.

$\text{Acme}_{Wright+Rapide} \rightarrow \textbf{Rapide}$

In this step, the goal is to translate Acme structures (i.e., components and connectors) annotated with Rapide fragments into native Rapide structures such as interfaces and modules. The basic idea behind the translation is that component interfaces in Acme become interfaces in Rapide. Component behavior (described by Wright property specifications) become module implementations in Rapide. The key difficulty is how to handle the fact that in Acme (as well as Wright and Aesop) new connectors may be defined and those connectors may have complex specifications, whereas in Rapide connectors are primitives.

There appeared to be two ways to handle the situation. One was to limit the class of architectural descriptions to just those that use the connector types provided by Rapide. The second was to represent complex connectors as modules in Rapide. We chose the latter, because it allows a much larger class of systems to be handled by the translation. (We will return to this issue in section 7.)

Thus to complete the translation, Acme connectors are translated into Rapide modules, and Acme attachments (between connectors and components) are translated into event bindings between the Rapide interfaces of modules representing Acme components and the Rapide interfaces of modules representing Acme connectors. Finally, we map an Acme top-level "System" into a Rapide top-level "Architecture".

5 Example

To illustrate how the pieces fit together for the integration of Wright and Rapide, consider the following deliberately simple (partial) Wright specification of a single reader attached to a pipe.

System Reader-Pipe:

Component Reader
    Port read $= read?x \rightarrow$ read
    Computation $= read.read?x \rightarrow$ Computation

Connector Pipe
    Role read $= read?x \rightarrow$ read
    Role write $= \overline{write!x} \rightarrow$ write
    Glue $= write.write?x \rightarrow \overline{read.read!x} \rightarrow$ Glue

Instances
    reader1 : Reader;
    pipe1 : Pipe;
    Attach pipe1.read **to** reader1.read

After the first translation step (b) we obtain an Acme description annotated with Wright processes. (The Acme description appears in Figure 4 at the end of this paper.) After the second translation step (c), the Acme description is almost the same, except that each component or connector now has a new Rapide property generated from the Wright properties. From this, we synthesize a native Rapide specification (d) to get:

```
type reader is interface
     action
          in          read_read(x : Params);
end interface reader

type pipe is interface
     action
          in          write_write(x : Params);
     action
          out         read_read(x : Params);
end interface pipe

module new_reader() return reader is

     while true
          await read_read(?x : Params);
          end await
end module
```

```
module new_pipe() return pipe is
    while true
        await write_write(?x : Params)
        ⇒ read_read(?x);
        end await
end module

Architecture system() return root is
    reader1 is new_reader();
    pipe1 is new_pipe();
connect
    (?x in Params) pipe1.read_read(?x)
to
    reader1.read_read(?x);
end system
```

The application of the translation rules can be seen by comparing the Rapide specification that is obtained from the original Wright specification. First, component *reader* is mapped into interface *reader*. Since its port process *read* only has a single observed event *read*, the reader interface only has an "in" event *read_read*[4]. Second, we generate module instances *reader1* and *pipe1* by calling module generators we get from component *reader* and connector *pipe*. Since we only have one attachment from port *read* to role *read* both of which only have one event, we need only one basic connection.

6 Recent Development

6.1 MetaH Acme Integration

The Software Engineering Institute at CMU has extended the analysis capabilities of an architectural definition language called MetaH by integrating MetaH with other ADLs through Acme [BW98]. MetaH supports the specification of process and communication structures of embedded real-time applications. Its toolset supports schedulability analysis as well as automatic generation of an executable application executive. A translation of system description in MetaH into Acme makes it possible to interchange MetaH specifications with other ADLs. Through architecture interchange, MetaH toolset are extended in a number of ways: Acme and Aesop based graphical editors, Acme based analysis tools, constraints analysis tools from Armani and Wright/Rapide control flow analysis.

A combination of MetaH-specific Acme types and properties are used to codify the structural concepts of MetaH as an Acme style. Additional semantic information embedded in MetaH descriptions such as error models is represented through a combination of structured property values and tailored component type refinements.

---

[4] the naming scheme is *port name_event name.*

6.2   Unicon Acme Integration

The UniCon model [SDK+95, K+] is based upon structural concepts that are very similar to those found in both Aesop and Acme. It includes components and first class connectors as well as explicit structures for describing ports (UniCon "players") and roles. It also supports hierarchical decomposition by allowing components to be defined in terms of either a sub-configuration or a concrete implementation. These can be encoded naturally as Acme representations. Like Aesop and Acme, UniCon also provides an open syntax that allows the specification of additional properties of elements of a description. These carry over directly to Acme.

However, UniCon places a number of constraints on the structure of a description that are left unrestricted by Acme. For example, components may have implementations, but players, roles and connectors may not. In contrast, Acme allows representations for these elements. The Acme to UniCon translator simply discards this additional specification. If a round-trip translation back to Acme were desired, the additional information has to be encoded using the UniCon property construct.

Acme also imposes a constraint on descriptions that UniCon does not: UniCon property lists may include multiple properties with the same name, in Acme property names must be unique; this problem is addressed by storing same-named properties as a single property whose value include all the values of the original properties.

Unlike Acme and Aesop, UniCon defines a built-in set of primitive component and connector types. Consequently it is only meaningful to translate an element of an Acme description, if it can be interpreted as one of these types. The Acme to UniCon translation tool addresses this problem by supporting plug-in semantic translators. New plug-ins can be created that can make sense of annotations generated by other tools, or particular type naming conventions used in an Acme description to choose the proper UniCon type to use. For example, a translator was defined that understands the types defined by several different styles defined in the Aesop environment. So for example, an Aesop pipe connector is translated as a "UniconPipe" connector.

Although a system in UniCon is described in terms of the same underlying concepts as those defined by Aesop (i.e. components, connectors, etc.), it differs in one basic way. In UniCon, all component and connector definitions are essentially templates that may be instantiated anywhere within a description. Consequently, the most natural way to encode Unicon component and connector structures in Acme are as types rather than as Acme instances. The UniCon to Acme translator then translates instantiations and extensions of components and connectors as instantiations of Acme types using the "extended with" clause to specialize it the new context (for example, choosing an implementation).

In 1997, an integrated design environment based on Aesop and UniCon was built, using Acme as an interchange language. Aesop was used for the front-end environment because it allowed us to easily create a customized UI environment tailored to a particular style, while we used UniCon as a backend compiler to generate executable code. The user was able to create designs using the Aesop GUI (storing the designs in the standard Aesop repository), edit implementation code associated with the design, and then run the UniCon compiler on the design to generate an executable system.

7 Discussion and Conclusion

Let us now return to the two key issues raised earlier: (1) How do we integrate diverse ADLs even in the presence of structural and semantic mismatches? (2) Does Acme help?

With respect to the problem of mismatched features in the ADLs, given the differences between the three ADLs (and especially between Wright and Rapide), it was clear from the outset that complete integration would not be possible. That is, we recognized that there would be certain kinds of system descriptions possible in one ADL that had no counterpart in one of the others. However, rather than attempting to get complete coverage, we attempted to find a scheme that would allow a significant subset of the systems to be mutually accessible in the integrated system. The key challenge was to make that subset as large as possible. To accomplish this we used three techniques that have general applicability to any integration effort of this kind.

1. **Limit the class of systems:** We avoided some of the difficulties in translation by excluding certain systems. In particular, we excluded Wright specifications that use nested parallelism. Ideally (as is the situation here), this does not impose a serious limitation on the class of system that can be handled.
2. **Limit the directionality:** A key factor in making the integration work was an early decision not to attempt to map Rapide specifications back to Wright. By avoiding the reverse translation problem, we avoided problems of handling features of Rapide that had no counterpart in Wright. For example, we did not have to handle the Rapide features for creating new architectural structures at runtime.
3. **Provide a semantics-based translator:** We were able to convert most Wright specifications into Rapide specifications using straightforward mappings. This helped us deal with a number of representational discrepancies that are likely to appear when attempting to integrate two arbitrary ADLs. These include: use (or not) of first class connectors; different treatments of non-determinism; different control structures (e.g., functional versus imperative descriptions); and different constraints on nesting (e.g., nested parallelism).

While each of these techniques is useful, it is worth noting that each has a downside that must be carefully considered. Limiting the class of systems makes the translation easier, but may exclude the very systems that one is hoping to analyze. Limiting the directionality clearly restricts the ability to incorporate native descriptions from ADL's that aren't mapped back. (For example, our system cannot handle native Rapide specifications directly – we can only exploit

Rapide tools on descriptions that are initially generated from Wright and Aesop.) Providing a translator helps bridge semantic gaps, but it also may make it difficult to relate the analyses produced by one ADL to the descriptions viewed in another.

With respect to the cost-effectiveness of Acme, we found that Acme reduced costs in two significant ways. The first was by providing useful infrastructure on which to build: The parsing and manipulating libraries substantially reduced the amount of code we had to write, and provided a convenient framework in which to apply the Wright-Rapide property translation tool. The second benefit was in providing a single representation that more than two ADLs could share. For example, we got Aesop compatibility (and hence a graphical front end) almost for free, since Aesop was already able to read and write Acme descriptions. Also although the issue of semantics mismatches among ADLs is independent of whether Acme is used an interchange language, Acme helps us focus on the semantics issues without getting side-tracked with syntactic detail.

In conclusion, we believe that while it is important not to generalize too far beyond the specific examples of this case study, the goal of integrating diverse ADLs through Acme shows considerable promise. Acme does not magically make semantic differences between ADLs disappear, but it does provide a framework within which one can achieve significant benefits by combining the toolsets of different ADLs. The primary challenge in doing this is to understand what classes of systems can be handled and what kinds of translation are required to map between the various ADL-specific tools. While the specific techniques will differ from ADL to ADL, there appear to be several general strategies for accomplishing the translation. We have illustrated several in this paper, but expect the repertoire to grow as others attempt similar integration efforts.

8   Acknowledgements

We would like to thank Peter Feiler and Andrew Kompanek for their comments on translating Unicon and MetaH into Acme. We are also grateful for anonymous referees, whose comments helped us improve this paper.

References

[AG97]   Robert Allen and David Garlan. A formal basis for architectural connection. *ACM Transactions on Software Engineering and Methodology*, July 1997.

[All97]   Robert Allen. *A Formal Approach to Software Architecture*. PhD thesis, Carnegie Mellon, School of Computer Science, January 1997. Issued as CMU Technical Report CMU-CS-97-144.

[BW98]   Mario Barbacci and Charles B. Weinstock. Mapping MetaH into Acme. *special report, CMU/SEI-98-SR-006*, July 1998.

[FDR92]   *Failures Divergence Refinement: User Manual and Tutorial*. Formal Systems (Europe) Ltd., Oxford, England, 1.2β edition, October 1992.

Acme Specification of the Reader-Pipe Example

```
System acmespec = component {
    ports : {
    };
    representations : {
        acmespec = configuration {
            components : {
                reader1 = component {
                    ports : {
                        read = port {
                            representations : {
                            external : CFamWrightRep = " {{ Name {WrightSpec1}}
                                {Data {spec1.wright}} {Tool {Component_editor}}}";
                            };
                        };
                    };
                    representations : {
                        external : CFamWrightRep = " {{ Name {WrightSpec1}}
                            {Data {spec1.wright}} {Tool {Component_editor}}};"
                    };
                };
            };
            connectors : {
                pipe1 = connector {
                    roles : {
                        read = role {
                            representations : {
                                external : CFamWrightRep = " {{ Name {WrightSpec1}}
                                {Data {spec2.wright}} {Tool {Connector_editor}}}";
                            };
                        };
                        write = role {
                            representations : {
                                external : CFamWrightRep = " {{ Name {WrightSpec1}}
                                {Data {spec2.wright}} {Tool {Connector_editor}}}";
                            };
                        };
                    };
                    representations : {
                        external : CFamWrightRep = " {{ Name {WrightSpec1}}
                            {Data {spec2.wright}} {Tool {Connector_editor}}}";
                    };
                };
            };
            Attachments : {
                pipe1.read to reader1.read
            };
        };
        bindings : {
        };
    };
};
```

Fig. 4. Acme Reader-Pipe System

[GAO94]   David Garlan, Robert Allen, and John Ockerbloom. Exploiting style in architectural design environments. In *Proceedings of SIGSOFT'94: The Second ACM SIGSOFT Symposium on the Foundations of Software Engineering*, pages 179–185. ACM Press, December 1994.

[GMW97]   David Garlan, Robert T. Monroe, and David Wile. ACME: An architecture description interchange language. In *Proceedings of CASCON'97*, Ontario, Canada, November 1997.

[K+]   Andrew Kompanek et al. Translating software architecture descriptions with Acme. *in preparation*.

[LAK+95]   David C Luckham, Lary M. Augustin, John J. Kenney, James Veera, Doug Bryan, and Walter Mann. Specification and analysis of system architecture using Rapide. *IEEE Transactions on Software Engineering, Special Issue on Software Architecture*, 21(4):336–355, April 1995.

[MDEK95]   J. Magee, N. Dulay, S. Eisenbach, and J. Kramer. Specifying distributed software architectures. In *Proceedings of the Fifth European Software Engineering Conference, ESEC'95*, September 1995.

[MT97]   Nenad Medvidovic and Richard N. Taylor. Architecture description languages. In *Software Engineering – ESEC/FSE'97*, volume 1301 of *Lecture Notes in Computer Science*, Zurich, Switzerland, September 1997. Springer.

[SDK+95]   Mary Shaw, Robert DeLine, Daniel V. Klein, Theodore L. Ross, David M. Young, and Gregory Zelesnik. Abstractions for software architecture and tools to support them. *IEEE Transactions on Software Engineering, Special Issue on Software Architecture*, 21(4):314–335, April 1995.

A Group Based Approach for Coordinating Active Objects

Juan Carlos Cruz, Stéphane Ducasse[1]

Abstract. Although coordination of concurrent objects is a fundamental aspect of object-oriented concurrent programming, there is only little support for its specification and abstraction at the language level. This is a problem because coordination is often buried in the code of the coordinated objects, leading to a lack of abstraction and reuse. Here we present CoLaS, a coordination model and its implementation based on the notion of Coordination Groups. By clearly identifying and separating the coordination from the coordinated objects CoLaS provides a better abstraction and reuse of the coordination and the coordinated objects. Moreover CoLaS's high dynamicity provides better support for coordination of active objects.

1 Introduction

Coordination technology addresses the construction of open, flexible systems from active and independent software entities in concurrent and distributed systems. Although coordination is a fundamental aspect of object-oriented programming languages for concurrent and distributed systems, existing object-oriented languages provide only limited support for its specification and abstraction [Frol93a, Aksi92a]. Furthermore, in these languages it is not possible to abstract coordination patterns from the representation of the coordinated objects. Coordination policies are generally hard-wired into applications making them difficult to understand, modify and customize. This is a serious problem when developing open and flexible systems. In those systems the coordination policies need to be adapted dynamically to respond to new coordination requirements.

In this paper we introduce a coordination model called CoLaS based on the notion of *coordination groups*. The CoLaS coordination model is based on the specification and *enforcement* of cooperation protocols, multi-action synchronizations, and proactive behaviour within groups of collaborating active objects. The current version of CoLaS is implemented in Smalltalk on top of the Actalk platform [Brio96a].

Coordination groups are high-level abstractions for managing the coordination aspect in concurrent object-oriented systems. We roughly define a *coordination group* as a set of policies that regulates the activities of a group of active objects — called *participants*. Groups are specified independently of the internal representation of their participants. This independence allows for a clear separation of computation and coordination concerns (as promoted by coordination languages [Gele92a]). Separation of concerns promotes design with a greater potential for reuse. Active objects may be reused independently of how they are coordinated, and coordination patterns can be reused in-

---

1. *Author's address:* Institut für Informatik (IAM), Universität Bern, Neubrückstrasse 10, CH-3012 Berne, Switzerland. *Tel:* +41 (31) 631.3315. *Fax:* +41 (31) 631.3965. *E-mail:* {cruz, ducasse}@iam.unibe.ch. *WWW:* http://www.iam.unibe.ch/~cruz.

dependently on different groups of active objects. Coordination groups support dynamic evolution of coordination in three distinct axes: (1) groups are created dynamically at any time; (2) participants join and leave the coordination groups whenever they want, and (3) their behaviour can be modified dynamically to adapt to new coordination requirements.

This paper is organized as follows: Section 2 discusses existing problems in the realization of the coordination in software systems, and establishes a list of requirements for an ideal coordination language for active objects. Section 3 introduces the CoLaS coordination model. Section 4 goes into the details by describing how CoLaS proposes a solution to the classical Gas Station example [Helm85a]. Section 5 presents some dynamic aspects of the approach. Section 6 illustrates proactive behaviour using the Electronic Vote example [Mins97a]. Section 7 evaluates the CoLaS model with respect to the problems and requirements defined in Section 2. Finally Section 8 concludes with a discussion evaluating our contributions compared with related work.

2 Language Support for Coordination in COO Systems

We consider that the primary tasks of coordination in concurrent object systems (COOs) are: (1) to support the creation of active objects, (2) to enforce cooperation actions between active objects, (3) to synchronise the occurrence of those actions in the system, and (4) to enforce proactive behaviour [And96b] on the system based on the state of the coordination. Providing a *high level* construct for explicitly specifying coordination separately from the computation and supporting dynamic evolution of the requirements addresses the following common problems:

No separation of computational and coordination concerns. In most concurrent object systems coordination policies are hard-coded into the actions of the cooperating objects [Frol93a, Lope97a] making understanding, modification and customisation difficult. This lack of separation of concerns promotes design with poor potential for reuse [Aksi92a]. In those systems objects cannot be reused independently of how they are coordinated and coordination patterns cannot be reused independently on different groups of objects.

Lack of high level coordination abstractions. Existing concurrent object-oriented languages (COOLs) offer low level support for the expression and abstraction of complex object cooperations and large scale synchronizations involving more than just a pair of objects [Aksi92a]. For example, in Java coordination can be modelled at a very low level of abstraction: threads model asynchronous activities; the synchronized keyword, the wait, notify and notifyAll methods are used to coordinate activities across threads. While the set of provided constructs can be used to solve non trivial coordination problems, in practise only expert programmers are able to handle them appropriately. Java programmers tend to rely on design patterns [Lea96a] to solve common coordination problems.

Dynamic Evolution of Coordination. The fact that coordination is mixed within the application code makes the coordination evolution difficult to realize. Indeed, three main changes in a coordination group can impact it: (1) the *creation* of new coordination groups, (2) the *addition/removal of new participants* to a coordination group (i.e. new objects come into play or leave the application), and (3) the *addition/removal of coordination policies*. The changes range broadly from local redefinition and recompilation of coordination and/or participants to the overall system redefinition and recompilation

The integration of coordination into a COOL should propose a solution to these problems. In the following we elaborate on the requirements for such an ideal language.

2.1 Requirements for a Coordination Language for Active Objects

Coordination Specification. Are the coordination policies fixed within the system? Can coordination policies be incrementally specified? Is the coordination expressed declaratively or procedurally?

It must be possible for programmers to define new coordination policies [Mins97a] within the system, their specification should be *user-defined*. Contrary to Synchronizers [Frol93a] that do not support incremental definition of the synchronization policies, the coordination policies should be defined *incrementally* from others like in [Aksi94a, Mukh95a, Duca98c]. Finally, as proposed in [Frol93a, Andr96b, Mins97a] policies should be *declarative* to avoid programmers deal with low-level details on how the coordination occurs.

Coordination Properties. Is the coordination: data-driven or control driven [Arbad96b]? Transparently integrated in the host languages? Non-intrusive? Is the coordination centralized (i.e. objects are coordinated using a central coordinator agent), decentralized (i.e. objects communicate explicitly to realize the coordination) or hybrid (i.e. achieved through the cooperation of both the objects and a coordinator agent) [Mukh95a]?

As COOLs promote data encapsulation and behaviour over data, the coordination in COOs must be *control driven* [Frol93a, Mukh95a, Arba96b, Mins97a].

Contrary to Linda based approaches [Kiel96a] where the coordinated objects are aware of the virtual shared space to which they communicate, coordination should be *transparent* from the point of view of the coordinated objects [Frol93a, Mukh95a, Mins97a]. Moreover, it should be *non-intrusive*: based on public interface of the coordinated object and not relying on their internal data.

Finally, the coordination must be based on a *hybrid* model [Frol93a, Aksi94b, Mukh95a, Mins97a]. The problem with centralized models [Agha93c, Andr96b] is that objects are forced to interact with a coordinator agent, and with decentralized models [Papa96a] is that objects must know other objects to realize coordination. The reusability of objects and coordination is limited in both cases.

Coordination Behaviour. Is coordination limited to synchronization of actions; or Can actions be enforced [Duca98c] and/or initiated [Andr96b] by the system? What kinds of information should be referred to by the coordination policies [Bloo79a]?

Coordination should not be limited (as in [Frol93a,Aksi94a]) to the synchronization of messages, it should be possible to enforce actions in coordinated objects as a reaction to certain messages received by the objects. Moreover, it should be possible to initiate actions in the system (i.e. proactive actions) depending on the state of the coordination [Andr96b, Mins97a]. The coordination state should take into account the state of the coordinated objects [Papa96a] and the history of the coordination.

Evolution. Can coordination policies be created and/or modified dynamically? Do coordination policies support the addition and removal of coordinated objects? Can we define new coordination patterns dynamically?

The coordination should be highly *dynamic*: objects must be able to join and/or leave the coordination at any time, coordination policies must be modifiable on the fly, and new coordination patterns must be able to be created at run-time [Andr96b]. A highly dynamic system will be able to respond to new coordination requirements.

Formal Properties. Can we prove that the behaviour of an object is compatible with the coordination policies of the system? Can we prove that the coordination will develop correctly (i.e. safe)?

Ideally we would like to have a formal model fully integrated to the coordination language that checks the ability of objects to be coordinated. Furthermore, we would like to be able to prove certain safety and liveness properties of the coordination like deadlock freeness, termination, etc. The formal model should not be limited to the specification and the verification of the coordination as in [Alle94c] but causally connected to the language in the sense of "executable specification".

A Quick Overview of CoLaS. According to these requirements, CoLaS is a *hybrid* model that supports *user-defined explicit* and *non-intrusive* object group coordination based on the *transparent* synchronisation and *enforcement* of exchanged messages. Moreover, coordination is not limited to coordinator state. CoLaS supports the *dynamic* evolution of the coordination.

3 The CoLaS Coordination Model

We propose a coordination model for COOs based on the notion of coordination groups. A coordination group specifies, encapsulates and enforces the coordination of a group of cooperating concurrent objects. The CoLaS model is built out of two kind of entities: the participants and the coordination groups.

3.1 Participants

In CoLaS the participants are *active objects* [Briot96a]: objects that have control over concurrent message invocations. Incoming messages are stored into a mailbox until the object is ready to process them. By default, an active object treats its incoming messages in a sequential way. In CoLaS active objects communicate by exchanging messages concurrently in an *asynchronous* way. Replies are managed using *explicit futures* so the objects are not blocked while waiting for their replies.

3.2 Coordination Groups

A *Coordination Group* (group in the following) is an entity that specifies and enforces the coordination of a group of participants to perform a common task. According to our notion of coordination the primary tasks of a group are: (1) to enforce cooperation actions between participants, (2) to synchronize the occurrence of those actions, and (3) to enforce proactive actions [Andr96b] (in the following proactions) in participants based on the state of the coordination.

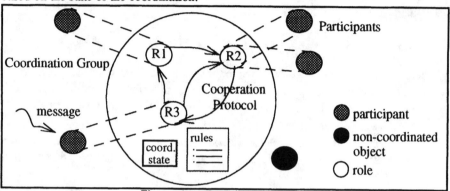

Figure 1 a Coordination Group

Coordination Specification. A group is composed of five elements: a Role Specification, a Coordination State, a Cooperation Protocol, Multi-Action Synchronizations and Proactions (Fig. 1).

- *The Role Specification:* defines the roles that participants may play in the group. Similar to connector roles [Alle94c], a role identifies abstractly entities sharing the same coordination behavioural specification within the group. Each role has an associated role interface.

- *The Coordination State:* defines information needed for the group coordination. It is global to the group and/or local to each participant in a given role.

- *The Cooperation Protocol:* defines implications between participant actions (e.g. the treatment of a message implies some other actions).

- *The Multi-Action Synchronizations:* specifies synchronisation constraints over messages exchanged by participants.

- *The Proactions:* specifies actions that must be executed by the group depending on the coordination state, independently of the messages exchanged by the participants.

The last three elements are specified using rules [Andr96b].

Object Group Participation. Objects join groups by enrolling to group *roles*. To play a role in a group, an object should possess at least the functionalities required by this role (interface compatibility). A role can be played by more than one object. Objects join and leave a group at any time without disturbing other participants.

Coordination Enforcement. When a participant handles a message waiting in its mailbox, the group checks if cooperation and/or multi-action synchronisation rules apply to this message. If so, the group enforces them (e.g. sends new messages, forbid others, etc.). Synchronisation rules are verified prior to the cooperation rules. They constrain the execution of the message and the actions specified in the cooperation rules. In contrast, as proaction rules do not depend on messages but on the state of coordination they are repeatedly checked. In every case, the group guarantees the consistency of participants during the enforcement process.

4 A Detailed View of the CoLaS Model

To help in understanding CoLaS, we present the classical Gas Station example [Helm85a]. Using this example we show the different elements of our model as well as their characteristics. This example illustrates the following coordination problems:

- *Transfer of information between entities:* car drivers communicate with cashiers to get authorizations to take gas from pumps. Pumps receive authorizations from cashiers to give fuel to drivers. Money and gas representations flow between participants.

- *Multi-action synchronizations:* there are different synchronisation constraints that have to be respected: cashiers must not authorize pumps to give fuel before being paid by drivers. Pumps must not give fuel to drivers before being authorized by cashiers.

- *Management of access to shared resources:* Cashiers must not authorize more drivers to take gas than there are pumps. They must prevent several drivers from getting gas from the same pump at the same time because there is only one hose per pump.

- *Dynamic evolution of the coordination.* New participants can leave or join the system (i.e. when a pump malfunctions or when new car drivers want to take gas).

4.1 A Case Study - The Gas Station System

Problem Description. The gas station consists of p pumps where car drivers can take gas for their cars. At a particular moment in time n car drivers can come to the gas station to obtain gas, but only p of them will be served at the same time. This is because each pump has only one hose to discharge gas. A car driver first has to pay an amount of money to one of the m cashiers. Then, the cashier orders a free pump to prepare to pump fuel. The driver receives an authorization from the cashier to take his gas, and finally he takes the amount of gas he paid for. In Fig. 2 we show the UML description of the different participants of the gas station as well as the interaction diagrams that describes the different cooperation actions that should be enforced during the coordination. Both actions pay(amount) and takeHose(pump) correspond to actions initiated by car-drivers. Note that this example does not really reflect reality: the cashier should be considered as an automatic machine but we follow the original example [Helm85a].

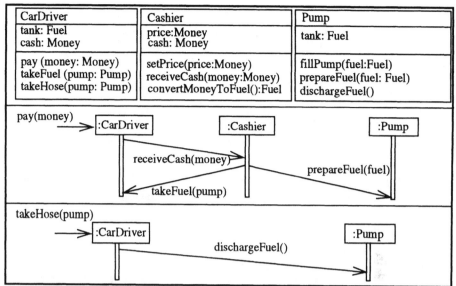

Figure 2 UML description of gas station classes, and interaction diagrams of the cooperation actions

4.2 Role Specification

In the gas station example, participants play one of the following roles: car-drivers, cashiers and pumps. Roles in a group are defined by sending the message defineRoles: to a coordination group (line 2 in Fig. 3). The minimal interface that an object should support to play a role is specified sending the message defineInterface:forRole: (e.g. an object that participates as a cashier should at least understand the messages receive-Cash: and convertMoneyToFuel:replyTo: line 4 in Fig. 3).

4.3 Coordination State

The coordination state of a group is specified by declaring   variables. It is global to the group (*group coordination variables*), and/or local to each participant (*per-role coordination variables*) in a role. Coordination state variables are created using the messages:defineVariable:initialValue: and/or defineParticipantVariable:forRole:initialValue: respectively (lines 7 and 8 in Fig. 3). In the example, the per-role variable represents the state of a pump (busy/free).The variable isFree is used to guarantee exclusive access of drivers to pumps.

```
1.    gasStation := CoordinationGroup new name: 'gas-station'.
2.    gasStation defineRoles: #('drivers' 'cashiers' 'pumps').
3.    gasStation defineInterface:#('pay:' 'takeFuel:' 'takeHose:') forRole: 'drivers'.
4.    gasStation defineInterface: #('receiveCash:' 'convertMoneyToFuel:replyTo:')
5.              forRole: 'cashiers'.
6.    gasStation defineInterface: #('prepareFuel:' 'dischargeFuel') forRole: 'pumps'.
7.    gasStation defineVariable:'whichPump' initialValue: nil.
8.    gasStation defineParticipantVariable: 'isFree' forRole: 'pumps' initialValue: true.
```

Figure 3 Role Specification and Coordination State of the Gas Station

4.4 Coordination Behaviour Specification

The coordination, i.e. the cooperation protocol, the multi-action synchronizations and the proactions, is specified using two different types of rules [Andr96b, Mins97a, Duca98c] as follows:

Rule1	= \<Message\> \<Operator\> \<Clauses\>
Message	= \<Role\> \<MethodSelector\> \<Arguments\>
Operator	= ImpliesBefore I ImpliesAfter I Disable I Ignore I Atomic
Rule2	= \<Condition\> \< ProOperator\> \<Clauses\>
ProOperator	= Once I Always

In Rule1 \<Message\> describes the message being treated (the symbol "*"can be used to specify any message). \<Operator\> specifies the semantics of the \<Clauses\>. Indeed for the operators ImpliesBefore or ImpliesAfter that specify a cooperation protocol, \<Clauses\> are possible *coordination actions* (like sending a message to another participant, changing the coordination state, etc.) that occurs before or after the message execution. For the operators Disable, Ignore and Atomic that specify multi-action synchronizations, \<Clauses\> are *synchronisation conditions* (referring to the state of the group, or to message information like the sender/receiver or arguments) that constrain the message execution (depending on the operator the message is ignored or delayed). For the Atomic operator, \<Message\> represents a set of messages that must be executed at the same time (i.e. those messages can refer to messages in different roles). In Message \<Role\> represents a role of the group and \<MethodSelector\> \<Arguments\> a message.

Rule2 specifies proactions [Andr96b]. For \<ProOperator\> operators Once and Always, the \<Clauses\> are the actions that are performed when the \<Condition\> referring to the state of the coordination holds. We explain these operators later in this paper. In CoLaS rules are added to a group by sending the message addRule:\<Rule\>.

4.4.1 Cooperation Protocol Specification

```
1.  [r1] drivers pay: money ImpliesAfter [ cashiers receiveCash: money ]
2.
3.  [r2] cashiers receiveCash: money ImpliesBefore [
4.          I quantityReply pump I
5.          quantityReply := CoordFuture new.
6.          receiver convertMoneyToFuel: money replyTo: quantityReply.
7.          pump := group selectAParticipantWithRole: 'pumps'
8.                      that: [ :participant I valueVariable: 'isFree' ofParticipant: participant ]
9.          group setVariable: 'isFree' ofParticipant: pump value: false.
10.         group setVariable: 'whichPump' value: pump.
11.         pump prepareFuel: ( quantityReply getValue).
12.         sender takeFuel: pump ]
13.
14. [r3] drivers takeHose: pump ImpliesAfter [ pump dischargeFuel ]
15.
16. [r4] pumps dischargeFuel ImpliesAfter [
17.         group setVariable: 'isFree' ofParticipant: receiver value: true ]
```

Figure 4 Cooperation Specification

A cooperation protocol is specified by a set of implication rules (operators ImpliesBefore and ImpliesAfter) that define *coordination actions* that must be triggered before or after the execution of a message. In the gas station example Fig. 4, four implication rules are defined:

Rule 1 (line 1): The driver invokes his method pay: specifying the amount of money of gas he wants to buy. This triggers a receiveCash: action at the cashier.

Rule 2 (line 3): The cashier receives a receiveCash: message from a driver. This triggers a set of actions. First, the cashier converts the money into an amount of gas (line 6). Then the group selects a free pump (line 7) and generates two messages: one to the selected pump to prepare to give fuel (line 11) and another to the driver to indicate that he can take his gas (line 12). Additionally the state of the pump is changed to indicate it is busy (line 9).

Rule 3 (line 14): The driver invokes its method takeHose indicating he will take gas from a pump. This triggers a dischargeFuel: action to the pump.

Rule 4 (line 16): The pump receives dischargeFuel: from a driver. After the gas is discharged the group coordination state is updated. The state of the pump is set to free.

Coordination Actions. As shown in the above rules, the coordination actions are the following:

- Manipulations of the coordination state (rules 2 and 4). Their value is accessed (resp. assigned) using valueVariable: (resp. setVariable:value:) for the group coordination variables and valueVariable:ofParticipant: (resp. setVariable:value:ofParticipant:) for per-role coordination state variables.

- Evaluation of participant state-predicates [Papa96a]: state predicates are used to check conditions based on internal participant state. These kinds of actions are not used in the gas-station example.

- Selection of a participant: a participant playing a role is selected by sending the message selectAParticipantWithRole: <aRole> that: <predicate> (line 7) to the group. This expression returns non-deterministically a participant playing the role <role> satisfying the condition <predicate>.

- Sending an *asynchronous message* to a participant: By default messages are sent asynchronously to participants (lines 11 and 12). If the receiver represents a role the message is multicasted to each object playing that role.

- Sending a *synchronous recursive message* to a participant: As in Actalk [Briot96a] where an active object may send a synchronous message to itself by using the pseudo-variable self. In ColaS the pseudo variable receiver is used to send a *synchronous message* to the receiver of the message triggering the rule (line 6).

4.4.2 Multi-Action Synchronizations

While the cooperation part of the group defines the cooperation protocol, multi-action synchronizations define constraints on how these cooperation actions occur. When a participant wants to treat a message the group verifies if synchronisation rules apply to this message. Depending on the rule semantics and the value of the conditions associated with the rules, messages are ignored or delayed. Because of the non-determinism in which participant actions may occur in the concurrent system, multi-action synchronisation constraints are necessary to ensure properties such as: (1) mutual exclusion, (2) temporal ordering and (3) atomicity of invocations processed by the group.

In CoLaS these three types of synchronizations are specified by combining rules using the operators Ignore, Disable and Atomic.

- Invocation exclusions are specified using Ignore and Disable operators. They ensure that if a certain *synchronisation condition* is not satisfied a message is ignored (i.e. not processed) or delayed. In Fig. 5 line 1 the variable isFree is used in a Disable rule to control exclusion of receiveCash: invocations from drivers when all pumps are busy.

- Temporal ordering is based on the past invocation history. The combination of coordination state variables keeping coordination historical information and Disable based rules allow one to express that invocations occur at the right time.

- Atomic based rules ensure the indivisible execution of messages in multiple objects. While the synchronisation condition is not satisfied and not all the messages in the atomic rule are ready to be processed, those message are delayed.

```
1.    [r5] cashiers receiveCash: money Disable: [
2.         | aParticipant |
3.         aParticipant := group selectAParticipantWithRole: 'pumps'
4.                        that: [:participant | group valueVariable: 'isFree'
5.                                            ofParticipant: participant ].
6.         (aParticipant isNil) ]
```

Figure 5 Multi-Action Synchronisations

Synchronisation Conditions. Inspired by [Bloo79a] CoLaS synchronisation conditions refer to the following information. Note that they are basically state queries whereas coordination actions in the cooperation protocol are state queries and changes (message sending and coordination variable assignment).

- the invoked message (its arguments, its sender, its receiver) accessed using the predefined variables msg, arguments, sender, and receiver lines (6,12,17 Fig. 4).

- the coordination state of the group and the coordination state of each participant as shown in coordination actions description section (line 4 Fig. 5).

- the keyword true is used to specify rules without conditions.

- the current time in the system: Time information is used to determine the relative order of invoked messages in participants. The current value of the time is obtained by sending the message now to the group (i.e. a centralized notion of time).

- historical information: historical information concerns information about whether a given action has occurred or not. This information differs from synchronisation state information in that it refers to actions that are already completed, as opposed to those still in progress. Historical information are stored using group and/ or per-role coordination variables. In Fig. 4 line 9 the per-role variable isFree is used to identify pumps already assigned to pump fuel.

4.4.3 Proactive Behaviour

Until now the coordination of the system has been purely reactive. *Coordination Actions* are done in response to the treatment of a message. But they cannot be initiated on their own. To introduce proactive behaviour [Andr96b] CoLaS supports proactions that ensure that certain Coordination actions are carried out by the group at a certain time, assuming that a certain coordination condition holds at that time. Two kinds of proactions are specified by the operators Once and Always. Once ensures that proactions are executed only one time when the condition is satisfied. Always ensures that the proactions are executed each time the condition is satisfied. The evaluation of the conditions is done periodically by the group.

4.5 Participants: Creation and Enrollment in Groups

After having specified a group we present how active objects are created and then how they join the groups.

```
1.   | drivers cashier pumps |
2.   drivers:= OrderedCollection with: (CarDriver new name: 'Dr1')
3.                           with: (CarDriver new name: 'Dr2')
4.                           with: (CarDriver new name: 'Dr3').
5.   cashier := Cashier new.
6.   pumps := OrderedCollection with: (Pump new name: 'P1') with: (Pump new name: 'P2').
7.
8.   gasStation addParticipants: drivers withRole: 'drivers'.
9.   gasStation addParticipant: cashier withRole: 'cashiers'.
10.  gasStation addParticipants: pumps withRole: 'pumps'.
```

Figure 6 Creation of participants and enrollment

Creation. In CoLaS active object classes are subclasses of the class ActiveObject. This special class manages transparently to programmers all aspects related with the internal activity of objects and their interaction with a group. Car drivers, cashiers and pumps are represented by classes Driver, Cashier, and Pump. Instances of these classes are created in lines 2, 5 and 6 in Fig. 6.

Enrollment. Active objects participate in a groups by playing a given role. An active object can join a group at any time by sending a message addParticipants:withRole: to a group. To enrol an object have to respect some interface obligations associated with the role. These obligations guarantee to the group the capacity of the object to play a such role in the cooperation enforced inside the group. They are verified during the enrollment process.

5 Dynamic Aspects

CoLaS supports three types of dynamic coordination changes: (1) new participants can *join or leave* the group at any time (as shown in Fig. 7), (2) new groups can be *created and destroyed* at any time, and (3) the *coordination behaviour* can be changed by adding and removing rules to the group (lines 1, 3, and 8 Fig. 8).

```
1.    (p := pumps withName: 'P1' ) outOfOrder.
2.    gasStation removeParticipant: p.
3.
4.    gasStation addParticipant: (Driver new withName: 'Dr4') withRole: 'drivers'.
```
Figure 7 Dynamic addition and removal of participants

New Members Joining The Group. As shown below new participants can join or leave a group at any time. When a pump malfunctions, drivers should not use it any more, so it is removed from the group (line 2 Fig. 7). Line 4 shows how a new driver is added to the group. Both operations are done transparently to the group without modifying the coordination behaviour.

Coordination behaviour changes-Managing Races. The rules 1, 2 and the rules 3,4 (Fig. 4) form two sets of cooperation actions. The first group handles the payment of the gas, and the notification and preparation of drivers and pumps. The second group the pumping of the fuel. Drivers can decide when they want to pay, and when they want to take their gas. In this solution it is possible that a driver pays before another, but that the other takes the hose before, thus getting the amount of gas purchased by the driver. In Fig. 8 we modify dynamically the coordination state and policies to avoid this race condition. To prevent it we define a new per-role variable called whoPayed in which we store the identification of the driver authorized to serve gas from that pump rule 5 (line 6). We include a Ignore synchronization rule (line 8) to ignore dischargeFuel invocations coming from drivers not authorized to take gas from that pump.

```
1.    gasStation defineParticipantVariable: 'whoPayed' forRole: 'pumps' initialValue: nil.
2.
3.    [r6] cashiers receiveCash: money ImpliesAfter[
4.        | pump |
5.        pump := group valueVariable:'whichPump'.
6.        group setVariable: 'whoPayed' ofParticipant: pump value: sender ]
7.
8.    [r7] pumps dischargeFuel
9.        Ignore: [
10.       | whoPayed |
11.       whoPayed := group valueVariable: 'whoPayed' ofParticipant: receiver.
```
Figure 8 Managing Races

6   Illustrating Proactive Behaviour - The Electronic Vote

Now we illustrate how CoLaS supports fairness in the Electronic Vote example proposed by [Mins97a]. With this example we show how proactive behavior is used in CoLaS to solve a coordination problem.

Problem Description. Assume that there is a specific issue on which an open group of participants is asked to vote. Every participant in the group can initiate a vote on any issue he chooses. Each voter *may* actually vote by sending a result of his vote back to the initiator. The system must guarantee that the vote is fair: (1) a participant can vote at most once, and only within the time period allotted for this vote, (2) the counting is done correctly, and (3) the result of the vote is sent to all the participants after the deadline expiration.

Coordination Specification. In the electronic vote example Fig. 9, four rules define the coordination: rules 1 and 2 define cooperation rules, rule 3 a multi-action synchronization rule, and rule 4 a proaction rule.

```
1.    | adminVote |
2.
3.    adminVote := CoordinationGroup new name: 'electronic-voting'.
4.    adminVote defineRoles: #('voters').
5.    adminVote defineVariables: #('deadline' 'numYes' 'numNot') initialValues: #(0 0 0).
6.    adminVote defineParticipantVariable: 'hasVoted' forRole: 'voters' initialValue: false.
7.    adminVote defineInterface: #('startVote:deadline:' ' voteOn:initiator:'
8.                                 'opinion:replyTo:' 'resultOf:' 'sendFinalResult:')
9.              forRole: 'voters'.
10.
11.   [r1] voters startVote: issue deadline: aDeadline ImpliesAfter: [
12.        group setVariable: 'deadline' value: aDeadline.
13.        voters voteOn: issue initiator: receiver ]
14.
15.   [r2] voters resultOf: vote ImpliesAfter: [
16.        (vote = 'Yes' )
17.              ifTrue: [ group incrVariable: 'numYes']
18.              ifFalse: [ group incrVariable: 'numNot'].
19.        group setVariable: 'hasVoted' ofParticipant: sender value: true. ]
20.
21.   [r3] voters resultOf: vote Ignore: [
22.        (group valueVariable: 'deadline' < Time now )
23.              or: [ group valueVariable: 'hasVoted' ofParticipant: sender]]
24.
25.   [r4] (Time now > (group valueVariable: 'deadline')) Once: [
26.              ((group valueVariable: 'numYes') >= (group valueVariable: 'numNot'))
27.                    ifTrue: [ voters sendFinalResult: 'Yes' ]
28.                    ifFalse: [ voters sendFinalResult: 'Not' ]]
```

Figure 9 Electronic Voting

Rule 1 (line 9): A voter initializes a vote by invoking his method startVote:deadline: and fixes a deadline. This triggers a multicasted message voteOn:initiator: to all members of the group by passing the initiator of the vote.

Rule 2 (line 19): When the vote initiator receives the votes of the group members he counts them. Positive and negative votes are counted using the global coordination variables NumYes and NumNot. The participant who voted is marked as "has voted" (the variable whoVoted associated with each voter is set to true).

Rule 3 (line 25): Results coming from voters marked as "has voted", or coming after deadline expiration are ignored by the initiator of the vote.

Rule 4 (line 26): Once the deadline has expired the system calculates and sends the result of the vote to all the participants.

As votes that arrived too late and votes sent twice by the same voter should not be counted they are ignored as shown in the rule 3 using the Ignore operator. The Proaction Once rule (rule 4) is used to send the final result of the vote once the deadline of the vote expires. Note that the presented solution does not support the confidentiality of the vote as in [Mins97a]. This situation is not linked to the CoLaS model but is just due to the way this example is expressed. To support vote confidentiality, the result of the vote should be returned to a new object dedicated to this task instead of the initiator.

7 Evaluation of the CoLaS Model

We now evaluate how CoLaS answers the problems and requirements we identified in Section 2. CoLaS evaluates positively for the following properties:

- *Separation of Concerns:* The coordination is not hard-wired any more into the co-ordinated objects. The coordination and computational aspects are specified separately in distinct entities: groups and participants.

- *Enforcing Encapsulation:* The coordination does not refer to the internals of co-ordinated objects. It is only expressed using the interface of the coordinated objects. Moreover, a group encapsulates the coordination information (state, behaviour) in a single and identifiable entity.

- *Multi Object Coordination Abstraction:* The coordination is not limited to two objects but to a group of objects. Moreover, the coordination specifies abstractly the different behaviour of the participants in terms of roles and their respective interfaces. Roles allows one to specify the coordination behaviour independently of the effective participant number. Thus roles specify *intentionally* the behaviour of a set of objects.

- *High-Level Abstraction:* The programmer no longer focuses on how to do the co-ordination but on how to express it. All the low-level operations concerning the coordination are managed by CoLaS. For example programmers do not lock or unlock participants to guarantee their consistency. The group protects participant states from third-party accesses by enforcing automatic locking policies.

- *Dynamic Evolution of Coordination:* The coordination behaviour specification is not rigid any more. CoLaS supports dynamic coordination changes in three distinct aspects: (1) coordination behaviour can be changed dynamically by adding/removing new rules, (2) new coordination groups can be created and destroyed at any time, and (3) new participants can join or leave the group at any time without disturbing other participants.

- *Coordination Specification:* Coordination is expressed declaratively in CoLaS by using rules. Coordination rules are specified by users that incrementally included them into groups. Rules are specified independently of the coordinated entities.

In the current state of CoLaS the following aspects are not supported:

- *Composability of Coordination:* Existing coordination patterns cannot be combined into new ones.

- *Formal Properties:* We do not have yet a formal model of CoLaS that we can use to formally validate properties of the coordination layer.

- *Incremental Definition of Groups.*

CoLaS a Language Independent Model. CoLaS is independent of any language. It is only based on the control of message passing. That's why it can be implemented in languages that provides such a functionality like CLOS, MetaAxa (a reflective extension of Java) or OpenC++ or using code instrumentation for trapping the messages.

8 Related Work and Conclusions

CoLaS. In this paper we introduced the CoLaS coordination model and its implementation in Smalltalk that supports coordination of active objects in concurrent object-oriented systems. CoLaS offers a high-level construct called Coordination Group that specifies and *enforces* the coordination of collaborating active objects by means of rules. Our approach mainly differs from similar approaches in that: (1) the cooperation is specified and enforced within the group; (2) the coordination state includes per-role information necessary to realize coordination; (3) the coordination includes the enforcement of permanent actions depending on the coordination state; (4) the state of participants is taken in account in the coordination; and (5) we support dynamic evolution of the coordination aspect: objects can join and leave the group at any time, coordination rules can be added and removed on the fly, and new groups can be created at run-time.

Related Work. Traditionally the coordination layer of concurrent object-oriented systems is developed using concurrent object-oriented languages. These languages provide only limited support for the specification of an abstraction of the coordination. In the last few years, a new set of so-called *coordination languages*: Linda [Gele92a], Gamma [Bana95a], Manifold [Arba96b], ActorSpace [Agha93c], Objective Linda [Kiel96a] to cite a few, have been developed to support the construction of coordination layers in software system. Due to space limitation we limit ourselves the approaches that support object-oriented concurrent programming and we focus on different comparisons than the ones we already made in Section 2.

In ObjectiveLinda [Kiel96a] objects are *aware* of the existence of a virtual shared space to which they must communicate. The coordination is not *transparent* to the coordinated objects. The same situation occurs with ACT [Aksit94a] contrary to CoLaS and [Frol93a, Mukh95a, Mins97a, Duca98c]. In CoLaS as in most of the approaches [Frol93a, Aksit94a, Mukh95a, Andr96b, Mins97a, Duca98c] the coordination is specified and encapsulated independently of the representation of the entities they coordinate. Concerning other coordination properties, CoLaS is a hybrid model (as in [Frol93a, Aksi92a, Mukh95a, Mins97a]), the coordination is achieved through the cooperation of both objects and a coordinator agent.

Groups behaviour not only constrains the treatment of messages as in [Frol93a, Aksi92a] but also enforces coordinated actions on participants. Such enforcements are done by reacting to certain messages or by *initiating* actions depending on the state of the coordination. In Moses [Mins97a] coordination actions can be enforced too but the actions only affect the receiver of the message (i.e. forward the message once it is received and modify the control state of the receiver). CoLaS coordination actions can be applied to any group participant. Moreover, CoLaS coordination rules may refer to different coordination information including participant states via state predicates. In Moses, coordination policies refer only to the local control state of object who has received the message, and in [Frol93a] they refer only to the state of the Synchronizer.

One the most important aspect of CoLaS is its support for dynamic evolution of the coordination. A group is a complete *dynamic* entity that can be created and destroyed at any time, and in which coordination rules can be added and removed, and participants can join or leave the group at any time. Approaches like [Frol93a, Aksi92a, Mins97a] do not manage the full dynamicity of the coordination.

Acknowledgment. The authors would like to thanks Oscar Nierstrasz, Tamar Richner, Serge Demeyer and the anonymous reviewers for their valuable comments.

References

[Agha93c] G. Agha and C. J. Callsen, ActorSpace: An Open Distributed Programming Paradigm, *Proc.4th ACM Conference on Principles and Practice of Parallel Programming, ACM SIGPLAN Notices*, vol. 28, no. 7, 1993, pp. 23-323.

[Aksi92a] M. Aksit and L. Bergmans, Obstacles in Object-Oriented Software Development, *OOPSLA '92, ACM SIGPLAN Notices*, vol. 27, no. 10, Oct. 1992, pp. 341-358.

[Aksi94a] M. Aksit, K. Wakita, J. Bosch, L. Bergmans and A. Yonezawa, Abstracting Object Interactions Using Composition Filters, LNCS 791, 1994, pp. 152-184.

[Alle94c] R. Allen and D. Garlan, Formalizing Architectural Connection, *ICSE'94*, May 1994.

[Andr96b] J.-M. Andreoli, S. Freeman and R. Pareschi, The Coordination Language Facility: Coordination of Distributed Objects, *TAPOS*, vol. 2, no. 2, 1996, pp. 635-667.

[Arba96b] F. Arbab, The IWIM Model for Coordination of Concurrent Activities, *COORDINATION'96*, LNCS 1061, Springer-Verlag, 1996, pp. 34-55.

[Bana95a] J.-P. Banâtre and Daniel Le Métayer, Gamma and the Chemical Reaction Model, *Coordination'95 Workshop*, IC Press, Londres, 1995.

[Bloo79a] T. Bloom, Evaluating Synchronization Mechanisms, *Proceedings of the Seventh Symposium on Operating Systems Principles*, 1979, pp. 24-32.

[Brio96a] J.-P. Briot, An Experiment in Classification and Specialization of Synchronization Schemes, *LNCS*, vol. 1049, Springer-Verlag, 1996, pp. 227-249.

[Duca98c] S. Ducasse and M. Guenter, Coordination of Active Objects by Means of Explicit Connectors, *DEXA workshops*, IEEE Computer Society Press, pp. 572-577.

[Frol93a] S. Frolund and G. Agha, A Language Framework for Multi-Object Coordination, *ECOOP'93*, LNCS 707, Springer-Verlag, July 1993, pp. 346-360.

[Gele92a] D. Gelernter and N. Carriero, Coordination Languages and their significance, *CACM*, vol. 35, no. 2, February 1992.

[Helm85a] D. Helmbold and D. Luckman. Debugging Ada Tasking Programs, *IEEE Software* vol. 2, no 2, March 1985, pp. 47-57.

[Kiel96a] T. Kielmann, Designing a Coordination Model for Open Systems,*COORDINATION'96*, LNCS 1061, Springer-Verlag, 1996, pp. 267-284.

[Lea96a] D. Lea, *Concurrent Programming in Java — Design principles and Patterns*, Addison-Wesley, 1996.

[Lope97a] C.V.Lopez and G. Kiczales, "D: A Language Framework for Distributed Programming", Tech. Rep. TR SPL97-010P9710047, Xerox Parc., 1997.

[Mins97a] N. Minsky and V. Ungureanu, Regulated Coordination in Open Distributed Systems,*COORDINATION'97*, LNCS 1282, Springer-Verlag, 1997, pp. 81-97.

[Mukh95a] M. Mukherji and D. Kafura, *Specification of Multi-Object Coordination Schemes Using Coordinating Environments R Draft*, Virgina Tech, 1995.

[Papa96a] M. Papathomas, ATOM: An Active object model for enhancing reuse in the development of concurrent software, RR 963-I-LSR-2, IMAG-LSR, Grenoble-France, 1996.

Introducing Connections Into Classes With Static Meta-Programming

Uwe Aßmann   Andreas Ludwig

Institut für Programmstrukturen und Datenorganisation
Universität Karlsruhe
Postfach 6980, Zirkel 2, 76128 Karlsruhe, Germany
fax:+49/721/30047, tel:+49/721/608-6088

Abstract. Connections can be inserted into classes transparently. Based on an open language with a static meta-object protocol, meta-operators can be constructed that work as connectors, mixing communication code into classes. Thereby, connectors become standard methods in the open language; connections are initiated by standard method calls, and connecting becomes a program transformation. This method paves the way for libraries of connectors which are easy to program, easy to understand, and easy to extend. Equipped with simple drivers, connectors become file-to-file transformation tools. Since connectors can be programmed in variants, architectures of large systems can be configured with the standard software production tooling.

1 Introduction

In software construction, it has become popular to separate architectural from application-specific aspects. Software engineers hope that both aspects can be exchanged independently of each other, improving reuse of components in different architectures and reuse of architecture with different components.

For this separation of aspects, *architectural description languages (ADL)* have been developed. Systems based on such languages provide tailored programming environments in which architectures are specified as a hierarchy of *components* [13] [2] [16] [11] [12]. Components are sets of classes or modules and provide abstract interfaces expressed in *ports*. Ports describe gates in and out of components through which data items flow. *Connectors* link the ports of different components together describing the communication. From those connector specifications, code can be generated so that applications consist of hand-written component code and generated architectural code. However, most systems only support fixed communication styles with a restricted set of connectors. This has begun to change only recently [17][1].

[8] extends this approach to *user-programmable connectors*. In the connector language FLO, connectors can be described in a lisp-like syntax enriched with some special programming constructs. From those specifications, the connector compiler can generate connection code. While this approach works well a user has to learn a new programming language for connectors. Instead it would be

advantageous to follow a library-based approach: if connectors were operators in a library for a standard programming language users would quickly understand how to write connectors. Since libraries are extensible per se it would be very easy to add new connectors to the system.

In this paper, we demonstrate how to program such a connector library with an open language that provides a meta-object protocol. In such a language, connectors become simple meta-programs extending classes and methods with architectural code [3]. As an example, an event-based connector is presented, an *observifier*, which substitutes a procedure call with an event-based communication, changing its connected classes transparently. The connector is implemented with OpenJava [18] and generates ordinary Java code (*static meta-programming*). In this setting, components correspond to sets of Java classes. Ports correspond to ordinary Java method calls, and connectors are meta-operators that replace calls by other communication mechanisms. Hence connector applications are program transformations, generating new versions of the software and specializing the components to specific communication styles.

Meta-programming connectors can modify components during their application. Current architectural systems and connector languages are only able to generate glue code between components, but leave components untouched during connection; this limits the range of reuse contexts [6]. Our approach enables *grey-box reuse*, i.e. a reuse that modifies components automatically according to the requirements of the reuse context. Additionally, since in our approach method calls play the role of ports existing legacy systems can be regarded as components and can be connected easily to other components.

Naturally, such connectors can be collected in libraries and we outline the structure of a library of connectors and composition operators, ℂ𝕠𝕞𝕡𝕠𝕤𝕥 [1], which is currently under development. Since ℂ𝕠𝕞𝕡𝕠𝕤𝕥 connectors are standard Java programs inheritance, code reuse, and factoring of common code into super classes can be used to extend them. ℂ𝕠𝕞𝕡𝕠𝕤𝕥 enables a system construction method which is based on composition. ℂ𝕠𝕞𝕡𝕠𝕤𝕥 operators and connectors may be called as programs from the shell which compose the final system from the basic components. Standard mechanisms to select variants of connectors help to configure the final communication and control flow architecture of the system. We believe that global system configurations and larger architectures can easily be specified with this approach.

Before we present the example connector *observifier*, we introduce the open language OpenJava. Then system construction with ℂ𝕠𝕞𝕡𝕠𝕤𝕥 is exemplified, showing how connectors can be invoked from a shell and exchanged by variant selection. Lastly, we outline the basic structure of the connector and composition library ℂ𝕠𝕞𝕡𝕠𝕤𝕥.

---

[1] ℂ𝕠𝕞𝕡𝕠𝕤𝕥 is a COMPOsition sySTem for Java classes.

2 The open language OpenJava

The OpenJava system is a Java preprocessor supporting a meta-object protocol. Calls to this protocol are resolved statically. In essence the protocol offers the abstract syntax tree to the user, and the meta-programs transform the abstract syntax tree of the program. Originally, OpenJava has been designed to develop Java language extensions, and the distribution contains extension examples, e.g. how to extend Java with templates. Language extension in OpenJava works as follows:

1. OpenJava allows the user to add new keywords to the language, i.e. to make small extensions to the grammar of the parser (e.g. the keyword *template*).
2. If the OpenJava compiler finds these keywords in a program, it calls a meta-program which handles the keyword. This meta-program overrides a method of a standard OpenJava compiler class and transforms one or more nodes in the abstract syntax tree to introduce the semantics of the keyword into the program. This process is repeated until the whole program has been investigated.
3. Finally, the OpenJava compiler pretty-prints the abstract syntax tree to an ordinary Java file or generates byte code.

In our case, the language extension facilities of OpenJava are not used. Instead we will only exploit the meta-programming interface for implementing the connector library COMPOST.

3 Applying a COMPOST connector

In our approach, connectors are program transformers which are implemented as meta-programming methods. Connector applications are program transformations, generating new versions of the software and configuring the components. This yields a system construction method in which connectors are operators composing the final system from the components. In the following, we give an overview how a COMPOST connector works.

Initialization phase First, all classes which should be connected must be determined. Either they are looked up in an existing abstract syntax tree or read from file.

Selection phase Then ports have to be identified where the connector connects classes. Since in our case ports are calls, calls in Java methods have to be identified which should be substituted. This can be supported by an interactive wizard.

Transformation phase This phase applies the selected connectors, transforming the classes and resulting in a modified abstract syntax tree. This is repeated until all ports are connected.

Emitting phase Finally, the abstract syntax tree is traversed by the standard OpenJava pretty printer to emit the final Java source code. The original classes and their modified versions should be put under version control.

3.1 The example: Towers of Hanoi

The following presents a simple example, attaching an event-based connection
to a procedure call port. The program solves Towers of Hanoi, recursively calling
itself with smaller problem size. The program prints a message about each move
with the method display. In terms of software architecture, Hanoi.compute
can be considered as a component which is connected to Hanoi.display by
a procedure call connector (Figure 1). Our example shows how the connector
observifier replaces this connection by an event-based connection.

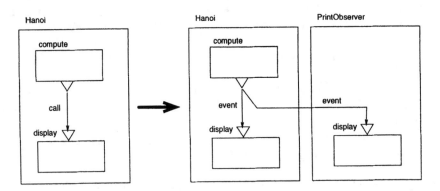

Fig. 1. Exchanging the method call to an event-based communication. A second observer listens to the events.

```java
public class Hanoi extends java.util.Observable implements java.util.Observer {

    public Hanoi() {}

    protected void compute(int n, String s, String t, String h) {
        if (n > 1) {
            compute(n - 1, s, h, t);
        }
        display(s, t);
        if (n > 1) {
            compute(n - 1, h, t, s);
        }
    }

    public void display( String s, String t ) {
        System.out.println(s + "␣-->␣" + t);
    }

    public static void main(String[] a) {
        Hanoi h = new Hanoi();
        h.compute(n, "Source", "Target", "Auxiliary");
    }
}
```

After applying the connector *observifier* from COMPOST, the program contains
the following modifications (underlined in the next listing).

1. In procedure `compute`, the call to `display` is exchanged to a notification of all listening observers.

2. These observers are attached to the `Hanoi` class in the constructor of the `Hanoi` class; one of them is `Hanoi` itself, another one is an object `PrintObserver` that prints some messages (we omit the class since it is trivial).

3. `compute` activates `display` with an event object containing all parameters of the old call. To this end, there is a new procedure `update` which acts as an observer: it receives the event, unpacks the parameters from the event object, and calls `display` via a procedure call.

```
public class Hanoi extends java.util.Observable implements java.util.Observer {

    public Hanoi() {
        addObserver(new PrintObserver());
        addObserver(this);
    }

    protected void compute(int n, String s, String t, String h) {
        if (n > 1) {
            compute(n−1, s, h, t);
        }
        setChanged();
        notifyObservers(new displayPack(s, t));
        if (n > 1) {
            compute(n−1, h, t, s);
        }
    }

    public void display(String s, String t) {
        System.out.println(s + "␣-->␣" + t);
    }

    public static void main(String[] a) {
        Hanoi h = new Hanoi();
        h.compute(n, "Source", "Target", "Auxiliary");
    }

    public void update(java.util.Observable o, Object arg) {
        this.display(((displayPack)arg).s, ((displayPack)arg).t);
        return;
    }
}
```

The output of the modified program is similar to the output of the original program. In addition, the listener procedure from `PrintObserver` prints a message for each move.

On the first sight, it seems awkward to substitute a call in a sequential program with an event-based communication. However, event communication allows that multiple observer procedures can be attached dynamically to the call, performing additional actions. For instance, a visualization algorithm may be attached that starts an incremental display of a data structure. Since this is transparent to the code, systems can be extended and adapted flexibly.

3.2 How the observification works

The observifier is a method which replaces a call to a event-signaling call sequence. On top of the meta-programming interface of OpenJava, the observifier becomes a simple routine with the following steps:

1. The interface of Hanoi is extended to implements the interface Observable as well as the interface Observer from JDK-1.0 (not shown here).[2]
2. The call is removed from its including statement list.
3. A call to a setChanged is inserted, signaling that an event has occured in the subject.
4. Since event communication in Java transfers single objects, the parameters of a call to method display have to be tupled into an event object. Hence another COMPOST operator *packify* creates a new class displayPack whose objects carry the attributes of such a call (see section 3.3).
5. A call to notifyObservers from java.util.Observable is inserted. This call transfers the event object and control to all observing objects. Its parameter is a new object of the pack class.
6. The packifier supports another method unpackify that creates statements to unpack the arguments from the event object. This operator is used to insert the unpacking of parameters into the update method of the observer.

```
package compost.connectors;

import openjava.ptree.*;
import openjava.util.*;
import openjava.*;
import compost.convenience.Packifier;
import compost.convenience.Find;


public class Observifier {

    /** Replace a call by an event-based communication. */

    public static ClassDeclaration observify(ClassDeclaration subject,
        StatementList statementList, int position, ClassDeclaration observer)
        throws PtreeException {

        // First of all, install the observation interface.
        createObservationInterface(subject, observer);

        // Remove the old method call
        MethodCall methodCall = (MethodCall)
            ((ExpressionStatement)statementList.elementAt(position)).getExpression();
        statementList.removeElementAt(position);
        Expression caller = methodCall.getExpression();
        statementList.insertElementAt(PartialParser.makeStatement("setChanged();"), position++);

        // Create a public packer class storing all arguments for observer.update().
        MethodDeclaration declaration = Find.findMethodDeclaration(observer,
            methodCall.getName().toString());
        ParameterList parameterList = declaration.getParameters();
        String packClassName = methodCall.getName().toString() + "Pack";
        ClassDeclaration packClass = Packifier.packify(packClassName, parameterList);

        // Create the notification call with the arguments of the original method call.
```

---

[2] The example uses the event model of the JDK-1.0. It would be no problem to write a connector for another event model, e.g. Java Beans.

```
  // Use the pack-method to put all arguments into an object vector.
  statementList.insertElementAt(
      new ExpressionStatement(
          new MethodCall(
              new Identifier("notifyObservers"),
              new ExpressionList(
                  new ConstructExpression(
                      new ClassType(new Identifier(packClassName)),
                      methodCall.getArguments()))))),
      position++);

  // Now insert the method call in observer.update().
  declaration = Find.findMethodDeclaration(observer, "update");
  declaration.getBody().insertElementAt(
      new ExpressionStatement(Packifier.unpackify(
          new Identifier(packClassName),
          declaration.getParameters().elementAt(1).getVariable(),
          methodCall.getName(),
          parameterList)),
      0);
  return packClass;
}

/** Create an attachment of an observer as first statement of the constructor. */
public static void createAttachmentInConstructor(ClassDeclaration subject,
    String insertString) throws PtreeException {

  ConstructorDeclaration declaration = Find.findConstructorDeclaration(
      subject, subject.getName().toString());
  declaration.getBody().insertElementAt(
      PartialParser.makeStatement("addObserver(" + insertString + ");"), 0);
}

}
```

3.3 Other composition operators: the packifier

The packifier is a support class in ComPost providing two simple composition operations. Its first method constructs a new class out of a parameter list, in which all parameters are attributes (the *pack class*). The pack class contains a constructor which packs a parameter list into an object. We call this process *packifying* a parameter list.

Second, an *unpackification* operation is supported. This meta-operation receives an object of a pack class and unpacks its attributes parameters back into a call.

```
package compost.convenience;

import openjava.ptree.*;
import openjava.util.*;
import openjava.*;

public class Packifier {

  public static ClassDeclaration packify(String className, ParameterList parameters) {

    // Turn parameter list into member list.
    MemberDeclarationList memberList = new MemberDeclarationList();
    for (ParameterList parList = parameters; ¬parList.isEmpty(); parList = parList.getRest()) {
      Parameter parameter = parList.getFirst();
      memberList.addElement(new FieldDeclaration(modifierlist,
          parameter.getTypeSpecifier(), parameter.getVariable(), null));
    }
```

```
// Add a constructor.
StatementList statements = new StatementList();
ConstructorDeclaration constructor = new ConstructorDeclaration(
    new ModifierList(new Modifier(Modifier.PUBLIC)),
    new Identifier(className), parameters, null, statement);

// Create the initialization statements.
for (ParameterList parList = parameters; ¬parList.isEmpty(); parList = parList.getRest()) {
    parameter = parList.getFirst();
    statements.addElement(new ExpressionStatement(
        new AssignmentExpression(
            new FieldAccess(
                new SpecialName(SpecialName.THIS),
                parameter.getVariable()),
            AssignmentExpression.EQUALS,
            new QualifiedName(parameter.getVariable()))));
}
memberList.addElement(constructor);

return new ClassDeclaration(
    new ModifierList(new Modifier(Modifier.PUBLIC)),
    new Identifier(className),
    new ClassType(new Identifier("Object")),
    new ClassTypeList(),
    memberList);
}

public static MethodCall unpackify(Identifier className, Identifier objectName,
    Identifier methodName, ParameterList parameters) {

    ExpressionList arguments = new ExpressionList();
    for (; ¬parameters.isEmpty(); parameters = parameters.getRest()) {
        arguments.addElement(
            new FieldAccess(
                new CastExpression(
                    new TypeSpecifier(new ClassType(className)),
                    new QualifiedName(objectName)),
                parameters.getFirst().getVariable()));
    }
    return new MethodCall(new SpecialName(SpecialName.THIS), methodName, arguments);
}
}
```

Of course, this design has still the disadvantage that for every packified call a new pack class is generated. This could be simplified such that a single pack class is generated for all calls that have the same signature. Then the library should maintain a table of pack classes which can be investigated whether a pack class with the right signature exist. However, since the packifier is a standard Java class, such improvements are rather simple. We expect that such design choices will lead to different designs of composition operators and libraries.

3.4 A simple driver

There are several alternatives how to invoke COMPOST connectors and composition operators. First, connectors could be called in OpenJava programs as standard procedures, using the meta-object protocol as a reflection interface.[3]

---

[3] This seems not to be possible with the current preliminary version of the OpenJava system; the classes have to be read in by a parser. This should be no problem as soon as lookup functions for meta-objects are provided.

Second, new keywords in OpenJava can activate connectors with its standard extension mechanism. In this way, connector languages such as FLO can be easily implemented on top of COMPOST. Third, connectors can be invoked by wizards in an integrated development environment (IDE). Fourth, simple driver programs may be written to start a connector from the shell.

The following listing shows such a driver for the observifier. It can be invoked from the shell with

```
$ java ObservifierMain -s Hanoi -o PrintObserver -c display
```

The driver analyzes its arguments, determining subject class name, the observer class name, and the name of the callee in the call that should be replaced. It reads the source file of the subject and object class and applies the observifier to the call.[4] Then observers are attached: The COMPOST operator `createAttachmentInConstructor` from the `Observifier` class extends the constructor of the subject class (in this case Hanoi) by a statement attaching the observer `PrintObserver` and the subject itself (again Hanoi). Finally the classes are pretty-printed as Java source code.

```java
import java.util.*;
import java.io.*;
import openjava.ptree.*;
import openjava.util.*;
import compost.convenience.*;
import compost.connectors.*;

public class ObservifierMain {

    /* Replace a call by an event connector. */
    public static void main(String[] argv) throws PtreeException {

        ClassDeclaration subject, observer, pack;
        String subjectname, observername, calleename;

        // Process command line
        subjectname = "noname"; observername = "noname"; calleename = "noname";
        for( int i = 0; i < argv.length; i++ ) {
            switch(argv[i].charAt(1)) {
            case 's' : subjectname = argv[++i]; observername = subjectname; break;
            case 'o' : observername = argv[++i]; break;
            case 'c' : calleename = argv[++i]; break;
            // here would be place for analyzing additional arguments to the
            // connector's main program, e.g. for variants of connectors
            }
        }

        // Read the classes
        subject = (ClassDeclaration)FileParsing.readClass("source/" + subjectname + ".java");
        observer = (subjectname ≡ observername) ? subject :
            (ClassDeclaration)FileParsing.readClass("source/" + observername + ".java");

        // Observify call port
        pack = Observifier.observify(subject,
            findCallToReplace(subject, calleename), 1, observer);

        // Add the attachment of the observers to the constructor of the subject
        Observifier.createAttachmentInConstructor(subject, "this");
        Observifier.createAttachmentInConstructor(subject, "new PrintObserver()");
```

---

[4] The replaced call is found by a convenience method `findCallToReplace` which we do not describe here.

```
    // Pretty print the classes
    FileParsing.writeClass(pack);
    FileParsing.writeClass(subject);
    if (subjectname ≠ observername) FileParsing.writeClass(observer);
  }
}
```

4 Integrating software architecture with conventional process and variant management

Connector drivers are file-to-file transformation tools which can be invoked by standard software process managers such as make or odin [7]. Since connectors can be programmed in various forms, specific variants can be selected by tools such as macro preprocessors (e.g. cpp or m4) and version management tools (e.g. rcs). Also the drivers may be parametrized by configuration switches:

```
$ java ObservifierMain -s Hanoi -o PrintObserver -c display -D sequential
$ java ObservifierMain -s Hanoi -o PrintObserver -c display -D thread_parallel
```

Both calls invoke variants of the observifier; the driver interprets the -D flag and invokes the corresponding variant. For instance, the first variant could start observers sequentially; the second variant could create threads for the observers, invoking them in parallel.

In this way, systems based on COMPOST connectors can be configured globally such that the software becomes scalable: the amount of parallelism, variations of structure, tight or loose coupling, all can be configured easily by the standard Unix software process tools. Additionally, the coarse-grain architecture of a system can be completely described by standard specifications, such as make-files. This provides software architecture specifications to the masses.

5 The COMPOST library of meta-operators

When meta-programming connectors are assembled, a library of program transformers results. Here we present an initial structure of such a library: COMPOST will not only contain connectors, but also other composition operators such as wrappers, control flow operators, or refactorings (see Figure 2).

convenience layer This layer directly relies on the meta-object protocol of OpenJava and provides standard functionality for all composition operators (finding and creating meta-objects, packification, file handling, etc.).

connectors Connectors extend application-specific code with communication code, connecting classes. Calls can be substituted by other connections; other connections can be substituted by calls.

control flow A meta-operator of this package determines for its parameters in which way their control flow is organized. For example, a sequential control flow operator may introduce sequential control flow with sequential method calls, whereas a data parallel operator may introduce data parallel threads.

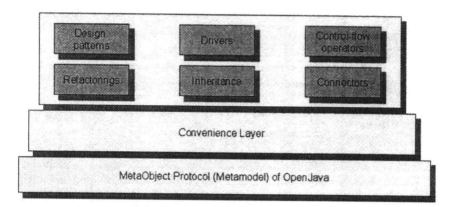

Fig. 2. The structure of the meta-operator library CoMPosT

If the meta-operators have the same interface they can be exchanged transparently.

design pattern operators Design patterns can be seen as transformers of class graphs which can be implementated with meta-programming [19] [10] [9] [3]. Patterns such as *proxy* or *bridge* become simple CoMPosT operators.

refactorings Refactorings are reengineering transformations that preserve program semantics [14] [15]. These transformations have to check semantic preconditions before they can be applied.

inheritance Several kinds of inheritance are well known. In CoMPosT, all of them can be provided as simple meta-operators.

drivers Meta-operators can be called from shell with simple drivers.

We expect that different designs for such operators will lead to a software market in which companies can compete with different designs and implementations of composition libraries.

6   Conclusion

This paper presents a method how to program connectors in an open language. Driven by an example, a connector meta-program is explained that introduces event-based observation into a standard object-oriented program. Since connectors are programmed in a standard programming language, new connectors can easily be developed. Connectors can modify components; this enables grey-box reuse. Since calls play the role of ports, legacy systems can be flexibly embedded. Connectors can be programmed in variants. When they are invoked from within a standard process management environment, architectures of large systems can be configured in a standard software production process.

We thank Daniel Pfeifer for providing the initial implementation of the observifier. A preliminary version of this paper was presented as position paper at [5]. ComPost can be found at [4].

References

1. Robert Allen and David Garlan. A formal basis for architectural connection. *ACM Transactions on Software Engineering and Methodology*, 6(3):213–49, July 1997.

2. M. Alt, U. Aßmann, and H. van Someren. Cosy Compiler Phase Embedding with the CoSy Compiler Model. In P. A. Fritzson, editor, *Compiler Construction (CC)*, volume 786 of *Lecture Notes in Computer Science*, pages 278–293, Heidelberg, April 1994. Springer.

3. Uwe Aßmann. Meta-programming composers in second-generation component systems. In J. Bishop and N. Horspool, editors, *Systems Implementation 2000 - Working Conference IFIP WG 2.4*, Berlin, February 1998. Chapman and Hall.

4. Uwe Aßmann and Andreas Ludwig. Compost home page. http://i44www.info.uni-karlsruhe.de/~assmann/compost.html, February 1999.

5. Uwe Aßmann, Andreas Ludwig, and Daniel Pfeifer. Programming connectors in an open language. In Web-Published Proceedings of Position Papers, WICSA 1, Working IFIP Conference on Software Architecture, IFIP WG 2.9, February 1999.

6. Martin Büchi and Wolfgang Weck. A plea for grey-box components. Technical Report TUCS-TR-122, Turku Centre for Computer Science, Finland, September 5, 1997.

7. Geoffrey M. Clemm. The Odin system. In Jacky Estublier, editor, *Software Configuration Management: Selected Papers of the ICSE SCM-4 and SCM-5 Workshops*, number 1005 in Lecture Notes in Computer Science, pages 241–2262. Springer-Verlag, October 1995.

8. S. Ducasse and T. Richner. Executable Connectors: Towards Reusable Design Elements. In M. Jazayeri and H. Schauer, editors, *Proc. 6th European Software Eng. Conf. (ESEC 97)*, volume 1301 of *Lecture Notes in Computer Science*, pages 483–499. Springer-Verlag, Berlin, 1997.

9. Amnon H. Eden and A. Yehudai. Tricks generate patterns. Technical Report Technical report 324/97, Department of Computer Science, Schriber School of Mathematics, Tel Aviv University, 1997.

10. Gert Florijn, Marco Meijers, and Pieter van Winsen. Tool support for object-oriented patterns. In Mehmet Aksit and Satoshi Matsuoka, editors, *ECOOP'97—Object-Oriented Programming, 11th European Conference*, volume 1241 of *Lecture Notes in Computer Science*, pages 472–495, Jyväskylä, Finland, 9–13 June 1997. Springer.

11. David Garlan, Robert Allen, and John Ockerbloom. Architectural mismatch: why reuse is so hard. *IEEE Software*, 12(6):17–26, November 1995.

12. David C. Luckham, John J. Kenney, Larry M. Augustin, James Vera, D. Bryan, and Walter Mann. Specification and analysis of system architecture using Rapide. *IEEE Transactions on Software Engineering*, 21(4):336–355, April 1995.

13. Jeff Magee, Naranker Dulay, and Jeffrey Kramer. Structuring parallel and distributed programs. In *Proceedings of the International Workshop on Configurable Distributed Systems*, London, March 1992.

14. William F. Opdyke. *Refactoring Object-Oriented Frameworks*. PhD thesis, University of Illinois at Urbana-Champaign, 1992.

15. Benedikt Schulz, Thomas Genßler, Berthold Mohr, and Walter Zimmer. On the computer aided introduction of design patterns into object-oriented systems. In *Proceedings of the 27th TOOLS conference*. IEEE CS Press, 1998.

16. Mary Shaw, Robert DeLine, D.V. Klein, T.L. Ross, D.M. Young, and G Zelesnik. Abstractions for software architecture and tools to support them. *IEEE Transactions on Software Engineering*, pages 314–335, April 1995.

17. Mary Shaw, Robert DeLine, and Gregory Zelesnik. Abstractions and implementations for architectural connections. In *3rd International Conference on Configurable Distribute systems*. IEEE Press, May 1996.

18. Michiaki Tatsubori. OpenJava language manual, version 0.2.3, January 1998. http://www.softlab.is.tsukuba.ac.jp/~mich/openjava/.

19. Walter Zimmer. *Frameworks und Entwurfsmuster*. PhD thesis, Universität Karlsruhe, February 1997.

TRUCE: Agent Coordination Through Concurrent Interpretation of Role-Based Protocols

Wilfred C. Jamison[1] and Douglas Lea[2]

[1] IBM Research Triangle Park, RTP NC 27709, USA
wjamison@us.ibm.com
[2] SUNY Oswego, Oswego NY 13126, USA
dl@cs.oswego.edu

Abstract. Established protocols for coordination are essential for implementing joint-action activities among collaborating software agents. Most existing agents, however, are designed only to support static protocols, limiting their interaction domain to specific sets of agents. We developed an agent collaboration framework for open systems that enables an agent to expand its acquaintance set and to adapt to various coordination protocols dynamically. This is achieved by writing coordination scripts that are interpreted at collaboration time. A script is a protocol specification for coordination. Proper synchronization is implemented via distributed rendezvous points. The concurrent interpretation of the same script constitutes the basic engine for enforcing coordination rules. In this paper, we present and demonstrate the major elements of the TRUCE language.

1 Introduction

The current methodologies for designing interacting agents in a cooperative problem solving (CPS) environment are tight, as most coordination protocols are either incorporated within an agent or fixed by the requirements of an application (In our context, an application is a composition of interacting tasks that needs to be coordinated). This method, however, often results to high coupling and limited flexibility. Thus, applications are more likely to require substantial rewriting when adapting to new collaborations.

Our goal is to develop a collaboration framework that will allow us to design and implement dynamic collaborative agent systems. This framework should meet three requirements over and above the basic requirements of open distributed systems, such as security, reliability, response time, *etc*. These are:

Adaptive Coordination. Agents adapt to varying coordination protocols resulting from working with different groups of agents.

Heterogeneity. Agents work in an open system and therefore interact with different kinds of agents running on different platforms.

Multiple Collaboration. Agents maximize their use by engaging in several collaboration activities simultaneously.

To achieve an adaptive and dynamic agent environment, the coordination logic embedded in an application is extracted, and the corresponding coordination rules are treated as subscribable services. The basic approach is to *separate* the coordination domain from the application domain in which coordination is carried out by special agents called *coordinators*. These coordinators implement higher-level coordination patterns that generalize interactive behaviors.

A major advantage of this approach is given by Gelernter and Carriero who stated that using a separate coordination language leads to portability, which in turn promotes *reusability* [13]. This is as a consequence of the lack of commitment by the coordinators to any base language used in the application programs. A coordination language can be used to link together (or glue) different applications written in different languages.

Coordination can be viewed as a set of coordination rules or *protocols*. Preprogrammed low-level fixed protocols such as TCP/IP do exist. Similarly, higher-level fixed protocols, such as blackboard systems, publish-subscribe systems, fault-tolerant services, and resource negotiation[22], are available. Dynamic coordination, however, implies *customizability* — that is, programmable coordination services that fit the needs of a particular group, and hence, requiring a special form of *protocol* programming. We do need to write coordination protocols, possibly more specialized and specific, that could best satisfy the needs of the problem being solved. Thus, we designed a general-purpose coordination language that will allow us to specify any arbitrary protocol.

TRUCE (Tasks and roles in a unified coordination environment) is a language framework that is currently applied in a bigger coordination system project. This system is called ACACIA (Agency-based Collaboration Architecture for Cooperating Intelligent Agents). TRUCE, however, is designed to be independent of other systems. In the succeeding sections, we present the essential concepts that define the language and provide an example for illustration.

2 Coordination Languages

There already exist a number of coordination languages introduced in this research area. These include languages based on *conversations, tuple-spaces, rules and events, logic systems* and others. Some examples are Linda [12], COOL [3], Finesse [4], CoLa [1] and PoLis [8]. TRUCE, however, is a small and yet powerful scripting language that is designed to support various kinds of multi-party actions and protocols that are necessary for agent coordination in an open system. Its salient properties include the following:

- It simplifies delegation of coordination tasks to *coordinator agents*. These coordination tasks can be developed independently of the functional components of agents.
- It contains a variety of primitive coordination constructs.
- It enables simple expression of coordination constructs that often translate to complex underlying actions.

- It simplifies the task of programming in a heterogeneous environment.
- It provides dynamic capabilities that are useful for dynamic collaboration.

The most significant contribution of the TRUCE language is a script-based coordination programming paradigm that supports dynamic coordination protocols. It also introduces a new coordination mechanism that relies upon the concurrent interpretation of a single script.

3 Collaboration Group

Central to any collaboration framework, and to an open system in general, is the notion of a group (or collaboration group). A collaboration group is a set of possibly heterogeneous agents that are engaged in a cooperative problem solving activity while being governed by a common set of coordination protocols. With the use of proxies (also called coordinators), a collaboration group can be made homogeneous.

A collaboration group is defined by the composition of its members, the problem being solved, and the coordination protocols being used. The protocols do not define a single thread of control – as control is distributed among the group members. This is necessary in an open system which operates asynchronously and in which agents may join and leave a group anytime.

Apart from the basic synchronization machinery, our coordination framework supports the following:

1. engagement in protocols that become known to agents dynamically in the course of their life-cycles;
2. separation of the identity of an agent from its *role(s)* in a protocol, allowing it to assume multiple roles in the same protocol and to engage simultaneously in multiple protocols;
3. accommodation for agents to join and leave collaboration groups and protocols dynamically;
4. encapsulation of coordination support as services whereby subscriptions are established when the support becomes necessary: details of coordination procedures are no longer the concern of the agents; and
5. availability of high-level supervisory capabilities without dependence upon fragile, centralized control mechanisms.

4 Coordination Protocols

Coordination among autonomous entities is easily implemented through the establishment of protocols. *Protocols* are rules or policies known to two or more parties who agree to comply with them. Protocols are created to address the set of dependencies imposed upon a collaborative task. Solutions to different problems mostly require different protocols. Some solutions, however, may use the same patterns of coordination for completely different problems. In such cases, coordination protocols can be shared and reused. We describe a familiar pattern below.

> A master agent sends the same message to a number of slave agents (mostly, by broadcasting). Each slave eventually sends its reply to the master. The master waits until it has collected all replies from the original set of slaves, at which point, it performs some processing on the messages received to come up with a single result.

One possible application that follows this protocol is *bidding* in which the master sends information about a sale item to the slaves. The latter reply with their price bids. After collecting all bids, the master determines the winner with the use of chosen criteria. Another application is *redundant programming*. In this case, the master solves a problem using some methods. To evaluate the quality of its solution, it sends the same problem to a number of slaves that can solve the same problem, but using different methods. It compares its own solution with those returned by the slaves. Having collected them all, the master determines its confidence-level of its own solution.

Some protocols are simple constraints. For example, "Task B cannot proceed without finishing task A." is a constraint imposed upon task B. This example is an instance of *order dependencies*. Another example is "Task C gets its inputs only from task D.". By applying such a constraint, task C becomes *data dependent* on task D. Task D, on the other hand, remains unconstrained. Some constraints are state-based, that is, certain restrictions are imposed upon the possible states of an entity. For example, "Agent A's buffer cannot exceed n items." is a constraint which A must observe. There are other types of dependencies. Interested readers can refer to Crowstron [11].

Some protocols may also come as guarded rules or triggers. These are rules or actions that are triggered whenever a particular condition is satisfied, for example, "When the temperature reaches 100 Farenheit, the boiler must be shut off.". The difference between a constraint and a trigger is that the former *imposes* a restriction, whereas the other *enables* a rule or an activity when certain conditions occur.

An agent may subscribe to a coordination service with different coordination protocols at various times. Since a collaboration group has no single locus of control (that is, each agent has its own thread), the only way that participants can follow an arbitrary protocol is by having a copy of a script that describes such protocol.

5 Concurrent Role-Based Interpretation

Concurrent Role-Based Interpretation constitutes TRUCE's primary mechanism for coordination. A script that describes a coordinated activity is given to all members of a collaboration group. Subsequently, they interpret the script in a concurrent fashion.

Role-based interpretation is a form of *selective* interpretation wherein an interpreter does not have to execute every instruction in the script. The fraction of the script to be interpreted is determined from the interpreter's *view* of the script. This view is defined by the interpreter's role in the overall activity. We explain these concepts in the following sections.

5.1 Roles

In a system of interacting components, Lea and Marlow [18] used roles to describe a *view* of one or more components by providing an *interface* specification of the messages expected. Thus, a role abstracts all other things about the components. In the same way, a role in TRUCE hides various details of an agent who reveals only its capabilities by performing the steps (or instructions) specified for that role. Application agents are individually mapped to a particular role.

Collaboration is about tasks and their coordination. While the completion of these tasks is necessary, the identities of the providing agents are irrelevant to the process. Referencing roles instead of the actual agents, not only hides these information, but is sufficient to describe a collaboration. Such an abstraction enables different providers to play the same role at different times without affecting the overall coordination protocols. Agents may also subcontract their tasks to other agents (including those that are not members of the group). Such a strategy is hidden and unimportant to other roles.

Agents carry out their individual tasks based on the roles assigned to them. Once the *role assignments* (also called *role-binding*) are established, all future references to the agents will occur through their role names. Knowledge about role assignment is hidden from other entities, including the users and other agents.

Roles may be viewed also as a language mechanism for dynamically binding agents to a set of coordination protocols. A role is a profile in terms of expertise, skills and responsibilities. Any agent that fits the profile is a *prospect* for the role. Willing prospects become *candidates*. An agent may fit a number of profiles, suggesting that simultaneous role assignments are possible.

5.2 Role-Based Programming

An instruction in a TRUCE script is called a *step*. A step has two components: the *action* that needs to be executed and a set of *collaborators* that participate in carrying out the action. Every collaborator has a specific role in a given step. Possible roles include the following:

1. *executor* — that initiates the action proactively
2. *receiver* — that receives the target result of the action directly
3. *object* — that is being used or manipulated by the action
4. *observer* — that is not involved at all but can sense and use the results of the action

The semantics of a given step may differ depending on which role the step is being viewed from. For example, let the pseudocode below represent a step:

producer.tell consumer about object X.

In this example, tell is an action used to specify the transmission of a message from a source to a destination. The performer of the action is producer, while the receiver is consumer. The object is X. The semantics of tell from the point of view of the producer can be described as follows:

> The tell action specifies that a message is placed in a packet containing at least the address of the destination, and sent to the destination.

Whereas, the viewpoint of the *consumer* role is given below:

> The tell action specifies that a message is expected to arrive, and therefore the receiver is suspended temporarily to wait for the message. When the packet finally arrives, the actual message is taken out of the packet and stored in a buffer, after which, the receiver resumes.

Thus, an interpreter for a *role-based* script behaves differently, depending on whose viewpoint it is performing the interpretation for.

A step implicitly describes the interaction involved among the collaborators. Therefore, the behavior of each collaborator is described through a sequence of steps. This sequence is what constitutes a protocol. A TRUCE script, also called a *truce*, can be viewed as a protocol specification.

The language is a simple collection of primitive or basic steps. Every such step has an associated set of specifiers or directives. The 15 TRUCE primitive steps are listed in Table 1. A user-defined step can be formulated from existing steps through composition. Optionally, it can be given a unique name. Other names may be introduced within the body of a step. The classification of names include *cast names, rule names, step names, packet names, property names* and *role names*.

A property is akin to a variable in traditional languages. A global property (prefixed by a dollar symbol) is one that can be accessed by all roles. Basic types includes *number, strings, boolean, role, date, time, list, packet*.

Every step has a *context* — a transient environment that consists of all names created within the step. A context also inherits the context of an immediately enclosing step, that is, when the step occurs inside another step. If collision occurs between a recently declared name and an inherited one, the former hides the latter until the current context is destroyed, which happens as soon as the interpretation of the step is completed.

5.3   Role Binding

TRUCE defines an arbitrarily large and unstructured *virtual agent space* with different agents coming from various places. Collaboration groups are formed

Primitive Steps	Description
truce	to declare and define a truce
cast	to declare a named set of roles
packet	to declare and define the format of a packet
protocol	to declare and define a set of event-based rules
set	to assign a value to a property
tell	to send information to another role
wait	to put a role in a waiting state
proceed	to tell a waiting role to resume its execution
retract	to undefine an existing property or rule
recover	to undo the retraction of a retracted name
trigger	to execute a truce, an episode or raise an event signal
step	to declare and define a named sequence of steps
if	to execute conditionally a sequence of steps
echo	to print out text on the standard output
break	to skip the current context

Table 1. TRUCE's Primitive Steps

from this agent space and coordinate themselves by interpreting a collaboration script. Hence, every agent becomes an independent interpreter. A role-based interpreter must assume one of the viewpoints (or role) in the step. It is therefore necessary to specify which agent has which role in every step. To do this, we maintain symbolic names or *ids* to represent every agent. We use these names to specify a collaborator's role in a step. The unique assignment of a symbolic name to an agent is called *role-binding*. Although we can perform role-binding before every step execution (thus allowing us to use different symbolic names every time), such method is not very efficient. Role-binding is done only once, – just before the first step is executed, – giving each collaborator only one symbolic name for the entire script. This symbolic name is used as the collaborator's *rolename*.

At any given step, a specific expertise/skill may be required for some of the roles in that step. The corresponding collaborators of those roles must therefore satisfy, directly or indirectly, the given requirement. In general, the requirements needed by a role, which a collaborator must be able to meet, is the sum of all expertise/skills required in all of the steps where that role appears. Role-binding is also the process of matching up the responsibilities of a role to an actual agent (a collaborator) that can and is willing to take these responsibilities. Furthermore, this binding serves as a *contract* between the collaborator and the collaboration group, obligating the former to fulfill all of its responsibilities. A collaborator may be bound to multiple roles only if it is able to meet the combined requirements of these roles. Roles and collaborators are bound dynamically, which means that roles need not be assigned to the same agent every time.

5.4 Concurrent Interpretation

We have seen the mechanics of role-based interpretation — how the semantics of a step is viewed by the interpreter based its role. However, role-based interpretation alone cannot accomplish the coordination process. In order to achieve the right coordination effect, a step must be interpreted from all of its viewpoints simultaneously, combining its semantics from all views. This process is called *concurrent interpretation*. By doing this, the coordination embedded within a step are extracted and executed properly. Hence, concurrent interpretation is, in effect, the application of coordination protocols. We extend this idea by applying concurrent interpretation to all steps in a script.

The combination of role-based and concurrent interpretation allows a coordination process to work without centralized control. It also avoids both performance and fault-tolerance problems associated with centralized mediation. Because each host has a copy of the complete script, the only communications necessary are those required by the steps. The key point is that *each agent knows exactly when to wait and to interact, and what to expect from other agents*. Since nothing can be assumed about the relative speeds of agents in a distributed environment, *rendezvous* points are used to synchronize agent interaction.

6 Implementation

The current implementation of TRUCE is Java-based along with the ACACIA system. A collaboration group is formed by ACACIA through the creation of proxies or coordinators for each of the participating agents. To drive the collaboration, a *truce* is submitted to the system where roles are also assigned to every agent. Their corresponding coordinators are given a copy of the *truce* and their viewpoints (that is, their roles). The communication between the agents and the coordinators are conducted via μKQML(a subset of KQML [19]). This is implemented using IBM JKQML [17]. These communications may occur anytime during the collaboration. Among the coordinators, the interaction is driven by the concurrent interpretation of the script. The global data space is implemented using Jada [9], a Java-based Linda system. Meanwhile, the overall communication infrastructure is built using iBus [20].

From a user agent's point of view, enabling TRUCE only requires that it speaks KQML and that it knows how to contact with a TRUCE interpreter, or an intermediate system like ACACIA, via TCP/IP or sockets communication. These interpreters are designed to be widely available by dispersing them to many hosts. Hence, the architecture is Internet-scalable.

7 Example

In the area of *electronic commerce*, electronic *auctioning* is a very promising application of agents. We illustrate how a simple auction may be carried out and coordinated using TRUCE.

7.1 Description

The *fisherman's auction* protocol is an old method normally used by fishermen to sell their fish to the middlemen. A fisherman presents his catch to the public. When the go-signal is given, any interested middleman can *whisper* his bid to the fisherman or to a representative. A bidder can only whisper once. After the last bidder, the highest price and the winner are announced.

We extend the scenario, generalizing *fishermen* to *sellers*, where there can be multiple items for sale. In this setting, only one seller can sell an item at a time. A seller can also bid for other sellers' items.

7.2 Solution

We shall introduce a facilitator to serve as a neutral party. This agent manages the bids by collecting them and announcing the highest price. The bidding goes through several rounds until nobody else can beat the current highest price. The sellers take turns in a round-robin fashion. The whole session finishes when all sellers have sold (or at least attempted) to sell their items.

The solution is composed of two parts. First, we write a truce for a bidding session involving only one item from a seller. Second, we extend the solution to include repetition of the truce developed in part 1, changing only the seller and item parameters.

First Part. Listing 1.0 gives us the complete solution codes for this part. We identify three roles in this coordination problem. These are facilitator, seller and some buyers. For brevity, we simplify the information domain by defining a sale item as consisting of the following information: *item code, current price, description*. Some other information needed would include the *bid price* of each interested buyer and the winning bid. Thus, we declare three packets (lines 3-6). Packets are data structures that are used to pass messages.

Buyers are not allowed to communicate with each other. Communication only flows from the facilitator to the buyers and vice-versa. TRUCE enables us to specify a communication topology for a given group. Each type of topology has primitive communication steps. These steps are separate from what we have given in Table 1 (User-defined topologies are supported by TRUCE). In this example, a *star* topology is ideal. This is specified in line 07 by using the *cast* step, which define a subgroup of the collaboration group. In a star topology, one of the roles become the center where communication can flow only between the center and all other roles. In this case, the facilitator is the center of the star.

There are 3 main activities that need to be accomplished.

- Declaration of item for sale
- bidding
- Declaration of the winning bid

For activity 1, we shall ask the seller to get the item information from the real collaborating agent (called its client). Then it relays the information to the facilitator (Line 32-34). Notice that a packet type must be specified explicitly (sell-item in this case) to determine the type of information being asked for. The symbol _client is reserved and pertains to the actual agent (thus, assigning values to it means these values are passed to the agent). Afterwards, the information is passed to the facilitator. The seller then waits until the facilitator notifies it with the outcome of the sale.

For activity 2, the item for sale is given to the buyers who in return would reply with their bids. The buyers take their bids from their corresponding collaborators. Later, the facilitator selects the highest bid and announces it to the bidders. It then calls for another round, giving them a chance to beat the current price. This procedure repeats until no bidder beats the current price.

In lines 10-16, the facilitator first relays the item information to all buyers using spread — a primitive operation for *star* in which the center broadcasts a message to the rest. This operation is followed by a block of TRUCE codes, called the callback actions. These are actions executed as soon as the receiver gets the message. In this example, a buyer executes the callback actions when it receives the item. The callback actions mainly describe the interaction between a buyer and the actual agent. The buyer gives the item information to the agent while the latter returns a bid. Necessarily, the facilitator collects all bids as shown in lines 18-26.

The property highest-price by the facilitator, which is initially set to zero, stores the current highest bid for the current round. The property winning-price stores the highest price that nobody else has beaten (hence, the winner). At this point, the facilitator collects the bids. *Collect* is another primitive operation in which the center receives messages from the other roles. The callback actions, which the facilitator executes whenever it receives a bid, tell us that the bid just received is compared with the current highest bid. The properties highest-price and winner (a role reference to the bidder of the highest price) are both updated depending on the result of the comparison. The predefined property _sender pertains to the role that sent the latest message (current bid, in this case). Notice that the specifier *synch* is set to true; This means that all members of the bidding-group waits until all bids have been collected and processed.

Now, we have to check whether another round is required. It happens when the current highest bid has changed. If so, a request for new bids from thebuyers is issued by the facilitator. Otherwise, the current highest price is declared as the winning price and the seller is notified.

Second Part. The second part of the solution considers the case where there are multiple sellers with multiple items to sell. We mentioned earlier that we shall use round-robin scheduling to coordinate them. We achieve this by structuring them into a ring - a different topology. A token is passed around so that the current bearer gets to sell one of its items. When a seller has nothing to sell, it simply passes the token to the next. This accomplishes the round-robin scheduling strategy.

Listing 1.0 Complete truce for Part 1

```
01 truce fisherman-auction { facilitator, seller, buyer[] } {
02 % Let's define the packets
03     packet sell-item { number {item-code, current-price},
04             text{descpn}},
05         bid-item { number {item-code, asking-price} },
06         winning-bid { number{price}, role{bidder} };
07     cast bidding-group { facilitator, buyer} struct=star;
08     episode auction {
09         initially { facilitator.set {highest-price} 0;};
10         step sell-and-bid {
11             bidding-group.spread { sell-item{item-for-sale} } {
12 % when the buyers receive the item, they tell their agents
13 % about the item and then ask them for a bid price.
14             set {_client} sell-item{item-for-sale};
15             set {my-bid} bid-item{_client};
16             }
17 % highest-price is initially set to zero;
18         set { winning-price} {highest-price};
19         bidding-group.collect { bid-item{my-bid} } synch=true
20                 timeout=5000 {
21 % For every replies received by the facilitator,
22 % it executes the following
23             if { highest-price < my-bid@asking-price } {
24                 set {highest-price} my-bid@asking-price;
25                 set {winner} _sender;
26             }
27             if { winning-price < highest-price } {
28                 facilitator.set {winning-price} highest-price;
29                 sell-and-bid;
30             }
31         } % end of step
32         seller.set {item-for-sale} sell-item {_client};
33         seller.tell {facilitator} data=item-for-sale target=item-for-sale;
34         seller.wait {facilitator};
35         bidding-group.sell-and-bid;
36 % facilitator announces the winner
37         facilitator.set {result} winning-bid{winning-price, winner};
38         facilitator.tell {seller, buyer} data=result synch=true
39                 target=result;
40         {seller, buyer}.set {_client} result;
41     } % end-of-episode
42 } % end-of-truce
```

Recall that we need to know when to stop the cycle. Once in a while, we should be able to test for the condition where all sellers did not attempt to sell. To accomplish this, we use the token as a counter. Initially set to 0, the counter is incremented everytime a seller sells an item. After travelling the whole ring, its value is tested by the facilitator. If the value remains at 0, the session is terminated. The whole listing is found in Listing 2.0. In line 3, we declare a cast with a ring topology.

To pass around the token, we use the **relay** communication protocol with the facilitator as the originator, as shown in lines 24-37. The token is set to 0 before the facilitator relays the token. In this topology, only one role receives the token at a time. The receiver can choose to sell or not (hence, the use of possibly). If not, the token is automatically passed to the next without modifying its value. Otherwise, it sets its flag myturn to indicate that it is going to sell something. A global property $selling is also set. The new seller waits while the selling is taking place. When it is over, the seller resets its flag and increments the token. The token is passed to the next seller in the ring.

The actual selling procedure is performed in a protocol named selling-protocol. Notice that all roles have to execute this protocol. The trigger involves a global property $selling, which is set by a seller in the sell step. See *selling-protocol* from lines 10-22. Only sellers test the value of their local property myturn. Recall that a receiver of the token sets this property. Thus, it gets to satisfy the condition and execute the step, **set $** "current-seller" $= \_me$. The property $\_me$ is predefined and refers to the role executing the step.

When such setting has been accomplished, the protocol is temporarily disabled so that no further trigger can take place. The truce we have written in part 1 is performed. The role facilitator is bound to the same facilitator in this imported truce. The role seller is bound to whoever is the current seller while both the buyers and the sellers become the buyers. Once finished with the selling, the protocol is switched back on.

The step sell is the entry point of the episode. We have discussed how this step works. The control loops through the same step sell. Observe that the termination condition is checked against the token value.

8 Conclusion

The major focus of our research work is towards the development of a framework for developing collaborative agents in a distributed environment such as the *Internet*. Multi-agent systems are attractive for collaborative problem solving, but support tools and frameworks for development are not wholly available. Although works are being done on developing methods for coordinating agents, our aim is to address the problems of preprogrammed coordination rules/protocols. Thus, we promote dynamic coordination by providing a way for specifying coordination protocols and for carrying them out. The former is accomplished through a coordination language while the latter is achieved with the use of proxies/coordinators.

Listing 2.0 Complete truce for Part 2

```
01 truce multiple-fisherman-auction { facilitator, sellers[], buyers[]}
02              import={fisherman-auction} {
03        cast selling-group{ facilitator,sellers} struct=ring;
04        packet token-type { number {counter} };
05        episode sell-and-buy {
06            initially  action
07                    facilitator.set {token} token-type{0};
08
09
10            protocol selling-protocol {
11                when { $selling = true } {
12                    sellers.if {myturn=true} {
13                        set $"current-seller"=_me;
14                    }
15                    retract {selling-protocol};
16                    facilitator.set {$selling} false;
17                    fisherman-auction {facilitator, $"current-seller",
18                        {buyers, sellers} };
19                    recover {selling-protocol};
20                    facilitator.proceed{$"current-seller"};
21                }
22            } % end-of-protocol
23        %%
24            step sell {
25                buyers.wait;
26                facilitator.set {token} token-type{0};
27                selling-group.relay {token} synch=true {
28                    sellers.{
29                        possibly {
30                            set {myturn} true;
31                            set {$selling}true;
32                            wait;
33                            set {myturn} false;
34                            set {token@counter} token@counter +1;
35                        }
36                    }
37                } % end-of-relay
38                facilitator.proceed{buyers};
39                {facilitator, buyers, sellers}.if {token@counter > 0 }
40                        { sell;}
42            } % end-of-sell
43            sell;
44        } %end-of-episode
45 } % end-of-truce
```

The most important properties of our framework include the following:

- Decentralization of the whole coordination process – since each collaborator becomes an independent interpreter and performs based on the given script, not by any other collaborator.
- Separation of coordination and computation concerns – since coordination protocols can be expressed in a *truce*, user agents can be written without regards to how it is going to coordinate at a later time.
- Services approach to coordination (advertise-subscribe collaboration model) – since coordination itself is provided as a service, and therefore coordinators behave like agents for agents.
- Dynamic coordination using protocol scripts – since it allows a user agent to participate in different collaboration groups using different scripts at any time.
- Reusable coordination protocols – since the "logic" of certain coordination protocols specified in a *truce* can be shared with any interested party.
- Support for simultaneous participation in multiple collaborations by a single agent – since an agent may be represented by different coordinators at the same time for different collaboration groups.

Finally, we expect for a significant increase in productivity by the agent developers, primarily because of the high-level abstraction provided by the language.

References

1. Aguilar, M., Hirsbrunner, B., and Krone, O., "The CoLa Approach: A Coordination Language for Massively Parallel Systems", http://www.cs.dartmouth.com Institut d'Informatique de Fribourgm Chemin du Musee, Sept. 28, 1994.
2. Arbab, F. "Coordination of Massively Concurrent Activities", *CS-R9565 1995* Computer Science/Department of Interactive Systems, Centrum voor Wiskunde en Informatica, Amsterdam, NL.
3. Barbuceanu, M. and Fox, M., "The Design of a Coordination Language for Multi-Agent Systems", *Technical Report*, Enterprise Integration Laboratory, University of Toronto.
4. Berry, A. and Kaplan, S.. "Open, Distributed Coordination with Finesse", *Technical Report*, School of Information Technology. The University of Queensland, Australia.
5. Biddle, Bruce J., *Role Theory: Expectations, Identities, and Behaviors*, Academic Press, Inc. , NY, 1979.
6. Bond, A. and Gasser, L.(editors) *Readings in Distributed Artificial Intelligence*, Morgan Kauffman Pub. Inc., San Mateo, California, 1988.
7. Castellani, S., and Ciancarini, P., "Enhancing Coordination and Modularity Mechanisms for a Language with Objects-as-Multisets", *Technical Report*, Department of Computer Science, University of Bologna, Italy.
8. Ciancarini, P., Jensen, K., and Yankelevich, D., "On the Operational Semantics of a Coordination Language", *Technical Report*, Department of Mathematics, University of Bologna, Bologna, Italy.

9. Ciancarini, P., Rossi, D., "Report C: Jada: A Coordination Toolkit for Java", *ESPRIT Open Long Term Research Project 20197 - Pagespace*, available at http://flp.cs.tu-berlin.de/ pagespc/.

10. Ciancarini, P., Vitali, F., and Tolksdorf, R., "Weaving the Web in a PageSpace Using Coordination", *Technical Report*, Department of Mathematics, University of Bologna, Bologna, Italy.

11. Crowston, Kevin (crowston@umich.edu), "A Taxonomy of Organizational Dependencies and Coordination Mechanisms", *Technical Report*, The University of Michigan, School of Business Administration.

12. Factor, M., Fertig, S. and Gelernter, D., "Using Linda to Build Parallel AI Applications", *TR-861*, Yale University Department of Computer Science, June 1991.

13. Gelernter, D., Carriero, N., "Coordination Languages and their Significance", *Communications of the ACM*, February 1992/Vol. 35, No. 2, pp. 97-107.

14. Haddadi, Afsaneh, "Communication and Cooperation in Agent System: A Pragmatic Theory", *Lecture Notes in Artificial Intelligence*, Vol. 1056, Springer-Verlag, 1995.

15. Jamison, W., "ACACIA: An Agency Based Collaboration Framework for Heterogeneous Multiagent Systems", *Multiagent Systems Methodologies and Applications*, *Lecture Notes in Artificial Intelligents* 1286, Springer-Verlag, 1996, pp. 76-91.

16. Jamison, W., "Approaching Interoperability for Heterogeneous Multiagent Systems Using High Order Agencies", *Cooperative Information Agents, First International Workshop, CIA'97, Kiel, Germany 1997 Proceedings*, Springer-Verlag, pp. 222-233.

17. JKQML, IBM Alphaworks, available at http://www.alphaWorks.ibm.com/formula/jkqml.

18. Lea, D. and Marlowe, J. "PSL: Protocols and Pragmatics for Open Systems", available at http://gee.cs.oswego.edu/dl.

19. Labrou, Y. and Finin, T., "A Proposal for a new KQML specification", *TR CS-97-03*, Computer Science and Electrical Engineering Department, University of Maryland at Baltimore, Maryland 21250.

20. Maffeis, Silvano. "iBus-The Java Intranet Software Bus", available at http://www.softwired.ch, 1998.

21. Malone, T. and Crowston, K., "The Interdisciplinary Study of Coordination", *ACM Computing Survey*, vol. 26. pp. 87-119, March 1994.

22. Rosenschein, J. and Zotkin, G., *Rules of Encounter, Designing Conventions for Automated Negotiation among Computers*, The MIT Press,, 1994.

23. Shoham, Y., "Agent-Oriented Programming",' *Artificial Intelligence* 60, pp 51-92, 1993.

24. Singh, Munindar P., "Multiagent Systemts, A Theoretical Framework for Intentions, Know-How, and Communications", *Lecture Notes in Artificial Intelligence*, Vol. 799, Springer-Verlag, 1994.

25. Wooldridge, Michael and Jennings, Nicholas R., "Agent Theories, Architectures and Languages: A Survey", in Wooldridge and Jennings (ed), *Intelligent Agent*, Springer-Verlag, 1-22.

The STL++ Coordination Language: A Base for Implementing Distributed Multi-agent Applications *

Michael Schumacher, Fabrice Chantemargue, Béat Hirsbrunner

University of Fribourg, Computer Science Department, PAI group
Ch. du Musée 3, CH-1700 Fribourg, Switzerland
URL: http://www-iiuf.unifr.ch/pai
Email: FirstName.LastName@unifr.ch

Abstract. This paper introduces the STL++ coordination language, a C++-based language binding of the ECM coordination model. STL++ applies theories and techniques known from coordination theory and languages in distributed computing to try to better formalize communication and coordination in distributed multi-agent applications. STL++, as such, may be seen as a preliminary agent language which allows the organizational structure or architecture of a multi-agent system to be described, with means to dynamically reconfigure it. It is aimed at giving basic constructs for distributed implementations of generic multi-agent platforms, to be run on a LAN of general-purpose workstations. STL++ uses an encapsulation mechanism as its primary abstraction, offering structured separate name spaces which can be hierarchically organized. Agents communicate anonymously within and/or across name spaces through connections, which are established by the matching of the communication interfaces of the participating agents. As an example, STL++ is used to simulate the automation of a trading system.
Keywords: Coordination, Distributed Systems, Concurrency, Communication Models, Agents, Multi-Agent Systems.

1 Introduction

Coordination can be defined as the process of *managing dependencies between activities* [29], or, in the field of Programming Languages, as the *process of building programs by gluing together active pieces*. To formalize and better describe these interdependencies, Gelernter and Carriero, in [9], propose to separate the two essential parts of a parallel application namely, *computation* and *coordination*. Because these two parts usually interfere with each other, the semantics of distributed applications is difficult to understand.

Gelernter and Carriero also state that a coordination language is orthogonal to a computation language and forms the *linguistic embodiment of a coordination*

---

* This work is financially supported by the Swiss National Foundation for Scientific Research, grant 20-05026.97.

model. Linguistic embodiment means that the language must provide language constructs either in form of library calls or in form of language extensions as a means to materialize the coordination model. Orthogonal to a computation language means that a coordination language extends a given computation language with additional functionalities which facilitate the implementation of distributed applications.

The most prominent representative coordination language is LINDA [8], which is based on a *tuple space abstraction* as the underlying coordination model. An application of this model has been realized in PIRANHA [7] (to mention one of its numerous applications) where LINDA's tuple space is used for networked based load balancing functionality. The PAGESPACE [15] effort extends LINDA's tuple space onto the World-Wide-Web and BONITA [34] addresses performance issues for the implementation of LINDA's in and out primitives. Some research tackles security issues of tuple spaces [38], [31]. Other models and languages are based on *control-oriented approaches* (IWIM/MANIFOLD [2], [3], CONCOORD [22], DARWIN [28]), *message passing paradigms* (ACTORS [1]), *object-oriented techniques* (OBJECTIVE LINDA [25], JAVASPACES [37]), *multi-set rewriting schemes* (BAUHAUS LINDA [11], GAMMA [4]) or *Linear Logic* (LINEAR OBJECTS [5]). A good overview on coordination models and languages can be found in [33].

Our work takes inspiration from control-oriented models and tuple-based abstractions, and focuses on coordination for purpose of Multi-Agent System (MAS) distributed implementations. This paper presents STL++, our C++-based coordination language. STL++ is an instantiation of the ECM coordination model which is a model for multi-grain distributed applications. For the time being, STL++ is built on top of PT-PVM [27], a software layer providing rich message passing facilities for light-weight processes (threads) over a LAN of general purpose workstations. STL++ can be considered as a platform which allows the organizational structure or architecture of a MAS to be described, with means to dynamically reconfigure it. It is conceived as a base for further multi-agent platforms. The rest of this paper is organized as follows. Section 2 examines the question of coordination in the field of MAS. Section 3 introduces the ECM model and gives a thorough description of STL++. Section 4 illustrates the application of STL++ to simulating the automation of a trading system. Section 5 is dedicated to a discussion of ECM and STL++. In the last section we draw some conclusions and outline future work.

2 Coordination in Multi-Agent Systems

As indicated by its name, a MAS is a macro system comprising multiple agents, each of which being a micro system. Numerous and various definitions on the notion of agent exist. Our aim here is not to cover all of them, but rather to introduce what we consider the most essential features of an agent for our concern. As said before, an agent is a system, which is situated within an environment: it senses in that environment and acts autonomously on it over time and in particular it is likely to exchange information with other agents. For more thorough definitions, refinements and variants, see [17] and [40]. Apart from defining what an agent is and what it is aimed at, communication between agents and hence coordination are given a lot of concern. This is the object of the subsequent sub-section.

2.1 Communication and Coordination between Agents

Communication between agents can be considered as composed of: i) the capacity to exchange information with other agents; ii) the intention or the type of message, which is often realized using illocutary speech acts [36] such as *request, deny* or *confirm*; iii) a common syntax for expressing the information exchanged; iv) and a common understanding of a message. The later can be achieved if agents that participate in the communication share a common information model (which is often referred to as ontology [20] or ontological commitments).

Research has resulted in several agent communication languages (ACL). The most representative is KQML [16], which is the de facto ACL standard. KQML comes along with KIF (Knowledge Interchange Format [19]) which provides a syntax for message content along with ontologies.

Exchange of information between agents can be realized at least with three basic paradigms: i) *Peer-to-peer communication*: messages are sent to specific agents; ii) *Multicast communication*: a message is sent to a group of agents; iii) *Generative communication*: communication is realized through the environment: agents generate persistent objects (messages) in the environment to be sensed by other agents.

An agent can communicate: i) *explicitly* by having an identifier of its partner of communication; or ii) *anonymously* by putting and getting messages on well defined ports (communication interfaces); these ports are connected to other ports belonging to other agents. This means that an agent has no identifier of other agents. For anonymous communication, connections between ports can be achieved by an external specialized agent (a coordinator agent, like in [2]) or as a result of the matching of ports which depends on port characteristics.

Distributed Artificial Intelligence (DAI) has developed several techniques for coordination [23], such as *Organizational Structuring* techniques (e.g. [39]), *Multi-Agent Planning* techniques (e.g. [24]) and *Negotiation* techniques ([6]).

Multi-agent planning and negotiation techniques are designed for applications that encompass the exchange of high-level information such as plans, knowledge, beliefs or intentions. Thus they suppose basic coordination involving the communication topology between agents, which constitutes the base of more complex strategies. Organizational structuring techniques try to provide this base by supplying an a priori organization by long-term relationships between agents. This technique has shown good results, especially with master/slave or client/server patterns, sometimes using blackboard architecture. STL++ tries to resolve weaknesses encountered in organizational structuring, especially by offering means for dynamical reconfiguration, and by using a locality principle for the management of agents (in blops), thus avoiding centralization. STL++ also

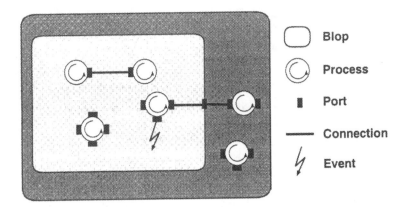

Fig. 1. The Coordination Model of ECM.

offers a complete set of communication primitives, that support peer-to-peer, group and blackboard communication.

3 STL++, a Coordination Language for Multi-Agent Systems

STL++ is a C++-based language binding of the ECM[1] coordination model [26], presented in the next section.

3.1 Coordination using Encapsulation: ECM

ECM uses an encapsulation mechanism as its primary abstraction (referred to as blops[2]), offering structured separate name spaces which can be hierarchically organized. Within them, active entities communicate anonymously within and/or across blops through connections, established by the matching of the communication interfaces of these entities.

ECM consists of five building blocks (see figure 1): i) *Processes*, as a representation of active entities; ii) *Blops*, as an abstraction and modularization mechanism for a group of processes and ports; iii) *Ports*, as the interface of processes/blops to the external world; iv) *Events*, a mechanism to support dynamicity (creation of new process or blop) inside a blop; v) *Connections*, as a representation of connected ports.

Blop. A blop is a mechanism to *encapsulate* a set of objects. Objects residing in a blop are by default only visible within their "home" blop. Blops have the same interface as processes, a (possibly empty) set of ports, and can be hierarchically structured. Blops serve as a separate name space for port objects, processes, and subordinated blops as well as an encapsulation mechanism for events.

---

[1] ECM stands for Encapsulation Coordination Model.

[2] This is a term we have coined.

Process. A process in ECM is a typed object with a (possibly empty) set of ports. Processes in the ECM model do not know any kind of process identification, instead a black box model is used. A process does not have to care about which process information will be transmitted to or received from. Process creation and termination are not part of the ECM model and are to be specified in the instance of the model.

Ports and Matching. Ports are the interface of processes and blops to establish connections to other processes/blops. Each ECM language binding must specify a minimal set of port *features*, each of which describing a port characteristics. The communication feature is mandatory and must support the following communication paradigms: point-to-point stream communication (with classical message-passing semantics), closed group (with multicast semantics) and blackboard communication. Additional features are available to refine the semantics of the communication between ports. The set of feature values of a port defines its *type*. A port is created with one or several *names*. Names are not to be used for identification, but for matching purposes. Names and type of a port are referred to as its *signature*.

The matching of ports is defined as a relationship between port signatures. Four general conditions must be fulfilled for two ports to match: i) both share at least a common name; ii) both belong to the same level of abstraction; iii) both belong to different objects (process or blop); and iv) both types must be compatible: a compliance relationship must be defined for every feature in the ECM instance. For the communication feature, ECM imposes that both ports have the same communication paradigm. Section 3 presents the features used for STL++ and the compliance relationship for each of them. The matching of ports is automatically established. This means that there exists no language construct to bind ports in order to establish a connection: the matching is therefore implicitly realized.

Connections. The matching of ports results in the following connections: i) *Point-to-point Stream*: 1:1, 1:n, n:1 and n:m communication patterns are possible; ii) *Group*: messages are broadcast to all members of the group. A closed group semantics is used, i.e. processes must be members of the group in order to distribute or receive information in it; iii) *Blackboard*: messages are placed on a blackboard used by several processes; they are persistent and can be retrieved more than once in a sequence defined by the processes.

Events. Events can be attached to conditions on ports of blops or processes. They are typically aimed at creating new processes. The conditions will determine when the event will be triggered in the blop. Condition checking is implementation dependent.

3.2 The Coordination Language STL++

We designed and implemented a first language binding of the ECM model, called STL[3] [26]. STL is applied to multi-threaded applications on a LAN of UNIX workstations. STL materializes the separation of concern as it uses a separate language exclusively reserved for coordination purposes and provides primitives which are used in a computation language to express interactions between the entities. The implementation of STL is based on PT-PVM [27], a library providing message passing and process management facilities at thread and process level for a cluster of workstations. In particular, blops are implemented as heavy-weight UNIX processes, and processes as light-weight processes (threads).

However, it turned out that the separation of *code* can not always be easily maintained. Although the black box process model of ECM is a good attempt to separate coordination and computation code, dynamic properties proved to be difficult to be expressed in a separate language. This is, for example, reflected in STL, where coordination primitives have to be present in the computation language, so as to offer dynamic coordination facilities; dynamic properties can not be totally separated from the actual program code. A duplication of code is therefore inevitable and, as a result, it may introduce some difficulties to manage a distributed application. Each process and its ports must indeed be declared both in the computation language and in the separate coordination language. These observations led us to the development of a new coordination language, called STL++. Starting from the experience acquired with STL, we adopted a single language approach: STL++ implements the conceptual model of ECM by enriching a given object oriented language (C++) with coordination primitives, realized in a library.

A STL++ application is a set of classes that inherit from the base classes of the library (see Figure 2). The main class of an application must inherit from WorldBlop, which is the default blop containing all other entities.

Blops. A blop inherits from the base class Blop and has to re-implement the start method. The user must call Blop::start() in order to initialize the blop. The creation of a blop results in the initialization of all enclosed blops, ports and agents (STL++ instantiations of ECM processes). Blops can be parameterized like normal objects.

A blop handles all its enclosed entities; thus, a blop creates agents as well as events, and binds events to its ports. In STL++, new blops can be dynamically created at runtime.

Agents. Agent classes inherit from the base class Agent and have to re-implement the start() method. Agents can be created directly by blops, through events or by other agents. An agent is initialized with Agent::start(). To communicate, agents dynamically create ports of predefined types through instantiation of a port C++-template class.

---

[3] Simple Thread Language.

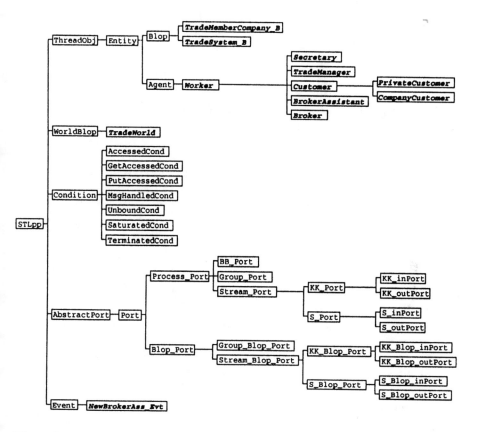

Fig. 2. STL++ user classes together with classes of the application presented in section 4 (bold italic).

Agent termination is implicit: the agent disappears along with its ports and data, when the corresponding `Agent` object terminates. Regarding the implementation, an `Agent` object is embedded in a light-weight process (thread).

Ports and Connections. In accordance with the ECM model, every port is endowed with one or several names and a set of features. STL++ distinguishes *Primary* and *Secondary Features* for ports.

Primary Features, which define the main semantics of a port, and therefore the basic port types, encompass: i) `Communication`: this feature captures ECM communication paradigms; ii) `Msg Synchronization`: this feature gives to the connection the usual semantics of message passing communication. Possible values are `synchron` and `asynchron`; iii) `Orientation`: this feature defines the direction of the data flow over a connection; there are three possible values, namely `in` (in-flowing), `out` (out-flowing) and `inout` (bi-directional).

Port Type	Communication	Msg Synchronization	Orientation
Blackboard	blackboard	asynchron	inout
Group	group	asynchron	inout
S-Stream	stream	synchron	in or out
KK-Stream	stream	asynchron	in or out

Table 1. Basic port types and values of their primary features.

Secondary Features, which define characteristics for specific types of ports, are: i) `Saturation`: this feature, ranging from 1 to INF (infinity) by integer values, defines the number of connections a port can have; ii) `Lifetime`: this feature, ranging from 1 to INF (infinity) by integer values, indicates the number of data units that can pass through a port before it decays; iii) `Data Type`: this feature defines the type of data authorized to pass through a port.

STL++ currently supports four basic port types, corresponding to the combinations of the primary features as displayed in Table 1. Note that, provided that ports match, it yields four basic connection types.

`Blackboard` **port type**. The resulting connection, as a result of the matching of ports of this type, has a blackboard semantics. The number of participating ports is unlimited. Messages are persistent objects which can be retrieved using a symbolic name. Moreover, messages are not ordered. To access the blackboard, the following LINDA-like primitives are provided: put (non-blocking), get (blocking) and read (blocking). Blackboard connections are persistent: if all the ports involved in a blackboard connection disappear, the connection still persists in the blop space with all the information it carries, so that new ports can later on reconnect to the blackboard and recover the pending information.

`Group` **port type**. The resulting connection has a closed group semantics. The number of participating ports is unlimited. Each member of the group can broadcast asynchronously messages to every participant in the group. Messages are stored at the receiver side. Thus, if a port in a group disappears, then the sequence of information that has not been read is lost. The primitives for accessing the group are: get (blocking) and put (non-blocking).

`S-Stream` **port type**. The semantics of a connection resulting from the matching of two S-Stream ports (S for synchronous) has the same semantics as the S-Channel defined in [2], in particular this connection is uni-directional. This connection always results from the matching of contradictory oriented ports, namely a producer and a consumer. In contrast to other connections, this connection never contains data, due to its synchronous nature. So the destruction of the producer or the consumer never causes loss of data. The primitives for accessing the port are get (blocking) and put (blocking).

`KK-Stream` **port type**. The semantics of a connection resulting from the matching of two KK-Stream ports (K for keep) is analogous to the asynchronous KK-Channel defined in [2], with its semantics (see below) when a port disappears from one end of the connection. As for S-Streams, this connection always results from the matching of contradictory oriented ports. If the connection is broken at

Feature F	Values	Compatibility
Communication	blackboard, stream, group	P1.F = P2.F
Msg. Synchronization	synchron, asynchron	P1.F = P2.F
Orientation	in, out, inout	(P1.F = in *and* P2.F = out) *or* (P1.F = P2.F = inout)
Saturation	{1,2,...,INF}	Always compatible
Data Type	Type	P1.F = P2.F
Lifetime	{1,2,...,INF}	Always compatible

Table 2. Compatibility for Features F for two Ports P1 and P2

its consuming port, the next new matching port will consume all pending data. If the connection is broken at its producing port, the consuming port will be able to continue to consume all data in the connection. If both ports are deleted, the connection disappears with its data. The primitives for accessing the port are get (blocking) and put (non-blocking).

Establishing Connections between Agents. Communication between agents is realized through connections which are the result of matched ports. In accordance with the ECM model, the matching is realized as a relation between port signatures. In STL++, in order to match, ports must belong to the same blop and must comply at name and type levels: i) *Name level.* Two ports match at name level if they share at least one name. A port may have several names; in this case, each name belongs to a different connection; ii) *Type level.* For two ports, values of the same feature must be compatible. Table 2 gives an overview of the compatibility functions used by the STL++ runtime system.

By introducing several names for each port, STL++ allows stream and group ports to be connected to different connections (blackboard ports cannot have multiple connections). Data written on such multiple connection ports are echoed on every connection. For stream connections, 1:1, 1:n, n:1 and n:m communication patterns can be built. Likewise, several groups can be connected to a single port.

Events. Event classes inherit from Event; the launch() method, which defines the acting of the event, must be re-implemented. Events are instantiated with a specific lifetime which determines how many times they can be triggered.

Conditions on ports (see table 3 for an overview) are checked when data flow through the port, or, in the case of saturatedCond condition, when a new connection is realized.

4 Simulation of a Trading System

The numerous activities that take place within a trading system are typically distributed and can be modeled by a multi-agent system. It has led solutions

Condition	Explanation
UnboundCond()	Port not connected.
SaturatedCond()	Port saturated.
MsgHandledCond(int n)	Port has handled n messages.
AccessedCond()	Port accessed.
PutAccessedCond()	Port accessed with **put** primitive.
GetAccessedCond()	Port accessed with **get** primitive.
TerminatedCond()	Port lifetime is over.

Table 3. Port Conditions

for agent-based electronic commerce; see for instance KASBAH [13], FISHMARKET [35], or a proposal based on the PAGESPACE platform [14]. If our goal is to fully automate a trading system, for the time being, we would rather concentrate on simulating the automation of such a system. Our aim, in this paper, is not to focus on the control algorithms of the different agents, nor on the negotiation techniques (see e.g. [21]) that are undertaken by the agents in order to process a transaction, but rather to concentrate on the basic coordination mechanisms that come into play in the interactions between agents, for which STL++ is precisely suitable. Thus, in this implementation, agents are endowed with a very basic autonomy [12] in the sense that they can make decisions on their own, without user intervention. More sophisticated autonomy-based control algorithms and smart negotiation techniques will be tackled in a further stage.

Figure 3 gives a scaled down graphical overview of the organization of the agents that compose our trading system, as well as their interactions. To avoid cluttering the graph, port names (on which the matching is based) have been intentionally omitted. The *TradeWorld* blop confines every activity in the trading simulation. Several *Trading System* blops (TSB) are accessible by *customers* (company or private customers), who are authorized members of a trading system that represent end-user agents. *Company* or *Private Customers* create queries to buy or sell goods. These queries, written by the customer on his query_P port (of KK_outPort type), are transmitted to a *Trading System Blop* (TSB).

In a TSB reside *Brokers*, each of whom is devoted to serve a particular customer, by handling his committed customer queries that came in. A pair of ports on the TSB, namely *name_query_gate_P* and *name_res_gate_P* (*name* being off1 or off2 in figure 3), serves as gates for each customer and his respective broker. Every query is then posted by the broker to his trade_P port (of BB_Port type), e.g., sell 100 securities at 1000 CHF and therefore published in the *Trade Unit Blackboard*. On the trade_P port is bound the event NewBrokerAss_Evt with the condition PutAccessedCond; the effect of the posting is that the NewBrokerAss_Evt event is triggered. The role of this event is to dynamically create a *Broker Assistant* that will be in charge of fulfilling the specific query, by establishing a dynamic connection with another broker assis-

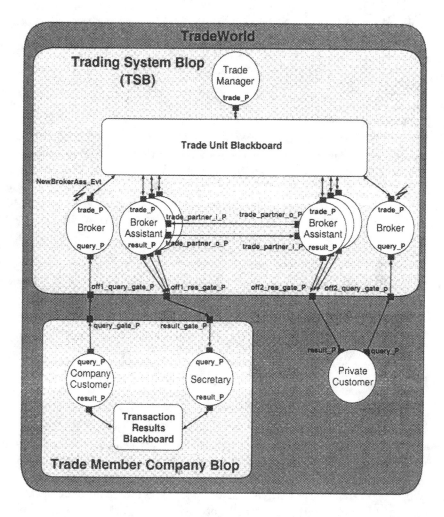

Fig. 3. Trading System with STL++.

tant interested in an (almost) symmetric query (e.g., buy 50 securities at 1000 CHF). This is possible on the basis of the information transmitted by the *Trade Manager*.

All queries are supervised by the *Trade Manager*; he knows who issued which query (through an identification contained in the query). For each new arrived query, the Trade Manager checks whether a possible matching between proposals can take place (e.g. case of a broker who wants to buy securities of type A and another broker who wants to sell securities of type A). If a kind of matching can somehow be issued between two *Broker Assistants*, the Trade Manager puts on the *Trade Unit Blackboard* two appropriate messages for each involved *Broker Assistant*. The information transmitted contains among others a specific

A newly created Broker Assistant has first to read from his trade_P port (of type BB_Port) in order to be informed of a specific transaction. In virtue of this information, he dynamically publishes two KK_Ports using the transaction id as port name (trade_partner_i_P and trade_partner_o_P ports). A new double connection is then established between these two partners. Both involved Broker Assistants exchange useful information so as to make their query successful (this is precisely where negotiation techniques appear).

When a successful transaction (the result of the agreement of two Broker Assistants) is issued, both Broker Assistants inform their committed customers by transmitting appropriate information on their result_P port (of type KK_outPort), and then terminate. On customer side, results about processed queries can be collected either directly or through a *Secretary Agent* (see figure 3). At regular intervals, non fulfilled queries are eliminated by the Trade Manager; all involved entities are kept posted.

5 Discussion

5.1 STL++ a Coordination Language

ECM, a coordination model for distributed programming, along with STL++ its instantiation, present some similarities with e.g. the IWIM [2] coordination model and its instance MANIFOLD [3], LINDA [8], DARWIN [28] or CONCO-ORD [22].

Though ECM shares many characteristics with IWIM, it however differs in several points: i) Blops are not coordinators like IWIM managers. Connections are not established explicitly by the blop (or by another agent), i.e. there is no language construct to bind ports in order to establish a connection: the establishment of connections is done implicitly, resulting from a matching mechanism between compatible ports within the same blop; the matching depends on the types and the states of the concerned ports. The main characteristics of blops is to encapsulate objects, thus forming a separate name-space for enclosed entities and an encapsulation mechanism for events; ii) ECM generalizes connection types, namely stream, blackboard or group, and does not restrict to channels; iii) In ECM, events are not signals broadcast in the environment, but objects that realize an action in a blop. Events are attached to ports with conditions on their state that determine when they are to be launched. They can create agents or blops, and their action area is limited to a blop.

ECM together with STL++ differ in the following points from LINDA: i) Like several further developments of the LINDA model (e.g. [25]), ECM uses a hierarchical multiple coordination space model [18], in contrast to the single flat tuple space of the original LINDA. But it has to be stressed that a blop is not a shared dataspace as a tuple space, but an abstraction mechanism of several agents that serves as a separate name space; ii) In STL++ agents get started through an event in a blop, or automatically upon initialization of a blop, or through a creation operation by another agent; LINDA uses a single mechanism:

`eval()`. The termination of an agent results in the loss of all its enclosed data and ports; it may as well result in the loss of pending data in the case of unbound connections. (see section 3). In Linda, a tuple replaces the terminated process; iii) In STL++ agents do not execute in a medium which is used to transfer data. Every communication is realized through connections established by the matching of ports. Only the engaged agents have access to those connections; iv) Blackboard connections allow for generative communication between the participating agents. For the time being, a string is used to introduce and retrieve data. Neither tuples, nor templates, nor pattern matching are supported for retrieving data. Blackboards are typed in the sense that only one type of data can be entered. There is also no kind of active tuples.

5.2 Implementing Coordination in MAS with STL++

STL++ can be considered as a preliminary language for constructing agent applications, stressing the coordination part of a MAS. In its purpose, STL++ is comparable to APRIL [30], conceived as a platform oriented towards the implementation of MAS, and to BAUHAUS LINDA [10], which has been applied to implementing Turingware, a superset of Groupware.

STL++ has some characteristics that make it a good candidate for implementing MAS: i) Blops constitute a mechanism which enables construction of a structured set of different environments, each of which is a closed private coordination space with communication interfaces to other environments. A set of complex interconnected and hierarchically organized spaces is indeed often desirable in MAS; ii) Autonomous agents are implemented as black boxes. An autonomous agent owns exclusive control over its internal state and behavior; it can define by itself its ports. It is seen from external views (its environment) as a delineated entity presenting clear interfaces. Being distinct from the outside (the environment), an agent is part of its environment composed by its surrounding blop and the agents living in it. iii) Sensing and acting capacities of agents are implemented with ports. Thus agents can perceive and act through different means, by virtue of the possibility to define port types and several instantiations of them. A port perceives specific data; this is enforced with the data type feature of ports. iv) As agents and environments may evolve over time, dynamicity is an important point in MAS. This has led to design STL++ so as to support blop reorganization, new port creation and destruction, thus yielding dynamic communication topologies.

6 Conclusion

In résumé, we presented the ECM coordination model and STL++, an instantiation that constitutes a platform to implement Multi-Agent Systems. An STL++ implementation of a simulation of a Trading System showed the potential of our coordination language.

Future work will consist of: i) Extending STL++ so as to support generic coordination patterns, yielding templates at disposal for general purpose implementations; ii) Enhancing the Trading System simulation so as to tackle more sophisticated autonomy-based control algorithms and smart negotiation techniques. We also work on a new ECM mapping in Java built on the ORBACUS Object Request Broker [32] and the JAVASPACES [37] API.

References

1. G. Agha. *ACTORS: A Model of Concurrent Computation in Distributed Systems.* MIT Press, 1986.
2. F. Arbab. The IWIM Model for Coordination of Concurrent Activities. In P. Ciancarini and C. Hankin, editors, *Proceedings of the First International Conference on Coordination Models, Languages and Applications*, number 1061 in LNCS. Springer Verlag, April 1996.
3. F. Arbab, I. Herman, and P. Spilling. An Overview of Manifold and its Implementation. *Concurrency: Practice and Experience*, 5(1):23–70, February 1993.
4. J.P. Banâtre and D. Le Métayer. Programming by Multiset Transformation. *Communications of the ACM*, 36(1):98–111, 1993.
5. M. Bourgois, J.M. Andreoli, and R. Pareschi. Extending Objects with Rules, Composition and Concurrency: the LO Experience. Technical report, European Computer Industry Research Centre, Munich, Germany, 1992.
6. S. Bussmann and J. Muller. A Negotiation Framework for Co-operating Agents. In S. M. Deen, editor, *Proceedings of CKBS-SIG*, pages 1–17. Dake Centre, University of Keele, 1992.
7. N. Carriero, E. Freeman, D. Gelernter, and D. Kaminsky. Adaptive Parallelism and Piranha. *IEEE Computer*, 28(1), January 1995.
8. N. Carriero and D. Gelernter. Linda in Context. *Communications of the ACM*, 32(4):444–458, 1989.
9. N. Carriero and D. Gelernter. Coordination Languages and Their Significance. *Communications of the ACM*, 35(2):97–107, February 1992.
10. N. Carriero, D. Gelernter, and S. Hupfer. Collaborative Applications Experience with the Bauhaus Coordination Language. In R. H. Sprague Jr., editor, *Proceedings of the 30th Hawaii International Conference on System Sciences*, volume 1, Wailea, Hawaii, 1997. IEEE. Minitrack on Coordination Languages, Systems and Applications.
11. N. Carriero, D. Gelernter, and L. Zuck. Bauhaus Linda. In P. Ciancarini, O. Nierstrasz, and A. Yonezawa, editors, *Object-Based Models and Languages for Concurrent Systems*, volume 924 of *Lecture Notes in Computer Science*, Berlin, 1995. Springer Verlag.
12. F. Chantemargue, O. Krone, M. Schumacher, T. Dagaeff, and B. Hirsbrunner. Autonomous Agents: from Concepts to Implementation. In *Proceedings of the Fourteenth European Meeting on Cybernetics and Systems Research (EMCSR'98)*, volume 2, pages 731–736, Vienna, Austria, April 14-17 1998.
13. A. Chavez and P. Maes. Kasbah: An Agent Marketplace for Buying and Selling Goods. In *Proceedings of the First International Conference on the Practical Application of Intelligent Agents and Multi-Agent Technology*, London, UK, April 1996. Lawrence Erlbaum.

14. P. Ciancarini, A. Knoche, D. Rossi, R. Tolksdorf, and F. Vitali. Coordinating Java agents for Financial Applications on the WWW. In *Proceedings of the Second International Conference and Exhibition on The Practical Application of Intelligent Agents and Multi-Agents, PAAM '97*, 1997.

15. P. Ciancarini, A. Knoche, R. Tolksdorf, and Fabio Vitali. PageSpace: An Architecture to Coordinate Distributed Applications on the Web. In *Proceedings of the Fifth International World Wide Web Conference*, volume 28 of *Computer Networks and ISDN Systems*, 1996.

16. T. Finin, R. Fritzon, D. McKay, and R. McEntire. KQML as an Agent Communication Language. In *Proceedings of the 3rd International Conference on Information and Knowledge Management (CIKM)*. ACM Press, 1994.

17. S. Franklin and A. Graesser. Is it an Agent or just a Program? A Taxonomy for Autonomous Agents. In J.P. Muller, M.J. Wooldridge, and N.R. Jennings, editors, *Proceedings of ECAI'96 Workshop (ATAL). Intelligent Agents III. Agent Theories, Architectures, and Languages*, number 1193 in LNAI, pages 21–35, August 1996.

18. D. Gelernter. Mulitiple Tuple Spaces in Linda. In E. Odijk, M. Rem, and J.Syre, editors, *Proceedings of the Conference on Parallel Architectures and Languages Europe (PARLE 89)*, volume 365 of *Lecture Notes in Computer Science*, pages 20–27, Berlin, 1989. Springer Verlag.

19. M.R. Genesereth and R.E. Fikes. Knowledge Interchange Format, Version 3.0. Reference Manual. Technical Report Logic-92-1, Computer Science Department, Stanford university, 1992.

20. T.R. Gruber. A Translation Approach to Portable Ontology Specifications. *Knowledge Acquisition*, 5:119–220, 1993.

21. R. Guttman and P. Maes. Cooperative vs. Competitive Multi-Agent Negotiations in Retail Electronic Commerce. In *Proceedings of the Second International Workshop on Cooperative Information Agents (CIA'98).*, July 1998.

22. A.A. Holzbacher. A Software Environment for Concurrent Coordinated Programming. In P. Ciancarini and C. Hankin, editors, *Proceedings of the First International Conference on Coordination Models, Languages and Applications*, number 1061 in LNCS. Springer Verlag, April 1996.

23. L. Lee H.S. Nwana and N.R. Jennings. Co-ordination in Multi-Agent Systems. In H. S. Nwana and N. Azarmi, editors, *Software Agents and Soft Computing*, number 1198 in LNAI. Springer Verlag, 1997.

24. Y. Jin and T. Koyoma. Multi-agent Planning through Expectation-based Negotiation. In *Proceedings of the 10th Int Workshop on DAI*, Texas, 1990.

25. T. Kielmann. *Objective Linda: A Coordination Model for Object-Oriented Parallel Programming*. PhD thesis, Dept. of Electrical Engineering and Computer Science, University of Siegen, Germany, 1997.

26. O. Krone, F. Chantemargue, T. Dagaeff, and M. Schumacher. Coordinating Autonomous Entities with STL. *The Applied Computing Review*, Special issue on Coordination Models Languages and Applications, 1998.

27. O. Krone, B. Hirsbrunner, and V.S. Sunderam. PT-PVM+: A Portable Platform for Multithreaded Coordination Languages. *Calculateurs Parallèles*, 8(2):167–182, 1996.

28. J. Magee, N.Dulay, and J. Kramer. Structuring parallel and distributed programs. *Software Engineering Journal*, pages 73–82, March 1993.

29. T.W. Malone and K. Crowston. The Interdisciplinary Study of Coordination. *ACM Computing Surveys*, 26(1):87–119, March 1994.

30. F.G. McCabe and K.L. Clark. April - agent process interaction language. In M. Wooldridge and N.R. Jennings, editors, *Intelligent Agents. Proceedings of First International Workshop on Agent Theories, Architectures, and Languages (ATAL'94)*, number 890 in LNAI. Springer Verlag, August 1994.

31. R. De Nicola, G. Ferrari, and R. Pugliese. Coordinating mobile agents via blackboards and access rights. In *Proceedings of the 2nd International Conference on Coordination Languages and Models (Coordination '97)*, number 1282 in LNCS. Springer Verlag, September 1997.

32. ORBacus Object Request Broker. Object Oriented Concepts, Inc., 1999. www.ooc.com.

33. G.A. Papadopoulos and F. Arbab. Coordination Models and Languages. In M. Zelkowitz, editor, *Advances in Computers, The Engineering of Large Systems*, volume 46. Academic Press, August 1998.

34. A. Rawston and A. Wood. BONITA: A Set of Tuple Space primitives for Distributed Coordination. In R. H. Sprague Jr., editor, *Proceedings of the 30th Hawaii International Conference on System Sciences*, volume 1, Wailea, Hawaii, 1997. IEEE. Minitrack on Coordination Languages, Systems and Applications.

35. J. A. Rodriguez-Aguilar, P. Noriega, C. Sierra, and J. Padget. Fm96.5 a java-based electronic auction house. In *Proceedings of the Second International Conference on The Practical Application of Intelligent Agents and Multi-Agent Technology (PAAM'97)*, 1997.

36. J. Searle. *Speech Acts*. Cambridge University Press, 1969.

37. Sun Microsystems, Inc. *JavaSpaces TM Specification, Revision 1.0*, March 1998.

38. R. van der Goot, J. Schaeffer, and G.V. Wilson. Safer tuple spaces. In *Proceedings of the 2nd International Conference on Coordination Languages and Models (Coordination '97)*, number 1282 in LNCS. Springer Verlag, September 1997.

39. K.J. Werkman. Knowledge-based Model of Negotiation using Shareable Perspectives. In *Proceedings of the 10th Int Workshop on DAI*, 1990.

40. M. Wooldridge and N.R. Jennings. Agent Theories, Architectures, and Languages: a Survey. In M. Wooldridge and N.R. Jennings, editors, *Intelligent Agents*, number 890 in LNCS, pages 1–39. Springer Verlag, 1995.

A Distributed Semantics for a IWIM-Based Coordination Language[*]

Mathieu Buffo[1], Didier Buchs[1]

[1] Software Engineering Laboratory, Swiss Federal Institute for Technology, 1015 Lausanne, Switzerland
{Mathieu.Buffo,Didier.Buchs}@epfl.ch

1 The Modelling Language CO-OPN$_{/2}$, and COIL

CO-OPN$_{/2}$ is a formal language allowing the modelling of object-oriented software systems. A CO-OPN$_{/2}$ model is composed of three kinds of entities, modelling three different parts of the global description, by three different formal semantics:

kind of entity	based on	kind of semantics
data types	algebraic data types	denotational semantics
classes, objects	algebraic Petri nets	structured operational semantics
components	IWIM coordination models	distributed compositional semantics

COIL is the part of CO-OPN$_{/2}$ allowing the model components and their coordination.

2 COIL is an IWIM-based Coordination Model

COIL, our coordination language, is a member of the *IWIM* (*Idealized Workers, Idealized Managers*) family of coordination models. Due to their intrinsic nature, IWIM models are particularly well suited for the modelling of coordination.

Indeed, coordination models can be categorised as either *exogenous* or *endogenous*. They can also be categorised as either *control-* or *data-driven*. IWIM is a family of coordination models which can be exactly characterised be the following two keywords: *exogenous* and *control-driven*. Typical IWIM-based coordination models includes Manifold and Darwin. On the opposite side, Linda is an *endogenous* and *data-driven* coordination model.

With regards to other IWIM coordination models, COIL can be characterised by two key points: it restricts the use of non-local interactions, and it allows high level abstractions of object migrations.

3 A Formal Distributed Semantics for COIL

This abstract is a summary of a technical report, in which we define a formal distributed semantics for COIL, as a set of interrelated transition systems, and we show that *COIL is a true coordination language*. This report can be found as:
Mathieu Buffo and Didier Buchs, *A Formal Component-Oriented Modelling Language for Building Distributed System*, technical report 99/308, LGL-DI-EPFL, 1999.

---

[*] This work has been partially sponsored by the Esprit Long Term Research Project 20072 "Design for Validation" (DeVa) with the financial support of the OFES, and by the Swiss National Science Foundation project "Formal Methods for Concurrent Systems".

Coordination in Context:
Authentication, Authorisation and Topology
in Mobile Agent Applications

Marco Cremonini[1], Andrea Omicini[1], and Franco Zambonelli[2]

[1] LIA - DEIS, Università di Bologna, Italy {mcremonini, aomicini}@deis.unibo.it
[2] DSI, Università di Modena, Italy franco.zambonelli@unimo.it

Adding the dimension of *mobility* to the engineering of complex software systems extends the scope of coordination. Since a mobile agent can roam a collection of different execution environments, physically distributed and possibly heterogeneous, interacting with both local resources and other mobile agents, both *topology* and *security* strictly relate to *coordination*. In this context, we propose an extension to the TuCSoN coordination model for Internet applications based on network-aware and mobile agents, which makes the coordination model coherently account for security and topology. TuCSoN defines a coordination space made up of a multiplicity of *tuple centres*, i.e., tuple spaces whose behaviour can be programmed to embed the laws of coordination, by means of *specification tuples* defining *reactions* to communication events.

While coordination deals with how software components interact, security deals with *(i)* how interacting entities are identified (*authentication*), and *(ii)* what they are allowed to do (*authorisation*). TuCSoN provides a simple yet expressive authorisation scheme, relying on the definition of a role-based access control model over tuples. So, *(i)* any communication operation on a tuple centre performed by an agent may either succeed or fail also according to the rights granted to the agent's role, and *(ii)* any reaction associated to the operation may either succeed or fail also according to the rights granted to the agent owning the corresponding specification tuple. As a result, the effect of a communication primitive is defined by the joint effects of both the coordination and authorisation policies.

As far as topology is concerned, two main problems have to be addressed in the coordination of network-aware mobile entities: *(i)* how the space roamed by agents is modelled (*network modelling*), and *(ii)* how the knowledge about the structure of that space is made available to the agents (*network knowledge*), when this knowledge is acquired dynamically by mobile entities (as typical in unpredictable environments like the Internet). So, we extend TuCSoN by making it explicitly model the Internet as a collection of *places*, *domains*, and *gateways*, where the place provides the abstraction for the mobile agent execution environment, the domain models (either logical or physical) groups of places belonging to the same application scenario, while the gateway is the main place of a domain, and is in charge of inter-domain routing for both incoming and outgoing agents. More precisely, each gateway *(i)* authenticates incoming agents on behalf of its associated domain, *(ii)* works as a *knowledge repository*, providing agents with information about the structure of its associated domain, filtered according to agent identity, thus working as the first authorisation level.

References
For general information, technical references, published papers, and updates on the current state of the research on the TuCSoN model, please refer to the TuCSoN Home Page, located at http://www-lia.deis.unibo.it/Research/TuCSoN/ .

Presence and Instant Messaging via HTTP/1.1: A Coordination Perspective

Mark Day

Lotus Development Corporation, Cambridge, MA, USA
Mark_Day@lotus.com

Colleague awareness tools are applications that allow a person to advertise their online presence and availability to others, as well as seeing the presence and availability of others on a network or internet. These tools typically provide two related services to users. We call these services *presence notification* and *instant messaging*.

Systems performing presence notification and instant messaging are currently provided by a variety of vendors, each with their own proprietary protocols. However, there is a strong incentive for developing interoperability among these different implementations. A number of proposals for such an interoperable protocol have been submitted to the IETF of which a majority have been based on HTTP [2]. We believe that presence and instant messaging are a poor match to HTTP: that in some sense, notification is unnatural for HTTP.

In our poster at the workshop and in a technical report[1], we show successively more elaborate CCS[3] models of HTTP/1.1's coordination functionality, including proxying, caching, and pipelining. We then develop CCS models of presence notification and instant messaging.

It is worth noting that our treatments of presence and instant messaging are quite similar, and that those treatments differ from those for HTTP/1.1 as it is currently defined. In particular, we had to introduce two features to support presence notification and instant messaging that were not present in all our previous elaborations of the HTTP interactions. First, we needed to index clients; this accounts for the fact that in presence notification and instant messaging, the recipient of a message and the initiator of a request are not necessarily the same client. In contrast, the only time that we needed to index any component in our HTTP models was to keep track of the depth of the intermediaries between client and server, or keep track of the number of pending requests with pipelining. Second, we needed to introduce a part of the client that is ready to accept an incoming message at any time.

It is interesting to see in a fairly concise way the way that the successive elaborations of HTTP correspond to increasingly complex models, and to see that efforts to embed notification in HTTP will further complicate its model.

References

1. Day, M. Presence and Instant Messaging via HTTP/1.1: A Coordination Perspective. Lotus Technical Report, 1999. *Available at http://www.lotus.com/research*
2. Fielding, R., Gettys, J., Mogul, J., Frystyk, H., Berners-Lee, T. Hypertext Transfer Protocol — HTTP/1.1. RFC 2068 (1997)
3. Milner, R.: Communication and Concurrency. Prentice-Hall (1989)

Towards a Periodic Table of Connectors

Dan Hirsch, Sebastián Uchitel, and Daniel Yankelevich *

Departamento de Computación, Universidad de Buenos Aires
{dhirsch, suchitel, dany}@dc.uba.ar

Connectors are the glue for combining components and are a critical aspect of software architecture design. Providing a framework similar in spirit to that of the periodic table of chemical elements, this work strives to obtain a set of high level canonical properties that can describe all possible connectors and allow operations to be defined over them. *Connector factorization* obtains a new connector characterized by the common subset of primitive properties of a given set of connectors. Also, a connector can be *specialized* by adding primitive properties to the set that characterizes it. This approach leads us to the notion of *connector class*. A connector class can be seen as a connector that does not define a criteria for a set of properties, these properties are viewed as optional by the class. In addition, we extend operations of specialization and factorization of connectors over classes. By explicitly defining the set of primitive properties to be included in the *periodic table*, it is also possible to explore the connector universe by contriving connectors as new combinations of properties. As in Mendeleev's original table, the periodic table of connector properties will require many refinements and additions. For instance, if one can characterize two known distinct connectors with the same set of properties, the table must be revised. Examples of properties that could be included in the initial table are, *Broadcast*, *Reliable*, *Typed* and *Synchronous*.

The ideas presented in this work are not completely new. In [1] the main goal is to understand operations over connectors but higher order connectors are used instead of reusing properties. [2] proposes a first sketch of the periodic table analogy only that it is based on low level properties not distinguishing between connectors and components.

Our work is in a preliminary stage and it would be very important to define a formal semantics for properties and to formalize this framework and its operations. But formal semantics may be difficult to establish until a complete understanding of relevant properties and an interesting canonical set has been defined. Our work is a first step in this direction.

References

1. Garlan, D.: Higher Order Connectors. Workshop on Compositional Software Architecture. 1998.
2. Kazman, R., Clements, P., Bass, L., Abowd, G.: Classifying Architectural Elements as a Foundation for Mechanism Matching. In Proceedings of COMPSAC'97. 1997.

* Partially supported by ARTE, PIC 11-00000-01856, ANPCyT and TW72, UBACyT.

Author Index

ecture Notes in Computer Science

r information about Vols. 1–1502

ase contact your bookseller or Springer-Verlag

Vol. 1539: O. Rüthing, Interacting Code Motion Transformations: Their Impact and Their Complexity. XXI,225 pages. 1998.

Vol. 1540: C. Beeri, P. Buneman (Eds.), Database Theory – ICDT'99. Proceedings, 1999. XI, 489 pages. 1999.

Vol. 1541: B. Kågström, J. Dongarra, E. Elmroth, J. Waśniewski (Eds.), Applied Parallel Computing. Proceedings, 1998. XIV, 586 pages. 1998.

Vol. 1542: H.I. Christensen (Ed.), Computer Vision Systems. Proceedings, 1999. XI, 554 pages. 1999.

Vol. 1543: S. Demeyer, J. Bosch (Eds.), Object-Oriented Technology ECOOP'98 Workshop Reader. 1998. XXII, 573 pages. 1998.

Vol. 1544: C. Zhang, D. Lukose (Eds.), Multi-Agent Systems. Proceedings, 1998. VII, 195 pages. 1998. (Subseries LNAI).

Vol. 1545: A. Birk, J. Demiris (Eds.), Learning Robots. Proceedings, 1996. IX, 188 pages. 1998. (Subseries LNAI).

Vol. 1546: B. Möller, J.V. Tucker (Eds.), Prospects for Hardware Foundations. Survey Chapters, 1998. X, 468 pages. 1998.

Vol. 1547: S.H. Whitesides (Ed.), Graph Drawing. Proceedings 1998. XII, 468 pages. 1998.

Vol. 1548: A.M. Haeberer (Ed.), Algebraic Methodology and Software Technology. Proceedings, 1999. XI, 531 pages. 1999.

Vol. 1550: B. Christianson, B. Crispo, W.S. Harbison, M. Roe (Eds.), Security Protocols. Proceedings, 1998. VIII, 241 pages. 1999.

Vol. 1551: G. Gupta (Ed.), Practical Aspects of Declarative Languages. Proceedings, 1999. VIII, 367 pgages. 1999.

Vol. 1552: Y. Kambayashi, D.L. Lee, E.-P. Lim, M.K. Mohania, Y. Masunaga (Eds.), Advances in Database Technologies. Proceedings, 1998. XIX, 592 pages. 1999.

Vol. 1553: S.F. Andler, J. Hansson (Eds.), Active, Real-Time, and Temporal Database Systems. Proceedings, 1997. VIII, 245 pages. 1998.

Vol. 1554: S. Nishio, F. Kishino (Eds.), Advanced Multimedia Content Processing. Proceedings, 1998. XIV, 454 pages. 1999.

Vol. 1555: J.P. Müller, M.P. Singh, A.S. Rao (Eds.), Intelligent Agents V. Proceedings, 1998. XXIV, 455 pages. 1999. (Subseries LNAI).

Vol. 1557: P. Zinterhof, M. Vajteršic, A. Uhl (Eds.), Parallel Computation. Proceedings, 1999. XV, 604 pages. 1999.

Vol. 1558: H. J.v.d. Herik, H. Iida (Eds.), Computers and Games. Proceedings, 1998. XVIII, 337 pages. 1999.

Vol. 1559: P. Flener (Ed.), Logic-Based Program Synthesis and Transformation. Proceedings, 1998. X, 331 pages. 1999.

Vol. 1560: K. Imai, Y. Zheng (Eds.), Public Key Cryptography. Proceedings, 1999. IX, 327 pages. 1999.

Vol. 1561: I. Damgård (Ed.), Lectures on Data Security. VII, 250 pages. 1999.

Vol. 1563: Ch. Meinel, S. Tison (Eds.), STACS 99. Proceedings, 1999. XIV, 582 pages. 1999.

Vol. 1567: P. Antsaklis, W. Kohn, M. Lemmon, Nerode, S. Sastry (Eds.), Hybrid Systems V. X, 445 page 1999.

Vol. 1568: G. Bertrand, M. Couprie, L. Perroton (Eds Discrete Geometry for Computer Imagery. Proceeding 1999. XI, 459 pages. 1999.

Vol. 1569: F.W. Vaandrager, J.H. van Schuppen (Eds Hybrid Systems: Computation and Control. Proceeding 1999. X, 271 pages. 1999.

Vol. 1570: F. Puppe (Ed.), XPS-99: Knowledge-Bas Systems. VIII, 227 pages. 1999. (Subseries LNAI).

Vol. 1572: P. Fischer, H.U. Simon (Eds.), Computatio Learning Theory. Proceedings, 1999. X, 301 pages. 19 (Subseries LNAI).

Vol. 1574: N. Zhong, L. Zhou (Eds.), Methodologies Knowledge Discovery and Data Mining. Proceedin 1999. XV, 533 pages. 1999. (Subseries LNAI).

Vol. 1575: S. Jähnichen (Ed.), Compiler Constructi Proceedings, 1999. X, 301 pages. 1999.

Vol. 1576: S.D. Swierstra (Ed.), Programming Langua and Systems. Proceedings, 1999. X, 307 pages. 1999.

Vol. 1577: J.-P. Finance (Ed.), Fundamental Approac to Software Engineering. Proceedings, 1999. X, 245 pag 1999.

Vol. 1578: W. Thomas (Ed.), Foundations of Softw Science and Computation Structures. Proceedings, 19 X, 323 pages. 1999.

Vol. 1579: W.R. Cleaveland (Ed.), Tools and Algorith for the Construction and Analysis of Systems. Proce ings, 1999. XI, 445 pages. 1999.

Vol. 1580: A. Včkovski, K.E. Brassel, H.-J. Schek (Ed Interoperating Geographic Information Systems. Proce ings, 1999. XI, 329 pages. 1999.

Vol. 1581: J.-Y. Girard (Ed.), Typed Lambda Calculi Applications. Proceedings, 1999. VIII, 397 pages. 19

Vol. 1582: A. Lecomte, F. Lamarche, G. Perrier (Ec Logical Aspects of Computational Linguistics. Proce ings, 1997. XI, 251 pages. 1999. (Subseries LNAI).

Vol. 1586: J. Rolim et al. (Eds.), Parallel and Distribu Processing. Proceedings, 1999. XVII, 1443 pages. 1

Vol. 1587: J. Pieprzyk, R. Safavi-Naini, J. Seberry (E Information Security and Privacy. Proceedings, 1999. 327 pages. 1999.

Vol. 1590: P. Atzeni, A. Mendelzon, G. Mecca (Ec The World Wide Web and Databases. Proceedings, 1 VIII, 213 pages. 1999.

Vol. 1592: J. Stern (Ed.), Advances in Cryptolog EUROCRYPT '99. Proceedings, 1999. XII, 475 pa 1999.

Vol. 1593: P. Sloot, M. Bubak, A. Hoekstra, B. Hertzb (Eds.), High-Performance Computing and Network Proceedings, 1999. XXIII, 1318 pages. 1999.

Vol. 1594: P. Ciancarini, A.L. Wolf (Eds.), Coordin Languages and Models. Proceedings, 1999. IX, 420 p 1999.

Vol. 1605: J. Billington, M. Diaz, G. Rozenberg (E Application of Petri Nets to Communication Netw IX, 303 pages. 1999.